A Prophet like Moses (Deut 18:15, 18)

Supplements to the Journal for the Study of Judaism

Editor

René Bloch (*Institut für Judaistik, Universität Bern*)
Karina Martin Hogan (*Department of Theology, Fordham University*)

Associate Editors

Hindy Najman (*Theology & Religion Faculty, University of Oxford*)
Eibert J.C. Tigchelaar (*Faculty of Theology and Religious Studies, KU Leuven*)
Benjamin G. Wright, III (*Department of Religion Studies, Lehigh University*)

Advisory Board

A.M. Berlin – K. Berthelot – J.J. Collins – B. Eckhardt – Y. Furstenberg
S. Kattan Gribetz – G. Anthony Keddie – L. Lehmhaus – O. Malka
A. Manekin – S. Mason – F. Mirguet – J.H. Newman – A.K. Petersen
M. Popović – P. Pouchelle – I. Rosen-Zvi – J.T.A.G.M. van Ruiten – M. Segal
J. Sievers – L.T. Stuckenbruck – L. Teugels – J.C. de Vos – Sharon Weisser

VOLUME 205

The titles published in this series are listed at *brill.com/jsjs*

A Prophet like Moses (Deut 18:15, 18)

The Origin, History, and Influence of the Mosaic Prophetic Succession

By

David N. DeJong

BRILL

LEIDEN | BOSTON

The Library of Congress Cataloging-in-Publication Data is available online at https://catalog.loc.gov
LC record available at https://lccn.loc.gov/2022026454

Typeface for the Latin, Greek, and Cyrillic scripts: "Brill". See and download: brill.com/brill-typeface.

ISSN 1384-2161
ISBN 978-90-04-52201-5 (hardback)
ISBN 978-90-04-52202-2 (e-book)

Copyright 2022 by David N. DeJong. Published by Koninklijke Brill NV, Leiden, The Netherlands.
Koninklijke Brill NV incorporates the imprints Brill, Brill Nijhoff, Brill Hotei, Brill Schöningh, Brill Fink, Brill mentis, Vandenhoeck & Ruprecht, Böhlau and V&R unipress.
Koninklijke Brill NV reserves the right to protect this publication against unauthorized use. Requests for re-use and/or translations must be addressed to Koninklijke Brill NV via brill.com or copyright.com.

This book is printed on acid-free paper and produced in a sustainable manner.

PRINTED BY DRUKKERIJ WILCO B.V. - AMERSFOORT, THE NETHERLANDS

In memory of my father, Jack, and dedicated to my mother, Margaret, who together instilled in me a love for the Scriptures

Contents

Acknowledgements XV
List of Tables XIII

Introduction 1
1 Origin and Rationale 1
2 Najman on Mosaic Discourse 8
3 Method and Overview 11

PART 1
Foundations: The Genealogical Model of Mosaic Prophecy

1 Is Moses among the Prophets? 17
   1 Introduction 17
   2 Designations for Moses in the Hebrew Bible 18
      2.1 *Overview of the Data* 18
      2.2 *Moses' Prophetic Status in the Pentateuch* 20
   3 The Obscure Origins of Mosaic Prophecy 25
   4 Conclusion 29

2 From Charisma to Canon: Deuteronomy's Redefinition of Moses and Prophecy 30
   1 Introduction 30
   2 The Relationship between Moses and Prophecy in Numbers 11–12 31
      2.1 *Introductory Comments* 31
      2.2 *The Redaction of Num 11:4–35* 32
      2.3 *Moses and Prophecy in Numbers 12* 40
      2.4 *Numbers 11–12 and the Charismatic Model of Mosaic Prophecy* 44
   3 The Characterization of Moses as a Prophet in Deut 18:9–22 46
      3.1 *Deuteronomy and Prophecy* 46
      3.2 *Deut 18:9–22: Restriction in Revelation* 49
         3.2.1 *Prolegomena*: Text, Structure, Unity, Date 49
         3.2.2 The Restriction in Mode of Revelation in Deut 18:9–15, 18 59

		3.2.3	The Restriction in Source of Revelation in Deut 18:15–18 64
	4	Conclusion: Moses in Numbers and Deuteronomy 18 70	

3 **"My Servants the Prophets," Part I: The Deuteronomistic Construction of a Mosaic Prophetic Succession**   72
   1   Introduction   72
   2   Yhwh's "Servants the Prophets" in the Deuteronomistic History   75
       2.1   *Overview of Data*   75
       2.2   *The Double Violation of Deuteronomy 18:9–22 in 2 Kings 17 and 21*   77
       2.3   *Prophecy and Fulfillment*   86
   3   Amos among Yhwh's "Servants the Prophets"   93
   4   Conclusion   96

4 **"My Servants the Prophets," Part II: Jeremiah as Culminating Figure in the Mosaic Prophetic Succession**   97
   1   Introduction   97
   2   Jeremiah and the Mosaic Prophetic Succession   98
       2.1   *Jeremiah among Yhwh's "Servants the Prophets"*   98
       2.2   *Jeremiah and Other Prophets*   103
   3   Jeremiah as Prophet like Moses   107
       3.1   *Jeremiah's Call Narrative*   107
       3.2   *Jeremiah as Moses' Equal*   109
       3.3   *Jeremiah as Final Prophet in the Pre-exilic Mosaic Succession*   114
   4   "My Servants the Prophets" as "Former Prophets" in Zechariah 1   118
   5   Conclusion   122

5 **"No Prophet like Moses": Deut 34:9–12 and the Creation of a Canonical Era**   123
   1   Introduction   123
   2   Deut 34:10–12: Hatchet or Hinge?   124
   3   Joshua as Moses' Successor in Deuteronomy   129
   4   Moses as Incomparable Prophet in Deut 34:10–12   132
   5   Unintended Consequences: An Eschatological Prophet like Moses?   137
   6   Conclusion   141

PART 2
Prophets Past and Future: The Periodization of Mosaic Prophecy

6   The Cessation of Prophecy in Second Temple Judaism: Previous Scholarship and a New Proposal   145
     1   Introduction   145
     2   The Status of Prophecy in Second Temple Judaism: A Selective Review   148

7   "I Will Send Elijah the Prophet": The Cessation and Deferral of the Mosaic Prophetic Succession   156
     1   Introduction   156
     2   A Scribal Colophon: The Conclusion to the Book of the Twelve   156
     3   The Mosaic Prophetic Succession in Ben Sira's *Laus Patrum*   167
         3.1   *Introduction*   167
         3.2   *Moses as Supreme Prophet in Sir 45:1–5*   168
         3.3   *Ben Sira's Construction of a Prophetic Succession*   170
     4   Conclusion   176

8   "Until the Prophet Comes": Past and Future Prophets like Moses in Hellenistic and Roman-Era Judaism   178
     1   Introduction   178
     2   The Prophet like Moses in the Historiographic Tradition   178
         2.1   *Joshua as the Prophet like Moses*   178
             2.1.1   Eupolemus   178
             2.1.2   The Joshua Apocryphon   179
             2.1.3   The *Testament of Moses*   180
             2.1.4   The *Biblical Antiquities* of Pseudo-Philo   181
         2.2   *Prophets Past and Future in 1 Maccabees*   183
     3   The Prophet like Moses at Qumran   186
         3.1   *Prophets and Prophecy at Qumran*   186
         3.2   *The Portrayal of Moses as Supreme Prophet in 4Q377*   187
         3.3   *Past Prophets as Legislators and Successors of Moses (4Q381; 1QS)*   191
         3.4   *The Eschatological Prophet like Moses at Qumran*   195
     4   The Prophet like Moses between Ben Sira and Josephus: Conclusion   203

9 "Moses and Those after Him": The Mosaic Prophetic Succession in the Writings of Flavius Josephus 205

1   Introduction 205
2   The "Exact Succession of the Prophets" in *Against Apion* 206
3   The Mosaic Prophetic Succession in the *Jewish Antiquities* 211
     3.1   *General Considerations* 211
     3.2   *Josephus's Interpretation of Deuteronomy* 214
     3.3   *Josephus's Portrait of Moses* 220
     3.4   *Joshua as the Prophet like Moses* 221
     3.5   *The Extent of the Mosaic Prophetic Succession* 223
4   Eschatological Prophets like Moses Reported on by Josephus 226
5   The Mosaic Prophetic Succession from Ben Sira to Josephus: Concluding Comments 234

10 Listening to a "Raised" Prophet: The Prophet like Moses in Luke-Acts 236

1   Introductory Comments on the Prophet like Moses in the New Testament 236
2   Prophets and Prophecy in Luke-Acts 239
3   Jesus as Prophet like Moses in Acts 3, 7 241
     3.1   *The Prophet like Moses in Luke-Acts: Scholarly Context* 241
     3.2   *The "Raised" Prophet: Acts 3:22–26* 245
     3.3   *The Rejected Prophet: Acts 7:37* 252
         3.3.1   Stephen's Speech in Narrative Context 252
         3.3.2   Parallels between Acts 3 and Acts 7 255
         3.3.3   Use of the Citation in Stephen's Speech 258
4   Listening to the Resurrected Prophet in Luke 265
5   Conclusion 272

PART 3
Mosaic Prophecy and Logos-Theology: The Triumph of Mosaic Discourse

11 Moses, the Prophetic Nature: The Incomparability of Moses in the Writings of Philo   277
   1   Introduction: The Triumph of Mosaic Discourse   277
   2   Philo of Alexandria and Mosaic Prophecy   278
       2.1   *Philo's Commentaries on Deut 18:9–22*   278
       2.2   *Moses' Prophetic Status in Philo*   282
       2.3   *Philo and the Mosaic Prophetic Succession*   287
   3   Conclusion   290

12 Like and unlike Moses: The Interpretation of Deut 18:15–18 in the Gospel according to John   291
   1   Introduction   291
   2   Previous Assessments of the Importance of the Prophet like Moses in John   293
   3   Martyn and the Moses-Jesus Relationship   298
   4   The Interpretation of Deut 18:15–18 in John's Gospel   300
       4.1   *References to "The Prophet" in John's Gospel*   300
       4.2   *The Prophetic Characterization of Jesus in John*   306
       4.3   *The Moses-Jesus Relationship in John: Four Controlling Passages*   312
   5   Conclusion: John and Luke-Acts on Deut 18:15–18   318

Conclusion: Retrospect and Prospect   320

Bibliography   325
Index of Modern Authors   354
Index of Ancient Sources   360
Index of Subjects   384

Acknowledgements

The idea for this book was hatched about a decade ago in a conversation in Jim VanderKam's office. Jim and I were discussing various options for a dissertation topic, and Jim encouraged me to look into the interpretation of the prophet like Moses in Jewish and early Christian texts. I am grateful to Jim for the encouragement to begin working on this important topic, as well as his guidance throughout the dissertation process. It was a privilege to work with a scholar who combines academic rigor and attention to detail with a breadth of interest in Hebrew Bible, ancient Judaism, and early Christianity. Jim's personal commitment to excellence, his integrity, and his dedication to service to the profession has made a lasting impact on me.

I am also grateful to other professors at Notre Dame who were invested in my work. In particular, I would like to thank Tzvi Novick, whose encouragement, advice, and feedback was important throughout the dissertation process. I want to thank Gary Anderson and John Meier, who served as readers of the dissertation. I would also like to mention two Notre Dame professors who have since passed away. Gary Knoppers' kindness and encouragement was impactful on me as I think about the type of professor that I would like to be. I have fond memories of going out to lunch with him to discuss my work, and I still occasionally return to his marked-up copies of various drafts. Finally, in the early stages of this project, it was a privilege to meet with Joseph Blenkinsopp. As the index of modern authors indicates, his intellectual influence is reflected throughout the work.

I have had various opportunities to present and discuss ideas in the book over the years, both as a doctoral student at the University of Notre Dame and later as a postdoctoral fellow at Saint Louis University. I am grateful to peers and colleagues at both institutions, too many to name, for engaging my ideas and helping me to clarify my arguments. I am grateful to friends who have provided support and advice throughout this process, particularly Justus Ghormley, whose encouragement helped me to the finish line.

I am grateful to my current colleagues in the Religion Department at Hope College, who have warmly welcomed me into the life of the Department and have provided a collegial and supportive academic environment.

I want to thank René Bloch and Karina Hogan, the general editors of the Journal for the Study of Judaism Supplement Series. They have been encouraging throughout the process of revising the dissertation into this book. I have appreciated their belief in the importance of the topic and their constructive comments, which have improved the book considerably.

The anonymous reviewers of the manuscript provided thorough and detailed comments on my first submission. The revision process strengthened and clarified my arguments, and also contributed to my personal growth as a scholar. I am deeply grateful for their commitment to scholarship and for their service to the profession in this way.

I am grateful to my family for their support. The finishing touches on the revised manuscript were completed over Christmas 2021 at my in-laws. I want to thank my parents-in-law for their encouragement, as well as Michael and Chantelle, who checked in on me regularly down in the basement to see how the writing was going. I want to thank my siblings Joanna, Tim, Esther, Nathan, Carina, and Brendan for tolerating and often embracing my love of argumentation and debate. It's undoubtedly the case that in our family home, preparation for life in academia began at a young age indeed. Thanks for supporting me in my goals over the years. As I think about my upbringing, I am particularly grateful for my parents, who created a loving home environment, one which combined a commitment to intellectual curiosity and academic endeavors with a deep rootedness in the Christian faith. It is to them that this book is dedicated, as a reflection of the profound influence they have had on me and on my life's work.

Most of all, I want to thank my wife, Crystal. I don't think either of us knew what embarking on this journey would entail when we moved to South Bend, Indiana, in August 2009. You have been unfailingly supportive though all of the ups and downs of academic life, and you have encouraged me not to give up even when the task seemed overwhelming. Thanks for keeping me grounded, and for doing life with me. I also want to thank my children, Luke and Aubrey. You bring joy and love and laughter to our lives every day. "Dad's book" is finally finished; thanks for being patient with a Dad who has worked on holidays, evenings, and weekends in order to complete this project. You have lived with this book, and encouraged me in the process in working on it, in ways you don't even realize. I'm so grateful for the love, support, and encouragement of you three; you fill my present with meaning and joy. I promise I'll take a little break before I write another one.

Tables

1. Moses' Prophetic Status in Deuteronomy   19
2. References to Divinatory Practices in the Hebrew Bible   61
3. The Appointment of Moses and the Prophet like Him as Mediators of the Divine Voice   67
4. Prohibited Divinatory Practices in Second Kings 17, 21   79
5. Prohibited Divinatory Practices in the DH   80
6. The Double Violation of Deut 18 in 2 Kings 17:13–17   83
7. The Double Violation of Deut 18 in 2 Kings 21:2, 6, 7–10   84
8. Yhwh's "Servants the Prophets" and the Prophecy-Fulfillment Schema of the DH   88
9. The Influence of Jeremiah in 2 Kings 21:12, 14   92
10. Jeremianic Terminology Associated with Yhwh's "Servants the Prophets"   102
11. The Influence of Deut 18:18 in Jeremiah 1   108
12. "Speaking" what Yhwh "Commands" in the Hebrew Bible   109
13. The Qualification of Deut 18:15, 18 in Deut 34:10   133
14. The Parallel Structure of Malachi 3:1, 23   163
15. The Mosaic Prophetic Succession in the *Laus Patrum*   171
16. Allusion to Elisha's Succession of Elijah in the *Laus Patrum*   174
17. The Eschatological Elijah in the *Laus Patrum*   175
18. Deuteronomy's Prophet-Laws in 4Q375   202
19. Josephus' Use of Prophet-Terminology in *Antiquities*   214
20. The Combined Citation in Acts 3:22–23   247
21. Parallels between the Speeches in Acts 3 and Acts 7   257
22. The Prophet's Rejection and Vindication in Acts   261
23. The Structure of Deut 18:15, 18–19; Acts 3:22–23; 7:37–39   264
24. Luke's Modification of Mark 6:15b; 8:28d   268
25. Allusions to and Echoes of Deut 18:15, 18 in John's Gospel   308

Introduction

"The connecting link between old and new, between Israel and Judaism, is everywhere Deuteronomy."[1]

∴

"What distinguishes prophecy in Israel is its tremendous ability to live on in ever new forms."[2]

∴

"Mosaic Discourse remains a living force in the imagination and in the soul of Judaism and Christianity throughout the centuries."[3]

∴

1   Origin and Rationale

The distinctiveness of Deuteronomy is found in its character as both deeply traditional and boldly innovative. It is a text that, more than most others in Jewish and Christian literature, self-consciously looks backward and forward, retrieving tradition and reshaping it. The rhetoric of reform often draws upon tradition even to justify departure from it, and the tension between Deuteronomy's interpretive and revisionary goals deeply shapes its theological character

---

1   Julius Wellhausen, *Prolegomena to the History of Ancient Israel*, trans. J. Black and A. Menzies, repr. (Gloucester, Mass.: Peter Smith, 1973 [1885]), 362. Quoted by Joseph Blenkinsopp, *Prophecy and Canon: A Contribution to the Study of Jewish Origins*, CSJCA 3 (Notre Dame: University of Notre Dame, 1977), 24: who provides his own explanatory gloss: "If this view of Wellhausen is correct, the authors of this book have better claim than anyone else to be considered the founders of Judaism. Deuteronomy stands at the beginning of the process which led Judaism, and afterwards Christianity and Islam, to be regarded as a religion of the book."
2   Rudolf Meyer, "Prophecy and Prophets in the Judaism of the Hellenistic-Roman Period," *TDNT* 6:812–828, here 828.
3   Hindy Najman, *Seconding Sinai: The Development of Mosaic Discourse in Second Temple Judaism*, JSJSup 77 (Leiden: Brill, 2003), 137.

and contribution. This monograph is an exploration of one such tension, that generated by the contrasting statements "a prophet like Moses" (Deut 18:15, 18) and "no prophet like Moses" (Deut 34:10).[4] The goal of this book is to examine how Deuteronomy functions as a tradition-mediating and tradition-shaping text with respect to the important concept of Mosaic prophecy.

This monograph represents a major revision of my University of Notre Dame dissertation, "A Prophet like Moses: Prophecy and Canon in Early Judaism and Christianity." It represents what is to my knowledge the first broad attempt to assess the reception-history of the concept of the prophet like Moses (Deut 18:15, 18; 34:10), covering the Hebrew Bible/Old Testament, ancient Judaism, and as a subset of ancient Judaism, nascent Christianity. For the intellectual genesis of this project, I am indebted to Joseph Blenkinsopp's slim volume *Prophecy and Canon*, published in 1977. In that work he indicated one significant direction in which biblical studies was headed when he wrote:

> Given the predominantly literary emphasis in Biblical studies, the result has been that the formation of the canon has not been seen as an important chapter in the religious and social history of early Judaism. *Indeed, it has not even been taken seriously by the practitioners of Biblical Studies as an essential aspect of the exegesis of texts.* Everyone knows about form criticism, redaction criticism, tradition-historical criticism and several other more recent and tentative approaches to the exegete's craft. But as yet few exegetes take seriously *what we may now call canon criticism as the study of the decisive phase in the development of the tradition and therefore in the religious history of which the individual text is a part.* This must be considered a serious omission if we are prepared to concede: first, the importance of the location of a text within an ongoing tradition; and second, that *canon implies the attempt to impose a definitive shape and meaning on the tradition as it comes to expression in texts.*[5]

Contemporaneous with Blenkinsopp, Brevard Childs was working out his own proposals for "canon criticism,"[6] so that in the forty years since these words

---

4 The phrase "prophet like Moses" will be used so often in this book that it would be distracting to continually place it in quotation marks. Thus, from this point it will be deployed without quotation marks, though the reference is to Deuteronomy's concept as found in 18:15, 18; 34:10.
5 Blenkinsopp, *Prophecy and Canon*, 10. Emphasis added.
6 Brevard Childs, *Introduction to the Old Testament as Scripture* (Philadelphia: Fortress, 1979).

were penned, this discipline has become its own sub-field, and there has been a flurry of publications on canon-related matters. Blenkinsopp's approach to canon criticism, however, differs significantly that of Childs. Influenced by Childs, the notion of canon criticism has become closely linked to "final form" readings of the biblical text, and also incorporates the history of reception. Blenkinsopp's study, however, focuses on how the final form of the biblical text (specifically, the tripartite Jewish canon) came to be, and does not engage extensively with synchronic readings of the text. That is, Blenkinsopp's approach to canon criticism ends where Childs' begins: Blenkinsopp interrogates the processes that led to the emergence of the canon; Childs and his followers undertake a reading of those texts in their final form and in their historical influence as unified texts. For this reason, as Ulrich puts it, "few have followed" Blenkinsopp in his understanding of the basic task and goals of canon criticism.[7]

This last statement requires qualification: though Blenkinsopp's definition of canon criticism has not been influential, his exegetical proposals have made a significant impact, particularly in the field of Hebrew Bible. It has not been noticed, however, that Blenkinsopp's working out of his proposal in *Prophecy and Canon*—which attempts to take seriously the concept of canon as "an essential aspect of the exegesis of texts" looks like what might be now called a reception-history of Deuteronomy 18. That is, Blenkinsopp locates the basic problem of canonicity in the coordination of prophecy to Moses in Deut 18:15–22, and he interprets later texts, such as Deut 34:10–12 and Mal 3:22–24, as hermeneutical comments further delineating the nature and shape of Mosaic prophecy.[8] Stephen Chapman's monograph *The Law and the Prophets*, which interacts extensively with Blenkinsopp's work, could also be re-described as a

---

7   Eugene Ulrich, "The Notion and Definition of Canon," in *The Canon Debate*, ed. L.M. McDonald and J.A. Sanders (Peabody, Mass: Hendrickson Publishers, 2002), 21–35, at 33: Blenkinsopp's approach to the study of the canonical process "constitutes an excellent and promising bellwether which, unfortunately, few have followed."
8   Consider various chapter and section headings in the work: "Prophecy in Deuteronomy" (39–46), which focuses on Deut 18:15–22; "Prophecy in the Deuteronomistic History," (47–53); "No Prophet like Moses" (Chapter 4, 80–95), "The Last Paragraph of *Nebî'îm*" (120–123). In these sections Blenkinsopp discusses the origin and interpretation of Deuteronomy's construal of Mosaic prophecy. Blenkinsopp sums up his conclusions, 147 (emphasis added): "To speak of the Bible as 'the word of God' is to affirm or imply its authoritative and prophetic character…. Such a claim, however, was made possible only by extending the concept of prophecy to cover all disclosures to the House of Israel, and in particular those communicated to it by Moses. *But it is precisely in this redefinition of prophecy, documented in detail in the present study, that we are to locate the basic problem of canonicity*."

reception history of Deuteronomy 18,[9] although neither Blenkinsopp nor Chapman present their work this way.

Reading these works suggested that such a reception history would be a useful contribution to scholarship, for three reasons. First, the discussion in which Blenkinsopp and Chapman have participated has largely been conducted in the field of Hebrew Bible, but their arguments about the hermeneutically contested relationship between Moses and prophecy have clear implications for Early Judaism and nascent Christianity. Indeed, it became clear that scholars of Hebrew Bible,[10] Early Judaism,[11] and the New Testament[12] were involved in discussions regarding the prophet like Moses and its influence in their respective fields, but that few had synthesized the results of such work in a more comprehensive fashion.[13] I therefore embarked on a project that would investigate the history of the concept of the prophet like Moses and highlight common themes in its reception "from Jeremiah to John," to coin a phrase. My original ambition to provide a full review of the influence of the prophet like Moses has been tempered by the abundance of material. There are areas for research not addressed

---

9   Stephen B. Chapman, *The Law and the Prophets: A Study in Old Testament Canon Formation*, FAT 27 (Tübingen: Mohr Siebeck, 2000). Note in particular chapter 3, "No Prophet Like Moses?" (111–149), and the discussions of Joshua (182–185) and Jeremiah (202–209) as "prophets like Moses."

10 See, e.g., Jeffrey Stackert, *A Prophet Like Moses: Prophecy, Law, and Israelite Religion* (New York: Oxford, 2014); Reinhard Achenbach, "'A Prophet like Moses' (Deuteronomy 18:15)—'No Prophet like Moses' (Deuteronomy 34:10): Some Observations on the Relation between the Pentateuch and the Latter Prophets," in *The Pentateuch: International Perspectives on Current Research*, ed. T.B. Dozeman, K. Schmid, and B. Schwarz, FAT 78 (Tübingen: Mohr Siebeck, 2011), 435–458; Christophe Nihan, "'Moses and the Prophets': Deuteronomy 18 and the Emergence of the Pentateuch as Torah," *SEÅ* 75 (2010): 21–55.

11 See, e.g., Howard M. Teeple, *The Mosaic Eschatological Prophet*, JBLMS 10 (Philadelphia: Society of Biblical Literature, 1957); John J. Collins, *The Scepter and the Star: Messianism in Light of the Dead Sea Scrolls*, 2nd ed. (Grand Rapids: Eerdmans, 2010), 128–141; Ferdinand Dexinger, "Der 'Prophet wie Mose' in Qumran und bei den Samaritanern," in *Mélanges bibliques et orientaux en l'honneur de M Mathias Delcor*, ed. A. Caquot, S. Légasse, and M. Tardieu, AOAT 215 (Neukirchen-Vluyn: Neukirchener Verlag, 1985), 97–111; John C. Poirier, "The Endtime Return of Elijah and Moses at Qumran," *DSD* 10 (2003): 221–242.

12 See, e.g., Dale C. Allison, *The New Moses: A Matthean Typology* (Minneapolis: Fortress Press, 1993); Wayne A. Meeks, *The Prophet-King: Moses Traditions and the Johannine Christology*, NovTSup 14 (Leiden: Brill, 1967); David P. Moessner, "Luke 9:1–50: Luke's Preview of the Journey of the Prophet like Moses of Deuteronomy," *JBL* 102 (1983): 575–605.

13 Allison, *New Moses*, does the most to examine comprehensively the theme, considering figures from the Hebrew Bible and Early Judaism that were represented as "like Moses" before focusing on the gospel of Matthew.

here, such as the potential influence of Deut 18:15–22 in Isaiah,[14] Ezekiel,[15] and the particular eschatological interpretation which developed among the Samaritans.[16] The truth of Wellhausen's dictum, quoted above, has become apparent, as in this project I have begun to gain an appreciation of Deuteronomy's far-reaching influence in Second Temple literature.

A second reason for the project was the tension between the passages in Deuteronomy that speak of a prophet like Moses: Deut 18:15, 18 affirms that God's intent is to send such a prophet, but Deut 34:10–12 eulogizes Moses by speaking of him as the greatest prophet of all, such that no prophet like Moses has since arisen in Israel. In Blenkinsopp's construal, this tension was a product of debate over the terms of canonicity, or normativity in revelation. This led me to inquire to what extent such a concern for normativity characterized the reception of Deuteronomy's prophet like Moses down through the centuries. As scholars such as Benjamin Sommer have shown,[17] historical-critical analysis and reception-history can and ought to be engaged in fruitful and productive dialogue, since in many instances later readers are animated by and respond to theological motifs at work in the formation of the text. Indeed, I argue that, from its origin in the seventh century BCE through its reception in the late first century CE, the concept of the prophet like Moses is utilized in the development of a normative discourse surrounding prophetic claims in ancient Judaism. This motif of normativity provides a key that unifies the origin of this text and its reception in antiquity. The architects of this Deuteronomic law articulated a principle by which claims to be authentic bearers and recipients of the prophetic word would be assessed, namely, coordination to Moses and the Mosaic Torah. The creation of this normative framework for prophetic claims would exert enormous influence in early Judaism and nascent Chris-

---

14 See, e.g., Martin O'Kane, "Isaiah: A Prophet in the Footsteps of Moses," *JSOT* 69 (1996): 29–51. The proposal that the עבד־יהוה of Second Isaiah is a prophet like Moses, supported by Gerhard von Rad (*Old Testament Theology*, trans. D.M.G. Stalker, 2 vols. [New York: Harper & Row, 1962], 2:260–262), ought also to be mentioned. See the discussion (and full bibliography) in Gordon P. Hugenberger, "The Servant of the Lord in the 'Servant Songs' of Isaiah," in *The Lord's Anointed: Interpretation of Old Testament Messianic Texts*, ed. P.E. Satterthwaite, R.S. Hess, and G.J. Wenham (Carlisle: Paternoster, 1995), 105–140.
15 E.g., Henry McKeating, "Ezekiel the 'Prophet Like Moses'," *JSOT* 61 (1994): 97–109.
16 See, e.g., Dexinger, "Der 'Prophet wie Mose'," Meeks, *Prophet-King*, 216–257; as well as Stanley J. Isser, *The Dositheans: A Samaritan Sect in Late Antiquity*, SJLA 17 (Leiden: Brill, 1976). Samaritan sources are late (4th century CE), but they may reflect interpretations of Deut 18:15 that go back to the Second Temple period.
17 Benjamin Sommer, *Revelation and Authority: Sinai in Jewish Scripture and Tradition*, AYBRL (New Haven: Yale University Press, 2015).

tianity. It provided a mode of legitimation that could be employed, contested, qualified, or disputed; it could not, however, be ignored.[18]

This leads to the third reason for the project, which is to contribute to the understanding of the development of this normative discourse and its relation to "canon." Blenkinsopp and Chapman discussed the concept of the prophet like Moses in the context of the eventual consequence it had for the structure of the Hebrew Bible. That is, they foregrounded the question of canon formation—the origin of "the law and the prophets," considered as literary collections—in their investigations.[19] As scholarship on canon has recognized, however, this privileges a category ("canon") that is much later than Deuteronomy and is anachronistic for most, if not all, of the Second Temple period.[20] The focus on the fixing of specific literary corpora poses the danger of putting questions to texts that they are not interested in answering.[21] Left relatively unexplored in Blenkinsopp and Chapman's work was the way that, in the time preceding fixed literary corpora, the concept of the prophet like Moses contributed to the re-shaping of prophecy itself in Second Temple Judaism, functioning as a normative index for the profile and perception of prophetic claimants. Also left unexplored was the way that the concept of the prophet like Moses was interpreted by the diverse movements of Second Temple Judaism, including early Christianity. This book, therefore, does not foreground the formation of literary collections as the telos of the project, but it does represent an attempt to describe the way that bids for religious normativity actually functioned in the era preceding the canon. In that sense, this book is not about the canon, but it is about the backstory to the canon. The thesis of this monograph is that Deuteronomy's prophet like Moses is the key building block utilized in the construction of normative tradition in early Judaism and Christianity.

---

18   Even when this legitimation procedure is rejected, it is not ignored. See, e.g., *GThom* 52: "His disciples said to him, 'Twenty-four prophets have spoken in Israel, and they all spoke of you.' He said to them, 'You have disregarded the living one who is in your presence, and have spoken of the dead.'"

19   Blenkinsopp, *Prophecy and Canon*, 147, speaks of "the emergence of a first canon with the book of Deuteronomy," an expression that today would generally be regarded as infelicitous, though it is consistent with his usage of the term. Between "the first canon" and the resulting canons of rabbinic Judaism, Samaritanism, and Christianity the norm-constructing potential of the concept of the prophet like Moses is continuously mined.

20   See, e.g., Eva Mroczek, *The Literary Imagination in Jewish Antiquity* (Oxford: Oxford University Press, 2016); Molly M. Zahn, *Genres of Rewriting in Second Temple Judaism: Scribal Composition and Transmission* (Cambridge: Cambridge University Press, 2020).

21   See on this point Mroczek, *Literary Imagination*, 12.

This claim perhaps seems to be out of step with current scholarship, which emphasizes the diversity and heterogeneity of Second Temple Judaism, and downplays notions of normativity. And indeed, one point I hope to register is that the notion that normativity (or canonicity) was simply undefined and "up for grabs" in Second Temple Judaism is as problematic as the notion that the canon was settled and binding.[22] Religious normativity in Early Judaism might be compared to currency in the modern world: there are many local currencies, but standard currencies such as the Euro or the American dollar are used as benchmarks for a medium of exchange, even in the context of cultural diversity. Early Jewish movements similarly developed local and specific practices, but that does not exclude the possibility that there were dominant religious media of exchange by which they legitimized themselves more broadly. Deuteronomy inaugurates a process in which the concept of the prophet like Moses becomes a fundamental unit of this religious currency.

To put it otherwise, the scholarly quest for definitional precision, which has led to the avoidance of the terms "canon" or "Bible" for Second Temple Judaism, might have the consequence of obscuring the actual character of this time period. Such scholarship emphasizes the discontinuity between Second Temple and rabbinic Judaism, so that the eventual emergence of a canon is a curious *novum*, unrelated to earlier developments.[23] In this respect, the key chapter in this book is the one on Flavius Josephus, which explores his comments on the extent of the Jewish scriptural corpus in light of what I argue is a long-standing priestly-scribal interpretive tradition regarding the Mosaic prophetic succession. His concerns may not be not our modern questions about the development of "canon" or "Bible," but they are not completely unre-

---

22 One example is found in Albert C. Sundberg's description of the Writings as "a wide religious literature without definite bounds" (*The Old Testament of the Early Church*, HTS 20 [Cambridge, MA: Harvard University Press, 1964]), which has been applied by Barton to the Prophets as well (see John Barton, *Oracles of God: Perceptions of Ancient Prophecy in Israel after the Exile* [London: Darton, Longman & Todd, 1986], 31, 33, 91: "Sundberg's 'wide religious literature without definite bounds' has proved to be, if anything, an understatement"). For a critique, see Stephen B. Chapman, "The Canon Debate: What It Is and Why It Matters," *JTI* 4 (2010): 273–294, at 291: "Jewish Scripture may not have been absolutely 'closed,' but it was not therefore merely an 'amorphous pool' or even 'anthology.' Missing in these proposals is the literary interrelatedness found among the various writings contained within the biblical corpus." Chapman is citing Barton, *Oracles of God*, 57 and Eugene Ulrich, *The Dead Sea Scrolls and the Origins of the Bible*, SDSSRL (Grand Rapids: Eerdmans, 1999), 60.

23 Zahn, *Genres of Rewriting*, 224, having deemphasized "canon" and authority throughout her book, attributes the rabbinic canon to the influence of "Greek ideas of authorship and textual authority."

lated to the emergence of such. What is required, then, is careful consideration of the discourse around normativity that actually developed in Second Temple Judaism and detailed analysis of how it was deployed. In my view, the most promising way forward in this respect is found in Hindy Najman's articulation of the development of Mosaic Discourse.[24] The next task, then, is to summarize Najman's description of Mosaic Discourse, as well as to explain how my contribution builds upon and modifies her analysis of it.

2 Najman on Mosaic Discourse

In her monograph *Seconding Sinai*, Najman introduces the concept of Mosaic Discourse, unpacks its key features, and investigates its influence in Jubilees, the Temple Scroll, and Philo of Alexandria. Najman is convinced of the broader importance of Mosaic Discourse for the character of Early Judaism, though initially she is circumspect in her claims:

> Mosaic Discourse … comes to play an increasingly important role in the development of Second Temple Judaism and, indeed, in the nascent periods of rabbinic Judaism and early Christianity. I do not claim that the discourse of Moses is the only discourse operative in ancient Judaism, or even that it is the most important one. Rather I hope to offer a new way of characterizing ancient biblical relationships to the esteemed past, and to lay the groundwork both for studies of other developments of Mosaic Discourse, and for studies of other discourses, tied to other founders.[25]

In a footnote, Najman mentions Davidic, Solomonic, and Enochic discourses as potential rivals to Mosaic Discourse in importance.[26] In this book I take up Najman's call to study "other developments" of Mosaic Discourse. Moreover, I also make a bolder claim for its centrality: in my view, it certainly is the "most important" discourse in Second Temple Judaism, even if it is not the only one.[27]

---

24 See Zahn, *Genres of Rewriting*, 202–204, for an appreciative assessment of the way Najman's work "can help us form a more nuanced picture" of concepts of authority in Second Temple Judaism.
25 Najman, *Seconding Sinai*, 17–18.
26 Najman, *Seconding Sinai*, 17–18n34.
27 To provide just one example: though he is not mentioned often in this book, the life and letters of Paul of Tarsus are inexplicable apart from the impressive normative weight exerted by Mosaic Discourse.

The main reason that Najman makes a fairly circumscribed claim for the significance of Mosaic Discourse is that she draws its boundaries somewhat narrowly. In Najman's analysis, Mosaic Discourse is characterized by four features:[28]

(1) The text claims the authority of older traditions "by reworking and expanding [them] through interpretation";
(2) The text ascribes to itself the status of Torah;
(3) The text re-presents Sinai: it provides access to revelation through a re-creation of the Sinai experience;
(4) The text is said to be associated with or produced by Moses.

These features arise from Deuteronomy, which she describes as "the origin of Mosaic Discourse and as a model for later instances of that Discourse."[29] As the first text to deploy Mosaic voicing consciously as a key part of its bid for authoritative status, Deuteronomy radically reshapes the terms for theological debate in Early Judaism. Najman sums up Deuteronomy's contribution in the conclusion to her first, foundational chapter:

> [Deuteronomy] marks the beginning of what I am calling Mosaic Discourse. Once there is a unity status of Torah to which all law and instruction can be said to belong, once rewriting—expository, expansive and even revisionary—may be authorized through the ever-present possibility of the re-presentation of Sinai, *once all that is sacred is linked to the incomparable Moses, once all that is authoritative must be linked to Moses as a founding figure*, then the operations performed by Deuteronomists upon earlier traditions may—indeed, must—be repeated by others upon those earlier traditions and upon Deuteronomic traditions themselves. *For the Deuteronomists have established a model for the authoritative interpretation of tradition and for its authoritative application to new circumstances.*[30]

Here Najman's language is stronger ("all law and instruction ... all that is sacred ... all that is authoritative") than her earlier claims would imply. Indeed, this rhetorical flourish is closer to the view that I will defend and unpack in this book. But the key question is, what is the model that the Deuteronomists have established to which Najman refers? In Najman's analysis, it is pseudepigraphic discourse tied to Moses that is its key feature, and so she goes on to discuss

---

28 Najman, *Seconding Sinai*, 16–17.
29 Najman, *Seconding Sinai*, 19.
30 Najman, *Seconding Sinai*, 39–40.

Jubilees and the Temple Scroll as "imitations" of Deuteronomy. However, this is not the model that Deuteronomy itself actually establishes for linking later authoritative discourse to that of Moses. Deuteronomy, through the category of the prophet like Moses, provides a mechanism for later texts and traditions to claim the heritage of Mosaic Discourse without direct imitation of its formal features (i.e., pseudepigraphy).[31] This framework allows many texts and authors to be explored as exemplars of Mosaic Discourse, a point that Najman acknowledges: she speaks of a "family of texts" and concludes her book with an acknowledgement of their diversity.[32]

In this respect, it is worth noting that Najman draws the boundaries of Mosaic Discourse more narrowly than Deuteronomy does. Mosaic Discourse, according to the parameters Deuteronomy establishes, might be characterized by the following features (it seems apposite for me to "re-write" Najman's features here, which I have indicated via italics):

(1) The text claims the authority of older traditions "by reworking and expanding [them] through interpretation";
(2) The text ascribes to itself the status of Torah *and/or prophecy*;
(3) The text provides access to revelation *through a mediator ultimately authorized by God in the Horeb theophany*;
(4) The text is said to be associated with or produced by Moses *or one of his legitimate successors and interpreters.*

To unpack this briefly: first, Najman's discussion is centered on Torah, but Deuteronomy also characterizes Moses' voice as prophetic, and as foretelling the vicissitudes of Israel's history of exile and return (cf. Deut 28–33). Second, it is too restrictive to assert that the text must re-present or re-create the Horeb (= Sinai) experience; however, it must establish a clear relationship of dependence between the figure for whom it is claiming Mosaic authority and that experience. Deuteronomy subordinates its discourse to the Horeb theophany, and it allows for Mosaic successors that are linked secondarily to that theophany. Finally, the texts discussed need not be restricted to those explicitly associated with Moses or Mosaic "authorship" (or transcription, in the case of Jubilees). Rather, it can also be associated with protagonists clearly identified as

---

31 Indeed, it would be fair to conclude that the authors of Deuteronomy do not want later texts to imitate its use of Mosaic Discourse directly: their attitude is "do as I say, not as I do" (cf Deut 4:2; 13:1). Jubilees and the Temple Scroll depart from Deuteronomy's model insofar as they deploy an even more authoritative angelic or directly divine revelatory mode of communication. Deuteronomy's model subordinates the prophet to Moses, whereas the pseudepigraphic model attempts to get "behind" Deuteronomy to the very words of Yhwh.

32 Najman, *Seconding Sinai*, 137: "One should expect this variation to be immense, far greater than the range I have considered in this book."

one of Moses' duly authorized successors, the prophets like him. Indeed, rather than consider texts that focus on Moses' own voice, all texts that claim to provide access to the voices of the prophet(s) like Moses can be considered to be participants in this Discourse. Thus, in this book I take up Najman's call to discuss other developments of Mosaic Discourse by considering how figures other than Moses (Jeremiah, Joshua, and Jesus, to name a few) are represented as heirs and interpreters of Mosaic tradition.

The phrase Mosaic Discourse will thus often occur on the following pages, but rarely will the speaker in view actually be Moses. Rather than employing contested canon-terminology, about which no agreement appears to be imminent, I intend in this book to explore the way in which Mosaic Discourse functioned as a legitimating framework in Early Judaism and Christianity. The concept of the prophet like Moses thus has a robust after-life, so much so that the following work will be limited to key moments in its story. This leads to a discussion of the limitations that I have established in order to decide which texts to consider in this study.

3   Method and Overview

It is important to be clear about what this book is and is not. Insofar as the book is about Moses, the Moses it is about is Deuteronomy's idealized and archetypal portrait of Moses. That is, the chapters below do not provide a full review of the concept of Mosaic prophecy or of the use of Mosaic typologies; such a project would extend the scope of the work beyond what is feasible. The following study interacts with the history of only that Mosaic prophecy that originates in and is dependent on the thought of Deut 18:9–22. Furthermore, in texts subsequent to Deut 18:9–22, my primary interest is not in Moses as *type*, but in Moses as a *standard* for authentic prophecy. The representation of Moses as a type is a literary device whereby narrative elements are designed to recall the life of Moses; one example is the gospel of Matthew's story of the baby Jesus' nearly fatal end at the hands of an evil king, which recalls Exodus 1–2. This investigation prescinds from such examples; thus, many texts that one might expect to be considered in a project on Moses (Matthew's gospel is a prominent example) are not treated. To focus on Moses as a *standard* is to examine the way the category of a prophet like Moses is invoked as a criterion of authentic prophecy in Second Temple Judaism and nascent Christianity.

Now to briefly summarize what the book is. The story of the prophet like Moses unfolds in several stages. In Part 1, "Foundations: The Genealogical Model of Mosaic Prophecy," I trace three foundational moments in the story.

First, after sketching the scriptural and scholarly context for Deuteronomy's portrayal of Moses as prophet (ch. 1), in chapter 2 I contrast the relationship between Moses and prophecy in Numbers 11–12 with that found in Deut 18:9–22. The argument, in brief, is that the charismatic model of prophecy assumed in Numbers 11–12 (in which it is associated with the presence of the divine spirit, is not subject to human or institutional control, and is available at Yhwh's sole prerogative) is deeply qualified, if not rejected, by Deuteronomy's stipulation that prophets must be like Moses and its prohibition of non-Mosaic claims to revelatory authority. The comparison with Numbers 11–12 allows the distinctiveness of Deuteronomy's genealogical model of prophecy entailed in the creation of the concept of the prophet like Moses to be delineated with clarity. In Deuteronomy's genealogical model, all prophecy, whether of Moses or of his successors, is originally rooted in the very words of God spoken at Horeb. Deuteronomy 18:9–22 thus creates an office of Mosaic prophecy as a part of its (perhaps theoretical and ideal) polity in order to "centralize" revelation and place strict limits on authorized divinatory specialists.

Second, in chapters 3 and 4, I trace the first and most influential interpretation of Deuteronomy's concept of the prophet like Moses, which occurs in the exilic, Deuteronomistic (Dtr) creation of the concept of Yhwh's "servants the prophets." This interpretation transforms a Mosaic office into a Mosaic succession. It is foundational insofar as it connects the concept of the prophet like Moses to a historiographic project. In the Dtr understanding, Mosaic prophecy consisted of an episodic, not continuous, succession (notable ruptures occur between Moses and Samuel, as well between Jeremiah and Zechariah). Jeremiah in particular becomes a Mosaic prophet *par excellence* as the final prophet in the pre-exilic Mosaic prophetic succession.

Third, in chapter 5, I argue that Deut 34:10–12 represents a further periodization of Mosaic prophecy. The final editors of Deuteronomy divide prophetic ages into the Mosaic and the post-Mosaic eras, the latter of which is now clearly marked as inferior to the former. This lays the foundation for the periodization of Mosaic prophecy traced in Part II, and provides an initial stimulus towards an eschatological interpretation of Deut 18:15–18.

In Part II, "Prophets Past and Future: The Periodization of Mosaic Prophecy," I explore how the construal of Mosaic prophecy in Second Temple Judaism sheds new light on the old question of the so-called cessation of prophecy (ch. 6). I discuss the influence of the Mosaic prophetic succession in texts such as Mal 3:22–24 and Ben Sira's *Laus Patrum* (ch. 7), the historiographic tradition and the Qumran texts (ch. 8), the writings of Flavius Josephus (ch. 9), and the early Christian historiographic work Luke-Acts (ch. 10). In these texts, I trace a priestly-scribal interpretive tradition in which the Mosaic prophetic succession is temporally delimited, increasingly aligned with a corpus of written scriptures, and occasionally expected to return in the eschatological future. That is, in these texts, the Mosaic prophetic succession (not prophecy as such, it should be noted) is considered to be a feature of the past and the future. In terms of the past, the ruptures in Mosaic prophecy attested in the Dtr corpus are forgotten, as a continuous history is posited for the Mosaic prophetic succession, stretching from the time of Moses to the Persian period. In terms of the future, various returns of Mosaic prophecy are contemplated: in the person of Elijah (so Malachi and Ben Sira), in a restoration of a national prophetic office (so 1 Maccabees), and in the earliest explicit eschatological interpretation of Deut 18:15 (so 1QS; 4Q175), which informs the early Christian portrayal of Jesus and the apostles (so Luke-Acts). It is in this time-period (and not in the scriptural narratives in which they figure prominently) that Joshua and Elijah become prophets like Moses in Deuteronomy's sense: Joshua is portrayed as the first prophet like Moses and represents Mosaic prophecy's scriptural past; Elijah is expected to restore the institution of Mosaic prophecy and represents its eschatological future.

Finally, in Part III, "Mosaic Prophecy and Logos-Theology: The Triumph of Mosaic Discourse," I consider two authors in which the charismatic model of prophecy is re-asserted, now combined with Deuteronomy's concept of the prophet like Moses, namely, Philo of Alexandria (ch. 11) and the anonymous author of the Fourth Gospel (ch. 12). I show that in these authors the supremacy of Mosaic Discourse as the legitimating norm *sine qua non* shapes their understanding of the vertical axis of divine-human communication. For Philo, this means there are in fact no prophets like Moses; for John, this means that Moses alone provides a commensurate scriptural touchstone for the claims the gospel develops about Jesus.

In sum, this book traces the origin and deployment of the concept of the prophet like Moses from the seventh century BCE to the end of the first century CE. I am mindful that the story of this passage and its interpretation does not end here. The rabbis have their own strategies for positioning themselves as heirs of the prophets and authoritative arbiters of Mosaic tradition. Moreover, Deuteronomy 18:15 will also go on to play a role in Islamic tradition—which puts its own unique twist on the passage, as the stipulation that the prophet will arise "from among your brothers" is taken to imply his Ishmaelite origin.[33] The norm-constructing potential of this text has continued to be mined through

---

33 See *Qurʾān* Sūrah 2:129; 7:157; and David E. Singh, "Muḥammad, 'the Prophet like Moses'?", *Journal of Ecumenical Studies* 43 (2008): 545–561 (at 556–557).

the centuries. My original aspiration to provide a full review of its influence has been tempered by the abundance of evidence. Nevertheless, I hope that this book will be a contribution to the study of prophecy, and the different forms that prophecy can take, particularly when subjected to the pressure of conformity to a normative tradition.

PART 1

Foundations: The Genealogical Model of Mosaic Prophecy

∴

CHAPTER 1

Is Moses among the Prophets?

1 Introduction

"Is Moses among the prophets?"[1] The very question seems strange, because of the ubiquity of the ascription of prophetic status to Moses in the monotheistic tradition. Yet, scholars who have considered the characterization of Moses in the Hebrew Bible have often been struck at the rarity of the ascription of prophetic status to him.[2] In fact, only two passages in the Hebrew Bible *explicitly* designate Moses as a prophet (נביא), Deut 18:15–18 (where the title occurs twice) and Deut 34:10–12—and, as we will see, there is some debate about Moses' prophetic status even in these passages. This book is about the origin, history, and influence of the coordination between Moses and prophecy posited in Deuteronomy's creation of the concept of the prophet like Moses. My fundamental thesis is that this coordination arises from Deuteronomy's concern for normativity in revelation, and that this feature of Deuteronomy's thought reverberates in the usages and interpretation of the passage throughout the centuries. This construction of a Mosaic norm for prophecy is a development of tremendous importance in the monotheistic tradition, ultimately resulting in the binomial phrase "the law and the prophets" becoming basic structural components of the Jewish and Christian canons. In this book I intend—as best as I can, conscious of the further terrain that could be navigated—to unpack the history of a revolutionary idea, Deuteronomy's concept of the prophet like Moses.

In this introductory chapter, I will provide some foundational data on the characterization of Moses in the Hebrew Bible, setting Deuteronomy's ascription of prophetic status to him in a broad context, and outline how my

---

1 Thomas C. Römer begins a recent study with this question, noting that it "may sound astonishing." See his "Moses, Israel's First Prophet, and the Formation of the Deuteronomistic and Prophetic Libraries," in *Israelite Prophecy and the Deuteronomistic History: Portrait, Reality, and the Formation of a History*, ed. Mignon R. Jacobs and Raymond F. Person Jr., AIL 14 (Atlanta: Society of Biblical Literature, 2013), 129–146.
2 Lothar Perlitt, "Mose als Prophet," *EvT* 31 (1971): 588–608, formulated the problem this way (590–591): "Mose spielt bei den Propheten keine Rolle, die Propheten spielen bei 'Mose' (im Pentateuch) keine Rolle." Christophe Nihan, " 'Moses and the Prophets': Deuteronomy 18 and the Emergence of the Pentateuch as Torah," *SEÅ* 75 (2010): 21–55, also calls attention to this issue, but suggests Perlitt's formulation is "too stark" (at 22n2).

approach is distinctive vis-à-vis two major scholarly treatments. I will also offer a few comments on the absolute historical origin of the idea of Moses as prophet, though this will take us into murky and debated areas. The discussion, however, will allow me to clarify the particular focus of this investigation.

2 Designations for Moses in the Hebrew Bible

2.1 Overview of the Data

The rarity of the ascription of prophetic status to Moses in the Hebrew Bible constitutes an intriguing conundrum. There are no straightforward, uncontroversial applications of the title נביא to Moses in the Hebrew Bible. Hosea 12:14 (Eng. 12:13) is perhaps the closest there is:

ובנביא העלה יהוה את־ישראל ממצרים ובנביא נשמר

> By a prophet the LORD brought Israel up from Egypt, and by a prophet he was guarded.[3]

The reference is implicit: Moses is probably meant but is not named in this passage (or, indeed, in the whole book of Hosea).[4] There are just three other references to Moses as a נביא in the Hebrew Bible, all in Deuteronomy. They are set out in Table 1 below, with the speaker indicated in parentheses. The scarcity of references to Moses' prophetic status is particularly surprising in view of the characterization of Moses in later Jewish and Christian tradition, in which he is often designated as a prophet and said to have prophesied.[5] The collocation "Moses the prophet" (משה הנביא) never occurs in the Hebrew Bible; nor is Moses ever the subject of the verb "to prophesy" (נבא). What was the nature of the ancient Judean scribal sensitivities that made "Jeremiah the prophet" (to provide one example) a natural designation, while "Moses the prophet" was not?

---

[3] Translations are based on the NRSV, with occasional modifications.
[4] Moses is named only once in the Book of the Twelve, in Mic 6:4. Nihan, "Moses and the Prophets," 33n30, therefore advocates caution in using this passage to develop Moses' portrait.
[5] Among many examples, see Wis 11:1; Philo, *Leg* 3.173; *Mos* 1.57, 2.3; *Assumption of Moses* 1:5, 3:11, 11:16; *Martyrdom and Ascension of Isaiah* 3:9; 2 Macc 1:29; John 5:46; Acts 26:22, 28:23; Hebr 3:5.

IS MOSES AMONG THE PROPHETS?

TABLE 1 Moses' prophetic status in deuteronomy

Deut 18:15 (Moses)	Deut 18:18a (Yhwh)	Deut 34:10 (post-Dtr editor)
נביא מקרבך מאחיך **כמני יקים** לך יהוה אלהיך אליו תשמעון	**נביא אקים** להם מקרב אחיהם **כמוך** ונתתי דברי בפיו	ולא־**קם נביא** עוד בישראל **כמשה** אשר ידעו יהוה פנים אל־פנים
The LORD your God **will raise up** for you a **prophet like me** from among you, from your people, to him you will listen.	**I will raise up** for them a **prophet like you** from among their own people, and I will put my words in his mouth	There has not **arisen** again a **prophet** in Israel **like Moses**, whom the LORD knew face to face.

Far outstripping any other epithet for Moses in the Hebrew Bible is the designation of Moses as the עבד יהוה, the "servant of Yhwh," which occurs forty times in various forms.[6] Other than this, the only designation to occur with some frequency is איש האלוהים, "man of God," which occurs six times, in mostly late texts.[7] Moses is once called a כהן, "priest" (Ps 99:6), highlighting his role as intercessor,[8] and once God's בחיר, "chosen one" (Ps 106:23). Prophet, נביא, occurs at most five times, in the texts cited above, a profile limited to Hos 12:14 and Deuteronomy. This data suggests that throughout the Hebrew Bible—in

---

6   The titles are: (1) משה עבד יהוה, which occurs 18× (Deut 34:5; Josh 1:1, 13, 15; 8:31, 33; 11:12; 12:6 [2×]; 13:8; 14:7; 18:7; 22:2, 4, 5; 2 Kgs 18:12; 2 Chr 1:3; 24:6); (2) משה עבדו, which occurs 5× (Exod 14:31, Josh 9:24, 11:15; 1 Kgs 8:56; Ps 105:26); (3) משה עבדי/עבדי משה, which occurs 6× (Num 12:7, 8; Josh 1:2, 7; 2 Kgs 21:8; Mal 3:22); (4) משה עבדך, which occurs 7× (Exod 4:10; Num 11:11; Deut 3:24; 1 Kgs 8:53; Neh 1:7, 8; 9:14); and (5) משה עבד האלוהים, which occurs 4× (Dan 9:11; Neh 10:30; 1 Chr 6:34; 2 Chr 24:9). See George W. Coats, *Moses: Heroic Man, Man of God*, JSOT-SupS 57 (Sheffield: JSOT Press, 1988), 182–185; Walther Zimmerli and Joachim Jeremias, *The Servant of God*, SBT 20 (Naperville, Ill.: A.R. Allenson, 1965), 21–22.

   The title is translated variously in the manuscripts of the LXX. Most common is παῖς (17×: Josh 1:7, 13; 9:24; 11:12, 15; 12:6 [1×; MT has 2×]; 13:8; 14:7; 18:7; 22:2, 5; Neh 1:7, 8; 1 Chr 6:34; 2 Chr 1:3; 24:9; Dan 9:11). Other translations include θεράπων (Exod 4:10; 14:31; Num 11:11; 12:7,8; Deut 3:24; Josh 1:2; 9:2 [2×: 8:31, 33 MT]); δοῦλος (1 Kgs 8:53, 56; 2 Kgs 18:12; 21:8; Neh 9:14; 10:30; Ps 104 [105]:26; Dan 9:11 [Theodotion]; Mal 3:22); οἰκέτης (Deut 34:5); ἀνθρώπου τοῦ θεοῦ (2 Chr 24:6).

7   Deut 33:1; Josh 14:6; Ps 90:1; 1 Chr 23:14; 2 Chr 30:10; Ezra 3:2. See Coats, *Moses*, 179–182.

8   As is clear from the parallelism the verse establishes: "Moses and Aaron were among his priests, Samuel also was among those who called on his name. They cried to the LORD, and he answered them." For the parallel between Moses and Samuel as effective intercessors, see also Jer 15:1.

various documents, early and late—"servant of God/Yhwh" was regarded as the most appropriate designation for Moses, all other epithets occurring only infrequently.

2.2 Moses' Prophetic Status in the Pentateuch

This survey of the data raises two initial questions. First, are the comparisons between Moses and "a prophet" in Deuteronomy (all using the preposition כ) designations of Moses as a prophet? Second, if this is answered in the affirmative, why in the Pentateuch does only Deuteronomy so designate Moses? Regarding the first: because of the paucity of data associating Moses with prophecy, some scholars have argued that "prophet" is not an appropriate title for Moses even in Deut 18:15, 18; 34:10. David Petersen suggests various alternatives:

> Deut 18:15 offers no unequivocal claim that Moses was thought to be a prophet. This verse, as the similar formulation in v. 18, may well mean that the prophet to come will be like Moses to the extent that people are to obey him—as they were supposed to obey Moses—or to the extent that the prophet is one of them—as was Moses. I think the latter is the more likely option.[9]

It is true that it is possible to understand the כמני, "like me," of Deut 18:15 as synonymous to the immediately preceding description of the prophet, מקרבך מאחיך, "from among you, from your own people." If this is the only sense in which the prophet is like Moses, it is not certain that Moses is here being given the title נביא.[10] On this read, it is *possible*, but not *necessary*, to understand Moses as a prophet in this passage.

It is, however, unlikely that "like me" (כמני) should be understood merely as a further explication of "from your midst, from your brothers" (מקרב מאחיך). In anticipation of the full discussion in the following chapter, three brief observations establish the initial probability of the hypothesis that Moses is under-

---

9   David L. Petersen, "The Ambiguous Role of Moses as Prophet," in *Israel's Prophets and Israel's Past: Essays on the Relationship of Prophetic Texts and Israelite History in Honor of John H. Hayes*, ed. Brad E. Kelle and Megan B. Moore, LHB/OTS 446 (New York: T&T Clark, 2006), 311–324; here 312.

10 See the questions posed by Jeffrey Stackert, *A Prophet Like Moses: Prophecy, Law, and Israelite Religion* (New York: Oxford, 2014), 37; see also Jeffrey H. Tigay, *Deuteronomy = [Devarim]: The Traditional Hebrew Text with the New JPS Translation*, JPSTC 5 (Philadelphia: Jewish Publication Society, 1996), 175: "the Torah never directly calls Moses a prophet."

stood as a prophet here. First, the etiology of prophecy offered in Deut 18:16–18 looks back to the authorization of Moses in Deut 5:23–31, and therefore grounds the appointments of Moses and the prophet like him respectively on the request of Israel at Horeb. Second, the prophet is said to be the one in whose mouth Yhwh will put words (18:18), and the bulk of Deuteronomy involves Moses' proclamation of Yhwh's words. Finally, if one resists the implication of Deut 18:15, 18 that Moses is a נביא, Deut 34:10 is particularly strange and inexplicable, for here Moses is definitely cast among the company of the prophets, even as his superiority over all other prophets is asserted.[11] As a preliminary hypothesis, therefore, it is safe to assert that Moses is called a prophet in Deut 18:15, 18; 34:10.

This leads to the second question above: why is Moses not designated a prophet in the rest of the Pentateuch? Why *only* Deuteronomy? The question of the relationship between Deuteronomy's characterization of Moses and that of other Pentateuch traditions has been variously construed. In his *Old Testament Theology*, Gerhard von Rad gave attention to the view of Moses in the Pentateuchal sources, representing Deuteronomy's portrayal as the logical culmination of earlier characterizations in the epic tradition.[12] In J Moses has a "prophetic commission" and speaks with a "prophetic style" (he uses the phrase "thus says the LORD;" cf. Exod 7:17; 8:1; 9:13).[13] Von Rad also cites Moses' role as intercessor, "for intercession was plainly the prophet's office *par excellence* in olden times."[14] Nevertheless von Rad settles on the designation "inspired shepherd" for the role of Moses in J. The role of Moses as נביא becomes more prominent in E; indeed, according to von Rad this is the first source to so explic-

---

11 Petersen, "Ambiguous Role," wants to downplay any characterization of Moses as a prophet in the Hebrew Bible. He therefore struggles particularly with Deut 34:10–12 (here 316):

> Deuteronomy 34 seems to imply that Moses was a prophet. The initial verse in this late coda to Deuteronomy, however, presents problems. First, the singularity of Moses, also attested in Num 12:6–8, is affirmed here .... Deut 34 challenges the expectation that may have been established by Deut 18 [note, Petersen says "may have been" because of his reading that Moses is *not* a prophet in Deut 18] .... What one might ... have expected to happen on the basis of Deut 18 has, according to Deut 34, not transpired. There has been no succession of prophets like Moses.

This is an over-reading of the tension between Deut 18 and 34. Tigay, *Deuteronomy*, 175, says that even Deut 34:10 does not claim prophetic status for Moses, but on this reading the verse is scarcely comprehensible.

12 Gerhard von Rad, *Old Testament Theology*, trans. D.M.G. Stalker, 2 vols. (New York: Harper & Row, 1962), 1:289–296.
13 von Rad, *Theology*, 1:292.
14 von Rad, *Theology*, 1:292, at footnote 9 he points to Gen 20:7; 1 Sam 7:5; 12:19, 23; 2 Kgs 19:1.

itly designate Moses—but his appeal is to Deut 34:10,[15] which we will see is from the hand of a late editor, not one of the early sources. Von Rad then comes to Deuteronomy:

> Deuteronomy's is the most rounded portrait of Moses, and probably has the most emphatic theological stamp on it. In it too Moses is נביא: indeed, he is the chief of the prophets (Deut 18:8 [sic]), in that he is the archetype and norm of all prophets, through whose coming Jahweh guaranteed the constant connexion between himself and his people.[16]

For von Rad, then, Deuteronomy's characterization of Moses represented a culmination of his prophetic profile in the earlier tradition.

More recently, Jeffrey Stackert has argued that Moses is a prophet in all the Pentateuchal sources: "the basic and persistent portrayal of Moses in each of the Torah sources is prophetic."[17] Stackert offers three reasons to consider Moses a prophet in each source: "the descriptions of his prophetic origins, his prophetic *modus operandi*, and his prophetic legitimation."[18] With respect to the first, Stackert argues that Moses' call narrative is prophetic.[19] As for the second, Moses is a conduit of divine messages, just as prophets were. And, lastly, Moses requires authenticating signs, which is a typical feature of ancient Near Eastern and Israelite prophets (Stackert, however, restricts this motif to J and E).

It is not to be doubted that there are prophetic features of Moses' career, as represented in the whole Torah; but it is at least questionable whether such overlap between Moses' activity and that of prophets constitutes a designation of Moses as a prophet. First, the comparative ancient Near Eastern evidence, helpfully summarized by Stackert, renders the identification of Israel's found-

---

15 von Rad, *Theology*, 1:293.
16 von Rad, *Theology*, 1:294.
17 Stackert, *Prophet like Moses*, 39.
18 Stackert, *Prophet like Moses*, 55; full discussion 55–69.
19 Stackert, *Prophet like Moses*, 55–62. The argument is largely based on the conformity of Moses' call narratives in Exod 3–4, 6–7 to a supposed "Gattung" or type scene. Stackert identifies six such narratives, four of which he claims (56) "stand unambiguously as examples of specifically prophetic commissioning." (Though he does not specify, presumably that of Gideon [Jdg 6:11b–17] and Second Isaiah [Isa 40:1–11] are excluded.) Of these four, only two (Jer 1:4–10; Ezek 1:1–3:11) explicitly designate their main character as נביא (the others are Exod 3:1–12; Isa 6:1–13). Since Stackert admits that such narratives are used for figures other than prophets (such as Gideon), the probative value of the supposed call narrative genre for establishing Moses' prophetic status is limited.

ing figure with the prophetic function dubious at best. Stackert argues that the various authentication procedures attested at Mari "emphasize the relatively low prestige and reliability conventionally ascribed to Mari prophets and prophecy."[20] More relevant than Mari to the formation of the Pentateuch is neo-Assyrian prophecy, which according to Stackert is also "viewed with suspicion"; indeed, with respect to various modes of divination, it "falls at the bottom of the hierarchy."[21] In the next chapter, we will see that the ambiguity attendant with prophecy also cautioned some biblical authors from associating Moses too closely with it.[22]

But ambiguity is not the most pressing reason to doubt this identification. In texts from the ancient Near East, "prophets" are consistently portrayed as functionaries with particular roles in an established social order: they are variously related to cult and king, and offer divine oracles for the welfare of society.[23] The stark difference from Moses' story is immediately apparent: Moses has no "official" role within Israelite society: he is not prophet, priest, or king. Rather, from the perspective of ancient Israel, Moses is associated with the founding acts that created the people.[24] As we have seen above, the most common des-

---

20   Stackert, *Prophet like Moses*, 48.
21   Stackert, *Prophet like Moses*, 49.
22   This is also the concern of Tigay, *Deuteronomy*, 175: "Apparently ... the title 'prophet' was felt to be too narrow and too restricted, at least in the popular mind, to oracular, divinatory, and magical functions ... to be applied to a figure as exalted and comprehensive as Moses."
23   See Martti Nissinen, "The Socio-religious Role of the Neo-Assyrian Prophets," in *Prophecy in its Ancient Near Eastern Context: Mesopotamian, Biblical, and Arabian Perspectives*, ed. Martti Nissinen, SBLSymS 13 (Atlanta: Society of Biblical Literature, 2000), 89–114; idem, "What is Prophecy?: An Ancient Near Eastern Perspective," in *Inspired Speech: Prophecy in the Ancient Near East: Essays in Honour of Herbert B. Huffmon*, ed. John Kaltner and Louis Stulman (London: T&T Clark, 2004), 17–37.
24   Coats, *Moses*, 185, argues that the tradition evinces a conscious avoidance of depicting Moses in terms of "any one particular office": "The epithets in the Moses tradition appear, therefore, to support the contention ... that the tradition depicts Moses, not in terms of prophet, priest, or king, portraits drawn from institutional offices operative in the time of the storyteller, but as the hero of the story, Israel's story." See also Petersen's conclusion ("Ambiguous Role," 323): "Moses is clearly not a model for any role within ancient Israelite society. He was neither paradigmatic prophet, priest, nor ruler. Rather, he was deemed to be the proverbial 'cult founder,' of which there can be only one." This statement is true for pre-Deuteronomic sources; with Deuteronomy, *contra* Petersen, Moses also becomes "paradigmatic prophet." Stackert, *Prophet like Moses*, 37, recognizes this point, as he says (emphasis original): Moses "functions in many ways beyond the stereotypically prophetic. Moses is, for example, the leader of the Israelite people, much like a monarch. He is also a priestly figure, performing sacrifices (Lev 8:14–23), declaiming *tôrôt*, and blessing the people (Exod 39:43). Moses is even portrayed as a heroic and saintly figure: he is at turns

ignation of Moses emphasizes his proximity to Israel's God: he is the "servant of Yhwh." This first occurs as a title for Moses in Exod 14:31, at the conclusion of the narrative of the crossing of the יַם־סוּף: "So the people feared the LORD and believed in the LORD and in his servant Moses (ויאמינו ביהוה ובמשה עבדו וייראו העם את־יהוה)."[25] The title associates Moses very closely with Yhwh: to believe in Yhwh is also to believe in "Moses his servant." It gives Moses a high status indeed, as the phrase אמן ב־ is ordinarily used only for God.[26] It is noteworthy that this title first occurs immediately after the narrative of the greatest miracle with which Moses is associated. This roots the title in the Exodus tradition, in which the lexeme עבד has tremendous thematic significance.[27]

In von Rad's analysis, Deuteronomy's characterization of Moses as a prophet represents an organic development that makes explicit what is already present in the earlier tradition. In Stackert's, it is an uncontroversial designation basic to all the Torah sources. In contrast to these assessments, my analysis will focus on what is innovative in Deuteronomy's construal of Moses as a prophet. It is not simply an organic development, nor is it a feature Deuteronomy shares with all the Torah sources. Rather, Deuteronomy's creation of the prophet like Moses constitutes a radical reshaping of the tradition of Mosaic prophecy.

---

vigorous advocate for the oppressed (Exod 2:11–12), incomparable wonder worker (Deut 34:10–12), and special object of YHWH's favor (Exod 33:17), all while also presenting as the humblest man on earth (Num 12:3). The label 'prophet' may thus be a *necessary* descriptor of Moses, but it is hardly a *sufficient* one."

25 Moses' self-designation as "your servant" in Exod 4:10 is not a titular usage. See *HALOT* 2:775.

26 The only other human figures to be the object of אמן ב־ in coordination with Yhwh are the prophets considered collectively, in Jehoshaphat's exhortation (2 Chron 20:20, האמינו ביהוה אלהיכם ותאמנו האמינו בנביאי והצליחו). The parallel is noted by Stephen B. Chapman, *The Law and the Prophets: a Study in Old Testament Canon Formation*, FAT 27 (Tübingen: Mohr Siebeck, 2000), 127. The phrase is also used of Moses in Exod 19:9; *Mekhilta Bahodesh* 2:105–106 (trans. Lauterbach) interprets: "'And may also believe thee forever,' in thee and also in the prophets that are to arise after thee." Other than this the only positive usage of the phrase with a human as an object occurs with Achish's trust in David (1 Sam 27:12).

27 The narrative is one in which Moses as the "servant" of Yhwh opposes Pharaoh and his "servants" (Exod 5:21; 7:10, 20; 8:3, 5, 7, 17, 20, 25, 27; 9:14, 20, 30, 34; 10:1, 6, 7; 11:3, 8; 12:30; 14:5), who have "enslaved" the people of Israel (Exod 1:13, 14; 2:23; 6:5, 9; 14:5; cf. 5:15, 16). Yhwh takes note of Israel's plight and "servitude" (Exod 6:5–7), and the divine plan for liberation includes an insistence that Israel must "serve" Yhwh in the wilderness (Exod 3:12; 4:23; 7:16, 26; 8:16; 9:1, 13; 10:3, 7, 8, 11, 24, 26; 12:31). Upon Israel's deliverance, Egypt is memorialized as the בית עבדים, "house of slavery" (Exod 13:3, 14; 20:2; Deut 5:6; 6:12; 7:8; 8:14; 13:5, 10; Josh 24:17; Jdg 6:8; Jer 34:13; Mic 6:4). The ubiquity of the lexeme עבד in the Exodus tradition is impressive, and this list of references is not exhaustive.

Deuteronomy inherits the concept of Mosaic prophecy, but also transforms it. Before defending this claim, however, it is necessary briefly to consider possible antecedents for Deuteronomy's view of Moses as prophet. This takes us back to the only other clue we have—Hos 12:14—and the disputed question of Deuteronomy's northern provenance.

3   The Obscure Origins of Mosaic Prophecy

> If we were to unravel all the traditions about Moses, tracing the different threads back to their beginnings, we might well find elements of a prophetic profile …. But the origins of the Moses tradition are, as they say, lost in the midst of time.[28]

As noted in the introduction, this book does not present a comprehensive analysis of Moses-typology or traditions about Moses. It does not even offer a full account of Mosaic prophecy, since important passages such as Exod 3–4 can be reasonably construed to provide Moses with a prophetic profile, even if they do not call him a prophet. Rather, in this book I tell the story of one limited or specific model of Mosaic prophecy, that of Deuteronomy's prophet like Moses. This Deuteronomic model of Mosaic prophecy circumscribes the prophetic function fairly narrowly: the prophet is not charismatic wonder-worker, but legislator and oracular guide.[29]

For this reason, I do not treat figures such as Samuel or Elijah in detail, though it has been argued that both are prophets like Moses.[30] The pre-deuter-

---

28 Joseph Blenkinsopp, *A History of Prophecy in Israel*, rev. and enl. (Louisville, Ky: Westminster John Knox Press, 1996), 50.

29 Throughout the book, I will follow the scholarly convention that distinguishes the adjectives "Deuteronomic" (also "D," pertaining to the pre-exilic law code) and "Deuteronomistic" (also "Dtr," pertaining to the historiographical and theological project of the late pre-exilic, exilic, and early post-exilic period).

30 For Samuel, see Roy L. Heller, *Power, Politics, and Prophecy: The Character of Samuel and the Deuteronomistic Evaluation of Prophecy*, LHB/OTS 440 (London: T&T Clark, 2006), 42–43, 47, 69–70. In his monograph, Heller does not distinguish sufficiently between the pre-D portrait of Samuel and the later Dtr perspective. On Elijah, Robert P. Carroll, "The Elijah-Elisha Sagas: Some Remarks on Prophetic Succession in Ancient Israel," *VT* 19 (1969): 400–415, argues with respect to the narratives of Elijah and Elisha (at 413): "part of the motivation behind the selection principles employed by the compiler of the volumes was the desire to present prophetic material shaped by the model of the Mosaic prophet. Therefore the sagas might almost be regarded as an experiment, or model, based on a dogma of the prophet being like Moses." Carroll presents considerable evidence concern-

onomic or non-deuteronomic character of the sources about Samuel, Elijah, and Elisha (which have, particularly in the case of Samuel, been overlaid with a Dtr layer) means that it is simply impossible for them to be prophets like Moses in the Deuteronomic sense, because the concept was not yet invented when the traditions about these figures originated.[31] Indeed, the legends surrounding such individuals reflect elements of the earliest prophetic movement in Israel, which was associated with prophetic conventicles (the so-called "sons of the prophets") and violent Yhwh-alone insurgency movements. Such "war prophets" and Nazirites may have looked back to figures such as Moses, Aaron, and Miriam as exemplars of charismatic divine action, particularly as justifications for violent acts.[32]

It is only late in the history of the northern kingdom that we encounter the earliest literary expression of the idea that Moses was a prophet, in the book of Hosea.[33] This is intriguing as a potential background for Deuteronomy's conception, as Hosea and Deuteronomy have long been linked in scholarship,[34] and the theory of a northern provenance for Deuteronomy or *Urdeuterono-*

---

ing Elijah's presentation as a Mosaic prophet (cf 408–413). However, the Mosaic typology employed is distinct from and, in my view, earlier than Deuteronomy's attempt to offer a bounded and normative construal of the phenomenon of prophecy. Elijah and Elisha might be described as Mosaic prophets, but not prophets like Moses in the Deuteronomic sense of the phrase.

31   The date of the Elijah narratives is highly contested, but their non-deuteronomic character (sacrifice offered at Carmel, no mention of the sin of Jeroboam) is generally recognized. For an early date (early 8th century BCE), see John Gray, *I & II Kings: A Commentary*, 2nd rev. ed, OTL (Louisville: Westminster/John Knox Press, 1971), 372. Gray (376) also argues that these narratives draw on early Moses traditions.

32   See the pre-deuteronomic Amos 2:11 for the association between "prophets" and Nazirites. On early war prophecy, see Blenkinsopp, *History of Prophecy in Israel*, 48–64. On Moses, Aaron, and Miriam, see Mic 6:4: "For I brought you up from the land of Egypt, and redeemed you from the house of slavery; and I sent before you Moses, Aaron, and Miriam." The relative equality of Moses, Aaron, and Miriam as agents of liberation is striking. One wonders if the three were already considered siblings at the time this was written.

33   See Blenkinsopp, *A History of Prophecy in Israel*, 50: "Hosea seems to have been the first to represent Moses as a prophet"; Hans W. Wolff, *Hosea: A Commentary on the Book of the Prophet Hosea*, trans. Gary Stansell, Hermeneia (Philadelphia: Fortress, 1974 [German original 1965]), "Apparently Moses was first called a 'prophet' by Hosea and his circle of supporters." In my view, A.A. MacIntosh, *A Critical and Exegetical Commentary on Hosea*, ICC (Edinburgh: T&T Clark, 1997), 513, correctly distinguishes between "the oldest literary reference to Moses as a prophet" and the origin of the concept itself ("That Hosea should have coined this title for Moses is questionable (so Rudolph *contra* Wolff)").

34   See the summary of scholarship in Brad E. Kelle, "Hosea 4–14 in Twentieth-Century Scholarship," *CBR* 8 (2010): 314–375, at 326–327.

mium still has adherents.³⁵ Moses' "debut" as a prophet in literature occurs in Hosea 12:14 (Eng. 12:13). The context is important: some relationship with the preceding verse is clearly intended, though the precise significance of this is obscure:

ויברח יעקב שדה ארם ויעבד ישראל באשה ובאשה שמר
ובנביא העלה יהוה את־ישראל ממצרים ובנביא נשמר

> Jacob fled to the land of Aram, there Israel served for a wife, and for a wife he guarded [sheep].
> By a prophet the LORD brought Israel up from Egypt, and by a prophet he was guarded.
>   Hos 12:13–14 [Eng. 12:12–13]

This first reference to Moses as a prophet is perhaps underwhelming, as he is not even named.³⁶ Despite the paucity of the data, a few observations can be made. First, the emphasis of the verse is on Yhwh's faithfulness to Israel, which Ephraim has spurned (12:15 [Eng. 12:14]). This is also the main point of comparison with the Jacob tradition. Although there is a division in scholarship over whether Jacob is a positive or negative example, I understand Jacob's "serving"

---

35 See, *inter alia*, the 2015 issue of *Hebrew Bible and Ancient Israel* devoted to the topic "Deuteronomy: a Judean or Samari(t)an Composition? Perspectives on Deuteronomy's Origins, Transmission, and Reception." Note the review of scholarship by Cynthia Edenburg and Reinhard Müller, "A Northern Provenance for Deuteronomy? A Critical Review," *HeBAI* 4 (2015): 148–161, and the argument for a northern provenance put forward by Gary N. Knoppers, "The Northern Context of the Law-Code in Deuteronomy," *HeBAI* 4 (2015): 162–183. See also the review of scholarship provided by Th.C. Vriezen and A.S. van der Woude, *Ancient Israelite and Early Jewish Literature*, trans. Brian Doyle (Leiden: Brill, 2005), 262–263, who discuss the formulation of this theory by influential scholars such as Vriezen, Bentzen, von Rad, and Alt; van der Woude indicates his agreement with this perspective on Deuteronomy's provenance as well (263: "The present author thus prefers to give priority to the thesis that Deuteronomy stems for the most part from Northern Israel"). See also the arguments of Sandra Lynn Richter, "The Question of Provenance and the Economics of Deuteronomy," *JSOT* 42 (2017): 23–50, for an approach which examines Deuteronomy's provenance from the perspective of the economic system assumed in the book, which leads to Richter to posit a rather early date for *Urdeuteronomium* (eleventh or tenth century BCE; with a northern provenance).

36 Nevertheless, most scholars affirm that the reference is to Moses. Heinz-Dieter Neef, *Die Heilstraditionen Israels in der Verkündigung des Propheten Hosea*, BZAW 169 (Berlin: de Gruyter, 1987), 234: "Durch den Bezug zur Herausführung aus Ägypten durch 'einen Propheten' kann kaum angezweifelt warden, daß damit Mose gemeint ist." So also MacIntosh, *Hosea*, 512: the prophet "is clearly Moses."

and "tending" for a wife as a positive expression of his love and, for the author, an image of Yhwh's commitment to Israel.³⁷ In Hos 12:14, Yhwh is the main actor, and Yhwh's constant efforts on Israel's behalf are represented by the repetition of the term "prophet" (נביא), just as Jacob's lengthy toil is underlined by the repetition of "wife" (אשה).

Second, the repetition of the term "prophet" has suggested to some scholars the possibility that Hosea has a nascent concept of a Mosaic prophetic succession in view, and even that he considered himself to be its rightful heir and exponent.³⁸ Indeed, though it seems most plausible to take both occurrences of "prophet" as a reference to Moses, some have argued that the second usage refers to Joshua or a later prophetic figure (on analogy with Jacob's multiple wives).³⁹ The verse then indicates Yhwh's *ongoing* provision of redemptive agents in Israel's history. MacIntosh criticizes this line of interpretation harshly: on this view, "it is hard to envisage on Hosea's part a more clumsy or obscure mode of communication."⁴⁰ To attribute a comprehensive concept of prophetic succession to Hosea is probably anachronistic, reading a later Dtr development into this earlier passage.

Third and most important, the "prophet" is associated with the Exodus tradition. The operative model of prophecy therefore is that of a charismatic savior figure.⁴¹ The *beth instrumenti* prefixed to the term נביא highlights the role of the prophet as the agent of Yhwh's powerful and liberating deeds; the prophet (נביא) functions as the *means* of deliverance.⁴² This conforms closely to the understanding of prophecy in the rest of Hosea, which is consistently

---

37 See Kelle, "Hosea 4–14," 325–326, as well as Martin Schott, "Die Jacobpassagen in Hosea 12," *ZThK* 112 (2015): 1–26, and the literature cited there, on the Jacob traditions and the division in scholarship on whether he is a positive or negative example. For Jacob as negative example, see Wolff, *Hosea*, 216; for the view I follow, see, e.g., Neef, *Die Heilstraditionen*, 234; MacIntosh, *Hosea*, 511; Dwight R. Daniels, *Hosea and Salvation History: The Early Traditions of Israel in Prophecy of Hosea*, BZAW 191 (Berlin: de Gruyter, 1990), 49.
38 See J. Andrew Dearman, *The Book of Hosea*, NICOT (Grand Rapids: Eerdmans, 2010), 314–315, and Daniels, *Hosea and Salvation History*, 49: "The prophets are the only true and faithful agents of Yahweh's protective guidance for his people. This care began with Moses as the prophet *par excellence* and, whether Hosea also referred to Samuel or not, he certainly viewed the office as continuing down to his own day (6:5)."
39 Francis I. Andersen and David Noel Freedman, *Hosea: A New Translation with Introduction and Commentary*, AB 24 (Garden City, N.Y.: Doubleday, 1980), 621, suggest Samuel or Elijah for the second figure; Dearman, *Hosea*, 314n73, suggests Joshua.
40 MacIntosh, *Hosea*, 513.
41 *Contra* Schott, "Die Jacobpassagen," 19: "Für den Verfasser von v. 14 sind die Propheten Gesetzesausleger und Mose der Prophet schlechthin."
42 MacIntosh, *Hosea*, 511, notes that this is a different usage of ב than in the preceding verse.

portrayed as charismatic and as an instrument of Yhwh's powerful deeds in history. Hosea 6:5 provides an important point of comparison: "Therefore I have hewn them by the prophets [בנביאים], I have killed them by the words of my mouth."[43] Prophets are associated here with violent action; Perlitt suggested that figures such as Elijah were in mind.[44] The fundamentally charismatic conception of prophecy is also evident in Hos 9:7, where the "prophet" is placed in parallel with the "man of the spirit (איש רוח)," and the popular perception that prophets were considered insane is reported. (Hosea, it might be said, did little to assuage such concerns in his personal life.) It is this charismatic model of Mosaic prophecy that Deuteronomy seeks to suppress (cf Deut 13:2–6) and replace with its own model for Mosaic prophecy.[45]

4   Conclusion

In sum, the origin of the concept of Mosaic prophecy is obscure, but the evidence is suggestive that it goes back to the Exodus traditions of the northern kingdom. The oldest conception of Mosaic prophecy is fundamentally charismatic and associated with military action, such as we see reflected in prophetic conventicles and early war prophets. Thus, while Hos 12:14 may influence Deuteronomy's later description of Moses as a prophet, the emphasis in what follows will be on Deuteronomy's innovation. Deuteronomy inherits the concept of Mosaic prophecy; it does not invent it out of thin air. In the next chapter, I will argue that the Pentateuch contains evidence of two responses to this charismatic model for Mosaic prophecy. The first, found in the final form of Num 11–12, assumes this model but dissociates Moses from other prophets. The second, found in Deuteronomy, seeks to replace the charismatic model of Mosaic prophecy with a genealogical one.

43   MacIntosh, *Hosea*, 211, argues that this is a *beth instrumenti*, which also occurs in Hos 12:14. JPS represents an alternate translation, where the ב is understood as object marker ("That is why I have hewn down the prophets"), but this makes a poor parallel with the second phrase ("by the words of my mouth"), as MacIntosh notes.
44   Perlitt, "Mose als Prophet," 604.
45   See Mark Leuchter, "Hosea's Exodus Mythology and the Book of the Twelve," in *Priests & Cults in the Book of the Twelve*, ed. Lena-Sofia Tiemeyer, ANEM 14 (Atlanta: SBL Press, 2016), 31–49, at 45–46, on Hos 12:14: "Here, we find an antecedent to Deuteronomy's similar view that a 'prophet like Moses' will arise in every successive generation. … the typology of a persistent Mosaic prophet originates in Hosea." Leuchter is correct that Hosea is an antecedent for Deuteronomy, but overstates the continuity between them.

CHAPTER 2

From Charisma to Canon: Deuteronomy's Redefinition of Moses and Prophecy

1   Introduction

In this chapter I compare and contrast two modes of relating Moses to prophecy in the final form of the Pentateuch, in order to delineate the innovative character of Deuteronomy's prophet like Moses. The relationship between Moses and prophecy has been a matter of considerable interest in recent scholarship,[1] but the distinctiveness of Deuteronomy's approach to Mosaic prophecy has not had the bearing it deserves on the discussion. I will argue that Deuteronomy's concept of the prophet like Moses is a theological *novum*, a creative redefinition of Moses in the interests of establishing a normative theological tradition. This re-characterization of Moses comes at the price of associating Israel's founder with the ambiguity of prophecy, a price that (as we will see) the editor of Num 11–12 was not willing to pay. The cost was worth it to the architects of Deuteronomy, because their ultimate goal was to overcome this ambiguity by redefining prophecy itself. The concept of the prophet like Moses originates as a re-characterization of Moses, but its goal is a redefinition of prophecy, one which subjects it to a Mosaic norm. The former is the subject of this chapter, the latter of the rest of this book.

---

1   See Jeffrey Stackert, *A Prophet Like Moses: Prophecy, Law, and Israelite Religion* (New York: Oxford, 2014); Reinhard Achenbach, "'A Prophet like Moses' (Deuteronomy 18:15)—'No Prophet like Moses' (Deuteronomy 34:10): Some Observations on the Relation between the Pentateuch and the Latter Prophets," in *The Pentateuch: International Perspectives on Current Research*, ed. T.B. Dozeman, K. Schmid, and B. Schwarz, FAT 78 (Tübingen: Mohr Siebeck, 2011), 435–458; Christophe Nihan, "'Moses and the Prophets': Deuteronomy 18 and the Emergence of the Pentateuch as Torah," *SEÅ* 75 (2010): 21–55; Dominik Markl, "Moses Prophetenrolle in Dtn 5; 18; 34. Structurelle Wendepunkte von rechtshermeneutischem Gewicht," in *Deuteronomium—Tora für eine neue Generation*, ed. G. Fischer, D. Markl, and S. Paganini, BZAR 17 (Wiesbaden: Harrassowitz Verlag, 2011), 51–68; Ernest W. Nicholson, "Deuteronomy 18.9–22, the Prophets and Scripture," in *Prophecy and Prophets in Ancient Israel*, ed. John Day, LHB/OTS 531 (London: T&T Clark, 2010), 151–171.

2 The Relationship between Moses and Prophecy in Numbers 11–12

2.1 *Introductory Comments*

The narratives of Numbers 11–12 provide the only sustained reflection on the relationship between Moses and prophecy in the Pentateuch outside of Deuteronomy.[2] The prophetic behavior of the seventy elders at the tent of meeting (Num 11:24–25), the prophesying of Eldad and Medad in the camp (11:26–27), Moses' apparently egalitarian wish that all God's people would be prophets (11:29), and the rebellion of Miriam and Aaron against Moses' prophetic authority (12:1–16) provide ample reflection on the relation between the authority of Moses and those considered "prophets," נביאים. I argue, however, that the redactor of these narratives was more interested in driving a wedge between Moses and prophecy than positing substantial continuity between them. In their final form, the goal of these narratives is to dissociate Moses from the ambiguity of prophecy. It therefore provides a sharp contrast to the Deuteronomic project, which brings Moses and prophecy together.

The analysis offered below investigates the relationship between Moses and prophecy as present in the final form of Num 11:4–12:16. I will argue that there is a consistent perspective on this relationship articulated by the redactor. This in itself is a controversial claim—many scholars see contradictions in these narratives—which will be sustained in light of a close reading. My attention to the final shape of the text is not intended to deny the fact that the compiler is working with traditional materials. Numbers 11–12 offers a series of narratives which recounts the wilderness journey of the people of Israel from Taberah (11:3) to the wilderness of Paran (12:16), from which spies are to be sent into the land (13:3). The compiler of this travelogue incorporates four "complaint" narratives: (1) an opening complaint story which provides the paradigmatic pattern for the episodes that follow (11:1–3); (2) the complaint of the people concerning their diet, with God's provision of quail and punishment of plague (Num 11:4–10, 13, 18–24a, 31–35);[3] (3) Moses' complaint that he cannot bear the people alone, with God's provision of leadership (Num 11:11–12, 14–17, 24b–30),[4] and (4) Miriam's complaint about Moses' Cushite wife, with God's punishment

---

2 Benjamin D. Sommer, "Reflecting on Moses: the Redaction of Numbers 11," *JBL* 118 (1999): 601–624; here 609, points out that these chapters "form a unity concerned with Moses' relation to the prophetic office, its roles, and its subsequent history."
3 Other versions of this story occur in Exod 16; Ps 78:18–31; Ps 105:40. The request for elders is not mentioned in any of these, supporting the original independence of the intertwined narratives.
4 Other versions of this story occur in Exod 18:13–26; Deut 1:9–18.

of leprosy (Num 12:1, 4–5, 9–16). These traditional stories, with their common structural features of the people's complaining, Mosaic intercession, and divine punishment, provided the redactor with raw material for reflection on his specific interest, namely, the nature of Mosaic revelation and its relationship to prophecy.

It is only the first brief narrative that was taken over untouched. The second and third are intertwined in the final form of the text, so that the exact delineation of each of them is disputed.[5] The fourth narrative has also been edited extensively: the original complaint story about Moses' Cushite wife has been transformed into a reflection on Moses' unique status.[6] In what follows, I will offer a proposal that explains both the intertwining of the stories in Num 11:4–35 and the redactional additions to Num 12:1–16 as mutually reinforcing aspects of an extended and careful reflection on the relationship between Moses and prophecy. The narratives have been edited with the goal of presenting the revelation given to Moses as vastly superior to that given to prophets.

2.2   The Redaction of Num 11:4–35

The episodes of the seventy prophesying elders and of Eldad and Medad have long been regarded as etiologies designed to give prophetic activity a Mosaic origin and imprimatur.[7] Gunneweg pointed out that this standard view is not specific enough: Num 11:4–35 is not simply an authorization of prophecy, but is concerned with the more precise question of how to characterize the relation-

---

5 My analysis of the division given above is also that of Philip J. Budd, *Numbers*, WBC 5 (Waco: Word, 1984), 124, as well as that of Stackert, *Prophet like Moses*, 91, and Joel Baden, *The Composition of the Pentateuch: Renewing the Documentary Hypothesis*, AYBRL (New Haven: Yale University Press, 2012), 82–102.

6 The traditional material, in this case, lacks parallel elsewhere. Jacob Milgrom, *Numbers = [Ba-midbar]: The Traditional Hebrew Text with the New JPS Translation*, JPSTC 4 (Philadelphia: Jewish Publication Society, 1990), 376, argues that an older complaint story in which Miriam complains about Moses' Cushite wife and receives punishment is clearly discernible; he detects it in 12:1–2, 4–5, 9–16. I doubt that 12:2 was part of the original complaint narrative: this introduces the issue of Moses as an exclusive channel of revelation into the original layer, which is needlessly complicated. The additions, then, would be found in 12:2–3 and 6–8. They are unified by a focus on Moses' unique status and authority and thus alter the story's import. Stackert, *Prophet like Moses*, 108, takes Num 12:1aα, 2–15 as a unified E narrative focused on Moses' prophetic status, but he does not explain the origin of the complaint about Moses' Cushite wife in 12:1aβb, nor how it intruded into the text.

7 E.g., Martin Noth, *A History of Pentateuchal Traditions*, trans. Bernhard W. Anderson (Englewood Cliffs, N.J.: Prentice-Hall, 1972; repr., Chico, Calif.: Scholars Press, 1981), 129; von Rad, *Theology*, 2:9.

ship between Moses and prophecy.[8] To understand this relationship, however, it is necessary to consider carefully both the portrayal of Moses in these narratives, as well as the role of prophecy.

In his analysis of the chapter, Sommer has given attention to the first aspect, the characterization of Moses. Sommer divides Num 11:4–35 into an "A" narrative ("Moses, the people, and plague"), and a "B" narrative ("Moses, the elders, and prophecy"), and argues that these contain two competing characterizations of Moses, one prophetic and one anti-prophetic.[9] The "prophetic" stories about Moses are unified in emphasizing Moses' "beneficence" and his humility:

> They depict him as good-hearted to the complaining people he leads and even to those who rival him, endowed with prophetic spirit greater than that of any human, unusually adept in all aspects of prophetic office, and humble in spite of it all.[10]

Sommer argues that the story of the request for quail and subsequent plague (the "A" narrative) has, in contrast, a radically different portrayal of Moses: "He is not humble but petulant, not beneficent but bitter. Instead of concern for his people, he displays contempt for them and for his unwanted role as their parent."[11] In this narrative, Sommer argues, Moses is self-centered and self-pitying (note his request to die, 11:15) and does not believe Yhwh's word (11:22); in

---

8   Antonius H.J. Gunneweg, "Das Gesetz und die Propheten: Eine Auslegung von Ex 33,7–11; Num 11,4–12,8; Dtn 31,14f.; 34,10," ZAW 102 (1990): 169–180; here 177.

9   It should be noted that Sommer, "Reflecting on Moses," divides Num 11:4–35 in a manner slightly different than the division I gave above. He names the first story "Moses, the people, and plague" and assigns to it 11:4–15, 18–24a, 31–35; the latter story, "Moses, the elders, and prophecy" he deems present only in 11:16–17, 24b–30. In my division above I have also assigned 11:11–12, 14–15 to the story of Moses' request for help with leadership. Incorporating Moses' complaint into this story naturally already mitigates Sommer's wholly positive characterization of Moses in this story and his negative characterization of Moses in the story of the quail. Sommer claims, "Reflecting on Moses," 608, that his division is advantageous because of "its elegance and simplicity …. It yields two sources and two complete stories." But this is questionable: in Sommer's story of the elders, Yhwh's command to assemble them at the tent of meeting is somewhat abrupt and does not respond to any request of Moses; it is simply the introduction to the story. Furthermore, the common vocabulary in 11:14, 17 suggests these verses belong in the same account (11:14, לא־אוכל אנוכי לבדי לשאת; 11:17, ולא־תשא אתה לבדך). See the response to Sommer given by Pamela Tamarkin Reis, "Numbers XI: Seeing Moses Plain," VT 55 (2005): 207–231.

10 Sommer, "Reflecting on Moses," 611.

11 Sommer, "Reflecting on Moses," 612.

short, he is an "anti-prophet."[12] Sommer takes note of exegetical efforts ancient and modern to harmonize the two portraits,[13] but believes that it cannot be done convincingly.[14] In contrast, I will argue that these private conversations between Moses and Yhwh are not an invitation by the narrator to judge Moses negatively; rather, they put the focus on Moses' singular role.[15] The problem of the positive and negative valences of Moses' character is resolved when attention is paid to the redactor's goal of contrasting Mosaic revelation with all forms of prophecy.

The solution to the enigma of Moses' character in these narratives and the unity of the final form of Num 11–12 comes via a clear understanding of the theological traditions upon which the author drew, particularly the specific conception of the "tent of meeting" (אהל מועד) that he inherited. This alternate tradition within the Pentateuch, delineated with clarity by Menahem Haran,[16]

---

12 Sommer, "Reflecting on Moses," 613. One wonders if the request to die would really be perceived as anti-prophetic; cf. 1 Kgs 19:4; Jonah 4:3.

13 Sommer, "Reflecting on Moses," 617 cites Milgrom, *Numbers*, 377 as an example of harmonizing the "two" Moses and finding the redactional unity in a movement from one to the other:

> [I]t is Moses' failure to "stand in the breach" (cf Ezek 22:30; Ps 106:23) that explains why the story of the elders is interwoven with the story of the quail: to provide punishment for Moses! ... Evidently the fusion of the two stories is an attempt to demonstrate that Moses was punished by the diminution of his spiritual powers (the story of the elders) for failing to intercede on Israel's behalf when it craved meat (the story of the quail) and for failing to believe that God could provide it.

Milgrom construes the "B" narrative as punishment for the negative actions of the Moses of "A" narrative. The problem with this theory is that nothing of the sort is stated or implied in the text: that Moses did not "stand in the breach" is not criticized, that Moses was being punished is nowhere implied, nor do we read that his spiritual powers were diminished.

14 For Sommer, this indeterminacy is the point; the redactor's purpose in combining the narratives was ("Reflecting on Moses," 621) "to ensure that all serious attempts to read this chapter present a debate between A ['Moses, the people, and the plague'] and B ['Moses, the elders, and prophecy'] .... [T]he redactor's insertion deliberately fosters a cycle of competing misreadings." Earlier (602), he states: "By bringing together two disparate stories, the redactor of Numbers 11 compels readers to contemplate several related motifs (in particular, images of Moses and of divinely sent רוח), but bars them from achieving interpretative closure." In evaluation, it must be noted that Sommer's redactor has a remarkably post-modern goal. Is it really the case that an ancient Israelite editor of traditional narratives about Moses would have the primary goal of promoting ambiguity?

15 Even Moses' request to die should be understood in terms of the burden of his isolating and singular role; compare the similar context for Elijah's request in 1 Kgs 19.

16 Menahem Haran, *Temples and Temple-Service in Ancient Israel: an Inquiry into the Character of Cult Phenomena and the Historical Setting of the Priestly School* (Oxford: Clarendon Press, 1977), 260–275. Haran argues that references to this understanding of the tent occur

is present in both the story about the elders and the complaint of Miriam and Aaron. This tradition portrays the tent of meeting (אהל מועד) as an oracular source of revelation.[17] Haran demonstrates the divergences from the priestly conception of the ten of meeting: it is situated outside the camp (Exod 33:7); it is not the divine abode, "but a place appointed for a fleeting prophetic vision;"[18] it is, in short, not a cultic site at all but an oracular one. Haran argues that this tradition was rooted in Israelite prophecy, comparing Moses' encounters with the divine to Elijah's theophany in 1 Kings 19.[19] The functioning of the oracular tent of meeting is described in Exod 33:7–11:

(7) Now Moses used to take the tent and pitch it outside the camp, far off from the camp; he called it the tent of meeting. And everyone who sought the LORD would go out to the tent of meeting, which was outside the camp. (8) Whenever Moses went out to the tent, all the people would rise and stand, each of them, at the entrance of their tents and watch

---

in Exod 33:5–11, Num 11:16–29, 12:4–10, and Deut 31:14–15. The unity of this tradition has been widely accepted in Pentateuchal scholarship, even though the date of these texts is disputed. Stackert, *Prophet like Moses*, 70 calls this the "'Tent of Meeting' cluster" and assigns all these texts to E (for Stackert, late eighth/early seventh century BCE). David M. Carr, *The Formation of the Hebrew Bible: A New Reconstruction* (New York: Oxford, 2011), 256–292, identifies the story of the elders and the oracle to Miriam and Aaron in Num 11–12 as "post-D insertions into non-P contexts" as part of the redaction of a post-D Hexateuch (see especially 267–271). A trend in European scholarship is to consider these texts post-priestly and date them to the Persian period. See Gunneweg, "Das Gesetz und die Propheten," 172–173, and especially Reinhard Achenbach, *Die Vollendung der Tora: Studien der Redaktionsgeschichte des Numeribuches im Kontext von Hexateuch und Pentateuch*, BZAR 3 (Wiesbaden: Harrassowitz Verlag, 2003), 219–301; further bibliography in Stackert, *Prophet like Moses*, 71n3. It seems unlikely to me that these texts are post-priestly: Gunneweg argues that they polemicize against the priestly tent of meeting by, e.g., insisting that the tent is not Yhwh's dwelling in the midst of the people but outside the camp. The problem with this is that the tradition has been first inserted precisely where it cannot contain such polemical force, i.e., *before* the construction of the priestly tent.

17 Haran, *Temples and Temple-Service*, 262.
18 Haran, *Temples and Temple-Service*, 266.
19 It should be noted that in this passage, Elijah's character has a negative valence, and, similarly to Moses in Num 11:15, Elijah requests to die (1 Kgs 19:4). Haran is followed in this by Israel Knohl, "Two Aspects of the 'Tent of Meeting,'" in *Tehillah le-Moshe: Biblical and Judaic Studies in Honor of Moshe Greenberg*, ed. Mordechai Cogan, Barry L. Eichler, and Jeffrey H. Tigay (Winona Lake, Ind.: Eisenbrauns, 1997), 73–79; who also thinks these passages reflect "the prophetic tradition of the Tent of Meeting" (74). It should be noted, however, that even if Haran and Knohl are correct that these passages originate in prophetic circles, the inference that Moses is characterized as a נביא in this tradition is not necessarily warranted (an inference Haran makes, see *Temples and Temple-Service*, 267n12).

Moses until he had gone into the tent. (9) When Moses entered the tent, the pillar of cloud would descend and stand at the entrance of the tent, and the LORD would speak with Moses. (10) When all the people saw the pillar of cloud standing at the entrance of the tent, all the people would rise and bow down, all of them, at the entrance of their tent. (11) Thus the LORD used to speak to Moses face to face, as one speaks to a friend. Then he would return to the camp; but his young assistant, Joshua son of Nun, would not leave the tent.

This is clearly the understanding of the tent of meeting in Num 11:4–12:16, as is clear from the setting of the tent of meeting outside the camp in both narratives (11:24–30; 12:4–5).[20] One might reasonably surmise, then, that the vehement conversation between Yhwh and Moses, in which Moses is in turn petulant and skeptical is a narrative instantiation of Exod 33:11, which says that at this tent of meeting Yahweh would speak to Moses "face to face, as one speaks to a friend (פנים אל־פנים כאשר ידבר איש אל־רעהו)."[21] The freedom with which Moses upbraids Yhwh, on this reading, serves to cast in sharp relief how close Moses is to Yhwh.

This hypothesis is confirmed by the structure of the redacted narrative. The final form has one feature that Sommer neglects: the two narratives have been combined in such a way that they now make a combined whole dividing neatly into speech and action.[22] In the first part (Num 11:4–24a), complaints get passed up the "chain of command" to Yhwh, who resolves on two specific courses of

---

20 A number of smaller details corroborate this picture. First, after the people's complaint, the narrative specifically notes that they stood weeping "at the entrances of their tents (איש לפתח אהלו)" (Num 11:10), which echoes the posture of the people in Exod 33:8 (so Gunneweg, "Das Gesetz und die Propheten," 179). Second, Haran, *Temples and Temple-Service*, 266 points out that the vocabulary of "standing" or presenting oneself is important in both passages (נצב: Exod 33:8; יצב: Num 11:16; עמד: Num 11:24; 12:5).

21 Joseph Blenkinsopp, *Prophecy and Canon: A Contribution to the Study of Jewish Origins*, CSJCA 3 (Notre Dame, Ind.: University of Notre Dame Press, 1977), 89, notes that Exod 33:11 suggests "the easy and unstinted familiarity existing between friends."

22 Here I adopt Milgrom's analysis of the passage's structure (*Numbers*, 376–380):
   A: the people complain about meat, Moses hears (4–10)
     B: Moses complains to God about leadership (11–15)
       X: God provides solutions in reverse order (B'A'), further dialogue (16–23)
     B': God executes plan regarding leadership (24–30)
   A': God executes plan regarding meat (31–35)
   The basic chiastic structure (ABB'A') repeats itself, first in Yhwh's announcing of the plan and then in its actual fulfillment. ABX are concerned with speech; B'A' with action. See Budd, *Numbers*, 130: "The whole story divides neatly into two between v. 23 and v. 24, a division indicating the movement from 'words' to 'action.'"

action. In the second (11:24b–35), these plans come to fruition by means of רוח ("spirit," 11:24–25; "wind," 11:31).[23] The redactor of Num 11:4–35 therefore transforms the traditional stories of the elders and the quail into fulfillments of oracular revelations given specifically to Moses. Indeed, the combination of two narratives that elsewhere occur independently is explained by the redactor's focus on the figure of Moses as the singular mediator between the Israelites and Yhwh, which can be schematized as follows:

Israel's Complaint → Moses' Complaint → Yhwh Reveals Plan to Moses → Moses' Complaint Resolved → Israel's Complaint Resolved

Further evidence that this is the structure of the redacted text is found in the conclusion of the dialogue between God and Moses. Moses expresses some doubt that God will be able to feed the entire people he is leading. To this God responds: "Is the LORD's power limited? Now you will see whether my word happens for you or not (היד יהוה תקצר עתה תראה היקרך דברי אם־לא)" (Num 11:23). The promised efficacy of the divine word is the hinge on which the stories turn. The singular suffix (היקרך) is somewhat strange here: why is Yhwh's word specifically fulfilled for Moses? The sense one gets is that the disagreement between Moses and Yhwh is akin to that of a wager between friends.[24] Therefore, in Num 11:4–35, Moses' "face to face" interaction with Yhwh is implicitly thematized by means of the interweaving of the stories.

Numbers 11:24b marks the shift in the narrative to the fulfillment of God's intentions. Prophecy plays a key role in the part of the narrative concerned with actions: it serves the function of demonstrating that Yhwh has done what he said he would do, namely, share Moses' spirit with the seventy elders. That is why it is not mentioned in Yhwh's plan (Num 11:17), but only in the fulfillment of that plan (Num 11:25). This episode is careful to distinguish between

---

23   Martin Buber, *Moses: The Revelation and the Covenant* (New York: Harper, 1958), 164–165: "In thus fusing the stories of the quail and the elders the purpose was to make the reader feel that both, the working in Nature and the working in the soul of human beings, are the one work from on high; and are indeed, in the last resort, the identical work from on high."

24   See Sommer, "Reflecting on Moses," 613: "The odd accusative in the word היקרך demonstrates that God afflicts the nation at least in part in order to demonstrate his might to his prophet"; also David Jobling, *The Sense of Biblical Narrative: Three Structural Analyses in the Old Testament (1 Samuel 13–31, Numbers 11–12, 1 Kings 17–18)* (JSOTSupS 7; Sheffield: University of Sheffield, 1978), 30; Milgrom, *Numbers*, 88: "From God's response (v. 23) to Moses' faltering faith (vv. 21–22), it would almost seem that the quail are brought to Israel in order to prove God's power to Moses!"

Yhwh's interaction with Moses and with the elders. Consider first Yhwh's stated intention:

> I will come down and talk with you (עמך) there; and I will take some of the spirit that is on you and put it on them (מן־הרוח אשר עליך ושמתי עליהם ואצלתי); and they shall bear the burden of the people along with you so that you will not bear it all by yourself.
> Num 11:17

Yhwh will speak directly only with Moses.[25] Furthermore, the partitive מן means that the elders, who temporarily prophesy, do not have direct interaction with Yhwh; their portion of the spirit comes from Moses' spirit.[26] And so it occurs:

> So Moses went out and told the people the words of the LORD; and he gathered seventy elders of the people, and placed them all around the tent. Then the LORD came down in the cloud and spoke to him (אליו), and took some (ויאצל) of the spirit that was on him and put it on the seventy elders; and when the spirit rested upon them, they prophesied (ויתנבאו). But they did not do so again.
> Num 11:24–25

Some have claimed that this reduction of Moses' spirit is a punishment of him.[27] Rather, the story accentuates Moses' unique relationship with God.[28] Because of the small portion of Moses' spirit that they received, the elders "behave like prophets" (ויתנבאו). The prophetic activity is probably ecstatic,[29] and its temporary nature highlights its role as confirmatory:[30] it is intended to

---

25 A point emphasized by Gunneweg, "Das Gesetz und die Propheten," 175.
26 See Milgrom, *Numbers*, 87.
27 E.g. Milgrom, *Numbers*, 377, based on the use of the word אצל.
28 See the perceptive comment of Jobling, *Sense of Biblical Narrative*, 32: "That the story is *affirming* Moses' uniqueness precisely at the moment of its 'dissipation' is hinted at by the otherwise inexplicable note that Yahweh *singles Moses out* for a conversation, of undisclosed content, immediately before the distribution of the spirit (vs. 25, 'and spoke to him,' cf. vs. 17)!"
29 Baruch A. Levine, *Numbers 1–20: A New Translation with Introduction and Commentary*, AB 4 (New York: Doubleday, 1993), 325, with references to 1 Sam 10:5, 10–11; 19:20–24; 1 Kgs 22:10. See also Noth, *Numbers*, 89. John R. Levison, "Prophecy in Ancient Israel: The Case of the Ecstatic Elders," *CBQ* 65 (2003): 503–21, contests this reading, which remains the most natural in view of the lexical evidence.
30 The fact that prophecy has the function of confirming the elders as having legitimately

demonstrate that the elders have been charismatically endowed with Moses' spirit, and are now ready to take up the task of governance. Their prophetic ecstasy, however, also emphasizes the gulf between Moses and prophetic activity. In this narrative, the presence of the spirit on Moses is so great that God can take a *part* of it, share that *part* with seventy others, who all engage in prophetic activity on the basis of the small portion of the spirit they receive. In this perspective, prophecy is something engaged in by one who has far less of the spirit than Moses. Moses has no need of such; the text specifies twice that God speaks directly to Moses.

The enigmatic episode of Eldad and Medad immediately follows. In context, this can also be primarily read as a further demonstration of the efficacy of the divine word: even those that did not come out to the tent of meeting prophesied. The redactor, however, is interested in the theological question of whether prophetic activity not derived from Moses' spirit threatens Moses' unique status. This issue is raised by Joshua, who begs Moses to stop Eldad and Medad; Moses, however, rejects any such worry (Num 11:29): "Would that all the LORD's people were prophets, and that the LORD would put his spirit on them!" Why does Moses not share Joshua's apprehension at non-Mosaic prophetic activity? It could be that Moses is portrayed here as an egalitarian wishing for the abolition of all hierarchy.[31] The statement is ambiguous, however, and does not

---

received Moses' spirit means that many scholars' criticism of this narrative (that it is unclear how falling into an ecstatic frenzy will enable the elders to share Moses' burden of leadership) is misplaced. See, among many, George B. Gray, *A Critical and Exegetical Commentary on Numbers*, ICC (Edinburgh: T&T Clark, 1903), 111; Martin Noth, *Numbers: A Commentary*, OTL (Philadelphia: Westminster, 1968), 89; Levison, "Ecstatic Elders?," 504; Gunneweg, "Das Gesetz und die Propheten," 176.

31 See Milgrom, *Numbers*, 91: "In effect, Moses proclaims that not only is it a desideratum that all of Israel qualify (through ecstasy) to become elders but that they may even attain a higher level—to be prophets like Moses himself." Milgrom rightly recognizes that Moses remains on a "higher level" than the prophesying elders. It is not clear from Moses' wish, however, that he actually desires the people to all be at his level: rather, he desires that they all be prophets like the elders. Stackert, *Prophet like Moses*, 106–107, advances a similar interpretation to that of Milgrom, rejecting the view that the elders were considered "prophets" (emphasis original):

> Moses's desideratum is *not* that all Israelites would be made prophets *like the elders were*. His wish is made with full knowledge that the elders *were not* appointed as prophets. He claims instead that, *even had the elders been so appointed*, he would seek an even more far-reaching remedy and one that Joshua would view as diminishing his distinctiveness even more than the actions of Eldad and Medad. That is, his wish is that all Israelites, including the elders, would be appointed prophets, *as he was*, so that they too might receive the divine spirit regularly, *as he does*. If this wish were fulfilled,

explicitly state that the provision of prophetic status would endanger Moses.³² In fact, in the final narrative, it serves as a transition between the resolution of Moses' complaint (11:24–29) and that of the people's (11:30–35). Moses' implication must be that if the people of Yhwh were prophets—to paraphrase, if the divine רוח rested on them in even a fraction of the amount that rests on Moses—then Moses' own burden would be substantially eased, as the people would not be so obstinate and refractory. It does not mean that Moses' unique status would be threatened. This conclusion is reinforced by Num 12, which makes clear that the revelation given to Moses is vastly superior to that received by prophets.

2.3 Moses and Prophecy in Numbers 12

There are three respects in which the following narrative, Num 12:1–16, is a culmination of the previous combined narrative in Num 11:4–35: (1) the protagonists, Miriam and Aaron, come from Moses' own immediate circle³³ and present a greater threat to Moses' status than either the seventy elders or Eldad and Medad;³⁴ (2) the types of prophecy envisioned, that of visions and

---

there would be no need even for the appointment of the elders, for there would be no need for oracular specialists or proxies for them.

Stackert's exegesis rests on a number of decisions. Particularly important is his contention that the elders were not prophets, but only behaved like prophets (103). This leads to the improbable result that in Num 11:29 Moses expresses the desire not that all the people would be prophets like Eldad and Medad (though it is their activity that provoked Joshua's concern), but like Moses himself. And this occurs in a text (E) that Stackert goes on to characterize as "zealously antiprophetic" (116)! It is more exegetically sound to conclude that Moses' wish is that all the people would receive the Spirit like Eldad and Medad had, and that this represents no threat to Moses' status, superior as he is to all prophets.

32 Budd's comments are apposite (*Numbers*, 130): "Joshua in this story represents a kind of sanctuary clericalism. The leadership must be prepared to hear the authentic voice of prophecy in such as Eldad and Medad who here represent the nonprofessional prophets." Being "prepared to hear" prophecy, it should be noted, does not imply abdication of leadership.

33 The precise date when a familial relationship for the triad of Moses, Aaron, and Miriam was asserted is unclear, and Noth, *Numbers*, 94 observes that it cannot be assumed in Numbers 12 (which implies for him that the narrative "cannot be dated too late"). Esther J. Hamori, *Women's Divination in Biblical Literature: Prophecy, Necromancy, and Other Arts of Knowledge*, AYBRL (New Haven: Yale University Press, 2015), 81, notes the significance of how this later tradition reshapes the narrative: "What new tension this adds to the story! Here she is, angry that her prophetic authority is being overlooked in comparison to that of Moses, that infant who owed his very life to her strategy. Who wouldn't object?"

34 Both have been given the title prophet(ess) earlier in the narrative: Miriam is called נביאה in Exod 15:20; Aaron is called נביא in Exod 7:1 (though this latter text is usually taken as late).

dreams (12:6, מראה and חלום), are legitimate modes of prophecy, and generally accorded greater respect in the Hebrew Bible than ecstatic prophecy, which is often associated with madness;[35] (3) the key phrase דבר ב־, which the redactor used to unify the older complaint story with the prophetic motif,[36] has been described as a "closer and more intimate conversation than דבר אל."[37] The narrative makes explicit what is implicit in Num 11:4–35, that Moses' "face to face" interaction with Yhwh sets him far above the ambiguity of prophetic revelation.

The redactor's additions to the original complaint story are mainly in Num 12:2–3, 6–8.[38] The accusation of Miriam against Moses for marrying a Cushite wife is a guise, and the real motives of Miriam and Aaron emerge in the form of two rhetorical questions: "Is it only through Moses that the LORD has spoken? Has he not also spoken through us? (הרק אך־במשה דבר יהוה הלא גם־בנו)" (Num 12:2).[39] The apparent question is whether Moses is the exclusive conduit of divine revelation. The episode of Eldad and Medad has acknowledged the legitimacy of non-Mosaic prophecy, so that Miriam and Aaron seem to be justified in their contention. However, the formulation of the questions, with the phrases "only through Moses" and "also through us" put in the position of emphasis, shows the real issue in play: Miriam and Aaron are challenging Moses' unique status and authority.[40]

---

35   See Milgrom, *Numbers*, 381: "the ecstatic is equated with a madman," with reference to Jer 29:26; Hos 9:7; 2 Kgs 9:11. But מראה is used with respect to Jacob (Gen 49:2), Samuel (1 Sam 3:15), and Ezekiel (Ezek 1:1, 8:3, 40:2), and חלום is frequently used, of both Israelites and non-Israelites (e.g. Abimelech [Gen 20:3, 6]; Pharaoh [Gen 41:7]). BDB, s.v. חלום, call dreams "the lowest grade of prophecy"; but given their widespread attestation and continued popularity even in late texts (e.g. Dan 1:17), this judgment seems unfounded.

36   The idiom דבר ב־ is used in 12:1, 8 to mean "speak against," and in 12:2, 6, 8 to mean "to speak through." It seems that the redactor purposely exploited the ambiguity of this phrase in order to transform the narrative into one about Moses' status vis-à-vis prophecy. See Levine, *Numbers 1–20*, 328, "It is likely that in this chapter a play on the ambiguity of *dibber b-* was intended."

37   See Gray, *Numbers*, 123; Milgrom, *Numbers*, 309n8 affirms this possibility and suggests that in the narrative the phrase implies "an intensity of speech, either of hostility (vv. 1, 8) or intimacy (vv. 2, 6, 8)."

38   On the intrusive character of vv. 6–8, see Hanna Tervanotko, "Speaking in Dreams: the Figure of Miriam and Prophecy," 147–167 in *Prophets Male and Female: Gender and Prophecy in the Hebrew Bible, the Eastern Mediterranean, and the Ancient Near East*, ed. J. Stökl and C. Carvalho, AIL 15 (Atlanta: SBL Press, 2013), 153–154.

39   My translation, which brings out the emphasis on רק, "only."

40   Hamori, *Women's Divination*, 76–77: "we should not assume that the problem is a general claim of prophetic ability. Rather, they suggest that Yahweh speaks through them just as he speaks through Moses. They claim equality." Hamori rightly notes (77) that the main

Yhwh summons Moses, Miriam, and Aaron to the tent of meeting outside of the camp. As Jobling points out, this summons may be deceptive: do Miriam and Aaron go to the tent of meeting anticipating that, like the elders, they will be elevated in the eyes of the people and have their high status confirmed?[41] Miriam and Aaron are singled out to hear Yhwh's words. Yhwh affirms what Miriam and Aaron have contended: there are others through whom God has spoken.[42] However, what is distinctive about Moses is the surpassing quality of the revelation given to him:

ויאמר שמעו־נא דברי אם־יהיה נביאכם יהוה במראה אליו אתודע בחלום אדבר־בו
לא־כן עבדי משה בכל־ביתי נאמן הוא פה אל־פה אדבר־בו ומראה ולא בחידת
ותמנת יהוה יביט ומדוע לא יראתם לדבר בעבדי במשה

> Hear my words: When there are prophets among you, [43] I the LORD make myself known to them in visions; I speak to them in dreams. Not so with my servant Moses; he is entrusted with all my house. With him I speak face to face—clearly, not in riddles; and he beholds the form of the LORD. Why then were you not afraid to speak against my servant Moses?
> Num 12:6–8

Sperling has called attention to the irony in the text: "Yhwh speaks to Miriam and Aaron directly and in utmost clarity."[44] They receive a "Mosaic-like" revelation concerning the superiority of Moses! Furthermore, this superiority is presented by means of an explicit re-articulation of the "face to face" tradi-

---

issue in the story is that of Moses' uniqueness. The editorial aside in 12:3 also highlights that is Moses' uniqueness that is at stake.

41   Jobling, *Sense of Biblical Narrative*, 35.
42   Hamori, *Women's Divination*, 75, puts it aptly: "Yahweh's response to this [i.e., the complaint] is a resounding 'Sort Of.'"
43   Literally, "If your prophets are Yhwh," which cannot be the sense, suggesting that the text is corrupt. See the discussion in Levine, *Numbers 1–20*, 329–331. Milgrom, *Numbers*, 309n23 suggests that a *mem* may have fallen out, its restoration would give the sense: "If your prophet is from the LORD." Stackert, *Prophet like Moses*, 109–110, argues that the Tetragrammaton originally stood in the beginning of the line, on the basis of 4Q27. But the text of 4Q27 does not preserve the full quotation, and Stackert acknowledges that it is unclear whether the Tetragrammaton also stood after נביאכם in that version. That is, its presence at the beginning of the line may not be re-location, but a variant edition with two occurrences of the Tetragrammaton. LXX attempts to make sense of MT by translating יהוה with a dative, κυρίῳ (i.e., "If your prophet belongs to the Lord").
44   S. David Sperling, "Miriam, Aaron and Moses: Sibling Rivalry," *HUCA* 70 (2000): 39–55; here 54.

FROM CHARISMA TO CANON 43

tion previously encountered in the context of the oracular tent of meeting in Exod 33:11. The implications for the standing of Moses vis-à-vis prophecy are clearly stated. Prophetic revelation is of lower and inferior quality to that given to Moses. Indeed, Moses is not called one of *"your* prophets" (נביאכם, 12:6);[45] rather, Yhwh calls Moses *"my* servant" (עבדי, 12:7). Prophets do not have such a rank. They are less trustworthy because prophecy itself is a weaker, less clear form of revelation, one that comes in dreams and visions.[46] Moses, however, speaks to God face to face or, literally, "mouth to mouth (פה אל־פה)"; he "beholds the form of the LORD." Yhwh's response to Miriam and Aaron thus does not deny the truth behind their question—Yhwh has indeed spoken to more people than just Moses[47]—but rejects their questioning of Moses' unique status and authority. Moses is distinguished from prophets in this oracle, not classified with them.

If Moses' status as the "servant of Yhwh" sharply distinguishes the revelation entrusted to him even from high-ranking figures such as Miriam and Aaron, how much more is Moses to be distinguished from the seventy elders and Eldad and Medad! This casts doubt on von Rad and Perlitt's construal of the relationship between Num 11 and 12. As Perlitt put it, "Num 11 wollte bestimmte Propheten mit Mose zusammenbringen, Num 12 will die Trennung von allen."[48] The attractiveness of this interpretation stems from the fact that the elders received a portion of Moses' spirit, רוח (Num 11:24). But it is inadequate precisely because even in Numbers 11 prophetic activity is a much weaker manifestation of the divine רוח than that experienced by Moses. In my view, the narratives in Num 11–12 are in basic agreement concerning the relationship between Moses and prophecy. The redactor takes up the oracular tent of meeting tradition in order to contrast Moses with those called "prophets," not

---

45 The use of נביאכם to mean "a prophet among you" is unusual but not in need of emendation; see the discussion in Stackert, *Prophet like Moses*, 110n98.

46 See Tervanotko, "Speaking in Dreams," 157–164, on the interpretation of Miriam as a prophet who dreams in reception history.

47 See Hamori, *Women's Divination*, 79 (emphasis original): "Yahweh does not actually disagree with Miriam. Miriam challenges the notion that Moses has *exclusive* access to Yahweh, and Yahweh responds by saying that Moses has *superior* access to him"; Sperling, "Miriam, Aaron, and Moses," 52–53: "The author does not deny the claims of Miriam and Aaron that Yhwh spoke to them as well as to Moses. Yhwh has indeed spoken to female and male prophets but, unfortunately, one cannot count on their reliability because Yhwh's revelation to them was through dreams and riddles. By their very nature dreams and riddles require solution and interpretation, which can be faulty. In contrast to all prophecies by all prophets, the prophecies of Moses require no interpretation."

48 Lothar Perlitt, "Mose als Prophet," *EvT* 31 (1971): 588–608; here 593. See von Rad, *Theology*, 2:9.

classify him among them. To this author, Moses is Yhwh's faithful servant, who has face to face interaction with the deity, as with a friend. To call him a נביא would be to suggest that the revelation given to him was more ambiguous and cryptic than it in fact was.[49]

2.4 Numbers 11–12 and the Charismatic Model of Mosaic Prophecy

If the preceding analysis of Num 11:4–12:16 is well-founded, the redactor of these passages reframed three traditional complaint narratives into an extended reflection on the superiority of Moses to that of prophets, whether contemporary or past.[50] The model of prophecy in view is fundamentally charismatic, that is, it depends on receipt of the divine רוח (cf. Num 11:29). As is often noted, the activity of the seventy elders and of Eldad and Medad has its closest parallel in pre-Deuteronomic narrative sources, in which the *hitpael* of נבא is consistently used. This may denote temporary ecstatic behavior that occurs under the influence of the "spirit of Yahweh." For example, Samuel's words closely associate the coming of the "spirit" with Saul's prophetic behavior: "Then the spirit of the LORD will overwhelm you (וצלחה עליך רוח יהוה), and you will behave like a prophet (והתנבית) along with them and be turned into a different person" (1 Sam 10:6). This narrative explicitly notes the end of Saul's ecstatic activity (1 Sam 10:13), which is also reported in the case of the seventy elders (Num 11:26).[51]

---

49 Levine, *Numbers 1–20*, 328, titles this section "Moses as a Unique Prophet." This is not necessarily objectionable, but it uses the term "prophet" differently than Numbers itself does here. The same feature is present in Sommer, "Reflecting on Moses," 608, "God himself sets Moses apart by announcing that from prophet to prophet there is none like this prophet." This terminology is pervasive in the commentaries, and tends to blur the distinction between Numbers' characterization of Moses and that in Deuteronomy by reading the latter into the former. See Perlitt, "Mose als Prophet," 596 (emphasis added): "Er is so über alles Maß hinausgewachsen, daß der Ehrentitel Prophet sein Größe nur an den unteren Rändern zu markieren vermag. *Ebendarum heißt er nicht Prophet, sondern Jahwesknecht!* An höheres Alter dieser Theologie ist auch deshalb schwer du denken, weil 'die Propheten' in einem distinktionslosen Plural zitiert werden." See also Noth, *History*, 129: "the story of the elders in Num 11 has motivated the insertion in Num 12, which portrays Moses as a prophet, or more correctly, as more than a prophet."

50 Stackert, *Prophet like Moses*, 109–117, argues that Num 12:6–8 "contextually must refer to habitual, non-Mosaic prophetic practice contemporary with Moses's oracular service" (116), which is in service of his broader claim that E (!) thought that prophecy ended with Moses. Not only does this interpretation involve a strange interpretation of the poetic oracle of Num 12:6–8 (which asserts a principle that is not restricted to prophets prior to Moses), it particularly founders on Deut 34:10, which Stackert assigns to E. Stackert does not address the issue of how E's hypothetical readers in the late eighth/early seventh century would have known that the comparison between Moses and prophets did not apply to contemporary prophetic figures, but only to those of Mosaic times.

51 Temporary ecstatic possession of the divine spirit is also reported of Saul in 1 Sam 19:23–24.

The redactor assumes the tradition of charismatic Mosaic prophecy such as is reflected in Hos 12:14 (see chapter 1), but reflects on this tradition by positing a radical distinction between Moses and all those who can properly be designated "prophets." This solution to the problem of the relationship between Moses and prophecy in effect makes Moses a "super-prophet," one who experiences a revelation so much greater than that given to regular prophets that it is fundamentally misleading to call it prophecy. This is an alternate and independent solution to the one that the Deuteronomic authors develop. I confess to a certain agnosticism as to when the redactor's efforts are to be dated in relation to Deuteronomy; in my view, these traditions represent two contrasting and independent modes of negotiating the relationship between Moses and prophecy.[52] The particularly salient feature of this model of prophecy is that, in the course of emphasizing Moses' superiority, the redactor acknowledges non-Mosaic prophecy. Prophecy is not necessarily connected to or dependent upon Mosaic revelation,[53] as the episode of Eldad and Medad shows, as well as Yhwh's strong affirmation of the divine prerogative to speak to prophets in dreams and visions (Num 12:6). The redactor blunts objections to Moses'

---

52   Noth, *Numbers*, 89: "the secondary additions in Num 11 come from circles of ecstatic 'prophecy.' To give even a comparably exact date to this is impossible; for this phenomenon is traceable from the time of Saul until the times of Jeremiah and Ezekiel." Noth, 94, cautions interpreters from ascribing "too late" of a date to Numbers 12, a caution that has been rejected in European scholarship, in which there is a tendency to assign a late date to the comparison between Moses and prophets in Num 11–12, and understand it as an allegory for the respective authority of the Law and the Prophets. So Nihan, "Moses and the Prophets," 39–41, considers Num 12:6–8 a post-Deuteronomic and even post-priestly expansion. In fact, he speaks of a *"comprehensive redaction* whose main objective was to establish the Pentateuch as *the* 'Torah'" (emphasis original, 39), of which Num 12:6–8 is a part (also Deut 34:10–12). Tervanotko, "Speaking in Dreams," 156 also argues that the connection with Deut 34:10 means that Num 12:6–8 "cannot be dated before the exile," though interestingly her interpretation does not see Miriam and Aaron as ciphers for the prophetic literature. I consider it unlikely that traditions about an alternate tent of meeting are post-priestly or post-exilic, and I am not convinced that such a comprehensive redaction of the Pentateuch as posited by Nihan, among others, is traceable. Moreover, in chapter 5 I will argue that Deut 34:10 interprets Num 12:6–8 (and therefore is not contemporaneous with it), precisely because it contains what Numbers lacks: a clear and defined relationship between Moses and the prophets. An early date for the oracle of Num 12:6–8 is proposed by Mark Leuchter, "Samuel: A Prophet Like Moses or a Priest Like Moses?," in *Israelite Prophecy and the Deuteronomistic History: Portrait, Reality, and the Formation of a History*, ed. Mignon R. Jacobs and Raymond F. Person Jr.; AIL 14 (Atlanta: Society of Biblical Literature, 2013), 147–168, who suggests that "an early form of this tradition—or at least the concept behind it—obtained among the Elides at Shiloh" (161).

53   *Contra* Gunneweg, "Das Gesetz und die Propheten," 177 and Nihan, "Moses and the prophets," 40–41.

authority by allowing for varied revelatory sources, weaker in quality, independent of Mosaic auspices. Deuteronomy, as we will see, will adopt a different course, in which any non-Mosaic revelation is prohibited. In order to accomplish this goal, Moses is classified among the prophets; indeed, as von Rad said, he becomes "the archetype and norm of all prophets."[54]

3   The Characterization of Moses as a Prophet in Deut 18:9–22

I will now consider the significant innovation in Deuteronomy's concept of the prophet like Moses. The creation of this concept is to be related to three of Deuteronomy's specific concerns: (1) the attempt to provide legislation that addresses the ambiguity in the phenomenon of prophecy; (2) the attempt to secure Israel's allegiance to a specifically *verbal* revelation: Israel is to be a community founded on the word of God, embodied in Deuteronomy itself; (3) the attempt to ensure that Israel can accurately identify and submit to the authorized custodians of that revelation. In comparison to the situation envisaged in Numbers, Deuteronomy is at pains to restrict what might be understood as legitimate revelation, both in mode and in source.

3.1   *Deuteronomy and Prophecy*

The depiction of prophecy in Num 11–12 as an ambiguous phenomenon is a viewpoint shared by the authors of Deuteronomy. Unlike other Pentateuchal sources, however, Deuteronomy takes a particular interest in this ambiguity as a *problem* and in its legislative program attempts to grapple with the issue of prophetic conflict and provide normative indicators for how the true spokesperson for Yhwh is to be discerned.[55] This undoubtedly reflects the time-period in which Deuteronomy was written and edited: the late Judean monarchy was marked by prophetic conflict, and the contradictory messages from different prophetic figures cannot have inspired confidence in the phenomenon as a whole (cf. Jer 23:9–40; 26–29).[56] Deuteronomy's legislative program addressing prophecy is concentrated in Deut 13:2–6, 18:15–22. Similar lan-

---

54   von Rad, *Theology*, 1:294.
55   See von Rad, *Theology*, 1:99: "what stands unmistakably in the forefront in Deuteronomy is an interest in prophecy and the problems which it set."
56   On the ambiguity of prophecy, see, *inter alia*, James L. Crenshaw, *Prophetic Conflict*, BZAW 124 (Berlin: de Gruyter, 1971); Robert P. Carroll, *When Prophecy Failed: Cognitive Dissonance in the Prophetic Traditions of the Old Testament* (New York: Seabury Press, 1979); Roy L. Heller, *Power, Politics, and Prophecy: The Character of Samuel and the Deuteronomistic Evaluation of Prophecy*, LHB/OTS 440 (London: T&T Clark, 2006), 1–44.

guage is used in these passages: both 13:2 and 18:15 speak of a נביא who will "arise" (קום) from "among you" (קרבך).⁵⁷ Israel is not to listen to the deceiving prophet, but is to listen to the prophet like Moses (לא תשמע, 13:4; אליו תשמעון, 18:15).⁵⁸ Both passages are also preceded by a strong contrast with the practices of the other nations, designating these as "abominations" (תועבה: 12:31; 18:12). Nihan therefore argues that Deut 18:9–22 "serves as a conclusion for chaps. 13–18, whose central topic is the exclusive worship of Yahweh."⁵⁹ Taken together, the passages offer Deuteronomy's "first sketch for a doctrine of prophecy,"⁶⁰ that is, its attempt to assess this phenomenon and provide some normative guidelines for it.

The first passage, Deut 13:2–6, authorizes a position of skepticism towards prophetic claimants.⁶¹ The similarity of the language here to the Vassal Treaties of Esarhaddon, specifically with respect to prohibitions of treasonous behavior, has often been noted.⁶² This suggests that those designated "prophet," נביא are appropriately viewed with a certain level of suspicion. But what sort of prophets are in view here? There are two main features of the seducer-prophet of Deut 13:2–6: this prophet summons Israel to the worship of other gods, whom Israel has not known (13:3), and the prophet offers confirmatory signs which in fact occur (13:2–3). In a provocative article, Jeffrey Stackert has noted that this description could fit the character of Moses in Exod 3–4.⁶³ It is this charismatic model of Mosaic prophecy that Deuteronomy's prophet-legislation seeks

---

57 נביא + קום is not frequent in the Hebrew Bible: it occurs only in Deut 13:2; 18:15, 18; 34:10; Amos 2:11 (though the formulation is slightly different, ואקים מבניכם לנביאים, "And I raised some of your children to be prophets"); Jer 29:15. Nihan, "Moses and the Prophets," 34, argues that Deut 18:15, Amos 2:11, Jer 29:15 "form a kind of a system" in which prophecy extends from Moses to Jeremiah and no further.

58 This parallel is noted by Jean-Pierre Sonnet, "Redefining the Plot of Deuteronomy—From End to Beginning. The Import of Deut 34:9," in *Deuteronomium—Tora für eine neue Generation*, ed. G. Fischer, D. Markl, and S. Paganini, BZAR 17 (Wiesbaden: Harrassowitz Verlag, 2011), 37–49; here 42.

59 Nihan, "Moses and the Prophets," 24; he supplies more arguments at 25n9, some of which are less credible (e.g., the use of בוא to refer to the fulfillment of prophetic sign in 13:4, 18:21–22). A similar observation is made by Markl, "Moses Prophetenrolle," 57, but he suggests that the relevant section is Deut 12–18.

60 Blenkinsopp, *A History of Prophecy in Israel*, 162.

61 See Heller, *Power, Politics, Prophecy*, 21–24.

62 See Eckart Otto, *Deuteronomium 12–34: Erster Teilband: 12,1–23,15*, HThKAT (Freiburg: Herder, 2016), 1241–1253.

63 Jeffrey Stackert, "Mosaic Prophecy and the Deuteronomic Source of the Torah," in *Deuteronomy in the Pentateuch, Hexateuch, and the Deuteronomistic History*, ed. Konrad Schmid and Raymond F. Person Jr., FAT 2:56 (Tübingen: Mohr Siebeck, 2012), 47–63, at 55–57 (see 56: "the extent of the similarities between the prophet in Deut 13 and the account of Moses

to displace with its model of genealogical prophecy: accredited prophets are "like Moses," and specifically like the Deuteronomic portrait of Moses.

The similarity between Moses as charismatic leader and the seducer-prophet of Deut 13:2–6 raises another problem, which is the epistemologically precarious position in which Deuteronomy places its readers. Despite the ambiguity of prophecy, Israel is expected to offer unquestioning obedience and loyalty to a genuine prophet, while accurately assessing and rejecting all prophetic charlatans. Israel has three options when it comes to adjudicating between prophetic claimants: (1) any prophet who, even if producing a sign or wonder (אות או מופת, Deut 13:2 [Eng.13:1]), attempts to lead the people to worship other gods is to be executed (Deut 13:2–6); (2) any prophet who speaks in the name of Yhwh but whose prophecy does not come true is not to be heeded, and the prophet will die in some unspecified manner (Deut 18:20–22); (3) Israel is to listen to and obey the prophet like Moses, upon pain of divine punishment (Deut 18:15–19). There is very little room for error: Israel will be held accountable for not listening to a genuine prophet, but also for listening to imposters.

In two places, the law-code acknowledges the difficult position into which it has placed its readers. First, Deut 13:4 calls attention to the fact that a prophet who produces a sign or wonder may indicate that Yhwh is testing the people.[64] Second, Deut 18:21 gives explicit voice to an objection by means of an interlocutor, who wonders: "How can we recognize a word that the LORD has not spoken?" Deuteronomy responds with the test of fulfillment, which seems inadequate for the moment of deciding whether to give adherence to a prophet. Deuteronomy's warning about a potential test from Yhwh and its attention to the question of fulfillment, however, are not the most important guides the book provides so that Israel may discern which prophet is a genuine spokesperson of God. Relevant to Deuteronomy's legislative interest in prophecy is the explicit designation of Moses as a נביא. Indeed, Deuteronomy offers its characterization of Moses as a prophet as a normative indicator by which genuine prophets may be discerned: Mosaic prophecy, as represented in Deuteronomy itself, is to become the touchstone and norm of all licit prophetic activity. Deuteronomy's concept of the prophet like Moses is therefore a creative characterization of Moses, in the interest of establishing a normative tradition. To make this case I turn to a detailed examination of Deut 18:9–22.

---

in Exod 3, including the reference to unfamiliar אלהים, suggests that Deut 13 is intentionally modeled on the E story").

64   Richard D. Nelson, *Deuteronomy: A Commentary*, OTL (Louisville, Ky.: Westminster John Knox, 2002), 166: this addition "seeks to counter potential resistance from readers who might otherwise respect such prophetic confirmatory signs."

3.2 Deut 18:9–22: Restriction in Revelation

3.2.1 Prolegomena: Text, Structure, Unity, Date

Here is the text and my translation of Deut 18:9–22 (MT):

(9) כי אתה בא אל־הארץ אשר־יהוה אלהיך נתן לך לא־תלמד לעשות כתועבת הגוים ההם: (10) לא־ימצא בך מעביר בנו־ובתו באש קסם קסמים מעונן ומנחש ומכשף: (11) וחבר חבר ושאל אוב וידעני ודרש אל־המתים: (12) כי־תועבת יהוה כל־עשה אלה ובגלל התועבת האלה יהוה אלהיך מוריש אותם מפניך: (13) תמים תהיה עם יהוה אלהיך: (14) כי הגוים האלה אשר אתה יורש אותם אל־מעננים ואל־קסמים ישמעו ואתה לא כן נתן לך יהוה אלהיך: (15) נביא מקרבך מאחיך כמני יקים לך יהוה אלהיך אליו תשמעון: (16) ככל אשר־שאלת מעם יהוה אלהיך בחרב ביום הקהל לאמר לא אסף לשמע את־קול יהוה אלהי ואת־האש הגדלה הזאת לא־אראה עוד ולא אמות: (17) ויאמר יהוה אלי היטיבו אשר דברו: (18) נביא אקים להם מקרב אחיהם כמוך ונתתי דברי בפיו ודבר אליהם את כל־אשר אצונו: (19) והיה האיש אשר לא־ישמע אל־דברי אשר ידבר בשמי אנכי אדרש מעמו: (20) אך הנביא אשר יזיד לדבר דבר בשמי את אשר לא־צויתיו לדבר ואשר ידבר בשם אלהים אחרים ומת הנביא ההוא: (21) וכי תאמר בלבבך איכה נדע את־הדבר אשר לא־דברו יהוה: (22) אשר ידבר הנביא בשם יהוה ולא־יהיה הדבר ולא יבוא הוא הדבר אשר לא־דברו יהוה בזדון דברו הנביא לא תגור ממנו

(9) When you come into the land which Yhwh your God is giving you, do not learn to imitate the abominations of those nations. (10) There is not to found among you one who causes his son or daughter to pass through the fire, a diviner, a conjurer, a soothsayer, a sorcerer, (11) one who casts a spell, a medium, a spiritist, or one who inquires of the dead. (12) For an abomination to Yhwh is everyone who does these, and on account of these abominations Yhwh your God is dispossessing them from before you. (13) You will be perfect with Yhwh your God. (14) For these nations whom you will dispossess listen to conjurers and to diviners, but to you Yhwh has not so given.

(15) Yhwh your God will raise up for you a prophet like me from among you, from your people, to him you will listen, (16) exactly[65] as you asked from Yhwh your God at Horeb, on the day of the assembly, saying, "Do not let me hear[66] the voice of Yhwh my God, and do not let me continue to see this great fire, lest I die." (17) And Yhwh said to me, "They have done well in

---

65 See Joüon-Muraoka 139eN: כל, in some contexts, practically leads to our adverbial idea of *totally, entirely, exactly*."
66 GKC 109d takes לא אסף as a jussive, as I have translated it. Joüon-Muraoka 114d, however, disputes this, saying it ought to be understood as an indicative ("I will not again").

what they have said. (18) A prophet I will raise for them from their people, like you, and I will put my words in his mouth, and he will speak to them all that I command him. (19) I will call to account the person who does not listen to my words, which he speaks in my name. (20) But the prophet who presumes to speak a word in my name which I have not commanded him to speak, or the one who speaks in the name of other gods, that prophet shall die."

(21) And if you say in your heart, "How will we recognize the word which Yhwh has not spoken?"—(22) that which the prophet speaks in the name of Yhwh, if the word does not happen, or the matter does not come to pass, that is a word which Yhwh has not spoken. The prophet spoke it in arrogance, do not fear him.

The textual tradition is stable; there are no major variants.[67] The passage can be divided into three sections: vv. 9–14 prohibit various foreign modes of revelation; vv. 15–20 speak of the institution of the prophet; vv. 21–22 provide a criterion for the discernment of prophets. In view of the careful way vv. 14–15 are tied together rhetorically, it is advisable not to understand this as a rigid three-fold division.[68] The three sections are unified by a fundamental concern with warrant in divine revelation: the divinatory practices of the nations are rejected (18:9–14), and only prophecy is admitted as a valid mode of divination for Israel (18:15–20). Prophecy, however, is also subject to certain provisions.

---

67 The following may be noted:

18:15: MT מקרבך מאחיך; SP אחיך מקרב and LXX ἐκ τῶν ἀδελφῶν σου adopt a smoother reading, harmonizing with 18:18.

18:16: LXX puts the people's request in first person plural instead of singular: οὐ προσθήσομεν ἀκοῦσαι τὴν φωνὴν κυρίου τοῦ θεοῦ ἡμῶν. LXX[B] (Vaticanus) has a further variant, reading σου instead of ἡμῶν; that is, it emphasizes Moses' role as mediator by having the people say that they can no longer hear the voice of *Moses*' God directly.

18:19: The LXX critical edition reads "his words" instead of אל־דברי "to my words": μὴ ἀκούσῃ [τῶν λόγων αὐτοῦ] ὅσα ἂν λαλήσῃ. The bracketed words, however, are missing in LXX[B] and a large number of Greek manuscripts. There is reason to prefer the reading of Vaticanus, as it could have occurred due to haplography in the LXX *Vorlage*, the scribe's eye jumping from one initial א to the next. LXX[B] represents a *lectio difficilor* in the Greek tradition, because ἀκούω lacks an indirect object and ὅσα lacks its antecedent. Also in this verse, LXX and 4Q175 1:7 include the noun ὁ προφήτης/הנביא respectively. This clarifies the subject of ידבר; in MT the antecedent is in v. 18. It is possible that הנביא originally stood in the text, but there is no trigger for haplography in MT, so the variants could represent a subsequent clarification.

68 Nihan, "Moses and the Prophets," 25, divides the passage into two units, vv. 9–13 and 14–22. This maintains the rhetorical unity of vv. 14–15, but also shows the overall unity of the passage, since v. 14 connects to the enumerated prohibited practices as well.

There are positive criteria: the prophet is to be *like Moses* (vv. 15, 18), is to be Israelite (vv. 15, 18), and is to speak only what Yhwh commands (vv. 18, 20). There are negative criteria: first, the prophet must not speak in the name of other gods (v. 20); second, if the prophet speaks in the name of Yhwh and the prediction fails, the prophet is judged to be presumptuous (vv. 21–22).

Scholarship is divided on the matter of the passage's unity. Mayes posits a series of accretions to an original Deuteronomic law in vv. 9–12: vv. 15–18 is a "late addition to the law," which includes v. 14 as a "connecting transitional link"; v. 13 and vv. 19–20, 21–22 represent other late additions.[69] Mayes thus reckons with at least four stages in the passage's growth. More circumspect is Udo Rütersworden, who divides the passage into two sections: vv. 9–15 represent the preexilic Deuteronomic law, while vv. 16–22 are exilic Dtr additions.[70] In defense of this view he rightly notes that the date of Deut 18:16–18 must be related to that of 5:22–31,[71] since both passages ground the activity of Israel's covenant mediator (Moses and the prophet like him) on the Horeb theophany. On the basis of an exilic dating of Deuteronomy 5, Rütersworden ascribes vv. 16–22 to a later hand than vv. 9–15. He adduces one additional consideration, which is that the phrase מקרב אחיהם in 18:18 represents a "smoothing" of the "grammatically not impossible" but awkward מקרבך מאחיך of 18:15.[72]

Nihan has countered this latter argument: the "distinct formulation of v. 15 is best explained in connection with v. 14: contrary to the diviners of the nations, the prophet 'like Moses' must absolutely be an Israelite 'from your middle, from your brothers.' In v. 18 the context is different and this contrast is no longer explicit."[73] Moreover, Nihan marshalls several arguments to support the literary unity of the entire pericope. He notes that vv. 9–12 and vv. 19–20, 21–22 point back to Deut 12:29–31, 13:2–6.[74] Indeed, Deut 12:29–31 transitions from the legislation concerning the central sanctuary by rooting this law in the contrast between the practices and the "abominations" of the nations (תועבה; Deut 12:31, 18:12); moreover, the passage specifically mentions the burning of one's children in fire, the first practice prohibited in Deut 18:10. In both Deut 12:29–13:6 and 18:9–22, Deuteronomy proceeds from the invoking of a strong contrast

---

69 Andrew D.H. Mayes, *Deuteronomy*, NCBC (Grand Rapids: Eerdmans, 1981), 279–280.
70 Udo Rütersworden, *Von der politischen Gemeinschaft zur Gemeinde: Studien zu Dt 16,18–18,22*, BBB 65 (Frankfurt am Main: Athenäum, 1987).
71 Rütersworden, *Von der politischen Gemeinschaft*, 85.
72 Rütersworden, *Von der politischen Gemeinschaft*, 85: "der Ausdruck in v. 18 ist eine Glättung des sperrigen, aber grammatisch nicht unmöglichen Ausdrucks in v. 15."
73 Nihan, "Moses and the Prophets," 28n16.
74 Nihan, "Moses and the Prophets," 25, "a sophisticated *inclusio* around the section comprising chapters 13–18 is thus created"; see also 29.

between Israel and the nations to a discussion of prophecy, including its potential pitfalls. Nihan's conclusion, one with which I concur, is that Deut 18:9–22 is substantially a unity.[75] It is possible, of course, that features such as the test of fulfilment were added as redactional glosses, but there are few clear signs of editorial reworking.

The date of Deut 18:9–22 is a contested issue which involves a variety of considerations. First, the passage occurs as the conclusion of Deuteronomy's so-called "constitutional polity" (16:18–18:22), which concerns the various offices in the land (judge, king, priest, prophet). Some attention must be paid to envisioning a *Sitz im Leben* for this polity. Second, Deut 18:16–18, with its recall of the Horeb revelation in Deuteronomy 5, plays a key role in the macro-structure of Deuteronomy.[76] It is therefore important to offer brief comments on the constitutional polity, as well as the composition of Deuteronomy as a whole and the scholarly quest for an *Urdeuteronomium* (though I can only touch on this latter issue).[77]

Deuteronomy 18:9–22 displays close lexical and thematic links with the constitutional polity as a whole, and cannot easily be extricated from it.[78] It is doubtful that this polity is a product of post-exilic Deuteronomistic scribes, as Nihan suggests,[79] or belongs to an exilic redaction of Deuteronomy, as Karel van

---

75 Nihan, "Moses and the Prophets," 29.
76 See particularly Markl, "Moses Prophetenrolle," 57.
77 For a full review of scholarship on the composition of Deuteronomy, see Eckart Otto, *Deuteronomium 1–11: Erster Teilband: 1,1–4,43*, HThKAT (Freiburg: Herder, 2012), 62–230.
78 To provide some examples: קרב + אח only occurs in Deut 15:11; 17:15, 20; 18:2, 15, 18; 19:19; 24:7; 1Sam 16:13; the warning against "presumption" is another motif, cf. זיד (17:13, 18:20) and זדון (17:12, 18:22). In terms of structure, Nihan, "Moses and the Prophets," 31–32, has also pointed to "the obvious gradation that the arrangement of the various offices in Deut 16:18–18:22 evinces." As Nihan shows, the office of judge is chosen by the people and is non-hereditary, that of king is requested by the people but chosen by Yhwh and is hereditary, that of priest is chosen by Yhwh and hereditary, and only prophecy is established by Yhwh and is non-hereditary (charismatic).
79 Nihan, "Moses and the Prophets," 31, dates Deut 18:9–22 to the post-exilic period: "For the Deuteronomistic scribes of the early Persian period the prophet has now replaced the king as the authoritative figure of the postexilic and post-monarchical community because he exemplarily illustrates the 'theocratic' ideal of that community." One wonders if the "prophet" would really be elevated over the priest as representing the "theocratic ideal" in the post-exilic era. All indications are that prophecy was held, if anything, in lower repute in this time (cf Zech 13:2–6; Neh 6:14). See Martti Nissinen, "The Dubious Image of Prophecy," in *Prophets, Prophecy, and Prophetic Texts in Second Temple Judaism*, ed. M.H. Floyd and R.D. Haak (LHB/OTS 427; New York: T&T Clark, 2006), 26–41.

der Toorn has argued.[80] This judgment is often based on the supposed utopian character of this constitution.[81] Whether it is in fact utopian is at least questionable;[82] even if it were, one could easily imagine an anti-Assyrian reform movement in the days of Manasseh composing an idealized polity.[83] Its commitment to a "theocratic ideal," as Nihan put it, is proof neither of exilic or post-exilic origin, nor, for that matter, of its utopian character.[84] More to the

---

80   Karel van der Toorn, *Scribal Culture and the Making of the Hebrew Bible* (Cambridge, Mass.: Harvard, 2007), 157.

81   This view was influentially promulgated by Norbert Lohfink, "Die Sicherung der Wirksamkeit des Gotteswortes durch das Prinzip der Schriftlichkeit der Tora und durch das Prinzip der Gewaltenteilung nach dem Ämtergesetzen des Buches Deuteronomiums (Dt 16,18–18,22)," in *Testimonium Veritati: Festschrift W. Kampf*, ed. H. Wolter, Frankfurter Theologische Studien 7 (Frankfurt am Main: Knecht, 1971), 143–155. See now van der Toorn, *Scribal Culture*, 157: "this constitution may be qualified as a Utopian document at home in a time in which dreams had to make up for lost realities. The temple vision of Ezekiel (Ezek 40–48) partakes of the same genre and belongs in the same period." I confess that I fail to see how Ezek 40–48 can be said to belong to the "same genre" as Deut 16:18–18:22; the supposed utopian character of this constitution is vastly overstated. The comparison to Ezek 40–48, with the ascription of an exilic date for the polity, is also made by Ernest Nicholson, *Deuteronomy and the Judaean Diaspora* (Oxford: Oxford, 2014), 106–107.

82   For an analysis of this text that focuses on its practical application in the pre-exilic period, see Mark A. O'Brien, "Deuteronomy 16.18–18.22: Meeting the Challenge of Towns and Nations," *JSOT* 33 (2008): 155–172.

83   On the possibility of Deuteronomy's origin in a clandestine movement, S.R. Driver, *A Critical and Exegetical Commentary on Deuteronomy*, ICC (Edinburgh: T&T Clark, 1895), li, is eloquent, if somewhat homiletic: "It may have been in the dark days of Manasseh, when the spiritual energy of prophecy, no longer able, as of yore, to make its voice heard openly among the people, nevertheless refused to be suppressed, and, hopeful of better times, provided in anticipation a spiritual rallying-point, round which the disorganized forces of the national religion might under happier auspices one day range themselves again." See also Nelson, *Deuteronomy*, 8: "Deuteronomy most likely began as a covert undertaking by dissident Jerusalem scribal circles during the reign of Manasseh and the minority of Josiah, with collaboration from aristocratic families, elements of the priesthood, and those schooled in wisdom." Bernard Levinson, *Deuteronomy and the Hermeneutics of Legal Innovation* (New York: Oxford, 1997), 151, raises the possibility that "the Deuteronomic authors represented a sectarian movement within late Judaean society," though he does not pursue it further due to concerns about potential anachronism.

84   Joseph Blenkinsopp, "Judaeans, Jews, Children of Abraham," in *Judah and the Judaeans in the Achaemenid Period: Negotiating Identity in an International Context*, ed. O. Lipschits, G. Knoppers, and M. Oeming (Winona Lake, Ind.: Eisenbrauns, 2011), 461–482, here 466, suggests that the architects of the polity "envisioned what we might call a constitutional monarchy, a monarchy not necessarily Davidic but one under the law interpreted by Levitical priests (Deut 17:14–20), somewhat analogous to the Iranian president who—at this writing—enjoys considerable power but is ultimately under the control of the Ayatollahs

point, the constitutional polity contains very little that could be characterized as Deuteronomistic.[85] The law of the king (Deut 17:14–20) is striking in this respect, as both Bernard Levinson and Gary Knoppers have shown.[86] Furthermore, Bernard Levinson has demonstrated that the laws concerning the administration of justice in 16:18–20, 17:2–13 reflect the same hermeneutical strategies vis-à-vis the Covenant Code and the same focus on centralization (and its consequences) as occur in the earliest strata of Deuteronomy, rendering unnecessary the view that these laws can only be understood as later additions to an original *Urdeuteronomium*.[87]

With respect to the law of the prophet, there is little to suggest the hand of a Dtr editor.[88] As is commonly agreed, the sense of the singular נביא in v. 15, 18 is distributive:[89] the passage promises not one particular prophet or even one succession of prophets; it authorizes an institution of prophecy.[90] (As we will see, the understanding of the prophet like Moses as the succession of singular figures to Moses emerges later, in the DH and Jeremiah.) Nothing in the passage implies that more than one prophet like Moses could not be operating simulta-

---

and the Sharia interpreted by them." Blenkinsopp's analogy to modern-day Iran is apposite: Deuteronomy's carefully calibrated division of powers is not necessarily as "utopian" as many scholars suppose, and certainly its polity need not be viewed as purely theoretical.

[85] This, however, is a debated point. See Gary N. Knoppers, "Rethinking the Relationship between Deuteronomy and the Deuteronomistic History: The Case of Kings," *CBQ* 63 (2001): 393–415, and his conclusion, 414: "However one dates the material in Deut 16 18–18:22—before, contemporaneous with, or after the work of the primary Deuteronomistic editor(s) of Kings—the disparities between the two works remain."

[86] Bernard Levinson, "The Reconceptualization of Kingship in Deuteronomy and the Deuteronomistic History's Transformation of Torah," *VT* 51 (2001): 511–534; Gary N. Knoppers, "The Deuteronomist and the Deuteronomic Law of the King: A Re-examination of a Relationship," *ZAW* 108 (1996): 329–346. On the law of the king, van der Toorn, *Scribal Culture*, 159, says "Josiah would not have consented to sponsor such views," but we can know very little about Josiah's personal inclinations; moreover, the law could have been written before Josiah's time (e.g., in the time of Manasseh, if the Deuteronomic reform movement emerged then).

[87] Levinson, *Deuteronomy and the Hermeneutics*, 98–143.

[88] *Pace* Brian Schmidt, "Canaanite Magic vs. Israelite Religion: Deuteronomy 18 and the Taxonomy of Taboo," in *Magic and Ritual in the Ancient World*, ed. Paul A. Mirecki and Marvin W. Meyer, RGRW 141 (Leiden: Brill, 2002), 242–259, who argues for the Dtr character of the text.

[89] The singular נביא can be compared to the singular מלך in 17:15, which is also similar to Deut 18:15, 18 in its specific requirement of endogeny (מקרב אחיך).

[90] See, e.g., Driver, *Deuteronomy*, 227; Tigay, *Deuteronomy*, 174–175; Nelson, *Deuteronomy*, 234–235.

neously, indeed, the admission that prophets are members of the broader class of diviners seems to demand this possibility. Though Driver's language is dated, his comments are apposite:

> The position assigned in this law to the prophet is a noticeable one. He appears in it as the representative in Israel of the heathen diviner; he is presented as the appointed agent for satisfying, in so far as they are legitimate, those cravings of humanity to unlock the secrets of the future, or to discover in some critical situation—as, for instance, that of Saul before the battle of Gilboaʿ (1 Sam 28:5 f.)—the purpose of Heaven, which gave birth in other nations to the arts of the diviner, and kindred superstitions …. A law prohibiting them [i.e., the "heathen" arts of divination], and at the same time placing the prophet in his true position in regard to them, would be in entire harmony with the scope of the Deuteronomic legislation.[91]

This mantic background suggests that the author would have deemed prophets to be part of an ancient institution, which Israelites could consult for guidance and advice (e.g., "where can I find my lost donkeys?" [1 Sam 9]).[92] Indeed, the verification principle presumes that prophets are primarily responding to inquiries that can easily be confirmed or disconfirmed.[93] The increasingly common assertion that Deut 18:9–22 is exilic or post-exilic ignores this mantic context, and incorporates alternate speculative assumptions.[94] Finally, given the Dtr association between disobedience to the prophets and exile, if this passage was late, one would expect Deut 18:19 to contain a threat of exile rather than the

---

[91] Driver, *Deuteronomy*, 221. Tigay, *Deuteronomy*, 173–174, also situates the law of the prophet in terms of the "universal human desire to learn the future and in some way control it." He goes on, "The Torah does not deprecate this desire but insists that it be pursued only by means chosen by God, particularly prophecy."

[92] Or more pressingly, "should we go to war or not?" (1 Kgs 22). For this and other examples of how prophecy was a part of ancient Israelite divinatory practices, see Rannfrid Thelle, "Reflections of Ancient Israelite Divination in the Former Prophets," in *Israelite Prophecy and the Deuteronomistic History: Portrait, Reality, and the Formation of a History*, ed. Mignon R. Jacobs and Raymond F. Person Jr., AIL 14 (Atlanta: Society of Biblical Literature, 2013), 7–33, at 14–23.

[93] See Stackert, "Mosaic Prophecy," 58–59, who emphasizes the consultative function of prophecy in the verification criterion in Deut 18:21–22.

[94] For example, Nihan, "Moses and the Prophets," 35, claims that the authors have only past, not present or future, prophets in view, and Nicholson, "Deut 18, Prophets, and Scripture," 163–167, argues that the author of this passage has *written* prophecy in view; nothing in the passage sustains either of these claims.

vague "call to account (דרש)."⁹⁵ Consistent with these observations, I will argue below that Deut 18:9–22 aims at accomplishing what might be called a "centralization" of revelation, and so in its ideology is closely allied to the purposes of *Urdeuterononium*, whatever its original extent.

It is beyond the scope of this study to investigate the precise contents of the pre-exilic *Urdeuteronomium* or develop a detailed proposal concerning the stages of Deuteronomy's composition.⁹⁶ The unity of Deut 18:9–22, and indeed its integral unity within both the constitutional polity and a pre-exilic *Urdeuteronomium*, fits well with the so-called "block model" of Deuteronomy's composition and growth, which has been argued for by Karel van der Toorn.⁹⁷ The rather limited number of occasions for scribal intervention into an authoritative text that has served as the public basis for a religious reform leads van der Toorn to conclude: "The odds are overwhelmingly in favor of a limited number of text editions, each new edition allowing the scribes to enrich the text with new material as it had accumulated over time."⁹⁸ He develops a proposal in which Deuteronomy develops in four editions, which he labels the Covenant, Torah, History, and Wisdom editions respectively.⁹⁹ In support, he claims that Deuteronomy has three beginnings ("rubrics," 1:1, 4:44, 4:45) and

---

95 See J.D. Atkins, "Reassessing the Origins of Deuteronomic Prophecy: Early Moses Traditions in Deuteronomy 18:15–22," *BBR* 23 (2013): 323–341, at 334: "Deut 18:15–19 lacks the quintessential Deuteronomistic perspective on prophecy and exile."

96 With the majority of scholars, I understand pre-exilic *Urdeuteronomium* to originate in the seventh century BCE, between 672 and 622 BCE. The *terminus post quem* depends on the generally recognized dependence of Deuteronomy on the vassal treaties of Esarhaddon. See Karin Finsterbusch, *Deuteronomium: Eine Einführung* (Göttingen: Vandenhoeck & Ruprecht, 2012), 21. Stackert, *Prophet like Moses*, 32, on the basis of this dependence, posits a date of 670 BCE for his D source, the precise contours of which he does not give. The *terminus a quo* depends on accepting the now heavily debated connection between Deuteronomy and Josiah's reform (2 Kgs 22–23). Some scholars deny this connection and posit an exilic origin for *Urdeuteronomium*, e.g., Finsterbusch, *Deuteronomium*, 24–27; Nicholson, *Deuteronomy and the Judaean Diaspora*; Juha Pakkala, "The Date of the Oldest Edition of Deuteronomy," *ZAW* 121 (2009): 388–401. A convincing rejection of Pakkala's arguments is found in the response article by Nathan MacDonald, "Issues in the Dating of Deuteronomy: A Response to Juha Pakkala," *ZAW* 122 (2010): 431–435.

97 van der Toorn, *Scribal Culture*, 146–147, argues that Deuteronomy's text would most probably not have been subject to countless small accretions over the two centuries of its expansion, suggesting three factors that would have to be present for Deuteronomy's revision: an occasion (provided, he suggests, by the need for a new master scroll), a motive ("the wish of scribes to attune the text to changing historical circumstances"), and a warrant, a formal authorization by the priests who were in charge of the Torah.

98 van der Toorn, *Scribal Culture*, 148.

99 van der Toorn, *Scribal Culture*, 150–172.

endings ("colophons," 28:69, 29:28, 34:10–12), which he associates with the first three stages in the book's growth.¹⁰⁰ It is striking that two of the proposed rubrics, 4:44–45, are next to each other in the final form of Deuteronomy. This raises the issue of how carefully his "Covenant" and "Torah" editions can be distinguished. Van der Toorn's *Urdeuteronomium*, his "covenant edition," has a rather slim profile, consisting of Deut 4:45; 6:4–9; 12:1–16:17; 26; 28, that is, it contains the prologue, stipulations, and blessings and curses of neo-Assyrian treaty texts.¹⁰¹ The Torah edition, which van der Toorn dates to the exilic period (590–570 BCE), opens with Deut 4:44 and includes as framing chapters Deut 5 and 29; moreover, directly pertinent to this investigation, it is in this edition that van der Toorn places the Deuteronomic Constitution.¹⁰²

Contrary to van der Toorn's proposal that 4:44, 45 represent two distinct rubrics, the theory that in fact there are two openings of the book was influentially advanced by S.R. Driver more than a century ago (1:1–5, 4:44–49).¹⁰³ Among modern commentators, Tigay, Nelson, and Weinfeld ascribe to its basic parameters.¹⁰⁴ According to Nelson, the majority of Deut 5–26, 28 constitute pre-exilic *Urdeuteronomium*; exilic additions are found first in chapters 4, 27, 29–30; later, as part of incorporation into the DH, chapters 1–3, 31, 34* are added;

---

100   van der Toorn, *Scribal Culture*, 151. For van der Toorn, the wisdom edition has no rubric or colophon; it substantively consists of Deut 4, 30; although van der Toorn suggests it may have included Deut 19–25 (162–166). This last suggestion is unlikely, which van der Toorn recognizes, and so he suggests that the wisdom edition at least included a number of interventions into the law of Deut 19–25 (165); here van der Toorn's proposal veers close to the "accretion" model that he pointedly rejects.
101   van der Toorn, *Scribal Culture*, 152–154.
102   van der Toorn, *Scribal Culture*, 157–158, see 158: "The effect of the addition is significant: what in the Covenant Edition had been a law code in the vein of earlier law codes became the constitution of a theocratic state; a reform document turned into a program for the establishment of a theocracy."
103   Driver, *Deuteronomy*, lxv: chapters 5–26, 28 "formed part of the law book found by Hilkiah: all are written in the same style, and all breathe the same spirit." In his recent commentary, Jack Lundbom, *Deuteronomy: A Commentary* (Grand Rapids: Eerdmans, 2013), 8, observes: "numerous scholars have followed Driver in viewing 1:1–5 and 4:44–49 as double superscriptions surviving in the present book."
104   Nelson, *Deuteronomy*, 4–9; Moshe Weinfeld, *Deuteronomy 1–11: A New Translation with Introduction and Commentary*, AB 5 (New York: Doubleday, 1991), 10: 4:44–28:68 "constituted the original book"; Jeffrey H. Tigay, *Deuteronomy = [Devarim]: The Traditional Hebrew Text with the New JPS Translation*, JPSTC 5 (Philadelphia: Jewish Publication Society, 1996), xxv: "the original book—'core-Deuteronomy'—probably consisted of something like 4:44 through chapter 28 or 30, the main sections of the book. Even within this core, there are later interpolations."

finally the Song and Blessing of Moses are incorporated (chapters 32–33). There is, in fact, a broad consensus in scholarship on the relative dating of the various sections of Deuteronomy; the disagreement consists in how much material to ascribe to pre-exilic Deuteronomy.[105] Scholars such as van der Toorn, Nelson, and Otto agree on the latest "blocks" to enter the book, but Nelson allows for a more extensive pre-exilic Deuteronomy, arguing that after it served as the basis of a reform movement, it is difficult to imagine Deuteronomy growing from a mere six chapters or so (van der Toorn's *Urdeuteronomium*) to the current thirty-four.[106]

Whatever the shape of *Urdeuteronomium*, it is important to note that the original law-code is not presented as Moses' valedictory on the day of his death. Rather, Deuteronomy is a "wilderness" law, given in Moab at some point after Israel came out of Egypt. Deuteronomy 28:69 [Eng. 29:1], which van der Toorn understands to be the original conclusion of the book,[107] presents Deuteronomy as a Mosaic speech that is supplementary to the Horeb covenant: "These are the words of the covenant that the LORD commanded Moses to make with the Israelites in the land of Moab, in addition to (מלבד) the covenant that he had made with them at Horeb." This forms an *inclusio* with Deut 5:2–3: "The LORD our God made a covenant with us at Horeb. Not with our ancestors did the LORD make this covenant, but with us, who are all of us here alive today." The first covenant was made by Yhwh with Israel at Horeb, the second via Moses in Moab. The Horeb covenant is spoken by Yhwh directly (Deut 5:6–21), after

---

105 Compare Eckart Otto, *Das Deuteronomium im Pentateuch und Hexateuch: Studien zur Literaturgeschichte von Pentateuch und Hexateuch im Lichte des Deuteronomiumrahmens*, FAT 30 (Tübingen: Mohr Siebeck, 2000), 233–242, who provides a brief overview of his understanding of Deuteronomy's development with a summary chart (242). Otto includes in dtn Deuteronomium 6:4f.; *12:13–28:44, but reckons with later exilic insertions into this block, including the prophet-law of 18:9–22.

106 Nelson, *Deuteronomy*, 8 notes that after "Deuteronomy became publicly accessible and respected, presumably as the foundation for Josiah's reform, its text would have remained more or less stable. For this reason, subsequent monarchic and exilic additions may be discerned without difficulty." Nelson's confidence ("without difficulty" [!]) is remarkable in view of the lack of scholarly agreement regarding the shape of an *Urdeuteronomium*.

107 Whether Deut 28:69 [Eng. 29:1] is a colophon or a superscription to what follows is a point of debate. The differing versification itself suggests the verse's ambiguity. Tigay, *Deuteronomy*, 274, points out that the phrase "words of the covenant" "applies to the laws, blessings, and curses of the preceding chapters much more readily than it does to the exhortation of chapters 29–30." Nelson, *Deuteronomy*, 338–339 provides a nice summary of arguments on both sides and concludes that "in the final form of Deuteronomy this verse looks both ways." This is certainly correct; however, Nelson maintains the possibility that it served as a concluding summary of an earlier edition of the book.

this (in distinction from the Covenant Code) Moses insists that Yhwh "added no more (ולא יסף)" (Deut 5:22).[108] Deuteronomy 6–26 then contains *Mosaic* law;[109] it is specifically marked as additional to Horeb (מלבד, 28:69). Levinson has seen the importance of the point: "Deuteronomy presents itself in narrative terms as the recapitulation of the story; in homiletical terms as exhortation to obey previously promulgated statutes; in legal terms as ancillary."[110] It is from this perspective that Deuteronomy's characterization of Moses as a נביא is to be seen, namely, as a manifestation of Deuteronomy's fundamental decision to use Mosaic Discourse as the vehicle of divine revelation, and to insist that all future revelation also be coordinated to the Mosaic touchstone. In this context, Deut 18:9–22 restricts authorized modes of revelation, both in mode and in source.

3.2.2 The Restriction in Mode of Revelation in Deut 18:9–15, 18

Deuteronomy 18:9–14 contains the fullest list of proscribed divinatory practices in the Hebrew Bible. The table below contains parallels between Deuteronomy's enumeration and the rest of the Hebrew Bible.[111] In compiling this com-

---

108 See Levinson, *Deuteronomy and the Hermeneutics*, 152: the statement is "a deliberate textual polemic" against the Covenant Code.

109 In my view, the use of Mosaic discourse is a feature of *Urdeuteronomium*, though this claim has been contested. Norbert Lohfink, "Das Deuteronomium: Jahwegesetz oder Mosegesetz?," *TP* 65 (1990): 387–391, finds a number of passages in Deuteronomy that refer to Yhwh as commanding the Israelites (4:13, 23; 5:32, 33; 6:17, 20, 24; 9:12, 16; 26:13–14, 16; 28:45). For Lohfink, particularly 6:17, 26:16, 28:45 are evidence that the law "am Anfange und am Ende metasprachliche Aussagen über sich selbst enthielt"; these "metasprachliche Aussagen" refer to Yhwh, not Moses, as commanding the law. He therefore argues that the use of Mosaic discourse belongs not to the earliest but to a later stage of the book. Lohfink acknowledges that this is no longer clear in the present form of the book, because Yhwh does not speak in first person, but concludes that in the oldest edition of the book it must have been "viel offensichtlicher" that it was the law of Yhwh, not Moses. Konrad Schmid, "Deuteronomy within the 'Deuteronomistic Histories' in Genesis–2 Kings," in *Deuteronomy in the Pentateuch, Hexateuch, and the Deuteronomistic History*, ed. Konrad Schmid and Raymond F. Person Jr., FAT 2:56 (Tübingen: Mohr Siebeck, 2012), 8–30, accepts Lohfink's argument ("the Mosaic fiction of Deuteronomy … is probably not primary" [16]), and says the view that "Deuteronomy is secondarily, not originally, an explanation of the Sinai legislation does not require special confirmation" (17–18). On the contrary, Deuteronomy's homiletic and hortatory style and its use of first person for its speaker, who makes consistent references to Yhwh in third person, suggests that the view that this is not original to the book would require considerably more evidence than Lohfink or Schmid provide.

110 Levinson, *Deuteronomy and the Hermeneutics*, 151.

111 See also H.L. Bosman, "Redefined Prophecy as Deuteronomic Alternative to Divination

prehensive list, the Deuteronomic code agrees with other legal collections, particularly H, but the relative date of these codes is disputed and beyond the purview of this analysis.¹¹² The precise distinctions between these terms for divinatory practices may be impossible to establish; Mayes even suggests that many of them may have already been synonymous to the Deuteronomic legislator.¹¹³ The paucity of non-polemical references to these practices suggests that Deuteronomy's authors were not entirely innovative in their negative view of these practices.¹¹⁴ Deuteronomy's innovation does not consist in the prohibition of these practices, but in its comprehensiveness.¹¹⁵ It is worth noting that Deuteronomy may also be dependent on prophetic sources. The only complete parallel to the final three practices listed is found in Isa 8:19–20:¹¹⁶

---

in Deut 18:9–22," *AcT* 16 (1996): 1–23; Driver, *Deuteronomy*, 221–226, provides a thorough discussion.

112 Most scholars assume D is prior to H. See, e.g., Christophe Nihan, "The Holiness Code Between D and P: Some Comments on the Function and Significance of Leviticus 17–26 in the Composition of the Torah," in *Das Deuteronomium zwischen Pentateuch und Deuteronomistischem Geschichtswerk*, ed. E. Otto and R. Achenbach, FRLANT 206 (Göttingen: Vandenhoeck & Ruprecht, 2004), 85–100. However, many scholars also do not assign Deut 18:9–22 to the D-code, so questions of textual dependence and direction are in this case, as always, complicated. For an argument for the priority of H, see Israel Knohl, *The Sanctuary of Silence: The Priestly Torah and the Holiness School* (Minneapolis: Fortress Press, 1995).

113 Mayes, *Deuteronomy*, 280. Thelle, "Israelite Divination," 26–27: "The exact references of each of these identifications of divinatory activity have been discussed and are not fully understood." The parallels in Leviticus (H) show that certain types of diviners were commonly grouped as sub-sets.

114 Schmidt, "Canaanite Magic," 250, emphasizes Isa 3:2 and Mic 3:6–7 as non-polemical, and concludes, 253: "In sum, none of the practices listed in Deuteronomy 18 were condemned in pre-exilic prophetic traditions." But, he arrives at this only by assuming Isa 8:19; 19:3; and 29:4 are "dtr redactional texts of First Isaiah" (247) and that other texts such as Isa 2:5–9 (250) and Mic 5:2 (252) are also Dtr. By this procedure one can prove anything.

115 See Nelson, *Deuteronomy*, 232–233: "The list intends to be exhaustive in order to emphasize a complete prohibition of every conceivable sort of such practices." *Pace* Schmidt, "Canaanite Magic," who argues that the passage is exilic, dtr, and innovative when compared to attitudes toward divinatory practices in pre-exilic Israelite religion.

116 Schmidt, "Canaanite Magic," 247, considers this a Dtr redactional text. However, the verb צפף occurs exclusively in First Isaiah (8:19; 10:14; 29:4; 38:14), rendering this thesis very unlikely. It should also be noted that the people "quoted" in Isa 8:19 have no knowledge of a prohibition of these practices, and that the prophetic polemic has more to do with their futility than with their betrayal of any particular law-code. As Thelle, "Israelite Divination," 31, points out, such divinatory methods are considered "foolish and for naught" in Isaiah, but "punishable by death" in Deuteronomy.

TABLE 2 References to divinatory practices in the Hebrew Bible

Divinatory Practice	Parallel Prohibition	Polemical References (selective)	Non-polemical References
מעביר בנו־ובתו באש	Deut 12:31; Lev 18:21, 20:2–5 (?):ᵃ ומזרעך לא־תתן להעביר למלך	2 Kgs 16:3; 17:17, 31; 21:6; 23:10; Jer 32:35; Ezek 20:31; 2 Chr 33:6	[See texts on child sacrifice, which do not use this precise terminology]
קסם		Josh 13:22; 1 Sam 15:23; 2 Kgs 17:17; Jer 14:14; 27:9; 29:8; Ezek 13:6, 23	Prov 16:10; Isa 3:2; Mic 3:6–7
מעונן	Lev 19:26	2 Kgs 21:6; Isa 2:6; 57:3; Jer 27:9; Mic 5:11; 2 Chr 33:6	
מנחש	Lev 19:26	2 Kgs 17:17; 21:6; 2 Chr 33:6	Gen 30:27; 44:5, 15
מכשף	Exod 22:18, מכשפה	2 Kgs 9:22; Isa 47:9, 12; Jer 27:9; Mic 5:11; Nah 3:4; 2 Chr 33:6	Dan 2:2
חבר חבר			Ps 58:6
שאל אוב	Lev 19:31, 20:6, 27	1 Sam 28:3; 2 Kgs 21:6; 23:24; Isa 8:19; 19:3; 1 Chr 10:13; 2 Chr 33:6	Isa 29:4
ידעני	Lev 19:31, 20:6, 27	1 Sam 28:3; 2 Kgs 21:6; 23:24; Isa 8:19; 19:3; 2 Chr 33:6	
דרש אל־המתים		Isa 8:19	

a See discussion in Tigay, *Deuteronomy*, 464–465.

וכי־יאמרו אליכם **דרשו** אל־האבות ואל־הידענים המצפצפים והמהגים הלוא־עם אל־
אלהיו **ידרש** בעד החיים אל־**המתים** לתורה ולתעודה אם־לא יאמרו כדבר הזה אשר
אין־לו שחר

> Now if people say to you, "Consult the ghosts and the familiar spirits that chirp and mutter; should not a people consult their gods, the dead on behalf of the living, for teaching and for instruction?" Surely, those who speak like this will have no dawn![117]

Deuteronomy's authors thus drew comprehensively on Israel's legal and prophetic traditions to prohibit all forms of divination, prophecy alone excepted.

---

117 So NRSV. The possibility of taking לתורה ולתעודה as the prophet's words, rather than as part of the quotation of the people, should be noted. If an early Deuteronomist author knew this oracle, and understood it in this way, it provides the same strong contrast between divinatory practices and obedience to a prophetic Torah that Deuteronomy itself promotes.

The provision of a prophet as ongoing bearer of revelation for Israel occurs in this context and is juxtaposed with the practices of the nations in the strongest possible way:

כי הגוים האלה אשר אתה יורש אותם אל־מעננים ואל־קסמים ישמעו **ואתה** לא כן נתן לך יהוה אלהיך **נביא** מקרבך מאחיך כמני יקים לך יהוה אלהיך אליו תשמעון

For these nations whom you will dispossess listen to conjurers and to diviners, but to you Yhwh has not so given. Yhwh your God will raise up for you a prophet like me from among you, from your people, to him you will listen.
    Deut 18:14–15, my translation

Both "but to you" (ואתה) and "prophet" (נביא) are placed in positions of emphasis: while the nations listen (שמע) to conjurers and diviners, Israel is to listen (שמע) to a native Israelite prophet, specifically one who is like Moses. Furthermore, the definition of prophecy in this context is supplied by Yhwh's quoted words in 18:18: "I will put my words in [the prophet's] mouth, and he will speak to them all that I command him." The prophet is the only legitimate conduit of divine revelation, which is for Deuteronomy fundamentally a matter of speech.[118]

As Deuteronomy was supplemented in the exilic and post-exilic periods, its scribal authors continued to return to this emphasis on the verbal character of divine revelation.[119] Deuteronomy 4 serves as a lengthy prologue to Moses' recounting of the moment when God spoke directly to the people, in the issuing of the Ten Words, and focuses on the verbal character of the revelation: "You heard the sound of words but saw no form; there was only a voice" (Deut 4:12).[120] Deuteronomy presents itself as a law-code that attempts to establish the community on the word of God,[121] which it insists is accessible to Israel, available to be obeyed:

---

118   That this may represent a limitation on prophetic activity is suggested by, e.g., Mic 3:11: נביאיה בכסף יקסמו. For the Deuteronomic authors, the main problem in that description would not be the issue of financial gain, as it was for Micah.

119   Consider the term דברים: used in 1:1, it also characterizes the divine law in 1:18; 4;10, 12, 13, 36; 5:22; 6:6; 9:10; 10:2, 4; 11:18; 12:28; 17:19; 18:18, 19; 27:3, 8, 26; 28:14, 58, 69; 29:8, 29; 31:24; 32:45, 46. The phrase "all the words of this law" (כל־דברי התורה הזאת) occurs only in Deuteronomy: 17:19, 27:3, 8; 28:58, 29:28; 31:12; 32:46.

120   תמונה is used; it also occurs in Num 12:8, where Yhwh says of Moses: "He sees the form of the LORD."

121   See Walther Eichrodt, *Theology of the Old Testament*, trans. J.A. Baker, 2 vols., OTL (Lon-

> The secret things belong to the LORD our God, but the revealed things belong to us and to our children forever, to observe all the words of this law (כל־דברי התורה הזאת).
>
> Deut 29:29

> Surely, this commandment that I am commanding you today is not too hard for you, nor is it too far away. It is not in heaven, that you should say, "Who will go up to heaven for us, and get it for us so that we may hear it and observe it?" Neither is it beyond the sea, that you should say, "Who will cross to the other side of the sea for us, and get it for us so that we may hear it and observe it?" No, the word is very near to you; it is in your mouth and in your heart for you to observe.
>
> Deut 30:11–14

This emphasis on the importance of the word of God, which is heightened as the book passes through its stages of transmission, has its origin in the Deuteronomic theology of unity. One Lord, one sanctuary, one people: to this needs to be added, one revelation, given to Israel at Horeb.[122] Because of this theological commitment, Deuteronomy prohibits all divinatory activity except prophecy, and restricts legitimate prophecy to speech, that is, to passing on the words of Yhwh.

---

don: SCM Press, 1961), "When, in Deuteronomy the term $d^e b\bar{a}r\bar{\imath}m$ is extended to cover every kind of legal material, the 'word,' as the comprehensive designation for the nation's law, acquires a heightened significance .... Thus the whole life of God's people is based on the word of God, in which is summed up the clear and unambiguous will of their sovereign Lord."

122 von Rad, *Theology*, 1:222, says of Deuteronomy's theological innovation: "The whole of the revelation of the will of Jahweh to Israel is now understood, in spite of the great variety of its contents, as a unity. It is seen as something indivisible and whole in which every part was co-ordinated with each and every other and where no detail could be understood except in relation to the whole. We can very well imagine that in her earlier days Israel was still a long way off the knowledge of this unifying principle for theological thought .... This view of Deuteronomy's of a theological unity presupposes a considerable capacity for theological reflexion .... Indeed, it is Deuteronomy's intention to be something like a totality of teaching. 'You shall not add to this, nor take from it.'" And later, at 1:229, von Rad sums up Deuteronomy's vision: "Thus in Deuteronomy everything is interrelated and gathered together to give a unified theological conspectus—one Jahweh, one (comprehensive) Israel, one revelation (תורה), one promised land (נחלה), one place of worship, one prophet. The core of Deuteronomy is the teaching, that is, the endeavor to make Israel listen to the revelation of the will of Jahweh in all circumstances."

3.2.3 The Restriction in Source of Revelation in Deut 18:15–18

Related to Deuteronomy's restriction in mode of revelation to speech is its restriction in source of revelation. The earliest articulations of the so-called "canonical" principle occur in Deuteronomy, in which Deuteronomy promotes its own status as an authoritative revelation, and warns against alternate polities or practices (Deut 4:2; 12:32 [MT 13:1]).[123] However, within the law-code itself, Deuteronomy includes provision for one authorized source of further revelation, namely the prophet like Moses. This is justified by an etiological narrative:

> This is what you requested of the LORD your God at Horeb on the day of the assembly when you said: "If I hear the voice of the LORD my God any more, or ever again see this great fire, I will die." Then the LORD replied to me: "They are right in what they have said. I will raise up for them a prophet like you from among their own people; I will put my words in the mouth of the prophet, who shall speak to them everything that I command."
> Deut 18:16–18

This etiology, as Markl has noted, grounds the continuing authority of the prophet on God's own words in the Horeb theophany.[124] Markl has also demonstrated the structural significance of this etiological narrative in Deuteronomy.[125] The book begins with Moses giving a historical summary of the people's journey to Sinai (1:6–3:29), which concludes with an exhortation to keep the law (4:1–40). The law proper then begins in Deut 5:1, as Moses reports the words that Yhwh spoke to the people at Horeb (Deut 5:1–22). Moses then recounts how the people, afraid that they would die due to their proximity to God, requested that Moses serve as their intercessor (Deut 5:23–27). God's positive response to this request serves to legitimate Moses as a vehicle of revelation.[126] Following

---

123 Nelson, *Deuteronomy*, 169, on Deut 13:1, "This command is often misconstrued as a 'canonical formula' intended to protect the text of Deuteronomy …. Adding and subtracting do not refer to accurate textual transmission, but to the commands one is to 'be careful to do.'" Taking Nelson's caution into advisement, it nevertheless seems that 4:2, 13:1 do reflect Deuteronomy's insistence on its own supreme authority, and in that sense alone the formula might be termed "canonical."

124 Markl, "Moses Prophetenrolle," 57.

125 The rest of this paragraph follows very closely the argument laid out by Markl, "Moses Prophetenrolle," 55–64. See also Nihan, "Moses and the Prophets," 27.

126 See Robert Polzin, *Moses and the Deuteronomist: A Literary Study of the Deuteronomic History* (New York: Seabury Press, 1980), 51: "5:28–31 are the authenticating words of God that

this, Deuteronomy presents its readers with the longest speech in the Hebrew Bible (chs. 6–26), spoken entirely by Moses. During the course of this speech, Moses returns to this etiology and specifies that it now also allows for one further authorized source of continuing revelation, namely, the prophet like Moses.

It follows from this that Deuteronomy's designation of Moses as a נביא is integrally bound up with the book's self-consciousness of its idiosyncratic character vis-à-vis other Pentateuchal law. While the rest of the Pentateuch ordinarily has God speaking the law *to Moses*; here in Deuteronomy Moses speaks the law *to Israel*. By the vehicle of Mosaic Discourse Deuteronomy reveals itself to be hermeneutically self-conscious:[127] the book's writers are keenly aware that they are presenting an updated interpretation of the "Mosaic" law for a new era, and they draw their portrait of Moses accordingly. At every stage in the book's composition, Moses is represented as a teacher (see למד in Deut 4:1, 5, 14; 5:31; 6:1; 31:19, 22) and interpreter of the law: he *expounds* Torah (see באר in Deut 1:5; 27:8).[128] Deuteronomy thus has a homiletic and hortatory character. Polzin, attentive to narratological considerations, puts it accurately:

> In Deuteronomy, Moses is pictured in his addresses as interpreting speeches that had taken place prior to his interpretive words .... Moses is pictured as setting the Deuteronomic lawcode *in context* by, among other things, interpreting past words, especially those of God's. What is immediately obvious here is the absolutely authoritarian, or at least authoritative, nature of Moses' interpretive function ....
>
> The principal role of Moses, as seen in the Book of Deuteronomy, is hermeneutic: he is the book's primary declarer (*maggîd*) and teacher (*mᵉlammed*) of God's word. He not only declares what God has said, he teaches or interprets what the divine words mean for Israel.[129]

---

show the basis for the unique teaching role Moses enjoys in the book of Deuteronomy." So also Nelson, *Deuteronomy*, 77.

127 See Ronald E. Clements, *Deuteronomy* (Sheffield: JSOT Press, 1989), 49: "The Deuteronomists were undoubtedly the most theologically self-conscious and ideologically aware of any of the major schools of writers who have contributed to the Old Testament."

128 William M. Schniedewind, "The Textualization of Torah in the Deuteronomic Tradition," in *Das Deuteronomium zwischen Pentateuch und Deuteronomistischem Geschichtswerk*, ed. Eckart Otto and Reinhard Achenbach, FRLANT 206 (Göttingen: Vandenhoeck & Ruprecht, 2004), 153–167; 159: "The unusual verb *b'r* 'to expound' or 'to make clear' points to the entire hermeneutic enterprise of Deuteronomy."

129 Polzin, *Moses and the Deuteronomist*, 9–10.

Deuteronomy's characterization of Moses as נביא is situated by the book in terms of this broader portrayal of Moses as an authorized interpreter of God's Word.[130]

The etiologies of Deut 5:23–31; 18:16–18 serve as a tacit acknowledgement that Deuteronomy is "rewritten" law, a post-mosaic iteration of mosaic tradition. Indeed, they suggest that Deuteronomy's self-understanding is—as Bernard Levinson has demonstrated—that of a legal project that is hermeneutical and revisionary: it revises and updates laws of the past, in accordance with its vision of Israel as a society that is devoted to Yhwh alone.[131] In this particular case, the narrative ingeniously used to accomplish this is that of Israel's request for a mediator at Sinai, first reported in Exod 20:19–21. Deuteronomy receives this tradition and transforms it into a story that authorizes ongoing legal revision to the mosaic tradition.[132]

---

130   So Schmid, "Deuteronomy within the 'Deuteronomistic Histories,'" 16: "the Mosaic fiction of Deuteronomy … becomes intelligible as part of a presentation that regards Deuteronomy already as an interpretive text." Sven Tengström's judgment is too stark ("Moses and the Prophets in the Deuteronomistic History," *SJOT* [1994]: 257–266; here 260): "Moses is portrayed in Deuteronomy essentially and originally as a *teacher*, not as a prophet."

131   This is the thesis of Levinson's *Deuteronomy and the Hermeneutics of Legal Innovation*. See, e.g., 4: "Deuteronomy was already a complex hermeneutical work from the beginning; it was the composition of authors who consciously reused and reinterpreted earlier texts to propound and justify their program of cultic and legal reform, even—or particularly—when those texts conflicted with the authors' agenda." I am in basic agreement with Levinson's exegetical conclusions, though at times his rhetoric, in my estimation, emphasizes too strongly the discontinuity between Deuteronomy and its sources (e.g., 15: "If the very notion of exegesis implies the continuity of the revising text with its source, I wish to underscore the opposite: the extent to which exegesis may make itself independent of the source text, challenging and even attempting to reverse or abrogate its substantive content, all the while under the hermeneutical mantle of consistency with or dependency upon its source"). See the criticisms of Levinson by Hindy Najman, *Seconding Sinai: the Development of Mosaic Discourse in Second Temple Judaism*, JSJSupS 77 (Leiden: Brill, 2003), 23–24.

132   See Thomas C. Römer, "Moses, Israel's First Prophet, and the Formation of the Deuteronomistic and Prophetic Libraries," in *Israelite Prophecy and the Deuteronomistic History: Portrait, Reality, and the Formation of a History*, ed. Mignon R. Jacobs and Raymond F. Person Jr., AIL 14 (Atlanta: Society of Biblical Literature, 2013), 129–146; at 132: "Apparently Deut 18 presupposes Exod 20:18–19 and Deut 5:23–29. The author of Deut 18:16–18 rewrites the older texts in order to root prophecy in the Horeb revelation."

FROM CHARISMA TO CANON

TABLE 3 The appointment of Moses and the prophet like him as mediators of the divine voice

Exod 20:[18], 19–21, 24:7	Deut 5:[23], 24–31	Deut 18:16–18
(19) וַיֹּאמְרוּ אֶל־מֹשֶׁה דַּבֵּר־אַתָּה עִמָּנוּ וְנִשְׁמָעָה וְאַל־יְדַבֵּר עִמָּנוּ אֱלֹהִים פֶּן־**נָמוּת** [Exod 24:7] וַיִּקַּח סֵפֶר הַבְּרִית וַיִּקְרָא בְּאָזְנֵי הָעָם וַיֹּאמְרוּ **כֹּל** **אֲשֶׁר־דִּבֶּר יְהוָה נַעֲשֶׂה** **וְנִשְׁמָע**] (20) וַיֹּאמֶר מֹשֶׁה אֶל־הָעָם אַל־תִּירָאוּ כִּי לְבַעֲבוּר נַסּוֹת אֶתְכֶם בָּא הָאֱלֹהִים וּבַעֲבוּר תִּהְיֶה יִרְאָתוֹ עַל־פְּנֵיכֶם לְבִלְתִּי תֶחֱטָאוּ (21) וַיַּ**עֲמֹד** הָעָם מֵרָחֹק וּמֹשֶׁה נִגַּשׁ אֶל־הָעֲרָפֶל אֲשֶׁר־שָׁם הָאֱלֹהִים	(24) וַ**תֹּאמְרוּ** הֵן הֶרְאָנוּ יְהוָה אֱלֹהֵינוּ אֶת־כְּבֹדוֹ וְאֶת־גָּדְלוֹ וְאֶת־קֹלוֹ שָׁמַעְנוּ מִתּוֹךְ הָאֵשׁ הַיּוֹם הַזֶּה רָאִינוּ כִּי־יְדַבֵּר אֱלֹהִים אֶת־הָאָדָם וָחָי (25) וְעַתָּה לָמָּה **נָמוּת** כִּי תֹאכְלֵנוּ הָאֵשׁ הַגְּדֹלָה הַזֹּאת אִם־יֹסְפִים אֲנַחְנוּ לִשְׁמֹעַ אֶת־**קוֹל יְהוָה אֱלֹהֵינוּ** **עוֹד וָמָתְנוּ** (26) כִּי מִי כָל־בָּשָׂר אֲשֶׁר שָׁמַע קוֹל אֱלֹהִים חַיִּים מְדַבֵּר מִתּוֹךְ־הָאֵשׁ כָּמֹנוּ וַיֶּחִי (27) קְרַב אַתָּה וּשֲׁמָע אֵת כָּל־אֲשֶׁר יֹאמַר יְהוָה אֱלֹהֵינוּ וְאַתְּ תְּדַבֵּר אֵלֵינוּ אֵת **כָּל־אֲשֶׁר יְדַבֵּר יְהוָה** אֱלֹהֵינוּ אֵלֶיךָ וְשָׁמַעְנוּ וְעָשִׂינוּ (28) וַיִּשְׁמַע יְהוָה אֶת־קוֹל דִּבְרֵיכֶם בְּדַבֶּרְכֶם אֵלָי **וַיֹּאמֶר יְהוָה אֵלַי** שָׁמַעְתִּי אֶת־קוֹל דִּבְרֵי הָעָם הַזֶּה אֲשֶׁר דִּבְּרוּ אֵלֶיךָ **הֵיטִיבוּ כָּל־אֲשֶׁר דִּבֵּרוּ** (29) מִי־יִתֵּן וְהָיָה לְבָבָם זֶה לָהֶם **לְיִרְאָה** אֹתִי וְלִשְׁמֹר אֶת־כָּל־מִצְוֺתַי כָּל־הַיָּמִים לְמַעַן יִיטַב לָהֶם וְלִבְנֵיהֶם לְעֹלָם (30) לֵךְ אֱמֹר לָהֶם שׁוּבוּ לָכֶם לְאָהֳלֵיכֶם (31) וְאַתָּה פֹּה **עֲמֹד** עִמָּדִי וַאֲדַבְּרָה אֵלֶיךָ אֵת כָּל־הַמִּצְוָה וְהַחֻקִּים וְהַמִּשְׁפָּטִים אֲשֶׁר תְּלַמְּדֵם וְעָשׂוּ בָאָרֶץ אֲשֶׁר אָנֹכִי נֹתֵן לָהֶם לְרִשְׁתָּהּ	(16) כְּכֹל אֲשֶׁר־שָׁאַלְתָּ מֵעִם יְהוָה אֱלֹהֶיךָ בְּחֹרֵב בְּיוֹם הַקָּהָל **לֵאמֹר** לֹא **אֹסֵף לִשְׁמֹעַ אֶת־קוֹל יְהוָה** **אֱלֹהָי** וְאֶת־הָאֵשׁ הַגְּדֹלָה הַזֹּאת לֹא־אֶרְאֶה **עוֹד** וְלֹא **אָמוּת** (17) **וַיֹּאמֶר יְהוָה אֵלָי** **הֵיטִיבוּ אֲשֶׁר דִּבֵּרוּ** (18) נָבִיא אָקִים לָהֶם מִקֶּרֶב אֲחֵיהֶם כָּמוֹךָ וְנָתַתִּי דְבָרַי בְּפִיו וְדִבֶּר אֲלֵיהֶם אֵת כָּל־אֲשֶׁר אֲצַוֶּנּוּ
(18) When all the people witnessed the thunder and lightning, the sound of the trumpet, and the mountain smoking, they were afraid and trembled and stood at a distance, (19) and **said to Moses** "You speak to us, and we will listen; but do not let God speak to us, or **we will die**."	(23) When you heard the voice out of the darkness, while the mountain was burning with fire, you approached me, all the heads of your tribes and your elders; (24) and you **said**, "Look, the LORD our God has shown us his glory and greatness, and we have heard his voice out of the fire. Today we have seen that God may speak to someone and the person may still live. (25) So now why should we die? For this great fire will consume us; **if we hear the voice of the LORD our God any longer, we shall die**. (26) For who is there of all flesh that has heard the	(16) This is what you requested of the LORD your God at Horeb on the day of the assembly when you **said**: "If I hear the voice of the LORD my God any more, or ever again see this great fire, **I will die**."

TABLE 3   The appointment of Moses and the prophet like him as mediators of the divine voice (*cont.*)

Exod 20:[18], 19–21, 24:7	Deut 5:[23], 24–31	Deut 18:16–18
〚Exod 24:7 Then he took the book of the covenant, and read it in the hearing of the people; and they said, "**All that the LORD has spoken we will do, and we will be obedient.**"〛 (20) Moses said to the people, "Do not be afraid; for God has come only to test you and to put the **fear** of him upon you so that you do not sin." (21) Then the people **stood** at a distance, while Moses drew near to the thick darkness where God was.	voice of the living God speaking out of fire, as we have, and remained alive? (27) Go near, you yourself, and hear all that the LORD our God will say. Then tell us **everything that the LORD our God tells you, and we will listen and do it**." (28) The LORD heard your words when you spoke to me, and **the LORD said to me**: "I have heard the words of this people, which they have spoken to you; **they are right in** all **that they have spoken**. (29) If only they had such a mind as this, to **fear** me and to keep all my commandments always, so that it might go well with them and with their children forever! (30) Go say to them, 'Return to your tents.' (31) But you, **stand** here by me, and I will tell you all the commandments, the statutes and the ordinances, that you shall teach them, so that they may do them in the land that I am giving them to possess."	(17) **Then the LORD replied to me: "They are right in what they have said.** (18) I will raise up for them a prophet like you from among their own people; I will put my words in the mouth of the prophet, who shall speak to them everything that I command."

In Exodus, Moses does not report divine affirmation of the people's request for a mediator. Nevertheless, in the following narrative, Moses alone speaks with God. The reader of Exodus might well conclude that such a narrative trajectory demands incorporating explicit divine acquiescence to the people's request. But Deuteronomy goes beyond this: God does not merely grant the request, but lauds it: that which the people have spoken is *good* (יטב: Deut 5:28; 18:17). Why does Deuteronomy insert this?

First, in Exod 20:20, Moses says that God came near and spoke directly to the people in order to test them. Perhaps Deuteronomy interprets the people's request for a mediator as an indication that they have passed a divine test. Indeed, this seems implied by the words of high praise Yhwh has for the people in Deuteronomy, including the wish that they would always fear Yhwh in this way (Deut 5:29).[133] The people's request, for Deuteronomy, is indicative of a desire to continue receiving the law even after exposure to the divine voice. Second, Deuteronomy greatly expands the people's request, and rewrites it to include the next words the people utter in the Exodus narrative, which occur several chapters later, in which they accept the obligation to obey the law (Exod 24:3, 7).[134] In Exodus, the request for the mediator is followed by Moses receiving the Covenant Code; only after this do the people accept the terms of the covenant. For Deuteronomy, however, the people's request for a mediator already included their acceptance of the terms of the covenant. Moses and the prophet like Moses are both secondary authorities to the very word of Yhwh as experienced at the Horeb theophany. Israel's request, however, it indicated their willingness to accept a covenant mediator as an ongoing authority in Israel's life.

Yhwh's voiced approval of the people's request may be relevant for understanding Deuteronomy's character as a self-conscious revision of the law. It is not often that God praises the people of Israel or acknowledges that they are right in what they have said. In fact, the only other times this occurs, it explicitly leads to a legal revision (Num 27:7; 36:5). In these two cases, the daughters of Zelophehad and the tribe of Joseph bring forward lacunae in the laws regarding inheritance. God approves of the objections brought forward and revises the law. One might suggest, then, that Deuteronomy's explicit attestation of divine approval of the people's request is then a significant hermeneutical marker. The successive appointments—first of Moses and then of the prophet like him—as mediators to speak on God's behalf constitute a legal revision to address the people's ongoing need for a source of authorized revelation.

These passages in Deuteronomy specify that the setting for the people's request and the divine response was the Horeb theophany.[135] This restricts

---

133   Weinfeld, *Deuteronomy 1–11*, 325, argues that the use of ירא in Deut 5:29 is taken from Exod 20:20, but that there are significant differences between the two: in Exodus the fear is "the divine terror;" in Deut 5:29 it is "inner religious feeling."
134   Weinfeld, *Deuteronomy 1–11*, 324, and Walter Brueggemann, *Deuteronomy*, AOTC (Nashville: Abingdon Press, 2001), 72, note the parallel between Exod 24:7 and Deut 5:27. The *Mekilta*, commenting on the Israelite request for a mediator, thus links this request with Deut 18:15, 18; see Bahodesh 9 (trans. Lauterbach): "'And they said to Moses: "Speak thou with us and we will hear."' ... From that time on the Israelites merited that prophets should be raised up for them, as it is said, 'I will raise thee up a prophet.'—I was going to raise up a prophet from among them in the future but by their merits they brought it about sooner." The theological logic is that of Deuteronomy: the request for a mediator itself indicates a willingness to obey, and is praiseworthy.
135   This resulted in some ancient versions, such as the Samaritan Pentatuech, including these passages in Exod 20. On such harmonizations, see Molly M. Zahn, *Rethinking Rewritten*

legitimate sources of divine revelation to those that were authorized at Horeb. That is why it is not redundant for Deuteronomy to attach Yhwh's affirmation of an intention to send a prophet like Moses to Moses' own promise of a such a prophet: Yhwh's words are the ultimate authority for Moses' words, both in the law-code as a whole (the long speech of Moses in Deut 6–26 is subordinated to the discourse of Deut 5, in which the words of Yhwh are cited) and in this specific scene.[136] Deuteronomy's specific attention to *voice* restricts all legitimate revelation to that based on the one revelation given by Yhwh to Israel at Horeb.

4 Conclusion: Moses in Numbers and Deuteronomy 18

Deuteronomy labels Moses a נביא in order to establish a coordination of various modes and sources of divine revelation. This provides a stark contrast to the solution of the relationship between Moses and prophecy opted for by the redactor of Numbers 11–12. The situation envisaged in Numbers 11–12 is that, while the revelation given to Moses is supreme, there are various other channels through whom Yhwh can act. Not all prophecy is under Mosaic auspices, and Yhwh does not assuage any concerns in this regard when coming to Moses' defense, affirming the divine prerogative to speak through prophets in visions and dreams. In short, what Numbers 11–12 lack is normativity in revelation, or canonicity: there is no clearly defined relationship between Moses and other channels of revelation.[137] Furthermore, there are no apparent restrictions on legitimate modes of revelation: Moses does not only talk with God, he also

---

Scripture: Composition and Exegesis in the 4QReworked Pentateuch Manuscripts, STDJ 95 (Leiden: Brill, 2011).

136   Markl, "Moses Prophetenrolle," 57.
137   *Contra* Nihan, "Moses and the Prophets," 40, on Num 12:6: "Other prophets, by contrast [to Moses, the servant], are only second rank officials standing between Moses and the people, whose task is to pass further the words received by Moses from Yahweh, i.e., the Torah;" later Nihan ("Moses and the Prophets," 42) says that prophets in this passage and Deut 34:10 are "mere commentators of the Mosaic Law—authorized, divinely inspired commentators, to be sure, but no longer the mediators of a distinct revelation from the Mosaic one, as per the situation still considered in Deut 18:9–22." Here, my position is directly the inverse of Nihan's: in Num 12:6–8, prophets are still considered mediators of an entirely distinct revelation. Deut 18:9–22 is precisely the passage that marks the significant shift towards subordinating prophetic revelation to that of Moses. Nihan's view results from interpreting Numbers' focus on Moses' uniqueness as though it were theologically equivalent to Deuteronomy's concern for normativity. The two traditions, however, should not be conflated: while Deuteronomy coordinates diverse sources of revelation, Numbers dissociates them.

beholds the form of Yhwh, which Deuteronomy is at pains to restrict (Num 12:8, cf. Deut 4:12). The situation that Numbers presents is one of a variety of modes of revelation, with Mosaic revelation being supreme.

Deuteronomy charts a different course. It attempts to replace this charismatic model with a genealogical model of prophecy, in which all genuine revelation has its originating moment in the Horeb theophany. Deuteronomy classifies Moses among the prophets, rather than dissociating him from them, in the interest of redefining prophecy itself. Non-Mosaic prophecy, which is viewed as unproblematic in the narratives of Numbers, is eliminated in the attempt to "centralize" revelation and bring it under the auspices of the Mosaic Torah. (In a way, the concept of the prophet like Moses represents the triumph of Joshua's jealousy; in Deuteronomy, Eldad and Medad are quieted at last.) The contrasting characterization of the relationship between Moses and prophecy casts the distinctiveness of Deuteronomy's portrayal of Moses as a prophet in sharp relief, as Deuteronomy inaugurates a shift from charism to canon in its transformation of prophecy.[138] Deuteronomy 18:9–22 is not the result of the reception of a corpus of "the law and the prophets;" rather, it instigates this process and itself provides its fundamental origin.[139] I now explore the next stage in this process, the construction of a series of prophets as heirs and successors of Moses in the Dtr historiographic project.

138   To be sure, Deuteronomy does not deny that prophets have a charismatic origin, but attempts to control this as much as possible. In this respect, the absence of the term רוח in Deuteronomy's prophet laws is significant.

139   Nicholson, "Deuteronomy 18.9–22," 158, argues that behind Deut 18:9–22 stands the reception of a prophetic corpus as scripture: "[T]his pericope already presupposes an emergent scripture embracing not only 'the book of the torah,' which already has such a standing in the Deuteronomistic corpus (cf. Deut 17:18–20; Josh 1:8), but also a core collection of prophetic books." He is even more specific, 162, "the prophet Jeremiah and the book bearing his name were in the mind of the author of Deut 18:15–18." This is based on Nicholson's view that Jer 1:9 is the source of Deut 18:18 rather than the reverse, a view I think unlikely, taking into consideration the generally accepted late Deuteronomistic redaction of the prose material in Jeremiah (more on this in chapter 4 below).

I agree with Tengström, "Moses and the Prophets," 266, who concludes his essay: "Deut 18:9–22, which establishes a coordinated hierarchy of authorities, appears to be at the origin of the bipartite division of the Hebrew scriptural canon into Moses *and* the Prophets." If this conclusion is correct, this passage has major importance in religious history. Markl, "Moses Prophetenrolle," 66, therefore justifiably says: "Das Zentrum des Buches Deuteronomium wurde so zu einer Schlüsselstelle für Weltreligionen," referring particularly to its influence in Judaism, Christianity, and Islam.

CHAPTER 3

"My Servants the Prophets," Part I: The Deuteronomistic Construction of a Mosaic Prophetic Succession

1 Introduction

The next stage in the story of the prophet like Moses is the role that it plays in the Deuteronomistic historiographical project. The Deuteronomic (D) emphasis on normativity is transformed into a Deuteronomistic (Dtr) construction of a company of Mosaic prophets, who speak with Moses's voice and represent his authority. In particular, the designation "servant of the LORD" (עבד־יהוה), which first occurs in the report of Moses' death (Deut 34:5), becomes important for the Dtr scribes as a title that coordinates Moses and the prophets in the Deuteronomistic History (DH). In this and the next chapter I will investigate more carefully the phrase "my/his [Yhwh's] servants the prophets," and argue that its usage in the DH, Jeremiah, and select other texts functions to position the prophets as "like Moses" by constructing an authorized succession of Mosaic prophets, one which extended from Moses to Jeremiah. In diachronic perspective, the establishing of a company of prophets as heirs to Moses is the first interpretation of the prophet like Moses, and it should be positioned between Deut 18:9–22 (which authorizes a prophetic *office*) and Deut 34:10–12 (which separates Moses from his prophetic *successors*). The motivation for this interpretation of Deut 18 was its key role in the theodicy of the exilic Dtr author and editor(s). Indeed, the positing of a Mosaic prophetic succession served as a device by which Yhwh's judgment of Israel and Judah was seen to be righteous. However, the Dtr construction of this succession furthered the project of redefining prophecy itself, as it exerted a pressure on post-exilic prophetic claimants to align their oracles with a specific prophetic tradition.

Before embarking on the detailed investigation, it may be useful to set out briefly the understanding of "Deuteronomism" that I employ. Scholars are rightly wary of so-called "pan-Deuteronomism,"[1] in which, as Coggins memorably stated, "the Deuteronomists have sometimes been praised or blamed

---

1 See *Those Elusive Deuteronomists: The Phenomenon of Pan-Deuteronomism*, ed. L.S. Schearing and S.L. McKenzie, JSOTSupS 268 (Sheffield: Sheffield Academic, 1999).

for virtually every significant development within ancient Israel's religious practice."[2] The view adopted here, informed by the proposals of Person and Albertz,[3] is that they represent the increasing influence of the scribal class in late pre-exilic Judah, in the Babylonian *golah*, and in early Persian period Yehud (that is, from the mid seventh to the early fifth centuries BCE). Historically, their emergence is associated with Josiah's reform, so that it is permissible to speak of a Dtr *movement* from 630–609 BCE, the death of Josiah.[4] It is probable that a version of the national history was produced at that time,[5] and was later thoroughly updated in the Babylonian exile as a history of sin and punishment.[6] The catastrophe of exile caused the Deuteronomists to revisit the oracles of the prophets, especially those who warned Israel and Judah of looming judgment. These oracle-collections were preserved, edited, and published; most notably, the Dtr scribes produced a book of sayings and deeds of the prophet Jeremiah. The basic Dtr corpus, then, consists of Deuteronomy, Joshua–2 Kings, and Jeremiah.[7] It seems likely, however, that some books ought to be added to this, including the so-called "Book of the Four" (Hosea, Amos, Micah, Zepha-

---

2   Linda Schearing quotes Coggins in the introduction to *Those Elusive Deuteronomists* (13). The original quotation is from R.J. Coggins, "Prophecy—True and False," in *Of Prophets' Visions and the Wisdom of Sages: Festschrift for R.N. Whybray*, ed. H.A. McKay and D.J.A. Clines, JSOTSupS 162 (Sheffield: JSOT Press, 1993), 80–94; here 85.
3   Raymond F. Person Jr., *The Deuteronomic School: History, Social Setting, and Literature*, SBL 2 (Atlanta: Society of Biblical Literature, 2002); Rainer Albertz, *Israel in Exile: The History and Literature of the Sixth Century BCE*, trans. David Green, SBL 3 (Atlanta: Society of Biblical Literature, 2003).
4   So Rainer Albertz, *The History of Israelite Religion in the Old Testament Period*, trans. J. Bowden (Louisville, Ky.: Westminster/John Knox Press, 1994); Norbert F. Lohfink, "Was There a Deuteronomistic Movement?," in *Those Elusive Deuteronomists*, ed. L.S. Schearing and S.L. McKenzie, JSOTSup 268 (Sheffield: Sheffield Academic, 1999), 36–66; here 57–59.
5   Following the theory proposed by Frank M. Cross, "The Themes of the Book of Kings and the Structure of the Deuteronomistic History," in *Canaanite Myth and Hebrew Epic* (Cambridge: Harvard University Press, 1973), 274–289, and elaborated and defended by Richard D. Nelson, *The Double Redaction of the Deuteronomistic History*, JSOTSup 18 (Sheffield: JSOT Press, 1981); Gary N. Knoppers, *Two Nations under God: The Deuteronomic History of Solomon and the Dual Monarchies*, 2 vols., HSM 52–53 (Atlanta: Scholars Press, 1993–1994).
6   By an individual or a group? Martin Noth, *Überlieferungsgeschichtliche Studien* (Tübingen: Niemeyer, 1943), thought of the Deuteronomist as a single historian, and the unity of perspective that stretches across the work makes this proposal not entirely implausible, despite the current climate of scholarly opposition. It should be noted that the theory of a single exilic historian is not incompatible with later scribal editing and expansions, such as we see in a comparison of MT and LXX versions of the books that make up the history.
7   This is the extent of the corpus argued for by Lohfink, "Was There a Deuteronomistic Movement?," who decries the ascription of much of the Hebrew Bible to anonymous Dtr scribes.

niah);[8] of these, we have evidence that Micah of Moresheth was known to the Dtr authors (Jer 26:18). Finally, Person has mounted an impressive argument for the redaction of the restoration prophets, Haggai and Zechariah 1–8, within the context of the Dtr school.[9]

The above picture suggests a national reform movement which was suspended with the fall of the Judean state but continued in the literary output of the elite class of scribes.[10] Even after the loss of independence, the Dtr scribes persisted in their goal, which was nothing less than the production of a religious identity; that is, they aspired to the establishment of a monolatrous political body. With the return of Zerubbabel (c. 520 BCE), and the Persian support of a rebuilt temple in Yehud, the Dtr school would have functioned as a scribal bureaucracy, serving as the administrative leaders and perhaps inculcating hopes of a restored Davidic monarchy. The dissolution of these hopes, the arrival of Ezra (458 BCE), and the hegemony of the priestly class and literature in the late fifth century may have led to the demise or transformation of the Dtr school.[11] If this proposal, put forth extensively by Person, is correct, then the texts to be treated in this chapter and the next were composed over the course of a century, from about 560–450 BCE, in both the Babylonian *golah* and early Persian period Yehud.[12]

---

8   For the theory of a "Book of the Four" as precursor to the Book of the Twelve, see David N. Freedman, "Headings in the Books of the Eighth-Century Prophets," in *Festschrift in Honor of Leona Glidden Running*, ed. W.H. Shea, AUSS 25 (Berrien Springs, Mich.: Andrews University Press, 1987), 9–26; James Nogalski, *Literary Precursors to the Book of the Twelve*, BZAW 217 (Berlin: de Gruyter, 1993); idem, *Redactional Processes in the Book of the Twelve*, BZAW 218 (Berlin: de Gruyter, 1993).

9   Person, *The Deuteronomic School*, 138–142.

10 So Lohfink, "Was There a Deuteronomistic Movement?," 61.

11 By the time of the Chronicler the priesthood was felt to be so vital to Judah's religious life that the Primary History was recast (partly) from this perspective. On this reconstruction, this occurs after the demise or transformation of the Dtr school. See Person, *The Deuteronomic School*, 142–144.

12 The minimum time-frame for the Dtr usages of the phrase "my/Yhwh's servants the prophets," from its early usages in 2 Kings to the final occurrence in Zech 1:6, would be about fifty years, if the dating of Albertz, *Israel in Exile*, 312–320, for the successive redactions of Jeremiah is accepted (he identifies three redactions, ca. 550, 540, and 520 BCE), and, for the prologue of Zechariah, the early date of Carol L. Meyers and Eric M. Meyers, *Haggai, Zechariah 1–8: A New Translation with Introduction and Commentary*, AB 25B (New York: Doubleday, 1987) is adopted (516/515 BCE; taking the view that the composite work of Hag–Zech 8 must have been published before the rededication of the temple). This time-frame seems, however, rather short in view of the editorial character of much of this material; there is no reason, e.g., to suppose that the oracles of First Zechariah were

On the basis of this historical outline, one can posit that the earliest descriptions of the prophets as a unified, collective body of Yhwh's "servants" are found in the work of the exilic Dtr authors (c. 560 BCE), who, by so doing, were coordinating the prophets to Moses, the paradigmatic "servant of Yhwh" (עבד־יהוה). My contention in what follows is that the phrase has a limited meaning, referring not to all of Israel's prophets but to an intermittent succession of Moses-like prophets from Moses to Jeremiah. In this chapter, I examine the foundational occurrences of this phrase in the DH; in the next, I explore Jeremiah's climactic role among the company of Yhwh's "servants the prophets."

2 Yhwh's "Servants the Prophets" in the Deuteronomistic History

2.1 *Overview of Data*

The designation of a collective body of prophets as Yhwh's "servants" occurs in the seventeen passages in the Hebrew Bible.[13] The profile suggests a Dtr provenance, as eleven of the occurrences are found in Second Kings and Jeremiah, the prophetic book that received more thorough Dtr redaction than any other. Two more of these occurrences, Amos 3:7 and Zech 1:6, can be ascribed to Dtr redaction with some confidence. The other four (Ezek 38:17; Ezra 9:11; Dan 9:6, 10) are late, Dtr-inspired usages, and will not figure prominently in my analysis.

The five collective references to the prophets as Yhwh's "servants" occur towards the end of the DH (2 Kgs 9:7; 17:13, 23; 21:10; 24:2). I argue below that the latter four of these occur in passages that have remarkable linkages to and dependency on Deut 18:9–22 and the concept of the "prophet like Moses." Deuteronomy 18:9–22 and Second Kings 17:5–23, 21:1–16 are three carefully interconnected passages in the DH that root a polemical contrast between Israelite prophecy and all other divinatory practices in the more fundamental contrast between Israel and the nations. A close examination of the relationship between these passages will justify the claim that they are mutually clarifying and illuminating, and that they provide a window into the import of the phrase "my servants the prophets" for the exilic Dtr author/redactor(s). The other passage, 2 Kgs 9:7, bears brief discussion, in order to explain why I exclude it from consideration in terms of the technical meaning that the phrase comes to acquire.

---

13   published in their present form within a few years of the historical prophet's activity, or that Jeremiah in its present form was substantially complete by 520 BCE.
2 Kgs 9:7; 17:13, 23; 21:10; 24:2; Jer 7:25; 25:4; 26:5; 29:19; 35:15; 44:4; Ezek 38:17; Amos 3:7; Zech 1:6; Ezra 9:11; Dan 9:6, 10.

In 2 Kgs 9:7, the narrative of the DH presents us with its first reference to the prophets as a collective body of Yhwh's servants. This comes via an unnamed prophet, who, commissioned by Elisha, anoints Jehu as king and says that through him Yhwh will "avenge on Jezebel the blood of my servants the prophets and the blood of all the servants of Yhwh (דמי עבדי הנביאים ודמי כל־עבדי יהוה)."[14] Second Kings 9:1–10:17 then recounts the destruction of the line of Ahab by Jehu, and refers several times to the fulfillment of Elijah's prophecy against the house of Ahab (9:26, 36–37; 10:10, 17). It is probable that 2 Kgs 9:7–10a is a Dtr addition to the original narrative, which has the function of emphasizing and reiterating Elijah's oracle against Ahab (1 Kgs 21:19–24; cf 1 Kgs 14:11; 16:4).[15] The phrase "my servants the prophets" occurs in the expanded speech and may even be a secondary addition to that speech, given the repetitiveness of the present MT, with דמי occurring twice.[16] The occurrence here, therefore, is probably a gloss that looks specifically back to the groups of prophets that Jezebel killed (1 Kgs 18:4, 13). It refers specifically to a company of prophets active in the days of Elijah. This is an anomalous usage of the phrase, which originally for the Dtr scribes referred not to a specific group of prophets of one particular time-period, but to the entire succession of prophets who had testified to Israel and Judah. Though later the rejection and killing of the prophets becomes an important motif,[17] within the DH its usage marks this text as anomalous. In this corpus, the description of the prophets as Yhwh's servants is related not to the prophets' violent fate but to a distillation of the prophetic message and the disobedience of Israel and Judah to that message.

---

14 All translations are based on the NRSV, with occasional modifications.
15 The literary grounds for this judgment are as follows: Elisha stresses in his command that the young prophet is to proclaim Jehu king and leave immediately (9:3–4); furthermore, Jehu's later reporting of the prophet's words cites only the first words of the prophet (9:12). Thus, e.g., Rudolf Smend, *Biblische Zeugnisse: Literatur des Alten Israel* (Fischer-Verlay, 1967), 168–171; Gwilym H. Jones, *1 & II Kings*, 2 vols., NCBC (Grand Rapids: Eerdmans, 1984), 2:450–451. T.R. Hobbs, *2 Kings*, WBC 13 (Dallas: Word, 1986), 114, says "most commentators regard vv 7–10 as a deuteronomistic insertion," but personally demurs from this view. On Elijah's prophecy, see John Gray, *I & II Kings: A Commentary*, 2nd rev. ed, OTL (Louisville: Westminster/John Knox Press, 1971), 433–436.
16 Graeme Auld, "Prophets and Prophecy in Jeremiah and Kings," *ZAW* 96 (1984), 66–82, at 81, on this passage: "It is easy to view *dmy 'bdy hnby'ym* an addition to an original *dmy (kl) 'bdy yhwh* to give precedence to Yahweh's 'prophetic' spokesmen."
17 See Odil Hannes Steck, *Israel und das gewaltsame Geschick der Propheten: Untersuchungen zur Überlieferung des deuteronomistischen Geschichtsbildes im Alten Testament, Spätjudentum und Urchristentum*, WMANT 23 (Neukirchen-Vluyn: Neukirchener Verlag, 1967); Betsy Halpern Amaru, "The Killing of the Prophets: Unraveling a Midrash," *HUCA* 54 (1983): 153–180.

In sum, it is doubtful that 2 Kgs 9:7 provides us with an early usage of the collective description of the prophets as Yhwh's servants or is a reliable guide to the original function of the phrase.

The remaining four occurrences of the phrase in the DH are in 2 Kgs 17:13, 23; 21:10; 24:2. These occurrences are bound tightly together; indeed, they form a deliberate system, which emphasizes the fulfillment of the prophetic message in the exiles of Israel (2 Kgs 17:13, 23) and Judah (2 Kgs 21:10, 24:2) respectively. A major theme of the DH is that Israel and Judah are responsible for the calamities that have come upon them, and that God has been just in judging their sins. It is the people's idolatry that led them to exile. I will show that the phrase "my servants the prophets" is originally used as a building block within this edifice, serving the purpose of vindicating Yhwh against objections to the divine commitment to Israel. The analysis below demonstrates that these four passages belong to the same editorial strand of an exilic redaction of the DH. These are collective descriptions of the prophets as a unified body of Yhwh's servants, through whom judgment was threatened and whose words brought that judgment into motion. My first task is to demonstrate the close relationship between this collective understanding of the prophets and the prophet-law of Deut 18:9–22, and I will now lay out in some detail its influence on this concept.

2.2   *The Double Violation of Deuteronomy 18:9–22 in 2 Kings 17 and 21*

Two passages in the DH, 2 Kgs 17:13–14 and 21:10–15, explicitly quote Yhwh's "servants the prophets." As I show below, these passages have been edited to emphasize Israel and Judah's transgressions of the law of the prophet in Deut 18:9–22. There are two ways in which explicit disobedience of Deut 18:9–22 is highlighted in these chapters: first, by citing from the prohibitions of divination, indicating Israel and Judah's disobedience to the law, and second, claiming that Israel did not "listen" (שמע) to the prophets or God.[18] With respect to the first of these, Nelson points out:

> The exilic editor … seems to have been deeply impressed by Deut 18:10, perhaps because of the popularity of divination among the neo-Babylonians. Upon this passage is based both the general accusation against Israel in 2 Kings 17:17 and the more specific one against Manasseh in 21:6.[19]

---

18   See Nelson, *Double Redaction*, 43 on these passages.
19   Nelson, *Double Redaction*, 59–60.

Table 4 below highlights the relationship between the prohibitions of divination in Deut 18:9–12 and the accusation against Israel (2 Kgs 17:17) and Manasseh of Judah (2 Kgs 21:2, 6) of engaging in such practices.

A number of factors suggest that the function of these passages is to render Israel's and Judah's (i.e., Manasseh's) disobedience explicit by citing the laws which they broke. First, the reports of proscribed divinatory practices are somewhat intrusive in their contexts. The charges that explicitly refer back to Deut 18:10 are in both cases appended to descriptions of Israel's and Judah's sin that focus almost entirely on the issue of the worship of other gods, and not divination *per se*. In 2 Kings 17, the litany of Israel's sin is described in vv. 7–12, 15–17. The citation of Deut 18:10 therefore serves as the conclusion of the Dtr historian's elaboration of Israel's infidelity. The issue of the worship of other gods dominates the preceding verses (17:7–12, 15–16), and the charge that Israel practiced divination is added on to this main indictment. The same is true of the account of Manasseh's sins: 2 Kgs 21:3–5 focuses on idolatry, and the grammar of the passage is suggestive of the secondary, intrusive character of the references to divination, that is, to Deut 18:10–11. Here are the verbs and their objects in 2 Kgs 21:3–6a:

(3) ויבן את־הבמות ... ויקם מזבחת ...ויעש אשרה ... וישתחו לכל־צבא השמים ויעבד אתם (4) ובנה מזבחת ... (5) ויבן מזבחות ... (6) והעביר את־בנו באש ועונן ונחש ועשה אוב

The narrative tense (*waw*-consecutive) is broken in 21:4 for a circumstantial clause describing the altars that Manasseh built. The passage resumes in narrative tense in 21:5, where the reader is informed that Manasseh also built altars for the host of heaven. The report about his engaging in divinatory practices, however, again breaks the narrative tense to use the *waw* + perfect formulation.[20] Eynikel therefore suggests that v. 6 was "added to the original account."[21] In any case, it is clear that in 2 Kgs 17:17 and 21:6, the charges that specifically allude to Deut 18:10–11 are ancillary to the main indictment of the worship of

---

20 Erik Eynikel, "The Portrait of Mannaseh and the Deuteronomistic History," in *Deuteronomy and Deuteronomic Literature: Festschrift C.H.W. Brekelmans*, ed. M. Vervenne and J. Lust (Louvain: Peeters, 1997), 233–261; here 237: "There seems to be no obvious reason why the narrative tense (*wayyiqtol*) should be interrupted here."

21 Eynikel, "Portrait of Mannaseh," 255; cf 244: "The accusation of Manasseh's practicing child sacrifice in combination with sorcery in 2 Kings 21,6 is very stereotypical, being similar to other late, exilic texts like Deut 12,31; 18,10 and 2 Kings 17,17."

TABLE 4   Prohibited divinatory practices in Second Kings 17, 21

Deut 18:9–12	2 Kings 17:17	2 Kings 21:2,6
(9) כי אתה בא אל־הארץ אשר־יהוה אלהיך נתן לך לא־תלמד **לעשות כתועבת הגוים** ההם (10) **לא־ימצא בך מעביר בנו־ובתו באש קסם קסמים מעונן** ו**מנחש** ו**מכשף** (11) ו**חבר חבר ושאל אוב וידעני ודרש אל־המתים** (12) כי־**תועבת** יהוה כל־**עשה** אלה ובגלל **התועבת** האלה יהוה אלהיך **מוריש אותם מפניך**	ויעבירו את־בניהם ואת־בנותיהם באש ויקסמו קסמים וינחשו ויתמכרו לעשות הרע בעיני יהוה להכעיסו	(2) **ויעש** הרע בעיני יהוה **כתועבת הגוים אשר הוריש יהוה מפני בני ישראל** (6) **והעביר את־בנו באש ועונן ונחש** ועשה **אוב וידענים** הרבה לעשות הרע בעיני יהוה להכעיס

(9) When you come into the land that the LORD your God is giving you, you must not learn to imitate the **abhorrent practices of** those **nations**.

(10) **No one shall be found among you who makes a son or daughter pass through fire, or who practices divination**, or is a soothsayer, **or an augur**, or a sorcerer, (11) or one who casts spells, or who consults **ghosts or spirits**, or who seeks oracles from the dead. (12) For whoever **does** these things is **abhorrent** to the LORD; it is because of such **abhorrent practices** that the LORD your **God is driving them out before you.**

They made their sons and their daughters pass through fire; they used divination and augury; and they sold themselves

to do evil in the sight of the LORD, provoking him to anger.

(2) He did what was evil in the sight of the LORD, following the **abominable practices of the nations** that the LORD **drove out before the people of Israel.**

(6) He made his son pass through fire; he practiced soothsaying and augury,

and dealt with **mediums and with wizards.** He *did* much *evil in the sight of the LORD, provoking him to anger.*

TABLE 5   Prohibited divinatory practices in the DH

	מעביר בנו־בתו באש	קסם	ענן	נחש	שאל (עשה) אוב	ידעני
Deut	18:10	18:10, 14	18:10, 14	18:10	18:11	18:11
Josh		13:22 (Balaam)				
Jdg			9:37			
1 Sam		6:2 (Philistine diviners) 28:8 (medium at Endor)			28:3, 7, 8, 9	28:3, 9
2 Sam						
1 Kgs				[20:33]		
2 Kgs	16:3 (Ahaz of Judah) 17:17 21:6 (Manasseh)	17:17 21:6	21:6	17:17 21:6	21:6 23:24 (Josiah)	21:6 23:24

other gods; in both instances they are a tacked-on conclusion. This suggests that they have been updated by an editor who wished to draw an explicit connection between the calamity of exile and the proscribed divinatory practices of Deut 18:9–14.

This judgment is reinforced by the absence of extensive preceding narration of such practices in the DH (Table 5). The proscribed divinatory practices are hardly mentioned with such frequency as to warrant their inclusion in a retrospective summary of Israel's sins. For example, "passing one's son/daughter through the fire" is not mentioned as occurring in the northern kingdom at all, yet is referred to in 2 Kgs 17:17 as a reason for judgment. The only times קסם, שאל (עשה) אוב, and ידעני occur in Israelite contexts are with reference to the account of the medium at Endor. Even more strikingly, the two concluding retrospectives furnish the *only* usages of נחש as a divinatory practice in the DH.[22] ענן is similarly rare, occurring only in Jdg 9:37 and 2 Kgs 21:6. In sum, the insertion of the proscribed divinatory practices into the Dtr editors' reports of the fall of the northern kingdom (2 Kgs 17:17) and of Manasseh's reign, the cause of the fall of the southern kingdom (2 Kgs 21:6), is not due to extensive reporting of such practices in the history, but as a way to make Israel's and Judah's violation of the law explicit. These verses are quotations from Deut 18:10–11, intended to

---

22   A point made by Nelson, *Double Redaction*, 59.

furnish a legal basis for the judgment of exile. They belong to the exilic redaction of the DH, which updates these texts from the perspective of Deut 18:9–22.

The observation that the exilic Deuteronomist was particularly taken with Deut 18:10 (cf Nelson's "deeply impressed" above) raises the possibility that the usage in this context of a formula "they did not listen" as a reference to Israel's abandoning of her covenant obligations stems from the law of the prophet (cf שמע in Deut 18:14, 15, 16, 19). Nelson has pointed to five occurrences in the DH in which Israel is charged in a summary fashion with not "listening" to Yhwh's voice, each time by specific appointed emissaries (Jdg 2:2; 6:10; 2 Kgs 17:14, 40; 21:9). As Nelson says, "it is *only* in these five places that this generalized accusation follows the citation of some generalized command of Yahweh designed to sum up the whole of the people's covenant responsibilities."[23] The third and fifth of the passages highlighted by Nelson are in context closely related to the sending of Yhwh's "servants the prophets" and the failure of the people to obey them. Second Kings 17:13–14 presents the Dtr reason for the fall of the northern kingdom (and Judah is not excluded):

(13) ויעד יהוה בישראל וביהודה ביד כל־נביאו כל־חזה לאמר שבו מדרכיכם הרעים ושמרו מצותי חקותי ככל־התורה אשר צויתי את־אבתיכם ואשר שלחתי אליכם ביד עבדי הנביאים (14) ולא שמעו ויקשו את־ערפם כערף אבותם אשר לא האמינו ביהוה אלהיהם

(13) Yet the LORD warned Israel and Judah by every prophet and every seer, saying, "Turn from your evil ways and keep my commandments [and] my statutes, in accordance with all the law that I commanded your ancestors and that I sent to you by my servants the prophets." (14) They would not listen but were stubborn, like their ancestors, who did not believe in the LORD their God.

This retrospective summary of the prophetic message immediately precedes the passage examined above, in which Israel's divinatory practices were condemned. The prophets have a juridical function here: the message of "every prophet and every seer" is summed up as the means by which Yhwh "warns" (עוד) Israel and Judah to repent and to live in accordance with "all the law (כל־התורה)."[24] This represents a redefinition of prophecy in light of Deuteron-

---

23 Nelson, *Double Redaction*, 51.
24 James Montgomery, *A Critical and Exegetical Commentary on the Books of Kings*, ed. H.S. Gehman, ICC (Edinburgh: T&T Clark, 1951): "The language is doubtless legal, denoting authoritative deposition at law;" Gerhard von Rad, *Studies in Deuteronomy*, trans.

omy 18: the prophets are conceptualized as proclaimers of Torah and, consequently, those who threaten judgment according to the sanctions of that law.²⁵ This phrase therefore links the prophets to Moses, the paradigmatic servant, and presents them as proclaimers of an essentially similar revelation.²⁶ Second Kings 17:14 goes on to specify that Israel "would not listen" to these prophets. This is in direct contradiction to the command concerning the prophet like Moses in Deut 18:15, 18–19, to whom Israel is commanded to listen. In sum, then, 2 Kgs 17:13–17 presents Israel as doubly violating the commands of Deut 18:9–15: not only did they do what they were forbidden to do, i.e., engage in the divinatory practices of the nations, they also did not do what they were commanded to do, i.e., listen to the prophets (see Table 6).²⁷

This conclusion is reinforced by an examination of 2 Kgs 21:1–15, the account of Manasseh's reign. The passage has three main divisions:

vv. 1–7a: indictment: Manasseh's sinful practices
vv. 7b–9:   Manasseh's practices held up to standard of Torah of Yhwh's servant Moses
vv. 10–15:   Judah's doom threatened by Yhwh's servants the prophets

Sections two and three are both quotations of Yhwh, whose "servants" Moses and the prophets are explicitly coordinated. The tripartite division, then, is one

---

D.M.G. Stalker (London: SCM Press, 1953), 83: "The Deuteronomist's own conception of the main element in the prophetic office comes to expression in 2 Kings 17:13: Jahweh gives testimony (העיד) through it, in virtue of which the prophets call for repentance and the keeping of the commandments."

25   Ernest Nicholson, *Deuteronomy and Tradition* (Philadelphia: Fortress, 1967), 118, comments on this verse: "What Moses did in Deuteronomy, so also did the prophets during the course of Israel's history." See also Ronald E. Clements, *Prophecy and Tradition* (Atlanta, Ga.: John Knox, 1975), 51–52: "There is good reason for believing that the Deuteronomic interpretation of prophecy contained in 2 Kings 17:13 ff. is related to that given in Deut 18:15 ff., and represents a significant Deuteronomic interpretation of the work of the great prophets as a role instituted by Yahweh to be a ministry of the covenant inaugurated by Moses. Thus it sets this preaching within a theological context of covenant ideas and vocabulary which it did not previously possess, and interprets it quite distinctly as *torah*, which is to be set alongside the *torah* of Moses." And later, 54: "By relating this message to the unique authority of the *torah* of Moses ... the basic groundwork of a canonically conceived work of 'the Law and the Prophets' was established."

26   Christophe Nihan, " 'Moses and the Prophets': Deuteronomy 18 and the Emergence of the Pentateuch as Torah," *SEÅ* 75 (2010): 21–55 (at 42), suggests that they become "mere commentators" on Torah.

27   Prof. Tzvi Novick has pointed out to me that the litany of Israel's sins is introduced in 2 Kgs 17:9 with the phrase דברים אשר לא כן, which could echo לא כן (Deut 18:14).

TABLE 6   The double violation of Deut 18 in 2 Kings 17:13–17

Deut 18:14–15, 9–10	2 Kgs 17:13–17
(14) Although these nations that you are about to dispossess do give heed to soothsayers and diviners, as for you, the LORD your God does not permit you to do so. (15) The LORD your God will raise up for you a **prophet** like me from among your own people; **to him you will listen** (אליו תשמעון).	(13) Yet the LORD warned Israel and Judah by every prophet and every seer, saying, "Turn from your evil ways and keep my commandments and my statutes, in accordance with all the law that I commanded your ancestors and that I sent to you by **my servants the prophets.**" (14) **They would not listen** (ולא שמעו) but were stubborn, as their ancestors had been, who did not believe in the LORD their God.
(9) When you come into the land that the LORD your God is giving you, you must not learn to imitate the abhorrent practices of those nations. (10) No one shall be found among you who **makes a son or daughter pass through fire, or who practices divination**, or is a soothsayer, or an **augur**, or a sorcerer	(15) They despised his statutes, and his covenant that he made with their ancestors, and the warnings that he gave them. They went after false idols and became false; they followed the nations that were around them, concerning whom the LORD had commanded them that they should not do as they did. (16) They rejected all the commandments of the LORD their God and made for themselves cast images of two calves; they made a sacred pole, worshiped all the host of heaven, and served Baal. (17) **They made their sons and their daughters pass through fire; they used divination and augury**; and they sold themselves to do evil in the sight of the LORD, provoking him to anger.

that closely reflects the logic of Deut 18, dealing in succession with proscribed divinatory practices (2 Kgs 21:6//Deut 18:10) and the authority of Moses and his prophetic successors. This suggests, again, that the phrase "they did not listen" in 2 Kgs 21:9 is not only a generalized indictment of Judah but also a specific allusion to the prophet-law of Deut 18. The "double violation" of Deut 18:9–22 that we have seen in 2 Kgs 17:13–17 is also present in 2 Kgs 21:1–10 (Table 7). There is some variation here from the pattern of 2 Kings 17. Specifically, Yhwh cites the law of "my servant Moses" as the standard to which Manasseh's practices are held and found wanting. Yhwh's "servants the prophets" are then introduced as the successors to Moses who enforce the sanctions of the covenant.

TABLE 7   The double violation of Deut 18 in 2 Kings 21:2, 6, 7–10

Deut 18:9–15	2 Kgs 21:2, 6, 7–10
(9) When you come into the land that the LORD your God is giving you, you must not learn to imitate the **abhorrent practices of** those **nations**.	(2) [Manasseh] did what was evil in the sight of the LORD, following **the abominable practices of the nations** that **the LORD drove out before the people of Israel.**
(10) **No one shall be found among you who makes a son or daughter pass through fire**, or who practices divination, or is a **soothsayer, or an augur**, or a sorcerer, (11) or one who casts spells, or who consults **ghosts or spirits**, or who seeks oracles from the dead. (12) For whoever does these things is abhorrent to the LORD; it is because of such abhorrent practices that **the LORD your God is driving them out before you.** (13) You must remain completely loyal to the LORD your God. (14) Although these nations that you are about to dispossess do give heed to soothsayers and diviners, as for you, the LORD your God does not permit you to do so.	(6) **He made his son pass through fire;** he practiced **soothsaying and augury**, and dealt with **mediums and with wizards**. He did much evil in the sight of the LORD, provoking him to anger. (7) The carved image of Asherah that he had made he set in the house of which the LORD said to David and to his son Solomon, "In this house, and in Jerusalem, which I have chosen out of all the tribes of Israel, I will put my name forever; (8) I will not cause the feet of Israel to wander any more out of the land that I gave to their ancestors, if only they will be careful to do according to all that I have commanded them, and according to all the law that **my servant Moses** commanded them." (9) **But they did not listen** (ולא שמעו); Manasseh misled them to do more evil than the nations had done that the LORD destroyed before the people of Israel. (10) The LORD said by **his servants the prophets** …
(15) The LORD your God will raise up for you a **prophet** like me from among your own people; **to him you will listen** (אליו תשמעון).	

In sum, the two passages in the DH that reflect upon the reasons for Israel's and Judah's successive exiles combine references to the proscribed divinatory practices of Deut 18:10–11, the phrase "my/Yhwh's servants the prophets," and the generalized phrase "they did not listen" as a summation of Israel's failure to maintain her covenantal obligations. That the last of these phrases is an allusion to the prophet-law of Deut 18 has not been widely recognized in scholarship, perhaps because the verb "to listen" is rather common. The Dtr historian(s) who edited these passages pressed Deut 18:9–22 in the service of their theodicy: God was just in punishing Israel and Judah, who had doubly sinned in practicing divination and in failing to listen to Yhwh's authorized representatives.

The law in Deuteronomy was a good candidate for this because of its own insistence that the proscribed divinatory practices listed served as the reason that Yhwh was driving out the nations from before Israel (Deut 18:12). In fact, this list of proscribed divinatory practices is the only *specific* reason adduced with respect to the justification of the conquest in the book of Deuteronomy. Elsewhere, where Deuteronomy proffers reasons for the conquest, it speaks generally of the nations' "wickedness" (Deut 9:4, 5) or service of other gods (Deut 8:19–20, 12:2–3); however, specific practices are rarely mentioned, and where they are, they parallel those in Deut 18:9–14 (12:31). In sum, Deut 18:9–15; 2 Kgs 17:13–17; 21:1–15 have the following similarities: 1) a focus on proscribed divinatory practices; 2) a contrast between these practices and the requirement to obey Moses and the prophets; 3) the proffering of an explanation for expulsion from the land, whether that be the original inhabitants (Deut 18:12), Israel (2 Kgs 17:18–20), or Judah (2 Kgs 21:10–15).

I am, of course, not the first to note the parallels between the proscribed divinatory practices in Deut 18:10–11 and the descriptions in 2 Kgs 17:17; 21:6; what is new in my analysis is the detailed elaboration of how this is related in context to the use of the phrase "my/Yhwh's servants the prophets." Schmidt, for example, draws upon these references to argue that Deut 18:10–11 is a part of the same Dtr redaction as the passages in 2 Kings.[28] In contrast, I characterize 2 Kgs 17:17; 21:6 as an *interpretation* of Deut 18, for several reasons. First, I noted above their intrusiveness in 2 Kings 17:17; 21:6. Second, the connection between the expulsion of the Canaanites and the exiles of Israel and Judah is best characterized as a later, exilic, reflection on the Deuteronomic law. Third, the language of "servants" is not present in the prophet-law, only in the later Dtr interpretation.[29]

---

28   Brian Schmidt, "Canaanite Magic vs. Israelite Religion: Deuteronomy 18 and the Taxonomy of Taboo," in *Magic and Ritual in the Ancient World*, ed. Paul A. Mirecki and Marvin W. Meyer; RGRW 141 (Leiden: Brill, 2002), 242–259.

29   I developed this thesis independently; however, I have now seen this claim made by Thomas C. Römer, "Moses, Israel's First Prophet, and the Formation of the Deuteronomistic and Prophetic Libraries," in *Israelite Prophecy and the Deuteronomistic History: Portrait, Reality, and the Formation of a History*, ed. Mignon R. Jacobs and Raymond F. Person Jr.; AIL 14 (Atlanta: Society of Biblical Literature, 2013), 129–146; at 134: "The use of the title 'ăbādîm for prophets may stem from Deut 18:14–22, where the prophets appear as Moses' successors." I have taken this suggestion and expanded upon it considerably.

Thus, though I consider these passages to be closely bound together through the *Fortschreibung* of 2 Kings from the perspective of Deuteronomy, I cannot concur that they are contemporaneous.

2.3   Prophecy and Fulfillment

The above considerations provide warrant for the claim that the collective description of the prophets as Yhwh's servants developed as an early exegesis of Deut 18:9–22. The binomial designation "my servants the prophets" therefore has no redundancy, as it seeks to coordinate a historical succession of prophets to the authority of Moses, the archetypal servant of Yhwh. Hitherto I have investigated the phrase only from the perspective of the Dtr concern with theodicy and exile. However, there is another (related) theme in the DH in which the phrase plays a role, that of prophecy and fulfillment. In fact, the four occurrences of the phrase "Yhwh's/my servants the prophets" towards the end of the DH (2 Kgs 17:13, 23; 21:10; 24:2) dovetail with a larger pattern in the DH, noticed by von Rad, in which the quotation of a (specific) prophet is paralleled later on by the notice of the fulfillment of that quotation.[30] Von Rad demonstrated the theological importance of this pattern:

> The Deuteronomist's conception is manifestly this: Jahweh revealed his commandments to Israel; in case of disobedience he threatened her with severe punishment, with the punishment of total destruction, in fact. That had now taken place. Jahweh's words had been "fulfilled" in history—they had not "failed," as the Deuteronomist is also fond of saying. There thus exists, the Deuteronomist means, an inter-relationship between the words of Jahweh and history in the sense that Jahweh's word, once uttered, reaches its goal under all circumstances in history by virtue of the power inherent in it. This conception can be reconstructed very clearly from the Deuteronomist's work. We refer to that system of prophetic predictions and exactly noted fulfillments which runs through the Deuteronomist's work.[31]

Von Rad then enumerates eleven prophecies and their corresponding "exactly noted fulfillments," from Nathan's prophecy of the construction of the temple (2 Sam 7:13, 1 Kgs 8:20) to Huldah's regarding Josiah (2 Kgs 22:15; 23:20). In all but

---

30   Von Rad, *Studies in Deuteronomy*, 78–81. Von Rad includes the second of these passages (2 Kings 21:10 and 24:2) in his series of eleven passages that highlight prophecy and fulfillment in the DH.

31   Von Rad, *Studies in Deuteronomy*, 78.

one of the examples von Rad cites, the prophecy in question is uttered by an individual figure, including Ahijah (1 Kgs 11:29–39 and 12:15b; 14:6–16 and 15:29), Micaiah ben Imlah (1 Kgs 22:17 and 22:35–38), and Elijah (1 Kgs 21:21–24 and 21:27–29; 2 Kgs 1:6, 17). The only exception to this rule occurs in 2 Kgs 21:10–15, which von Rad describes as spoken by "unknown prophets."[32] Von Rad, however, is not interested in the anomalous character of this last prophecy, later referring to it as an oracle delivered by an "unknown prophet [singular!]."[33] His work focused on establishing the importance of the prophecy-fulfillment motif for the Deuteronomist, particularly with respect to the promises to David. It is worth asking, though, why in the case of Manasseh the prophets quoted are both plural and anonymous. The only parallel to this, omitted by von Rad in his list, is the generalized prophetic warning against Israel in 2 Kgs 17:13, with the subsequent noted fulfillment. Table 8 presents these passages in their interrelationship according to the pattern von Rad highlighted.[34]

The pattern von Rad isolated, in which individual, named prophets were quoted and the fulfillment of their words was later noted, is used for discrete events that are narrated within the DH. In these passages, however, Dtr is reflecting not on discrete events within the history, but *on the history as a whole*. Specific, named prophets are related to specific events within the history; in contrast, the prophetic witness considered generally is related to the lives of Israel and Judah considered generally, that is, to the entire covenantal narrative. Dtr could have ascribed the oracle against Manasseh to a specific named prophet. But the fact that it is instead attributed to a generalized plural collective—Yhwh's servants the prophets—suggests that its communicative intent is to refer to the entire succession of prophets from Moses to the exile, inclusive of Moses at its origin and Jeremiah at its conclusion. By this phrase the Dtr editors deliberately distill and sum up the prophetic message in order to emphasize that the inter-relationship between the prophetic word and history governs not only discrete events within the history, but the life of Israel and Judah as a whole.

In this connection, Robert Polzin's narrative-critical work deserves attention. Examining the DH from the perspective of its "ultimate semantic authority," Polzin has developed an intriguing proposal: the prophet like Moses is the narrator of the DH, the "voice" which succeeds Moses in authoritatively narrat-

---

32   Von Rad, *Studies in Deuteronomy*, 81.
33   Von Rad, *Studies in Deuteronomy*, 83.
34   Michael Fishbane, *Biblical Interpretation in Ancient Israel* (Oxford: Oxford University, 1988), 469, has also noted the importance of these passages in the prophecy-fulfillment schema of the DH.

TABLE 8 Yhwh's "servants the prophets" and the prophecy-fulfillment schema of the DH

	Quotation:	Fulfillment:
Israel (2 Kgs 17)	(13) Yet the LORD warned Israel and Judah by every prophet and every seer [כל־נביאו כל־חזה] saying, "Turn from your evil ways and keep my commandments and my statutes, in accordance with all the law that I commanded your ancestors and that I sent to you by **my servants the prophets**."	(22) The people of Israel continued in all the sins that Jeroboam committed; they did not depart from them (23) until the LORD removed Israel out of his sight, as he had foretold through all **his servants the prophets**. So Israel was exiled from their own land to Assyria until this day.
Judah	*2 Kgs 21:10–15* (10) The LORD said by **his servants the prophets**, (11) "Because King Manasseh of Judah has committed these abominations, has done things more wicked than all that the Amorites did, who were before him, and has caused Judah also to sin with his idols; (12) therefore thus says the LORD, the God of Israel, I am bringing upon Jerusalem and Judah such evil that the ears of everyone who hears of it will tingle. (13) I will stretch over Jerusalem the measuring line for Samaria, and the plummet for the house of Ahab; I will wipe Jerusalem as one wipes a dish, wiping it and turning it upside down. (14) I will cast off the remnant of my heritage, and give them into the hand of their enemies; they shall become a prey and a spoil to all their enemies, (15) because they have done what is evil in my sight and have provoked me to anger, since the day their ancestors came out of Egypt, even to this day."	*2 Kgs 24:2–4* (2) The LORD sent against him [Jehoiakim] bands of the Chaldeans, bands of the Arameans, bands of the Moabites, and bands of the Ammonites; he sent them against Judah to destroy it, according to the word of the LORD that he spoke by **his servants the prophets**. (3) Surely this came upon Judah at the command of the LORD, to remove them out of his sight, for the sins of Manasseh, for all that he had committed, (4) and also for the innocent blood that he had shed; for he filled Jerusalem with innocent blood, and the LORD was not willing to pardon.

ing Israel's story. The proposal seems implausible, yet Polzin marshalls several arguments to bolster his case. First, building on the work of von Rad, Polzin notes the balance established between Deuteronomy and Joshua–2 Kings:

> It has long been emphasized that basic to the viewpoint of the Deuteronomist is "that system of prophetic prediction and its exactly observed fulfillment which pervades the whole work of this writer" .... We thereby see that Deuteronomy, in that it is almost totally a number of Mosaic speeches, functions as an expression of the prophetic word of God, and that Joshua–2 Kings mainly recount events that constitute "its exactly observed fulfillment."[35]

In Deuteronomy, Polzin observes, the dominant voice is that of Moses; only fifty-six verses are given to the narrator. In Joshua–2 Kings, the narrator's voice takes over, describing the fulfillment of Moses' prophecies.[36] The DH is therefore the vindication of Moses' prophetic status, according to his own criterion of fulfillment: his prophecies of Israel's apostasy and exile have in fact come true.[37] The narrator of the DH is, according to Polzin, the voice which succeeds Moses and provides access to his prophecies: "If the path to God is through Moses, the path to Moses is through the text's narrator"; "as the word of God is to the word of Moses, so the word of Moses is to the word of the Deuteronomic narrator."[38] This leads to Polzin's unconventional conclusion:

> The "prophet like Moses" is the narrator of the Deuteronomic History, and through him, the Deuteronomist himself .... [W]e can be very precise concerning the words of God referred to in 18:14–22 .... [T]hese words begin

---

35   Robert Polzin, *Moses and the Deuteronomist: A Literary Study of the Deuteronomic History* (New York: Seabury Press, 1980), 18–19. The quotation is from von Rad, *Studies in Deuteronomy*, 78.
36   Polzin, *Moses and the Deuteronomist*, 19.
37   See Sven Tengström, "Moses and the Prophets in the Deuteronomistic History," *SJOT* [1994]: 257–266, 264: "Thus, the criterion established in Deut 18:20–22, which characterizes the true prophet as the one whose words are fulfilled, should not be understood as a practical rule among the others, because on a practical level the true prophet must be recognized before his predictions are realized; rather the criterion was meant as the basic principle of the deuteronomistic theology of history." The comments are apposite; however, I would reframe this to suggest that the original function of the criterion as a practical rule for consultative prophecy is transformed in the Dtr historiographical project into an authentication of Moses as the prophet *par excellence*.
38   Polzin, *Moses and the Deuteronomist*, 27, 57.

with the narrator's report in Joshua 1:1 … and end with the final words of 2 Kings 25:30.[39]

I agree with Polzin that the editors of the DH—who melded various traditions into a national narrative containing recurring patterns of election and salvation, sin and judgment—are conscious of a distinction between history and History, that is, between the discrete events composing the history and the overall arc of Israel's and Judah's story. It is unconvincing, however, to posit that the narrator assumes the authoritative role of the prophet like Moses; this would require that the texts of the DH were intentionally composed as scripture or the "word of God," which seems anachronistic. Polzin's insights should be reframed: the generalized references to Yhwh's "servants the prophets" and the summative distillations of their message are the vehicle that the Dtr historian uses to demonstrate that the entire story is subordinated to the divine word spoken by Moses in Deuteronomy.

To make this somewhat abstract hypothesis concrete: what actual prophets does the Dtr historian have in view in 2 Kgs 17:13, 23; 21:10; 24:2? The phrase is not only a reference to the individual prophets that figure prominently in the DH, such as Samuel, Nathan, Elijah or Elisha. Some of these are portrayed as issuing stern prophecies of doom (e.g., Elijah, 1 Kgs 21:19–24); however, a statement of warning such as 2 Kgs 17:13 scarcely suffices as a characterization of their prophetic activity. Nicholson points out, "Among the prophetic figures who are representative of 'old prophecy,' only Ahijah at the foundation of the northern state of Israel announces judgment on such a scale upon this newly founded kingdom" (cf 1 Kgs 14:15–16).[40] He therefore argues that the "prophetic announcement of judgment against Israel and Judah" must "embrace some at least of the line of prophets from the eighth century onwards, beginning with Amos."[41]

Indeed, both passages support the hypothesis that the prophets included in the phrase go beyond the ones explicitly named in the DH. The reference to "every prophet and every seer (כל־נביאו כל־חזה)"[42] in 2 Kgs 17:13 suggests that Dtr

---

39   Polzin, *Moses and the Deuteronomist*, 61.
40   Ernest W. Nicholson, "Deuteronomy 18:9–22, the Prophets and Scripture," in *Prophecy and Prophets in Ancient Israel*, ed. John Day, LHB/OTS 531 (London: T&T Clark, 2010), 151–171; here 153.
41   Nicholson, "Deut 18:9–22," 153. It should be noted that the redaction of Ahijah's prophecies is thoroughly Deuteronomistic.
42   There appears to be an error in MT, the ו is not a suffix but should be prefixed to כל. The parallelism between prophets and seers is not foreign to pre-exilic literature (cf Isa 29:10, 30:10), but its usage here is perhaps suggestive of the Chroniclers' representation

is attempting to provide a comprehensive summary of the prophetic message in Israel. The term חזה may be included with the recognition that Isa 1:1 labels the oracles associated with Isaiah as his vision, חזון (cf Obad 1). The mention of Judah in a passage on the downfall of the northern kingdom (17:13, cf v. 19) implies that the author includes Judean prophets in his purview.[43] The charge that Israel "went after false idols and became false" (2 Kgs 17:15) is dependent on Jer 2:5; the wording is identical (וילכו אחרי ההבל ויהבלו).[44] The prophetic speech in 2 Kgs 21:11–15 is an amalgam of prophetic sayings.[45] Distinctive elements include the metaphor of the "measuring line" and the "plummet," which probably derives from Isa 28:17 (cf Amos 7:7–8).[46] In particular, the dominant inter-text is Jeremiah, which has striking parallels to the phrases in 2 Kgs 21:12, 14;[47] the use of the term "God of Israel" in a prophetic formula, the reference to tingling ears (cf 1 Sam 3:11),[48] and overlap between the language of 21:14 and Jer 12:7 (see Table 9). Clearly, then, more prophets than those mentioned in the DH are in view; Dtr constructs a prophetic succession that extends from Moses to Jeremiah, inclusive of prophetic figures in both Israel and Judah.

These exilic usages of the phrase "my/Yhwh's servants the prophets" establish its association with direct speech. Yhwh's "servants the prophets" are quoted in a summary fashion, which has the function of distilling the variegated phenomenon of pre-exilic prophecy to a unified message of repentance:

---

of prophets and seers who attended various monarchs (cf 1 Chr 29:29; 2 Chr 9:29, 12:15, 29:25).

43 Lohfink "Was there a Deuteronomistic Movement?," 45 has argued for the dependence of this summative chapter on the oracles of Amos (while rejecting the characterization of Amos as "Deuteronomistic"): "[T]here is only one chapter of the basic Deuteronomistic canon that has several passages parallel to Amos: 2 Kings 17. Therefore, we can ask whether, in this chapter which speaks of Israel's rejection of the Torah preached by the prophets, the Deuteronomistic authors have not systematically made allusions to earlier prophetic writings, including Amos 2.4."

44 William Holladay, *Jeremiah 2: A Commentary on the Book of the Prophet Jeremiah Chapters 26–52*, Hermeneia (Minneapolis: Fortress, 1989), 85. Holladay also notes the dependence of 2 Kgs 17:10 on Jer 2:20 ("on every high hill and under every leafy tree").

45 Hobbs, *2 Kings*, 307, takes the speech as a "Deuteronomistic summary of the prophetic preaching"; Burke O. Long, *2 Kings*, FOTL 10 (Grand Rapids: Eerdmans, 1991), 249: "As though summarizing the substance of many oracles, the writer presents in stylized Dtr language the reason for judgment (v. 11), the proclamation of punishment itself (vv. 12–14), and, as a framing closure he repeats the justification for coming disaster (v. 15)."

46 Jones, *I & II Kings*, 2:599.

47 Jones, *I & II Kings*, 2:599–600.

48 On the potential relationship with Samuel traditions, see Graeme Auld, "Jeremiah–Manasseh–Samuel: Significant Triangle? Or Vicious Circle?," in *Prophecy in the Book of Jeremiah*, ed. H.M. Barstad and R.G. Kratz (BZAW 388; Berlin: Walter de Gruyter, 2009), 1–9.

TABLE 9   The influence of Jeremiah in 2 Kings 21:12, 14

Jer 19:3; 12:7	2 Kgs 21:12,14
ואמרת שמעו דבר־יהוה מלכי יהודה וישבי ירושלם **כה־אמר יהוה צבאות אלהי ישראל הנני מביא רעה** **על־המקום הזה אשר כל־שמעה תצלנה אזניו** עזבתי את־ביתי **נטשתי** את־**נחלתי נתתי** את־ידדות נפשי בכף **איביה**	לכן **כה־אמר יהוה אלהי ישראל הנני מביא רעה** **על־ירושלם** ויהודה **אשר כל־שמעיו תצלנה** שתי **אזניו** **ונטשתי** את שארית **נחלתי ונתתים** ביד **איביהם** והיו לבז ולמשסה לכל־איביהם
You shall say: Hear the word of the LORD, O kings of Judah and inhabitants of Jerusalem. **Thus says the LORD of hosts, the God of Israel: I am going to bring such disaster upon** this place **that the ears of everyone who hears of it will tingle.** I have forsaken my house, I have **abandoned my heritage**; I have **given** the beloved of my heart into the hands of her **enemies**.	Therefore **thus says the LORD, the God of Israel, I am bringing upon** Jerusalem and Judah **such evil that the ears of everyone who hears of it will tingle.** I will **cast off** the remnant of **my heritage**, and **give** them into the hand of their **enemies**; they shall become a prey and a spoil to all their **enemies**.

the prophets are represented, quite literally, as speaking with one voice.[49] The usage of this phrase in the context of quotation persists: in its seventeen occurrences, direct quotation of Yhwh's "servants the prophets" occurs in five passages;[50] in eleven of the passages, the speech of these prophets is referred to, without direct quotation.[51] In Jeremiah, the phrase always occurs in one of Jeremiah's "sermons," so that it is always set in the context of direct speech, and on the occasions that Jeremiah "quotes" the collective body of prophets, their direct speech is set within his.[52] In light of the connections with Deut 18:9–22,

---

49   Stephen B. Chapman, *The Law and the Prophets: a Study in Old Testament Canon Formation*, FzAT 27 (Tübingen: Mohr Siebeck, 2000), 206, on Jer 25:4–6 and 2 Kgs 17:13: "In both cases a succession of prophets is not only cited, but quoted, as if one single message could be distilled from the immense variety of prophetic actions and oracles throughout Israel's history."
50   2 Kgs 21:10; Jer 25:4–6, 35:15, 44:4; Ezra 9:11.
51   2 Kgs 17:13, 23, 24:2; Jer 7:25, 26:5, 29:19; Ezek 38:17; Amos 3:7–8; Zech 1:6; Dan 9:6, 10.
52   It is only in one of the passages (2 Kgs 9:7) that the phrase is not connected to a distillation

it seems permissible to postulate that the close association of the phrase with speech-acts is dependent on Deuteronomy's restriction of prophetic activity to passing along the words of Yhwh (Deut 18:18). Yhwh's "servants the prophets" are therefore portrayed as authoritative exponents and interpreters of Mosaic Discourse.

The main import of these allusions to the writing prophets in 2 Kgs 17 and 21, in my view, is a belated recognition within the DH that prophets of doom were also authentic exponents of Mosaic Discourse.[53] It is interesting that such prophets, who presented themselves as sharp critics of Israel's and Judah's ruling classes, are nowhere mentioned by name in the DH, and may even, in the case of Amos, have been deliberately omitted.[54] Thus, it is not coincidental that the non-DH usages of the phrase Yhwh's "servants the prophets" occur in the scrolls of the prophets of doom *par excellence*, Amos and Jeremiah. I will consider Jeremiah's role in the Mosaic prophetic succession in more detail in the next chapter; at this juncture, it is appropriate to highlight the deliberate incorporation of Amos into the company of Mosaic prophets.

3 Amos among Yhwh's "Servants the Prophets"

In contrast to Amos' famous claim that he was not a prophet (Amos 7:14), the oracle of Amos 3:3–8 situates him among Yhwh's "servants the prophets." Amos 3:7 interrupts a poetic series of rhetorical questions with a parenthetical prose remark concerning the importance of Yhwh's prophets in the divine council:

כי לא יעשה אדני יהוה דבר כי אם־גלה סודו אל־עבדיו הנביאים

---

of the prophetic message by reference or by summary quotation, a fact that confirms its designation as anomalous.

53 The only "writing prophet" who does figure in the DH is Isaiah, prophet of Jerusalem's salvation. On the hypothesis of a pro-Davidic Josianic edition of the DH, the prophets originally included would have been those that conformed to a nationalistic commitment to the southern kingdom. See Albertz, *Israel in Exile*, 279–282, for such a perspective (albeit one that demurs from the hypothesis of a Josianic edition).

54 Joseph Blenkinsopp, *A History of Prophecy in Israel*, rev. and enl. (Louisville, Ky: Westminster John Knox Press, 1996), 248n6, argues that 2 Kgs 14:27 may be a polemical rejection of the prophecies of Amos ("But the LORD had not said that he would blot out the name of Israel from under heaven [ולא דבר יהוה למחות את שם ישראל מתחת השמים], so he saved them by the hand of Jeroboam son of Joash"); cf. Amos 9:8a.

> Surely the Sovereign LORD does not speak without revealing his council to his servants the prophets.

The context contains vivid usage of imagery and metaphor (the lion, vv. 4, 8; the bird, the snare, v. 5; the trumpet, v. 6). In the poetic series of rhetorical questions, the prose explanatory remark of v. 7 seems intrusive.[55] Indeed, Auld has pointed out that there is tension between the emphasis on the prophets' indispensable role in Yhwh's council here and the rhetorical questions of 3:8, which suggest that prophecy is compelled from anyone who hears Yhwh's voice.[56] Moreover—and this is closely related to the perspective on Yhwh's "servants the prophets" developed in Jeremiah—the character of Amos 3:3–8 is an oracle of doom is surely significant. The rhetorical question preceding the insertion would have struck Amos' Dtr editors as a prophecy or warning of Jerusalem's devastation ("Does disaster befall a city, unless Yhwh has done it?"), leading to this reverential statement.

Christophe Nihan has observed that the Dtr editors of Amos' oracles may have been influenced by Amos 2:11, which, other than Deut 18:15, 18 and Jer 29:15, contains the only occurrence of Yhwh "raising" (קום) up prophets in the Hebrew Scriptures.[57] Nihan argues:

---

[55] *Pace* Francis I. Andersen and David Noel Freedman, *Amos: A New Translation with Introduction and Commentary*, AB 24A (Garden City: Doubleday, 1989), 391–392, who argue for its originality on the basis that there are other prose interjections into Amos' poetic oracles (they adduce 1:6, 1:13, 2:1). Nevertheless, they say of the phrase "servants of Yahweh," 399: "All occurrences can hardly be assigned to a Deuteronomistic editor, but except for the present instance, they are late"—which seems to be an admission that the evidence does not favor the phrase's originality to the oracle. On the phrase as a Dtr insertion, see Graeme Auld, *Amos*, OTG (Sheffield: JSOT Press, 1986), 30 (emphasis original): "Scholars have normally argued that the phrase is a part of 'Deuteronomistic' usage: that is, an element of the terminology of those ancient scholars who edited the books of Joshua to Kings, and perhaps Jeremiah too ... who were probably active at the time of the Exile of Jerusalem and Judah in Babylon in the sixth century BCE .... Amos 3.7, if early would be the *sole* and striking exception to this pattern."

[56] Auld, *Amos*, 31: "who ever found himself face to face with a lion without his stomach turning around and his knees shaking? Then the second question presses the conclusion home. So it is with prophesying. *No-one* ever heard the divine voice without prophesying. And the implication is surely there that hearing the divine voice is no more the prerogative of official prophets than fear of wild beasts or air raid sirens requires special capacities or accreditation. It is just that strong point which is undercut or neutralized by v. 7 with its class of prophetic servants who are made privy to the Lord's purposes."

[57] The parallel between prophets and nazirites suggests a pre-deuteronomic view of prophecy (Andersen and Freedman, *Amos*, 331–332). Later, the Deuteronomistic editors of Amos may have had figures such as Samson and Samuel in mind. Here endogenous prophecy

> [T]he three passages form a kind of system: Deut 18 connects the origin of this tradition with Moses at Mount Horeb; Amos 2 demonstrates that Yahweh continued to establish prophets at regular intervals throughout the preexilic period; finally, Jer 29 asserts that this tradition has come to an end with the Babylonian exile. Even though Amos 2:11 is probably pre-Deuteronomistic … it seems that this passage was reused by the Deuteronomists after the exile in order to establish a comprehensive theory regarding the history of prophecy from Moses to Jeremiah.[58]

Indeed, it seems likely that the Deuteronomists may have interpreted Amos 2:11 in terms of a Mosaic prophetic succession. This is particularly plausible in the light of the way Amos situates the sending of prophets by Yhwh within a summary of the salvation-history:

> (9) Yet I destroyed the Amorite before them, whose height was like the height of cedars, and who was as strong as oaks; I destroyed his fruit above, and his roots beneath. (10) Also I brought you up (העליתי) out of the land of Egypt, and led you forty years in the wilderness, to possess (לרשת) the land of the Amorite. (11) And I raised up some of your children to be prophets and some of your youths to be nazirites. Is it not indeed so, O people of Israel? says the LORD. (12) But you made the nazirites drink wine, and commanded the prophets, saying, "You shall not prophesy."
> Amos 2:9–12

The link between the Exodus (2:10), the destruction of the inhabitants of the land and possession of it (ירש: Deut 18:14; Amos 2:10), and the raising up of prophets (Deut 18:15; Amos 2:11) may have caused this passage to be interpreted in light of Deuteronomy 18's promised prophet like Moses. Amos, willingly or not (cf. Amos 7:14–15), is thus incorporated into a prophetic class that stretches back to Israel's originating moments. The significance of the inclusion of Amos in the company of "Yhwh's servants the prophets" reflects the exilic Dtr conclusion that prophets who pronounced judgement, such as Amos, Micah (cf Jer 26:18), and Jeremiah, were indeed to be classified among the company of Mosaic prophets.

("from your sons") is a manifestation of a divine gift, not a stipulation against foreign divination, as in Deuteronomy.

58   Nihan, "'Moses and the Prophets,'" 34.

4 Conclusion

In sum, the Dtr neologism Yhwh's "servants the prophets" represents the earliest, exilic interpretation of Deuteronomy's prophet like Moses. These prophets were understood as a succession of spokespersons for Yhwh, which culminated in the warnings issued in the final period of Israel's and Judah's history, from the eighth century to the exile. Moreover, for the Deuteronomists, this succession included not only the great prophets of the DH, mainly active in the northern kingdom, but also included prophets from or active in Judah such as Amos and Jeremiah. This brings us to a consideration of the Dtr portrayal of Jeremiah as a figure of particular significance in the Mosaic prophetic succession.

CHAPTER 4

"My Servants the Prophets," Part II: Jeremiah as Culminating Figure in the Mosaic Prophetic Succession

1   Introduction

Before moving on from the Dtr interpretation of the prophet like Moses, it is important to consider the way in which the Dtr scribes portray Jeremiah as a culminating figure in the pre-exilic Mosaic prophetic succession. In Dtr thought, Jeremiah was the Mosaic prophet *par excellence*.[1] But how did the scribes understand Jeremiah's precise relationship to Moses on the one hand and the Mosaic prophetic succession on the other? In recent years these questions have been a matter of considerable interest in scholarship. Regarding the first, some have claimed that Jeremiah was regarded as Moses' equal, or per-

---

1   On the relationship between Jeremiah and Deuteronomy, see Nathan Mastnjak, *Deuteronomy and the Emergence of Textual Authority in Jeremiah*, FzAT 2/87 (Tübingen: Mohr Siebeck, 2016). Important earlier studies include J. Philip Hyatt, "Jeremiah and Deuteronomy," in *A Prophet to the Nations: Essays in Jeremiah Studies*, ed. L.G. Perdue and B.W. Kovacs (Winona Lake: Eisenbrauns, 1984 [1942]), 113–127; idem, "The Deuteronomic Edition of Jeremiah," in *A Prophet to the Nations: Essays in Jeremiah Studies*, ed. L.G. Perdue and B.W. Kovacs (Winona Lake: Eisenbrauns, 1984), 247–267; Ernest W. Nicholson, *Preaching to the Exiles: A Study of the Prose Tradition in the Book of Jeremiah* (New York: Schocken Books, 1970); Winfried Thiel, *Die deuteronomische Redaktion von Jeremia 1–25*, WMANT 41 (Neukirehen: Neukirchener Verlag, 1973); idem, *Die deuteronomische Redaktion von Jeremia 26–45*, WMANT 52 (Neukirehen: Neukirchener Verlag, 1981). Commentaries in support of Dtr influence on Jeremiah include William McKane, *A Critical and Exegetical Commentary on Jeremiah*, 2 vols., ICC (Edinburgh: T&T Clark, 1986–1996); Robert P. Carroll, *Jeremiah: A Commentary*, OTL (Philadelphia: Westminster, 1986). The main dissenters, who argue that Jeremianic and Dtr language belong to the common prose of the late seventh century, are William L. Holladay, *Jeremiah 1: A Commentary on the Book of the Prophet Chapters 1–25*, Hermeneia (Philadelphia: Fortress, 1986); idem, *Jeremiah 2: A Commentary on the Book of the Prophet Jeremiah Chapters 26–52*, Hermeneia (Minneapolis: Fortress, 1989); Helga Weippert, *Die Prosareden des Jeremiasbuches*, BZAW 132 (Berlin: de Gruyter, 1973). This theory, however, fails to explain why the relationship between Jeremiah and the DH is so much closer than that between the DH and other prophetic literature of the late monarchy. See Thomas C. Römer, "How Did Jeremiah Become a Convert to Deuteronomistic Ideology?" in *Those Elusive Deuteronomists: The Phenomenon of Pan-Deuteronomism*, ed. L.S. Schearing and S.L. McKenzie, JSOTSupS 268 (Sheffield: Sheffield Academic, 1999), 189–199, who provides survey of research and hypothesizes a first Dtr redaction of Jer 7–35 in the exilic period.

haps even his superior. Regarding the second, some have claimed that for the Dtr school, Jeremiah represented an end or final point in Mosaic prophecy. My contribution will be to clarify and sharpen such claims: in both cases they offer important insights regarding the Dtr construal of Jeremiah as a Mosaic prophet, but require important qualifications. To state my conclusion at the outset: Jeremiah is understood to be a final prophet specifically in the sense that for the Dtr scribes he was the last prophet in the pre-exilic Mosaic prophetic succession. Jeremiah becomes an important locus for scribal reflection on prophecy; indeed, he is transformed by the scribal authors of the book into a paradigmatic Mosaic prophet, who becomes the legitimate conduit of the Mosaic tradition, and who is portrayed as having the authority to modify and reshape that tradition.

2   Jeremiah and the Mosaic Prophetic Succession

2.1   *Jeremiah among Yhwh's "Servants the Prophets"*

The Dtr redaction of Jeremiah evinces tremendous interest in prophets and prophecy.[2] Salient here is that six of the seventeen occurrences of the Dtr phrase Yhwh's "servants the prophets" are in Jeremiah, all in Dtr-influenced passages.[3] Moreover, all of the occurrences have been put in *speeches* made

---

2   James T. Hibbard, "True and False Prophecy: Jeremiah's Revision of Deuteronomy," *JSOT* 35 (2011): 339–358; here 342: "An examination of the concordance reveals that Jeremiah has more to say about נביאים by a considerable margin than any other book among the latter prophets: the term נביא occurs in Isaiah seven times; in Ezekiel 17 times, but the term occurs 95 times in Jeremiah." The disparity is striking, but it is important to note that Hibbard's analysis is based on the MT. It is widely acknowledged that the Hebrew *Vorlage* of the LXX represents an earlier version of Jeremiah than that represented by MT, and there the noun "prophet" occurs 57 times—still considerably more than in Isaiah and Ezekiel, but considerably less than in MT. Of the 38 occurrences in MT that are not represented in LXX, 27 are the addition of הנביא to Jeremiah's name; see J. Gerald Janzen, *Studies in the Text of Jeremiah* (HSM 9; Cambridge: Harvard University Press, 1973), 145–148. Jeremiah's prophetic status is hardly emphasized in the earliest material in the book—rather, he is a dissident figure who opposes the "prophets" collectively—but is increasingly emphasized through the stages of redaction. On this, see Matthijs J. de Jong, "Why Jeremiah is Not Among the Prophets: An Analysis of the Terms נביא and נבאים in the Book of Jeremiah," *JSOT* 35 (2011): 483–510.

3   The phrase occurs in 7:25; 25:4; 26:5; 29:19; 35:15; 44:4; all but one (26:5) of these passages are considered "C" material and typically assigned to the Deuteronomists. The division of Jeremiah into A (poetry), B (biographical prose), and C (prose sermons) material originated with Sigmund Mowinckel, *Zur Komposition des Buches Jeremia* (Kristiania: Jacob Dybwad, 1914).

by Jeremiah as the Dtr movement represented him: Jeremiah is portrayed as an exponent and interpreter of Mosaic Discourse.[4]

There are two references to the prophets as Yhwh's servants in the prose traditions within Jer 1–25. The first of these occurs in the temple sermon, and the second in Jeremiah's concluding prophecy, in which he indicates for the first time that the inexorably approaching exile will last seventy years (Jer 25:11–12). Key phrases associated with the concept of Yhwh's "servants the prophets" in Jeremiah are underlined in the quotations below:

(25) למן־היום אשר יצאו אבותיכם מארץ מצרים עד היום הזה ואשלח אליכם
את־כל־עבדי הנביאים יום השכם ושלח (26) ולוא שמעו אלי ולא הטו את־אזנם ויקשו
את־ערפם הרעו מאבותם

(25) From the day that your ancestors came out of the land of Egypt until this day, I have persistently sent all my servants the prophets to them, day after day; (26) yet they did not listen to me, or pay attention, but they stiffened their necks. They did worse than their ancestors did.

Jer 7:25–26

(3) מן־שלש עשרה שנה ליאשיהו בן־אמון מלך יהודה ועד היום הזה זה שלש ועשרים
שנה היה דבר־יהוה אלי ואדבר אליכם אשכים ודבר ולא שמעתם (4) ושלח יהוה אליכם
את־כל־עבדיו הנבאים השכם ושלח ולא שמעתם ולא־הטיתם את־אזנכם לשמע

(3) For twenty-three years, from the thirteenth year of King Josiah son of Amon of Judah, to this day, the word of the LORD has come to me, and I have spoken persistently to you, but you have not listened. (4) And though the LORD persistently sent you all his servants the prophets, you have neither listened nor inclined your ears to hear.

Jer 25:3–4

Both passages situate prophetic activity within a temporal framework: in Jer 7:25, this framework extends from the "day" of the Exodus until "this day," that is, until Jeremiah's time; in 25:3, it extends for twenty-three years, from the thirteenth year of Josiah to "this day," that is, the fourth year of Jehoiakim, 605/604 BCE (cf 25:1). Moreover, both passages use a construction which includes a finite verb, its corresponding infinitive absolute, and another infinitive

---

4 The historical accuracy of this portrayal is ancillary to my main purpose. When I refer to "Jeremiah" in the discussion below, I refer to the prophet as a character in Dtr prose, and not the historical figure Jeremiah.

absolute to which the first is joined by a conjunction.[5] Williams classifies this as a use of the infinitive absolute that expresses continuous or repetitive action.[6] Such a construal of their force would amount to an insistence that Yhwh was continuously sending prophets (7:25; 25:4), and that Jeremiah has been speaking throughout the entire twenty-three year range to which he refers (25:3). These passages present the earliest articulation of the concept of the *continuous* sending of prophets to Israel from Moses onwards;[7] this is one of the only occurrences of this concept in the Hebrew Bible (cf Jer 11:7; 2 Chr 36:15–16). The idea of a continuous Mosaic prophetic succession becomes important in the Hellenistic and Roman periods, particularly in the writing of Josephus. Here it should not be understood literally, as though the Dtr authors thought there was a Mosaic prophet in every generation. The positing of a continuous succession of prophets is a hyperbolic claim, motivated by theodicy. Yhwh's righteousness is stressed by the insistence that the prophets were sent repeatedly, from the time of the Exodus until the days of Jeremiah.[8]

In the second of these passages, Jeremiah's ministry is presented as a microcosm of the prophetic tradition: he has spoken persistently over a specific temporal range, just as Mosaic prophets have from the time of the Exodus.[9] This

---

5 A literal translation of this construction would be as follows: "And I sent to you all of my servants the prophets, rising early and sending [**השכם** יום הנביאים עבדי־כל־את אליכם **ואשלח** **ושלח**]" (Jer 7:25); "And I spoke to you, rising early and speaking [**ודבר אשכים אליכם ואדבר**]" (Jer 25:3); "And the LORD sent to you all of his servants the prophets, rising early and sending [**ושלח השכם** הנבאים עבדיו־כל־את אליכם יהוה **ושלח**]" (Jer 25:4).

6 Ronald J. Williams, *Hebrew Syntax: An Outline*, 2nd ed. (Toronto: Univ. of Toronto, 1976), 38; cf 1 Sam 6:12, וגעו הלך הלכו, "they went, lowing as they went." There is dispute about whether the concept of continuous or repetitive action can be applied as a general rule to similar occurrences of coordinated infinitive absolutes. On the construction, see Waltke-O'Connor 35.3.2b–d; GKC 113s. In these cases, the use of temporally delimited phrases in the near context of the verbs strongly suggests that such an interpretation is warranted.

7 See Holladay, *Jeremiah 1*, 263: "What is emphasized here in the present verse is the steady, persistent effort of Yahweh to communicate with his people through a long series of prophets"; McKane, *Jeremiah*, 1:175: "the meaning is that there has been a continuous and insistent ... prophetic witness from the earliest period to the present"; Nicholson, "Deuteronomy 18:9–22," 152: "as though they constituted an unbroken succession."

8 Christl Maier, *Jeremia als Lehrer der Tora: Soziale Gebote des Deuteronomiums in Fortschreibungen des Jeremiabuches*, FRLANT 196 (Göttingen: Vandenhoeck & Ruprecht, 2002), 111, speaks of "die Ausweitung der Prophetenreihe vom Exodus bis Jeremia [the expansion of the prophetic succession from Exodus to Jeremiah]." And later she links this to Deut 18:15, 18 (112): "Die Vorstellung, daß JHWH seit der Zeit des Exodus ProphetInnen sandte, basiert auf derjenigen, die bereits Mose als Propheten, ja als *den* Propheten überhaupt sieht (Dtn 18,15.18)."

9 It should be noted that this is true of Jer 25:3–4 MT; LXX presents the passage as words of Yhwh.

aligns Jeremiah with the Mosaic prophetic succession and presents him as a culminating figure within it. The twenty-three years of Jeremiah's prophetic proclamation are the final link in the chain of the proclamation by Yhwh's "servants the prophets," and Jeremiah has joined them in both preaching to and experiencing the rejection of the people. The Dtr editors thus emphasize Jeremiah's unique and significant role in the prophetic succession. In fact, they reserve the hyperbolic language noted above for Jeremiah (it does not occur in the DH), precisely because of their conviction that Jeremiah played a *climactic* role in the prophetic succession that began with Moses.

Underlined in the citations of Jer 7:25; 25:3–4 above are three phrases which serve to clarify the Dtr redactors' usage of the phrase "Yhwh's/my servants the prophets" in Jeremiah. Two of these phrases, "rising early and sending" (השכם ושלח) and "they did not incline their ears" (ולא הטו את אזנם), are "common C diction" not found in the DH, that is, they are unique to Jeremiah.[10] Nevertheless, in Jeremiah they occur in close connection to the concept of Yhwh's "servants the prophets" (Table 10). The presence of unique Jeremianic terminology in commonly accepted "Dtr" sections of Jeremiah has led scholars to distinguish between Dtr redaction of the DH (Dtr or DtrH) and that of Jeremiah (DtrJ).[11] This is a literary designation, and should not be used to posit the existence of a DtrJ "school," which would be distinguished from the Dtr scribes.[12] In my view, the reason this language occurs in Jeremiah and not the DH is due to the Dtr scribes' understanding of Jeremiah's climactic role within the institution of Mosaic prophecy.

See McKane, *Jeremiah*, 1:618–623, and the observation that the goal of MT's modifications is "to represent that 25:1–7 is prophetic reminiscence rather than prophetic proclamation" (622).

10 Louis Stulman, *The Prose Sermons of the Book of Jeremiah: A Redescription of the Correspondences with Deuteronomistic Literature in the Light of Recent Text-Critical Research*, SBLDS 83 (Atlanta: Scholars Press, 1986), 42. Stulman categorizes C diction according to how frequently it is attested in the Dtr corpus; these two phrases are unattested, other than in the prose of Jeremiah.

11 For a helpful summary of DtrJ and its characteristics, see Mastnjak, *Deuteronomy*, 21–26. For a summary of the debate over the designation, see Carolyn J. Sharp, *Prophecy and Ideology in Jeremiah: Struggles for Authority in Deutero-Jeremianic Prose*, OTS (London; New York: T&T Clark, 2003), 21–23.

12 Sharp, *Prophecy and Ideology*, 26: "Deutero-Jeremiah" and Dtr may belong to the "same redactor or editorial group" which has "responded flexibly to the requirements of varied literary and thematic contexts."

TABLE 10 Jeremianic terminology associated with Yhwh's "servants the prophets"[a]

Passage	עבדי הנבאים	השכם ושלח	לא שמעו	ולא הטו את־אזנם
7:25–26	Y	Y	Y	Y
25:3–4	Y	Y	Y	Y
26:5	Y	Y	Y	
29:19 (MT)	Y	Y	Y	
35:15	Y	Y	Y	Y
44:4–5	Y	Y	Y	Y

a See Maier, *Jeremia als Lehrer der Tora*, 110, for a more comprehensive table highlighting the similarities between these passages.

The phrase "rising early and sending" (השכם ושלח) occurs eleven times in Jeremiah, mostly in "passages explicitly having to do with the LORD's servants the prophets."[13] This phrase extends and emphasizes the motif of theodicy already encountered in the DH: the scribes take up Jeremiah's voice in order to insist emphatically that Yhwh has taken the initiative in repeatedly sending prophets, so that Judah is without excuse. The other phrase also serves the overall goal of theodicy, in this case by magnifying the people's sin: they did not listen and did not "incline their ears" despite the repeated and ongoing warnings of the prophets. This phrase occurs eight times in Jeremiah.[14] Four of these are in close relation to the concept of Yhwh's "servants the prophets;" the other four serve to detail Judah's disobedience to various covenantal laws (Jer 7:24, 11:8 [summaries of the covenant]; Jer 17:23 [Sabbath]; Jer 34:14 [freedom for slaves]). Overall, then, the phrase serves to emphasize and compound Judah's guilt, and the references to specific matters of Torah suggest that the model of prophecy assumed by it is precisely one in which prophets are proclaimers of ethics, per Deut 18.

Thus, despite the fact that two of the phrases associated closely with the motif of Yhwh's "servants the prophets" in Jeremiah are not found in the DH,

13 Sharp, *Prophecy and Ideology*, 21, appeals to Jer 7:13, 25; 25:3, 4; 26:5; 29:19; 35:14, 15; 44:4. This list accounts for 9 of the 11 occurrences in Jeremiah; the other two are in 11:7, 32:33, and according to Sharp "can nevertheless be read as implying prophetic warning." The only other occurrence in the Hebrew Bible is in 2 Chr 36:15, which is dependent on Jeremiah for the formulation.

14 See Jer 7:24, 26; 11:8; 17:23; 25:4; 34:14; 35:15; 44:5; Stulman, *Prose Sermons*, 42.

they serve to emphasize and strengthen a theme found there. They underline Yhwh's righteousness by insisting that prophets were sent persistently, and Judah's guilt by the charge that they failed to be good students of the prophetic Torah.[15] The Jeremiah scroll contains hyperbolic and emphatic expansion of a DH motif, namely, that Yhwh was righteous in punishing Israel and Judah. This hyperbole is a direct function of the Dtr conception of Jeremiah's role as the final link in a prophetic chain that has warned Israel and Judah about the consequences of disobedience: with Jeremiah, both Yhwh's warning and Judah's guilt come to their climactic point.

2.2 Jeremiah and Other Prophets

For the scribal editors of the Jeremiah scroll, Jeremiah was therefore no ordinary prophet. He was an authorized exponent of Mosaic tradition, who stood in the company of Yhwh's "servants the prophets." Moreover, even within that succession, he is a figure of special significance. Before turning to discussion of the Jeremiah-Moses relationship, it is important to note the way the tradents of the Jeremiah materials take a particular interest in his relationship to other prophets, both those incorporated into the authorized succession (Micah of Moresheth; Uriah ben Shemaiah) and those excluded from it (Hananiah of Gibeon).

The episode of Jeremiah's "trial" (ch. 26) contains connections to Jeremiah's relationship both to the norms for prophecy in Deut 18:9–22 as well as to other prophets in the Mosaic prophetic succession. Jeremiah's speech in this chapter is a précis of the Temple sermon (vv. 4b–6; cf. "Shiloh" in 7:12, 14; 26:6),[16] to which the people and religious leadership respond negatively and assemble for the trial of Jeremiah as a presumptuous prophet.[17] The formulation "you

---

15 For the pedagogical use of "incline one's ear," cf, e.g., Prov 5:1, 13; 22:17.
16 Notably, the speech is preceded by God's charge to Jeremiah that he not "hold back a word" (26:2), one of only three occurrences of גרע with דבר as object. The other two are found in the so-called "canonical" formulae of Deut 4:2, 13:1, where Moses commands the people not to omit a word from the Torah. The parallel is noted by Holladay, *Jeremiah 2*, 104; Jack R. Lundbom, *Jeremiah 21–36: A New Translation with Introduction and Commentary*, AB 21B (New York: Doubleday, 2004), 287. Mastnjak, *Deuteronomy*, 64–70, draws out implications for Jeremiah's standing vis-à-vis Moses (65): "The allusion to Deut 13:1 in Jer 26:2 elevates the words of Jeremiah to the level of Moses. Just as the words of Moses are inviolable and must be obeyed, so also the words of Jeremiah."
17 McKane, *Jeremiah*, 2:676–681, is a rare voice opposed to this interpretation (cf 2:678: "The interpretation of v. 10 as an inauguration of legal proceedings should be called into question despite the unanimous approval which is given to it"). According to McKane, the officials are "trouble-shooters ... conducting a fact-finding enquiry" who decide "that there

shall die" (מות תמות, v. 11) is a legal phrase indicating Jeremiah deserves the capital penalty, with Deut 18:20 as the basis of the charge.[18] In his defense, Jeremiah insists that Yhwh is speaking through him, and that the community's condemnation of him will only implicate them further in guilt (Jer 26:12, 15). Jeremiah's words sway the officials, and the ruling is that he is not to be killed (Jer 26:16).[19] After this verdict has been reached, "some of the elders of the land" (guardians of the community's memory) step forward and assert that there is historical precedent for a Yhwh-prophet speaking doom, quoting the oracle of Micah against Zion (Jer 26:18; cf. Mic 3:12). This is the only instance of the direct quotation of one prophet in another in the Hebrew Bible, which provides an indication of the Dtr authors' interest in situating Jeremiah within a prophetic tradition. Micah, too, is hereby incorporated into the company of Yhwh's "servants the prophets." Importantly, Micah provided precedent for a Yhwh-prophet to be a prophet of doom. Finally, Micah appeared to be invalidated by Deuteronomy's norms for prophecy: what he said had not, in fact, come to pass (at least, at the time of the narrative). The Dtr editors emphasize that the possibility of Yhwh's change of heart qualifies a strict application of

---

is no case for Jeremiah to answer and that he should not be put on trial" (2:680). Whether a trial or a pre-trial hearing, it seems that the law of the prophet is being invoked.

18 Holladay, *Jeremiah 2*, 105: "it is the formula by which a death sentence is pronounced." Michael Fishbane, *Biblical Interpretation in Ancient Israel* (Oxford: Oxford University, 1988), 246; Anthony C. Osuji, *Where is the Truth?: Narrative Exegesis and the Question of True and False Prophecy in Jer 26–29 (MT)*, BETL 214 (Leuven: Peeters, 2010), 136: Deut 18:20 is the "main issue of the trial." Holladay, *Jeremiah 2*, 106, has an apt comment: "What one sees here then is not so much mob hysteria as a theological judgment anchored in the tradition."

19 In all probability, this should be understood as a suspension of judgment, rather than a declaration of Jeremiah's authenticity. The view that this amounts to a recognition of Jeremiah's authenticity is represented by, among others, Leslie Allen, *Jeremiah: A Commentary*, OTL (Louisville, Westminster John Knox, 2008), 26n10, Nicholson, *Preaching*, 300 ("a deafening silence is maintained about the deeper issue of the content of Jeremiah's prophesying, now that its divine source was granted"); Carroll, *Jeremiah*, 517 (Jeremiah has "acquired public recognition of his authenticity"); Osuji, *Where is the Truth?*, 143 ("the court scene leaves no question that Jeremiah is a true prophet of YHWH"). In view of the difficulties such an interpretation introduces (particularly, why then did Jeremiah continue to go unheeded?), it is preferable to hold that this involves only the suspension of judgment. See Walter Brueggemann, *A Commentary on Jeremiah: Exile and Homecoming* (Grand Rapids: Eerdmans, 1998), 236 ("The princes do not assert that Jeremiah's word is true"); Holladay, *Jeremiah 2*, 107; Frank L. Hossfeld and Ivo Meyer, *Prophet gegen Prophet: Eine Analyse der alttestamentlichen Texte zum Thema: Wahre und falsche Propheten*, BibB 9 (Fribourg: Verlag Schweizerisches Katholisches Bibelwerk, 1973), 43: the officials accepted his right to speak as a Yhwh-prophet but not the truth of his message.

the criterion of fulfillment (cf. 26:3, 13).[20] Indeed, the elders refer to a tradition in which doom was averted in the days of Hezekiah (normally associated with the prophet Isaiah).

The other prophet that Jeremiah is related to in this chapter is the less well-known Uriah ben Shemaiah, who prophesied against the city, fled to Egypt, and was extradited and put to death by Jehoiakim (26:20–23).[21] The episode serves to highlight the contrasting responses to the prophetic warning by the two Davidides, Hezekiah and Jehoiakim, and reinforces the peril of Jeremiah's situation. These points are often noted in the commentaries; however, the passage has a third function that is rarely discussed: it presents Jeremiah as the norm of authentic prophecy. Uriah is described as one who "prophesied against this city and against this land in words exactly *like* those of Jeremiah (ינבא על־העיר הזאת ועל־הארץ הזאת ככל דברי ירמיהו)" (26:20). The coordinating conjunction "like" (cf. Deut 18:15, 18) is here employed to portray Uriah as a "prophet like Jeremiah." Jeremiah's words are determinative for the authentic prophetic tradition, and so they were the words according to which Uriah prophesied.[22]

Finally, this leads us to consider briefly the famous and much-discussed episode of Jeremiah's conflict with Hananiah. In the confines of my argument, I cannot do justice to the importance of this passage in discussions of prophetic conflict;[23] I do, however, want to highlight critical points germane to the argument being laid out here. Hananiah's prophecy of the imminent return of the exiles and the temple vessels (28:2–4) directly contradicts Jeremiah's own proclamation of a long-term exile (Jer 25:11–12). Jeremiah's response to Hananiah juxtaposes an appeal to the Deuteronomic norms for prophecy with the situating of Jeremiah within a prophetic tradition:

---

20 See Hibbard, "True and False Prophecy," 349–354.
21 Carroll, *Jeremiah*, 520, is unnecessarily merciless in his evaluation of Uriah's flight: "Like a fool Uriah fled to Egypt, where (could he not have known?) the authorities supported Jehoiakim because he was their vassal. Uriah was extradited from Egypt (as he must have known he would be, unless he was an exceptionally ignorant prophet!), returned to the court and was there executed."
22 Even in his flight to Egypt, Uriah was preemptively like Jeremiah (cf 43:1–7).
23 The discussion on the pericope is immense. James L. Crenshaw, *Prophetic Conflict: Its Effect upon Israelite Religion*, BZAW 124 (Berlin: De Gruyter, 1971), represented an important turning point in the "rehabilitation" of Hananiah. See also Osuji, *Where is the Truth?*; R.W.L. Moberly, *Prophecy and Discernment* (Cambridge: Cambridge University, 2006); Daniel Epp-Tiessen, *Concerning the Prophets: True and False Prophecy in Jeremiah 23:9–29:32* (Eugene, Ore.: Pickwick, 2012); Seth B. Tarrer, *Reading with the Faithful: Interpretation of True and False Prophecy in the book of Jeremiah from Ancient Times to Modern*, JTISup 6 (Winona Lake, In.: Eisenbrauns, 2013). On the way Deuteronomy's norms for true and false prophecy are employed in Jer 28–29, see Mastnjak, *Deuteronomy*, 80–90.

> (8) The prophets who preceded you and me from ancient times (מן־העולם) prophesied war, famine, and pestilence against many countries and great kingdoms. (9) As for the prophet who prophesies peace, when the word of that prophet comes true (בבא דבר הנביא), then it will be known that the LORD has truly sent the prophet.
>
> Jer 28:8–9

To many, Jeremiah seems to be grasping for an answer to Hananiah.[24] In fact, the logic of Deut 18:15–22 is operative in the construction of this response: Jeremiah is the authorized recipient of the prophetic tradition (v. 8), and so he reminds Hananiah of the Mosaic test for authentic prophecy (v. 9).[25] The prophets of v. 8 include figures such as Micah, quoted above, and also other noteworthy prophets of doom, such as Amos. In the narrative, the apparently intractable debate between Jeremiah and Hananiah is resolved by Jeremiah's prediction of Hananiah's death (28:10). This has the dual function of serving as a sentence on Hananiah for speaking presumptuously and of confirming Jeremiah's status as a genuine spokesperson of Yhwh.[26] Jeremiah's affinity to authentic prophets like Micah and his declarations of judgment against presumptuous prophets like Hananiah emphasize that Jeremiah was a figure of particular significance in the Mosaic prophetic succession. Indeed, it is fair to say, for the Dtr scribes of this book, Jeremiah was superior to most, if not all,

---

[24] So, e.g., Gerhard von Rad, *Old Testament Theology*, trans. D.M.G. Stalker, 2 vols. (New York: Harper & Row, 1962), 2:209–210: "It is surprising to see a prophet so much at sea with a problem. At times in his famous encounter with Hananiah Jeremiah's arguments are almost groping."

[25] The standard interpretation of this passage applies v. 8 to Jeremiah and v. 9 to Hananiah. In a provocative article, Matthijs J. de Jong, "The Fallacy of True and False in Prophecy Illustrated by Jer 28:8–9," *JHS* 12.10 (2012): 1–29, challenges this "full scholarly consensus" (6) and argues instead that Jeremiah is the prophet of "peace" (for Babylon) and Hananiah the prophet of doom (for Babylon). However, de Jong acknowledges that Jeremiah is presented as a prophet of doom in a later literary layer, which he says is related to "a later, scribal depiction of prophecy, and not to prophecy as a historical phenomenon" (5). Since my argument focuses on the scribal reception of Jeremiah, and not the historical prophet, I will not consider de Jong's arguments in detail, which are bracing but ultimately unpersuasive (for example, Jer 37:19 suggests Jeremiah's opponents were saying that the king of Babylon would not come, which sounds more like a prophecy of peace than of war).

[26] Holladay, *Jeremiah 2*, 129, sets these options in unnecessary opposition to each other: "Jrm's announcement of the coming death of Hananiah is not foreknowledge, but a death sentence based on Deut 18:20 ... a false prophet must die." See, rightly, Rannfrid I. Thelle, "MT Jeremiah: Reflections of a Discourse on Prophecy in the Persian Period," in *The Production of Prophecy: Constructing Prophecy and Prophets in Yehud*, ed. D.V. Edelman and E. Ben Zvi (London: Equinox, 2009), 184–207; here 193.

his predecessors, so that the best point of comparison for Jeremiah was none other than Moses himself. I now turn to a discussion of the Jeremiah-Moses relationship and its significance for the Dtr understanding of history.

3 Jeremiah as Prophet like Moses

3.1 *Jeremiah's Call Narrative*

The strongest evidence for the conscious scribal portrayal of Jeremiah as the prophet like Moses occurs in Jeremiah's call narrative (1:4–10). There are two parallels with Deut 18:18b in this narrative, in 1:7 and 1:9 (Table 11).[27] As Holladay points out, the usual construction of the phrase "to put [God's] words in the mouth" of the prophet is with שׂום, not נתן.[28] The construction occurs with נתן only in Deut 18:18b; Jer 1:9; 5:14. Many scholars have therefore accepted the influence of Deuteronomy on Jeremiah's call narrative here.[29] Recently, however, a number of scholars have questioned this, claiming that Deut 18:18 is dependent on Jer 1:7, 9; that is, in Deuteronomy Moses is presented as a "prophet like Jeremiah."[30] Nicholson argues that Jer 5:14 (הנני נתן דברי בפיך לאשׁ) is the source of Jer 1:9, which renders superfluous the posited dependence on Deut 18:18. However, the parallel between Jer 1:7 and Deut 18:18 still requires explanation. Holladay points out that the conjunction between "command" (צוה) and (דבר) attested here occurs in only three texts, in two of which the figure of Moses

---

27 This chart below is modelled on the one in Thomas Römer, "The Formation of the Book of Jeremiah as a Supplement to the So-called Deuteronomistic History," in *The Production of Prophecy: Constructing Prophecy and Prophets in Yehud*, ed. Diana V. Edelman and Ehud Ben Zvi (London: Equinox, 2009), 168–183; here 173.

28 William L. Holladay, "The Background of Jeremiah's Self-Understanding: Moses, Samuel, and Psalm 22," *JBL* 83 (1964): 153–164; here 155. Thiel, *Jeremiah 1–25*, 67–68, provides a detailed list of references.

29 Allen, *Jeremiah*, 113–115; Louis Stulman, *Jeremiah*, AOTC (Nashville: Abingdon, 2005), 42. McKane, *Jeremiah*, 1:13, says "the correspondence between the Jeremiah passages and the Deuteronomy passages is not sufficiently exact to establish literary dependence," which seems too skeptical.

30 Ernest Nicholson, *Deuteronomy and the Judaean Diaspora* (Oxford: Oxford, 2014), 79–82; Werner H. Schmidt, "Das Prophetengesetz Dtn 18:9–22 im Kontext erzählender Literatur," in *Deuteronomy and Deuteronomic Literature: Festschrift C.H.W. Brekelmans*, ed. M. Vervenne and J. Lust, BETL 133 (Leuven: Leuven University Press, 1997), 55–69. Mastnjak, *Deuteronomy*, 54, rightly raises the question of what the meaning of this "supposed reuse of Jer 1" in Deut 18 would be: does it undercut the commonly accepted distributive meaning of "prophet" in Deut 18:15, 18, understanding the passage instead as a cryptic reference to Jeremiah?

TABLE 11   The influence of Deut 18:18 in Jeremiah 1

Deut 18:18b	Jer 1:7, 9
ונתתי דברי בפיו ודבר אליהם את כל־אשר אצונו	v. 9 נתתי דברי בפיך v. 7c ואת כל־אשר אצוך תדבר
And I will put my words in his mouth And he will speak to them all that I command	v. 9: I will put my words in your mouth v. 7c: and all that I command you will speak

looms large (Table 12).[31] Nicholson posits that Jer 1:7 is also the source of Deut 18:18, but does not interact with Exod 7:2 or offer grounds to accept this claim.[32] Nicholson also fails to consider the literary parallels drawn between Jeremiah and Moses: both are set apart from birth (Jer 1:5; Exod 2:1–10), and both protest their inadequacy as a vehicle for the divine message, specifically referring to their inability to speak effectively (Jer 1:6; Exod 4:10).[33] Therefore, even though the concept of Yhwh "putting his words in the mouth" of the prophet is present in Jeremianic poetry, it is likely that the Dtr authors of this passage intended to allude to Deut 18:18 in this passage, presenting Jeremiah at the outset as a prophet like Moses.[34] Indeed, one might go further and postulate that the combination of the allusion to Deut 18:18 in Jer 1:7, 9 and the positioning of Jeremiah among Yhwh's "servants the prophets" in 25:3–4 provides corroborative evidence for the influence of Deut 18:9–22 on this Dtr theological neologism. These pericopes form an *inclusio* at the bookends of the first half of the book (see the dates in 1:2, 25:3), establishing Jeremiah's important role in the company of Mosaic prophets.[35]

---

31 Holladay, "Background," 155; so also Römer, "Formation," 173.
32 Nicholson, *Deuteronomy and the Judaean Diaspora*, 80.
33 So Allen, *Jeremiah*, 26.
34 Sharp, *Prophecy and Ideology*, 152, has questioned this interpretation, on less than convincing grounds. She rejects the allusion to Deut 18:18 in Jer 1:9, but ignores the שׂום/נתן distinction in her counter-argument. She appeals to Num 22:38 (in which Balaam says he can speak only what God "puts" [שׂום] in his mouth), and says it would be "absurd" on this basis to view Balaam as "prophet like Moses." This argument fails because in Jeremiah's call narrative there are a number of corroborating motifs that suggest he is being portrayed in Mosaic terms; the allusion (with נתן) is but one of them. For further arguments for the dependence of Jer 1:7, 9 on Deut 18:18, see William Holladay, "Elusive Deuteronomists, Jeremiah, and Proto-Deuteronomy," *CBQ* 66 (2004): 55–77, at 66–69; Mastnjak, *Deuteronomy*, 51–59.
35 On Jer 1 and 25 as "bookends" of the first half of Jeremiah, see Stulman, *Jeremiah*, 223–226.

TABLE 12   "Speaking" what Yhwh "commands" in the Hebrew Bible

Exod 7:2a	Deut 18:18c	Jer 1:7c
אתה תדבר את כל־אשר אצוך	ודבר אליהם את כל־אשר אצונו	ואת כל־אשר אצוך תדבר
You [Moses] shall speak all that I command you,	who [the prophet like Moses] shall speak to them everything that I command	you [Jeremiah] shall speak whatever I command you.

Jeremiah is the only prophet to have a call narrative so clearly marked by allusions to Moses and to the concept of the prophet like Moses. Why did he loom so large in the Dtr understanding of prophecy? A figure such as Isaiah of Jerusalem could have been a locus of Dtr admiration and alignment to Moses; such re-writing, however, is not predominant in First Isaiah. There are two strikingly opposed hypotheses in scholarship regarding the precise significance of this portrayal of Jeremiah. Some have argued that it is intended to validate ongoing post-Mosaic prophecy, and present Jeremiah as a figure equal to or even greater than Moses. Others have claimed that Jeremiah was thought to be the final prophet like Moses. In my view, both of these views have important contributions to make, though both overstate their case. I will address each of these in turn.

3.2 *Jeremiah as Moses' Equal*

Some scholars have argued that the scribal authors of Jeremiah thought of him as a figure equal to or even greater than Moses in authority.[36] For example, Maier has claimed that the prohibition of intercession positions Jeremiah as "a more potent intercessor than Moses," since Yhwh seems to consider the possibility that Jeremiah would succeed where even figures such as Moses and Samuel would fail (cf Jer 15:1).[37] Maier also points out that in his halakhic role, Jeremiah is portrayed as one who teaches and enforces the terms of Mosaic law.[38] For example, with respect to the Sabbath in Jer 17, "the prophet teaches

---

36 Georg Fischer, "Jeremiah—'The Prophet like Moses?'" in *The Book of Jeremiah: Composition, Reception and Interpretation*, ed. Lundbom, Evans, and Anderson, VTSup 178 (Leiden: Brill, 2018), 45–66, at 48: "Jer, in its very first chapter, claims Jeremiah as the *announced successor of Moses*, and equal to him."

37 Christl Maier, "Jeremiah as Teacher of Torah," *Int* 62 (2008): 22–32, here 31.

38 Maier, "Jeremiah as Teacher of Torah," 24–30, discusses examples from Jer 7:5–8; 17:19–27; 22:1–5; 34:13–17.

the significance and correct execution of a single commandment in the divine Torah."³⁹ Maier dates this passage to the mid-fifth century BCE, which would imply that at quite a late period, post-Mosaic prophets rather than Moses himself were employed as the authority to update divine legislation. As an interpreter of Mosaic law, Jeremiah is portrayed as a tradition-mediating and tradition-generating figure: he receives and reshapes Mosaic tradition.⁴⁰ This robust halakhic role underlines the significance of the Moses-Jeremiah relationship for the authors of this scroll.

Benedetta Rossi has argued that within the editing of the Jeremiah scroll, Jeremiah is transformed from a prophet within the Mosaic succession to one that is superior to other Mosaic prophets; indeed, superior to even Moses himself.⁴¹ That is, in Rossi's view, there are multiple engagements with the concept of the prophet like Moses reflected in the Jeremiah scroll. First, Jeremiah is placed among the company of Mosaic prophets. Later, in response to Deut 34:10–12's assertion of Moses' superiority,⁴² the tradents of the Jeremiah scroll elevate his status, so that he transcends the Mosaic prophetic succession:

> Jeremiah is no longer one of the prophets in the line of the Mosaic succession (cf. Jer. 26.5; 28.28) or merely an announcer of the Torah as mediated by Moses (cf. for instance, 7.5–9). *Indeed, he is portrayed as the prophet like Moses, being placed on the same level.* Reference to Deut. 18.18 in Jer. 1.7d, 9c suggests that the prophetic succession … has been superseded. This marks a subsequent shift towards a prophetic authority directly attributed to God that aims to parallel and potentially replace the mediatory role of Moses.⁴³

According to Rossi, the scribes did this in order to buttress and support the new covenant prophecy (Jer 31:31–34), which placed Jeremiah on the same level as Moses.⁴⁴ Thus, "Jeremiah is depicted not as successor but rather as a substitute

---

39   Maier, "Jeremiah as Teacher of Torah," 27.
40   Cf also Ezek 40–48. See also Mastnjak, *Deuteronomy*, 185, who argues that the expansion of the Sabbath law in Jer 17 is part of DtrJ's concern "to depict Jeremiah as of equal status and authority with D's Moses."
41   Benedetta Rossi, "Reshaping Jeremiah: Scribal Strategies and the *Prophet like Moses*," *JSOT* 44 (2020): 575–593.
42   Rossi, "Reshaping Jeremiah," *JSOT* 44 (2020): 575–593, at 576 (emphasis original): "[T]he depiction of Jeremiah as *a prophet like Moses* develops in Jer. in response to Deut. 34.10–12."
43   Rossi, "Reshaping Jeremiah," 586–587. Emphasis added.
44   See her article "Conflicting Patterns of Revelation: Jer 31,33–34 and its Challenge to the

for Moses himself."[45] Ultimately, she argues that the project to replace Moses' authority with that of Jeremiah failed; in reception history, Jeremiah continues to be assimilated to Moses, but does not replace him.[46]

Maier and Rossi have demonstrated that the tradents of the Jeremiah tradition had a high view of Jeremiah, so much so that the question of his equality to Moses cannot be ruled out in principle. This is a startling observation, as it reminds readers of the way later editorial judgments continue to inform contemporary interpretations, for example, in the assumption of Moses' superiority as prophet. That said, Rossi does not give enough attention to methodological issues in her proposal. She claims: "the scribal strategy at work in reshaping Jeremiah apparently aims to build a parallel (i.e. Jeremiah as the prophet *like Moses*) in order to replace the paralleled character (i.e. Moses)."[47] How one discerns that a parallel intends at *replacement* rather than *alignment* would require fuller clarification than Rossi provides. Important for Rossi's argument is the claim that the development of Jeremiah as a prophet like Moses is a response to Deut 34:10–12. Thus, it has a polemical edge: it asserts a vaunted status for Jeremiah to combat the notion of Moses' superiority as prophet. But, if Rossi has the diachronic relationship incorrect—that is, if Deut 34:10–12 is later than the portrayal of Jeremiah as a prophet like Moses—then the scribal authors of Jeremiah are not necessarily polemical or reacting negatively to the assertion of Mosaic superiority. In the next chapter I will argue that the separation of Moses from all subsequent prophets in Deut 34:10–12 is precisely a response to the dynamic that Maier and Rossi have noted, that is, the ambiguity present in the text about the relative status of Moses and prophets after him such as Jeremiah.

Post-Mosaic Revelation Program," *Bib* 99 (2018): 202–225. Here Rossi argues that the new covenant prophecy is a challenge to Deut 31:9–13; 34:10–12. Thus, the tradition-historical development she argues for can be schematized as: Deut 18:15–18 → Deut 34:10–12 → Jer 31:31–34 → Jeremiah as the prophet like Moses.

45 Rossi, "Reshaping Jeremiah," 576.
46 Rossi attempts to answer an interesting question: why is there an underwhelming reception of Jeremiah's "new covenant" prophecy in Second Temple literature? Her solution is that the creation of Jeremiah as prophet like Moses, intended to support the replacing of Moses with Jeremiah, ended up eclipsing the significance of Jer 31:31–34 ("Reshaping Jeremiah," 593, emphasis original): "Jeremiah, the *prophet like Moses*: this parallel, set up presumably in order to legitimise the promise of the new covenant throughout the book, seems, paradoxically, to have been fatal to its reception." But a simpler hypothesis is that it is Deut 34:10–12 that intervenes in the tradition and undercuts the robust reception of Jer 31:31–34.
47 Rossi, "Reshaping Jeremiah," 588. Emphasis original.

In his work, Mastnjak too claims that the scribal authors of Jeremiah use the concept of the prophet like Moses to portray Jeremiah as Moses' equal.[48] Moreover, he similarly discerns a polemical motive behind this move: he argues that the portrayal of Jeremiah as Mosaic prophet is intended to respond to the strictures imposed by Deuteronomy on prophecy and retain a more robust role for ongoing prophetic revelation. Mastnjak posits greater tension between DtrJ and Deuteronomy than is warranted by the evidence.[49] A representative example will clarify this point. Mastnjak argues for an allusion to Deut 5:33 in Jer 7:23, which indeed is plausible:

> **You must follow exactly the path that the Lord your God has commanded you,** so that you may live, and **that it may go well with you,** and that you may live long in the land that you are to possess.
> Deut 5:33

> But this command I gave them, "Obey my voice, and I will be your God, and you shall be my people; and **walk only in the way that I command you, so that it may be well with you.**
> Jer 7:23[50]

On the surface, the DtrJ passage appears to be a straightforward re-use of Deut 5:33, but Mastnjak discerns a polemical motive. He does this by reading Deut 5:33 in the strongest possible manner, and positioning Jeremiah as responding to it:

> Deuteronomy 5:33 … asserts that the final authoritative set of divine commands are those that were given to Moses at Horeb and transmitted to the people in Moab. Jeremiah 7:22–23 has taken a passage in which D asserts its own final authority, *transformed it into a command to obey the succession of prophets* [cf. Jer 7:25, "my servants the prophets"], and presented this new formulation as the Mosaic command given in the wilderness.

---

48 Mastnjak, *Deuteronomy*, 40–41: "the DtrJ layer of the book had an acute interest in the relationship between the prophetic authority of Moses and that of Jeremiah. Through a series of literary allusions to the D source, the DtrJ authors portray Jeremiah's prophetic authority as equivalent to the authority of Moses. This claim can be observed in Jer 1:4–9; 7:22–23; 11:1–5; 21:8–10; and 26:2. A similar effort appears in the non-DtrJ Jer 36:28."
49 It should be noted that on the historical level, it seems implausible to think of post-exilic Yehud as supporting multiple scribal schools with strong opposition between them.
50 Mastnjak, *Deuteronomy*, 42–43, details the clause-level connections between these passages.

Rather than simply disagreeing with D's presentation of its own authority as ultimate, Jer 7:23 projects its own view of prophecy back to Moses and does so by transforming the words of its source.[51]

In fact, D does not assert its own "final authority" in 5:33; rather, it asserts the final authority of the Horeb theophany, to which D itself is the first authoritative commentary, *following* 5:33. Mastnjak's argument is problematic, since Deuteronomy already contains a command to obey the prophet-successors of Moses, whereas Mastnjak presents this as DtrJ's innovation *against* Deuteronomy![52]

Rossi's and Mastnjak's ascription of a polemical motive to the scribes of the Jeremiah scroll has the distinct advantage of attempting to offer an explanation as to why there is such thorough redaction of the Jeremiah scroll to present him as a prophet like Moses. It also helpfully emphasizes that the question of Jeremiah's potential equality to Moses is not resolved in the Jeremiah scroll. I now turn to an opposite understanding of the Moses-Jeremiah relationship, which is that Jeremiah is portrayed as a prophet like Moses precisely in order to bring prophecy to a close. Though in my view it is closer to portraying accurately the intentions of the Jeremiah tradents, it too overstates the case.

---

51 Mastnjak, *Deuteronomy*, 45. Emphasis added.
52 Mastnjak's construal of D plays a vital role here: the more limited a role he can claim for the prophet like Moses, the more plausible will appear the claim that DtrJ pushes back against these strictures. In fact, Mastnjak's analysis of D's view of prophecy (Mastnjak, *Deuteronomy*, 37–40), while solid, is inaccurate precisely on this point. He claims that D only allows for prophecy that is consultative divination for matters of individual concern—e.g., what happened to my lost donkeys?, as in 1 Sam 9—and not Mosaic prophecy in the sense of providing normative ethical instruction that is of national importance (Mastnjak, *Deuteronomy*, 38):

> [A]s Deut 18:9–22 describes and legislates post-Mosaic prophecy, it describes forms of prophecy that are *vastly different* from the forms employed by Moses. It neither imagines nor allows post-Mosaic prophecy in a Mosaic form …. The intermediaries that Deut 18 imagines as prophets "like Moses" are expected to give prophetic revelations that are starkly different from what D attributes to Moses.

This interpretation is contradicted by one of the most striking features of Deut 18:9–22, the re-use of the etiology justifying a prophetic intermediary for the prophet like Moses (Deut 5:23–27; 18:16–18). The repetition of the people's request for a mediator places Moses and the prophet like him in parallel, implying that the revelation they convey is analogous. Indeed, Mosaic prophecy in D consists primarily of two things: ethical instruction and prediction of the future, and Deut 18:9–22 does not reject either of these roles for the prophet like Moses. On the importance of the etiology for the equality of Moses and the prophet like him, see Rossi, "Reshaping Jeremiah," 579–580.

3.3 *Jeremiah as Final Prophet in the Pre-exilic Mosaic Succession*

Several scholars have argued that Jeremiah is represented by the Deuteronomists as the final prophet like Moses, the last prophet in the chain of the prophets. The conjunction between Jeremiah being a prophet like Moses and a final prophet is an interesting one, particularly since its first occurrence is in *Pesiqta de Rab Kahana*. Commenting on Jer 1:9, R. Judah bar Simon enumerates parallels between Moses and Jeremiah:

> R. Judah bar Simon opened discourse by citing this verse: [Deut 18:18–19]. It is written, "There arose no prophet again in Israel like Moses," (Deut 34:10), and yet you say, "a prophet like you." But the sense is, like you in giving rebuke. You find that whatever is written about this one [Moses] is written about that one [Jeremiah]. This one prophesied for forty years and that one prophesied for forty years. This one prophesied concerning Judah and Israel, and that one prophesied concerning Judah and Israel. As to this one, the members of his tribe opposed him, and as to that one, the members of his tribe opposed him. This one was thrown into the river, and that one was thrown into a pit. This one was saved by a slave girl, and that one was saved by a slave boy. This one came with words of rebuke, and that one came with words of rebuke.[53]

Later, the same text offers the apparently unrelated claim that Jeremiah was the last of the prophets:

> Further: just as Benjamin was the last among all tribes, so Jeremiah was the last among all the prophets. But did not Haggai, Zechariah, and Malachi prophecy [sic] after him? R. Eleazar and R. Samuel bar Nahman: R. Eleazar said, "Their prophecy was cut short." R. Samuel bar Nahman said, "The prophecy [that they later on delivered] was already put in storage in their possession [in the time of Jeremiah]."[54]

To R. Samuel is attributed the position that later prophecies were made known in the time of Jeremiah and only subsequently published in the times of the post-exilic prophets. Though the rabbis do not make the connection between Jeremiah as prophet like Moses and Jeremiah as final prophet explicit, their association of these two concepts is paralleled in modern scholarship.

---

53 *Pesiq. Rab Kah.* 13:6 (trans. Neusner).
54 *Pesiq. Rab Kah.* 13:14 (trans. Neusner). See also *Abot R. Nat. A* 1; *Qoh. Rab.* 12.7.

The understanding of Jeremiah as a final prophet has a robust history in critical scholarship. For Wellhausen, the introduction of a public law code in 622 BCE was the beginning of the end of prophecy: "There was now in existence an authority as objective as could be; and this was the death of prophecy."[55] He therefore asserts: "We may call Jeremiah the last of the prophets: those who came after him were prophets only in name."[56] Wellhausen's sharp contrast between (early and authentic) prophecy and (late and stifling) law has generally been rejected, but L. Stephen Cook's analysis shows that many have followed Wellhausen in viewing Jeremiah as a key transition or even terminal point in prophecy.[57] One influential proposal is related to the view that I will advance below, namely, that the succession of prophets ceased with the loss of the monarchy.[58] I will argue below that for the Dtr historians, the exile was a

---

55 Julius Wellhausen, *Prolegomena to the History of Ancient Israel*, trans. J. Black and A. Menzies, repr. (Gloucester, Mass.: Peter Smith, 1973 [1885]), 402.
56 Wellhausen, *Prolegomena*, 403.
57 L. Stephen Cook, *On the Question of the "Cessation of Prophecy" in Ancient Judaism*, TSAJ 145 (Tübingen: Mohr Siebeck, 2011), 10–42, 195–196.
58 See David L. Petersen, *Late Israelite Prophecy: Studies in Deutero-Prophetic Literature and in Chronicles*, SBLMS 23 (Missoula, Mont.: Scholars Press, 1977), 5–6, 97–102; Frank Moore Cross, *Canaanite Myth and Hebrew Epic* (Cambridge, Mass.: Harvard University, 1973), 223–229, 343–346, and discussion in Cook, *Cessation of Prophecy*, 28–29. On the relationship of divinatory practices in the ancient Near East to the institution of the monarchy, see Michael H. Floyd, "The Production of Prophetic Books in the Early Second Temple Period," in *Prophets, Prophecy, and Prophetic Texts in Second Temple Judaism*, ed. M.H. Floyd and R.D. Haak, LHB/OTS 427 (New York: T&T Clark, 2006), 276–297, at 280–281:
> The cultural context in which Israel emerged and existed as a nation was defined in terms of a common ancient Near Eastern worldview, the basic features of which are well known. The cosmos is defined in terms of a heavenly reality above and an earthly realm below, delimited by the ruling god's control of the otherwise chaotic waters .... This cosmic reality is represented on earth by the corresponding figure of the human king .... When the human king governs in accord with the will of the divine king, the people are blessed with peace, justice, and plenty; but when he does not, the people are cursed with conflict, oppression, and want .... [D]ivination presumes the correspondence between heaven and earth that is represented by the human king .... Much of ancient Near Eastern divination gravitated around the monarchy.

> Later, Floyd draws the implications of exile for prophecy (285): "The effect of exile and restoration on the practice of prophecy can be correlated with the effect of this momentous transition on Israel's worldview. The overthrow of the monarchy and the destruction of Jerusalem ripped a hole, as it were, in the middle of the cosmos. The *axis mundi* represented by these central institutions was radically destabilized. The correspondence between the earthly and the heavenly king, which provided the epistemological basis for describing interaction between the human and divine realms, had disintegrated. One response would have been to question whether prophecy would continue at all .... However, other possibilities could also be imagined [Floyd goes on to situate the production of prophetic literature in this context]."

significant rupture not only in the monarchy, but also in the Mosaic prophetic succession. Jeremiah, therefore, was not thought by them to be the last prophet *as such*, but the last prophet in the pre-exilic Mosaic prophetic succession, which was understood to be the technical or precise meaning of the phrase "Yhwh's/my servants the prophets."

Joseph Blenkinsopp, Christopher Seitz, and Armin Lange have argued that for the Dtr scribes, Jeremiah ends prophecy altogether.[59] Blenkinsopp appeals to a number of features of Jeremiah to support this claim, including the overlap between the conclusion of Kings and of Jeremiah (2 Kgs 24:18–25:30; Jer 52), and the parallels between Moses and Jeremiah in their calls and in their forty-year prophetic careers.[60] Seitz adduces more specific considerations. The key plank in his understanding of Jeremiah as the final Mosaic prophet is the command from Yhwh that Jeremiah not intercede for the people (Jer 7:16, 11:14, 14:11, 15:1). Seitz comments:

> What we see is the prophetic office breaking down in the man Jeremiah. In a sense, it implodes because Jeremiah is forbidden to exercise his intercessory responsibility …. The inevitable result will be doom and destruction, and Jeremiah must share this fate. The office of Mosaic prophet is breaking down for a divine purpose: that Israel might be judged, wholly and completely, and a new beginning set in motion.[61]

Seitz also points to the conclusion of the book, in which Jeremiah is taken against his will to Egypt with Judeans who remained in the land (cf Jer 43): "With this action the book signals that prophecy has come full circle. The succession of prophets following Moses comes to an end in Jeremiah, with the

---

59 Joseph Blenkinsopp, "'We Pay No Heed to Heavenly Voices': the 'End of Prophecy' and the Formation of the Canon," in *Biblical and Humane: A Festschrift for John F. Priest*, ed. L.B. Elder et al. (Atlanta: Scholars Press, 1996), 19–31; at 26, claims that the Deuteronomists "thought of him [Jeremiah] as standing at the end of the prophetic *didache* as Moses stands at its beginning." I quote the text as given, though Blenkinsopp probably meant *diadoche*. Christopher R. Seitz, "The Prophet Moses and the Canonical Shape of Jeremiah," *ZAW* 101 (1989): 3–27, at 12: "Those who shaped the book of Jeremiah saw him as the last Mosaic prophet"; Armin Lange, *Vom prophetischen Wort zur prophetischen Tradition: Studien zur Traditions- und Redaktionsgeschichte innerprophetischer Konflikte in der Hebräischen Bibel*, FAT 34 (Tübingen: Mohr Siebeck, 2002), 266 (emphasis added): "Dabei dürfte Jeremia, wie die Ablehnung aller nachfolgenden Prophetie zeigt, von der dtrJer *als der letzte Prophet in dieser Kette Gott gesandter Propheten* verstanden worden sein."
60 Blenkinsopp, "We Pay No Heed," 26–27.
61 Seitz, "Prophet Moses and Shape of Jeremiah," 11.

return to Egypt."⁶² Finally, Lange's argument for this view is based on diachronic considerations: he contends that the Dtr editors of Jeremiah were opposing the rebuilding of the temple and, specifically, the prophets of restoration, Haggai and Zechariah.⁶³ He reads narratives of prophetic conflict in Jeremiah allegorically, substituting Haggai and Zechariah for Jeremiah's prophetic opponents. Lange presses the point that Jeremiah's polemic is consistently addressed against "prophets" in general (cf., e.g., Jer 23), and so argues that the editors of Jeremiah were aiming at nothing less than the eclipse of prophecy itself.⁶⁴

It must be acknowledged that the Dtr scribes saw Jeremiah as arising at a particularly significant, even "final," point in Judah's national life. Nevertheless, I am not convinced that the Dtr scribes saw Jeremiah as the final Mosaic prophet *as such*. Rather, Jeremiah for them ended a *particular prophetic succession*, one that had stretched from the Exodus to the Exile. The scribal authors of Jeremiah do position the prophet as final, but this has to do with the rupture in national life caused by the exile: Jeremiah is the last warning before the judgment occurs. It does not have to do with a theory of the end of prophecy *per se*. There is a sense, then, in which Jeremiah is the first eschatological prophet like Moses, to use the term "eschatological" somewhat loosely. The *telos* or eschatological horizon of unheeded Mosaic prophecy is exile, and this is determined by the logic of Deuteronomy: the Mosaic prophet stipulates the conditions that pertain to life in the land, and warns that disobedience will lead to dispossession, as it had for the previous inhabitants (cf. Deut 18:12).⁶⁵ The reason that the Dtr

---

62 Seitz, "Prophet Moses and Shape of Jeremiah," 12. At 14–18 Seitz also proffers a number of significant parallels between Jeremiah and Moses that do not of themselves amount to the claim that Jeremiah is a *final* prophet: the burning and rewriting of the scroll in Jer 36 is paralleled to the rewriting of the tablets of the covenant (cf Deut 10:1–2); two men in their generations are found righteous and escape judgment (Joshua/Caleb and Baruch/Ebed-Melech, respectively); both had forty-year careers.

63 Lange, *Vom prophetischen Wort*, 241–243, takes the dispute over the return of the temple vessels in Jer 27:16–22 as one which aligns the salvation-prophets in Jeremiah's day with Haggai and Zechariah: both confidently claimed that the temple vessels would return. In contrast, he believes that the editors of Jeremiah opposed such efforts. He concludes (243): "Auf dieser Weise versucht die dtr Redaktion nicht nur, die falsche Heilsprophetie neben dem Frevel des Volkes als einen wesentlichen Anlaß für die Katastrophe von 587 v.Chr. zu verstehen, sondern auch das damals Erlebte mahnend den Bemühungen ihrer eigenen Gegenwart, den Tempel wiederaufzubauen, entgegenzuhalten." Later, at 266–267, Lange argues that the polemic against the prophets who "dream" (Jer 23:9–40) is directed against Zechariah's night visions.

64 Lange, *Vom prophetischen Wort*, 262: the Dtr editors' criticism is not aimed at "einer bestimmten prophetischen Gruppe … sondern die Prophetie als solche."

65 I am grateful to Prof. Tzvi Novick for helping me to clarify this point. As he put it in a comment in personal communication: "the very logic of Mosaic prophecy implies an expiration date."

scribes developed Jeremiah's prophetic profile at such length is that, for them, Jeremiah brought the pre-exilic company of Yhwh's "servants the prophets" to a close.

Importantly, the Dtr construction of a pre-exilic Mosaic prophetic succession, culminating in Jeremiah, does not prohibit ongoing prophetic activity. It does, however, construct a normative prophetic tradition, and so creates pressure for future prophetic claimants to align themselves with this tradition. As is well-known in scholarship, in the post-exilic period there is an increasing turn to intertextuality in prophetic oracles, as the sayings of the pre-exilic prophets are mined and applied to new situations. The Dtr construction of a Mosaic succession will ultimately lead later authors in Second Temple Judaism to posit a cessation of Mosaic prophecy, but initially it contributes to its ongoing redefinition and adaptation in post-exilic Yehud. To clarify these claims, and indeed to support my contention that Jeremiah ends not prophecy itself but the pre-exilic Mosaic succession, I turn in conclusion to the Dtr portrayal of Zechariah as renewing Mosaic prophecy, albeit in a belated and derivative manner.

4   "My Servants the Prophets" as "Former Prophets" in Zechariah 1

The oracles of First Zechariah are surrounded by a Dtr editorial framework in Zech 1:1–6; 7–8.[66] In this context the phrase "my servants the prophets" recurs (1:6), and is synonymous with a new description that emphasizes the temporally delimited meaning of the term: "my servants the prophets" become, in Zechariah, the "former prophets" (1:4; 7:7, 12). The prologue intends to legitimate Zechariah as an heir of this prophetic succession:[67]

> (1) In the eighth month, in the second year of Darius, the word of the LORD came to the prophet Zechariah son of Berechiah son of Iddo, saying: (2) The LORD was very angry with your ancestors. (3) Therefore say to them,[68]

---

66   So Raymond F. Person Jr., *The Deuteronomic School: History, Social Setting, and Literature*, SBL 2 (Atlanta: Society of Biblical Literature, 2002), 138–142.

67   David L. Petersen, *Haggai and Zechariah 1–8: A Commentary*, OTL (London: SCM Press, 1984), 110.

68   In light of the preceding argument concerning repeated prophetic testimony in Jeremiah, Michael H. Floyd's comments on ואמרת (v. 3) are suggestive (*Minor Prophets, Part 2*, FOTL 22 [Grand Rapids: Eerdmans, 2000], 318–319), where he argues that against the NRSV translation as an imperative, "there is no compelling reason to take this verb as anything but a description of habitual or past repeated action .... 1:2–3 should thus be translated: 'Yahweh was very angry with your forebears, and you [repeatedly] said to them ....'"

> Thus says the LORD of hosts: Return to me, says the LORD of hosts, and I will return to you, says the LORD of hosts. (4) Do not be like your ancestors, to whom the former prophets [הנביאים הראשנים] proclaimed, "Thus says the LORD of hosts, Return from your evil ways and from your evil deeds." But they did not hear or heed me, says the LORD. (5) Your ancestors, where are they? And the prophets, do they live forever? (6) But my words and my statutes, which I commanded my servants the prophets, did they not overtake your ancestors? [אך דברי וחקי אשר צויתי את־עבדי הנביאים הלוא השיגו אבתיכם] So they repented and said, "The LORD of hosts has dealt with us according to our ways and deeds, just as he planned to do."
> Zech 1:1–6

The model of prophecy operative within this passage is Deuteronomy's genealogical model, in which there has been a pre-exilic succession of Mosaic prophets. Key language from Deut 18:15 ("to him you will listen") and 18:18 ("command") is present: the people have not "listened" to the prophets (שמע, v. 4), who were "commanded" (צוה, v. 6) Yhwh's "words" and "statutes";[69] thus, their words eventually "overtook" Israel and Judah (v. 6).[70]

Zechariah is portrayed as a qualified heir and interpreter of Mosaic Discourse, but what this means for the Dtr scribes is that the concept of a pre-exilic Mosaic succession exerts normative pressure as a tradition into which he is incorporated.[71] Mosaic Discourse thus becomes somewhat cumbersome: in their commentary, Meyers and Meyers highlight the "excessive use of internal and layered quotations"[72] in Zech 1:1–6. Indeed, the "word of the LORD" that comes to Zechariah quotes the "thus says the LORD" that the "former prophets" spoke. Here Yhwh's "servants the prophets" belong not to the present but the past, which has led some to conclude that for the tradents of this book, all

---

[69] Carol L. Meyers and Eric M. Meyers, *Haggai, Zechariah 1–8: A New Translation with Introduction and Commentary*, AB 25B (New York: Doubleday, 1987), 101, suggest the phrasing here "seems to indicate an awareness of both a corpus of earlier prophetic materials and a body of covenant materials which together would have constituted the nucleus of the first two divisions of Scripture, and Law and the Prophets."

[70] Meyers and Meyers, *Haggai and Zechariah 1–8*, 96, refer to the word as a "hunting term" which "reflects the language of Deuteronomy." The most relevant parallels are found in Deut 28:2, 15, 45.

[71] Meyers and Meyers, *Haggai and Zechariah 1–8*, 101: "Both the prophet and his followers saw themselves as belonging to the long line of true prophets."

[72] Meyers and Meyers, *Haggai and Zechariah 1–8*, 101; cf. 100: "At least five internal quotations can be discerned …. Not only is this section replete with quoted speech, but also the quotes are layered: there are quotes within quotes within quotes."

authentic prophecy was in the past.[73] This is too strong: Yhwh's "servants the prophets" does not denote the entire class of prophets, but refers to a specific pre-exilic prophetic succession. This clarifies how it is that Zechariah can also be called a נביא (1:1).[74] One might go so far as to say that the new designation juxtaposed to Yhwh's "servants the prophets," namely, "former prophets," implies that the prophetic status of Zechariah and others among his contemporaries is assumed. Zechariah is thus presented as a new beginning in prophecy: the dormant prophetic succession, interrupted by the trauma of exile, is again restored. The passage refers to the failing of the prophetic succession with the rhetorical questions of v. 5: "Your ancestors, where are they? And the prophets, do they live forever?" The Meyers comment: "Curiously, the prophets who are usually linked with God or God's word are here on the opposite side; they are paired with the ancestors in their mortality."[75] For the editors of First Zechariah, the phrase Yhwh's "servants the prophets" specifically denotes a pre-exilic Mosaic prophetic succession.

To push this point further, it can be argued that the editors of Zechariah believed this succession had specifically come to end in Jeremiah. Petersen compares Zechariah's summary quotation of the message of the "former prophets" to key passages from Jeremiah:[76]

> Zech 1:4: "Return [שובו נא] from your evil ways [מדרכיכם הרעים] and from your evil deeds [מעלליכם הרעים]."
> Jer 18:11: "Turn now [שובו נא], all of you from your evil way [מדרכו הרעה], and amend your ways and your doings [מעלליכם]."
> Jer 25:5: "Turn now [שובו־נא], every one of you, from your evil way and wicked doings [מדרכו הרעה ומרע מעלליכם]."
> Jer 35:15: "Turn now [שבו־נא] every one of you from your evil way [מדרכו הרעה], and amend your doings [מעלליכם]."

---

73 Second Zechariah's hostile attitude to prophecy is also occasionally taken as evidence for this view (Zech 13:2–6). See, e.g., R.J. Coggins, *Haggai, Zechariah, Malachi*, OTG (Sheffield: JSOT Press, 1987), 21, and later, 83–84: "Prophets are now figures from the past (1.4–6), and those who claim such status in the present are to be distrusted (13.2–6); the words of those past prophets were, for the community to which Zechariah was addressed, threats and promises whose exact implications God would in his own good time reveal."

74 Floyd, *Minor Prophets, Part 2*, 322, points out that mentioning of Zechariah's father and grandfather (1:1) suggests that "Zechariah's prophetic role has some kind of transgenerational dimension." Even as there is a sharp distinction from the pre-exilic prophets, the text endeavors to trace lines of continuity as well.

75 Meyers and Meyers, *Haggai and Zechariah 1–8*, 95.

76 Petersen, *Haggai and Zechariah 1–8*, 132.

These parallels have also been cited by Tollington, who concludes:

> [I]t was the prophecies of Jeremiah threatening the disaster of the exile which were in the mind of the originator of Zech. 1.2–6. The exile is being presented as the punishment of Yahweh on his people in the past because of their failure to heed his words delivered by the prophet Jeremiah.[77]

The parallels are quite precise in terms of formulation and structure. However, there is one further similarity: in the latter two passages, Jer 25:5 and 35:15, Dtr Jeremiah is presented as doing the same thing as Zechariah in this prologue, namely, quoting Yhwh's "servants the prophets."[78] These words are not only chosen because Zechariah is taking up Jeremiah's words; rather, they represent a Dtr distillation of the prophetic message, and they position Jeremiah and Zechariah respectively as exponents of Mosaic Discourse.[79] It therefore seems plausible that by their coining of the phrase "former prophets" as a parallel to the concept of Yhwh's "servants the prophets," the redactors of Zechariah specifically draw on the concept of a pre-exilic prophetic succession, extending from Moses to Jeremiah, which had come to an end and now was being rekindled in the visions of Zechariah.[80] Indeed, even very late post-Dtr occurrences of the phrase Yhwh's "servants the prophets" seem to reflect the awareness of the technical meaning given this phrase by Dtr authors, namely, its designation of a pre-exilic prophetic succession extending from Moses to Jeremiah.[81]

---

77 Janet E. Tollington, *Tradition and Innovation in Haggai and Zechariah 1–8*, JSOTSup 150 (Sheffield: JSOT Press, 1993), 206; see also A. Petitjean, *Les Oracles du Proto-Zacharie*, EBib (Paris: Gabalda, 1969), 39.
78 See Heiko Wenzel, *Reading Zechariah with Zechariah 1:1–6 as the Introduction to the Entire Book*, CBET 59 (Leuven: Peeters, 2011), 45–85, who argues that Zech 1:4 specifically draws on Jer 25:5, 7, and that Zechariah is "quoting Jeremiah's summary" (73) of the prophetic message.
79 Petersen, *Haggai and Zechariah 1–8*, 133, rightly notes: "Zechariah 1:4b comprises not so much a single quotation but the sort of thing people in 520 would have expected such prophets to say."
80 So also Floyd, *Minor Prophets, Part 2*, 324–325.
81 Ezek 38:17; Ezra 9:11; Dan 9:6, 10; Bar 2:20, 24. In Ezek 38:17, the activity of Yhwh's "servants the prophets" is linked with "former days" (קדמונים בימים). Even in the late passage Dan 9, the phrase has a technical meaning, referring a pre-exilic prophetic succession from Moses to Jeremiah (cf. Dan 9:2, 6, 10, 11). 1QS 1:1–3 may be the earliest use of this phrase that includes post-exilic prophets.

5 Conclusion

This chapter and the preceding one have traced the earliest interpretation of Deut 18:9–22, which presents the prophets as a unified class of Yhwh's servants, who were like Moses in proclaiming Torah and warning of divine judgment. In this way, the Dtr scribes secure the concept of the prophet like Moses as an element in their theodicy: not only did Israel and Judah not listen to the prophets who were repeatedly sent by Yhwh; but in so doing they were also disobeying the Torah, which specified that Israel would face sanctions for not listening. In constructing this prophetic tradition, however, the Dtr scribes also furthered the redefinition of prophecy in post-exilic Yehud, as the concept of the Mosaic prophetic succession exerted a normative pressure on future prophetic claimants, such as Zechariah. In particular, Jeremiah becomes an important tradition-mediating figure in the Dtr view: he is represented as a prophet like Moses and has an important place in the Dtr school's understanding of history, as the last and climactic prophet before the calamity of exile. The construction of a temporally delimited prophetic tradition would lead to another major shift in the view of Mosaic prophecy in the Second Temple period. In Part II of this book, I examine the establishing of chronological boundaries for Mosaic prophecy. Before doing so, however, it is necessary to turn to the conclusion of the Pentateuch (Deut 34:10–12), which provides a further comment on the relationship between Moses and prophecy, and which would be foundational for the later periodization of Mosaic prophecy.

CHAPTER 5

"No Prophet like Moses": Deut 34:9–12 and the Creation of a Canonical Era

1 Introduction

The next stop in the story of the prophet like Moses brings us back to Deuteronomy, and specifically to its concluding encomium, which denies that there have been any prophets like Moses:

(10) ולא־קם נביא עוד בישראל כמשה אשר ידעו יהוה פנים אל־פנים (11) לכל־האתות
והמופתים אשר שלחו יהוה לעשות בארץ מצרים לפרעה ולכל־עבדיו ולכל־ארצו (12)
ולכל היד החזקה ולכל המורא הגדול אשר עשה משה לעיני כל־ישראל

(10) Never since has there arisen a prophet in Israel like Moses, whom Yhwh knew face to face, (11) with respect to all the signs and wonders that the Lord sent him to do in the land of Egypt, against Pharaoh and all his servants and his entire land, (12) and with respect to all the mighty deeds and all the awe-inspiring greatness that Moses displayed before the eyes of all Israel.

Deut 34:10–12

The authors of this passage take up and refine the shift from charism to canon that we have already seen featured in Deuteronomy. In so doing, they strive for a delicate balance, carefully calibrating the respective authority of Moses and his prophetic successors. This balance will ultimately render the conclusion of the Pentateuch susceptible of two radically different interpretations: read diachronically, it seeks to mark out the Mosaic era as normative, enshrining Moses as the prophet *par excellence*; read synchronically, however, its denial that a prophet like Moses has arisen provides an opening for an eschatological interpretation of Deut 18:15, 18. This passage therefore adumbrates the main exegetical options that will be canvassed in the remainder of this book.

In my view, Deut 34:10 is both dependent on and a qualification of the promise of the prophet like Moses of Deut 18:15–18.[1] First, these texts are the only passages in the Hebrew Bible that explicitly designate Moses as a

---

[1] This is the majority view that has emerged concerning this passage. Skepticism that there is

"prophet," נביא.² Second, the passages use the uncommon formulation of נביא + קום, along with a comparison to Moses.³ Third, in Deut 18:15, 18, Moses and Yhwh unambiguously affirm the possibility and the future coming of a such a prophet; in Moses' eulogy at the conclusion of the book, the narrator strikes a different tone, averring in a retrospective analysis that such a prophet has not arisen. The fact that a clear tension exists between the emphases of these texts strengthens the probability that there is some intended interpretive relationship between them. The precise nature of this relationship, however, has been a matter of considerable debate in recent scholarship. It has become common to connect the qualification of the promise of Deut 18:15 in this passage to the creation of the Pentateuch itself: by marking out Moses as prophet *par excellence*, the Torah is established as "canonical" and normative. In what follows, I develop the proposal that the authors' goal is not to establish precise literary collections as such, but to separate Moses from his prophetic successors and demarcate the life of Moses (i.e., Exodus–Deuteronomy) as a uniquely authoritative and normative epoch in Israel's history.

2   Deut 34:10–12: Hatchet or Hinge?

The perhaps infelicitous alliterative section heading provides metaphors for the two main functions scholars have attributed to Deut 34:10–12. When understood as a hatchet, the focus is on how it divides Moses from his successors; the

---

any interpretive relationship between them is expressed by Philip Y. Yoo, "The Four Moses Death Accounts," *JBL* 131 (2012): 423–441, at 437 ("Deut 34:10 is unrelated to the document that contains Deut 18:15"); Ernest W. Nicholson, "Deuteronomy 18.9–22, the Prophets and Scripture," in *Prophecy and Prophets in Ancient Israel*, ed. John Day, LHB/OTS 531 (London: T&T Clark, 2010), 151–171, at 159n20; Robert R. Wilson, *Prophecy and Society in Ancient Israel* (Philadelphia: Fortress Press, 1980), 162n52 ("the glorification of a hero by stressing his incomparability is common in folkloristic death accounts"). Jeffrey Stackert, *A Prophet Like Moses: Prophecy, Law, and Israelite Religion* (New York: Oxford, 2014), 136–138, accepts the relationship between these texts, but has argued that Deut 18:15, 18 is dependent on Deut 34:10, which he assigns to E. Gerhard von Rad, *Old Testament Theology*, trans. D.M.G. Stalker; 2 vols. (New York: Harper & Row, 1962), 1:293, also assigned Deut 34:10 to E. This is a problematic interpretation of a text that is clearly retrospective. The narrator's self-conscious temporal distance from the events of the Pentateuch suggests that the passage should not be assigned to one of the oldest epic sources. Stackert also does not address the problem that, on his reading, the title נביא is conferred on Moses only at the conclusion of this source, and nowhere else in it.

2 See the discussion on pp. 20–21 above on the designation of Moses as "prophet" here.
3 Other than here, the only times prophets are said to "arise" are Deut 13:2; Amos 2:11; Jer 29:15. See the discussion above (pp. 46–47).

contrasting image of a hinge, however, highlights how the passage joins Moses to the prophets that follow him. The sharpest of divisions is found in the claim of some scholars that the passage contradicts and nullifies the promise of Deut 18:15, 18: it is an attempt to enshrine the authority of the Torah and do away with the prophetic word.[4] Driver observed that the two passages on the prophet like Moses can be harmonized, as the point of comparison to Moses in each is different: in the first, the prophet is said to be like Moses in passing on the word of Yhwh; in the second, all prophets are unlike Moses in terms of the quality of revelation they receive.[5] Harmonization, however, overlooks the true significance of these passages, which construct and contest the possibility of a prophet like Moses. Beginning with the work of Joseph Blenkinsopp, recent scholarship has emphasized the hermeneutical function of this conclusion: it neither nullifies nor endorses the promise of Deut 18:15–18, but extends its emphasis on normative authority by more precisely delineating the contours of the relationship between Moses and prophecy.[6]

Blenkinsopp's specific contribution was to propose that the conclusions of the canonical corpora of the Torah and Prophets (Deut 34:10–12 and Mal 3:22–24 respectively), were precisely written as *conclusions*:[7] the editors who drafted these words intended them not only as conclusions to their specific books, but also to mark off distinct sections in Israel's revealed literature. Chapman summarizes as follows:

---

[4] E.g., Antonius H.J. Gunneweg, "Das Gesetz und die Propheten: Eine Auslegung von Ex 33,7–11; Num 11,4–12,8; Dtn 31,14 f.; 34,10," ZAW 102 (1990): 169–180, at 180; Konrad Schmid, "The Late Persian Formation of the Torah: Observations on Deuteronomy 34," in *Judah and the Judeans in the Fourth Century BCE*, ed. O. Lipschits, G.N. Knoppers, and R. Albertz (Winona Lake, Ind.: Eisenbrauns, 2007), 237–250, speaks of the promise of Deut 18:15 being "essentially abrogated" (244).

[5] S.R. Driver, *A Critical and Exegetical Commentary on Deuteronomy*, ICC (Edinburgh: T&T Clark, 1895), 425; cf Richard D. Nelson, *Deuteronomy: A Commentary*, OTL (Louisville, Ky.: Westminster John Knox, 2002), 235.

[6] Joseph Blenkinsopp, *Prophecy and Canon: A Contribution to the Study of Jewish Origins*, CSJCA 3 (University of Notre Dame Press, 1977), 80–95. Jeffrey H. Tigay, *Deuteronomy = [Devarim]: The Traditional Hebrew Text with the New JPS Translation*, JPSTC 5 (Philadelphia: Jewish Publication Society, 1996), 339, notes that medieval Jewish writers already deployed this text to reject the claims to prophetic authority made by Christianity and Islam.

[7] The implications of this have been to place canon not only on the agenda of critics who offer literary, final-form readings of the text, but to interrogate the extent to which the concept of canon influenced the writing and redaction of the biblical texts themselves. That is, if the editors of the Torah and the Prophets respectively wrote self-conscious conclusions to these collections, then canon as a concept must be taken seriously for the historical-critical exegesis of texts (not only for theological analysis). See Blenkinsopp, *Prophecy and Canon*, 10.

On this theory, historical investigation reveals that the literary shape of the present Old Testament canon has arisen not by accident but as the intentional design of those editors who established the canon's major divisions and total organization.⁸

The implication is that these passages have primarily a hermeneutical function: they reflect the attempt to provide a normative shape to Israel's scriptures, what Chapman has called a "theological grammar."⁹ This meta-textual function means that these passages offer interpretive indicators for how the collection they conclude is to be read.

Blenkinsopp's proposal was that the editors responsible for the conclusion of Deuteronomy essentially created the Pentateuch by limiting the period of normative revelation to Moses. They did so in order to end the confusion that had arisen over the status of various prophetic claimants.¹⁰ As Blenkinsopp says,

> The last paragraph of the Pentateuch gives an impression of finality. By denying parity between the age of Moses and that of the prophets, it in effect defines a period of Israel's history as normative, and does so in such a way as to exclude the likelihood of any addition to this canonical narrative.¹¹

This hypothesis has become very influential indeed, and has been taken up in recent years by scholars such as Konrad Schmid, Thomas Römer, and Mark Brettler. Schmid speaks of this passage as the product of a "Pentateuchal redaction" or "Pentateuchal redactor":

> The Torah was deliberately shaped as Torah by several textual insertions in Deuteronomy 34 with a distinct theological profile. In other words, it is

---

8   Stephen B. Chapman, "A Canonical Approach to Old Testament Theology? Deuteronomy 34:10–12 and Malachi 3:22–24 as Programmatic Conclusions," *HBT* 25 (2003): 121–145; here 122.
9   Stephen B. Chapman, *The Law and the Prophets: a Study in Old Testament Canon Formation*, FAT 27 (Tübingen: Mohr Siebeck, 2000), 71–110.
10 Blenkinsopp, *Prophecy and Canon*, 94: "the Torah-canon, to which no addition was contemplated, represented a very definite solution to the problem of conflicting authority-claims created by free prophecy."
11 Blenkinsopp, *Prophecy and Canon*, 96. See Chapman's summary, "Canonical Approach," 123: "Blenkinsopp attributes this act of intentional literary subordination to a postexilic priestly theocracy concerned to safeguard its position in the face of prophetic claims to religious authority."

possible to detect elements of a clear "Torah" redaction or "Pentateuchal redaction" in Deut 34 .... This text separates the Torah in a qualitative way from the subsequent reading of the "Former Prophets" and thus establishes the Torah as a textual authority of "archtypal-prophecy [sic]" over against the books of the regular "prophets."[12]

Similarly, Römer and Brettler assert: "Deuteronomy 34:10–12, along with v. 4, should thus be seen as redactional, created as part of a conscious effort to 'create' a Pentateuch."[13]

For other scholars, the conclusion of Deuteronomy does not create a Mosaic canon, but is evidence for an incipient notion of a bipartite scriptural collection, an antecedent to "the law and the prophets." For example, Chapman has argued that the incomparability formula ("no prophet like Moses"), as elsewhere in the DH,[14] does "not claim that an individual is *sui generis*, but *primus inter pares*"; it is "better understood as preeminence than uniqueness."[15] He further contends that Moses has a prophetic profile in this passage, both in terms of his status as covenant mediator and with respect to the signs and wonders he performed.[16] Chapman concludes: "Rather than driving a wedge between Law and Prophets, Deut 34:10–12 construes the significance of Moses in such a way as to connect his work theologically with the work of the prophets who follow him."[17] For Chapman, the conclusion to Deuteronomy does not overrule prophecy with law but establishes a hermeneutical framework in which Mosaic law and prophecy emerge together as a bipartite collection of authoritative scriptures.[18]

---

12 Schmid, "Late Persian Formation," 239–241.
13 Thomas Römer and Marc Z. Brettler, "Deuteronomy 34 and the Case for a Persian Hexateuch," *JBL* 119 (2000): 401–419; at 404. On their inclusion of v. 4, see further below.
14 Here Chapman draws upon the work of Gary N. Knoppers, " 'There Was None Like Him': Incomparability in the Books of Kings," *CBQ* 54 (1992): 411–431.
15 Chapman, *The Law and the Prophets*, 119.
16 Chapman, *The Law and the Prophets*, 120–127.
17 Chapman, *The Law and the Prophets*, 127.
18 In this bipartite collection, it might seem natural to designate Mosaic Law as preeminent, but Chapman resists this implication. See his chapter, "The Preeminence of Torah?" in *The Law and the Prophets*, 241–292. Similar to Chapman, Hans-Christoph Schmitt argues that Deut 34:10–12 is a "Verbindungsstück" between the Tetrateuch and the DH which creates an "Enneateuch" from Genesis to 2 Kings; see his "Dtn 34 als Verbindungsstück zwischen Tetrateuch und Deuteronomistischem Geschichtswerk," in *Das Deuteronomium zwischen Pentateuch und Deuteronomistischem Geschichtswerk*, ed. E. Otto and R. Achenbach, FRLANT 206 (Göttingen: Vandenhoeck & Ruprecht, 2004), 181–192; at 182–183:

There are thus two scholarly traditions that can be traced: some interpret the passage as that which *separates* Moses from the prophets and establishes the Pentateuch as normative (so, it is a hatchet); others emphasize the way this conclusion *joins* the law and the prophets (so, it is a hinge). What unifies these proposals, however, is the view that Deut 34:10–12 is framed particularly with reference to textual corpora, though they differ on the details of which texts are in view.[19] In contrast to all of these proposals, I would argue that the editors have a chronological, and not a canonical, division in view here:

> Trotz der Betonung der einzigartigen Stellung des Mose in Dtn 34,10–12 trennt dies "Epitaph" auf Mose den Pentateuch nicht ab, sondern teilt die Geschichte des Enneateuch in "ein Vorher und ein Nachher" …: Die einzigartige durch Mose vermittelte Offenbarung Jahwes wird hier zum unübertreffbaren Leitbild für die gesamte weitere Geschichte Israels, wie es für das spätdeuteronomistische Geschichtswerk Gen 1–2 Kön 25 (DtrS) charakteristisch ist. Die im weiteren Enneateuch auftretenden Propheten müssen sich daher dem Urpropheten Mose, mit dem Jahwe 'von Angesicht zu Angesicht' verkehrt, unterordnen.

My translation:
> Despite the emphasis on the unique role of Moses in Deut 34:10–12, this "epitaph" of Moses does not partition off the Pentateuch, but divides the history of the Enneateuch into a "before and after": the revelation uniquely mediated through Moses becomes here an unsurpassable model for the entire later history of Israel, as is characteristic for the late deuteronomistic history Gen 1–2 Kgs 25 (DtrS). The prophets treated later in the Enneateuch must therefore be subordinated to the Urprophet Moses, with whom Yhwh spoke "face to face."

19 The view that the editors have texts in view is shared by all the scholars mentioned above. Chapman, *The Law and the Prophets*, 129 does not commit to a specific list: "[T]he editors responsible for Deut 34:10–12 were aware of some form of prophetic scripture in addition to the Torah, and therefore sought to express in these verses a theological framework which would undergird and illuminate the meaning and the authority of both more fully." Schmid, "Late Persian Formation," 245, asserts that the Former Prophets are in view: "Moses must be separated from the prophets as soon as the Torah is seen as superior to the Prophets (that is, Joshua–Malachi as a section of the canon referred to as the "Prophets")." The problem with this view is that it reverses historical causality: rather than providing the *historical origin* of these editorial comments, the divisions of the canon arose later than these comments, influenced by them. Römer and Brettler's distinct thesis is that the Pentateuch was created with reference to one prophetic text alone, the book of Joshua ("Deuteronomy 34," 416): "Confronted with this valorization of Joshua by the D-P Hexateuch redactors, the Pentateuch redactors put Deut 34:10–12 at the end of the Torah, insisting thereby that no one can be compared to Moses. Joshua 24 came from an attempt to compare Joshua to Moses, but this was countered in Deut 34:10–12, by insisting that Moses was *sui generis*, since Moses, and only Moses, could come so very close to God." This thesis too is problematic; there is no evidence for the categories of "Pentateuch" or "Hexateuch" as closed corpora in the Persian period.

Moses, the preeminent "servant of Yhwh," is separated from his prophetic successors. That is, the "prophets" in view are not to be understood in the first place as prophetic *scriptures*, but as all the historical prophets who arose in Israel between Moses and the post-exilic situation of the framers of the Pentateuch. Deuteronomy 34:10–12 participates in a historiographic project, and further refines the periodization of prophecy begun by the creation of the class of "servants of Yhwh" in the DH. It refines this by creating two distinct prophetic eras: Mosaic prophecy, which is supreme, and post-Mosaic prophecy, which includes all of Moses' inferior prophetic successors.[20] Indeed, in its immediate context, the insistence that no prophet like Moses has arisen in Deut 34:10–12 occurs as a comment on Joshua's accession to leadership within Deuteronomy (Deut 34:9). This is strong evidence for a chronological rather than canonical interpretation of the import of Deuteronomy's concluding denial of parity between Moses and the prophets. I will now explore Joshua's role as Moses' successor in Deuteronomy, before turning to other features of Deut 34:10–12.

3 Joshua as Moses' Successor in Deuteronomy

In its final form, the designation of Joshua as Moses' successor is particularly important within Deuteronomy.[21] In his concluding prose words, Moses calls on the people to submit to Joshua's leadership and exhorts Joshua to be strong and courageous (Deut 31:1–8). Moses then writes down the book of the law, giving it to the priests and arranging for its public reading (Deut 31:9–13). Joshua then receives an official commission:

> The LORD said to Moses, "Your time to die is near; call Joshua and present yourselves in the tent of meeting, so that I may commission him." So Moses and Joshua went and presented themselves in the tent of meeting, and the LORD appeared (וירא) at the tent in a pillar of cloud; the pillar of cloud stood at the entrance to the tent …. Then the LORD commissioned

---

20   See Schmid, "Late Persian Formation," 245 (emphasis original): "Why does Deut 34:10 stand out against Deut 18:15? The reason is most likely the need to break up the chain of prophetic succession beginning with Moses. Whereas Deut 18:15 *envisions* Moses as an arch-prophet and envisions a *succession* of prophets, Deut 34:10 wants to *separate* Moses from all other prophets."

21   Moshe Weinfeld, *Deuteronomy 1–11: A New Translation with Introduction and Commentary*, AB 5 (New York: Doubleday, 1991), 14, claims that this is the "central concern" of the Dtr framework in Deut 1–3; 31:1–8, pointing to Deut 1:38; 3:21–22, 28; 31:3, 7–8, and noting the resonance of these passages with phrases that occur in Josh 1:5–6, 7, 9.

Joshua son of Nun and said, "Be strong and bold, for you shall bring the Israelites into the land that I promised them; I will be with you."

> Deut 31:14–15, 23

Haran designates this passage as part of the non-priestly tent of meeting tradition,[22] which thematizes Moses' "face to face" interaction with Yhwh. It is significant, then, that it is here stated that Yhwh "appeared" (ראה) to Joshua. Joshua has taken over the leadership of the people, and he will now receive direct commands from Yhwh.

Deuteronomy's presentation of Joshua as Moses' successor is complete at the conclusion of the book:

ויהושע בן־נון מלא רוח חכמה כי־סמך משה את־ידיו עליו וישמעו אליו בני־ישראל ויעשו כאשר צוה יהוה את־משה

Joshua son of Nun was full of the spirit of wisdom, because Moses had laid his hands on him; and the Israelites obeyed him, doing as the LORD had commanded Moses.

> Deut 34:9

This follows the account of Moses' death in Deut 34:5–8, and summarizes the longer priestly account, in which God commands Moses to prepare for death (Num 27:12–14; cf Deut 32:48–52) and Moses commissions Joshua as his successor (Num 27:15–23).[23] Specific parallels are found in Yhwh's description of Joshua in Numbers 27:18 as a "man in whom is the spirit [איש אשר־רוח בו]" and the reference to the laying of Moses' hands on Joshua (Num 27:18, 23). The difference between the accounts is subtle but important: in Numbers, Moses commissions Joshua because he has the spirit; in Deuteronomy, Joshua has the spirit because Moses commissioned him.[24] That is, in line with what we have

---

22 Menahem Haran, *Temples and Temple-Service in Ancient Israel: an Inquiry into the Character of Cult Phenomena and the Historical Setting of the Priestly School* (Oxford: Clarendon Press, 1977), 262.

23 The source-critical divisions of Deut 34 and its relationship to other chapters in the Pentateuch are vigorously disputed. I am sympathetic to the argument of Phillip Stoellger, "Deuteronomium 34 ohne Priesterschrift," *ZAW* 105 (1993): 26–51, that all of Deut 34 is late and (post)-Deuteronomistic. See also Félix García López, "Deut 34, Dtr History and the Pentateuch," in *Studies in Deuteronomy: In Honour of C.J. Labuschagne on the Occasion of His 65th Birthday*, ed. Florentino García Martínez et al., VTSup 53 (Leiden: Brill, 1994), 47–61. Yoo, "Four Moses Death Accounts," argues (unconvincingly, in my view), that all four Pentateuchal sources are present in Deut 34.

24 See Blenkinsopp, *Prophecy and Canon*, 87.

seen in non-P material in Num 11–12, in P Joshua is qualified to be Moses' successor because of his charismatic authority as one endowed with the divine רוח. Deuteronomy downplays Joshua's charismatic authority by specifying that the spirit was a רוח חכמה,²⁵ and it insists that Joshua's possession of this spirit is posterior, not prior, to Moses' laying on of hands. This reversal in logic is reflective of Deuteronomy's concern to subordinate and bring all religious authority under Moses: the theological view that produced the coordination between Moses and prophecy now gives way to the first embodiment of this paradigm.²⁶

The second half of Deut 34:9 specifies that the Israelites "obeyed" (שׁמע) Joshua, "doing" (עשׂה) all that the LORD has commanded Moses. Joshua is thus marked—in a sense—as the "prophet" of Deut 18:15, to whom the Israelites are to listen (שׁמע).²⁷ The parallelism of שׁמע and עשׂה picks up on the theme traced in chapter two above, from Israel's acceptance of the terms of the covenant in Exod 24:7 to the reframing of that acceptance in terms of submission to the covenant mediator in Deut 5:27.²⁸ This makes it indisputably clear that Joshua is Moses' legitimate successor and that in submitting to Joshua the Israelites indicate their willingness to continue to receive divine instruction via an authorized mediator. As Sonnet has pointed out, the promise of a prophet like Moses therefore receives an initial fulfillment within the narrative arc of Deuteronomy itself.²⁹ The description of Joshua as Moses' "successor in prophecy" found in the *Laus Patrum* (διάδοχος Μωυσῆ ἐν προφητείαις, Sir 46:1), then, is a defensible exegesis of the final form of Deuteronomy (more on this in chapter seven below).

Here it is important to be precise. Simply because the identification of Joshua with the promised prophet like Moses is a defensible or plausible reading does not mean it was intended by the editors of Deuteronomy, either in the formulation of the original prophet-law,³⁰ or in the later Dtr transformation

---

25 I owe this observation to Tzvi Novick.
26 It is for this reason that Eleazar the priest, so important in Num 27:15–23, is not mentioned in the closing chapter of the Pentateuch.
27 Jean-Pierre Sonnet, "Redefining the Plot of Deuteronomy—From End to Beginning. The Import of Deut 34:9," in *Deuteronomium—Tora für eine neue Generation*, ed. G. Fischer, D. Markl, and S. Paganini, BZAR 17 (Wiesbaden: Harrassowitz Verlag, 2011), 37–49, at 41–43: "Deuteronomy is thus the stage of an effective and literal fulfillment of a word formulated by Moses in God's name, and this confirms Moses' quality as a prophet—according to the criterion he has himself taught."
28 Sonnet, "Redefining the Plot of Deuteronomy," 44.
29 Sonnet, "Redefining the Plot of Deuteronomy," 42.
30 *Contra* Hans M. Barstad, "The Understanding of the Prophets in Deuteronomy," *SJOT* 8 (1994): 236–251, who adopts the idiosyncratic view that Joshua is the *only* figure intended in the promise of a prophet like Moses, based on the claim that the Deuteronomists were hostile towards prophecy.

of the prophet-law into a historical Mosaic prophetic succession. Nevertheless, the Second Temple understanding of Joshua as the prophet like Moses emerges implicitly here, and explicitly, as we will see later, in Hellenistic and Roman-era texts. I now turn to a brief consideration of the way the editors of Deuteronomy formulate its conclusion in order to separate the Mosaic era from all subsequent epochs in Israel's history.

4   Moses as Incomparable Prophet in Deut 34:10–12

Immediately following the portrayal of Joshua as the one to whom the Israelites listened, Deuteronomy denies parity between any subsequent נביא and Moses the archetypal prophet:

ולא־קם נביא עוד בישׂראל כמשה אשר ידעו יהוה פנים אל־פנים

> There has not arisen again a prophet in Israel like Moses, whom the LORD knew face to face.
> Deut 34:10

This retrospective assertion that no prophet like Moses has arisen is a denial that the investiture of Joshua, related in the preceding verse, implies Joshua's equality with Moses.[31] In the broader context, however, it is not Joshua's debatable status as a prophet, but the title עבד יהוה that informs the editors' concluding denial of parity between Moses and Joshua. The passage is surrounded by references to Moses not as נביא but as עבד יהוה (Deut 34:5, Josh 1:1). These are the first two occurrences of the full title עבד יהוה, with the divine name included (eighteen of its twenty-three total occurrences refer to Moses).[32] Indeed, the most densely packed collection of biblical references to Moses as the "servant of Yhwh" are found here, at the transition from Deuteronomy to Joshua, where

---

31   So David M. Carr, *The Formation of the Hebrew Bible: A New Reconstruction* (New York: Oxford, 2011), 271: "Deut 34:10–12 can be taken as a post-D element designed to reinforce Moses's unique authority precisely at the point of transition to Joshua where one might (mis)understand Joshua as Moses's full successor." One of the problems with Stackert's (*Prophet like Moses*, 117–123) interpretation of the passage is that, as a part of "E," Deut 34:10 has no relation to the appointment of Joshua as Moses' successor in Deut 34:9 (for him, P).

32   See p. 19 above, note 6, for the data on titles for Moses. In later literature, Moses is called עבד האלוהים 4× (Dan 9:11; Neh 10:30; 1 Chron 6:34; 2 Chr 24:9); he is the only figure to receive this title.

TABLE 13 The qualification of Deut 18:15, 18 in Deut 34:10

Deut 18:15abα	Deut 18:18a	Deut 34:10a
נביא מקרבך מאחיך כמני יקים לך יהוה אלהיך	נביא אקים להם מקרב אחיהם כמוך	ולא־קם נביא עוד בישראל כמשה

the title occurs in various forms no less than six times in a short span (Deut 34:5; Josh 1:1–2, 7–8, 13, 15b). It is into this text, replete with the characterization of Moses as "servant of Yhwh," that the post-exilic editors of the Torah insert the conclusion with the title נביא.[33] In connection with the immediate context of Deut 34:10, Joshua's investiture, it is particularly important that in biblical narrative, Joshua is the only other character who receives the full designation עבד יהוה (Josh 24:29; Jdg 2:8).[34]

As we have seen, for the Dtr historians, the title "servant of Yhwh" established a *link* between Moses and his successors, from Joshua to Jeremiah. The authors

---

33 See García López, "Deut 34," 53: "The title *nby'* applied to Moses is surprising, specially [sic] for the contrast it supposes with *'bd yhwh* of v. 5; a contrast which is accentuated if compared to Jos 1:1,2,7, the continuation of Deut 34, where Moses continues to be given the title of *'bd yhwh*."

34 The title occurs in two psalm headings, applied to David (Ps 18:1, 36:1), and it also occurs in Isa 42:19 as a reference to the Servant of Deutero-Isaiah.

On Joshua, see Walther Zimmerli and Joachim Jeremias, *The Servant of God*, SBT 20 (Naperville, Ill.: A.R. Allenson, 1965), 22n44: "In the afterglow of the story of Moses, Joshua can also once (Josh 24:29 = Jdg 2:8), as the one who completes the work of Moses, be called 'Servant of Yahweh'." See also Joshua's statement to the tribes of Transjordan: "You have observed all that Moses the servant of the LORD commanded you, and have obeyed me (ותשמעו בקולי) in all that I have commanded you" (Josh 22:2), and the narrator's concluding observation that Israel served Yhwh all the days of Joshua, and all the days of the elders who outlived Joshua (Josh 24:31).

Based on an analysis of Deut 34 and Josh 24, Römer and Brettler, "Deuteronomy 34," have argued that Deut 34:7–9 belongs, along with Josh 24, to a "Hexateuch" redaction. Interestingly, their language suggests that their proposed Hexateuch redactor was influenced by Deut 18:15, 18 (though they do not make this claim): he wanted (416, emphasis added) "to stress that, *like Moses*, Joshua concludes a covenant, *like Moses* he enacts laws and decrees [Josh 24:25], and *like Moses* he is concerned with a book [Josh 24:26]." I am persuaded that Joshua was cast in Moses' image, but not that this necessarily belonged to a Hexateuch redaction that is to be distinguished from (and is later than) the DH. In terms of interpretation, however, their construal of the function of Deut 34:10–12 in the context of this "Hexateuch" is similar to mine (416): "Joshua 24 came from an attempt to compare Joshua to Moses, but this was countered in Deut 34:10–12, by insisting that Moses was *sui generis*, since Moses, and only Moses, could come so very close to God."

of Deut 34:10–12 presuppose the coordination between the titles עבד and נביא that is established throughout the DH. Their intervention here is therefore a post-Dtr clarification of the relationship between Moses and his prophetic successors, one which defines the era of Mosaic revelation as supreme. As we have seen, the Jeremiah scroll leaves the question of the relative status of Jeremiah in relation to Moses ambiguous. The goal of this clarification is to ensure that Deut 18:15, 18 is correctly interpreted: Joshua and Jeremiah and any other subsequent "servants of Yhwh," whose continuity with Moses is stressed, in fact were not truly *like* Moses at all! The strong tension, which verges on contradiction,[35] between Deut 34:10a and 18:15, 18 is deliberate, as the כמשה of Deut 34:10 looks directly back to Deut 18:15, 18.[36] Furthermore, the specification that such a prophet has not arisen "in Israel" (בישראל) is not a limitation, allowing that such prophets may have arisen outside Israel; rather, it refers to the endogenous qualification of the prophet in Deut 18:15, 18.[37] This interpretive clarification has the goal of establishing the Mosaic age as the definitive era of revelation.

The editors go on to specify three features of Moses's career that make him the prophet *par excellence*, which have to do with the quality of revelation he received, the signs and wonders he performed, and his connection to Israel's founding narrative. The first of these is drawn from the tent of meeting tradition traced above, particularly Exod 33:11 and Num 12:6–8.[38] Here, however, the language is fuller: those passages refer to Yhwh *speaking* with Moses "face to face," but here it states that Yhwh "*knew*" him face to face (ידעו יהוה פנים

---

35 Christophe Nihan, " 'Moses and the Prophets': Deuteronomy 18 and the Emergence of the Pentateuch as Torah," *SEÅ* 75 (2010): 21–55, at 38, speaks of the passage as an "unmistakable correction" of Deut 18:15, 18.

36 Stackert, *Prophet like Moses*, 119–120, reads the verse: "Never again did a prophet arise in Israel, as Moses (did)"; that is, he takes the preposition *kāp* as a conjunction. This leads to an overly strong interpretation that no prophet arose after Moses. For this use of *kāp*, he appeals (119n119) to Joüon 158n2; 174d; Isa 11:9, 61:11; Ps 42:2. In these poetic texts, however, the *kāp* stands at the beginning of its clause, which is coordinated to another clause by the use of כי (Isa 11:9) or כן (Isa 61:11; Ps 42:2). These are not parallels to the use of *kāp* within its clause in Deut 34:10a. Therefore, Stackert's reading of the verse lacks grammatical warrant, and insofar as this serves as the exegetical basis for his claim that E attempted to end prophecy, it undermines his larger thesis.

37 Although the rabbis add that Balaam was Moses' equal among the nations, see *Sifre Deut*; *Vayikra R.* 1.13; *Bamidbar R.* 14.20.

38 So also Andrew D.H. Mayes, *Deuteronomy*, NCBC (Grand Rapids: Eerdmans, 1981), 414: the verse is a post-dtr "reflection on Moses based on tradition concerning him in the Tetrateuch," appealing to Exod 33:11 and Num 12:6–8. The LXX amplifies the allusion to Num 12:6–8 by translating עבד with οἰκέτης instead of the usual παῖς (cf. Josh 1:13).

אל־פנים)." As Perlitt noticed, Deut 34:10b combines two concepts that are ordinarily kept separate, and each of which constitutes a distinct honor in its own right, that of Yhwh "knowing" an individual and that of Yhwh speaking or appearing to someone directly.[39] The combined expression may be understood as a sort of exegetical "overkill" in praise of Moses.[40] Deuteronomy 34:10 harmonizes the competing representations of the relationship between Moses and prophecy in the Pentateuch: it draws on Num 12:6–8, which asserted the supremacy of Moses' direct interaction with Yhwh over the vagaries of prophetic revelation, but combines this with the tradition in Deut 18:15, 18, in which Moses is a נביא and all prophetic activity is to be coordinated to his archetypal role.[41]

Deuteronomy 34:11–12 features the other two respects in which Moses' uniqueness is asserted, namely, his "signs and wonders" and his role in the Exodus narrative. Blenkinsopp has questioned the grammatical and logical connection of these verses to Deut 34:10: "Introducing as they do a different and distracting idea of prophecy, they must derive from a different source, and this is also apparent in the awkward syntax resulting from the combination."[42] The "awkward syntax" to which Blenkinsopp refers is the use of the preposition

---

39 Lothar Perlitt, "Mose als Prophet," *EvT* 31 (1971): 588–608, at 592 (emphasis original): *"Darin war Mose inkommensurabel, daß Jahwe ihn 'kannte von Angesicht zu Angesicht'. Das aber ist sprachlich beinahe zuviel des Guten. Daß Jahwe jemanden 'kennt,' ist sonst Glückes genug* [with references to Jer 1:5; 2 Sam 7:20; Gen 18:19] .... *'Von Angesicht zu Angesicht' kann man reden oder sogar, wie im Fall Gideons* (Jdg 6:22), *Jahwes Engel sehen, nicht aber 'erkennen' oder 'erwählen.' Die Herkunft dieser überfüllenden Wendung ist indes nich zweifelhaft* [Perlitt goes on to point to Exod 33:11; Num 12:6–8]."
40 Alternatively, Stackert, *Prophet like Moses*, 117–123, translates the phrase "the one whom YHWH selected directly," appealing to Jer 1:5 for this sense of ידע, and understanding the phrase to refer back to Moses' commission in Exod 3–4. The story of Moses' call, however, contains no reference to God speaking "face to face" to Moses.
41 A number of scholars, including, e.g., Carr, *Formation of the Hebrew Bible*, 273; Nihan, "Moses and the Prophets," 36–42, now assert that Num 12:6–8 and Deut 34:10–12 are a part of the same redaction of the Pentateuch, because of their common focus on Moses' incomparability. While it is true that they share this motif, they accomplish it in different ways: in Deut 34:10–12 Moses is incomparable *prophet*; in Num 12:6–8 he is God's servant, set apart from all prophets. Moreover, in Num 12:6–8, other prophets are not necessarily dependent on or connected to Moses, whereas Deut 34:10–12 assumes the connection between Moses and prophets established by Deut 18:15, 18. Finally, Deut 34:10–12 has a clear retrospective and editorial voice; its perspective is quite different from that of Num 12:6–8. Thus, it should be understood as a later interpretation of Num 12:6–8.
42 Blenkinsopp, *Prophecy and Canon*, 87; Driver, *Deuteronomy*, 425 assigns the verses to "a later (and inferior) Deut. writer." So also Chapman, *The Law and the Prophets*, 123.

lāmed to introduce these phrases. In this "liturgical" conclusion,⁴³ the absolute supremacy of Moses is emphasized by the repetition of לכל:

לכל־האתות והמופתים אשר שלחו יהוה לעשות בארץ מצרים
לפרעה ולכל־עבדיו ולכל־ארצו
ולכל היד החזקה ולכל המורא הגדול
אשר עשה משה לעיני כל־ישראל

> [He was unequaled] **for all** the signs and wonders that the LORD sent him to perform in the land of Egypt,
>> **against** Pharaoh and **against all** his servants and **against all** his land,
>
> and **for all** the mighty deeds and **for all** the terrifying displays of power that Moses performed **before** the eyes of **all** Israel.
>> Deut 34:11–12

The preposition *lāmed* is used in a number of ways in these verses. In the indented lines occur relatively common usages, as the text speaks of the deeds Moses did "to" Pharaoh and all Egypt and "before" all Israel. Governing these clauses, however, are phrases introduced with the *"lāmed* of specification," which has the sense "with regard to."⁴⁴ It is likely that these prepositions are to be understood not in relation to ידע in 34:10b, but to קום in 34:10a; that is, they represent further qualifications of the sense in which no prophet like Moses has arisen.⁴⁵ Though this is not a common usage, it is not ungrammatical, as the parallel in Pharaoh's words to Joseph clarifies:⁴⁶

לא־ראיתי כהנה בכל־ארץ מצרים לרע

> I had **not** seen **like** these in all the land of Egypt **for** [with respect to] ugliness.
>> Gen 41:19b

---

43 Blenkinsopp, *Prophecy and Canon*, 88, suggests that the closest parallels to these phrases are in "liturgical hymns."
44 See Nelson, *Deuteronomy*, 394; Chapman, *Law and the Prophets*, 123.
45 This is reflected in the NRSV insertion "He was unequaled." So also Chapman, *The Law and the Prophets*, 123: "Beginning with לכל־, the Hebrew text seems to use a form of the *lamed* of specification ('with respect to') to modify the main clause in Deut 34:10a." *Contra* Stackert, *Prophet like Moses*, 121–122, who takes the ל preposition as objects of ידע, and cites as parallel Jeremiah's appointment as prophet "for the nations (לגוים)" in Jer 1:5.
46 Waltke-O'Connor 11.2.10d describe this usage as a *"lāmed* of specification." See also 1 Kgs

ולא־קם נביא עוד בישראל כמשה ... לכל־האתות והמופתים

> There did **not** arise again a prophet in Israel **like** Moses ... **for** [with respect to] all the signs and wonders
>
> Deut 34:10a, 11aα

Further supporting the unity of Deut 34:10–12 is the ascription of "signs and wonders" to *Moses* in Deut 34:11 ("which Yhwh sent him to do"). As many have pointed out, this conclusion asserts Mosaic agency for actions that are normally said to be done by Yhwh (cf., e.g., Deut 4:34; 7:19; 29:2).[47] Nihan therefore suggests that it belongs to the same tradition as that found in Deut 34:10b, namely, that which asserts Moses "unique intimacy with God" and so "justifies ... the separation of Moses' revelation from all further revelations."[48] Indeed, with Nihan, I agree that there is no need to posit that Deut 34:11–12 is later than or subsequent to Deut 34:10. The eulogy is unified and consistent; it is a paean to Moses. By elaborating with a flourish on Moses' unique power in defeating Pharaoh and liberating Israel, the editors of Deuteronomy define the Mosaic era as canonical and normative, and distinguish him from all of his successors.

5   Unintended Consequences: An Eschatological Prophet like Moses?

The juxtaposition of the titles עבד יהוה and נביא at the end of Deuteronomy both joins and divides: it joins Moses to the following era which tells of the his-

---

10:10bα: לא־בא כבשׂם ההוא עוד לרב, "there did not come again such spice for [with respect to] abundance."

47   See, e.g., Nihan, "Moses and the Prophets," 38 ("Moses thus achieves quasi-divine status"); Schmid, "Late Persian Formation," 246 ("divine predicates are very boldly transferred to Moses himself"); Dennis Olson, *Deuteronomy and the Death of Moses: A Theological Reading* (Minneapolis: Fortress Press, 1994), 169–170; Mayes, *Deuteronomy*, 414; Jeffrey Stackert, "Mosaic Prophecy and the Deuteronomic Source of the Torah," in *Deuteronomy in the Pentateuch, Hexateuch, and the Deuteronomistic History*, ed. Konrad Schmid and Raymond F. Person Jr., FAT 2:56 (Tübingen: Mohr Siebeck, 2012), 47–63, at 53. Nelson, *Deuteronomy*, 397, has observed that this creates some tension in the final form of Deuteronomy, because the only two human agents said to perform signs and wonders (את and מופת) are the deceiving prophet of Deut 13:2–6 and Moses, the incomparable prophet. The authors, perhaps aware of the tension, pile up synonyms for "miracle" and insist on the public character of Moses' deeds; see Tigay, *Deuteronomy*, 340: "No prophet so thoroughly proved his authenticity as Moses did .... The Israelites do not have to rely on secondhand reports. They witnessed the events and are certain of the truth they prove: the indisputable authenticity of Moses."

48   Nihan, "Moses and the Prophets," 38–39; cf. Schmid, "Late Persian Formation," 245–246.

tory of Yhwh's "servants the prophets," but it also divides the Mosaic era from this history as a special and normative epoch by insisting on Moses' incomparability. Read diachronically, Deut 34:10–12 is not an assertion of eschatological hope for a future prophet like Moses, and it is doubtful that those who composed it intended to convey such a hope. That said, the insertion of Deut 34:10 into Deuteronomy allows for a synchronic, final-form reading of Deuteronomy which might generate and intensify an eschatological interpretation of Deut 18:15, 18. Such an interpretation would represent an alternate way to harmonize the apparent conflict between these two passages: if a prophet like Moses has not yet arisen, then the specific promise of Deut 18:15, 18 that a prophet like Moses will arise remains unfulfilled.[49] Blenkinsopp rejects this possibility, arguing that עוד in Deut 34:10 cannot mean "yet" (i.e., "no prophet like Moses has yet arisen"), but must mean "since" ("no prophet like Moses has since arisen"). As he says:

> [W]here this particular construction occurs in the Hebrew Bible (לא ... עוד with the past tense) it never means "not yet" with the implication "it hasn't happened yet but it will later." Following attested usage it must on the contrary be translated "never again," "never since" or "no longer" with no limitation of time unless expressly stated.[50]

Even if this was correct, it would not rule out an eschatological exegesis of the final form of Deuteronomy, because the assertion that there has "never again" arisen a prophet like Moses might be understood to place greater pressure on Yhwh's (18:18) and Moses' (18:15) affirmation of the divine intention to send such a prophet.[51]

---

49   The earliest explicit articulation of this logic that I have discovered is found in Eusebius, *Demonstration of the Gospel*, III.2. See also Patrick D. Miller, "Moses My Servant: the Deuteronomic Portrait of Moses," *Int* 41 (1987): 245–255; at 249.

50   Blenkinsopp, *Prophecy and Canon*, 86: At 176n14 Blenkinsopp provides sixteen references to support this: 2 Chr 13:20 ("Jeroboam never again recovered his power"); Exod 2:3; Josh 2:11; 5:1, 12; Jdg 2:14; 1 Sam 1:18; 2 Sam 3:11; 14:10; 1 Kgs 10:5, 10; 2 Kgs 2:12; 1 Chr 19:19; 2 Chr 9:4; Jer 44:22; Ezek 33:22. In this list, 1 Kgs 10:5 (//2 Chr 9:4) may be a counter-example. It is said there that Solomon's wealth "took the breath away" of the queen of Sheba (ולא־היה בה עוד רוח), which surely does not mean that she died! Rather, it means that her "spirit was not still in her," but would return, presumably in time for her to give her laudatory speech.

51   If the editors had truly wished to rule out an eschatological reading, they would have used the imperfect instead of perfect of קום: "never again *will* a prophet like Moses arise"; cf. Gen 8:21 ("I will not again curse the ground"); 9:11, 15; 17:5.

The allusions to Genesis in Deut 34 strengthen the possibility of an eschatological interpretation, as they highlight the open-ended and incomplete character of the narrative. Schmid, Römer and Brettler argue that the link to the promises to the patriarchs in this chapter are a part of the deliberate creation of a Pentateuch; in contrast, I argue that they function to tie the chapter to what follows and are resistant to closure and finality. Consider first the recurrence of the language of Gen 12:1 in Deut 34:1:

> Then Moses went up from the plains of Moab to Mount Nebo, to the top of Pisgah, which is opposite Jericho, and the LORD showed him (ויראהו יהוה את־כל־הארץ) the whole land: Gilead as far as Dan.

The use of ראה in the Hif'il alludes back to God's command to Abram: "Go to the land I will show you" (Gen 12:1).[52] The passage goes on to state that God showed Moses "all the land (את־כל־הארץ)": this is an allusion to Gen 13:15, where God says to Abram: "all the land (את־כל־הארץ) that you see I will give to you and your offspring forever." The emphasis on "all" the land continues in the description of Deut 34:2–3 ("all Naphtali," "all the land of Judah"). In Deut 34:4, Yhwh (perhaps somewhat insensitively) belabors the point: "This is the land (זאת הארץ) of which I swore to Abraham, to Isaac, and to Jacob, saying, 'I will give it to your descendants' (לזרעך אתננה); I have let you see it with your eyes, but you shall not cross over there" (Deut 34:4).[53] Schmid, Römer and Brettler have argued that this verse in particular stems from the same author as Deut 34:10–12 and creates a deliberate *inclusio* with Gen 12:7b: "To your descendants I will give this land (לזרעך אתן את הארץ הזאת)."[54] I concur with the proposed allusion, but not with their construal of its significance. Römer and Brettler say of v. 4:

> It belongs to a redactional layer that aims to strengthen the coherence of the Pentateuch ... By slightly revising vv. 1–3 and creating the reference to Abraham, Isaac, and Jacob in v. 4, the book of Deuteronomy becomes the end of the Pentateuch.[55]

---

52   Schmid, "Late Persian Formation," 242–244, notes this parallel to Gen 12:1 as well as those discussed below.
53   On the allusion to Gen 12:7 here, see Eckart Otto, *Das Deuteronomium im Pentateuch und Hexateuch: Studien zur Literaturgeschichte von Pentateuch und Hexateuch im Lichte des Deuteronomiumrahmens*, FAT 30 (Tübingen: Mohr Siebeck, 2000), 217; Nelson, *Deuteronomy*, 395.
54   Schmid, "Late Persian Formation," 243; Römer and Brettler, "Deuteronomy 34," 405.
55   Römer and Brettler, "Deuteronomy 34," 405–406.

In my view, it is more plausible to understand the various allusions to Genesis 12–13 in Deut 34:1–4 as stemming from the same redactional layer, which is prior to Deut 34:10–12, rather than argue that the allusion to Gen 12:7 in v. 4 alone stems from a later author.[56] By means of these allusions, the strongest possible emphasis is placed on the fact that the promises to the patriarchs are on the verge of fulfillment, yet remain unfulfilled: Moses is permitted to see the land but not cross over there. Surely the poignancy of this scene serves to link Deut 34 to the narrative that follows, not separate it and create a Pentateuch. In diachronic perspective, the insertion of Deut 34:10–12 marks out the Mosaic era (Exodus–Deuteronomy) as normative;[57] in synchronic perspective, the chapter as a whole emphasizes that the story is not complete. The conviction that the final prophet has not yet arrived would be in harmony with this latter synchronic perspective.

There are two additional arguments for an eschatological reading of Deut 34:10–12 in synchronic perspective. First, Markl has noted to the differing levels of the authority of the voices in Deuteronomy that promise a prophet like Moses.[58] The promise is given by Moses and further anchored in the word of Yhwh at Horeb (Deut 18:15, 18). The denial that such a prophet has arisen, however, is given in the narrator's voice. This ascribes greater authority to the promise of the coming of a prophet like Moses than to its denial. In fact, Markl argues that if there is no such future prophet, Moses himself will fall victim to his criterion of fulfillment.

---

56 So García López, "Deut 34," 55–56: "Deut 34:1b–4 is due, at least in part, to an author who knows the story of Abraham, especially Gen 12:1–4a, 6–8 and 13:14–17, passages which belong to the same literary composition." Schmid, "Late Persian Formation," 242, and Römer and Brettler, "Deuteronomy 34," 405, make much of the naming of the three patriarchs, taking this as evidence that v. 4 is later than the surrounding material in vv. 1–6. They also note the grammatical problems that the quotation of Gen 12:7 creates, with its singular suffix (because, in the quoted passage, only Abram is in view). I am not confident that the naming of the patriarchs here necessitates the conclusion that this passage is later than and separable from the surrounding material.

57 Schmid, "Late Persian Formation," 251 and Römer and Brettler, "Deuteronomy 34," 407 both acknowledge that the literary horizon of Deut 34:10–12 is Exodus–Deuteronomy. Thus, their thesis of a Pentateuchal redactor demands that earlier verses in the chapter be ascribed to the same hand, in order to ensure Genesis too is incorporated into the purview of this redactor. I find it to be a simpler, more economical thesis (and less vulnerable to charges of anachronism) to understand the closure in view in Deut 34 as chronological, marking out the Mosaic era, and not canonical, marking out a specific literary five-book corpus.

58 Dominik Markl, "Moses Prophetenrolle in Dtn 5; 18; 34. Structurelle Wendepunkte von rechtshermeneutischem Gewicht," in *Deuteronomium—Tora für eine neue Generation*, ed. G. Fischer, D. Markl, and S. Paganini, BZAR 17 (Wiesbaden: Harrassowitz Verlag, 2011), 51–68, at 58–59.

Second, the narrative horizons of Deuteronomy and of the DH do not meet up. Second Kings concludes in exile, but the prophecies of Moses in Deuteronomy (cf. Deut 30:1–10), move beyond the end of exile and look to future restoration. At the end of Deuteronomy and Second Kings, the people are outside the land, awaiting the leadership of an authorized Mosaic successor to bring about the fulfillment of the promises.[59] The assertion that no prophet like Moses has arisen could be understood in this context as an expression of hope: in the normative period of Moses, the people awaited the fulfillment of the promises to the patriarchs, *as is the case today* (cf. Deut 29:27 [Eng. 29:28]). In fact, in Second Temple Judaism the expectation of an eschatological prophet like Moses emerges among various groups, including at Qumran and in early Christianity, which we will examine later in this study. This provides a plausible resolution of the tension between Deut 18:15, 18; 34:10, though it was not intended by the editors who inserted Deut 34:10–12. Methodologically, it is important to note that reception history ought to take into account not only the interpretation of biblical texts, but also the way that their incorporation into a broader context exerts its own influence later in the tradition.

6 Conclusion

Subsequent to the Dtr use of the title "servant" in order to link Moses and his prophetic successors, the authors of Deut 34:10–12 provide a further clarification of Deut 18:15, in which Moses' superiority to all prophets that have arisen thus far (i.e., until the late Persian period) is emphasized. Thus, these authors create a distinction between two prophetic eras, the age of Moses and the age of post-Mosaic prophets. They do not insist that the post-Mosaic prophetic era has come to an end; presumably, further prophets are possible, even though their inferiority to Moses is stressed. The next stage in the interpretation of Deut 18:15, 18 posits a temporary cessation in the Mosaic prophetic succession, while amplifying the possibility of an eschatological interpretation adumbrated above. In this period the Mosaic prophetic succession is extended

---

[59] It is perhaps worth mentioning von Rad's proposal that the "servant of the LORD" (עבד־יהוה) of Second Isaiah represents an interpretation of Deuteronomy's prophet like Moses (*Old Testament Theology*, trans. D.M.G. Stalker, 2 vols. [New York: Harper & Row, 1962], 2:260–262). See the discussion and literature in Gordon P. Hugenberger, "The Servant of the Lord in the 'Servant Songs' of Isaiah," in *The Lord's Anointed: Interpretation of Old Testament Messianic Texts*, ed. P.E. Satterthwaite, R.S. Hess, and G.J. Wenham (Carlisle: Paternoster, 1995), 105–140.

backward and forward: on the one hand, Joshua is now explicitly presented as a prophet like Moses in order to establish an ancient *continuous* prophetic succession; on the other hand, an eschatological interpretation of Deut 18:15 is authorized by the priestly custodians of Israel's scriptures and ultimately adopted by various Jewish groups. The next stage in the story of Deut 18:15, 18 examines how the prophet like Moses becomes a figure of the past and the future, and not the present.

PART 2

*Prophets Past and Future:
The Periodization of Mosaic Prophecy*

∴

CHAPTER 6

The Cessation of Prophecy in Second Temple Judaism: Previous Scholarship and a New Proposal

1   Introduction

The division of Mosaic prophecy into separate eras—the life of Moses, the pre-exilic Mosaic succession culminating in Jeremiah, and the resumption of Mosaic prophecy in the Second Commonwealth—provides an initial periodization of prophecy that will be taken up by Hellenistic and Roman-era authors. This periodization of prophecy is not systematically applied throughout the Dtr's disparate sources; it remains schematic. There is no sense of the end of prophecy *as such*, nor is there any attempt work out a theory of a continuous prophetic succession from Moses onwards. The only clear instance of prophetic succession is the transition from Elijah to Elisha (1 Kgs 19:16, 19; 2 Kgs 2:9, 15). On the basis of this solitary occurrence, some have argued that the idea of prophetic succession was present in ancient Israel, but the lack of evidence renders the thesis difficult.[1]

Over the course of the next several chapters, I will argue that a number of authors in the Hellenistic and Roman periods demonstrate an interest in "filling in the gaps" in the Mosaic prophetic succession; that is, they emphasize the continuity in Israel's prophetic institution from Moses onwards. The increased ascription of prophetic activity to the past is related to a conviction that this particular prophetic succession has come to an end in the present.

---

1   Robert P. Carroll, "The Elijah-Elisha Sagas: Some Remarks on Prophetic Succession in Ancient Israel," *VT* 19 (1969): 400–415, suggests on the basis of Deut 18:15–22 and Elisha's succession of Elijah that "there are indications in the Old Testament to support the idea of prophetic succession in ancient Israel" (408), and suggests as a "possibility" that the Elijah-Elisha "legends arose in the northern kingdom already shaped by a myth of a prophetic succession of a Mosaic order" (413). See the criticism of Carroll by David T. Lamb, "'A Prophet Instead of You' (1 Kings 19.16): Elijah, Elisha, and Prophetic Succession," in *Prophecy and Prophets in Ancient Israel: Proceedings of the Oxford Old Testament Seminar*, ed. John Day, LHB/OTS 531 (London: T&T Clark, 2010), 172–187, who refers to Carroll and several others, commenting (at 172): "Scholars who conclude that prophecy in Israel was a permanent institution [i.e., on the basis of Deut 18:15–22] speak, almost synonymously, of a continual office or an unbroken succession of prophets. However, the conjecture of a permanent prophetic institution is not supported by the general evidence of the Deuteronomistic History (DH), or by the specific evidence of the prophetic transition of Elijah and Elisha."

The activity of Mosaic prophets, therefore, is thought at this time to occur in a bounded epoch in Israel's past, and occasionally also as a hope for Israel's future. The sense that the prophetic succession has ended is balanced by the ascription of prophetic status to an increasing number of figures from Israel's past, most notably Joshua, but also others. Such an interpretation derives from a historicizing reading of Deut 18:15–22: understood as an actual speech of Moses to the Israelites on the plains of Moab, the prophet who is "among" the Israelites is surely none other than Moses's successor Joshua.[2] Moses, therefore, established a prophetic office, which would continue uninterrupted for many generations. Yet, as the concluding verses of Deuteronomy averred, none of these were truly Moses's equal, and so an eschatological interpretation of Moses's promise was maintained by some factions within Second Temple Judaism.

In my view, this construal of Mosaic prophecy as past and future phenomenon emerges from a specific social location, that of the priestly-scribal class.[3] The antiquarian and historiographic interests of priestly literature are well-attested, represented in texts such as the genealogies in Genesis and the production of Chronicles in the Hellenistic period. In line with this, Mosaic prophecy was understood to be a phenomenon belonging to Israel's sacred history, but also one that might return in the future. These interests are not merely antiquarian, however: the priestly-scribal class circumscribed the bounds of Mosaic prophecy in the past in order to secure their place as the authorized heirs and interpreters of the prophets in the present.

---

2 The identification of Joshua as the prophet like Moses is also made by the medieval exegete Abraham ibn Ezra (1089–1167).
3 On Second Temple scribes and scribalism, see, *inter alia*, Martin S. Jaffee, *Torah in the Mouth: Writing and Oral Tradition in Palestinian Judaism, 200 BCE–400 CE* (Oxford: University Press, 2001), 20–27; on the phrase "priestly-scribal", note Jaffee's discussion (20–22, emphasis added):

> For most of the Second Temple period, the primary employer of various sorts of literary scribes was the Jerusalem Temple itself, which served as the political and economic, as well as the cultic, center of the country .... [P]olitical or theological objections to the Hasmonean Temple state do not entitle us to assume that the dissidents were themselves antipriestly in outlook or nonpriestly in family origins .... [A] significant nonpriestly literary community beyond the reach of Temple authorities, and functioning as an independent center of literary or intellectual tradition among a growing class of urbanized intellectuals, is difficult to account for in economic terms .... We are left with the impression that the extension of a genuine literary culture was socially confined to the Temple scribal administration, a small nonscribal elite, and dissident, scribally trained groups who stood in political opposition to the Hasmonean state. *In other words, scribal literary culture was largely a phenomenon associated with priests or those trained in priestly milieus.*

This relates closely to a key feature of the concept of the Mosaic prophetic succession in the Hellenistic and Roman eras, which is that it increasingly overlaps with a collection of normative scriptures, and thus contributes to the emergence of canon. Scholars have recognized that to speak of "canon" as a closed list of normative books is anachronistic at least before the end of the first century CE.[4] Indeed, the phrase "the law and the prophets," often used to refer to authoritative scriptures in Second Temple Judaism, does not in itself indicate that either of these collections were closed, or limited to what we now call the first two sections of the Tanakh. John Barton questioned whether the "prophets" could be said to be closed in Second Temple Judaism, pointing to the wide array of literature that was treated as prophetic.[5] But not even the Pentateuch is secure: in a number of publications, James VanderKam has pointed out that the number of compositions received as authoritative Torah in this time period may not have been limited to five.[6] An implication of my argument over these chapters, which would need to be tested in greater detail, is that in this time period normative status accrued not to a defined list of books, but to authorized exponents of Mosaic Discourse, that is, to Moses and his successors.[7] Thus, some groups in Second Temple Judaism may have accepted the books of Jubilees or 4QReworked Pentateuch as scriptural compositions, pre-

---

4   See, e.g., Eugene Ulrich, *The Dead Sea Scrolls and the Origins of the Bible*, SDSSRL (Grand Rapids: Eerdmans, 1999), 53–61; James C. VanderKam, "Questions of Canon Viewed through the Dead Sea Scrolls," in *The Canon Debate*, ed. L.M. McDonald and J.A. Sanders (Peabody, Mass.: Hendrickson, 2002), 91–109.
5   See John Barton, *Oracles of God: Perceptions of Ancient Prophecy in Israel after the Exile*, 2nd ed. (New York: Oxford, 2007 [1986]), 35–95.
6   VanderKam, "Questions of Canon," 93: "it is inappropriate to use the word *Bible* for our books Genesis through Deuteronomy, or to assume that *Torah* and *Moses* means just these five when talking about the Qumran group and its time"; at 96, he refers to works such as Reworked Pentateuch, the Temple Scroll, and Jubilees as examples of Mosaic scriptures. See also idem, *From Revelation to Canon: Studies in the Hebrew Bible and Second Temple Literature*, JSJSup 62 (Leiden: Brill, 2000), 1–30; idem, *The Dead Sea Scrolls and the Bible* (Grand Rapids: Eerdmans, 2012), 49–71. On this point, see also Eva Mroczek, *The Literary Imagination in Jewish Antiquity* (Oxford: Oxford University Press, 2016), 161. On the Reworked Pentateuch texts in particular, see Molly M. Zahn, *Rethinking Rewritten Scripture: Composition and Exegesis in the 4QReworked Pentateuch Manuscripts*, STDJ 95 (Leiden and Boston: Brill, 2011).
7   The Enochic literature may be the exception that proves the rule: it is possible that the choice of antediluvian Enoch as its primary agent of revelation is particularly constructed in opposition to the normative status attributed to Mosaic prophecy. See John J. Collins, *Apocalypse, Prophecy, and Pseudepigraphy: On Jewish Apocalyptic Literature* (Grand Rapids: Eerdmans, 2015), 78–81, who refers also to George Nickelsburg, "Enochic Wisdom: An Alternative to the Mosaic Torah?" in *Ḥesed ve-Emet: Studies in Honor of Ernest S. Frerichs*, ed. J. Magness and S. Gitin, BJS 320 (Atlanta: Scholars Press, 1998), 123–132.

cisely because normative authority was not associated with Torah, considered as a defined list of literary works, but with Torah, considered as Moses's own prophecy.[8] Similarly, the Apocryphon of Joshua could be quoted alongside passages from the Pentateuch in 4QTestimonia, because normative status accrued to Joshua as Moses's successor in prophecy.[9]

For the Deuteronomists, the exile constituted a rupture in the prophetic line: it marked a terminal point in Mosaic prophecy, and subsequent prophets were interpreted as picking up the mantle of the pre-exilic prophets. By the time of the Hellenistic and Roman periods, Mosaic prophecy is seen to have a continuous history that begins with Moses and ends at some point in the Persian period. The line of prophets is increasingly identified with the authorship of a collection of scriptures, so that its terminal point is co-extensive with the chronological extent of those writings. Thus, the Hellenistic and Roman periods witness what might be called the "scripturalization" or "scribalization" of the Mosaic prophetic succession, which would eventually lead to its function as providing the basic structure of the emerging canon. This is a priestly-scribal interpretive tradition that will reach its culmination in the writings of Josephus, but it is one that, as I will argue in the next chapter, already emerges in the conclusion of Malachi and the Wisdom of Ben Sira.

2   The Status of Prophecy in Second Temple Judaism: A Selective Review

The foregoing comments may suggest that I will hew closely to what may be described as the traditional position concerning the status of prophecy in Second Temple Judaism, namely, that prophecy was widely thought to have ceased at some point in the past, sometime after the return from the Babylonian exile.[10] This once dominant paradigm for the study of prophecy has come

---

8   This dynamic clarifies the ambiguous status of Genesis, which is both Mosaic and not Mosaic. On the one hand, it is interesting that the *Letter of Aristeas* does not mention Genesis specifically, but considers Mosaic Torah normative, without precisely indicating its boundaries. On the other hand, *Jubilees* overcomes the ambiguity by insisting that Genesis too is part of the revelation given to Moses on Sinai.

9   On the Apocryphon of Joshua, see Ariel Feldman, *The Rewritten Joshua Scrolls from Qumran: Texts, Translations, and Commentary*, BZAW 438 (Berlin: De Gruyter, 2013).

10 The varied contributions on this question have been synthesized and analyzed in L. Stephen Cook, *On the Question of the "Cessation of Prophecy" in Ancient Judaism*, TSAJ 145 (Tübingen: Mohr Siebeck, 2011), 10–42. Cook's own perspective represents a re-assertion of this traditional perspective. Important earlier studies advocating this perspective include

under siege since the mid-twentieth century, with many scholars now insisting on the vitality of prophecy throughout the Second Temple period.¹¹ The position I wish to develop over the next few chapters admittedly does have certain affinities with the former consensus, but it is not identical to it, and my argument fully acknowledges one of the chief planks of the newer position, namely, that no text before the rabbinic period claims that prophecy *as such* has ceased.¹² In my view, prior to the rabbinic period, not all prophecy, but only one sort of prophecy, was thought to have ceased, that of the national institution of prophets who succeeded Moses in unbroken succession, per Deut 18:15–22.¹³ There is evidence that this particular prophetic succession was thought to have ceased, but not permanently: the prophet like Moses is in this time period consigned to the past and deferred to the (eschatological) future.

Ragnar Leivestad, "Das Dogma von der prophetenlosen Zeit," *NTS* 19 (1972–1973): 288–299 (who affirms that the cessation of prophecy is rabbinic, but claims that Jews in the Second Temple period believed they were living in a *Zwischenzeit*, a period between prophetic activity); Barton, *Oracles of God*, 105–116; Benjamin Sommer, "Did Prophecy Cease? Evaluating a Reevaluation," *JBL* 115 (1996): 31–47.

11   Important contributions include Ephraim Urbach, "When Did Prophecy Cease?" *Tarbiz* 17 (1946): 1–11 [Hebrew]; Rudolf Meyer, "Prophets and Prophecy in the Judaism of the Hellenistic-Roman Period," *TDNT* 6:812–828 [s.v., "προφήτης"]; Frederick Greenspahn, "Why Prophecy Ceased," *JBL* 108 (1989): 37–49; John R. Levison, "Did the Spirit Withdraw from Israel? An Evaluation of the Earliest Jewish Data," *NTS* 43 (1997): 35–57. See also the essays in Kristin De Troyer, Armin Lange and Lucas Schulte, eds., *Prophecy after the Prophets? The Contribution of the Dead Sea Scrolls to the Understanding of Biblical and Extra-biblical Prophecy*, CBET 52 (Leuven: Peeters, 2009); Michael H. Floyd and Robert D. Haak, eds., *Prophets, Prophecy, and Prophetic Texts in Second Temple Judaism*, LHB/OTS 427 (New York: T&T Clark, 2006).

12   The classic text in this connection is *t. Sotah* 13:2 (trans. Neusner): "When the latter prophets died, that is, Haggai, Zechariah, and Malachi, then the Holy Spirit came to an end in Israel. But even so, they made them hear through an echo (בת קול)." The text goes to narrate accounts in which a בת קול indicates that Hillel the elder and Samuel the Small would have been worthy of the Spirit of prophecy, but their generation was not worthy. Levison, "Did the Spirit Withdraw from Israel?," 47–50, argues that even this passage does not refer to an "end of prophecy," since it belongs to a larger unit which speaks of the good things that leave the world upon the death of righteous men, with no sense that such withdrawal is permanent. He is right to focus on the rhetoric of decline in the broader context, but does not notice that none of the parallels he cites provide a way to mitigate the loss with a substitute, as happens in *t. Sotah* 13:2. That is, Levison does not sufficiently take into account the relationship of the בת קול to prophecy, and the way it provides an attenuated mode of revelation after prophecy has ceased.

13   Compare Barton, *Oracles of God*, 109: "Certainly the distinction is not drawn at all neatly, but the texts do surely preserve an awareness that all 'prophets' are not quite the same kind of thing."

Cook establishes that, with a few exceptions,[14] scholarship until the mid-twentieth century accepted that prophecy had ceased at some point in the post-exilic period. He cites a 1949 article by Franklin Young as representative of the consensus that had reigned until that point: "It is a fact generally acknowledged by biblical scholars that long before Jesus's day the Jews believed prophecy had ceased in Israel and the prophetic spirit had withdrawn. We need not labor this point."[15] Contemporaneous with Young's assertion, this point was in fact labored in articles by Ephraim Urbach and Rudolf Meyer, both of whom sharply questioned this consensus.[16] Urbach's distinctive contribution was to argue that the concept of the cessation of prophecy originated as rabbinic doctrine. More speculatively, he claimed that it was a polemic against Christian claims to ongoing prophetic activity. The retrojection of prophetic activity to the distant past served to undercut contemporary claims to divine revelation. Meyer's treatment has been more influential than Urbach's, and is foundational for the approach of many scholars today: he argues that prophecy did not cease, but was transformed.[17] Urbach and Meyer's articles marked the beginning of a trend, so that by the end of the twentieth century the traditional position was no longer the consensus of scholarship.[18]

---

14 Cook, *Cessation of Prophecy*, 16–17, discusses Harnack's views as a notable exception; see Adolf von Harnack, *The Mission and Expansion of Christianity in the First Three Centuries*, trans. James Moffatt, 2nd ed., 2 vols. (New York: G.P. Putnam's Sons, 1908 [German original 1902]), 1:331: "The common idea is that prophets had died out in Judaism long before the age of Jesus and the apostles, but the New Testament itself protests against this erroneous idea [e.g., Anna, Luke 2:36]"; 1:332: "the wealth of contemporary Jewish apocalypses, oracular utterances, and so forth shows that, so far from being extinct, prophecy was in luxuriant bloom, and also that prophets were numerous, and secured both adherents and readers." As Cook points out, Harnack goes on to acknowledge a distinction between "canonical" prophets and prophecy as such (1:332–333n5: "although the line of the 'canonical' prophets had been broken off before the appearance of Jesus, prophets need not therefore have been extinguished"). Cook, *Cessation of Prophecy*, 18–19, also refers to C.C. Torrey, *The Second Isaiah* (New York: Charles Scribner's Sons, 1928) as an early adopter of the view that prophecy did not cease.
15 Cook, *Cessation of Prophecy*, 19, citing Young, "Jesus the Prophet: A Re-examination," *JBL* 68 (1949): 286.
16 Urbach, "When Did Prophecy Cease?"; Meyer, "Prophets and Prophecy." See Cook's discussion, *Cessation of Prophecy*, 20–25.
17 Cook, *Cessation of Prophecy*, 25, citing Meyer, "Prophets and Prophecy," 828: "What distinguishes prophecy in Israel is its tremendous ability to live on in ever new forms."
18 As is evident from a perusal of the essays in De Troyer, Lange, and Schulte, eds., *Prophecy after the Prophets?*, as well as Floyd and Haak, eds., *Prophets, Prophecy, and Prophetic Texts*, in which most of the contributors assent to the persistence of prophecy and reject the traditional view.

Yehezkel Kaufmann's contribution on this theme is a polemical rejection of Wellhausen's thesis that prophecy was supplanted by law.[19] Kaufmann positions his discussion as an affirmation of the traditional position, but a rejection of the dominant (Wellhausian) articulation of that position. On the one hand, Kaufmann seems to affirm the traditional rabbinic position with complete confidence:

> That Malachi marks the end of an era is an historic fact which is beyond doubt ... Malachi is the last in the succession of these men [i.e. prophets], the last prophet known to us by name .... Malachi is the watershed between two ages, and the difference between them is great.[20]

On the other hand, he acknowledges that prophecy underwent a transformation in the Persian period, speaking in this context of the "aftergrowths of prophecy," including apocalyptic literature, prophetic predictions and dreams among the Essenes, and the prophetic activity reported of some high priests.[21] In what sense, then, does Malachi end prophecy for Kaufmann? Particularly in the sense that with Malachi a particular type of prophecy came to an end, prophecy as a "national mantic institution":

> There are prophetic gleanings, there is "prophetic" divination, but no recognized prophecy to which people repair in order to know by its spoken word the will of God and His command .... Certainly there were in the Hasmonean period inspired individuals of the type of Josephus or the Essene prophets. But there was no prophet according to whose word it was possible to decide what to do with the stones of the altar which the Greeks had polluted (1 Macc 4:46) .... [P]rophecy was no longer a national mantic institution, it could not now, as it had in the past, function as an institutionalized means of inquiring God's will in matters of private concern.[22]

For Kaufmann, the period of prophecy as a "national mantic institution" was the period between Moses and Malachi: "Moses is the master of the prophets ... Malachi is the last prophet."[23]

---

19   Yehezkel Kaufmann, *History of the Religion of Israel*, trans. C.W. Efroymson, 4 vols. (New York: Ktav, 1977), 4:449–484.
20   Kaufmann, *History*, 4:452.
21   Kaufmann, *History*, 4:453, speaks of the "transformation which occurred in prophecy in the Persian period."
22   Kaufmann, *History*, 4:454.
23   Kaufmann, *History*, 4:450; see discussion 4:449–451.

Kaufmann's older contribution remains useful precisely because of his fidelity to the ideology of his sources. He harmonizes Dtr and rabbinic thought in order to present a schematization of the history of prophecy in the Second Temple period. He proposes four periods in the history of Second Temple prophecy: first, a period without prophecy (586–538 BCE); second, "a period of brief rebirth, Deutero-Isaiah to Malachi" (538–c. 400 BCE); third, from Nehemiah to the Hasmonean age, a period without prophecy; fourth, from the Hasmonean age to the destruction of the Second Temple, a period of apocalyptic and messianic prophecy.[24] This schematization is tendentious, in the sense that it assumes the ideology represented in the sources conforms rather neatly to the history which lies behind them, but it does synthesize many of the views present in these sources. It also makes clear that there is a sense in which it is true for Kaufmann that prophecy can be said to have both ceased and not ceased. His solution—that not all prophecy ceased, but prophecy as a "national mantic institution" did—remains attractive, particularly when it is understood not as a statement of historical fact but as representing one ideological strand in Second Temple Judaism, that of the priestly-scribal establishment.

In his 1986 monograph *Oracles of God*, John Barton follows Kaufmann in two important respects: first, he rejects Wellhausen's notion that the decline of prophecy could have had anything to do with the increased authority of Torah (precisely because in this time period prophets were understood as transmitters of Mosaic revelation); second, he underscores this distinction between different types of prophecy: "when we encounter the doctrine that prophecy has ceased it does not mean that there is no longer anything at all that can be called 'prophecy,' but rather that there are no longer 'great' prophets like those of old."[25] In my view, this can be formulated with greater precision: there are longer authorized Mosaic prophets, per the institution of Deut 18:15–22.

I will not discuss all of the texts marshalled in this debate, since they do not all interact with Mosaic prophecy and Deut 18:9–22.[26] However, the texts that do interpret Deut 18:15, 18 suggest, in my view, an alternative approach that may be helpful. Instead of construing the question in general terms ("did prophecy cease"?), one might hypothesize—building on the proposals of Kaufmann and

---

24 Kaufmann, *History*, 4:463.
25 Barton, *Oracles of God*, 114–115.
26 Cook, *Cessation of Prophecy*, 5–9, cites the following: Amos 8:11; Mic 3:6–7; Isa 63:11; Ps 74:9; Lam 2:9; Zech 13:2–3; 1 Macc 4:45b–46; 9:27; 14:41; Pr Azar 15; 1QS IX 9–11; 1QpHab II 6–10; VII 4–5; 2 *Apoc Bar* 85:1–3; Matt 11:13; Mark 6:15; John 8:52; Acts 19:2; Hebr 1:1–2; Josephus, *Ag. Ap.* 1.41; *t. Sot.* 13:3; *y. Sot.* 24b; *b. Sanh.* 11a; *Cant. Rab.* 8:9; *S. Olam Rab.* 30; *Abot R. Nat. A* 1; *Qoh. Rab* 12:7; *Pesiq. Rb. Kah.* 13:14; Justin, *Dial.* 53:3–4; 82:1; Origen, *Cels.* 7.8; Athanasius, *Inc.* 39–40.

Barton—that in this time-period it was believed that the authorized succession of Mosaic prophets had come to an end. This does not imply a judgment about prophecy in general: Josephus, who holds to the failure of the exact succession of Mosaic prophets, also believes that the Essenes, and indeed he himself, were recipients of prophetic revelations.[27] This thesis affirms important points made by both sides of the debate: with the traditional position, it affirms that a prophetic institution was understood to have (perhaps temporarily) ceased; with the conclusions of Urbach, Meyer, and those following in their wake, this position agrees that no Second Temple period text asserts the end of prophecy *per se* and that prophetic revelations were still thought to be possible. My contribution over the next several chapters, therefore, will suggest a way forward which incorporates the strengths of the traditional and more recent views.

Such a way forward has been provided by Karel van der Toorn's proposal, which also mediates between the traditional and newer perspectives on the question of prophecy's continuation, and attempts to provide greater specificity regarding the historical context for the emergence of the notion of an "end of prophecy." He hypothesizes that between 300 and 200 BCE, temple scribes formulated what he calls "the doctrine of the closure of the prophetic era."[28] Though there is no explicit attestation of such a doctrine, van der Toorn infers it from his exegesis of key texts, particularly the conclusion to the Book of the Twelve (Mal 3:22–24) and Ben Sira's *Laus Patrum*. He articulates the hypothesis as follows:

> Around 250 BCE ... the Jerusalem scribes decided to publish all the Minor Prophets on a single scroll. Moreover, they artificially turned their number into twelve by inventing a prophet by the name of Malachi .... The scribes' motive for creating a twelfth prophetic book had to do with the number twelve: twelve stood for plenitude and, by implication, for closure. The publication of the Twelve Minor Prophets as a single scroll conveyed the message that the time of the prophets had come to an end; no new prophet would thenceforth arise.[29]

---

27 On various Essenes, see *J.W.* 1.78–80//*Ant.* 13.311–313; *Ant.* 15.373–379; *J.W.* 2.111–113//*Ant.* 17.346–348; see also his summary comment (*J.W.* 2.159) that Essenes "seldom ... err in their predictions." On Josephus himself, see *J.W.* 3.352–353; 3.399–408.

28 Karel van der Toorn, *Scribal Culture and the Making of the Hebrew Bible* (Cambridge, Ma.: Harvard, 2007), 252–262; here 252. An important precursor to this view is provided by Barton, *Oracles of God*, 115 (emphasis original): "there was no prophetic *canon*, but there was a prophetic *age*."

29 van der Toorn, *Scribal Culture*, 252–253. The date 250 BCE is posited based on references to Greece in the prophetic corpus (255).

Thus, with the traditional perspective, he argues that, among priestly-scribal circles at least, prophecy was thought to have temporarily ceased. With the more recent view, however, van der Toorn acknowledges the ongoing presence of contemporary prophetic claimants; indeed, he argues that scribes did this precisely to undercut the claims of such figures:

> The edge of the doctrine lay in the rejection of claims of inspiration by people from the post-prophetic era. The scribal establishment of Jerusalem attempted to secure its moral leadership by disqualifying contemporaneous visionaries and ecstatics as empty chatterboxes; the real prophets were the Books of the Prophets, to whose interpretation the scribes held the keys.[30]

For van der Toorn, the positing of a breach in the Mosaic prophetic succession was intended to secure the social prestige of the "scribal establishment," namely, the Jerusalem-centered hieratic interpreters of the Scriptures.[31]

Van der Toorn's proposal represents a promising way forward, particularly as it attempts to provide specific answers to the questions when, why, and by whom a cessation in Mosaic prophecy might have been postulated. One of the significant problems in the history of this particular debate is that the question has been posed in general terms ("did prophecy cease?"), and the proposed solutions have correspondingly attempted to distill what Second Temple Jews *in general* believed about prophecy. I would argue that much of the textual evidence that was taken to support the so-called "end of prophecy" needs to be understood with greater specificity: it does not reflect widespread views in Second Temple Judaism, but reflects the historiographic and antiquarian interests of the priestly-scribal class, and their self-understanding as the heirs and interpreters of the prophets.

There is one speculative feature of van der Toorn's hypothesis, however, from which I demur. He suggests that the so-called dogma of the prophetic era was explicitly promulgated as an "act of authority."[32] The notion that any such decree was issued seems incongruent with scribal self-understanding

---

30   van der Toorn, *Scribal Culture*, 263.
31   Here van der Toorn's argumentation echoes that of Greenspahn, "Why Prophecy Ceased."
32   van der Toorn, *Scribal Culture*, 263: "The canonization of the Hebrew scriptures has come about on account of two decisions carried out by persons or institutions in a position of authority. One decision was the promulgation of the Torah as the law of the land … enforced by Ezra and Nehemiah …. The second act of authority, occurring about two centuries later, was the enunciation of the dogma of the prophetic era."

about how their authority was to be exercised. In Judaism of the Hellenistic and Roman periods, the scribal elite—specifically those scribes who were learned in the sacred texts and authorized to expound them—were recognized as having a hermeneutical authority.[33] Ben Sira describes the cultural prestige acquired by the wise scribe: it is those who devote themselves to Torah that have the standing to dispense justice and rule the people (Sir 38:24–34). To the extent that the scribes held and promulgated a doctrine of the closure of the prophetic era, this was accomplished by and through the interpretation of Scripture. This is evident in the way Deuteronomy's promise of a future prophet is taken up in the conclusion of Malachi, and also in Ben Sira's reflections on the concept of a Mosaic prophetic succession, the subject of our next chapter.

33   The term "scribe" does not, of course, convey this authority in itself, as there were many types of scribes in Second Temple Judaism. Nevertheless, there is evidence that some scribes—probably, specifically those entrusted with copying the Scriptures—were looked to as authorities in matters of Torah and of the interpretation of Scripture. See Martin Goodman, "Texts, Scribes, and Power in Roman Judaea," in *Literacy and Power in the Ancient World*, ed. A. Bowman and G. Woolf (Cambridge: Cambridge, 1994), 99–108.

CHAPTER 7

"I Will Send Elijah the Prophet": The Cessation and Deferral of the Mosaic Prophetic Succession

1   Introduction

The next development in the story of the prophet like Moses includes the earliest attested eschatological interpretation of Moses's promise, in the person of the returning Elijah (Mal 3:22–24; Eng. 4:4–6). This is an important development, one that will reverberate through the centuries in Judaism and Christianity, creating its own interpretive trajectories, many of which I cannot examine within the scope of this book. In this chapter I argue that the earliest articulations of the eschatological Elijah tradition, present in Mal 3:24 and Sir 48:10, reflect a Hellenistic-era scribal interpretation of Deut 18:15, 18, which asserts that the Mosaic prophetic succession has been provisionally closed in the present, and is therefore deferred to the eschatological future. The thesis that I wish to test—that prophecy did not cease, but that the Mosaic prophetic succession was thought to have ceased—finds its earliest evidence in these authors' assigning of the activity of Mosaic prophets to the past and the future. In terms of past prophecy, the figure of Joshua emerges as an important referent of Moses' promise that God would raise up a prophet like him. In terms of future prophecy, the scribes dampen eschatological expectation by creating a new prerequisite for the "day of the LORD," the return of Mosaic prophecy in the great Mosaic prophet Elijah.

2   A Scribal Colophon: The Conclusion to the Book of the Twelve

The earliest reference to the Twelve Prophets as a unified collection (i.e., a "Book of the Twelve") is found in Ben Sira's *Laus Patrum*:

> May the bones of the Twelve Prophets send forth new life from where they lie, for they comforted the people of Jacob and delivered them with confident hope.
> Sir 49:10

The critical point for our purposes is the relationship between the concept of a closed series of twelve prophets on the one hand, and the conclusion of the book of the Twelve on the other, which holds out the promise of the return of prophecy in the person of Elijah. That these concepts are not unrelated is suggested by the fact that Ben Sira also furnishes the earliest extant citation of Mal 3:23–24 (Sir 48:10). That is, in the *Laus Patrum* occurs both the reference to the Twelve as a unity, and to Elijah's role as prophet who is destined to return. Ben Sira's work therefore provides a *terminus ad quem* for both the publication of the book of the Twelve and the composition of Mal 3:22–24. It seems safe to hypothesize, therefore, that this latter passage is a product of Hellenistic-era Jerusalem scribes.[1] I now turn to a sustained examination of the closure and deferral of Mosaic prophecy in the colophon to the Book of the Twelve.

Earlier we have considered at length the coordination between the titles "servant" (עבד) and "prophet" (נביא), evidenced in the phrase "Yhwh's/my servants the prophets," as well as in the hinge of the Torah and the DH, in which Moses's status as "servant of Yhwh" and incomparable prophet are juxtaposed. A Dtr-inspired coordination of these terms occurs in the coda to the book of Malachi, though here an eschatological prophet is meant, and is associated with the figure of Elijah:

(22) זכרו תורת משה **עבדי** אשר צויתי אותו בחרב על־כל־ישראל חקים ומשפטים
(23) הנה אנכי שלח לכם את אליה **הנביא** לפני בוא יום יהוה הגדול והנורא (24) והשיב
לב־אבות על־בנים ולב בנים על־אבותם פן־אבוא והכיתי את־הארץ חרם

(22) καὶ ἰδοὺ ἐγὼ ἀποστέλλω ὑμῖν Ηλίαν τὸν Θεσβίτην πρὶν ἐλθεῖν ἡμέραν κυρίου τὴν μεγάλην καὶ ἐπιφανῆ (23) ὃς ἀποκαταστήσει καρδίαν πατρὸς πρὸς υἱὸν καὶ καρδίαν ἀνθρώπου πρὸς τὸν πλησίον αὐτοῦ μὴ ἔλθω καὶ πατάξω τὴν γῆν ἄρδην (24) μνήσθητε νόμου Μωυσῆ τοῦ δούλου μου καθότι ἐνετειλάμην αὐτῷ ἐν Χωρηβ πρὸς πάντα τὸν Ισραηλ προστάγματα καὶ δικαιώματα

Remember the teaching of **my servant** Moses, the statutes and ordinances that I commanded him at Horeb for all Israel. Lo, I will send you **the prophet** Elijah before the great and terrible day of the LORD comes. He

---

1 On the formation of the Book of the Twelve, see the review of scholarship in Barry Alan Jones, *The Formation of the Book of the Twelve: A Study in Text and Canon*, SBLDS 149 (Atlanta: Scholars Press, 1995), 13–42; see also James Nogalski, *Redactional Processes in the Book of the Twelve*, BZAW 218 (Berlin: de Gruyter, 1993).

will turn the hearts of parents to their children and the hearts of children to their parents, so that I will not come and strike the land with a curse.

Mal 3:22–24 (Eng. 4:4–6)

Karel van der Toorn claims that this passage represents the earliest eschatological interpretation of Deut 18:15, in which the promised prophet like Moses is associated with the "day of Yhwh."[2] Indeed, it is defensible to posit that Elijah is here and elsewhere understood as a Mosaic figure, though explicit interaction with Deuteronomy 18 is not in evidence in the Elijah tradition.[3] If this pas-

---

2 Karel van der Toorn, *Scribal Culture and the Making of the Hebrew Bible* (Cambridge, Ma.: Harvard, 2007), 253–254, 331n48. See also Joseph Blenkinsopp, *Prophecy and Canon: A Contribution to the Study of Jewish Origins*, CSJCA 3 (University of Notre Dame Press, 1977), 87: "Given the close thematic links between the Moses and Elijah of Jewish tradition, it is not impossible that the eschatological messenger identified in Mal 3:23–24 with Elijah was thought to be the Mosaic prophet, though this cannot be proved"; Christophe Nihan, " 'Moses and the Prophets': Deuteronomy 18 and the Emergence of the Pentateuch as Torah," *SEÅ* 75 (2010): 21–55, at 51: "Here, as it appears, the promise of Deut 18 is maintained despite the revision in Deut 34:10–12 by being reinterpreted in a strictly *eschatological* sense"; Beth Glazier-McDonald, *Malachi: The Divine Messenger*, SBLDS 68 (Atlanta: Scholars Press, 1987), 267: "Cognizant of the Deuteronomic tradition, it is likely that Malachi was influenced by the claim that Yahweh would send another prophet 'like Moses' .... Elijah is to be the agent of this return. Indeed, 'like Moses,' he functions as the means by which Israel can be assured of the most intimate association with its God"; Andrew E. Hill, *Malachi: A New Translation with Introduction and Commentary*, AB 25D (New York: Doubleday, 1998), 384 (emphasis original): "The juxtaposition of the two ideal figures, Moses and Elijah, may be a conflation of two interrelated texts from the Primary History: Deut 18:15–22 (the forecast of a prophet *like* Moses) and 2 Kgs 17:13–14 (linking the prophetic ministry of Elijah to the stipulations of the Mosaic covenant)." Dale Allison, *The New Moses: A Matthean Typology* (Minneapolis: Fortress, 1993), 76–77, has more bibliography (at 76–77n179) and a critical discussion of the issue. He rightly points out that in NT texts the eschatological Elijah is usually distinguished from the prophet like Moses; however, one needs to distinguish the *reception* of Mal 3:22–24 from its *origin* as, most probably, a comment on Mosaic prophecy and specifically the return of Mosaic prophecy in Elijah.

3 On Elijah as the prophet like Moses, see Robert P. Carroll, "The Elijah-Elisha Sagas: Some Remarks on Prophetic Succession in Ancient Israel," *VT* 19 (1969): 400–415, at 408–413; Robert R. Wilson, *Prophecy and Society in Ancient Israel* (Philadelphia: Fortress, 1980), 197–199; Nihan, "Moses and the Prophets," 51. In this monograph, I discuss the origin of the expectation of an eschatological Elijah tradition (in Mal 3:23–24; Sir 48:10), but do not deal substantially with the Elijah-tradition (both in 1–2 Kgs and in later interpretation) for three reasons. First, I can discern no clear interpretive relationship to the prophet-law of Deut 18:9–22 in the Elijah tradition of 1–2 Kings. Second, it would expand the scope of the monograph beyond what is feasible to incorporate a full discussion of Elijah as eschatological prophet. Third, the eschatological Elijah tradition acquires a life of its own in NT and rabbinic interpretation: even if it originates in relation to Deut 18:15, it does not remain bound to this context.

sage represents the re-interpretation of Deut 18:15 as an eschatological promise, a question arises as to the precise relationship between this interpretation of Deut 18:15 and the earlier one attested in Deut 34:10, which denied parity between Moses and any other prophet. Blenkinsopp, who was one of the earliest scholars to read both these passages precisely as intentional *conclusions* to specific literary collections (that is, as "intentionally placed hermeneutical markers" guiding the reading of Torah and Prophets respectively),[4] also argued that there was a marked tension in their emphases: Deut 34:10–12 asserts the primacy of Torah, but Mal 3:22–24 restores the balance, maintaining an eschatological hope and subverting the attempt to limit the era of normative revelation to the Mosaic epoch. In line with this, the mission of the eschatological Elijah to restore the twelve tribes of Israel (cf. Sir 48:10) is taken by Blenkinsopp to reflect "the tendency within the prophetic tradition itself to embody the ancient charismatic Israel."[5] This re-assertion of the "millenarian hope" leads Blenkinsopp to conclude: "the tension which seemed to have been resolved in favor of the claims of the past at the conclusion of the Pentateuch is now restored."[6]

I am dependent on Blenkinsopp's recognition that the passage is deliberately composed as a conclusion that further delineates the relationship between the prophecy of Moses and that of his authorized successors, but I am not entirely convinced of his construal of its force. Where Blenkinsopp finds the hand of an eschatologically oriented editor, I suggest that there is an extension of the increasing insistence on textual authority. Present-day Mosaic prophecy is negated in two ways. First, in Malachi, its function is assigned to the priesthood:

(6) True instruction was in his mouth (בפיהו), and no wrong was found on his lips. He walked with me in integrity and uprightness, and he turned many from iniquity. (7) For the lips of a priest should guard knowledge,

---

4 The phrase is that of Stephen B. Chapman, "A Canonical Approach to Old Testament Theology? Deuteronomy 34:10–12 and Malachi 3:22–24 as Programmatic Conclusions," *HBT* 25 (2003): 121–145; here 121.
5 Blenkinsopp, *Prophecy and Canon*, 122. Blenkinsopp cites Sir 48:10 and Isa 49:5–6 to justify understanding the inter-generational reconciliation depicted in Mal 3:23 as bringing about "the final reintegration of Israel represented by the twelve sons of Jacob."
6 Blenkinsopp, *Prophecy and Canon*, 123. Stephen B. Chapman, *The Law and the Prophets: A Study in Old Testament Canon Formation*, FAT 27 (Tübingen: Mohr Siebeck, 2000), 132, in my view rightly comments: "This assessment derives more, however, from his thorough-going acceptance of O. Plöger's 'bipolar model' [i.e. theocratic vs. eschatological] of post-exilic society than from the text itself."

and people should seek instruction from his mouth, for he is the messenger of the Lord of hosts (ותורה יבקשו מפיהו כי מלאך יהוה צבאות הוא).
Mal 2:6–7

Second, the coming of a Mosaic prophet is deferred to the eschatological future.[7] A scribal colophon that calls for obedience to the law of Moses in the present and defers prophetic activity to the future "day of Yhwh" is a sharply circumscribed eschatology indeed. The colophon to Malachi reflects not "millenarian hope," but a scribal closure of the Mosaic prophetic succession. To develop this view, there are three main questions that must be addressed. First, is the passage a unity? Second, why in particular is Elijah mentioned and what function is attributed to him? Third, what is the nature of the concluding function of Mal 3:22–24?

With respect to the first issue, many scholars have argued that the call to observe the law of Moses and the promise of Elijah's return were successive redactions.[8] The text-critical evidence might favor the suggestion that these two sentences are separable and possibly distinct additions. In the LXX, the promise of Elijah occurs first, and the book ends with the reminder to observe the law of Moses. It seems, however, that there is a simpler explanation for the transposition. It most likely occurred to avoid ending the Book of the Twelve with the word חרם, "curse." On the principle that MT represents the more difficult reading, it is likely that it preserves the original order, and that the LXX represents a later rearrangement, which ends the work with a positive command instead of a threat.[9] Thus, the textual variants are not relevant to the question of the passage's original unity.

Blenkinsopp regards these as successive additions, the latter being motivated by the hand of an eschatological editor.[10] Kessler, on the other hand, argues that the promise of Elijah's return is the first addition, followed by the

---

[7] This is nearly the opposite strategy to the one employed in the earlier polemic against prophecy in Zech 13:2–6, which attempts to negate its authority in the present by envisioning an eschaton without prophecy. "If you can't beat 'em, join 'em," may sum up the attempt to "end" prophecy by deferring it in Mal 3:22–24.

[8] E.g., Rainer Kessler, *Maleachi*, HThKAT (Freiburg: Herder, 2011), 304.

[9] So Hill, *Malachi*, 366. Jones, *Formation of the Book of the Twelve*, 118–125, provides a full discussion of the text-critical differences. He argues that the LXX order was primary and that the MT revised the order, "conforming the text to the 'canonical' order of the careers of Moses and Elijah" (122). I wonder if this consideration would have weighed heavily in this instance: the accent is not on Elijah's past, but on his future.

[10] Blenkinsopp, *Prophecy and Canon*, 121.

nomistic appeal to Moses.[11] In my view, there are compelling reasons to regard the appeal to Moses and Elijah not as successive additions but as a unity. The appendix contains a balanced appeal to two prominent figures from Israel's scriptural narratives, Moses and Elijah. This invocation of two named characters is a major factor that supports the internal unity and coherence of this appendix. A second observation has to do with the term "at Horeb" (בחרב) in 3:22, which looks ahead to the promise of Elijah, a prophet who also experienced a theophany at Horeb.[12] Third, and decisive in my view, is the observation that both sentences have a temporal focus: the first looks back to Moses; the second looks forward to Elijah. Christoph Nihan has argued that this temporal focus is the key to understanding the passage's contribution as a conclusion that "works a 'compromise' of sorts between 'Moses' and the 'Prophets' … which involves one more reinterpretation of Deut 18 and Deut 34 respectively."[13] Nihan summarizes his view:

> [T]he compromise achieved between "Moses" and the "Prophets" rests first and foremost upon a neat distinction between *present history* and *eschatological times*. *For the interval between Malachi (the last prophet) and the return of Elijah (the eschatological prophet) the Torah of Moses is absolutely normative* … As far as the end of times is concerned, however, there is a place for the revelations contained in the "classical" prophets, who, contrary to Moses, have all announced the coming "Day of Yahweh."[14]

The use of the term "compromise" to describe this passage blunts Blenkinsopp's characterization of Mal 3:22–24 as a reassertion of eschatological hope against the theocratic priestly class. In fact, the conclusion to Malachi ensures that in the "present time" the Law of Moses remains the normative ideal, and

---

11   Kessler, *Maleachi*, 304.
12   See Hill, *Malachi*, 372: "the place name 'Horeb' yokes the two appendixes of Malachi by connecting the ideal figures of Moses and Elijah with a site they had in common—the 'mountain of God.'" So also Elie Assis, "Moses, Elijah, and the Messianic Hope: A New Reading of Mal 3:22–24," *ZAW* 123 (2011): 207–220; at 211; Nihan, "Moses and the Prophets," 49n65.
13   Nihan, "Moses and the Prophets," 48.
14   Nihan, "Moses and the Prophets," 52 (emphasis original). The phrase "contrary to Moses" implies greater tension between Moses and the prophets than would have been perceived; other than this quibble, this statement by Nihan represents in my view a promising approach to the passage.

it defers prophecy to the eschatological future. Thus this text represents the scribal attempt to declare the Mosaic prophetic succession provisionally but not finally closed.

In my estimation, the term "compromise" also has potential to shed light on the role of Elijah in the text. The introduction of this character from the DH is somewhat abrupt and has occasioned many theories.[15] There is widespread agreement that Mal 3:23–24 is an interpretive gloss, specifying the identity of the "messenger of the covenant" (מלאך הברית) of 3:1–5.[16] This is supported by the parallel structure of 3:1aα and 3:23 (Table 14). Hill observes that Malachi revises the eschatological time-table by introducing the coming of a preparatory figure.[17] This amounts to a deferral of the "day of Yhwh," and is perhaps suggestive of a waning eschatological enthusiasm. In particular, the sense of immediacy that pervades 3:1–5 (in 3:1, see חפצים, מבקשים, פתאם, and the repetition of הנה; in 3:5, note ממהר) is dramatically lessened in the conclusion of Malachi.[18] The selection of a figure from hoary antiquity as the future prophet would have underlined the sense that the day of Yhwh is not a feature of the present or even the imminent future.[19] The contemplation of the possibility that the eschatological Elijah might fail in his mission—resulting in the land being struck with a curse—is a striking indication of the dampened expectation of this passage.[20] Indeed, the studied scribal character of this eschatological

---

15   Assis, "Moses, Elijah," 211 reviews some of the main options (because of Elijah's heavenly ascent, or his affinity to Moses, or to Malachi) and suggests a theory of his own (which seems speculative): "The fact that Elijah had then [i.e., in 1 Kings] failed to renew the covenant between God and the people was what allowed a later prophet to foresee his return to complete his life's work, correcting what he had failed to do."

16   See Glazier-McDonald, *Malachi*, 259: "The scholarly consensus is that Mal 3:23–24 are a gloss upon 3:1–5." Hill, *Malachi*, 383, defends this consensus, tracing the interpretation back as far as Calvin. Allison, *New Moses*, 76–77n179, notes that the equation seems to be present in the gospels: "Matt 11:10 and Mark 1:12 [*sic*, 1:2 is meant] apply Mal 3:1 to John the Baptist, who in Matthew and Mark is the eschatological Elijah."

17   Hill, *Malachi*, 385: "Malachi modifies the eschatological teaching of Haggai and First and Second Zechariah (e.g., introducing the preparatory role of the *messenger* prior to the Day of Yahweh)."

18   This is not contradicted by the use of הנה + participle, which can indicate "a long-term state of affairs." See Waltke-O'Connor, § 37.6d.

19   The LXX variant, which reads "Elijah the Tishbite" (Ηλιαν τὸν Θεσβίτην) as opposed to MT's "Elijah the prophet," should be noted here. It is possible that the translator wished to specify clearly that the reference was to the Elijah of the narratives of 1–2 Kings, and not some other future Elijah.

20   See David L. Petersen, *Late Israelite Prophecy: Studies in Deutero-Prophetic Literature and in Chronicles*, SBLMS 23 (Missoula, Mont.: Scholars Press, 1977), 44–45: "The curse, v. 24b,

TABLE 14   The parallel structure of Malachi 3:1, 23

Structure:	Mal 3:1aα	Mal 3:23
a) Exclamatory particle, first person	הנני	הנה אנכי
b) Verb "to send", object (prophet)	שלח מלאכי	שלח לכם את אליה הנביא
c) Preparatory function	ופנה־דרך לפני	לפני בוא יום יהוה הגדול והנורא

promise marks it as maintaining prophetic hope by reinterpreting it in light of Israel's scriptures and her history of covenant with Yhwh.[21]

With respect to the figure of Elijah, it should also be noted that the "compromise" (to return to Nihan's characterization) is not only between the claims of Torah and those of prophecy, represented in the figures of Moses and Elijah, but also between the Dtr prophetic tradition and the so-called "writing prophets."[22] The singling out of Elijah, and the setting of Elijah's return before the "great and terrible day of Yhwh" (יום יהוה הגדול והנורא, 3:23), juxtaposes a major theme of classical prophecy (the coming day of Yhwh) with one of the most prominent prophets of the DH. Thus, the choice of Elijah, besides being related to the tradition of his ascent to heaven, reflects an intertextual commingling of prophetic traditions, also observable in other late prophetic texts such as Zech 13:2–6.[23] There is a literary shape to the coda of Malachi, as the promise of a future prophet is positioned as a compromise between what scholars now describe as the traditions of Dtr and "classical" prophecy respectively.

Finally, Nihan's observation that the passage is unified by its distinctions between the past, present, and eschatological future provides a new perspective on its concluding function. The corpora of literature to which Mal 3:22–24 has been understood as the colophon has been a subject of vigorous debate. The proposals can be listed as a continuously broadening range: it concludes

---

recognizes the possibility that the prophet will be unable to create the requisite ritual and ethical cleanliness for Yahweh's coming to be safe for Israel."

21   See Hill, *Malachi*, 377–378, who notes that it is a combination of Exod 23:20 and Joel 2:31b. On the use of Exod 23:20, see Petersen, *Late Israelite Prophecy*, 43.

22   Hill, *Malachi*, 365: "the two appendices bridge two literary collections: the Primary History and the Latter Prophets. … the two anthologies were intended to be read together."

23   The prophet in Zech 13:4–5 no longer puts on the "hairy mantle" (v. 4, אדרת שער; cf 1 Kgs 19:13, 19; 2 Kgs 2:8, 13, 14) and protests, in the famous words of Amos, "I am not a prophet" (v. 5, לא נביא, cf Amos 7:14).

Malachi alone,[24] the Book of the Twelve,[25] the Latter Prophets,[26] the prophetic collection as a whole,[27] or, most broadly, an early collection of Torah and Prophets.[28] Elie Assis has argued for the first view listed, emphasizing the conclusion's intertextual connections with the rest of the book. He appeals to the feature discussed above, namely, the status of 3:23 as an explanatory clarification concerning the identity of the messenger of Mal 3:1.[29] He also points to parallels between Mal 3:24 and 1:6 ("fathers" and "children"), and argues that the concept of "return" in 3:24 (שׁוּב) is anticipated in 3:7, 2:6.[30] Finally, Assis advances the (idiosyncratic) interpretation that the mention of "fathers" in Mal 3:24 is a reference to God, meaning that the function of Elijah will be to restore the covenantal relationship between God and Israel.[31] It is certainly the case that some of the features of Malachi's conclusion can be explained with reference to the book itself. Nevertheless, Assis does not adequately treat the many differences between the conclusion and the remainder of the book. While most of Malachi is in dialogue form, the conclusion is direct speech.[32] Moreover, the

---

24 Assis, "Moses, Elijah," 207–220; Glazier-McDonald, *Malachi*, 243–270; Marvin Sweeney, *The Twelve Prophets*, 2 vols., Berit Olam (Collegeville, Minn.: Liturgical Press, 2000), 2:714; Michael H. Floyd, *Minor Prophets, Part Two*, FOTL 22 (Grand Rapids: Eerdmans, 2000), 568–571, 612–614; Brevard Childs, *Introduction to the Old Testament as Scripture* (Philadelphia: Fortress, 1979), 495.

25 E.g., R.J. Coggins, *Haggai, Zechariah, Malachi*, OTG (Sheffield: JSOT Press, 1987), 84; Paul Redditt, "The Book of Malachi in its Social Setting," *CBQ* 56 (1994): 240–255; here 243.

26 Blenkinsopp, *Prophecy and Canon*, 121, suggests that the Latter Prophets have a deliberate 3+12 structure, modelled on the patriarchs. If such a structure is deliberate, the concluding function of this pericope would encompass the latter prophets.

27 For the colophon as conclusion to the נביאים from Joshua—Malachi, see Wilhelm Rudolph, *Haggai, Sacharja 1–8, Sacharja 9–14, Maleachi*, KAT 13/4 (Gutersloh: Mohn, 1976), 291–293; Rex Mason, *The Books of Haggai, Zechariah, and Malachi* (Cambridge: Cambridge University, 1977), 238; Jones, *Formation of the Book of the Twelve*, 59–63.

28 David L. Petersen, *Zechariah 9–14 and Malachi: A Commentary*, OTL (Louisville: Westminster John Knox, 1995), 232–233. Hill, *Malachi*, 365, argues that it links the Primary History and a prophetic collection. Julia M. O'Brien, *Nahum, Habakkuk, Zephaniah, Haggai, Zechariah, Malachi*, AOTC (Nashville: Abingdon, 2004), 316–317, supports these broad views of the conclusion's function.

29 Assis, "Moses, Elijah," 209.

30 Assis, "Moses, Elijah," 209.

31 Assis, "Moses, Elijah," 212–214; he bases this on Mal 1:6, and appeals to other plural terms for God.

32 Chapman, *Law and the Prophets*, 134–135. Floyd, *Minor Prophets*, 563–568, attempts to mitigate the force of this point by emphasizing the variegated character of the rest of Malachi, 568: "3:22 and 3:23–24 cannot be relegated to the status of appendices just because they fail to fit the generic mold that is supposedly normative for all units in the main body, for no one particular generic mold is in fact normative for all units in the main body."

conclusion contains a number of striking terminological departures from the phraseology of the main part of Malachi, as summarized already by Smith in his 1912 commentary:

> Malachi's term is not יום יהוה, nor יום הגדול והנורא, but היום הבא ... Malachi speaks of התורה, but not of תורת משה. Malachi constantly cites אמר יהוה; these verses never. אנוכי stands here as against אני elsewhere in Malachi.[33]

Not only are differing phrases used for concepts already mentioned in the book, but the conclusion is replete with stereotyped Dtr terminology that suggests the hand of a later editor.[34]

Chapman, constrained on the one hand by the observation that the promise of Elijah responds to Mal 3:1, and on the other hand by the terminological indications that the scope of the conclusion goes beyond Malachi alone, cannot decide, and affirms both positions:

> In my view, the appendices in Mal 3:22–24 [4:4–6] were originally designed to close the book of Malachi alone, but exercised such literary force by the power of their canon-conscious allusions that they retained their status as a conclusion (at the same time broadening their scope) during the formation of the book of the Twelve and the prophetic corpus.[35]

Chapman is hesitant to ascribe to the authors of this colophon the intent to conclude more than Malachi, though he, along with many other authors who take this position, seems to recognize the fittingness of this conclusion for a broader literary corpus.[36] One of the points that gives Chapman pause is

---

33   J.M.P. Smith, *A Critical and Exegetical Commentary on Haggai, Zechariah, Malachi, and Jonah*, ICC (Edinburgh: T&T Clark, 1912), book 2, 85. See also Glazier-McDonald, *Malachi*, 244, 252: אני/אנכי is particularly striking as אני occurs often in Malachi (1:4, 6 [2×], 14; 2:9; 3:6, 17, 21).

34   Chapman, *The Law and the Prophets*, 134: " 'Remember,' 'the law of my servant Moses,' 'statutes and ordinances,' 'Horeb' and 'all Israel' are familiar deuteronomistic expressions." In addition to these, O'Brien, *Nahum*, 315 also points to the concluding term, חרם.

35   Chapman, *The Law and the Prophets*, 144.

36   See also Assis, "Moses, Elijah," 209: "[T]hese verses were written from the outset as the closing to the Book of Malachi, though admittedly they would also serve as a fitting closing to the Pentateuch and Prophets"; Sweeney, *Twelve Prophets*, 714: "Although the concluding verses of Malachi might be read in relation to the Torah and the Prophets, there is little indication that they were composed with this role in mind"; Floyd, *Minor Prophets*, 612: "By ending in this way Malachi may also provide a suitable ending for the Book of the Twelve or for the prophetic section of the canon, but … there is no reason to assume that

the fact that no set canonical order in which the Book of Twelve closes the prophetic collection is in evidence in Second Temple times, so that these verses could hardly be understood as the conclusion to a literary collection broader than the Book of the Twelve.[37] Indeed, there is no set order of the Book of the Twelve itself, and one important Qumran manuscript has the book of Jonah in the final position.[38] The lack of importance of canonical order in this time-period is indeed an important datum that provokes a reconsideration of the nature of the concluding function of Mal 3:22–24. On balance, it seems that the specific references to Moses and Elijah are invoking a broader frame of reference than that supplied by merely the book of Malachi or indeed even the Book of the Twelve.[39] In my view, however, this broader scope should not be defined with respect to a specific literary corpus, but in terms of a chronological prophetic succession. This view is suggested by the past- and future-oriented character of the coda, and it can be clarified by a consideration of another proposed intertextual allusion in Mal 3:22–24.

In his commentary, Rudolph was the first to argue extensively for an allusion to Josh 1:2, 7 in the conclusion of Malachi, and thus claimed that these passages consciously bounded a corpus of נביאים considered as a literary collection.[40] The terminological overlap is striking: both passages describe Moses as Yhwh's "servant" (משה עדדי, Josh 1:2, 7; Mal 3:22), and both refer to his תורה (Josh 1:7; Mal 3:22) which he "commanded" (צוה: Josh 1:7; Mal 3:22) "all" Israel (כל־ישראל, Mal 3:22; כל־העם הזה, Josh 1:2). The composer of Mal 3:22 used language strikingly reminiscent of the opening verses of Joshua. Because the Second Temple period evidence does not permit confidence that there was a set canonical order, Chapman thinks the only conclusion that can be drawn from this allusion is that the colophon is an example of Dtr-inspired "scribal prophecy" (*Schriftprophetie*).[41] It goes beyond the evidence to assert, with Rudolph, that

---

this concluding passage or any part of it was designed primarily for either of these other purposes." It is striking that in these authors' denial of the broader force of this conclusion, they must simply ascribe its fittingness as such to coincidence—it is simply one way the conclusion can be read, no more.

37 Chapman, *The Law and the Prophets*, 136–139.
38 See Jones, *Formation of the Book of the Twelve*.
39 See Hill's (somewhat plaintive) rhetorical question, in response to scholars such as Glazier-McDonald who restrict the scope of this conclusion, *Malachi*, 366: "Surely this appeal to Moses at the conclusion of Malachi has significance beyond the prophet's own message?"
40 Rudolph, *Haggai*, 291. See also Erich Bosshard and Reinhold G. Kratz, "Maleachi im Zwölfprophetenbuch," *BN* 52 (1990): 27–46; here 46.
41 Chapman, *The Law and the Prophets*, 139.

the existence of the "Prophets" (נביאים) as a closed literary corpus can be established on these rather slender grounds. That said, Nihan proposes an intriguing possibility, between the minimalism of Chapman and the maximalism of Rudolph: the allusion to Josh 1:2, 7 "established a *chronological* delineation, not a canonical one: Just like Joshua is the first 'prophet' after Moses, Malachi is the last prophet before the eschatological prophet [i.e., Elijah]."[42] Nihan has thus side-stepped the debate about what range of works this colophon concludes by arguing that the closure in view is not literary but chronological. In formulating the colophon to Malachi, the scribes deliberately looked back to the beginning of the institution of Mosaic prophecy, asserted the temporary conclusion of this institution in the figure of Malachi (the final prophet in a series of twelve), and held out hope for the return of the Mosaic succession in the person of one of the most prominent individuals in that office, Elijah the Tishbite. On this account, the scribal colophon to Malachi, which is most likely to be dated to the Hellenistic period, indicated that the Mosaic prophetic succession was provisionally, but not finally, closed. I will now turn to Ben Sira's *Laus Patrum*, a text from the Hellenistic period that supports and clarifies this hypothesis.

3   The Mosaic Prophetic Succession in Ben Sira's *Laus Patrum*

3.1   Introduction

It has often been pointed out that Ben Sira wrote in the crossroads of cultural confluence between Judaism and Hellenism. In the context of the dominance of Greek thought and culture, Ben Sira writes to inculcate a love and respect for Israel's own ancestral traditions. His grandson and translator captures Ben Sira's goal when he says that his grandfather wrote "so that by becoming familiar also with his book those who love learning might make even greater progress in living according to the law" (Prologue). In the context of the cultural pressure brought to bear by Hellenism, Ben Sira insists on the antiquity and prestige of Israel's traditions and offices, including its prophets, understood as successors to Moses.[43]

At the outset of his *Laus Patrum*, Ben Sira indicates that one of the groups he will praise consists of "those who spoke in prophetic oracles" (44:3). A more literal translation might be: "seers of all in their prophecy" (חוזי כל בנבואתם; Greek:

---

42 Nihan, "Moses and the Prophets," 50.
43 For this perspective on the book, see Martin Hengel, *Judaism and Hellenism: Studies in their Encounter in Palestine during the Early Hellenistic Period*, trans. J. Bowden, 2 vols. (Philadelphia, Fortress Press, 1974), 1:131–153.

ἀπηγγελκότες ἐν προφητείαις).[44] The noun נבואה, "prophecy" or "prophetic office," is a feature of late Biblical Hebrew.[45] In the narration of Israel's heroes that follow, Ben Sira praises Moses as prophet *par excellence*, puts particular emphasis on the concept of prophetic succession, and closely relates this succession with a literary corpus of prophetic works.

3.2 Moses as Supreme Prophet in Sir 45:1–5

Ben Sira's description of Moses focuses on his function as the unsurpassed mediator of divine revelation, particularly in 45:3b–5. The text is presented here in the nine bicola into which it is divided:[46]

> (23b) From his [Jacob's] descendants the Lord brought forth a godly man, who found favor in the sight of all
> (1) and was beloved by God and people, Moses, whose memory is blessed.
> (2) He made him equal in glory to the holy ones [Heb. אלוהים], and made him great, to the terror of his enemies.
> (3) By his words he performed swift miracles; the Lord glorified him in the presence of kings.
> He gave him commandments for his people, and revealed to him his glory.
> (4) For his faithfulness and meekness he consecrated him, choosing him out of all humankind.
> He allowed him to hear his voice, and led him into the dark cloud,
> (5) and gave him the commandments face to face, the law of life and knowledge,
> so that he might teach Jacob the covenant, and Israel his decrees.
>   Sir 44:23b–45:5

Ben Sira transitions from Jacob directly to Moses, emphasizing not his Levitical but his Israelite origin. Moses was "brought out from him" (ἐξήγαγεν ἐξ αὐτοῦ), that is, from Jacob. The Hebrew text is fragmentary here, but Manuscript

---

44   For the Hebrew text, see Pancratius Beentjes, *The Book of Ben Sira in Hebrew: A Text Edition of All Extant Hebrew Manuscripts and a Synopsis of all Parallel Hebrew Ben Sira Texts*, VTSup 68 (Leiden: Brill, 1997). The LXX is cited according to the critical edition of Joseph Ziegler, *Septuaginta: Vetus Testamentum Graecum Auctoritate Academiae Litterarum Gottingensis editum XII.2: Sapientia Iesu Filii Sirach* (Göttingen: Vandenhoeck & Ruprecht, 1965).
45   See 2 Chr 9:29; 15:8; Neh 6:12.
46   See Jeremy Corley, "A Numerical Structure in Sirach 44:1–50:24," *CBQ* 69 (2007): 43–63.

B contains the words ממנו איש. Ben Sira thus introduces Moses by referring to his status as an Israelite prophet.[47] In the final five bicola, Ben Sira interweaves scriptural traditions regarding Moses's status as supreme revelatory agent, which are synthesized to present Moses as the prophet *par excellence*.[48] In particular, vv. 4–5 combine motifs from Pentateuchal passages relating to Moses as prophet:

(4) באמונתו ובענותו ויבחר בו מכל ... וישמיעהו את קולו ויגישהו לערפל

(5) וישם בידו מצוה תורת חיים ותבונה ללמד ביעקב חקיו ועדותיו ומשפטיו לישראל

(4) ἐν πίστει καὶ πραΰτητι αὐτὸν ἡγίασεν ἐξελέξατο αὐτὸν ἐκ πάσης σαρκός
(5) ἠκούτισεν αὐτὸν τῆς φωνῆς αὐτοῦ καὶ εἰσήγαγεν αὐτὸν εἰς τὸν γνόφον καὶ ἔδωκεν αὐτῷ **κατὰ πρόσωπον** ἐντολάς, νόμον ζωῆς καὶ ἐπιστήμης, διδάξαι τὸν Ιακωβ διαθήκην καὶ κρίματα αὐτοῦ τὸν Ισραηλ

Verse 4a clearly refers to Num 12:3, 7 in attributing to Moses "faithfulness and meekness" (12:3, ענו; 12:7, נאמן). As in Num 12:6–8, Sir 45:4 specifies that these attributes of Moses qualified him for unparalleled access to the divine. The "choosing" of Moses "from all flesh" does not refer generally to his appointment out of humanity, but specifically to the narratives of the appointment of Moses from the Israelites as the covenant mediator.[49] This is clear from the phrases that immediately follow: "He caused him to hear his voice" and "led

---

47 Cf Deut 18:15: מקרבך מאחיך כמני.
48 The relevant passages are particularly Exod 33:7–11; Num 12:6–8; Deut 5:23–31; 34:10–12. Patrick Skehan and Alexander Di Lella, *The Wisdom of Ben Sira: A New Translation with Notes, Introduction, and Commentary*, AB 39 (New York: Doubleday, 1987), 510, refer to Exod 33:11; Num 12:7–8; Deut 34:11 with respect to the description of Moses as "beloved to God and humans" in 45:1 and his hearing of God's voice, 45:5. Benjamin Wright, *No Small Difference: Sirach's Relationship to its Hebrew Parent Text*, SBLSCS 26 (Atlanta: Scholars Press, 1989), 169–170, disputes the influence of scriptural language on Sir 45:1–5 on grounds that it is a "summary composition." This seems to me to be a false dilemma. A similar skepticism about tracing specific allusions in Ben Sira is expressed by Richard Horsley, *Scribes, Visionaries, and the Politics of Second Temple Judea* (Louisville: Westminster John Knox, 2007), 109–149. Horsley makes some remarkable and what seem to me to be highly improbable claims, e.g., 120, "There is ... no basis for arguing he [Ben Sira] is engaged in the interpretation of the (books of) the Pentateuch"; 131: "Ben Sira was not an interpreter of the Torah/law of Moses or other 'Scripture'" (the description of Sirach as such an interpreter by his grandson and translator is dismissed by Horsley as a "projection" [119]). Detailed study of the *Laus Patrum* casts serious doubt on such an approach to Ben Sira.
49 See Exod 20:18–21; Deut 5:23–31; 18:16–18; Skehan and Di Lella, *Wisdom of Ben Sira*, 511.

him into the cloud."[50] Ben Sira highlights Moses's personal agency in receiving divine revelation with the phrase בידו, rather than פנים בפנים or one of its variants. One wonders if Ben Sira felt some discomfort—already evident in some scriptural texts—at the implication that Moses saw God, as he specifies in v. 3b that Moses saw God's *glory*. Ben Sira's grandson, in any case, has no such qualms, and makes the allusion to this motif explicit by translating בידו with κατὰ πρόσωπον (45:5). Thus Ben Sira's praise of Moses focuses predominantly on his status as prophet without equal, one who was "like God" (45:2; cf Exod 7:1) and had unparalleled access to the divine.

3.3   Ben Sira's Construction of a Prophetic Succession

Ben Sira's interest in succession is evident with respect to each of Israel's offices.[51] Aaron and David are specifically mentioned as the recipients of "everlasting covenants" (Aaron: 45:7, 15, 25; David: 45:25), thereby establishing a genealogical principle for the offices of priest and king respectively (45:25). Ben Sira also emphasizes continuity in Israel's prophetic leadership, and draws on the language of Deuteronomy to do so.[52] Table 15 details Ben Sira's interest in prophetic succession in the *Laus Patrum*. Key terminology pertaining to the concept of prophetic succession and reflecting the influence of Moses's promise that a prophet like him would be "raised up" (קום/ἀνίστημι) is underlined. In constructing this prophetic chain, Ben Sira draws on scriptural terminology. He is both traditional and innovative, alluding to key phrases but utilizing them in a new context, in which the concept of a chronological Mosaic prophetic succession that begins with Joshua is more fully developed than in his sources. In his base text, it is only the last case (Elijah-Elisha) that is clearly marked as a transferal of the prophetic office; Ben Sira, however, has incorporated this solitary instance into a broader chronological framework for Mosaic prophecy.

---

50   On his "voice," see Deut 5:25, 27, 31; 18:16; on the "cloud," see Exod 20:21: ומשה נגש אל־הערפל.

51   See the comments of Burton L. Mack, *Wisdom and the Hebrew Epic: Ben Sira's Hymn in Praise of the Fathers*, CSHJ (Chicago: University of Chicago, 1985), 47–48; Hengel, *Judaism and Hellenism*, 1:136, calls this interest in succession "a striking feature ... by which the continuity of salvation history is guaranteed.... The continuity of the tradition, like the idea of inspiration, is meant to provide rational backing for the ancestral heritage and to support its authority."

52   See Pancratius Beentjes, "Prophets and Prophecy in the Book of Ben Sira," in *"Happy the One who Meditates on Wisdom" (Sir. 14,20): Collected Essays on the Book of Ben Sira*, CBET 43 (Leuven: Peeters, 2006), 207–229; here 213: "Chapters 46–49 in the Book of Ben Sira have been structured as a continuous story of prophets: Joshua (46:1), Samuel (46:13), Nathan (47:1), Elijah (48:1), Elisha (48:12)."

TABLE 15 The Mosaic prophetic succession in the *Laus Patrum*

Passage	Prophet(s)	Hebrew	Greek	English
46:1	Moses-Joshua	גבור בן חיל יהושע בן נון משרת משה בנבואה	κραταιὸς ἐν πολέμῳ Ἰησοῦς Ναυη καὶ διάδοχος Μωυσῆ ἐν προφητείαις	Joshua son of Nun was mighty in war, and was the successor of Moses in the prophetic office.
47:1	Samuel-Nathan	וגם אחרי עמד נתן להתיצב לפני דוד	καὶ μετὰ τοῦτον ἀνέστη Ναθαν προφητεύειν ἐν ἡμέραις Δαυιδ	After him Nathan rose up to prophesy in the days of David.
48:1a	Elijah	עד אשר קם נביא כאש	καὶ ἀνέστη Ηλιας προφήτης ὡς πῦρ	Then Elijah arose, a prophet like fire
48:8b, 12a	Elijah-Elisha	ונביא תחליף תחתיך	καὶ προφήτας διαδόχους μετ' αὐτόν	and prophets to succeed you.
			Ηλιας ὃς ἐν λαίλαπι ἐσκεπάσθη καὶ Ελισαιε ἐνεπλήσθη πνεύματος αὐτοῦ	When Elijah was enveloped in the whirlwind, Elisha was filled with his spirit.

The first departure from scriptural precedent occurs in Ben Sira's description of Joshua as Moses's successor in prophecy in 46:1. As Corley says, the description of Joshua's activity as "prophecy" is "rather unexpected," because the scriptural texts never refer to him as a "prophet," נביא.[53] Ben Sira does use a scriptural title for Joshua when he refers to him as "aide of Moses," משרת משה.[54] This title, moreover, has prophetic connotations, and it is used for Joshua in the context of the perceived threat to Moses's prophetic status posed by Eldad and Medad's prophesying (Num 11:28). Importantly, the verb שרת is also used after Elijah throws his mantle over Elisha (1 Kgs 19:19), summoning him as his successor: "Then he set out and followed Elijah, and became his servant (וישרתהו)" (1 Kgs 19:21bβ).[55] This helps to explain a peculiar feature of the grandson's translation

---

53 Corley, "Numerical Structure," 61.
54 See Exod 24:13; 33:11; Num 11:28; Josh 1:1. For a roughly contemporary usage of this title for Joshua, see also 4Q378 Frg. 22 i 2: ישוע משרת עבדך משה. See Carol Newsom, "Apocryphon of Joshua," in *Qumran Cave 4 XVII: Parabiblical Texts, Part 3*, DJD 22 (Oxford: Clarendon, 1996), 237–288, here 259.
55 Jeremy Corley, "Canonical Assimilation in Ben Sira's Portrayal of Joshua and Samuel," in *Rewriting Biblical History: Essays on Chronicles and Ben Sira in Honor of Pancratius C. Beentjes*, ed. J. Corley and H. van Grol, DCLS 7 (Berlin: De Gruyter, 2011), 57–77 (at 62), calls attention to this parallel, and cites Rudolf Smend, *Die Weisheit des Jesus Sirach erklärt* (Berlin: Reimer, 1906), 439 (trans. Corley): "the servant and helper of the prophet in his office is, like Elisha, also his successor."

of Sir 46:1, as διάδοχος does not represent משרת in any of the passages where that title is used for Joshua.[56] First Kings 19:21, however, provides precedent for understanding "aide" to connote "prophetic successor."[57]

What impetus is there for the description of Joshua as a prophet in this text? One explanation, offered by Beentjes, is that this is due to the ascription of the book of Joshua to a corpus of prophetic literature. As he says, "the description of Joshua in Sir 46:1 ... is a piece of evidence that in Ben Sira's time reckoning the Books of Joshua, Judges, Samuel and Kings to the 'Prophets' was already in the air."[58] The problem with this hypothesis is that it explains one conundrum (the description of Joshua as prophet) with reference to a literary classification that is not clearly articulated until a later period (as is evidenced by his phrase, "in the air"). If a causal relationship is to be posited here, it is more likely that the description of Joshua in prophetic terms (for which we have considerable evidence in the Second Temple period, as we will see) influenced the literary classification of the book, rather than *vice versa*.[59]

In my view, rather than resulting from the so-called prophetic "genre" of the book of Joshua, the combination in Sir 46:1 of two ideas, Joshua as prophet and Joshua as aide/successor to Moses, is a Hellenistic period interpretation of Deut 18:15.[60] Several considerations are important here. First, as shown above, Ben Sira's portrayal of Moses focuses on his role as unsurpassed prophet. His richly textured poetry contains subtle allusions to a wide range of biblical texts that emphasize Moses's role as Israel's divinely appointed intermediary. In this respect, it is important that in Sir 46:1 the noun נבואה primarily applies to

---

56 See Wright, *No Small Difference*, 153: "The use of διάδοχος by the grandson seems to reflect an idea about the continuance of the prophetic line. In this verse, Joshua succeeds Moses. Later in 47:1, Nathan follows Samuel, and in 48:12, Elisha follows Elijah. The presence of this scheme in Greek Sir precludes the notion of a different parent text for the grandson in this verse." It is interesting to note that the grandson may have amplified Ben Sira's emphasis on the concept of a prophetic succession.

57 Though it can also simply mean "attendant" (2 Kgs 4:43; 6:15).

58 Beentjes, "Prophets and Prophecy," 213.

59 Ariel Feldman, *The Rewritten Joshua Scrolls from Qumran: Texts, Translations, and Commentary*, BZAW 438 (Berlin: DeGruyter, 2013), 126–127, has made this point with respect to 4QTestimonia, which cites the *Joshua Apocryphon* (4Q379): "Perhaps, one could posit that 4QTestimonia's citation of Joshua's expanded curse reflects the widely accepted notion of Joshua as a prophet, rather than the Torah-like authority of the work preserved in 4Q379."

60 So Corley "Canonical Assimilation," 63; Helge Stadelmann, *Ben Sira als Schriftgelehrter: Eine Untersuchung zum Berufsbild des vor-makkabäischen Sōfēr unter Berücksichtigung seines Verhältnisses zu Priester-, Propheten- und Weisheitslehrertum*, WUNT 2/6 (Tübingen: Mohr [Paul Siebeck], 1980), 191: "hinter der Aussage Ben Siras in v. 1b eine Auslegung von Dt 18:15 steht, ... die jenen Vers in Josua erfüllt sein läßt: Er ist der angekündigte Nachfolger des sich hier also Propheten bezeichnenden Mose."

Moses's office, and secondarily to Joshua's. This ascription of prophetic status to Moses is most likely based on Deut 18:15, 18; 34:10, the only passages in the Hebrew Bible to explicitly use the prophetic title with reference to Moses. Second, because Ben Sira uses an abstract noun (that is, he does not call Joshua the aide to Moses "the prophet," but the aide to Moses "in prophecy"), he also meant this term to cover Joshua's role as Moses's successor.[61] In fact, Ben Sira inaugurates a tradition in which Joshua's prophetic status is asserted, in which it is intertwined with the issue of succession to Moses, often with the key term διάδοχος.

Ben Sira's interest in the continuity of this prophetic succession is signaled when he transitions from praise of Samuel to that of David by giving one verse to Nathan:

וגם אחרי עמד נתן להתיצב לפני דוד

καὶ μετὰ τοῦτον ἀνέστη Ναθαν προφητεύειν ἐν ἡμέραις Δαυιδ
Sir 47:1

Nathan is explicitly designated as "after him," i.e., Samuel. Ben Sira goes beyond his scriptural source by describing Nathan as Samuel's successor. Moreover, Ben Sira uses terminology reminiscent of Deut 18:15, 18 to position Nathan within a continuous succession of Mosaic prophets.[62] In keeping with this focus on this succession, Ben Sira incorporates allusions to the scriptural narratives pertaining to the transfer of Elijah's prophetic office to Elisha (Table 16).[63] In Sir 48:8b, Ben Sira refers to the singular instance of Elisha following Elijah, with נביא in the singular. His grandson, however, translates with a plural (προφήτας), suggesting a line of successors (διαδόχους). Further, in Sir 48:12, Ben Sira provides

---

61 Stadelmann, *Ben Sira als Schriftgelehrter*, 191.
62 Cf. Skehan and Di Lella, *Wisdom of Ben Sira*, 525: "By mentioning Nathan at the head of this part, Ben Sira calls attention to the succession of prophets in Israel from the time of Moses." It might be pointed out that Ben Sira uses עמד, not קום (cf. Deut 18:15, 18). For this substitution in Late Biblical Hebrew, see BDB, s.v. עמד 6a; see also Avi Hurvitz, "The Linguistic Status of Ben Sira as a Link between the Biblical and the Mishnaic Hebrew: Lexicographical Aspects," in *The Hebrew of the Dead Sea Scrolls and Ben Sira*, ed. T. Muraoka and J.F. Elwolde, STDJ 26 (Leiden: Brill, 1997), 71–85. Hurvitz compares Sir 47:1 with the use of קום in Deut 34:10 (78); see also his citation of *Mek.* to Exod 20:19, where קום is used in the lemma (Deut 18:18) and עמד in the surrounding commentary (83).
63 For this feature of Ben Sira's *Laus Patrum*, and other examples, see John G. Snaith, "Biblical Quotations in the Hebrew of Ecclesiasticus," *JTS* 18 (1967): 1–12; see 7–8: "In several places, and especially in the 'Praise of the Fathers,' Ben Sira used key words and phrases from the canonical passages to remind readers of the original, classical passage."

TABLE 16   Allusion to Elisha's succession of Elijah in the *Laus Patrum*

1 Kings 19:16b; 2 Kings 2:15aβ	Sir 48:8b, 12a
ואת־אלישע בן־שפט מאבל מחולה תמשח לנביא תחתיך	ונביא תחליף[a] תחתיך καὶ προφήτας διαδόχους μετ' αὐτόν
ויאמרו נחה רוח אליהו על־אלישע	Ηλιας ὃς ἐν λαίλαπι ἐσκεπάσθη καὶ Ελισαιε ἐνεπλήσθη πνεύματος αὐτοῦ
and you shall anoint Elisha son of Shaphat of Abel-meholah as prophet in your place	and a prophet as successor in your place and prophets as successors after him
And they said, "The spirit of Elijah rests on Elisha."	When Elijah was enveloped in the whirlwind, Elisha was filled with his spirit.

a   Mack, *Wisdom and the Hebrew Epic*, 46. On the term תחליף, Mack observes: "The double connotation of successor (in relation to the predecessor) and effective agent (in relation to contemporaries and descendents) is noteworthy as an indication of the principle of power or influence that is understood to reside in the meaning of succession itself."

an allusion to the biblical language of Elijah's "spirit" resting on or filling Elisha. Ben Sira therefore situates Elisha's succession of Elijah in the context of a much longer tradition of Mosaic prophecy. Indeed, Elijah himself, who appears on the scene rather suddenly and without warning in the DH (cf 1 Kgs 17:1), "arises" in turn as a Mosaic prophet in the *Laus Patrum* (עד אשר קם נביא כאש, 48:1a). Ben Sira situates Elijah in this succession and provides evidence of the view that the prophetic succession would return with Elijah's appearance at the "appointed time" (48:10). He signals this eschatological role at the outset of his portrayal of Elijah by alluding to Mal 3:19 in 48:1, and makes it explicit by the citation of Mal 3:24 in 48:10 (Table 17).[64]

Like the editors of the Book of the Twelve, Ben Sira holds that prophecy is a Mosaic institution that extended chronologically from Moses to Malachi. This succession seems to be closed in the present, so that Ben Sira's own teaching is said to be "like prophecy" (Sir 24:33): it is through reflection upon and interpretation of Scripture that prophecy is available in his day.[65] This is related to

---

64   So Snaith, "Biblical Quotations," 8.
65   See Hengel, *Judaism and Hellenism*, 1:134 (emphasis original): "On the one side he is a wisdom teacher who is to a strong degree indebted to the tradition, but on the other side his self-awareness goes beyond that of a mere trident and assumes *prophetic features* …. Just

TABLE 17   The eschatological Elijah in the *Laus Patrum*

Mal 3:19aα, 24a [Eng. 4:1aα, 6a]	Sir 48:1, 10abα
כי־הנה היום בא בער כתנור	עד אשר קם נביא כאש ודבריו כתנור בוער
	הכתוב נכון לעת להשבית אף לפנ[...]
והשיב לב־אבות על־בנים ולב בנים על־אבותם	להשיב לב אבות על בנים
See, the day is coming, burning like an oven	Until there arose a prophet like fire, and his words burned like an oven
He will turn the hearts of parents to their children and the hearts of children to their parents	At the appointed time, it is written, to calm the wrath before ... to turn the hearts of parents to their children

another motif that we find in Ben Sira, namely, the increasing tendency to align the prophetic succession with a scriptural corpus. This assimilation works in two ways. First, as Corley has noted, Ben Sira portrays figures that arise in the succession in light of each other: so Joshua's image is connected to Samuel's (and Moses's) by making him a prophet and intercessor, and Samuel's is aligned to Joshua's by emphasizing his military endeavors.[66] Corley also argues that Ben Sira "assimilates Joshua and Samuel backward to Moses and forward to David," and describes this as "the developing process of the formation of an authoritative tradition of Israelite religious heroes."[67] Second, it is noteworthy that Ben Sira's succession of prophets follows precisely those later included in the literary corpus of "prophets," נביאים (unless the textually uncertain reference to Job in 49:9 is meant to incorporate him into this succession).[68] Ben Sira's

---

as Simon the Just stands at the end of a series of the priestly and royal rulers of Israel, so the author himself concludes the sequence of prophets and wise men of the people." Similarly, Timothy H. Lim, *The Formation of the Jewish Canon*, AYBRL (New Haven: Yale University, 2011), 102–106, suggests on the basis of Sir 50:27 that Ben Sira may have included his own work in the prophetic collection.

66   See also Beentjes, "Prophets and Prophecy," 213: "It is significant that נבואה ... is the *first* characterization which Ben Sira uses to portray Samuel [cf. 46:13]. So doing the author reminds of the same noun that he used referring to Joshua and Moses (46:1)."
67   Corley, "Canonical Assimilation," 73.
68   He first discusses the so-called "former prophets," mentioning figures such as Joshua (46:1–8), the judges (46:11–12), Samuel (46:13–20), Elijah (48:1–10), and Elisha (48:12–14), and

"prophets," then, are at least co-extensive with the later division of נביאים. However, Ben Sira does not assert this as a "canonical" distinction, or assert that his corpus of prophetic literature was closed—that is to read his work with a question in mind that he has no interest in answering.[69] Rather, Ben Sira articulates the scribal doctrine implicit in the construction of Mal 3:22–24, namely, the authorized Mosaic prophetic succession is a matter of the past and future, not present, reality. In this period, the prophetic succession becomes increasingly scripturally aligned, but it is not yet considered definitively closed, either historically or canonically.

4 Conclusion

Malachi and Ben Sira redescribe two important earlier figures as prophets like Moses, Joshua and Elijah, even though they are not clearly marked as such (at least, in the Deuteronomic sense) in the scriptural narratives in which they appear. The redescription of Joshua in these terms reflects the scribal tendency in the Hellenistic and Roman era to assert that the Mosaic prophetic succession was continuously operative in Israel's scriptural past. This expansion of the concept of the Mosaic prophetic succession in the past will reach its zenith in Josephus's claim that there was an unbroken succession of prophets from Moses to Artaxerxes. By contrast, the incorporation of Elijah into the succession reflects the deferral of Mosaic prophecy to the eschatological future. In the

---

concluding this survey with a summary statement that is distinctly reminiscent of the Dtr view of prophecy (48:15–16; cf 2 Kgs 17:13–14). He then mentions Isaiah (48:23–25), Jeremiah (49:6–7), Ezekiel (49:8) and the Twelve (49:10).

69 See David M. Carr, *The Formation of the Hebrew Bible: A New Reconstruction* (New York: Oxford, 2011), 193 (emphasis added): "Ben Sira is not offering a summary of a sharply defined Scriptural canon of books. Instead, in his 'praise of our fathers,' Ben Sira praises a series of teaching father-figures of Israel's history organized *chronologically*, a series that ultimately leads up to his extensive praise of a more contemporary high priest, probably Simon the Second." See also Mack, *Wisdom and the Hebrew Epic*, 224–225. An opposing perspective is argued by Alon Goshen-Gottstein, "Ben Sira's Praise of the Fathers: A Canon-Conscious Reading," in *Ben Sira's God: Proceedings of the International Ben Sira Conference Durham—Ushaw College 2001*, ed. O. Kaiser, BZAW 321 (Berlin: de Gruyter, 2002), 235–267 (e.g., 243: "It seems to me that canonical awareness is the framework in which the Praise is best understood, rather than historical awareness .... [B]oth pedagogy and history are secondary to Ben Sira's true concern, which is to describe and reflect on the meaning of the canon"). Goshen-Gottstein makes a number of stimulating exegetical observations but falls short of fully sustaining this thesis; see the critical comments of Alexander Di Lella, "Ben Sira's Praise of the Ancestors of Old (Sir 44–49)," in *History and Identity: How Israel's Later Authors Viewed its Earlier History*, DCLY (Berlin: de Gruyter, 2006), 151–170, at 153.

next chapter, we will consider how both of these features of the priestly-scribal periodization of Mosaic prophecy influence other works of the Hellenistic and Roman era, including but not limited to 1 Maccabees and the texts from Qumran.

CHAPTER 8

"Until the Prophet Comes": Past and Future Prophets like Moses in Hellenistic and Roman-Era Judaism

1   Introduction

The priestly-scribal construct of the temporary cessation of the Mosaic prophetic succession is marked by a tendency to amplify the importance of Mosaic prophets in Israel's ancient past and to authorize a return of Mosaic prophecy in the eschatological future. In this chapter I explore the influence of this construct after its earliest articulations in Malachi and Ben Sira. In terms of the amplification of the Mosaic prophetic succession in the past, I highlight select texts subsequent to Ben Sira that portray Joshua as the prophet like Moses. I will also consider the classic texts from 1 Maccabees about the cessation and future return of Mosaic prophecy, and consider what evidence the Qumran corpus sheds on the idea of the past and future Mosaic prophet. This latter corpus provides evidence of the eschatological interpretation of Deut 18:15, 18, but I will argue that it does so in a highly circumscribed manner, within the framework of the priestly-scribal approach to past Mosaic prophecy.

2   The Prophet like Moses in the Historiographic Tradition

2.1   *Joshua as the Prophet like Moses*
2.1.1   Eupolemus

The characterization of Joshua in prophetic terms, often using the key word "successor" (διάδοχος),[1] recurs in a number of texts subsequent to Ben Sira.[2] To be sure, not all of these texts are priestly, but they reflect the influence of

---

1   Cf also Philo, *Virt.* 68.
2   On the characterization of Joshua, see Zev I. Farber, *Images of Joshua in the Bible and Their Reception* BZAW 457 (Berlin: De Gruyter, 2016). The Hellenistic period characterization of Joshua as a prophet has been discussed by Ed Noort, "Joshua: The History of Reception and Hermeneutics," in *Past, Present, Future: The Deuteronomistic History and the Prophets*, ed. J.C. de Moor and H.F. van Rooy, OtSt 44 (Leiden: Brill, 2000), 199–215; Katell Berthelot, "The Image of Joshua in Jewish Sources from the Second Temple Period," *Meghillot* 8–9 (2010): 97–112 [Hebrew].

the priestly-scribal construal of Mosaic prophecy in Hellenistic and Roman-era Judaism. The earliest occurs a generation after Ben Sira, in a quotation from Eupolemus, a Hellenistic Jewish historian who probably wrote in the middle of the second century.[3] The quotation comes to Eusebius via Alexander Polyhistor's "On the Jews"; and despite misunderstandings which may have emerged in the tradition, it seems to give access to Eupolemus' history.

> And Eupolemus says in a certain "On the Prophecy of Elijah" that Moses prophesied for forty years. Then Joshua the son of Nun prophesied for thirty years; he lived one hundred and ten years and pitched the sacred tabernacle in Shiloh. After this Samuel was prophet. (Eusebius, *Prep. Ev.* 9.30.1–2)[4]

Here the earliest leaders of Israel are characterized as prophets, so that before there was any king in Israel the succession of leaders was one of prophets. As Fallon notes, the "omission of the period of the judges is striking."[5] Though it is hazardous to venture a hypothesis about why this is, it has the effect of emphasizing the continuity in Israel's pre-monarchic prophetic leadership.[6]

2.1.2 The Joshua Apocryphon

The Apocryphon of Joshua is a text preserved in various fragments at Qumran. Though the exact number of fragments included in the work is debated, it seems to preserve a rewriting of the transition between Deuteronomy and Joshua, as well as portions of the book of Joshua. Feldman has identified two features of this rewriting that are significant for our purposes: its levitical-priestly milieu, and its portrayal of Joshua as the prophet like Moses of Deut 18:15, 18.[7] It is noteworthy that the prophetic profile of Joshua is not limited to one part of the work, but is found in fragments from multiple scrolls (4Q378, 4Q379, 5Q22). In the first of these, Joshua becomes an exponent of Mosaic Discourse, as he is portrayed as speaking to the people in messages largely taken

---

3 F. Fallon, "Eupolemus: A New Translation and Introduction," in *The Old Testament Pseudepigrapha*, ed. J. Charlesworth (Garden City: Doubleday, 1983), 2:861–872, dates Eupolemus' composition to 158/7 BCE.
4 The translation is that of Fallon, "Eupolemus."
5 Fallon, "Eupolemus," 866.
6 So Wayne Meeks, *The Prophet-King: Moses Traditions and the Johannine Christology*, NovTSup 14 (Leiden: Brill, 1967), 150.
7 See Ariel Feldman, *The Rewritten Joshua Scrolls from Qumran: Texts, Translations, and Commentary*, BZAW 438 (Berlin: De Gruyter, 2013), 69, 73, on Joshua's portrayal as prophet like Moses; 126, 199, on the levitical-priestly milieu.

from Deuteronomy.⁸ Though the text is fragmentary, it appears to emphasize both Joshua's role as prophetic agent of salvation and successor to Moses:

2 ביד ישוע משרת משה 3 [...] דך ביד משה על ישוע למען עמך

through the hand of Joshua, minister of your servant Moses ... your ... through the hand of Moses to Joshua, on behalf of your people
4Q378 frag 22 lines 2–3⁹

The portrayal of Joshua in prophetic terms is also found in 4Q379. He utters an intercessory prayer, possibly in response to the sin of Achan.¹⁰ More importantly, it contains the rewriting of Joshua's curse upon the rebuilder of Jericho (Josh 6:24–26), which is quoted as an authoritative prophecy in 4Q175, a text that also includes an eschatological interpretation of Deut 18:15, 18.¹¹ Finally, in 5Q22 frag. 9 Joshua prophesies about the coming of David and provides a prophetic justification for why the tabernacle was not located at Jerusalem immediately after the conquest.¹² Although much remains unclear regarding the overall scope and purpose of the composition, it provides important documentation of the tradition of Joshua's prophetic status traced here.

2.1.3 The *Testament of Moses*

The *Testament of Moses* does not call Joshua a prophet, but it does draw a prophetic portrait of Moses and draws on the concept of a Mosaic succession (διαδοχή), so that its evidence is worthy of inclusion here. The text understands Moses in prophetic terms (cf. 11:16) and specifically refers to Deuteronomy as Moses's prophetic discourse (1:5). In this context, the *Testament of Moses* refers to the succession of Moses by Joshua: "Moses called to himself Joshua, the son of Nun, a man approved by the Lord, that Joshua might become the minister for the people in the tent of testimony" (*Test. Mos.* 1:6–7).¹³ Priest translates

---

8   See Devorah Dimant, "Two Discourses from the Apocryphon of Joshua and Their Context (4Q378 3 i–ii)," *RevQ* 23 (2007): 43–61, at 58 she speaks of "the author's wish to link Joshua's words, both thematically and ideologically, to the legacy of his mentor Moses."
9   See Feldman, *Rewritten Joshua Scrolls*, 59.
10 See 4Q379 frag 18; Feldman, *Rewritten Joshua Scrolls*, 95–97.
11 Feldman, *Rewritten Joshua Scrolls*, 119, notes that the rewritten text presents the curse as a prophecy rather than an oath.
12 For the text and translation, see Feldman, *Rewritten Joshua Scrolls*, 142–144.
13 Translations from the *Testament of Moses* are taken from J. Priest, "Testament of Moses: A New Translation and Introduction," in *The Old Testament Pseudepigrapha*, ed. J. Charlesworth (Garden City: Doubleday, 1983), 1:920–934.

the Latin "successor" with the term "minister," but notes that the Greek διάδοχος probably lies behind this term.[14] Moses returns to the characterization of Joshua as his successor at the conclusion of his prophetic speech that details the future course of history, saying, "Therefore, you, Joshua son of Nun, be strong; for God has chosen you to be my successor in the same covenant (te elegit deus esse mihi successorem eiusdem testamenti)" (*Test. Mos.* 10:15). Following this, Joshua laments his inadequacy for the task in comparison with the great Moses, who is "the divine prophet for the whole earth" (*Test. Mos* 11:16). The text's portrayal of Moses in prophetic terms and its emphasis on Joshua as Moses's successor suggests that it provides auxiliary evidence for this interpretive tradition.

2.1.4   The *Biblical Antiquities* of Pseudo-Philo

The *Biblical Antiquities* of Pseudo-Philo also understand Joshua as Moses's successor in prophecy. Moses himself is understood as the "first of all the prophets" (*L.A.B.* 35:6; cf 53:8).[15] And in his farewell speech, Moses tells the Israelites that they will despair of having a leader like him:

> But then you and all your sons and all your generations will rise up after you and lament the day of my death and say in their heart, "Who will give us another shepherd like Moses or such a judge for the sons of Israel to pray always for our sins and be heard for our iniquities?"
>
> *L.A.B.* 19:3

In Pseudo-Philo's account, however, the cry for a shepherd "like Moses" is answered in the person of Joshua, whose stature is elevated,[16] and who is given

---

14   Priest, "Testament," 1:927. Howard M. Teeple, *The Mosaic Eschatological Prophet*, JBLMS 10 (Philadelphia: Society of Biblical Literature, 1957), 50, suggests dependence on Deut 18:15 here, and also cites R.H. Charles as holding this view, see his *The Apocrypha and Pseudepigrapha of the Old Testament*, 2 vols. (Oxford: Clarendon Press, 1913), 2:412, 423.

15   Translations of Pseudo-Philo are taken from Daniel J. Harrington, "Pseudo-Philo: A New Translation and Introduction," in *The Old Testament Pseudepigrapha* (ed. J. Charlesworth; Garden City: Doubleday, 1983), 2:297–377. For the Latin text, see Howard Jacobson, *A Commentary on Pseudo-Philo's* Liber Antiquitatum Biblicarum: *With Latin Text and English Translation*, 2 vols., AGJU 31 (Leiden: Brill, 1996). With respect to this phrase, Jacobson comments (2:918): "Perhaps LAB simply means 'foremost' (cf especially Deut 34:10). But he may well have written and meant 'first,' in spite of passages like Gen 20:7 referring to Abraham as a prophet." As we will see in the next chapter, Josephus also downplays prophecy before Moses.

16   So Noort, "Joshua," 204 (emphasis original): "With Pseudo-Philo Joshua is revalued. He is the ideal, *equivalent* successor to Moses."

a distinctly prophetic characterization.[17] Indeed, God's first words to Joshua after the death of Moses develop this profile:

> Then God said to Joshua the son of Nun, "Why do you mourn and why do you hope in vain that Moses yet lives? And now you wait to no purpose, because Moses is dead. Take his garments of wisdom and clothe yourself, and with his belt of knowledge gird your loins, and you will be changed and become another man."
>
> L.A.B. 20:2

The biblical idiom of being changed and becoming another man is an allusion to 1Sam 10:6, which says of Saul: "Then the Spirit of the LORD will be strong on you and you will prophesy with them and be changed to another man (צלחה עליך רוח יהוה והתנבית עמם ונהפכת לאיש אחר)."[18] L.A.B.'s use of the motif here is therefore an indication that the author understands Joshua to be a prophet. However, in Pseudo-Philo, this prophetic characterization is linked to and dependent on Joshua's taking up of Moses's "garments of wisdom": it is as the successor of Moses that he becomes a prophet.[19] L.A.B. goes on to develop its (brief) account of Joshua by portraying him in Moses's image, for example, adding a prayer in which he intercedes for Israel on account of their sinfulness (L.A.B. 21:2–6).[20] Later, before Joshua dies, God appears to him in a dream (L.A.B. 23:3), so that Joshua's final speech is reframed as a prophetic discourse. Finally, after Joshua dies, the Israelites lament him, concluding their

---

17 See Feldman, *Rewritten Joshua Scrolls*, 14.
18 Zev Farber, "Images of Joshua: the Construction of Memory in Cultural Identities" (Ph.D. Diss.: Emory, 2013), 222, notes the allusion to 1Sam 10:6, but fails to perceive its relevance for Joshua's prophetic characterization, instead interpreting in light of his suggestion that Joshua feels unprepared for his task. Jacobson, *Commentary*, 2:661, also notes the allusion but does not interpret in terms of prophetic status.
19 Farber, "Images of Joshua," 221: "God … suggests that Joshua can become a second Moses if he puts on Moses's clothes, a suggestion as bizarre as it is unprecedented." It is not unprecedented, in terms of prophetic succession, as the story of Elijah throwing his mantle over Elisha shows (1Kgs 19:19). John Levison, *The Spirit in First Century Judaism*, AGJU 29 (Leiden: Brill, 1997), 99–101, recognizes the significance of the allusion to 1Sam 10:6 for Joshua's prophetic status, and also claims that the "metaphor of clothing in this scene ought also to be interpreted as a signal for the spirit," pointing to L.A.B. 27:10, 36:2; Jdg 6:34.
20 On Joshua as intercessor, see also Sir 46:5; Jeremy Corley, "Canonical Assimilation in Ben Sira's Portrayal of Joshua and Samuel," in *Rewriting Biblical History: Essays on Chronicles and Ben Sira in Honor of Pancratius C. Beentjes*, ed. J. Corley and H. van Grol, DCLS 7 (Berlin: De Gruyter, 2011), 57–77, at 64–67.

speech with the following question: "And who will go and tell the just Moses that we have had a leader like him [*ducem simil ei*] for forty years?" (*L.A.B.* 24:6).[21] Joshua is therefore understood as the prophet like Moses who leads the people as the successor of Moses, the servant of God.[22]

In sum, the portrayal of Joshua as the prophet like Moses is one of the most striking features of the periodization of Mosaic prophecy. It reflects its antiquarian and historiographic orientation, as well as the tendency towards the "scripturalization" of the Mosaic succession, that is to say, its delimitation by the priestly-scribal class. I will argue in the next chapter that Josephus inherits and expands upon this tradition identifying Joshua as the first prophet like Moses. Before turning to Josephus, however, I turn to other evidence that the Mosaic prophetic succession was viewed as a past and future phenomenon by considering 1 Maccabees and the Qumran corpus.

2.2 Prophets Past and Future in 1 Maccabees

The three passages from 1 Maccabees quoted below have played an important role in the discussion of the so-called cessation of prophecy in ancient Judaism. They are also particularly salient in terms of reflecting the influence of Deut 18:15, 18, especially with respect to a future expected prophet. Here are the texts:

> (44) They deliberated what to do about the altar of burnt offering, which had been profaned. (45) And they thought it best to tear it down, so that it would not be a lasting shame to them that the Gentiles had defiled it. So they tore down the altar, (46) and stored the stones in a convenient place on the temple hill until a prophet should come to tell what to do with them (μέχρι τοῦ παραγενηθῆναι προφήτην τοῦ ἀποκριθῆναι περὶ αὐτῶν).
> 1 Macc 4:44–46

> So there was great distress in Israel, such as had not been since the time that prophets ceased to appear among them (ἀφ' ἧς ἡμέρας οὐκ ὤφθη προφήτης αὐτοῖς).
> 1 Macc 9:27[23]

---

21 Farber, "Images of Joshua," 219: "Clearly, the author would like to draw a parallel between the leadership of Joshua and the leadership of Moses"; Jacobson, *Commentary*, 2:735: "There is probably some influence here from Deut 18:15, 18."
22 It is worth pointing out that in *L.A.B.* there is, if not a "continuous succession," a definite increase in prophetic activity between Moses and Samuel, relative to its biblical sources. For example, Kenaz, the leader after Joshua, has a prophetic profile (28:6), and there are other prophets attested in his time (e.g., 28:1, 3; 30:5).
23 1 Macc 9:27 is a rather strange passage. It is unclear what it means to date a period of time

> The Jews and their priests have resolved that Simon should be their leader and high priest forever, until a trustworthy prophet should arise (ἕως τοῦ ἀναστῆναι προφήτην πιστόν)
>
> 1 Macc 14:41

An allusion to Deut 18:15, 18 appears in the last passage,[24] which speaks of a trustworthy prophet "arising" (MT: קום; LXX: ανιστήμι) and stipulates that this prophet will be "trustworthy" (πιστός), reminiscent of Moses and of significant prophets after him (Num 12:7; 1 Sam 3:20).[25]

---

from the *absence* of something; moreover, the precise temporal indicator (the Babylonian exile? the work of Haggai and Zechariah? [cf 9:54]) remains unclear (see discussion, with references, in L. Stephen Cook, *On the Question of the "Cessation of Prophecy" in Ancient Judaism*, TSAJ 145 [Tübingen: Mohr Siebeck, 2011], 68–70). John R. Levison, "Did the Spirit Withdraw from Israel? An Evaluation of the Earliest Jewish Data," *NTS* 43 (1997): 35–57, at 39–40, argues that the time period since the failure of a prophet to appear is marked by tranquility, not by a complete absence of prophets (here 40):

> The translation of 1 Macc 9:27, therefore, to indicate "… the disappearance of prophecy among them" (NJB) is due to a confusion of the events of a particular moment in time and the events which took place thereafter. In 1 Macc 9:27, the detail that a prophet did not appear enables the readers to identify the particular day of distress to which the author refers, from which point relative tranquility can be dated.

A similar interpretation to Levison's is advanced by Frederick Greenspahn, "Why Prophecy Ceased," *JBL* 108 (1989): 37–49, at 40. Levison is certainly right that NJB's translation is too strong (so also Cook, *Cessation of Prophecy*, 70n79). What Levison does not point out is that this temporal specification presupposes that in the time since "a prophet did not appear," no prophet has in fact appeared—otherwise the readers would not in fact know what time is meant. Jonathan Goldstein, *1 Maccabees: A New Translation with Introduction and Commentary*, AB 41 (Garden City, N.Y.: Doubleday, 1976), 48, takes the mention of a "time of distress" as an allusion to Dan 12:1, and therefore thinks the reference to a prophet failing to appear is an attack against Daniel's failed oracle of resurrection. The verse is therefore a "bitter attack against false prophets" (376). This interpretation is speculative.

24 See M. Philonenko, " 'Jusqu' à ce que lève un prophète digne de confiance' (1 Maccabées 14,41)," in *Messiah and Christos. Studies in the Jewish Origins of Christianity Presented to David Flusser*, ed. I. Gruenwald, S. Shaked, and G. Stroumsa (Tübingen: Mohr Siebeck, 1992), 95–98. Philonenko argues that the title προφήτης πιστός derives from the "rapprochement" of Deut 18:15, 18 and Num 12:7.

25 Matthias Henze, "Invoking the Prophets in Zechariah and Ben Sira," in *Prophets, Prophecy, and Prophetic Texts in Second Temple Judaism*, ed. M.H. Floyd and R.D. Haak, LHB/OTS 427 (New York: T&T Clark, 2006), 120–134, notes (121), "The emphasis here is on 'trustworthy'." This statement should thus be considered within the framework of the general tendency within Hellenistic Judaism to address the ambiguity inherent in the Hebrew term נביא. The most well-known example of this is the LXX neologism ψευδοπροφήτης, which occurs

Building on this allusion, several considerations suggest that the author is referring in these passages to the temporary cessation and future return of the Mosaic prophetic succession. First, these three passages all occur within temporal clauses (μέχρι, 4:46; ἀφ' ἧς ἡμέρας, 9:27; ἕως, 14:41), which taken together understand prophecy as a phenomenon of the past and potentially the future. Second, it should be noted that they each occur at significant transitional moments in the narrative: the rededication of the temple (4:36–60), the death of Judas and conferral of leadership upon his younger brother Jonathan (9:18–31), and the decree confirming Simon as "leader and high priest forever" (14:27–45). The author is aware of the absence of prophets particularly when decisions of national importance were being made. These decisions are both halakhic (4:44–46) and political (9:28–31; 14:41). A prophet that can declaim Torah and bestow legitimacy on Israel's authorized ruler (cf, e.g., 1 Kgs 1:45–46, 19:15–16) is the prophet who fills the Mosaic office of Deut 18:15–22 and serves within the framework of Israel's political leadership.[26]

The final reference to the future prophet ought to be understood in light of the author's recognition that acquiescence to the legitimacy of Hasmonean leadership was far from universal among his contemporaries. The author is stridently pro-Hasmonean, portraying figures such as Judas as a leader analogous to heroic biblical figures of the past, especially David.[27] This repristination of the ancient ideal made the contemporary absence of trustworthy prophets particularly problematic. The author allows that Simon's leadership may be qualified (or confirmed) by the ruling of a future prophet—perhaps hoping to mollify critics of the Hasmoneans—and portrays the potential arising of a prophet as an expected and possible feature of the present order.[28] Therefore, the expectation of a future prophet is not an eschatological interpretation of

---

ten times (Jer 6:13, 33:7, 8, 11, 16; 34:9; 35:1; 36:1, 8; Zech 13:2) and is taken up in the NT (Matt 7:15; 24:11, 24; Mark 13:22; Luke 6:26; Acts 13:6; 2 Pet 2:1; 1 John 4:1; Rev 16:13; 19:20; 20:10). See also the similar phenomenon at Qumran, e.g., נביאי כזב in 1QHª 12:16.

26 See David Aune, *Prophecy in Early Christianity and the Ancient Mediterranean World* (Grand Rapids: Eerdmans, 1983), 105: "The type of prophecy reflected in 1 Macc 4:45b–46 and 14:41 is 'clerical' prophecy, i.e. a type of early Jewish prophecy which assumes that prophetic gifts are coextensive with the priestly-political leadership of the nation."

27 See, e.g., 1 Macc 2:29–30, 51–68; 3:1–9, 18–22, 58–60; 4:8–11, 17–18, 24–25. On 1 Maccabees "biblical" style, see Goldstein, *1 Maccabees*, 77–78, and his judgment (at 78): "First Maccabees is both a presumptuous work and a stylistic tour de force."

28 Goldstein, *1 Maccabees*, 508: "The proviso, 'until a true prophet should arise,' represents a compromise between the Hasmonaean party and other sects .... The proviso here also surely reflects the practice in the times of the Israelite kingdoms: the founder of an Israelite dynasty should receive designation from a true prophet."

Deut 18:15, 18.[29] Rather, in light of the author's pro-Hasmonean agenda, the coming of a prophet would be a natural feature of Israel's re-constitution as an independent state. The restoration of the Mosaic office is expected as eminently possible within the near future, as a decision about what to do with the stones of the defiled altar is deferred to the judgment of that figure. 1 Maccabees provides evidence of the interpretation of Deut 18:15, 18 as referring to past and future prophets, but does not associate the return of a Mosaic prophet with the day of Yhwh, as Malachi does.

3   The Prophet like Moses at Qumran

3.1   *Prophets and Prophecy at Qumran*

The finds from Cave One included the remarkable *pesher* to Habakkuk, and so from its beginning Qumran scholarship has been aware of the importance of prophets and prophecy in the thought of the Qumran community. As Barstad rightly says, "Qumran society was altogether saturated with prophecy."[30] Though a comprehensive distillation of the data pertaining to prophecy at Qumran was long a *desideratum* for scholarship, this would await the published dissertation of Alex Jassen, who thoroughly surveys Qumran material relevant to prophecy and situates it in its broader Early Jewish context.[31] Jassen comments on the somewhat restricted use of the term נביא at Qumran, a usage that is consonant with the priestly-scribal tradition traced above, in which Mosaic prophets are a feature of the past and potentially the future, but not typically the present:

> The Qumran library ... rarely contains any explicit reference to contemporary prophets and their assumed prophetic roles. Rather, the overwhelming majority of references to individuals with prophetic designations are to prophets from Israel's biblical heritage.[32]

---

29   So Aune, *Prophecy in Early Christianity*, 105; John Barton, *Oracles of God: Perceptions of Ancient Prophecy in Israel after the Exile*, 2nd ed. (New York: Oxford, 2007 [1986]), 107; Levison, "Did the Spirit Withdraw," 41–42; Cook, *Cessation of Prophecy*, 68.

30   Hans Barstad, "Prophecy at Qumran?" in *In the Last Days: On Jewish and Christian Apocalyptic and its Period*, ed. K. Jeppesen, K. Nielsen, and B. Rosendal (Aarhus: Aarhus University, 1994), 104–120; here 104.

31   Alex P. Jassen, *Mediating the Divine: Prophecy and Revelation in the Dead Sea Scrolls and Second Temple Judaism*, STDJ 68 (Leiden: Brill, 2007).

32   Jassen, *Mediating the Divine*, 25.

Similarly, Hans Barstad's full review of the term נביא in the Qumran corpus shows that it is predominantly used to refer to prophets of Israel's past.[33] In the confines of my limited focus, I will discuss here only those Qumran texts that cite or allude to Deut 18:15–22. How was Moses' promise that God would raise up a prophet like him understood at Qumran? The profile of Deut 18:15,18 is perhaps not as prominent as we might expect in the Dead Sea Scrolls, given the importance of prophecy to the community's self-understanding. Nevertheless, the text does exert influence at Qumran, first of all on the portrayal of Moses himself, but also on the view of past prophets at Qumran and in the expectation of a future, eschatological prophet attested there.

3.2   The Portrayal of Moses as Supreme Prophet in 4Q377

According to James Bowley, Moses is the biblical figure mentioned most often in the sectarian texts at Qumran.[34] In view of this, his later observation that there is comparatively little interest in Moses' biography at Qumran is rather striking.[35] Moses' role as the charismatic leader of Israel's exodus is undoubtedly assumed, but not reflected on or asserted as a normative pattern. Rather, at Qumran Moses' status as chief revelatory agent—that is, his prophetic role as bearer of the words of God—has come to outstrip by far all other roles in importance.[36] The texts contain ample references to God speaking to (and through)

---

33   Barstad, "Prophecy at Qumran?," 120: "Our main conclusion, then, must be that we have hardly found one single text which unambiguously supports the information provided by Josephus: that there were some people among the Essenes 'who engage in the foretelling of things to come'." It should be noted, however, that the circumspect use of the term נביא in the Qumran corpus is precisely paralleled by Josephus.

34   James E. Bowley, "Moses in the Dead Sea Scrolls: Living in the Shadow of God's Anointed," in *The Bible at Qumran: Text, Shape, and Interpretation*, ed. P. Flint, SDSSRL (Grand Rapids: Eerdmans, 2001), 159–181, here 159. George J. Brooke, "Moses in the Dead Sea Scrolls: Looking at Mount Nebo from Qumran," in *La Construction de la Figure de Moïse/The Construction of the Figure of Moses*, ed. T. Römer, *Transeuphratène* Supplement 13 (Paris: Gabalda, 2007), 209–221, (at 209–210) provides a review of the data and claims, "it is easy to conclude that relatively speaking there is far more interest in Moses in the Qumran non-biblical literary corpus, than there is in David who plays such a statistically prominent role in the Hebrew Bible" (210).

35   Bowley, "Moses," 171: "What we do not observe is a biographical interest in Moses, recounting his role in the history of Israel or his position among ancient lawgivers such as we have among Greco-Jewish writers of the same period. We find no interest in Moses' childhood, with its intriguing narratives of survival via a miniature ark on the Nile and life in the Egyptian palace." See also Brooke, "Moses," 216.

36   The few examples Bowley, "Moses," 170–173, gives of interest in Moses' biography conform to this. He notes CD 5:17–19, which contrasts Moses and Aaron to the magicians Jannes and Jambres; 4Q374 frg. 2 2:6, which refers to Moses as being made "like God" to Pharaoh

Moses.[37] In many of these texts the phrase "by the hand of Moses," ביד מושה, is used, which indicates his prophetic instrumentality as conduit of the divine commands.[38]

Specific titles are not often applied to Moses in the Qumran corpus. 4Q377, which dates to the first century BCE,[39] is a unique text in this regard, containing several epithets in close connection: Messiah (משיח, line 5), man of God (איש האלוהים, line 10), angel (מלאך, line 11), messenger (מבשר, line 11), and man of piety (איש חסדים, line 12). This text makes explicit assumptions about Moses' status and role that otherwise often remain implicit.[40] Though scholars have focused on the possible deification of Moses in this work, it in fact rewrites scriptural topoi that reflect on Moses' status as supreme prophet.[41] Here is the DJD text and translation of 4Q377 frg. 2 2:2–12:

2 יבינו בחוקות מושה vacat [   ]
3 ויען אליבֿחֿ[ ] ויֿ[אמר שמ֗]עיֿ [עֿדת יהוה והקשב כול הקהל]oooo[ ]ם֗[ ]
4 לֿ [ ]oo [ ]oošoo[ ]יֿ[ ] vacat ארור האיש אשר לוא יעמוד וישמור ויעֿ[שה]
5 לכול מ֗[ ]oo[ ]oo בפי מושה משיחו וללכת אחר יהוה אלוהי אבותינו המֿ[   ]oo[
6 לנו מהר סינ]יֿ[ ] vacat וֿיֿדֿבֿרֿ עֿ[ם]קהל ישראל פנים עם אל פנים כאשר ידבר

(cf Exod 7:1); and 4Q504 frg. 1 2:7–10, which refers to Moses' intercession for Israel. These three examples of interest in Moses' "biography" also highlight his prophetic role. See also Brooke, "Moses," 212: "Over against the Enoch literature, which can be read as deliberately anti-Mosaic, the majority view of Moses in the Qumran library is one in which he acts as a pivotal focus as a mediator of the Law and a channel of the covenant."

37 See Bowley, "Moses," 169–170, with references to 1QM 10:6, 1QS 1:2–3, 8:15; CD 5:21; 4Q252 frg. 1 4:2; 4Q377 frg. 2 2:5.

38 See, e.g., 1QHa 4:24; 4Q382 frg. 104 2:7; 4Q504 frg. 4 2:8; 4Q504 frg. 3 2:14; 4Q504 frg. 1–2 5:14.

39 James C. VanderKam and Monica Brady, "4QApocryphal Pentateuch B," in *Qumran Cave 4 XXVIII: Miscellanea, Part 2*, DJD 28 (Oxford: Clarendon, 2001), 205–217, here 206: "100–50 BCE, with a date earlier in this period more likely."

40 To illustrate: if we did not have 4Q377, there would no precedent for calling Moses a משיח at Qumran. But the thought is surely implicit in CD 5:21–6:1: ביד משה וגם במשיחו הקודש. See the comments on this title in VanderKam and Brady, "4QApocryphal Pentateuch B," 215.

41 For a discussion of the divine/angelic attributes of Moses, see Crispin H.T. Fletcher-Louis, *All the Glory of Adam: Liturgical Anthropology in the Dead Sea Scrolls*, STDJ 42 (Leiden: Brill, 2002), 136–149. See the criticisms of Fletcher-Louis by Brooke, "Moses," 214–215, 221; Wido van Peursen, "Who was Standing on the Mountain? The Portrait of Moses in 4Q377," in *Moses in Biblical and Extra-Biblical Traditions*, ed. A. Graupner and M. Wolter, BZAW 372 (Berlin: de Gruyter, 2007), 99–114; Phoebe Makiello, "Was Moses Considered to be an Angel by those at Qumran?" in *Moses in Biblical and Extra-Biblical Traditions*, ed. A. Graupner and M. Wolter, BZAW 372 (Berlin: de Gruyter, 2007), 115–127. In agreement with these latter scholars, my view is that the text does not assert such status for Moses.

7 איש עם רעהו וכא̇[ש]ר̇ [ ]ש̇oo [ ]ר̇ הראני באש בעורה ממעלה [מ]שמים
[ ] vacat
8 ועל הא̇ר̇ץ עמד על ההר להודיע̇ כיא אין אלוה מ̇ב̇לעדיו ואין צור כמוהו [ ]
9 הקהל{ה̇ע̇ד̇}ה̇ [ע̇]נ̇ו ורעדודיה אתזתם מלפני כבוד אלוהים ומקולו̇ת הפלא
10 ויעמודו מרוחק vacat ומושה איש האלוהים עם אלוהים בענן ויכס
11 עליו הענן כיא [ ]o [בהקדשו וכמלאך ידבר מפיהו כיא מי מבש]ר̇ [כמ̇ו̇ה̇ו
12 איש חסדים ויו[ ]o [ם אשר לוא נבראו̇ {ל}מעולם ולע̇ד̇]oooo [ ]ooo

2 and they will have understanding in the statutes of Moses *vacat* [ ]

3 And Elibah[ ]answered [and] said: He[ar], congregation of Yhwh, and pay attention, all the assembly [ ]

4 to [ ] [ ][ ] *vacat* Cursed is the one who will not stand and keep and d[o]

5 all *m*[ ]⁴² though the mouth of Moses his anointed one, and to follow Yhwh, the God of our fathers, who [ ]

6 to us from Mount Sin[ai] *vacat* And he spoke wi[th]the assembly of Israel face to face as a man speaks

7 with his friend and a[s] [ ] He showed us in a fire burning above [from] heaven *vacat* [ ]

8 and on the earth; he stood on the mountain, to make known that there is no god beside him and there is no rock like him. [ ]

9 the assembly {the congrega[tion}]they answered. Trembling seized them before the glory of God and because of the wondrous sounds, [ ]

10 and they stood at a distance. *vacat* And Moses, the man of God, was with God in the cloud. And the cloud covered

11 him because [ ] when he was sanctified, and like a messenger he would speak from his mouth, for who is a mess[enger]⁴³ like him,

---

42 Ariel Feldman, "The Sinai Revelation according to 4Q377 (*Apocryphal Pentateuch B*)," DSD 18 (2011): 155–172, at 157, restores "commandments of Yhwh" here.

43 VanderKam and Brady, "4QApocryphal Pentateuch B," 214, and Fletcher-Louis, *All the Glory of Adam*, 142, translate "who of fles[h]." See the comments of VanderKam and Brady, "4QApocryphal Pentateuch B," 216: "If the word at the end of line 11 is correctly deciphered, it expresses the incomparability of Moses .... In the context this seems more likely than understanding מבש]ר as a *Pi'el* participle." In my view, the prolific use of titles for Moses in the text favors reading "messenger," rather than "from flesh." More speculatively, one could suggest that מכל should have been used, if the comparison was with humanity in general (see מכל [בשר] in Sir 45:4). See Géza G. Xeravits, *King, Priest, Prophet: Positive Eschatological Protagonists of the Qumran Library*, STDJ 47 (Leiden: Brill, 2003), 126, on מבשר as a prophetic designation.

12 a man of faithfulness and [   ] who were not created {to} from eternity and forever [ ]

The text is a speech of Elibah, אליבח (line 3). This otherwise unknown figure reminds the congregation of the obligations they took on in the Sinai revelation, specifically, "to keep and to do" the law (line 4; cf. Exod 24:7; Deut 4:6, 7:12). The speech goes on to reflect on Israel's inability to receive continued exposure to the divine presence, and their concomitant need for Mosaic mediation, which is a theme both in Deuteronomy's appointment of Moses to speak God's word to the people and in its subsequent provision for a prophet like Moses (Deut 5:23–31; 18:16–17). Initially the people hear the words of God directly, and 4Q377 applies to the assembled Israelites what in the Pentateuch is a description of Moses, namely that he spoke with God "as a man speaks with his friend" (lines 6–7; cf Exod 33:11).[44] After this, the text recounts the appointment of Moses, whom it has already identified as God's Messiah (line 5):

> And they stood at a distance. And Moses, the man of God, was with God in the cloud. And the cloud covered him because [ ] when he was sanctified, and like an angel he spoke from his mouth (וכמלאך ידבר מפיהו). For who is a messenger like him (כמוהו)?
>
> 4Q377 2 ii 10–11

Particularly of interest for our purposes is the text's usage of כ־, "like," to indicate Moses' incomparable status as prophet. Positively, Moses is said to be "like an angel" as the mediator of the words of God.[45] Moses' incomparability as a prophet is also reflected in the rhetorical question "who is a messenger like him"? These comparisons with כ־ represent an echo of the "like Moses" language of Deut 18:15, 18; 34:10.[46] This judgment is confirmed by the specifications in line 5 that the commandments come "though the mouth of Moses" (בפי מושה) and in line 11 that Moses spoke "from his mouth" (מפיהו), which are further indications of this text's reflection on Moses' prophetic status and his

---

44 Fletcher-Louis, *All the Glory of Adam*, 144–145, notes that this is an assimilation of the language of Exod 33:11 to the context of Deut 5:4, where God is said to speak to Israel "face to face."

45 van Peursen, "Portrait of Moses," 111: "It indicates ... his role as a trustworthy messenger who passed God's words on to the people"; note 111n57, where he connects this role to the description of the prophet in Deut 18:18 as one in whose mouth God puts words.

46 See the references to Deut 18:18, 34:10 in VanderKam and Brady, "4QApocryphal Pentateuch B," 216.

characterization as unsurpassed in fulfilling that office.⁴⁷ Indeed, a number of scholars have interpreted Moses' designation as "Messiah" in this text specifically in terms of his prophetic status.⁴⁸ Because the emphasis here is on Moses' status as supreme revelatory agent, the text reflects the influence of Deut 34:10–12 more than Deut 18:15–18. In 4Q377, Moses is not really comparable to other prophets after all. In that sense, this text provides a parallel to the interactions with Mosaic prophecy that we will consider later, in the writings of Philo and the gospel according to John. The text is somewhat anomalous at Qumran, as it separates Moses from other prophets, rather than emphasizing the role of the prophets as Moses' duly authorized successors and interpreters.

3.3 Past Prophets as Legislators and Successors of Moses (4Q381; 1QS)

In the Qumran corpus, the past prophets are often conceptualized as heirs and successors of Moses, and tradents of Mosaic Torah. I first consider in this connection one of the non-sectarian psalms from Qumran. Eileen Schuller observes that the collection of psalms in 4Q381 is ascribed to various biblical figures, and suggests a date in the Persian or early Hellenistic period for it.⁴⁹ Fragment 69 seems to be set in the time of Israel's conquest of the land. I set out below the first six lines (5a being supralinear in the manuscript):⁵⁰

1 [ ] לכם כי ת̇ȯ [ ]ȯm [ ]לם בראותו כי התעיבו עמי [הא]ר̇ץ
2 היתה [ ] כל הארץ לנדת טמאה בנדת טמאה והפלא מראשונה
3 ז̇[ו]עץ אל לבו להשמידם מעליה ולעשות עליה עם
4 [..]בכם ויתנם לכם ברוחו נביאים להשכיל וללמד אתכם
5a o[·כם מן שמים ירד וידברעמכם להשכיל אתכם ולהשיב ממעשי ישבי
5 ·נתן ח[ק]ים תורות ומצות בברית העמיד ביד̇ [משה] ooo

---

47 See VanderKam and Brady, "4QApocryphal Pentateuch B," 215. See also Jassen, *Mediating the Divine*, 118–119 for discussion of this passage in terms of Moses' status as prophet.

48 So van Peursen, "Portrait of Moses," 113, see also Heinz-Josef Fabry, "Mose, der 'Gesalbte JHWHs': Messianische Aspekte der Mose-Interpretation in Qumran," in *Moses in Biblical and Extra-Biblical Traditions*, ed. A. Graupner and M. Wolter, BZAW 372 (Berlin: de Gruyter, 2007), 129–142; here 141: "Die in 4Q377 dem Mose verliehene Bezeichnung 'sein Gesalbter' besagt weder eine königliche noch eine priesterliche Funktion des Mose. Sie ist nach allem nur als Attribut des Mose zu verstehen, das ihn als prophetischen Geistträger ausweisen soll"; Feldman, "Sinai Revelation," 160: "The appellation 'his anointed one' (משיחו) may also point to his role as the bearer of God's word" (appealing to 1 Kgs 19:16; Isa 61:1; Ps 105:15; 1 Chr 16:22).

49 Eileen M. Schuller, "4QNon-Canonical Psalms B," in *Qumran Cave 4 VI: Poetical and Liturgical Texts, Part 1*, DJD 11 (Oxford: Clarendon, 1998), 87–172; here 90.

50 Schuller, "4QNon-Canonical Psalms B," 149–150.

1]*lkm* because *t.*[ ]*lm*. When he saw that the peoples of [the la]nd acted abominably
2] all the land [became] total unclean defilement. And marvelously from the first
3 he to]ok counsel with himself to destroy them from upon it, and to make upon it a people
4]*bkm*, and he gave them to you by his spirit, prophets to instruct and to teach you
5a]*km* from heaven he came down, and he spoke with you to instruct you, and to turn (you) away from the deeds of the inhabitants of
5 He gave la]ws, instructions and commandments by the covenant he established through [Moses]

The use of the term "prophets," נביאים, in line 4, and particularly its situating before the Sinai theophany, has struck Schuller as "odd."[51] I wish to suggest that this psalm includes all authorized exponents of Mosaic Discourse—Moses and his prophetic successors—in this term, so that it understands Israelite prophecy to have its originating point in the theophany at Horeb. The chief inter-texts Schuller discusses with respect to this psalm are Ezra 9:11 and Neh 9:13–14, 20, 24, 30.[52] I would propose another, one that also lies behind Ezra 9:11, namely, Deut 18:12, 15–18. Deuteronomy 18:9–11 catalogues examples of foreign divination, which are characterized as abominations, and are said to be the reason that Yhwh will drive them out before Israel (ובגלל התועבת האלה יהוה אלהיך מוריש אותם מפניך; Deut 18:12b). The passage goes on to promise Israel the institution of endogenous prophecy—Moses and his successors—as their continued means of access to the divine will, to ensure that they continue to obey Yhwh's commands. This is also the progression of thought reflected in 4Q381 frag 69 1–4: God decided to destroy the inhabitants of the land because of their "abominations" and send prophets to Israel to "instruct and to teach you." Schuller notes that this latter phrase "echoes the deuteronomistic description of the role of Moses (e.g., Deut 4:1, 5, 14; 6:1; et al.)."[53] Thus, as in Ezra 9:11, the term

---

51 Schuller, "4QNon-Canonical Psalms B," 151.
52 Eileen M. Schuller, *Non-Canonical Psalms from Qumran: a Pseudepigraphic Collection*, HSS 28 (Atlanta: Scholars Press, 1986), 209. While there is much shared vocabulary with these prayer texts, the clear setting of the Horeb theophany (line 5a) favors, in my view, the conclusion that the chief scriptural basis for this psalm is in fact Deut 18:12–18, though certainly the influence of Ezra 9; Neh 9 is not to be discounted.
53 Schuller, "4QNon-Canonical Psalms B," 151.

"prophets" includes both Moses and his prophetic successors, which clarifies its placement before the description of the Horeb theophany.

The function of the past "prophets" in 4Q381 is to mediate Torah. In this context, it is also important to consider the view of the prophets in the *Community Rule* (specifically, 1QS).[54] The genealogical model of prophecy, which subordinates all prophets to Moses, is pronounced in the *Community Rule*. Two references are particularly important here: first, the opening of the document, and second, 1QS 8:15–16, which begins the section in which the expectation of an eschatological prophet like Moses is attested. The *Community Rule* begins as follows:

> For [the Instructor …] … for his life, [book of the Ru]le of the Community: in order to seek God with [all (one's) heart and] with a[ll (one's) soul;] in order to do what is good and just (הטוב והישר) in his presence, as he commanded by the hand of Moses and by the hand of all his servants the prophets (כאשר צוה ביד מושה וביד כול עבדיו הנביאים).
>
> 1QS 1:1–3abα

Moses and the prophets are represented as a succession of lawgivers, in accordance with Deuteronomy's claim that prophecy originates with Moses at Horeb, and that prophets after Moses would be authorized to bring an updated legislative word from God. Indebtedness to Deuteronomic thought is pervasive in the passage. Line 3 uses the Dtr expression "his servants the prophets," which, as we have seen above, is in its scriptural occurrences a technical phrase specifically marking the pre-exilic succession of prophets, and coordinating the authority of those prophets to that of Moses. Moreover, according to Jassen, "the language of doing what is 'good and right' is clearly drawn from Deuteronomy (6:18; 12:28; 13:19)."[55] Additionally, the verb, "command" (צוה)—with God as subject and Moses or his prophet-successor as object—is important for Deuteronomy, both in the appointment of Moses as lawgiver (Deut 6:1–2) and that of his prophet-successor (Deut 18:18).[56]

---

54 For the text of the *Community Rule*, see Sarianna Metso, *The Community Rule: A Critical Edition with Translation*, EJL 51 (Atlanta: SBL Press, 2019). For the textual history of the document, see idem, *The Textual Development of the Qumran Community Rule*, STDJ 21 (Leiden: Brill, 1997); Alison Schofield, *From Qumran to the Yaḥad: A New Paradigm of Textual Development for The Community Rule*, STDJ 77 (Leiden: Brill, 2009).

55 Alex Jassen, "The Presentation of the Ancient Prophets as Lawgivers at Qumran," *JBL* 127 (2008): 307–337; here 314. See also Jassen's full analysis of this expression at Qumran, 315n20.

56 John Lübbe, "A Reinterpretation of 4QTestimonia," *RevQ* 12 (1986): 187–197, at 190–191, thus

A similar perspective on the function of the prophets as successors of Moses is found in column 8, after the quotation of Isa 40:3:

> This is the study of the law wh[i]ch he commanded through the hand of Moses (צוה ביד מושה), in order to act in compliance with all that has been revealed from age to age, and according to what the prophets have revealed through his holy spirit (גלו הנביאים ברח קודשו).
>
> 1QS 8:15–16

Here the prophets gain some independence from Moses even as they continue to be represented as his successors. Because God's revelation comes from "age to age" (עת בעת), the prophets are not mere interpreters of Mosaic law, but can genuinely add to and update Torah by means of new revelation. On the one hand, this might seem to be a robust view of the past prophets' halakhic authority. On the other hand, it is a prophetic authority that is mediated by priestly interpretation. As Jassen has shown, the closest parallel in the community's present to the prophets' legislative activity in the past is found in the description of sectarian legislation in 1QS 5:8b–9:[57]

> He shall undertake by a binding oath to return to the law of Moses with all his heart and soul, following all that he has commanded and in accordance with all that has been revealed from it to the sons of Zadok the priests who keep the covenant [לכול הנגלה ממנה לבני צדוק הכוהנים שומרי הברית] and seek his will, and to the multitude of the men of their covenant who together willingly offer themselves for his truth and to walk according to his will.

Jassen concludes of that the community "viewed itself as the immediate heir to the classical prophetic lawgivers and its own experience as a direct continuation of this prophetic activity."[58] To refine this point, in 1QS it is not just the "community" in general that has legislative authority, but the "sons of Zadok." By contrast, 4QS^d, an earlier manuscript of the *Community Rule*, refers in this passage not to the "sons of Zadok" but to the "council of the men [of] the community" (עצת אנשי היחד).[59] On the social level, Vermes has argued that the

---

concluded that the concept of "Moses and the prophets" in the opening of 1QS reflects in the influence of Deut 18:18; Jassen, *Mediating the Divine*, 173, concurs.

57 See Jassen, "Ancient Prophets as Lawgivers," 328–335, and especially the chart at 331.
58 Jassen, "Ancient Prophets as Lawgivers," 329.
59 See Metso, *Community Rule*, 26–27. See also James H. Charlesworth, "Challenging the

emphasis on priestly authority in 1QS represents a change in leadership structure in the community due to a takeover by Jerusalem Zadokites.⁶⁰ Whether this can be sustained or not, on the *ideological* level, the *Community Rule* increases its emphasis on priestly authority precisely in the version of the text, 1QS, that includes the reference to the coming of the prophet and the Messiahs of Aaron and Israel.⁶¹ To the development of this eschatological interpretation I now turn.

3.4   The Eschatological Prophet like Moses at Qumran

This brings us to the only unambiguous reference to the expectation of an eschatological prophet like Moses in the Qumran corpus, found in 1QS 9:11. The reference to the future prophet occurs in the context of regulations for the community life (starting in 8:20). These communal regulations are provisional laws for the present time, subject to revision in the eschaton. Here is the text in context:

> They should not depart from any counsel of the law in order to walk in complete stubbornness of their heart, but instead shall be ruled by the first directives (במשפטים הרשונים) which the men of the community began to be taught until the prophet comes, and the Messiahs of Aaron and Israel (עד בוא נביא ומשיחי אהרון וישראל).
>
>   1QS 9:9–11

As Jassen observes, the immediate context (9:3–9) looks back to the formation of the sectarian community and contains laws that "are uniquely focused on matters that serve to establish borders between communities."⁶² In the period prior to the coming of the prophet and the messiahs of Aaron and Israel, the

---

Consensus Communis Regarding Qumran Messianism (1QS; 4QS MSS)," in *Qumran-Messianism: Studies on the Messianic Expectations in the Dead Sea Scrolls*, ed. Charlesworth, Lichtenberger, and Oegema (Tubingen: Mohr Siebeck, 1998), 120–134, at 131, who argues that the "reaffirmation of the unparalleled supremacy of the Sons of Zadok [in 1QS] seems a later redaction."

60   Geza Vermes, "The Leadership of the Qumran Community: Sons of Zadok—Priests—Congregation," in *Geschichte, Tradition, Reflexion: Festschrift für Martin Hengel zum 70. Geburtstag*, ed. P. Schäfer (Tübingen: Mohr Siebeck, 1996), 375–384.

61   Speculatively, one might posit if such a takeover as hypothesized by Vermes did occur, it would be an effective rhetorical strategy for this leadership to assure the community that this takeover was temporary, until the arrival of new leadership in the messianic era.

62   Jassen, *Mediating the Divine*, 166–167.

members of the community must follow the "former precepts,"[63] that is, the sectarian interpretation of Torah. When the awaited trio arrives, new laws may be implemented.

The identity of this future prophet with the prophet like Moses is confirmed by 4Q175, which was written by the same scribe as 1QS and furnishes the scriptural testimony for the expected messianic trio.[64] This text is a series of quotations about eschatological figures: first, it contains first Deut 5:28–29 and 18:18–19, concerning the eschatological prophet (Exod 20:21 in the proto-Samaritan tradition); second, Num 24:15–17 is quoted about a political messiah; third, it cites Deut 33:8–11, which pertains to the eschatological priestly messiah. Fourth, the passage quotes a lengthy section from the Apocryphon of Joshua, which takes up Joshua's curse of the rebuilder of Jericho in Josh 6:26 and transforms it into a prophecy of an eschatological antagonist, an "accursed man of Belial" (line 23) who will arise.

This eschatological interpretation would appear to be a development of great significance in the story of the prophet like Moses, as this passage is the earliest *explicit* eschatological interpretation of Deut 18:15. I argued above that the Elijah-expectation in Mal 3:22–24; Sir 48:10 is related to the concept of the Mosaic prophet, but the passages refer to Deut 18:15, 18 only implicitly. The earliest documentation of the expectation of a future prophet like Moses as a figure distinguishable from Elijah-expectation occurs here, in these sectarian Qumran texts.[65] Differing lines of evidence converge that suggest a first century BCE date for the emergence of this eschatological interpretation. First, 4QSᵉ, an earlier manuscript of the *Community Rule*, contains no parallel to 1QS 8:15b–9:11, the key passage in which the eschatological interpretation of Deut 18:15, 18 is

---

63 See Jassen's discussion of this phrase, *Mediating the Divine*, 165–171.
64 Jassen, *Mediating the Divine*, 161n18, and note the references to the paleographical work of Allegro and Cross there.
65 Elijah-expectation continues to develop in its own trajectory, and it is beyond the scope of this investigation to consider the relevant texts in detail. However, three comments should be made. First, at Qumran the Elijah texts are non-sectarian (4Q521; 4Q558), while the eschatological interpretation of Deut 18:15 occurs exclusively in sectarian texts. Second, the eschatological prophet like Moses appears in conjunction with other messianic figures—the Messiahs of Aaron and Israel—pointing to the hope for a reestablishing of an Israelite polity or constitution. In contrast, the eschatological Elijah is often a sole agent acting immediately prior to the day of Yhwh. Third, the eschatological Elijah has a rather robust role (in 4Q521, it includes raising the dead), while the eschatological prophet like Moses is a cryptic figure whose role remains unclear. It remains unclear how the Qumran community reconciled these differing eschatological expectations, or whether they thought they even needed to be reconciled.

first attested.⁶⁶ Second, Berthelot and Feldman have convincingly argued that 4Q175 was written to provide a polemical response to the prophetic claims of John Hyrcanus.⁶⁷

The apparent significance of this development in the story of the prophet like Moses, however, is blunted by the observation that the precise role that this prophet was expected to play in the eschatological future remains unclear. John Collins, writing on the messianism of the scrolls, asserts: "The eschatological prophet is a shadowy figure, not only in the Scrolls, but generally in the Judaism of the time."⁶⁸ Horsley strongly downplays this figure's significance:

> For the currency in Jewish society at the time of Jesus of an expectation of an eschatological prophet like Moses there is almost no evidence. The idea, probably presupposed in the *4QTestim*, which quotes Deut 18:18, is present but not prominent or central in one Jewish group that had withdrawn from the rest of society.⁶⁹

Early Qumran scholarship was indeed puzzled at the paucity of references to the eschatological prophet like Moses in the Qumran texts. This silence was turned to good effect by scholars such as Geza Vermes, who argued that the sect viewed the Teacher of Righteousness as the eschatological prophet, and other documents, such as CD, failed to mention this figure because he had already

---

66 On the various editions of the *Community Rule* and their significance for the development of sectarian eschatology, see Harmut Stegemann, "Some Remarks to 1QSa, to 1QSb, and to Qumran Messianism," *RevQ* 17 (1996): 479–505. Stegemann concludes that the community's expectation of coming messianic figures is to be situated not in the first stages of the community, but only later, in response to disappointing events in the life of the community (such as the death of the Teacher). See also Charlesworth, "Challenging the *Consensus Communis*," who argues on the basis of the text-critical evidence of the *Community Rule* manuscripts for the comparatively minor significance of messianic expectations at Qumran.

67 See Katell Berthelot, "4QTestimonia as a Polemic Against the Prophetic Claims of John Hyrcanus," in *Prophecy after the Prophets? The Contribution of the Dead Sea Scrolls to the Understanding of Biblical and Extra-biblical Prophecy*, ed. K. De Troyer, A. Lange, and L. Schulte, CBET 52 (Leuven: Peeters, 2009), 99–116. Berthelot argues that the unity of 4Q175 is in its character as a polemic against John Hyrcanus, who claimed to combine prophetic, priestly, and royal honors (cf Josephus, *Ant.* 13.299). See also 4Q379 frag 22 lines 7–12; Feldman, *Rewritten Joshua Scrolls*, 99–104, 119–125.

68 John Collins, *The Scepter and the Star: Messianism in Light of the Dead Sea Scrolls*, 2nd ed. (Grand Rapids: Eerdmans, 2010), 128.

69 Richard Horsley, "'Like One of the Prophets of Old': Two Types of Popular Prophets at the Time of Jesus," *CBQ* 47 (1985): 435–463, at 443.

come.⁷⁰ The problem with this argument is that 1QS, which speaks of the future prophet, dates to a time in the community's history after the Teacher's death.⁷¹

The opacity of the texts and their view of the prophet's role is a theme of Jassen's discussion of the eschatological prophet at Qumran, which ranges over several chapters.⁷² Jassen's thorough investigation attempts to overcome this textual recalcitrance by examining every possible clue regarding the prophet's role. That said, Jassen's discussion, which presses the evidence as far as it can go, provokes the more fundamental question of *why* the evidence is so sparse. We are faced with the perplexing situation that the first articulation of an independent eschatological interpretation of Deut 18:15, 18 occurs in the context of an eschatological scenario in which this figure's role is unclear or marginal at best. In my view, the solution to this problem is found in the broader priestly-scribal construal of Mosaic prophecy attested at Qumran. I will return to this possibility below; first, however, it is important to consider what might be said about the functions of the eschatological prophet like Moses at Qumran.

Jassen argues that the eschatological prophet like Moses at Qumran has three main roles: a preparatory role, a halakhic role, and a role in comforting the righteous. The first of these is based on the observation that in both 1QS and 4Q175, the prophet is the figure mentioned first, before the two messiahs. He characterizes the evidence from order as "highly suggestive" but ultimately "inconclusive"; nevertheless, on the basis of parallels to Elijah-expectation, Jassen concludes that the prophet was thought to arrive before the Messiahs and exercise a preparatory function.⁷³ If Jassen is correct, this the earliest evidence for the concept of the eschatological prophet as a precursor of the Messiah. But the evidence from order is surely inconclusive; the trio of figures in 1QS 9:11 may have been expected all at once.

---

70 See Geza Vermes, *An Introduction to the Complete Dead Sea Scrolls* (Minneapolis: Fortress, 1999), 166. See Jassen, *Mediating the Divine*, 188–189n38, for an extensive list of references to early Qumran scholarship that accepted this identification.

71 Jassen, *Mediating the Divine*, 188–190, provides a review and assessment of this interpretive tradition, which has fallen out of favor in scholarship.

72 Jassen, *Mediating the Divine*: the relevant texts are "prohibitively opaque" (157) and "extremely vague" (161); they are "extremely opaque and leave much to be reconstructed" due to the fact that "very little evidence is provided with which to construct a full prophetic portrait of the eschatological prophet" (194); the "texts outlining the sectarian belief in the prophet at the end of days ... are unfortunately very unforthcoming about the specific responsibilities associated with the eschatological prophet" (195).

73 Jassen, *Mediating the Divine*, 162–165; see 165: "The prophet comes before the messiahs in the Rule of the Community and 4QTestimonia and presumably performs various actions in preparation for the imminent arrival of the messiahs."

Jassen is on firmer ground when he argues that the eschatological prophet was expected to serve as a legislator in the messianic era. As we have seen, a juridical function is ascribed to "prophets" (נביאים) in 1QS 1:1–3 and 8:15–16; it would be consistent with the document's perspective on the function of prophets for the eschatological prophet to be the legislator that updates the community's regulations.[74] Jassen further argues that even if 1QS is ambiguous regarding which eschatological figure would serve as legislator, 4Q175 makes the prophet's halakhic role "patently clear."[75] The fact that 4Q175 draws upon the Samaritan tradition, in which the promise of Deut 18:15–18 is placed immediately after the Decalogue (or, Ennealogue), and adjoined to the Israelites' request that Moses serve as mediator of the divine law (Exod 20:21 proto-SP), is for Jassen a deliberate authorial choice emphasizing the prophet's juridical role.[76] The argument seems sound; however, when considered in the light of the sect's broader eschatology, questions emerge. With respect to 4Q175, the quotation of Deut 33:8–11, pertaining to the eschatological priest, could equally be taken as evidence that it is the "Messiah of Aaron" who will play the key role in adjudicating Torah for the new age.[77] In my view, the eschatological prophet's juridical role was a possibility in the event that issues not previously addressed in Torah might arise. Nevertheless, the primary halakhic role in the eschatological community would belong to the priestly Messiah, identified elsewhere as the "Interpreter of the Law" (דורש התורה; cf CD 7:18; 4Q174 i 11–12).[78] In

---

74 So Jassen, *Mediating the Divine*, 174: "In this sense, the allusions to the eschatological prophet in 4QTestimonia and the ancient biblical prophets (including Moses) in the Rule of the Community mirror each other. Each presents the mediation of divine law as the prerogative of the prophet." In connection with this, Meeks, *Prophet-King*, 169, has compared the עד of 1QS 9:11 with the μέχρι of 1 Macc 4:46 and the ἕως of 1 Macc 14:41, which also look forward to a prophet's future halakhic or legislative activity.

75 Jassen, *Mediating the Divine*, 171–172.

76 Jassen, *Mediating the Divine*, 173, concludes: "the author of 4QTestimonia uses the scriptural tradition reflected in the Samaritan text in order to highlight the juridical function of the prophet expected at the end of days." The way this is phrased seems to go beyond the evidence: one should not imagine the author choosing between the proto-MT and SamP and selecting the text that most appeals to him. From the author's perspective, the SamP makes explicit what is implied in Deut 18:16–17 MT, namely, that the request for a prophet like Moses occurred at the Horeb theophany, after the giving of the Ten Words.

77 Cf 4Q175 lines 17–18: "They have made your judgments shine for Jacob/your law for Israel."

78 Some have identified the דורש התורה precisely as the eschatological prophet like Moses, which would certainly undermine my argument. See the discussion of Michael A. Knibb, "Apocalypticism and Messianism," in *The Oxford Handbook of the Dead Sea Scrolls*, ed. T.H. Lim and J.J. Collins (Oxford: Oxford University, 2010), 403–432 (at 423), and bibliography cited there. That said, the דורש התורה is most likely not the eschatological prophet like Moses, but the expected priestly messiah (so Xeravits, *King, Priest, Prophet*, 169–171;

sum, though Jassen has built as strong a case as one could, both the proposed preparatory and legislative functions of the eschatological prophet like Moses are at least open to question.

The third role is based on Jassen's identification of the prophet mentioned in 11QMelchizedek with the eschatological prophet like Moses.[79] This figure is introduced in the context of a pesher exegesis of Isa 52:7 ("How beautiful on the mountains are the feet of the messenger who announces peace"). After quoting the verse, the interpretation is as follows:

(17) פשרו ההרים [המה] הנביא[ים] ...
(18) המבשר הו[אה] משיח הרו[ח] ...

(17) Its interpretation: the mountains [are] the prophet[s] ...
(18) the messenger [is] the anointed one of the Spiri[t] ...[80]

The scriptural precedents for this latter figure, "the anointed one of the Spirit," are found in Isa 61:1 and Dan 9:26. Is this also a reference to the eschatological prophet like Moses, who is then identified as the figure referred to in Isaiah and Daniel? In light of my broader argument, it is indeed appealing to understand the prophets of the past Mosaic succession as the "mountains" and the "anointed of the Spirit" as the prophet like Moses who rekindles the dormant succession.[81] That said, Deut 18:15, 18 is not alluded to in this passage, so this

---

James C. VanderKam, "Messianism in the Scrolls," in *The Community of the New Covenant: The Notre Dame Symposium on the Dead Sea Scrolls*, ed. E. Ulrich and J.C. VanderKam, CJAS 10 [Notre Dame: University of Notre Dame, 1994], 211–234, at 227, 229, 233). In both the texts in which this figure appears, it is closely associated with a royal or Davidic eschatological protagonist. Thus, this figure fits naturally into the dyadic messianism of the scrolls, and should be regarded as a priestly rather than prophetic eschatological agent, based on scriptural precedents such as Zech 4.

79 Jassen, *Mediating the Divine*, 177–185, on 11QMelch, and 186–188 on the identification of this prophet with the prophet like Moses. Jassen (187n35) cites Xeravits, *King, Priest, Prophet*, 182–183, as providing support for this identification. However, Jassen misunderstands Xeravits' claim: Xeravits argues that the prophet of 11Q13 is Moses *redivivus*, which he distinguishes from the expectation of a prophet like Moses. Xeravits bases this on the combination of terms מבשר and משיח, which are in 4Q377 applied to Moses. This argument is unpersuasive, since in 11QMelch these titles derive from the passages of Isaiah under consideration (Isa 52:7 in 2:16–17; 61:1 in 2:20).

80 11QMelch ii 17–18. For the text and translation, see Xeravits, *King, Priest, Prophet*, 70–72.

81 Jassen, *Mediating the Divine*, 179, argues that the plural prophets of line 17 are also eschatological prophets, so that the passage has "multiple eschatological prophets" in view. The imagery of Isa 52:7, in which the "messenger" runs on the "mountains," suggests rather to me that the plural "prophets" mentioned are those of the scriptural past.

identification remains uncertain. In any case, even if we were to accept it, the passage does not add much to the prophet's role. As Jassen puts it, this prophet "announces the impending eschatological tumult" and later "shifts into the role of comforting the 'mourners' who have survived the eschatological upheaval."[82] Essentially, the prophet has insight into the divine plan for history, and draws upon that insight to console the righteous. This role is not necessarily entirely unimportant, particularly in view of the sect's keen interest in the eschatological timetable, but neither it is particularly robust.

This brings us to the question: why such a delimited role for the eschatological prophet? I would argue that this is a consequence of the dyadic messianism of the sectarian scrolls, in which the primary innovation (relative to contemporary eschatological expectations) is the expanded role of the eschatological priest. This is resonant with the broader context of 1QS 9:11, which places strong emphasis on the priestly character of the community.[83] At Qumran (and, as we will see, in Josephus), prophets may be associated with the *origin* of divine law, but priests control its *interpretation* and *application*. In this connection, it is worthwhile to highlight another Qumran text that supports this line of interpretation, one which has not often been discussed in relation to the eschatological prophet like Moses.[84] This text, 4Q375, presents itself as an updated law of the prophet from Deuteronomy, and provides an avenue of appeal for cases in which people are divided on whether the prophet is genuine. In Table 18, I have set out the text of 4Q375 and its quotations of Deuteronomy's prophet-laws, along with the (slightly adapted) DJD translation.[85]

First, the text contains instructions to listen to the accredited prophet like Moses, based on Deut 18:15–18, with allusions to that passage. Second, in lines 4–5 the text refers to the prophet who leads Israel astray (Deut 13:2–6).[86] However, the text goes on in a third part to augment Deuteronomy's law concerning prophets by adding recourse for appeal to the central sanctuary. This update is modelled on Deuteronomy's law of the "supreme court" found in Deut 17:8–

---

82   Jassen, *Mediating the Divine*, 185.
83   See the sacrificial language in 1QS 9:4–5, as well as the descriptions of the community as "a holy house for Aaron" (בית קודש לאהרון) and a "holy of holies" (קודש קודשים) in 9:6.
84   In his treatment of the text, Jassen (*Mediating the Divine*, 301–304), discusses it as an interpretation of Deut 13:2–6, but not of Deut 18:18.
85   For the text and (adapted) translation of 4Q375, see J. Strugnell, "4QApocryphon of Moses^a," in *Qumran Cave 4 XIV: Parabiblical Texts, Part 2*, DJD 19 (Oxford: Clarendon, 1995), 121–136, here 113–114.
86   So also Gershon Brin, "The Laws of the Prophets in the Sect of the Judaean Desert: Studies in 4Q375," *JSP* 10 (1992): 19–51, at 22.

TABLE 18   Deuteronomy's prophet-laws in 4Q375

4Q375 B 1:1–9	Deut 18:18, 13:2a, 6
1 [את כול אשר] יצוה אלוהיכה אליכה מפי הנביא ושמרתה	18:18 ונתתי דברי בפיו ודבר אליהם את כל-אשר אצונו
2 [את כול החו]קים האלה ושבתה עד יהוה אלוהיכה בכול	
3 לבכה ובכו[ל נפשכה ושב אלוהיכה מחרון אפו הגדול	
4 להושיעכ[ה ממצוקותיכה . והנביא אשר **יקום** ו**דבר** בכה	13:2a כי-**יקום** בקרבך **נביא**
5 **סרה** להש[יבכה מאחרי אלוהיכה **יומת**] [. וכיא יקום השבט	13:6 והנביא ההוא או חלם החלום ההוא **יומת כי דבר-סרה** על-יהוה אלהיכם ...
6] אשר [הואה ממנו ואמר לוא יומת כיא צדיק הואה נביא	להדיחך מן-הדרך אשר צוך יהוה אלהיך
7 נ[אמן הואה ובאתה עם השבט ההואה וזקניכה ושופטיכה	ללכת בה
8 א[ל המקום אשר יבחר אלוהיכה באחד שבטיכה] [. לפני	
9 ה[כוהן המשיח אשר יוצק על ר[ו]אשו שמן המשיחה	

1 [all that] your God commands you by the prophet's mouth, and you shall keep
2 [all] these [pre]cepts, and shall return to Yhwh, your God with all
3 [your heart and with al]l you soul, and your God will repent of the fury of his great wrath
4 [in order to save y]ou from your trials. However, the prophet who rises up to preach
5 [apostasy] to you, [to make] you [tu]rn away from God, shall die. And if the tribe
6 from [which] he comes should rise up and say: "He is not to die, for he is a just man, he is a
7 [tr]ustworthy prophet," you shall come with that tribe and your elders and your judges
8 [t]o the place which your God will choose in one of your tribes before
9 [the] anointed priest upon whose head the oil of anointing has been poured

13.[87] There are verbal links between these passages that may have encouraged this association.[88] The tribe from whom the prophet comes has the option of attesting to the veracity of the prophet. If they do so, the prophetic claimant—prophet like Moses or seducer prophet?—will have to undergo an ordeal before the high priest in order for the prophet's genuineness to be tested.[89] The right

---

87   Brin, "Laws of the Prophets," 32: "from I 7 onwards the basic text is Deuteronomy 17, the law of the supreme court"; 49–50: "This text introduces the issue of the seducer prophet on the basis of Deuteronomy 13 with an innovation regarding the option of an appeal given to the tribe, whose prophet stands at the center of the crisis."
88   Cf זדון: Deut 17:12, 18:22; זיד: 17:13, 18:20.
89   See the attempt to reconstruct some of the stages of this process by John Strugnell, "Moses-Pseudepigrapha at Qumran: 4Q375, 4Q376, and Similar Works," in *Archaeology and History in the Dead Sea Scrolls: The New York University Conference in Memory of Yigael Yadin*, ed. L.H. Schiffman, JSPSup 8 (Sheffield: JSOT Press, 1990), 221– 56, at 231–232. *Contra*, Jassen, *Mediating the Divine*, 301–303, who contends that the trial has nothing to do with the

of the anointed priest to make a final determination as to the authenticity of a prophet is a notable feature of this legislation. In this construal of the Mosaic prophetic succession, contemporary prophetic claimants were subject to priestly scrutiny and verification.

In conclusion, the evidence for expectation of an eschatological prophet like Moses is less prominent than that for other messianic figures at Qumran. It has a relatively minor role within the Qumran corpus, and may not even have been present in the *Community Rule* at every stage of its composition. It can be concluded, however, that the priestly-scribal construal of Mosaic prophecy, in which the past prophets were viewed as tradents and interpreters of Mosaic Torah, exercised influence at Qumran, and that this provided the context for the eschatological interpretation of Deut 18:15 that emerged there.

4 The Prophet like Moses between Ben Sira and Josephus: Conclusion

In this chapter I have traced two tendencies in the developing understanding of the Mosaic prophetic succession: the amplification of the role of Mosaic prophets in the scriptural past, and the deferral of Mosaic prophecy to the future. With respect to the first point, we have seen a considerable body of evidence emerging that Joshua, Moses's successor, was regarded as the first prophet like Moses. The "scripturalization" of the Mosaic prophetic succession is a reflection of its periodization by the priestly-scribal class, with their well-documented historiographic interests. With respect to the second point, texts such as 1 Maccabees and the *Community Rule* expect the future restoration of Mosaic prophecy. The role this figure was expected to play, however, is unclear or somewhat marginal. One consequence of this discussion is that the notion of the eschatological prophet like Moses at Qumran does not provide a clear parallel to early Christian identifications of this prophet with Jesus, in which the prophet clearly has a more authoritative and prominent role. How does the more robust view, in which the prophet like Moses could be identified with the Messiah and liberator, come about in Early Judaism? It may be that we observe

---

prophet *qua* prophet, it merely has do with the prophet's violation of Mosaic law; cf. 302: "Neither Deuteronomy nor 4Q375 impugns the prophetic character of the seducer prophet .... There is no concern with ascertaining the reliability of the prophet's oracular ability (as in Deut 18:15–22). The perceived danger is the prophet's advocacy of defiance of God's law." In fact, the tribe's defense of the prophet does include the prophet's trustworthiness (cf נאמן, line 7). Jassen's attempt to explain this away is unconvincing (303: "Even with this clause, the tribal intervention is not guided by a desire to vouch for this individual's prophetic ability. Rather, they are claiming that the individual is falsely accused").

this not in the first century BCE, as at Qumran, but only in the first century CE, and not only in nascent Christianity, but also in various prophetic movements reported on by Josephus. With this, we turn to Josephus' understanding of the Mosaic prophetic succession, as well as the evidence his writings provide for the currency of an expectation of an eschatological Mosaic prophet.

CHAPTER 9

"Moses and Those after Him": The Mosaic Prophetic Succession in the Writings of Flavius Josephus

1   Introduction

The writings of Flavius Josephus continue to be some of the most important sources for the tumultuous and factious world of Second Temple Judaism, and the scholarly interpretation of his understanding of prophets and prophecy parallels precisely the broader debate about the vitality and persistence of prophecy in the Second Temple period. For a long time, the settled consensus was that Josephus believed that prophecy had ceased in the Persian period, so that he reserved prophet-terminology for biblical prophets. As the broader consensus was challenged, so too was the interpretation of Josephus, and some scholars claim not only that Josephus allowed for contemporary prophets, but also that he considered himself to be one.[1] The issues raised are complex, and cannot all be treated in the parameters of this study; that said, I will situate Josephus's understanding of the Mosaic prophetic succession within the broader context of his views on prophecy. I will argue that Josephus is a witness to and exponent of a scribal and hieratic interpretation of Deut 18:15–22, which understood Joshua to be the first prophet like Moses and postulated a continuous succession of Mosaic prophets into the Persian period, one that was aligned with and responsible for the production of Israel's scriptures. Furthermore, I will discuss the indirect evidence for the eschatological interpretation of Deut 18:15–22 in the first century CE found in Josephus' writings, and show that in his construal of various eschatological movements his self-presentation is as one who adheres to the Deuteronomic norms for the evaluation of prophetic claimants.

---

1   Rebecca Gray, *Prophetic Figures in Late Second Temple Jewish Palestine: The Evidence from Josephus* (New York: Oxford University Press, 1993), 35–79; Lester L. Grabbe, "Thus Spake the Prophet Josephus …: The Jewish Historian on Prophets and Prophecy," in *Prophets, Prophecy, and Prophetic Texts in Second Temple Judaism*, ed. M.H. Floyd and R.D. Haak, LHB/OTS 427 (New York: T&T Clark, 2006), 240–247; Per Bilde, "Josephus and Jewish Apocalypticism," in *Understanding Josephus: Seven Perspectives*, ed. S. Mason, JSPSup 32 (Sheffield: Sheffield Academic, 1998), 35–61, see especially 42–48, 52–56. A nuanced understanding of Josephus's "prophetic" self-understanding is put forward by Joseph Blenkinsopp, "Prophecy and Priesthood in Josephus," *JJS* 25 (1974): 239–262.

2 The "Exact Succession of the Prophets" in *Against Apion*

Josephus' most explicit statement on prophecy[2] occurs in the much-discussed passage on the twenty-two book corpus of Hebrew Scriptures in *Against Apion* 1.37–41. This pericope is a *locus classicus* in scholarship on the history of the canon; my interest in the text, however, has to do with its account of a prophetic succession (διαδοχή), rather than its potential status as evidence for an emerging tripartite canonical structure. There has been a noteworthy shift in Josephan scholarship to understanding the Jewish historian first of all as an author in his own right, with his own agenda and biases, rather than simply mining his works for historical information about Second Temple Judaism.[3] This shift is certainly relevant to this famous passage in *Against Apion*, as the scholarly focus on the canon obscures Josephus' own interests, which have to do not with canonical closure but with the priestly and prophetic successions and their relationship. For Josephus, it is important that the priestly succession extends into the present and focuses on the preservation and interpretation of the scriptural records, whereas the prophetic succession is located in the past and associated with their origin. To clarify these claims, I turn first to a consideration of the broader context of Josephus's statement about the end of the Mosaic prophetic succession.

In *Against Apion*, Josephus contrasts the recent, contradictory, and numerous records of the Greeks (1.6–27) with the ancient, harmonious, and carefully delimited literary patrimony of the Judeans.[4] This literary record has been kept "with scrupulous accuracy" (μετὰ πολλῆς ἀκριβείας),[5] because it has been bequeathed to divinely appointed superintendents, namely, "chief priests and prophets" (*Ag. Ap.* 1.29). Josephus emphasizes both the divine origin and the careful preservation of the Judean records, which taken together guarantee that the history related in his *Antiquities* is unimpeachable.

The concept of succession is no less important for Josephus with respect to the priestly preservation of Israel's scriptures than it is in relation to their prophetic origin. Indeed, in the section on the continuity of the priestly office

---

2 See also *Ant.* 8.148.
3 See the shift in scholarship noted by Steve Mason, "Introduction: Josephus as Author and Thinker," in *Understanding Josephus: Seven Perspectives*, ed. S. Mason, JSPSupS 32 (Sheffield: Sheffield Academic, 1998), 11–18.
4 A nice summary of the context is given in Gray, *Prophetic Figures*, 9–10.
5 Citations from Josephus are taken from the LCL translations by Thackeray, unless otherwise noted.

(1.30–36), Josephus uses the key term "exact" twice (τὸ ἀκριβὲς, 1.32; τῆς ἀκριβείας, 1.36), both with respect to the careful preservation of records regarding priestly marriages and genealogy, and the continuous preservation of the high-priestly office for two thousand years. Josephus also insists that the care taken with respect to the priestly genealogy has been rigorously followed in diaspora communities (1.32–34). Though he does not mention Rome as one of these communities, the reader cannot fail to be reminded that Josephus is himself a diaspora priest, who considers himself a qualified interpreter of the prophetic scriptures (see *Vita* 1–6).[6] It is worth citing here from the narrative of his encounter with Nicanor, envoy of Vespasian, who compelled him to surrender:

> (351) But as Nicanor was urgently pressing his proposals and Josephus overheard the threats of the hostile crowd, suddenly there came back into his mind those nightly dreams, in which God had foretold to him the impending fate of the Jews and the destinies of the Roman sovereigns. (352) He was an interpreter of dreams and skilled in divining the meaning of ambiguous utterances of the Deity (ἱκανὸς συμβαλεῖν τὰ ἀμφιβόλως ὑπὸ τοῦ θείου λεγόμενα); a priest himself and of priestly descent, he was not ignorant of the prophecies in the sacred books (τῶν γε μὴν ἱερῶν βίβλων οὐκ ἠγνόει τὰς προφητείας ὡς ἂν αὐτός τε ὢν ἱερεὺς καὶ ἱερέων ἔγγονος). (353) At that hour he was inspired to read their meaning, and, recalling the dreadful images of his recent dreams, he offered up a silent prayer to God. (354) "Since it pleases thee," so it ran, "who didst create the Jewish nation, to break thy work, since fortune has wholly passed to the Romans, and since thou hast made choice of my spirit to announce the things that are to come, I willingly surrender to the Romans and consent to live; but I take thee to witness that I go, not as a traitor, but as thy minister (ἀλλὰ σὸς ἄπειμι διάκονος)."
>
> *Jewish War* 3.351–354

As in *Against Apion*, here it is the prerogative of the priestly class—including Josephus himself—to interpret the prophetic scriptures.[7] Indeed, interpretation is itself a charismatic and prophetic gift, which allows Josephus to perceive that Vespasian will become emperor (*War* 3.400–403). Though Josephus

---

6 On Josephus' priestly status and its implications, see James S. McLaren, "Josephus and the Priesthood," in *A Companion to Josephus*, ed. H.H. Chapman and Z. Rodgers, Blackwell Companions to the Ancient World (Chicester, West Sussex, UK: John Wiley & Sons, 2016), 273–281.

7 See Blenkinsopp, "Prophecy and Priesthood in Josephus."

does not consider himself a prophet in the technical sense, he certainly has a prophetic self-understanding, and considers himself a member of the class legitimately appointed to supervise and interpret the sacred oracles. He therefore surrenders to Vespasian as God's "servant" (διάκονος; Hebr. עבד), a title with prophetic associations.

Returning to *Against Apion*, Josephus transitions from the legitimate priestly preservation of the Judaean records to their divine origin, specifically their prophetic authorship:

> (37) It therefore naturally, or rather necessarily, follows (seeing that with us it is not open to everybody to write the records, and that there is no discrepancy in what is written; seeing that, on the contrary, the prophets alone (ἀλλὰ μόνον τῶν προφητῶν) had this privilege, obtaining their knowledge of the most remote and ancient history though the inspiration which they owed to God, and committing to writing a clear account of the events of their own times just as they occurred)—it follows, I say, that (38) we do not possess myriads of inconsistent books, conflicting with each other. Our books, those which are justly accredited, are but two and twenty, and contain the record of all time. (39) Of these, five are the books of Moses, comprising the law and the traditional history from the birth of man down to the death of the lawgiver. This period falls only a little short of three thousand years. (40) From the death of Moses until Artaxerxes, who succeeded Xerxes as king of Persia, the prophets subsequent to Moses (οἱ μετὰ Μωυσῆν προφῆται) wrote the history of the events of their own times in thirteen books. The remaining four books contain hymns to God and precepts for the conduct of human life. (41) From Artaxerxes to our own time the complete history has been written,[8] but has not been deemed worthy of equal credit with the earlier records, because of the failure of the exact succession of the prophets (διὰ τὸ μὴ γενέσθαι τὴν τῶν προφητῶν ἀκριβῆ διαδοχήν).
>
> *Ag. Ap.* 1:37–41

---

[8] Thackeray translates γέγραπται ... ἕκαστα in 1.41 as "the complete history has been written," but this may go beyond Josephus. Steve Mason, "Josephus and His Twenty-Two Book Canon," in *The Canon Debate*, ed. L.M. McDonald and J.A. Sanders (Peabody, Mass.: Hendrickson, 2002), 110–127, at 113, translates "all sorts of things have been written." See also the comments of Gray, *Prophetic Figures*, 13: "there was enough material to string together a story, but not enough to write a completely comprehensive history of the period."

This text is often mined as an early source for a tripartite Hebrew canon;[9] however, as Mason has shown, the problem with such readings is that Josephus's primary interest here was not the structure of the Hebrew scriptures.[10] For Josephus, *all Scripture* was prophetic—Moses wrote as the first and greatest of the prophets, and the later prophetic writings included historiography and poetry. The prophetic literary heritage is divided into two authorial voices— Moses and prophets after him—and into various genres, including history, poetry, and law.[11] Moses—the greatest of prophets—was given divine insight into the "most remote and ancient history," covering in his own writings a span of three thousand years. The subsequent prophets (οἱ μετὰ Μωυσῆν προφῆται) accomplished the more modest but nevertheless significant goal of producing completely accurate contemporary records.[12] Since the Persian period, how-

---

9   See the brief discussion in James VanderKam and Peter Flint, *The Meaning of the Dead Sea Scrolls: Their Significance for Understanding the Bible, Judaism, Jesus, and Christianity* (New York: HarperCollins, 2002), 165–167, with a table indicating divergent scholarly reckonings of the books in Josephus's canon. My own view (following Barton, *Oracles of God*) is that Josephus's primary distinction is between the five books of Moses and seventeen books written by prophets who lived between Moses and Artaxerxes. Of these latter seventeen, thirteen can be said be said to be concerned with history. Josephus is aware of four other sacred books (probably Job, Psalms, Proverbs, Ecclesiastes) that do not fit within the framework of his main interest, which is historical and chronological, and is constrained to include reference to them. But the numbers thirteen and four should not be taken to indicate a firm distinction between נביאים and כתובים at the time of Josephus.

10 Mason, "Josephus," 114 (emphasis original): "His most comprehensive criterion for classifying the Judean records here is that of *genre* .... Moses wrote in two genres; other prophets wrote historical tradition; and the final group (of prophets!) wrote both hymns to God and advice to mortals .... Contrary to virtually universal opinion, then, Josephus does not arrange the Judean sacred text in divisions, whether two or three." Blenkinsopp, "Prophecy and Priesthood," 241, is not correct to state that Josephus's periodization of history (from creation to Moses, from Moses to Artaxerxes, from Artaxerxes to his day) "corresponds to the three divisions of the Jewish canon."

11 Mason, "Josephus," 114: "Still less is there a division called 'prophets' in this passage, for *all* of the authors—and this is basic to his entire argument—are prophets .... Josephus mentions two authorial entities, so to speak, Moses and not-Moses." Barton, *Oracles of God*, 49 (emphasis original): "At all events the primary idea to which Josephus is a witness is not that the books of Scripture were organized in a tripartite form, but that they derived from either of *two* sources: Moses and the prophets."

12 Gray, *Prophetic Figures*, 11: "Josephus here [in 1.37] distinguishes between the writing of 'the most remote and ancient history' ... , and the writing of the history of the events of one's own day .... This distinction corresponds to the one he draws between Moses and his successors in 1.39–40." An interesting consequence of this is that not all prophetic writing was necessarily "inspired" according to Josephus: prophets would certainly depend on divine inspiration to know events of the distant past and future, but when writing about their own times they wrote σαφῶς, "clearly, distinctly" (1.37).

ever, even this standard has not been possible to attain, because of the failure of the exact succession of the prophets after Moses.

Neither here nor anywhere else in his writings does Josephus assert that prophecy as such has ceased. Rather, an *exact succession* of prophets (ἀκριβῆ διαδοχή) came to an end in the Persian period, which does not rule out the occasional occurrence of later prophets or prophetic activity (such as the flash of prophetic insight Josephus believed that he had been granted).[13] Indeed, though much of the scholarly debate revolves around the disputed question of prophecy's cessation at some point in the Persian period, Josephus delimits the "exact succession" at both its beginning and its end, and does not rule out the intermittent occurrence of prophets before or after it. Thus, Josephus held that the patriarch Jacob was a prophet (*Ant.* 2.194), and that John Hyrcanus had prophetic gifts (*Ant.* 13.299), but the exact succession begins with Moses and continues until Artaxerxes. At the risk of tautology, one might suggest that the succession begins with Moses because it is the Mosaic prophetic succession (that is, the institution of Deut 18:15–22) that Josephus has in mind. Mason's observation that Josephus here distinguishes two (not three) authorial entities—"Moses and not-Moses,"[14] as he puts it—makes the same point from another angle: the succession Josephus is describing includes Moses, the greatest of all prophets, and those who inherited his office in direct continuity.

This leads to the hypothesis that Josephus is an heir and prime exemplar of a Second Temple period scribal and priestly interpretation of Deut 18:15–22, one whose origins can be traced at least as far back as Ben Sira's *Laus Patrum*. This interpretation does not assert that prophecy as such has ceased, or that there are or can be no prophets in the present. Rather, it historicizes the promise

---

13 See Louis Feldman, "Prophets and Prophecy in Josephus," *JTS* 41 (1990): 386–422, 400: "He speaks not of the cessation of prophecy as such but rather of the failure of the exact succession of the prophets." So also Willem C. van Unnik, *Flavius Josephus als historischer Schriftsteller* (Heidelberg: Verlag Lambert Schneider, 1978), 48: "Hier wird als nicht gesagt, daß mit der Zeit des Artaxerxes der Prophetie an sich ein Ende gesetzt wurde und daß sie seitdem nicht mehr bestand. Nein, die Prophetie besteht noch; nur gibt es keine genaue Sukzession (ἀκριβὴς διαδοχή) mehr." *Contra* Barton, *Oracles of God*, 106 ("For Josephus it is evidently important to stress that true prophets lived only between Moses and Artaxerxes"). Per Bilde, "*Contra Apionem* 1.28–56: Josephus' View of his Own Work in the Context of the Jewish Canon," in *Josephus' Contra Apionem: Studies in its Character and Context with a Latin Concordance to the Portion Missing in Greek*, ed. L.H. Feldman and J.R. Levison, AGJU 34 (Leiden: Brill, 1996), 94–114, at 103, pushes this point too far when he claims that Josephus also regarded historians subsequent to Artaxerxes as prophets: "Josephus also regarded these authors as 'prophets'. The problem, as he saw it, was only that these 'prophets' did not succeed each other without interruption."

14 Mason, "Josephus," 114.

of Deut 18:15, 18, applying it to Joshua as Moses' immediate successor and also to the succession of prophets that inherited Moses' office. (This interpretation makes good sense if Deuteronomy is understood as a testamentary speech that actually took place on the plains of Moab.) Moreover, this interpretation has a tendency to increase markedly (relative to the scriptural sources) the number of Mosaic prophets from Moses to the Persian period. Finally, the (perhaps temporary) cessation of this prophetic succession provides an opening for asserting hieratic control over the interpretation of the prophetic scriptures in the present.

3 The Mosaic Prophetic Succession in the *Jewish Antiquities*

3.1 General Considerations

How seriously should we take Josephus's postulation of an unbroken prophetic succession in *Against Apion*? If he believed such a succession was operative, is this conviction reflected in his account of Israel's history, the *Antiquities*? It must be granted that Josephus's claim could be hyperbolic, made as it is in the context of an apologetic document.[15] There are reasons to doubt such an interpretation, however. First, as noted above, in the near context Josephus demonstrates the importance of the concept of continuous succession to him, with his reference to the priestly genealogies. Moreover, the hypothesis of hyperbole sits at odds with the chronological precision with which he bounds the succession: if he did not really believe it was exact, why would he demarcate its boundaries so specifically? It seems then that he believed there was at least one Mosaic prophet in every generation from Moses until Artaxerxes. Josephus' claim to stand in a long-standing tradition in his views about the origin and extent of the Jewish scriptures (*Ag. Ap.* 1.38, 42–43) is difficult to assess (as there exists no earlier enumeration of scriptural books),[16] but it seems likely that he is not

---

15 Finn Damgaard, "Brothers in Arms: Josephus' Portrait of Moses in the 'Jewish Antiquities' in the Light of His Own Self-Portraits in the 'Jewish War' and the 'Life,'" *JJS* 59 (2008): 218–235, has shown that on such matters as the portrayal of Israel's obedience to Moses, the *Antiquities* and *Against Apion* are scarcely reconcilable.

16 It is striking, and perhaps not coincidental, that the two earliest canonical notices that explicitly number the books of the Jewish scriptures date to the late first century CE. Josephus and the author of Fourth Ezra offer a roughly similar "public" canon (4 Ezra 14:45 speaks of 24 books), but the latter author also refers to 70 secret books. Perhaps Josephus's limited canon is part of a polemical debate going on within Judaism about the proliferation of writings claiming to be scriptural. In that case, his claim to be standing in a long-standing tradition should be situated in that context, and not be taken as evidence

original in his view concerning the failure of the Mosaic prophetic succession, given the evidence traced in previous chapters from Ben Sira onwards.

If this hypothesis is sound, the concept of a prophetic succession ought to be reflected in Josephus's *Jewish Antiquities*. Rebecca Gray has argued that it is not: "Apart from the passage in *Against Apion* … there is no evidence that Josephus had a well-developed notion of a continuous prophetic 'succession' (διαδοχή) stretching from the time of Moses into the Persian period."[17] On this basis she argues that Josephus's postulation of an exact succession is not a core conviction, but is a corollary of his acceptance of a delimited scriptural corpus.[18] Cook has criticized Gray, claiming the observations she adduces "do not seem sufficient to necessitate the conclusion that Josephus's direction of logic runs in any direction other than the one he states."[19] He suggests that Gray requires more evidence than is necessary: a continuous prophetic succession might only require prophets in each generation, not strict transference from master to student.[20] Mason, too, highlights counter-evidence to Gray's claim, citing Joshua's succession of Moses as one of the "clues that this category was already in his thoughts as he wrote *Antiquities*."[21] In what follows I plan to build on Mason's suggestion and show that the *Antiquities* do provide a witness to Josephus's concept of an exact Mosaic prophetic succession.

A first general consideration pertains to Josephus's use of prophetic terminology in the *Antiquities*, which supports the thesis that this concept was important to his understanding of Israel's political history. On the one hand, relative to his base text, Josephus dramatically increases the number of references to "prophets," "prophesying" and "prophecy" in Books 1–11 of *Antiquities*. Louis Feldman has tabulated 169 occurrences where Josephus has added prophet-

---

that an enumerated canon predates him considerably. See the contrasting perspectives on these texts in Eva Mroczek, *The Literary Imagination in Jewish Antiquity* (Oxford: Oxford University Press, 2016), 161–171, who understands them as symbolic, not literal, and Juan Carlos Ossandón Widow, *The Origins of the Canon of the Hebrew Bible: An Analysis of Josephus and 4 Ezra*, JSJSup 186 (Leiden: Brill, 2018), who argues that they provide evidence for an act of canonization in the first century CE.

17   Gray, *Prophetic Figures*, 12.
18   Gray, *Prophetic Figures*, 12: "[T]he theory of a continuous prophetic succession seems to be *derived from* the existence of such a set of [completely accurate] writings, in something like the following way: Josephus believed that only prophets, inspired by God, were capable of writing perfectly accurate history; there existed what he regarded as perfectly accurate histories …; therefore, he concluded, there must have been a prophet in each successive generation."
19   L. Stephen Cook, *On the Question of the "Cessation of Prophecy" in Ancient Judaism*, TSAJ 145 (Tübingen: Mohr Siebeck, 2011), 135.
20   Cook, *Cessation of Prophecy*, 135.
21   Mason, "Josephus," 118–119; quotation from 119.

terminology where it is not present in his biblical source text.²² On the other hand, Josephus is reticent to use the term for contemporary and recent figures, with few uses of these terms from Book 12 onwards. In Table 19, I tabulate the occurrences according to Niese's critical edition (the bolded numerals indicate the period from Moses to Artaxerxes). Gray's pronouncement that the passage in *Against Apion* is the only evidence for the notion of the continuous prophetic succession is belied by the distribution of prophet-terminology in the *Antiquities*, which is abundant precisely in the time-period in which the prophetic succession was operative. Far from failing to confirm the view that Josephus expresses in *Against Apion*, his use of terms for prophets and prophecy in *Antiquities* conforms very closely to it.

A second general consideration is that in his *Antiquities* Josephus is concerned throughout with Israel's form of government and the particular offices of its leaders.²³ At the outset, he promises that his *magnum opus* will include both Judean antiquities (ἀρχαιολογία) and "the constitution of our government" (διάταξιν τοῦ πολιτεύματος, *Ant* 1.5). Josephus envisions Jewish history as a narrative which includes many unexpected changes of fortune, chances of war, great actions of the commanders (στρατηγῶν ἀνδραγαθίαι), and also changes of the form of government (πολιτευμάτων μεταβολαί, 1.13). Josephus thus signals at the beginning of his work his attentiveness to Israel's changing political leadership and constitutions over the centuries, and he continues to return to this

---

22   Feldman, "Prophets and Prophecy," 389–391, e.g., Josephus refers to Samuel as a prophet forty-five times, the Bible does so just once (1 Sam 3:20). Feldman's footnote noting the rare occurrences of the opposite phenomenon (mention of prophet/prophecy in the Bible that is not paralleled in Josephus) is illuminating (391n27):

> If we ask why, on the contrary, Josephus (*Ant* 1.208) omits the biblical statement (Gen 20:7) which speaks of Abraham as a prophet, and likewise why he omits (*Ant.* 2.293 ff.) the biblical statement (Exod 7:1) which speaks of Aaron as a prophet, we may suggest that both of these passages occur before the revelation at Sinai, and that Josephus wished, in general, to reserve the term "prophet" for those through whom God speaks after this revelation.

This is another way of saying that Josephus's prophetic terminology is focused on and informed by the succession promised in Deut 18:15–22.

23   See Steve Mason, " 'Should Any Wish to Enquire Further' (*Ant.* 1.25): The Aim and Audience of Josephus' *Judean Antiquities/Life*," in *Understanding Josephus: Seven Perspectives*, ed. S. Mason, JSPSupS 32 (Sheffield: Sheffield Academic, 1998), 64–103, especially 80–87; Yehoshua Amir, "Josephus on the Mosaic 'Constitution,'" in *Politics and Theopolitics in the Bible and Postbiblical Literature*, ed. H.G. Reventlow et al. (JSOTSup 171; Sheffield: Sheffield Academic, 1994), 13–27; Daniel Schwartz, "Josephus on Jewish Constitutions and Community," *Scripta Classica Israelica* 7 (1983–1984): 30–52; idem, "Josephus's *Jewish Antiquities*," in *A Companion to Josephus*, ed. H.H. Chapman and Z. Rodgers, Blackwell Companions to the Ancient World (Chicester, West Sussex, UK: John Wiley & Sons, 2016), 36–58; at 54.

TABLE 19   Josephus' use of prophet-terminology in *Antiquities*

Book	Προφήτης	Προφητεύω	Προφητεία	Total
1	1	0	0	1
2	1	0	1	2
3	1	1	1	3
4	2	2	2	6
5	5	5	0	10
6	50	13	4	67
7	24	4	3	31
8	66	9	6	81
9	63	10	8	81
10	52	8	6	66
11	4	2	1	7
12	1	0	1	2
13	3	1	1	5
14	0	0	0	0
15	0	0	0	0
16	0	0	0	0
17	0	0	0	0
18	1	0	0	1
19	0	0	0	0
20	2	0	0	2

theme.[24] In light of Josephus's attentiveness to the varied offices held by Israel's leaders and the changing forms of that leadership throughout Israel's history, his assertion of a continuous prophetic succession that is delimited fairly precisely ought to be understood as a component of his understanding of Jewish political history.

3.2   *Josephus's Interpretation of Deuteronomy*

My thesis, however, is more specific than these general considerations can establish: I am claiming that Josephus inherits and transmits a priestly-scribal interpretation of the concept of the prophet like Moses. This hypothesis faces the challenge that Josephus omits Deut 18:9–22 in his paraphrase of Deuteron-

---

24   Cf. esp. *Ant.* 1.10; 3.84; 4.194–198; 4.223–224; 4.302; 5.120; 6.36; 6.83; 20.261.

omy, which is found in *Ant.* 4.176–331.²⁵ Nevertheless, a careful reading of Josephus' rewriting of Deuteronomy provides an indication of the role of the Mosaic prophet in Israel's political leadership.

Josephus understands Deuteronomy as providing a normative guideline for the ideal Israelite πολιτεία. Indeed, the majority of his uses of this term occur in the context of his paraphrase of Deuteronomy (*Ant.* 4.176–331).²⁶ McBride comments on Josephus's use of this term as follows:

> Most noteworthy here is Josephus' choice of the Greek term *politeia*, rather than *nomos* or the like, to describe the juridical substance of Deuteronomy; there is no reason to doubt that he understood *politeia* to represent Hebrew *tôrâ* in its characteristically Deuteronomic usage .... The association of Torah with *politeia* invokes the heady realm of Hellenistic philosophical debate regarding the origins and evolution of human statecraft and, above all, about whose state had attained the most sublime form of government. By identifying the Mosaic Torah of Deuteronomy as the ancient Israelite *politeia*, Josephus boldly advanced the case for Jewish priority in the history of civilized political thought and practice.²⁷

Influenced by Deuteronomy, Josephus regards the monarchy as a change in constitution which was not desirable (4.223–224; 6.36); rather, he idealized the "aristocracy" that he traced to Mosaic times (4.223; 6.84; 6.268; 20.229). Jose-

---

25   Josephus's retelling includes an initial epitome of its contents (4.176–193), followed by an interlude (4.194–198), after which Josephus provides his own summary of Israel's constitution (4.199–301). Finally, it concludes with the exhortations (blessings and curses), poetry, and narrative material paralleled in Deut 27–34 (4.301–331). Josephus does not preserve the character of Deuteronomy as a sustained Mosaic speech; rather, he summarizes Moses's discourse at the outset (4.176–193) and also gives Moses the last words as well (4.312–319). In separating Moses's speech from his own free adaptation of Deuteronomy's legislation, Josephus attempts to do justice to Deuteronomy's complex character as both farewell discourse—Moses's hortatory words spoken on his last day—and divine lawcode. David Lincicum, *Paul and the Early Jewish Encounter with Deuteronomy*, WUNT 2/384 (Tübingen: Mohr Siebeck, 2010), 172–180, notes three features of Josephus's understanding of Deuteronomy: his interpretation of its function as a constitution (πολιτεία), as law, and as the last words and deeds of Moses.
26   Thirteen of Josephus's eighteen uses of πολιτεία in Books 1–4 occur in his rewriting of Deuteronomy: *Ant* 4.184, 191, 193, 194, 195, 196, 198, 223, 230, 292, 302, 310, 312; other occurrences are *Ant.* 1.10, 121; 3.84, 213; 4.45.
27   S. Dean McBride, "Polity of the Covenant People: The Book of Deuteronomy," *Int* 41 (1987): 229–244; here 229–230. A similar perspective is advanced by Mason, "Aim and Audience," 80–87.

phus therefore has Moses introduce the law of the king (Deut 17:14–20) by emphasizing that such an institution is unnecessary and not to be preferred:[28]

> Aristocracy (Ἀριστοκρατία), with the life that is lived thereunder, is indeed the best: let no craving possess you for another polity (ἄλλης πολιτείας), but be content with this, having the laws for your masters (δεσπότας) and governing all your actions by them; for God suffices for your ruler (ἡγεμών). But should you become enamored of a king (βασιλέως δ' εἰ γένοιτο ἔρως ὑμῖν) …
>
> *Ant.* 4.223

Though, as mentioned, Josephus does not directly restate the laws of priest (Deut 18:1–8) and prophet (Deut 18:9–22) in his summary of Deuteronomy,[29] the "aristocratic" constitution he has in mind involves rule by the leadership of a prophet, a high priest, and a council—at least in its original form.[30] These

---

28 For Josephus's views of the monarchy, see Paul Spilsbury, *The Image of the Jew in Flavius Josephus' Paraphrase of the Bible*, TSAJ 69 (Tübingen: Mohr Siebeck, 1998), 160–188.

29 Though I see an echo of Deut 18:15, 18, 19 in *Ant.* 4.186, and Louis Feldman, "Parallel Lives of Two Lawgivers: Josephus' Moses and Plutarch's Lycurgus," in *Flavius Josephus and Flavian Rome*, ed. J. Edmondson et al. (Oxford: Oxford University, 2005), 209–242, at 227, argues that Deut 18:10–11 is reflected in *Ant.* 4.279, where Josephus's Moses prescribes the capital penalty for those who keep poison (φάρμακον and θανάσιμον are used). Somewhat speculatively, it may be suggested that Josephus does not directly refer to Moses's promise of a future prophet precisely because of its usage in the eschatological movements that he believed had contributed directly to the calamity of 70 CE. Perhaps more likely, he may have been cognizant of the tension between his incorporation of the Balaam narrative (*Ant.* 4.104–130) and the strong invective against foreign divination in Deut 18:9–14. In Josephus's account, Moses was magnanimous to the Gentile seer, since he could have claimed Balaam's prophecies for himself (4.156–158). It is hard to reconcile this image of Moses with the Moses who proclaims Deut 18:9–14; accordingly, Josephus may have not included the latter passage in his distillation of Deuteronomy, though he certainly observes the rule that prophecy is properly endogenous (cf. Mason, "Josephus," 118, on Josephus's "ethnic criterion for prophets").

30 Schwartz, "Josephus on Jewish Constitutions," 32–34, argues that by "aristocracy" Josephus means government by council, which he (too rigidly, in my view) distinguishes from hierocracy. Louis Feldman, *Judean Antiquities 1–4, Translation and Commentary*, Vol. 3 of *Flavius Josephus: Translation and Commentary*, ed. S. Mason (Leiden: Brill, 2000), 414, takes "aristocracy" as meaning that "κρατία (government) by laws is best (κράτιστον = ἄριστον)," which he also equates to theocracy; the same construal is given by Spilsbury, *Image of the Jew*, 162. This interpretation assumes that the rest of Josephus's comments in *Ant.* 4.223 serve as an elaboration of what he means by Ἀριστοκρατία. But this does not fit well with Josephus's later usages of the term (e.g., *Ant.* 6.84). Mason, "Aim and Audience," 82–83, summarizes "aristocracy" purely in terms of priestly rule: "This aristocracy comprises a high priest and

are archetypically symbolized in Moses, Aaron, and the elders (cf Exod 18:13–27; Num 11:16–25). In this understanding, Moses and Aaron were succeeded by Joshua and Eleazar respectively: Aaron and Eleazar represent the continuity of priestly leadership; Moses and Joshua the prophetic.

Moses's farewell speech is crafted by Josephus as a call to the Israelites to obey the leaders appointed to succeed him. Moses' imminent death looms over the narrative, and Josephus portrays the people as despairing that they will ever have another leader like Moses (*Ant.* 4.194; cf *L.A.B.* 19:3). In this context, Moses tells the Israelites: "only obey those whom God wills you to follow" (μόνον οἷς ὁ θεὸς ὑμᾶς ἕπεσθαι βούλεται τούτοις πειθαρχεῖτε; *Ant.* 4.181).[31] After speaking of his own departure (*Ant.* 4.184), he specifies that these are Eleazar the priest, Joshua, and the elders:

> Moreover the best of counsels, by following which you will attain felicity, will be put before you by Eleazar the high priest and Joshua, as also by the council of elders and the magistrates of the tribes; to whom give ear ungrudgingly (ὧν ἀκροᾶσθε μὴ χαλεπῶς), recognizing that all who known well how to obey will know also how to rule, should they reach the authority of office.
> *Ant.* 4.186

The charge that the Israelites are to "give ear" to these leaders (ὧν ἀκροᾶσθε) may reflect the influence of Deut 18:15, which speaks of the prophet to whom Israel

---

a priestly senate (γερουσία)." There is evidence for Josephus speaking in terms of priestly rule (*Ag. Ap.* 2.185), which, of course, would make him a member of Israel's aristocracy. It is possible that with the failure of the exact prophetic succession Josephus thought that the aristocracy had become chiefly a matter of priestly rule (according to Josephus, the high priest is the one constant in Jewish political history, cf. *Ant.* 20.224–251). But in Israel's archaic or original aristocracy, the γερουσία is not exclusively composed of priests, but is regularly distinguished from them (e.g., *Ant.* 5.23, 12.142). Second, in the ideal or archetypal πολιτεία, a prophet is included in the ruling body, and Mason does not adequately account for this feature (for example, he says, at 83, "Josephus alters the biblical narrative to make Moses' great successor Joshua consult his *gerousia* several times [5.15, 43, 55]," implying that Joshua seeks the elders' approval, which is inaccurate—in the cited passages, Joshua, as the prophet, is keeping the elders informed, not "consulting").

31 The referent for the relative pronoun οἷς is ambiguous, as both Thackeray and Feldman note in their translations. Thackeray (LCL) translates, "Only obey those precepts which God would have you follow," on the grounds that the command to follow rulers comes later, in 4.186. Feldman (Brill) tentatively proceeds in the same direction: "Only obey those [rules] that God wishes you to follow." Admittedly certainty is impossible here; my interpretation is informed by the fact that the pending death of Moses looms over the speech (cf 4.177, 184, 194), so that most likely his human successors are in view.

must listen (αὐτοῦ ἀκούσεσθε). One might object that this exhortation makes no mention of a prophet, but rather a variety of leaders. Sarah Pearce, however, has demonstrated that the triad of Eleazar, Joshua, and the council (γερουσία), represents for Josephus the offices instituted by Moses in the ideal and archetypal *politeia*, and that in this grouping Joshua fills the role of the prophet.[32] As she points out, this triad returns in Josephus's version of the legislation regarding the central court of appeal, based on Deut 17:8–12:[33]

> But if the judges see not how to pronounce upon the matters set before them—and with men such things oft befall—let them send up the case entire to the holy city and let the high priest and the prophet and the council of elders (ὅ τε ἀρχιερεὺς καὶ ὁ προφήτης καὶ ἡ γερουσία) meet and pronounce as they think fit.
>
> *Ant.* 4.218

This text is quite important for our purposes: only here in his restatement of Deuteronomy does Josephus refer to "the prophet" (ὁ προφήτης) as one of Israel's instituted offices.[34] The prophet in mind must be the one authorized by Deut 18:15–22. In fact, this passage restates the triad encountered above, but

---

[32] See Sarah J.K. Pearce, "Josephus as Interpreter of Biblical Law: The Representation of the High Court of Deut 17:8–12 according to Jewish Antiquities 4.218," *JJS* 46 (1995): 30–42; idem, *The Words of Moses: Studies in the Reception of Deuteronomy in the Second Temple Period*, TSAJ 152 (Tübingen: Mohr Siebeck, 2013), 306–320. See also Spilsbury, *Image of the Jew*, 165: "The one period of which Josephus writes unequivocally as an 'aristocracy' in that of the life-times of Moses and Joshua. It is there that our attention must turn for further insight into Josephus' ideal constitution."

[33] In Deuteronomy, the appellants are directed to the Levitical priests and the judge (17:9), and later to the priest (sg.) or the judge (17:12). Josephus interprets this as the high priest and the prophet and the council. What justifies this change? Some interpreters have argued that Josephus here reflects knowledge of Second Temple institutions. Against this, Pearce, *Words of Moses*, 310–324, has claimed that there is an exegetical basis for Josephus's triad: these were the offices established in Mosaic times (the elders, the prophet, and the priests), and in fact Josephus would have specific referents in mind for these roles: Joshua as the prophet, Eleazar as the priest, and the elders (established in the narratives of Exod 18 and Num 11) as the council.

[34] See Wayne Meeks, *The Prophet-King: Moses Traditions and the Johannine Christology*, NovTSup 14 (Leiden: Brill, 1967), 142, on Josephus's substitution of προφήτης for שׁוֹפֵט/κριτής: "The implication is that 'the prophet' is regarded as a regular administrative office, comparable to the High Priesthood on one hand and the Council of Elders on the other. Obviously this notion is not derived from contemporary practice. It must instead be connected with the idea of a prophetic succession, stemming from Moses' prophetic and ruling offices." In this connection Meeks, 143–144, also refers to Justin, *Dial.*, 52.3 (trans. Falls):

generalizes for a time when Eleazar the high priest and Joshua (the prophet) are no longer present.³⁵ Subsequently, the triad of Joshua, Eleazar, and the elders (γερουσία) recurs often in the following narrative.³⁶ Therefore, in Josephus's account, which is sensitive to the various forms of Israel's πολιτεία, the Mosaic ideal of aristocracy (*Ant.* 4.223) was embodied in the collaborative rule of the high priest, the prophet, and the council. Joshua, Eleazar, and the council of elders represent an archetypal "historical" instantiation of Deuteronomy's ideal polity, in which Joshua functions as prophet-successor to Moses. To confirm

> You will not have the nerve to assert, nor could you prove it if you did, that your race did not always have a prophet or king from the beginning until the time when Jesus Christ was born and suffered. Although you claim that Herod, after whose reign Christ suffered, was from Ashkelon, you still must admit that you then had a high priest of your own race, so that even then you had one who offered sacrifices and observed the other legal ceremonies of the Mosaic Law. And since you also had a continuous succession of prophets down to John (καὶ προφητῶν κατὰ διαδοχὴν μέχρις Ἰωάννου γεγενημένων) (even when your people were led captive into Babylon, your lands ravaged by war, and your sacred vessels carried away), there never ceased to be a prophet in your midst who was lord and leader and ruler of your people (μὴ παύσασθαι ἐξ ὑμῶν προφήτην, ὃς κύριος καὶ ἡγούμενος καὶ ἄρχων τοῦ λαοῦ ὑμῶν ἦν). Indeed, even your kings were appointed and anointed by the spirit in these prophets.
>
> In my first encounter with this passage, I was skeptical of whether it provided evidence for the concept of a prophetic succession in early Judaism, since (as Meeks notes), Justin is clearly dependent on the thought of Luke 16:16 ("The law and the prophets were until John"), and may only reflect a (garbled) understanding of that saying of Jesus. Meeks has forced me to reconsider. Two points are worth noting. First, even if Justin is dependent on Luke 16:16//Matt 11:13, it is interesting that he appears to have interpreted that logion not primarily in terms of a closed corpus of literature, but in terms of a continuously operative prophetic succession. Second, Meeks points to the elevated titles Justin uses for the prophet ("Lord" and "ruler" and "prince"). He believes this must have "some scriptural or traditional basis" (143), and concludes (144)
>
>> The succession of prophets must have been traced back to Moses.... Cryptic as are the passages in Justin's *Dialogue* and Josephus' *Antiquities*, therefore, they can be taken as evidence for some tradition that a continuous succession of prophets, extending from Moses until the close of the age, would exercise for Israel both Moses's prophetic office and his rulership.
>
> Though I am unsure why Meeks uses the expression "the close of the age" in this context, I now believe that this comment is substantially correct, and that Justin's comment is not only informed by Luke 16:16//Matt 11:13, but also reflects the tradition of a continuous Mosaic prophetic succession.

35 Pearce, *Words of Moses*, 320, "The fact that Josephus does not name Eleazar or Joshua [in *Ant.* 4.218] may be motivated by the desire to represent this body as valid for a timeless present."

36 In *Ant.* 4.324 this group accompanies Moses on the mountain to the place of his departure, and it is also mentioned in *Ant.* 5.15, 55, 57, 80, 103. See discussion in Pearce, *Words of Moses*, 314–316.

this hypothesis, I now turn to consider Josephus's prophetic characterizations of Moses and Joshua, as well as his increasing of the role of Mosaic prophet in his narration of Israel's history relative to his scriptural sources.

3.3 *Josephus's Portrait of Moses*

Josephus's portrait of Moses is both creative and traditional. With respect to the first of these, his favored term for Moses in the re-telling of his life is, perhaps surprisingly, "general."[37] At the burning bush, Moses is appointed "general and leader of the Hebrews" (στρατηγὸν καὶ ἡγεμόνα τῆς Ἑβραίων; *Ant.* 2.268). These terms encapsulate Moses's political role while avoiding any suggestion that he was a king.[38] As for the traditional element, Josephus utilizes Deuteronomy's depiction of Moses as the supreme prophet, even though (like the Torah) he uses the title προφήτης sparingly for Moses (*Ant.* 2.327; 4.329). This combination of creative and traditional elements in Moses's portrait is exemplified in Josephus's rewriting of Deut 34:10, which describes Moses's incomparability as a prophet:

> As general he had few to equal him, and as prophet none, insomuch that in all his utterances one seemed to hear the speech of God himself (καὶ στρατηγὸς μὲν ἐν ὀλίγοις προφήτης δὲ οἷος οὐκ ἄλλος ὥσθ' ὅ τι ἂν φθέγξαιτο δοκεῖν αὐτοῦ λέγοντος ἀκροᾶσθαι τοῦ θεοῦ).
>
> *Ant.* 4.329

Josephus departs from his source by incorporating a comment on Moses's military prowess into Moses' eulogy; he is faithful to it, however, in his acknowledgment that as a prophet Moses surpassed all others. Josephus clarifies this prophetic ability by adverting to a motif that plays a substantial role in Deuteronomy, namely the authorization of Moses as God's divinely accredited spokesperson, who speaks so that Israel will not need to hear the divine voice directly.[39]

---

37 Josephus uses στρατηγός (*Ant.* 2.241, 268; 3.2, 11, 12, 28, 65, 67, 78, 102, 105; 4.82, 194, 329) and ὑποστράτηγος in *Ant.* 4.317. See Spilsbury, *Image of the Jew*, 97n9; Damgaard, "Josephus' Portrait of Moses," 221, 228 on this designation for Moses. Another favored term for Moses, though one that does not occur as frequently in Josephus' narration of Moses' life, is νομοθέτης (*Ant.* 2.6, 18, 20, 23, 24; 3.180; 4.13, 150, 156). On this designation, see Spilsbury, *Image of the Jew*, 101–103.

38 Meeks, *Prophet-King*, 132–134, emphasizes Josephus's avoidance of the term "king" for Moses (see, in contrast, Philo's extensive employment of it in his *Life of Moses*, and Meeks' discussion in *Prophet-King*, 107–117).

39 Compare Meeks, *Prophet-King*, 137: "Moses's prophecy consists for Josephus precisely in the fact that in his words it was not he himself who spoke, but God."

One feature of Moses's status as supreme prophet for Josephus was that his powers of prognostication were unequalled. Speaking of Deut 32, Josephus writes:

> Then he recited to them a poem in hexameter verse, which he has moreover bequeathed in a book preserved in the temple, containing a prediction of future events, in accordance with which all has come and is coming to pass (καθ' ἣν καὶ γέγονε τὰ πάντα καὶ γίνεται), the seer having in no whit strayed from the truth.
>
>   *Ant.* 4.303

Josephus specifies that Deut 32 contains prophecies that were being fulfilled up to his own day,[40] and goes on to suggest that Moses foresaw not only the Babylonian exile but also the Roman conquest and destruction of the second temple (*Ant.* 4.313–314). Moses therefore was a prophet with a particular long-range prowess, which for Josephus establishes him as Israel's unrivaled and supreme prophet.[41]

3.4 *Joshua as the Prophet like Moses*

The scriptural text does not ascribe the title נביא/προφήτης to Joshua. In his interpretive retelling, Josephus refers to Joshua as a prophet three times, two of which occur specifically in the context of his succession to Moses. The first instance occurs in *Ant.* 4.165:

> Moses, already advanced in years, now appointed Joshua to succeed him both in his prophetical functions and as commander-in-chief (διάδοχον ἑαυτοῦ Ἰησοῦν καθίστησιν ἐπί τε ταῖς προφητείαις καὶ στρατηγὸν), whensoever the need should arise, under orders from God himself to entrust the direction of affairs to him. Joshua had already received a thorough training in the laws and in divine lore under the tuition of Moses.

Josephus's base text, Num 27:18–20, suggested the prophetic characterization by referring to Joshua as a "man in whom is the spirit (איש אשר רוח בו)" (Num

---

40 See also Philo, *Mos.* 2.288.
41 According to Josephus, Jeremiah (*Ant.* 10.79), and Daniel (*Ant.* 10.276) were also prophets who also had particular long-range prowess, and foretold the destruction of the Second Temple. See Blenkinsopp, "Prophecy and Priesthood in Josephus," 242: "for Josephus prophecy consists principally in prediction."

27:18).⁴² In this text, Joshua's authority is curtailed in favor of Eleazar's (cf. Num 27:21), but Josephus omits the references to Eleazar here and emphasizes Joshua's prophetic and military role: he is Moses's successor as προφήτης and στρατηγός.⁴³ The key term διάδοχος is used, which links this passage to Josephus's mentioning of the "exact succession" (ἀκριβῆ διαδοχήν) in *Ag. Ap.* 1.41, as well as to Sir 46:1, on which Josephus may be dependent:

> κραταιὸς ἐν πολέμῳ Ἰησοῦς Ναυη καὶ **διάδοχος** Μωυσῆ ἐν **προφητείαις**
> Sir 46:1a LXX

> **διάδοχον** ἑαυτοῦ Ἰησοῦν καθίστησιν ἐπί τε ταῖς **προφητείαις** καὶ **στρατηγὸν**
> *Ant.* 4.165

Both passages refer to Joshua's prophetic ability and military prowess as the key features of his role as Moses's successor.

The second reference to Joshua's prophetic status occurs as an aside towards the end of Josephus's retelling of Deuteronomy:

> He taught them, too, how their sacrifices might be made the more acceptable to God, and how the troops when taking the field should consult the oracular stones, as I have previously indicated. Joshua also prophesied in the presence of Moses (προεφήτευσε δὲ καὶ Ἰησοῦς Μωυσέος παρόντος).
> *Ant.* 4.311

Joshua's prophetic status is once again closely linked to his role as Moses's successor: he prophesies in Moses's presence. This is an extra-biblical addition; Feldman suggests that it too is based on the description of Joshua in Num 27:18.⁴⁴ It seems more likely that it is an expansion based on Deut 31:14–15:

> The LORD said to Moses, "Your time to die is near; call Joshua and present yourselves in the tent of meeting, so that I may commission him." So Moses and Joshua went and presented themselves in the tent of meet-

---

42 So also Pearce, *Words of Moses*, 316.
43 See Feldman, *Judean Antiquities 1–4*, 388n478: "By omitting this [i.e. Eleazar] Josephus lessens the subordination of Joshua to the high priest, or he wishes to minimize the role of the Urim." The former is the more likely possibility; Josephus does not minimize the Urim (cf *Ant.* 3.214–218).
44 Feldman, *Judean Antiquities 1–4*, 470n1089.

ing, and the LORD appeared at the tent in a pillar of cloud; the pillar of cloud stood at the entrance to the tent.

On the basis of analogy with the account in Numbers 11, it would be logical for Joshua to prophesy when he is commissioned as Moses' successor at the tent of meeting.

The third and final reference to Joshua as prophet occurs in *Ant.* 5.20:

> And Joshua, with the stones which each of the tribal leaders had, by the prophet's orders (τοῦ προφήτου κελεύσαντος), taken up from the river-bed, erected that altar that was to serve as a token of the stoppage of the stream, and sacrificed thereon to God.
>
> *Ant.* 5.20

The title is used here in the specific context of Joshua's authority to establish an altar (1 Macc 4:46 is comparable, in terms of the prophetic function envisaged). This passage does not directly have to do with Joshua's succession of Moses, but does imply that he inherited Moses's legal authority. This halakhic authority is one of the main distinguishing features of the model of prophecy presupposed in Deut 18:15–22: the prophet like Moses serves the people's need for an updated legislative word from God.[45] As modern biblical scholarship has emphasized, the multiplicity of altars in the narratives of Joshua and Samuel stand in stark contrast to Deuteronomy's vision of a single sanctuary and a single altar. Josephus therefore stresses that the altar at the Jordan was indeed authorized by the command of a Mosaic prophet. The Jordan becomes "a place which the LORD your God has chosen," via the prophet's commands. Josephus addresses the tension present in the scriptural text by deferring to the halakhic authority implied in the institution of the Mosaic prophetic succession.

3.5 *The Extent of the Mosaic Prophetic Succession*

The foregoing considerations, I believe, establish fairly conclusively that Josephus interpreted Deut 18:15–22 in terms of Joshua's succession of Moses. Josephus envisaged that Deuteronomy took place as an actual speech of Moses on his last day, and that Joshua was the prophet who was "among" the Israelites, raised up to lead them. However, does the concept of an "exact succession" (ἀκριβῆ διαδοχήν, *Ag. Ap.* 1.41) continue in the *Antiquities*?

---

45 *Pace* Jonathan Klawans, *Josephus and the Theologies of Ancient Judaism* (New York: Oxford University, 2012), 159–161 (see 160: "In Josephus's world, not once does a post-Mosaic prophet address, let alone solve, a legal matter").

Though space precludes a detailed consideration of Books 5–11 (with the hundreds of references to prophets and prophecy contained therein), there is evidence that Josephus downplayed any prophetic "silences" in the period from Moses onwards, in favor of the notion of a continuous prophetic office. Indeed, a careful reading of the *Antiquities* suggests that Josephus did as much as he could to posit an exact succession of the prophets. Josephus describes the deaths and burial places of Joshua and Eleazar in *Ant* 5.119, and continues: "After the death of these, Phinehas prophesied (Μετὰ δὲ τὴν τούτων τελευτὴν Φινεέσης προφητεύει)" (*Ant.* 5.120). Phinehas is not called a prophet in the scriptural text. Later, Josephus calls Deborah a "certain prophetess (τινα προφῆτιν)" (*Ant.* 5.200), picking up on the reference to Deborah as a prophetess, נביאה (Jdg 4:4). He calls Samson a prophet (*Ant.* 5.285), and then has the succession of Israel's leadership proceed from Samson to Eli (*Ant.* 5.318), who also exercised a prophetic role (*Ant.* 5.340, 345). After Eli, the leadership passes on to Samuel: from this point onwards, Josephus's base texts are more conducive to positing an "exact" succession of prophets. Relatedly, Josephus omits the biblical description of the time before Samuel as one in which prophetic activity was rare (1 Sam 3:1; cf *Ant.* 5.351). In sum, if Josephus held a doctrine of the "exact succession of the prophets" conceived of as a chain stretching from Moses onwards, the time-period that would be the least conducive to this claim would be the death of Moses to the time of Samuel, as it has a complete absence of named prophets other than Deborah.[46] Josephus, however, describes figures such as Joshua, Phinehas, and Samson in prophetic terms, often introducing "prophets" into this phase of the history. Gray is therefore incorrect to suggest that the *Antiquities* gives no evidence of Josephus's holding a consistent doctrine of the exact succession of the prophets; on the contrary, it seems his chronological indications in *Ap.* 1.40–41 is intentionally quite precise: there was always *at least one* prophet in Israel from the time of Moses until Artaxerxes of Persia.

Concluding this exact succession with the time of Artaxerxes has occasioned several interpretations: Barton held that it was a reference to the time of Ezra,[47] while Cook maintains that Josephus refers to the Ahasuerus of the book of Esther.[48] The latter seems the most probable hypothesis, for several

---

[46] At Jdg 7:7–10, the MT includes an account of an anonymous prophet. This is a late intrusion that may (similarly to Josephus) respond to the perceived absence of prophets in this time-period.

[47] Barton, *Oracles of God*, 106.

[48] Cook, *Cessation of Prophecy*, 132n289; also Gray, *Prophetic Figures*, 26.

reasons. "Artaxerxes" is only otherwise mentioned by Josephus in his retelling of the book of Esther (*Ant.* 11.184–296). Second, Josephus's retelling of Esther marks the conclusion of his dependence on scriptural base texts in *Antiquities*, which conforms to the statement that this period marks the conclusion of the exact prophetic succession in *Ag. Ap.* 1.41. Third, it seems likely that Esther was included among his thirteen historiographic prophetic works, given that it figures prominently in his *Antiquities* and that it is certainly not one of the four prophetic works of poetry and wisdom.[49] Therefore, though Josephus does not clearly signal the end of the "exact succession" in his *Antiquities*, the evidence that we have suggests that this category was in his mind as he wrote it—indeed, it is only on the basis of knowledge of *Antiquities* that one can understand why Josephus chose the reign of Artaxerxes as the moment of the failure of the exact prophetic succession.[50] Like Ben Sira, Josephus aligns the Mosaic prophetic succession with an authoritative scriptural record; unlike Ben Sira, there is a pronounced sense that he considers both the prophetic line and the prophetic literature to be closed, and subject to the interpretive authority of the ancient succession that has persisted to his present, namely, that of the priesthood. But is this cessation of Mosaic prophecy temporary? I now turn to evidence in Josephus for the eschatological interpretation of Deut 18:15, 18, which may have reached the height of its influence in Early Judaism in the first century CE.

---

49   It is possible to harmonize Josephus's twenty-two books with those of the Tanakh, but this involves counting multiple books together (Judges-Ruth, Samuel, Kings, Chronicles, Ezra-Nehemiah, Jeremiah-Lamentations). Counting all these as six books would leave seven others: Joshua, Isaiah, Ezekiel, Daniel, the Twelve, Job, and Esther. The four non-historiographic prophetic works would be Psalms, Proverbs, Ecclesiastes, and Song of Songs. Whether such harmonization is plausible, however, is at least questionable. I doubt that Josephus's canon can be accurately reconstructed. That said, educated guesses can be made, and given Job's absence from the historiographic prophetic succession (compare the *Antiquities*), it seems probable that Song of Songs should give way to Job in the four non-historiographic prophetic works (allowing at least one of the combinations above to count as two books, perhaps Judges and Ruth). On all this, however, see Mroczek, *Literary Imagination*, 161–167, who argues that all such endeavors are beside the point; the number 22 is symbolic, not literal.

50   Gray, *Prophetic Figures*, 26, recognizes that Artaxerxes is specifically associated with Esther, but claims that Josephus's "treatment of John Hyrcanus shows more clearly that the limits of the prophetic age were flexible .... Josephus was able to extend the golden age of the great prophets to include his own personal hero, John Hyrcanus." This is mistaken: Josephus is well aware that Hyrcanus's exercise of the prophetic office took place much later than the failure of the "exact succession."

4 Eschatological Prophets like Moses Reported on by Josephus

In both his *Jewish War* and his *Antiquities*, Josephus describes a number of prophetic movements of the first century CE.[51] Scholars are divided as to which figures exactly to include; the list below follows that given by Gray (where there are parallel accounts, they do not always agree and so are treated separately).[52]

1. Theudas, in the time of Fadus, 44–48 CE (*Ant.* 20.97–98; cf Acts 5:36)[53]
    This imposter (γόης) claimed to be a prophet (προφήτης γὰρ ἔλεγεν εἶναι), and persuaded many to take their possessions and follow him to the Jordan, which he claimed he would divide. Many of his followers were killed, and Theudas was captured and beheaded.

2. Unnamed figures in time of Felix, 52–60 CE (*War* 2.258–260, *Ant.* 20.167–168)
    War: "Deceivers and seducers" (πλάνοι γὰρ ἄνθρωποι καὶ ἀπατεῶνες) who claimed to be divinely inspired (προσχήματι θειασμοῦ) led a crowd into the wilderness (εἰς τὴν ἐρημίαν), promising that God would there show them "signs of freedom" (σημεῖα ἐλευθερίας). Felix killed many of them.
    Ant.: Multiple "imposters and deceivers" (γόητες καὶ ἀπατεῶνες) persuaded a crowd to follow them into the wilderness (εἰς τὴν ἐρημίαν ἔπεσθαι), promising "wonders and signs" (τέρατα καὶ σημεῖα). They were punished (in an unspecified manner) by Felix.

3. The Egyptian, c. 55 CE (*War* 2.261–263; *Ant.* 20.169–172; cf Acts 21:38)[54]
    War: An Egyptian false prophet (ψευδοπροφήτης) led 30,000 men from the wilderness (ἐκ τῆς ἐρημίας) to the Mount of Olives, and planned an attack

---

51 These are occasionally called the "sign prophets," following the article of Paul W. Barnett, "The Jewish Sign Prophets—A.D. 40–70: Their Intentions and Origin," *NTS* 27 (1980–1981): 679–697. See also Gray, *Prophetic Figures*, 112–144; Richard A. Horsley and John S. Hanson, *Bandits, Prophets, and Messiahs: Popular Movements in the Time of Jesus* (Minneapolis: Winston, 1985), 160–172; Robert L. Webb, *John the Baptizer and Prophet: A Sociohistorical Study*, JSNTSup 62 (Sheffield: JSOT Press, 1991), 333–348; David M. Miller, "Whom Do You Follow? The Jewish Politeia and the Maccabean Background of Josephus's Sign Prophets," in *Common Judaism: Explorations in Second Temple Judaism*, ed. A. Reinhartz and W. McCready (Minneapolis: Fortress, 2008), 173–183.
52 Gray, *Prophetic Figures*, 112.
53 The reference in Acts is chronologically confused (since Gamaliel gives his speech prior to Theudas' movement), and adds no information other than specifying that Theudas attracted 400 followers.
54 Gray, *Prophetic Figures*, 116–117, points to the discrepancies between the two accounts

on Jerusalem. Felix engaged him in battle; his followers were dispersed or killed, while the Egyptian fled.

Ant. One who said he was a prophet (προφήτης εἶναι λέγων) came from Egypt to Jerusalem. He promised his follower that at his command the walls of Jerusalem would fall down (ὡς κελεύσαντος αὐτοῦ πίπτοι τὰ τῶν Ἱεροσολυμιτῶν τείχη). Felix killed 400 of his followers and captured 200.

4. Unnamed figure under Festus, 60–62 CE (*Ant.* 20.188)
   A certain imposter (γόης) promised salvation (σωτηρίαν) and freedom from misery (παῦλαν κακῶν) if people would follow him to the wilderness (ἕπεσθαι μέχρι τῆς ἐρημίας). Both he and his followers were killed.

5. Unnamed figure led followers to temple, 70 CE (*War* 6.285–287)
   A "false prophet" (ψευδοπροφήτης) proclaimed that God commanded (κελεύει) the people to go into the Temple court, where they would receive "signs of deliverance" (σημεῖα τῆς σωτηρίας). He was one of many prophets proclaiming that the people should "wait for help from God" (προσμένειν τὴν ἀπὸ τοῦ θεοῦ βοήθειαν).

6. Jonathan (*War* 7.437–450, *Life* 424–425)
   War: He led "not a few of the poor ... into the desert" (οὐκ ὀλίγους τῶν ἀπόρων ... εἰς τὴν ἔρημον), promising "signs and apparitions" (σημεῖα καὶ φάσματα). He was captured, and falsely accused prominent Jews in order to save himself, including Josephus. When these claims were brought to Rome, Jonathan was punished by Titus (tortured, and burnt alive).
   Life: He had "raised a tumult" (στάσιν ἐξεγείρας), attracting some two thousand followers. He falsely accused Josephus, and was put to death by Vespasian.

In Josephus' narrative, these rebellions indicated that Judaea was headed for a decisive and disastrous confrontation with Rome. They vindicate his understanding of the calamity that befell Judaea: the people should have listened to Josephus, a lonely Jeremiah telling them to submit to the pagan oppres-

---

of the Egyptian. In *War* and *Antiquites*, he gathers his following in different locales (the wilderness and Jerusalem respectively), has a different military strategy (only in *Antiquities* do we hear of his promised miracle), and has wildly different numbers of followers. Acts 21:38 says that the Egyptian led 4000 *Sicarii* into the wilderness, providing still a third tradition.

sor, rather than putting their vain hopes in prophetic charlatans.[55] His reports of these movements are stereotyped, following a pattern that consistently includes the prophetic claimant leading followers into the wilderness, promising that God would manifest signs and wonders through them, and subsequently being brutally put down by the Romans.

The combination of prophetic claimants, the wilderness, miraculous signs, and political deliverance has caused some scholars to conclude that a Moses-Joshua typology lies behind the self-understanding of these figures.[56] Indeed, Dale Allison has argued that they provide evidence for the vitality of an eschatological interpretation of Deut 18:15 in the first century CE. After reviewing the evidence, he concludes:

> [T]he expectation of an eschatological prophet like Moses, founded upon Deut 18:15 and 18, was not little known, or just the esoteric property of the Qumran coventicle and Jewish-Christian churches. It was instead very much in the air in first-century Palestine and helped to instigate several short-lived revolutionary movements. Jesus was far from being the only individual thought of as the eschatological fulfillment of Deut 18:15 and 18. Indeed, there were several men who bravely, if in the event foolishly, set out to hasten divine intervention by imitating Moses in their deeds.[57]

Allison's conviction is shared, in varying degrees, by others,[58] though the dominant emphasis in contemporary scholarship is on the relatively minor role of

---

55 So Gray, *Prophetic Figures*, 144: "Like Jeremiah, Josephus … preached an unpopular message of submission to foreign rule and was abused and maligned by his own people. And like Jeremiah, he too had to contend with deceivers and false prophets who promised the people that God would deliver them."

56 Jeremias, "Μωϋσῆς," *TDNT* 4:862: "All these messiahs follow the example of Moses by calling for an exodus into the wilderness and promising signs and wonders, and also deliverance. The series is an impressive testimony to the strength with which the idea that the Messiah would be a second Moses was anchored in popular expectation"; Dale C. Allison, "Q's New Exodus and the Historical Jesus," in *The Sayings Source Q and the Historical Jesus*, ed. A. Lindemann (Leuven: Leuven University, 2001), 395–428, at 427–428, suggests Theudas and the Egyptian "held a Mosaic self-conception."

57 Dale Allison, *The New Moses: A Matthean Typology* (Minneapolis: Fortress, 1993), 83.

58 Geza Vermes, *Jesus the Jew: A Historian's Reading of the Gospels* (Philadelphia: Fortress, 1973), 94, says that the expectation of an eschatological prophet was "prevalent in inter-Testamental Judaism"; Oscar Cullmann, *The Christology of the New Testament*, trans. S.C. Guthrie and C.A. Hall, rev. ed. (Philadelphia: Westminster, 1963), 15–16, asserts (emphasis original): "The expectation of the prophet who would appear at the end of days must have been common in New Testament times. In view of the success of the Baptist, the Jews ask

specific eschatological or messianic expectations in Second Temple Judaism.[59] Nevertheless, it is worth posing the question: do these movements provide indirect evidence for the vitality of an eschatological interpretation of Deut 18:15 in the first century CE?

It is perhaps tempting to conclude as much, and to relate these prophetic movements to the evidence of the NT and Qumran regarding the expectation of an eschatological prophet like Moses. That said, we lack clear evidence regarding these figures' self-understanding and goals. Our main witness, Josephus, is unquestionably hostile.[60] The two that are particularly promising in terms of a Mosaic self-understanding are Theudas and the Egyptian. Only in these two cases does Josephus explicitly state that they claimed prophetic status.[61] It is perhaps not coincidental that it is only in these two instances that the promised "sign" is reported with specificity, and is directly connected to the agency of the prophetic claimant: Theudas claimed that the Jordan would divide "at his command" (προστάγματι, *Ant.* 20.97), and the Egyptian that he would order the walls of Jerusalem to collapse (ὡς κελεύσαντος αὐτοῦ, *Ant.* 20.170).[62] Although

---

him in John 1:21, 'Are you *the* prophet?' It is assumed that everyone knows who is meant thereby"; Richard Bauckham, "Messianism According to the Gospel of John," in *Challenging Perspectives on the Gospel of John*, ed. J. Lierman, WUNT 2/219 (Tübingen: Mohr Siebeck, 2006), 34–68, at 48: "For several decades before the revolt, Davidic messianism, it seemed, produced no popular movements, but the hope of Moses-like prophetic leader spawned several."

59   See the chapter on eschatology in E.P. Sanders, *Judaism: Practice and Belief, 63 BCE–66 CE* (Philadelphia: Trinity, 1992), 279–303.

60   See Helen K. Bond, "Josephus and the New Testament," in *A Companion to Josephus*, ed. H.H. Chapman and Z. Rodgers, Blackwell Companions to the Ancient World (Chicester, West Sussex, UK: John Wiley & Sons, 2016), 147–158, at 151: "It is clear that Josephus detests these men … and the depth of his scorn makes any reconstruction of their aims and promises difficult in the extreme." Perhaps Luke is less hostile, but he scarcely seems to have reliable independent information about Theudas. His information about the Egyptian suggests, like *War*, a wilderness movement, but offers no other point of contact with Josephus' accounts (unless the tribune's confusion of Paul with this figure reflects knowledge that the Egyptian was planning an assault on Jerusalem).

61   Theudas: προφήτης γὰρ ἔλεγεν εἶναι, *Ant.* 20.97; the Eygptian: προφήτης εἶναι λέγων, *Ant.* 20.169.

62   In contrast, in some of the other movements reported by Josephus, the promised "signs of freedom" (σημεῖα ἐλευθερίας, *War* 2.258) or "deliverance" (σημεῖα τῆς σωτηρίας, *War* 6.285) may not have been expected to come about through prophetic agency, but instead would be wrought directly by God. Consider the counsel of the "false prophet" that the people should "wait for help from God (προσμένειν τὴν ἀπὸ τοῦ θεοῦ βοήθειαν)" (*War* 6.286). See Sanders, *Judaism: Practice and Belief*, 286: "They [the followers of these movements] probably thought that, by stepping boldly forth and risking their lives, they would hasten the day of their deliverance, but they looked to God as the commander-in-chief who would

the miracles promised are more reminiscent of Joshua than Moses, this has not deterred Allison, who considers this a logical extension of the promise of a prophet like Moses. With respect to Theudas, he says, "To cross the Jordan once again was to repeat the exodus again, and to be like Joshua was to be like Moses."[63] As far as the "Egyptian" is concerned, Allison sums up the data with a rhetorical question:

> Now an individual who came from Egypt, who led the people in the desert, who made himself out to be a prophet, and who sought to rule Israel—how could such a one not have been perceived as another prophet-king like Moses?[64]

It is indeed striking that these figures appear in the only time-period in which we have a documented eschatological interpretation of Deut 18:15. In this connection, it is useful to draw upon Richard Horsley's adaptation of anthropologist James C. Scott's distinction between "great tradition" and "little tradition":

> [T]he "little tradition" refers to the distinctive patterns of belief and behavior which are valued by the peasantry. The "great tradition" refers to the corresponding patterns among the aristocracy and their intellectual-scribal retainers, sometimes to a degree embodied in written documents. Depending on the historical development of the traditions, there is considerable parallel and a degree of interaction among them.[65]

Horsley argues that this "little" or "popular" tradition would not have been directly influenced by scripture; rather, they were informed by broader patterns

---

strike the decisive blow. Their vision of the future probably differed from that of the readers of the *War Rule* only in degree .... In all these instances redemption was basically up to God."

63 Allison, "Q's New Exodus," 428. More speculatively, he adds: "Josephus's remark that Theudas ... persuaded 'the majority of the masses' to take up their possessions reminds one of nothing so much as Exodus 12, where the Israelites pack their possessions for the wilderness (vv. 32–36)."

64 Allison, "Q's New Exodus," 428. See also Richard Horsley, " 'Like One of the Prophets of Old': Two Types of Popular Prophets at the Time of Jesus," *CBQ* 47 (1985): 435–463, at 458: "Is he simply an Egyptian Jew who had at some point returned to Palestine (as Hillel had returned from Babylon)? Or is the name more symbolic, in the typological sense of a leader like Moses and Joshua: having come out of Egypt, he was now leading the people."

65 Richard Horsley, "A Prophet like Moses and Elijah: Popular Memory and Cultural Patterns in Mark," in *Performing the Gospel: Orality, Memory, and Mark*, ed. R.A. Horsley, J.M. Draper, and J.M. Foley (Minneapolis: Fortress, 2006), 166–190; here 175.

of Israelite cultural memory.⁶⁶ Indeed, this lies behind his curious insistence that, on the one hand, the eschatological interpretation of Deut 18:15 was not widely attested in Second Temple Judaism, but that, on the other, Theudas and the Egyptian were eschatological prophets in a Mosaic mold—a combination of views that is rather striking.⁶⁷ I would allow for mutual influence and overlap between "official" and "popular" traditions, and not define them as separately as Horsley does. In the confines of this study, the implications of this distinction would be to insist that even if Theudas and the Egyptian represented themselves as eschatological prophets like Moses, they did not necessarily do so on the basis of the priestly-scribal construct of the cessation and deferral of the Mosaic prophetic succession.⁶⁸ They may, however, have been influenced by scribal teaching about a return of prophecy, and the notion that a prophetic claimant needed to represent himself in terms of the great figures of Israel's past seems to have informed their self-understanding. Indeed, in view of the evidence discussed above that Joshua was viewed as the original and perhaps paradigmatic prophet like Moses, the fact that Theudas and the Egyptian patterned their promised signs after Joshua is highly suggestive, if ultimately inconclusive.

---

66   Horsley, "A Prophet like Moses and Elijah," 182–183.
67   See Horsley and Hanson, *Bandits, Prophets, and Messiahs*, 160, where these views are immediately juxtaposed with no acknowledgement of any tension between them
> Indeed, during the first century C.E., the memory of ancient prophetic movements of liberation informed new prophetic movements, and traditional oracular prophecy was revived among the people. [New Paragraph] As indicated in the first part of this chapter, however, there is simply very little evidence for Jewish expectations of an eschatological prophet prior to the time of Jesus. There is no documentation whatsoever for expectations of *the* eschatological prophet, and very little for expectations of the prophet like Moses based on Deut 18:18.

Having claimed the expectation does not exist, Horsley and Hanson will go on to describe a first-century Samaritan prophet as "Moses' eschatological counterpart" (164) and Theudas as both a "new Joshua" and "as leading a new Exodus," analogous to Moses (166). This is all rather confusing, but it is clarified in one illuminating comment (161): "The point to be recognized is that with the popular prophets who appeared at the time, we are dealing with more than simply a fulfillment of some particular expectation. Prophecy was very much alive among the Jewish people." That is, because Horsley and Hanson do not want to allow the theological construct of prophecy's cessation to play a role in their interpretation of the evidence (see 146–147), they refuse to correlate the reported eschatological movements with the scripturally-based hopes for the eschatological revival of a dormant tradition.
68   See also Bauckham, "Messianism," 53, on the "distinction between popular and learned views of the Moses-like prophet," in which the former is associated with eschatological liberator and the latter with the teacher of Deut 18:15–19.

There is, however, one positive conclusion that can be drawn from these accounts of the sign prophets, which in my view has not been registered with sufficient clarity in scholarship, and that has to do with Josephus' self-presentation as a priest who is well-versed in the scriptural norms for adjudicating prophetic claimants. That is, though it is unclear whether all of the sign prophets self-identified as prophets (much less prophets like Moses),[69] it is absolutely clear that Josephus rejects the whole lot of them as false prophets or charlatans. Indeed, he indicates that such figures are to be understood not as the Mosaic prophet of Deut 18:15–22, but in terms of the deceiving prophet of Deut 13:2–6, whom Israel is to reject. Thus, though the influence of Deuteronomy's norms for prophets in these figures self-understanding is uncertain, it can be affirmed more confidently in Josephus' self-presentation.

Josephus' preferred term for these prophetic claimants is γόης ("imposter, charlatan"), which he uses not only for Theudas (*Ant.* 20.97) and the Egyptian prophet (*War* 2.261), but also for anonymous general deceivers (*Ant.* 20.160, 167) and another unnamed imposter (*Ant.* 20.188). Additionally, Josephus regularly employs the language of deception to describe these figures. Regarding Theudas, he says, "many were deluded (ἠπάτησεν) by his words" (*Ant.* 20.98). Later he says that general imposters "deluded the multitude (τὸν ὄχλον ἠπάτων)" (*Ant.* 20.160). The Egyptian "got together thirty thousand men that were deluded by him (τῶν ἠπατημένων)" (*War* 2.261).[70] It is noteworthy that Philo uses the same vocabulary precisely in the context of discussing the seducer-prophet of Deut 13:2–6:[71]

> And if, indeed, any one assuming the name and appearance of a prophet, appearing to be inspired and possessed by the Holy Spirit, were to seek to lead the people to the worship of those who are accounted gods in the different cities, it would not be fitting for the people to attend to him being deceived (ἀπατωμένους) by the name of a prophet. For such an one is an impostor and not a prophet (γόης γὰρ ἀλλ' οὐ προφήτης ἐστὶν ὁ τοιοῦτος), since he has been inventing speeches and oracles full of falsehood.
>
> *De Spec. Leg.* 1.315

---

69 *Contra* Bauckham, "Messianism," 43.
70 See also *War* 6.287, where with respect to the false prophets at the temple's destruction Josephus makes the general observation: "Now, a man that is in adversity does easily comply (πείθεται δὲ ταχέως) with such promises; for when such a seducer (ἐξαπατῶν) makes him believe that he shall be delivered from those miseries which oppress him, then it is that the patient is full of hopes of such his deliverance."
71 See Gray, *Prophetic Figures*, 207–208n103.

Thus, in drawing upon the language of deception (cf. Deut 13:6), Josephus presents himself, for those who know the scriptures, as one who has evaluated these movements according to the standards of Torah and found them wanting.

There is another piece of evidence that may contribute to Josephus' understanding of these figures in terms of a contrast between the true prophet of Deut 18:15, 18 and the seducer prophet of Deut 13:2–6. In *Against Apion*, Josephus attributes to anti-Jewish writers (Apollonios Molon, Lysimachus, and certain others) the charge that Moses was both charlatan and deceiver (γόης καὶ ἀπατεών; *Ag. Ap.* 2.145, 161). René Bloch has argued that Josephus projects an inner-Jewish debate onto these Greek anti-Jewish writers. Indeed, Bloch claims that when Josephus defends Moses from the charge of being a "charlatan," he first of all has in mind the various "charlatans" of his own time.[72] Josephus' main point is to assert that Moses has nothing in common with these religious frauds: "Mose ist kein Johannes von Gischala .... Mose ist kein Theudas."[73] Though Bloch does not speculate regarding these figures' self-understanding, it is possible that one of the reasons for Josephus to defend Moses using the same terminology with which he castigated prophetic charlatans would be a way to respond to claims by such figures to be the agents of Mosaic prophetic authority.

This line of interpretation is also supported by the stereotyped character of Josephus' reports. It is evident that he views these figures as conforming to a standard or type. Moreover, these reports often include a specific notice of the death of the prophetic claimant and many of his followers.[74] Death, of course, is the punishment of any false prophet (Deut 13:6; 18:20). Josephus shows no dismay at the brutal tactics of the Romans against these movements, because he regards the Romans as instruments of divine justice against false prophets. In keeping with his self-understanding as priest and qualified interpreter of Israel's prophetic scriptures, Josephus presents himself as obedient to the Deuteronomic norms in identifying and castigating these charlatans. Whether or not they all claimed prophetic status, Josephus denounces them

---

[72] René Bloch, "Mose und die Scharlatane: Zum Vorwurf γόης καὶ ἀπατεών in *Contra Apionem* 2:145.161," in *Internationales Josephus-Kolloquium, Bruxelles 1998*, ed. F. Siegert and J.U. Kalms, Münsteraner judaistische Studien 4 (Münster, Lit, 1999), 142–157; at 153: "Wenn er Moses gegen den Vorwurf der γοητεία verteidigt, denkt er in erster Linie an die Goeten seiner Zeit!"

[73] Bloch, "Mose und die Scharlatane," 153.

[74] Theudas: *Ant.* 20.98; Jonathan of Cyrene: *War* 7.450; *Life* 425; unnamed imposter, *Ant.* 20.188; cf. also *Ant.* 20.161, 167; *War* 2.258–260. In the cases of the Egyptian (*Ant.* 20.171; *War* 2.263) and of an unnamed prophet at the temple's destruction (*War* 6.284–285), Josephus does not report the death of the leader, but does mention that of many of their followers.

as seducers who led Israel astray, and who played a significant role in bringing about the calamity of the Jewish War. The currency of the Deuteronomic norms for prophecy, then, are manifest in Josephus' self-presentation, even if only uncertainly in the prophetic movements themselves.

5 The Mosaic Prophetic Succession from Ben Sira to Josephus: Concluding Comments

In conclusion, Josephus is an heir and exemplar of an interpretive tradition in which there is an increased scriptural alignment of the Mosaic prophetic succession in the Second Temple period. Beginning with Ben Sira in Hellenistic Jerusalem, scribal authors posited that this particular prophetic succession (not prophecy as such) had provisionally ceased, and they carved out a space in the present in which the prerogative to interpret the prophetic scriptures belonged to the priestly-scribal establishment. The "prophets," then, were mainly those figures represented in the scriptures of Israel, and indeed an increasing number of them.[75] I have particularly emphasized the prophetic status of Joshua, because there is considerable evidence that he was understood to be the primary referent of Moses's promise, made in his farewell speech on the plains of Moab, that God would raise up from among the Israelites a prophet like him. The ascription of prophetic status to Joshua, however, illustrates two of the tendencies in this time period: first, the "scripturalization" of the Mosaic prophetic succession, witnessed from Ben Sira to Josephus; and second, the developing sense that such a succession was continuously operative in Israel's past, extending directly from Moses through the Persian period, with the various ruptures indicated in the Deuteronomistic oeuvre completely forgotten.

The hope or expectation of a future Mosaic prophet is not nearly so pronounced as the view that Mosaic prophets properly speaking belonged to the past, but it is not entirely marginal, and emerges in different ways in texts from the time of Malachi and Ben Sira to that of the Qumran community and the emergence of Christianity. The evidence that such expectations influenced sev-

---

75 Interestingly, Eugene Ulrich, "The Bible in the Making: The Scriptures Found at Qumran," in *The Bible at Qumran: Text, Shape, and Interpretation*, ed. P. Flint, SDSSRL (Grand Rapids: Eerdmans, 2001), 51–66, at 56, suggests that the third category of the "Writings" emerged as a reaction to the proliferation of literature claiming to be prophetic (emphasis original): "[A]pparently the category of 'Prophets' was gradually perceived as being *stretched too far* .... [T]he book of Psalms, which had been counted among the Prophets, began to establish a new category that eventually would be called the Ketubim or the Hagiographa."

eral revolutionary movements is suggestive, though to what extent remains unknown. Given the little that is known about figures such as Theudas and the Egyptian, it is striking that the available evidence, meagre though it is, conforms with the notion that a prophetic claim had to be staked with reference to a Mosaic norm. If written sources from any of these prophets' followers had survived, we might be better informed as to how they articulated their self-understanding. In the case of ancient Christianity, we do have such documents. Here we can observe how one messianic movement in ancient Judaism, nascent Christianity, responded to the pressure exerted by the Mosaic norm for prophecy. I now turn to Luke-Acts, and consider how its author responded to and incorporated the priestly-scribal concept of the Mosaic prophetic succession in its narrative of Christian origins.

CHAPTER 10

Listening to a "Raised" Prophet: The Prophet like Moses in Luke-Acts

1 Introductory Comments on the Prophet like Moses in the New Testament

The thesis that the expectation of a prophet like Moses according to Deut 18:15 strongly influenced the NT writings might seem to be belied by the infrequency of references to this passage. The index of scripture citations and allusions in the twenty-seventh edition of Nestle-Aland's Greek New Testament suggests a rather slim profile: the only two quotations occur in occur in the early chapters of Acts, in speeches of Peter (3:22–23) and Stephen (7:37), and the editors propose allusions in Matt 17:5; Mark 9:4, 7; Luke 7:39; 9:35; 24:25; John 1:21; 5:46. Notably, there are no citations or allusions in some of the earliest Christian texts, such as Paul's epistles. In accordance with this restricted profile, Howard Teeple argued that the influence of Deut 18:15, 18 was relatively minor in the NT:

> It must be emphasized ... that only a portion of Judaism entertained this expectation, and therefore it is not surprising that there were also many Jewish Christians who did *not* interpret Jesus in that manner. Although Jesus is presented as a prophet in all the canonical gospels, the only New Testament books which definitely present him as the Prophet *like Moses* are the Gospels of Matthew and the Book of Acts.[1]

Oscar Cullman's roughly contemporaneous *Christology of the New Testament* makes a similarly limited claim, although he substitutes John's gospel for that of Matthew: "Except for the Gospel of John and the first (Jewish Christian) part of Acts, no New Testament writing considers Jesus the eschatological Prophet who prepares the way for God."[2] These minimalist conclusions have

---

1 Howard M. Teeple, *The Mosaic Eschatological Prophet*, JBLMS 10 (Philadelphia: Society of Biblical Literature, 1957), 78. Emphasis original.
2 Oscar Cullmann, *The Christology of the New Testament*, trans. S.C. Guthrie and C.A. Hall, rev. ed. (Philadelphia: Westminster, 1963 [German original: 1957]), 38. David Aune, *Prophecy in Early Christianity and the Ancient Mediterranean World* (Grand Rapids: Eerdmans, 1983), 156, also claims the identification of Jesus as the prophet like Moses is limited to Acts and John.

been redressed by scholars who identify the importance of Moses typology in other gospel material. Wayne Meeks highlighted the importance of Moses traditions for John's christology,[3] while scholars such as David Moessner and Jocelyn McWhirter, among others, have argued for its extensive presence in Luke-Acts.[4] Dale Allison has extended Teeple's initial work by showing how pervasive Moses typology is in Matthew, and in his detailed study he also pays attention to Mark as one of Matthew's sources.[5]

Methodologically, it is critical to register the point that scholars reach different assessments of the importance of the prophet like Moses depending on how expansively they define this concept. This book deals with the story of the prophet like Moses, not Moses typology in general. The former concept has limited influence in the NT; the latter is extensive.[6] Not all Moses typology has authorized succession to Moses in view; much of it has to do with a general appeal to the Exodus tradition as an archetypal salvation story. Matthew's gospel is perhaps the most prominent example of an early Christian text that draws heavily upon Moses typology, but makes little explicit use of Deut 18:15.[7]

---

3 Wayne A. Meeks, *The Prophet-King: Moses Traditions and the Johannine Christology*, NovTSup 14 (Leiden: Brill, 1967); see also Christopher A. Maronde, "Moses in the Gospel of John," *CTQ* 77 (2013): 23–44.

4 David P. Moessner, *Lord of the Banquet: The Literary and Theological Significance of the Lukan Travel Narrative* (Minneapolis, Fortress, 1989); idem, "Luke 9:1–50: Luke's Preview of the Journey of the Prophet Like Moses of Deuteronomy," *JBL* 102 (1983): 575–605; idem, "Paul and the Pattern of the Prophet Like Moses in Acts," *Society of Biblical Literature Seminar Papers* 22 (1983): 203–212; idem, "Good News for the 'Wilderness Generation': The Death of the Prophet Like Moses According to Luke," in *Good News in History: Essays in Honor of Bo Reicke*, ed. Ed. L. Miller (Atlanta: Scholars Press, 1993), 1–34; Jocelyn McWhirter, *Rejected Prophets: Jesus and his Witnesses in Luke-Acts* (Minneapolis: Fortress, 2013). See also J. Severino Croatto, "Jesus, Prophet Like Elijah, and Prophet-Teacher Like Moses in Luke-Acts," *JBL* 124 (2005): 451–465.

5 Dale C. Allison, *The New Moses: a Matthean Typology* (Minneapolis: Fortress Press, 1993).

6 For a study of every reference to Moses in the New Testament, see John Lierman, *The New Testament Moses: Christian Perceptions of Moses and Israel in the Setting of Jewish Religion*, WUNT 2/173 (Tübingen: Mohr Siebeck, 2004).

7 Outside of the Transfiguration account (which is dependent on Mark), there are no citations of or allusions to Deut 18:15, 18 in Matthew's gospel. Aune, *Prophecy in Early Christianity*, 154–155, therefore rightly distinguishes between the two: "although Matthew uses a number of literary devices and theological motifs to depict Jesus as a new Moses, he never attempts to identify Jesus with the eschatological Mosaic prophet." Allison, *New Moses*, 315, concedes that Deut 18:15–22 is not a major source of theological reflection for Matthew, while rightly insisting that Moses-typology is broader than just interaction with this text: "even if 'the prophet like Moses' does not appear at all, the significance for Matthean theology of Jesus' likeness to Moses is not thereby settled." Earlier, he appeals to "*anagnorisis*, the pleasure of recognition" (286), which suggests that Matthew may deliberately leave it to the reader to make the identification between Jesus and Deut 18:15, 18—see his sharply worded comments, 284:

In terms of this more limited focus, the list above points to Luke-Acts as the primary locus of reflection on Deut 18:15–22: it is here that the only two citations occur, and the only proposed allusions in the Synoptic gospels outside of the Transfiguration account occur in material that is unique to Luke.

In my view, this distribution of references is no mere coincidence. In the foregoing, I have traced a hieratic scribal historiographic interpretation of the concept of the prophet like Moses, one which culminates in the writings of Josephus, and one which puts forward the priestly-scribal establishment as the authorized arbiters of prophetic claims. In this chapter, I will argue that Luke-Acts, the earliest Christian historiographic work, which is roughly contemporary to Josephus,[8] is influenced by this tradition; moreover, so situating the work has the potential to clarify key features of the author's understanding of prophets and prophecy.

    The First Gospel has this apparent defect, that its author did not trumpet all his intentions [Allison cites as an example the inclusion of the women in the genealogy of Matthew 1] .... This means that it is, in a fundamental sense, an incomplete utterance, a book full of holes. Readers must make present what is absent; they must become actively engaged and bring to the Gospel knowledge of what it presupposes.

While this may be the gospel writer's intention with respect to the identification of Jesus as the prophet like Moses, in the absence of allusions and citations, such a conclusion can only remain speculative.

8 Luke-Acts is typically dated between 70 CE–125 CE. The precise date is not particularly important for my argument. Steve Mason (*Josephus and the New Testament*, 2nd ed. [Peabody, Mass.: Hendrickson, 2003], 251–298) has proposed that the author knew of Josephus' work, at least via public readings of it, which would suggest a date rather towards the end of this spectrum, and is an intriguing possibility in view of the argument I am going to lay out in this chapter. For an earlier date (shortly before 70 CE), see I.H. Marshall, *The Book of Acts: An Introduction and Commentary*, TNTC (Downers Grove: InterVarsity, 1980), 46–48. For a second-century date, see Richard Pervo, *Acts: A Commentary* (Hermeneia; Minneapolis: Fortress, 2009), 5–7. A key consideration is that the author represents himself as the erstwhile travelling companion of Paul in the so-called "we"-passages (Acts 16:10–17; 20:5–21:18; 27:1–28:16). Though a variety of solutions to this have been proposed, the simplest possibility is that the author is claiming personal knowledge of these parts of the narrative (so Martin Hengel, *Acts and the History of Earliest Christianity*, trans. John Bowden [Philadelphia: Fortress, 1980], 66; Joseph Fitzmyer, *The Acts of the Apostles*, AB 31 [New York: Doubleday, 1998], 103). Probably the most influential alternate theory has been the "travel diary" proposed by Martin Dibelius, *Studies in the Acts of the Apostles*, trans. Mary Ling (London: SCM Press, 1956), 196–197, 199–206. The author's potential personal knowledge of Paul (as well as his hagiographic treatment of him, which is not incompatible with personal acquaintance some decades earlier, but does preclude dating Acts too early), combined with the gathering and use of sources that date to c. 70 CE, suggests a date between 80–100 CE.

2 Prophets and Prophecy in Luke-Acts

Luke-Acts evinces tremendous interest in prophets and prophecy.[9] The only two quotations from Deut 18:15, 18 in the NT occur in early speeches in Acts; moreover, Peter's Pentecost speech includes a lengthy quotation regarding the diffusion of prophecy in the eschatological age (Acts 2:16–21; cf Joel 2:28–32 [MT 3:1–5]). Early Christian prophecy is a heterogenous phenomenon, and in this chapter I cannot comprehensively treat the subject of prophets and prophecy in Luke-Acts in relation to the development of early Christianity. That said, the evidence is suggestive that Luke seeks to harmonize or combine two models of prophecy: a charismatic model, such as we find reflected in early Christian texts such as Paul's epistles,[10] and a genealogical model, such as I have traced above. Though Luke does not exclusively deploy the priestly-scribal construal of Mosaic prophecy, I will argue that he is aware of this line of interpretation of Deut 18:15–22, and incorporates it into his "apologetic historiography" for the early Christian movement.[11]

The hypothesis of Luke's familiarity with the priestly-scribal construal of the Mosaic prophetic succession illuminates his usage of prophet-terminology, which is otherwise confusing and seemingly inconsistent. On the one hand, a number of Luke's references to prophets and prophecy seem to imply that prophets are figures of the past, and are associated with Israel's scriptural traditions. Luke regularly uses the phrase "all the prophets" to refer to a past (and presumably now closed) prophetic succession; indeed, he is the only NT writer to refer consistently to prophets in this way.[12] On the other hand, Luke-Acts is unique in the New Testament for references to contemporary prophets and prophetic activity.[13] This use of prophet-terminology is explicable on the hypothesis that Luke had the view that prophecy in general did not cease, but

---

9   For a brief summary of scholarship on prophets and prophecy in Luke-Acts, see McWhirter, *Rejected Prophets*, 11–13.
10 See 1 Thess 5:20–21; 1 Cor 11–14. On early Christian prophecy, see Aune, *Prophecy in Early Christianity*; Christopher Forbes, *Prophecy and Inspired Speech in Early Christianity and its Hellenistic Environment*, WUNT 2/75 (Tübingen: Mohr Siebeck, 1995); Laura Nasrallah, *An Ecstasy of Folly: Prophecy and Authority in Early Christianity*, HTS 52 (Cambridge, Mass.: Harvard University Press, 2004).
11 For the category of "apologetic historiography," see Gregory E. Sterling, *Historiography and Self-Definition: Josephos, Luke-Acts, and Apologetic Historiography*, NovTSup 64 (Leiden: Brill, 1992).
12 See, e.g., πάντων τῶν προφητῶν, Luke 11:50; see also Luke 13:28; 24:27; Acts 3:18, 24; 10:43. Elsewhere in the NT, the phrase "all the prophets" for past prophets occurs only at Matt 11:13.
13 Named prophets include John the Baptist (Luke 1:76; 7:26; 20:6), Anna (Luke 2:36), Jesus

an authorized succession of Mosaic prophets did. Relatedly, other than John the Baptist and Jesus, contemporary figures referred to as prophets are typically minor characters in Luke's narrative. This observation, too, suggests that Luke distinguished between "great prophets" (cf Luke 7:16), that is, authorized heirs of the Mosaic prophetic succession, and regular, less significant prophets. Luke describes the prophets of the Mosaic succession in reverential terms: they are the "holy prophets of old" (τῶν ἁγίων τῶν ἀπ' αἰῶνος προφητῶν; Luke 1:70); they are associated with "Abraham and Isaac and Jacob" (Luke 13:28) and also the "kings" (Luke 10:24). For Luke, it is not contemporary prophets, such as Agabus (Acts 11:27; 21:10), that inherit the mantle of the Mosaic succession; rather, this role is bequeathed to prominent early Christian leaders, such as Peter and Stephen. These leaders are not called "prophets" in Luke's narrative; they are portrayed in priestly terms as authorized and inspired interpreters of the prophetic scriptures.[14] Indeed, Luke's portrayal of Peter and Stephen is strongly reminiscent of Josephus's self-presentation as a priest who was skilled in interpreting the sacred oracles.

Strelan has adduced significant evidence to support the contention that the author of Luke-Acts has a priestly, temple-centered perspective, though he does not incorporate Luke's view of prophecy into his argument.[15] In fact, he goes so far as to claim that Luke was a Jewish priest himself, and compares this to Josephus's self-presentation as priest and historian.[16] Strelan acknowledges

---

(Luke 7:16; 9:8, 19), Agabus (Acts 11:27; 21:10), prophets in the church at Antioch (Acts 13:1), Judas and Silas (Acts 15:32), and the daughters of Philip (Acts 21:9).

14 This feature of Luke's use of prophet-terminology is not sufficiently noted by McWhirter, *Rejected Prophets*, who refers throughout to the apostles as "prophets" (see 11, 87–94; e.g.: "Peter and the apostles are Spirit-filled prophets, ready—like Elisha—to carry on the ministry of their mentor" [93]), and does not discuss at any length Luke's "minor" prophets such as Anna, Agabus, and the daughters of Philip. The parallels she highlights between between Elijah-Elisha and Jesus-the apostles are indeed apt, but it remains significant that Luke does not explicitly call the apostles "prophets," and in fact reserves this title for different characters in Acts. In my view, McWhirter's insightful study explicates not Luke's view of prophets and prophecy in general, but Luke's view of the Mosaic prophetic succession more specifically.

15 Rick Strelan, *Luke the Priest: The Authority of the Author of the Third Gospel* (London: Routledge, 2016), 130–144, details the interest of Luke-Acts in such priestly themes as teaching, scriptural interpretation, halakhah/Torah (such as circumcision), repentance and forgiveness, pronouncing of blessings, and liturgy (hyms and worship).

16 Strelan, *Luke the Priest*, 2: "It was the author's status as priest that gave him the authority to interpret the various traditions he deals with and to write his interpretations as authoritative texts for his audiences"; for comparisons to Josephus, see Strelan, *Luke the Priest*, 39–40. Strelan's thesis is intriguing; that said, in my view the author does not represent himself in priestly terms, but his main protagonists.

that his thesis is ultimately unprovable; nevertheless, he advances a number of compelling arguments demonstrating the author's self-understanding as a custodian and interpreter of Israel's scriptural traditions and of early Christian traditions about figures such as Jesus and Paul.[17] There is first of all the point that only Luke-Acts among the earliest Christian writings represents itself as historiography: it is a two-volume narrative telling of the origins of "the Way" (cf. Acts 9:2; 18:25–26; 19:9, 23; 24:14, 22). In Early Judaism, providing a normative historical account was particularly the prerogative of the priestly-scribal tradition. Second, Luke-Acts is not temple- or Torah-critical, as has often been alleged;[18] rather, Luke-Acts is Jerusalem- and temple-centered.[19] Though I make no claim that Luke was a Jewish priest, I hope to show that Luke-Acts situates its view of Jesus' identity as the eschatological prophet like Moses within the priestly-scribal, historiographic tradition that I have traced from Ben Sira to Josephus, in which the question of succession to Moses is understood in fundamentally genealogical terms.

3 Jesus as Prophet like Moses in Acts 3, 7

3.1 *The Prophet like Moses in Luke-Acts: Scholarly Context*

In the quotations above, Teeple and Cullman agree on the presence of Jesus as eschatological Mosaic prophet in one book only, namely the Acts of the Apostles. It is striking that both are also agreed on denying the theme for Luke. Indeed, Teeple is vehement on this point: "Although Luke and Acts were written by the same author and Acts clearly contains the idea that Jesus is the

---

17 Strelan, *Luke the Priest*, 145: "Luke writes not as an editor simply regurgitating a tradition that he has learned or received from elsewhere, but as an authoritative teacher with a clear agenda including that of controlling how the Scriptures and other traditions, both Jewish and Christian, are to be interpreted."

18 See on this topic Steve Smith, *The Fate of the Jerusalem Temple in Luke-Acts: An Intertextual Approach to Jesus' Laments over Jerusalem and Stephen's Speech*, LNTS 553 (London: T&T Clark, 2017), and the literature cited there.

19 Strelan, *Luke the Priest*, 139: "Jerusalem remains, for Luke, the *axis mundi*." This is particularly clear from the prominence of the temple in the beginning and end of Luke (e.g. Luke 1:8–23; 2:22–52; 24:50–53), and the opening scenes of Acts (Acts 2–5; 7). On the centrality of the temple in Luke-Acts, see also Paula Fredriksen, *From Jesus to Christ: The Origins of the New Testament Images of Christ*, 2nd ed. (New Haven: Yale University Press, 2000), 32–33; 197. *Contra* Amy-Jill Levine, "Luke and the Jewish Religion," *Int* 68 (2014): 389–402 (at 393–394): "Following the nativity material in first two chapters, the sacred quality of Israel, Jerusalem, and the temple is gradually eroded …. Jerusalem may be the 'holy city' for Matthew, … but it is not for Luke."

eschatological prophet like Moses, one looks in vain in Luke for evidence that the author has altered or inserted traditions to support this doctrine."[20] In this respect, the parentheses in the quotation from Cullmann are signficant: it is only "the first (Jewish Christian) *part* of Acts" that views Jesus as the prophet like Moses. The presuppositions here are somewhat jarring when compared to the trend in scholarship to view Luke-Acts as a literary and theological unity. Before detailed analysis of Luke-Acts, it is worthwhile to discuss the opposed viewpoints in scholarship concerning whether the identification of Jesus as the prophet like Moses was indeed important for Luke, the late first-century historian and theologian.

Teeple and Cullmann's judgment lies in the shadow of the twentieth-century exegete Rudolf Bultmann. In his *Theology of the New Testament*, Bultmann ascribed considerable importance to the so-called "Hellenist" church (cf Acts 6:1), the early community of Greek-speaking Jews (such as Stephen) that, in Bultmann's view, was a tremendously important locus of theological creativity and an important precursor to Paul.[21] In this vein, and in what was perhaps the most influential New Testament christology written in this time period, Ferdinand Hahn argued that the quotations in Acts 3 and 7 represented a "pre-Lukan Moses-Jesus typology that had its origin in Hellenistic Jewish Christianity."[22] To be sure, Hahn raised the possibly that the citations of Jesus as the prophet like Moses belong to Luke's theologizing, before rejecting it and insisting on their early and traditional character.[23] Reginald Fuller, too, ascribed these citations to the "primitive" christology of the earliest church, not to Luke himself.[24]

---

20 Teeple, *Mosaic Eschatological Prophet*, 87–88. Teeple allows that Luke 7:16 represents a "possible example."

21 Bultmann (*Theology of the New Testament*, trans. Kendrick Grobel, 2 vols. [New York: Charles Scribner's Sons, 1951]), 1:189, proclaims: "The so often and so passionately debated question, 'Jesus and Paul,' is at bottom the question: 'Jesus and Hellenistic Christianity.'"

22 Ferdinand Hahn, *The Titles of Jesus in Christology: Their History in Early Christianity*, trans. H. Knight and G. Ogg (London: Lutterworth, 1969), 374. See criticism in Meeks, *Prophet-King*, 28: "he would be on safer ground to assume that the third evangelist has constructed this 'prophetic christology' in its present form."

23 Hahn, *Titles*, 378: "The decisive question now is whether the idea, clearly palpable in these texts, of Jesus as the eschatological prophet like Moses reaches back to the early Palestinian stratum of the New Testament tradition .... Otherwise the objection may be made that it is palpable exclusively in the Lukan writings and in consequence of that ought to be regarded as a Lukan *theologumenon*." Hahn rejects this latter possibility, and later asks (386–387, emphasis mine): "In the Gospel of Luke is an *after-effect* of the conception of Jesus as the eschatological prophet discernable?" Hahn only allows for this in the Lukan travel narrative, "with traits in its construction that have parallels in Deuteronomy," but offers no specifics.

24 Reginald H. Fuller, *The Foundations of New Testament Christology* (New York: Charles Scrib-

Two trends in Luke-Acts scholarship have led to increased attention on the importance of the concept of the prophet like Moses for the author of Luke-Acts. First, since the mid-twentieth century, there has been an increased emphasis on the author's role as theologian, with the concomitant view that the two volumes are closely unified in *Tendenz* and theological outlook. This trend was inaugurated by Hans Conzelmann's *Die Mitte der Zeit*, which worked out a consistent theological program for Luke-Acts based on the delay of the *Parousia* (Christ's return) in early Christianity.[25] Interestingly, Conzelmann himself held that Deut 18:15 was of no importance to the author: "Luke has simply taken it over from the tradition without reflecting on it."[26] Subsequently, there has been division on this point: some scholars have argued that a prophet like Moses christology is of central importance for Luke;[27] other scholars acknowledge it, but restrict it to a subsidiary or supporting role;[28] still others

---

ner's Sons, 1965), 158–159; so also C.K. Barrett, *A Critical and Exegetical Commentary on the Acts of the Apostles*, 2 vols., ICC (Edinburgh: T&T Clark, 1998), 1:189–190, 337. Similar language was used by Richard F. Zehnle, *Peter's Pentecost Discourse: Tradition and Lukan Reinterpretation in Peter's Speeches of Acts 2 and 3*, SBLMS 15 (Nashville: Abingdon, 1971), 94: "The discourse of Acts 3 is the most primitive and undeveloped christological statement in the New Testament." The use of pejorative adjectives such as "primitive" for what was regarded as a Jewish prophet-christology is a scholarly construct that requires critical scrutiny. Luke's theology is here judged deficient by a standard that is foreign to it, namely, the Logos-christology of John's gospel. Also, "Jewish" Christianity is here considered early and "primitive"; whereas it is now recognized in scholarship that the categories "Jewish" and "Christian" were not neatly separable in the first century CE and well beyond; see, e.g., Adam H. Becker and Annette Y. Reed, ed., *The Ways that Never Parted: Jews and Christians in Late Antiquity and in the Early Middle Ages* (Minneapolis: Fortress Press, 2007); Daniel Boyarin, *Border Lines: The Partition of Judaeo-Christianity* (Philadelphia: University of Pennsylvania Press, 2004).

25 Hans Conzelmann, *Die Mitte der Zeit* (Tübingen: J.C.B. Mohr [Paul Siebeck], 1953); ET: *The Theology of St. Luke*, trans. Geoffrey Buswell (New York: Harper & Row, 1961).
26 Conzelmann, *Theology*, 167n3.
27 This is an important theme of McWhirter, *Rejected Prophets* and Moessner, *Lord of the Banquet*. So also Croatto, "Jesus, Prophet like Elijah"; Richard J. Dillon, *From Eye-Witnesses to Ministers of the Word: Tradition and Composition in Luke 24*, AnBib 82 (Rome: Biblical Institute Press, 1978); Luke Timothy Johnson, *The Literary Function of Possessions in Luke-Acts*, SBLDS 39 (Missoula, Mont.: Scholars Press, 1977); David L. Tiede, *Prophecy and History in Luke-Acts* (Philadelphia: Fortress, 1980).
28 Robert F. O'Toole, *Luke's Presentation of Jesus: A Christology*, SubBi 25 (Rome: Pontificio Istituto Biblico, 2004), 54: " 'prophet' is not Luke's dominant title for Jesus"; Jack Dean Kingsbury, "Jesus As the 'Prophetic Messiah' in Luke's Gospel," in *The Future of Christology: Essays in Honor of Leander E. Keck*, ed. A.J. Malherbe and W.A. Meeks (Philadelphia: Fortress, 1993), 29–42; Robert C. Tannehill, *The Narrative Unity of Luke-Acts: A Literary Interpretation*, 2 vols. (Minneapolis: Fortress, 1990), 97: "Those who speak of Jesus as a

consider it an inadequate view of Jesus, one that Luke reports but himself rejects.[29]

A second important and related trend has been to understand the speeches of Acts as creations of the author, expressing his theological outlook.[30] According to Soards' historical review, it was in early nineteenth-century German criticism that this position was first put forward by J.G. Eichhorn, and it was firmly established by the turn of the twentieth century.[31] It was challenged in the mid-twentieth century, when (in line with the interests noted above) the speeches were mined not for the theology of Luke the historian and theologian, but for the apostolic preaching of the earliest church.[32] The tide began to turn against this view of the speeches with the work of Martin Dibelius, who emphasized their Lukan character and insisted that the task of scholarship was to understand them in relation to the narrative development of Acts.[33] The speeches of Acts then represent not the teaching of the earliest Jerusalem church, but a late-first century author's attempt to make sense of his present circumstances, that is, the development and success of the Gentile mission and the comparative failure of the mission to the Jews.[34] The speeches build upon each other, interpreting the story that the author is telling as the proclamation about Jesus moves from Jerusalem, to Judea and Samaria, and then to the "ends of the earth"

---

prophet in Luke may not understand him completely, but this title does not represent a distortion to be rejected."

29   Kingsbury, "Jesus," 30, says rightly that this position "has largely fallen into disfavor today," but provides references to a number of exponents (30n5). Joseph Verheyden, "Calling Jesus a Prophet, as Seen by Luke," in *Prophets and Prophecy in Jewish and Early Christian Literature*, ed. J. Verheyden, K. Zamfir, and T. Nicklas, WUNT II/286 (Tübingen: Mohr Siebeck, 2010), 177–210, has questioned the identification of Jesus as a prophet for Luke.

30   See the review of nineteenth and twentieth century scholarship in Marion Soards, *The Speeches of Acts: Their Content, Context, and Concerns* (Louisville, Ky.: Westminster/John Knox, 1994), 1–11.

31   Soards cites A. Jülicher, *Einleitung in das Neue Testament*, 5th/6th eds., Grundriss der Theologischen Wissenschaften 3/1 (Tübingen: J.C.B. Mohr [Paul Siebeck], 1913), 404, who calls the speeches "free inventions [freie Erfindungen] of the author."

32   Particularly influential here was C.H. Dodd, *The Apostolic Preaching and its Developments* (London: Hodder, 1936). See also the summary of François Bovon, *Luke the Theologian: Fifty-Five Years of Research (1950–2005)*, 2nd rev. ed. (Waco: Baylor University Press, 2006), 137: "until 1950, the majority of exegetes … used Acts as a witness to primitive Christology …. [T]hey all insisted on the traditional nature of the Christological statements imbedded in the missionary speeches of Acts …. [E]ach considered the Christology of the apostles, the eyewitnesses, more important than Luke's."

33   Dibelius, *Studies*, 138–185.

34   Tiede, *Prophecy and History*, 7, speaks of Luke-Acts an "*intra-family* struggle … over who is really the faithful 'Israel.'" See also McWhirter, *Rejected Prophets*, 6–7, 57, 123–126.

(1:8). In my view, it is indeed no coincidence that citations of Deut 18:15 occur precisely in two of the Jerusalem speeches in Acts, delivered to a Jewish audience.[35] Luke, as we will see, utilizes Deut 18:15 in order to suggest that the Jewish people have rejected one of their own, a prophet whom their greatest teacher promised, who would come from among them. The motif of the prophet like Moses was useful in late first-century Christian apologetic precisely as a lens by which Luke understood the unfolding of history, and as a way of situating the early Christian community within the framework of a normative tradition.[36]

3.2 The "Raised" Prophet: Acts 3:22–26

Luke's first quotation of Deut 18:15 occurs in the context of a healing narrative that takes place in the temple precincts. After healing a man "lame from birth" (3:2), Peter seizes the opportunity to preach to the astonished crowd (3:12–26). In this temple sermon, Luke portrays Peter as an inspired exegete, an authoritative interpreter of Israel's sacred traditions, proclaiming the message about Jesus at the locale of priestly power. After proclaiming the resurrection, Peter goes on to focus on the fulfillment of prophecy in Jesus:

> (18) In this way God fulfilled what he had foretold through all the prophets (πάντων τῶν προφητῶν), that his Messiah would suffer. (19) Repent therefore, and turn to God so that your sins may be wiped out, (20) so that times of refreshing may come from the presence of the Lord, and that he may send the Messiah appointed for you, that is, Jesus, (21) who must remain in heaven until the time of the restoration of all things, that God announced long ago through his holy prophets (ὧν ἐλάλησεν ὁ θεὸς διὰ στόματος τῶν ἁγίων ἀπ' αἰῶνος αὐτοῦ προφητῶν). (22) Moses said, "The Lord your God will raise up for you from your own people a prophet like me. You must listen to whatever he tells you. (23) And it will be that everyone who does not listen to that prophet will be utterly rooted out of the people." (24) And all the prophets, as many as have spoken, from Samuel and those after him (πάντες δὲ οἱ προφῆται ἀπὸ Σαμουὴλ καὶ τῶν καθεξῆς ὅσοι ἐλάλησαν), also predicted these days. (25) You are the descendants of

---

35 In fact the citations of Scripture in Acts mostly occur in speeches addressed to Jewish audiences. See Fitzmyer, *Acts*, 90–91.

36 See Dulcinea Boesenberg, "Moses in Luke-Acts" (PhD diss., University of Notre Dame, 2013), 312: "Not only does Luke use the figure of Moses as a means of demonstrating continuity between the Israelites and the followers of Jesus, but, more significantly, he uses Moses as a means of causing division among Jews and drawing new boundaries around Israel."

the prophets and of the covenant that God gave to your ancestors (ὑμεῖς ἐστε οἱ υἱοὶ τῶν προφητῶν καὶ τῆς διαθήκης ἧς διέθετο ὁ θεὸς πρὸς τοὺς πατέρας), saying to Abraham, "And in your descendants all the families of the earth shall be blessed." (26) When God raised up (ἀναστήσας) his servant, he sent him first to you, to bless you by turning each of you from your wicked ways.

Acts 3:18–26[37]

The quotation of "Moses" in Acts 3:22–23 is somewhat odd. It amounts to a paraphrase that follows Deut 18:15 LXX fairly closely, continues by picking up key words and phrases from Deut 18:18–19, and replacing the rather anodyne threat found there with a more specific proclamation of judgment, to which the closest parallel is found in Lev 23:29 (see Table 20).[38]

The text follows Deut 18:15 LXX, not MT, as is clear from the absence of a phrase corresponding to מקרבך, "from your midst."[39] But it follows the LXX rather imprecisely: the order of the middle clauses has been transposed, the prounous have been changed from singular to plural, and the first of these is moved before the verb in Acts.[40] The change in the pronoun from singular to plural is contextually appropriate, as Peter has been addressing his audience with "you" (pl.) throughout the speech.[41] The transposition of the pronoun ὑμῖν into a place of emphasis is also done for rhetorical purposes, and provides a clue that Peter is not merely quoting Deut 18:15; rather, the entire scene is a reiteration of it. Peter addressed the gathered Israelites as an authorized interpreter of Scripture, calling them to "listen" to the prophets raised up by God. The other effect of the transposition of the middle clauses, besides the way it places the

---

37 Barrett, *Acts*, 1:189–190, lists eleven "special features" of this speech to demonstrate its pre-Lukan provenance, but six of these have parallels elsewhere in Acts, which Barrett then downplays, e.g.: "the word ἀρχηγός occurs elsewhere in Acts *only* at 5.31"; "Deut 18.15, 16 (v. 23) is quoted elsewhere in Acts *only* at 7.37" (emphasis added). Ernst Haenchen, *The Acts of the Apostles: A Commentary*, trans. Bernard Noble and Gerald Shinn (Philadelphia: Westminster, 1971), 204n1, 211 regards the speech as basically Lukan composition.

38 So Barrett, *Acts*, 1:209; Luke Timothy Johnson, *The Acts of the Apostles*, SP 5 (Collegeville: Liturgical Press, 1992), 70; Gert J. Steyn, *Septuagint Quotations in the Context of the Petrine and Pauline Speeches of the Acta Apostolorumi*, CBET 12 (Kampen: Kok Pharos, 1995), 148–149.

39 See the comparison with MT in Steyn, *Septuagint Quotations*, 143. Was this removed because of its possibly overly specific reference to the assembly of Israel on the plains of Moab?

40 See Boesenberg, "Moses in Luke-Acts," 323, with respect to the pronouns; Steyn, *Septuagint Quotations*, 144, on the order of clauses.

41 Steyn, *Septuagint Quotations*, 146.

TABLE 20   The combined citation in Acts 3:22–23

Deut 18:15–16a, 18b–19; Lev 23:29 LXX	Acts 3:22–23
	(22) Μωϋσῆς μὲν εἶπεν ὅτι
(15a) προφήτην	(a) προφήτην
(b) ἐκ τῶν ἀδελφῶν σου ὡς ἐμὲ	(c) ὑμῖν ἀναστήσει κύριος ὁ θεὸς ὑμῶν
(c) ἀναστήσει σοι κύριος ὁ θεός σου	(b) ἐκ τῶν ἀδελφῶν ὑμῶν ὡς ἐμέ·
(d) αὐτοῦ ἀκούσεσθε (16) κατὰ πάντα ὅσα ...	(d) αὐτοῦ ἀκούσεσθε κατὰ πάντα ὅσα ἂν
(18b) καὶ δώσω τὸ ῥῆμά μου ἐν τῷ στόματι αὐτοῦ καὶ λαλήσει αὐτοῖς καθότι ἂν ἐντείλωμαι αὐτῷ	λαλήσῃ πρὸς ὑμᾶς.
(19) καὶ ὁ ἄνθρωπος ὃς ἐὰν μὴ ἀκούσῃ ὅσα ἐὰν λαλήσῃ ὁ προφήτης ἐπὶ τῷ ὀνόματί μου ἐγὼ ἐκδικήσω ἐξ αὐτοῦ	(23) ἔσται δὲ πᾶσα ψυχὴ ἥτις ἐὰν μὴ ἀκούσῃ τοῦ προφήτου ἐκείνου ἐξολεθρευθήσεται ἐκ τοῦ λαοῦ ....
Lev 23:29 πᾶσα ψυχὴ ἥτις μὴ ταπεινωθήσεται ἐν αὐτῇ τῇ ἡμέρᾳ ταύτῃ ἐξολεθρευθήσεται ἐκ τοῦ λαοῦ αὐτῆς	

adverbial phrase "for you" in a significant position, is the way it places emphasis on the verb ἀνίστημι, "to raise up." As we will see, this verb is important for Luke's distinctive interpretation of Deut 18:15 as a cryptic reference to Christ's resurrection.

The remainder of Peter's quotation of Moses distills Deut 18:18–19 into two main thoughts: the prophet will speak (λαλέω) God's words to the people, and whoever does not listen to the prophet will be liable to judgment. Again, the text is handled with considerable freedom, as is exemplified in the introduction of a judgment formula from Lev 23:29.[42] It seems unnecessarily complicated to argue, as some have,[43] that Deut 18:15–19 and Lev 23:29 were juxtaposed as part of a pre-Lukan *catena* or *florilegium*.[44] Indeed, it is inaccurate to speak of Luke "quoting" any specific secondary passage here; the phrase "will be cut off from

---

42   McWhirter, *Rejected Prophets*, 101n9, sees the second passage as a conflation of Gen 17:14; Exod 12:15, 19.
43   Wolfgang Kraus, "Die Bedeutung von Dtn 18,15–18 für das Verständnis Jesu als Prophet," ZNW 90 (1999): 153–176, here 158; Richard J. Dillon, "The Prophecy of Christ and his Witnesses according to the Discourses of Acts," NTS 32 (1986): 544–556, here 549.
44   The matter is put forcefully by Steyn, *Septuagint Quotations*, 142: "To assume that these

the people" is common Pentateuchal parlance for exclusion from the assembly.[45] Luke has replaced the vague threat of judgment found in Deut 18:19 ("I will exact vengeance from him [ἐγὼ ἐκδικήσω ἐξ αὐτοῦ]") with one that is more specific, and one that reflects his conviction that Israel has become "the divided people of God."[46] Particularly noteworthy here is the freedom and authority that Luke ascribes to Peter to depart from the scriptural text in order to expound it.

The majority of commentaries assume that the quotation of Deut 18:15 in Acts 3:22 represents the expectation of an eschatological prophet like Moses, and that this prophet is identified with Jesus. Luke's quotation is then explained with reference to 1QS 9:11 and 4Q175, and occasionally Samaritan expectation of such a prophet.[47] Nevertheless, the words preceding and following the quotation suggest the possibility that Luke may have adopted a standard interpretation of Deut 18:15, that is, as a reference to a non-eschatological Mosaic prophetic succession.[48] Luke introduces the quotation by speaking of the universal restoration that "God announced long ago through his holy prophets (ὧν ἐλάλησεν ὁ θεὸς διὰ στόματος τῶν ἁγίων ἀπ' αἰῶνος αὐτοῦ προφητῶν)" (3:21) and follows it with a reference to a succession of prophets, starting with Samuel:

---

phrases (in Acts 3:22–23) were to be found already combined before Luke's time, remains problematic, questionable, and unprovable."

45 The phrase uses the passive voice of the verb ἐξολεθρεύω (LXX, consistently translating the *Niphal* of כרת); see Gen 17:14; Exod 12:19, 30:33, 31:14; Lev 17:4, 9, 14; 18:29, 19:8, 20:17, 18; 22:3; 23:29; Num 9:13, 15:30, 19:20.

46 The phrase is that of Jacob Jervell, *The Theology of the Acts of the Apostles* (Cambridge: Cambridge University, 1996), 34–43.

47 E.g., Johnson, *Acts*, 70; Fitzmyer, *Acts*, 290.

48 John Calvin struggles with Peter's interpretation of Deut 18:15, and seeks to harmonize it with the standard interpretation which authorizes a prophetic office. See his *Commentary on the Acts of the Apostles*, trans. H. Beveridge, repr., 2 vols. (Grand Rapids: Baker, 1979 [1848]), 1:154–157: "But here ariseth a question, which hath in it great difficulty; to wit, in that Peter applieth that unto the person of Christ which Moses spake generally of the prophets .... [T]here is no cause why we should set ourselves to be laughed to scorn by the Jews, by wresting the words of Moses violently, as if he spake of Christ alone in this place. Yet we must see whether Peter doth cite the testimony fitly, whose authority ought to serve for a sound reason. I say, that in Peter's speech there is nothing which is not most convenient. For he saw that which all men ought to grant, that this testimony doth so appertain unto the other prophets, that yet notwithstanding it doth chiefly commend Christ, not only because he is the prince and chief of all the prophets, but because all other former prophecies were directed toward him, and because God did at length speak absolutely by his mouth .... Therefore, Peter did not wrest this place, or abuse the same through ignorance." Beveridge's nineteenth-century translation is a revision of that of Christopher Fetherstone, 1585.

"And all the prophets, as many as have spoken, from Samuel and those after him, also predicted these days (καὶ πάντες δὲ οἱ προφῆται ἀπὸ Σαμουὴλ καὶ τῶν καθεξῆς ὅσοι ἐλάλησαν καὶ κατήγγειλαν τὰς ἡμέρας ταύτας)" (3:24). This latter verse has been regarded as a *"crux interpretum"*:[49] Luke Timothy Johnson formulates two questions that have bothered interpreters: "Left unclear are questions such as: why 'from Samuel onwards,' and why 'whosoever spoke'?"[50] Both questions are neatly answered on the hypothesis that Luke understands Deut 18:15 to refer to the Mosaic prophetic succession, in which the first great prophet to arise after Moses was Samuel (in accordance with the DH's own presentation, though not, as we have seen, the most prevalent view in Second Temple Judaism),[51] and in which what is particularly characteristic about these prophets is that, like Moses, it is in their mouths that God put words so that they speak (λαλέω, Deut 18:18) to the people. That Luke has this concept in mind is particularly clear from his usage of the adverb καθεξῆς, "in a row, one after another."[52] Moreover, Luke has used a μέν ... δέ construction to link verses 22 and 24; that is, he brings together the speech of Moses with that of the prophets who succeeded him.[53] It seems likely, then, that Luke recognizes an initial fulfillment of Deut 18:15 in the witness of the Mosaic prophetic succession to "these days" (v. 24)—that is, to the eschatological events of the death and resurrection of Jesus and the outpouring of the Spirit. Finally, v. 25 reinforces the sense that the "prophets" Luke has in mind are the past prophets of the Mosaic prophetic succession, with its appeal to the hearers: "You are the descendents of the prophets and of the covenant that God gave to your ancestors (ὑμεῖς ἐστε οἱ υἱοὶ τῶν προφητῶν καὶ τῆς διαθήκης ἧς διέθετο ὁ θεὸς πρὸς τοὺς πατέρας)."[54]

Indeed, if Peter's speech ended after v. 25, it would have to be reconsidered whether the citation of Deut 18:15 in 3:22 includes any support for the notion of the coming eschatological prophet like Moses. The thought of the speech

---

49 So Haenchen, *Acts*, 209.
50 Johnson, *Acts*, 70.
51 So Fitzmyer, *Acts*, 290.
52 See Barrett, *Acts*, 1:211. The adverb is only used in Luke-Acts in the NT or LXX, it appears most prominently in Luke's stated ambition to narrate the gospel story "in order" (Luke 1:3), and also occurs in Luke 8:1; Acts 11:4; 18:23. Yet another clue that the speech in Acts 3 is hardly pre-Lukan!
53 Dillon, "Prophecy of Christ," 548, argues that this construction links vv. 22, 24 (and not vv. 22–23).
54 See Tob 4:12 for a similar usage of the phrase "sons of the prophets"; in the Hebrew scriptures, the phrase typically refers to members of prophetic guild (cf, e.g., 2 Kgs 2:3, 5, 7, 11, 15; Amos 7:14).

could be summarized as follows: Jesus, God's servant (3:13, 26), has suffered, been raised from the dead, and is now in heaven awaiting the "restoration of all things" (3:18–21), in accordance with what "all the prophets," from Moses onward, have spoken (3:22–24), to whom the people were commanded to listen. The eschatological interpretation emerges only in the last sentence of the speech, as Luke positions Jesus as a climactic prophet like Moses in v. 26: "When God raised up (ἀναστήσας) his servant, he sent (ἀπέστειλεν) him first to you, to bless you by turning each of you from your wicked ways."⁵⁵ The use of ἀνίστημι for the "raising" of Jesus looks back to the citation of Deut 18:15 in 3:22, linking the sending of Jesus to the succession of Mosaic prophets.

There are two main options for the interpretation of the speech's concluding sentence. One is that the verb ἀνίστημι in Deut 18:15 struck Luke, so that he discerned in it a cryptic, deeper meaning: Jesus is the prophet who was "raised up" by God, that is, resurrected from the dead. A number of scholars, however, argue that by ἀνίστημι in 3:26, Luke refers to Jesus' ministry, and not to his resurrection.⁵⁶ On this account, God's "raising up" of his servant is the sending of Jesus as a prophet. The attractiveness of this latter view stems not only from the fact that it accords with the plain sense of Deut 18:15, but also because it seems to make better sense of the subsequent reference to the "sending" of Jesus in v. 26. It seems improbable to these interpreters that Luke would refer to the post-resurrection proclamation by the apostles as God's "sending" of Jesus.⁵⁷ This, however, fails to pay sufficient attention to the narrative context of Peter's speech, that is, the miraculous healing of the lame man, which Peter repeatedly insists was not done by his power or piety (3:12), but in fact was done by Jesus: it is "his name" which strengthened the man (3:16).⁵⁸ So, there is ample reason

---

55 Rightly Dillon, "Prophecy of Christ," 548: "the murdered Messiah, now resurrected preacher of repentance, can be presented by Luke as the climax of a prophets' line running all the way back to Moses."
56 So, e.g., Haenchen, *Acts*, 210; Fuller, *Foundations*, 168; Barrett, *Acts*, 1:213: it refers not to resurrection but "that God brought him on to the stage of history." See the full discussion in David Miller, "Luke's Conception of Prophets Considered in the Context of Second Temple Literature" (PhD diss., McMaster University, 2004), 243–259.
57 Miller, "Luke's Conception of Prophets," 246: "But is it really likely that Luke's implied readers ... would judge from the evidence in Peter's sermon that Peter was referring to *himself* as the agent of blessing when he said that God "raised up his servant" and "sent him to bless [the people] by turning [them] from their evil ways" (3:26)? ... Although ἀνίστημι can denote resurrection and although Luke can speak of Jesus working through his disciples, a reference to the sending of Jesus through his disciples is surely not the most obvious interpretation of Acts 3:26 when the verse is considered on its own."
58 Tannehill, *Narrative Unity*, 2:53: "Acts 3:16 is an overloaded and awkward sentence, but

in the context to suppose that Luke would ascribe an action apparently done by Peter to the risen Jesus.⁵⁹

In my view, it is preferable to understand ἀνίστημι in v. 26 as both a reference back to the citation of Deut 18:15 in v. 22 and to the resurrection. First, the adverbial phrase "first to you" in v. 26 does not demand a reference to Jesus' prophetic career; rather, it fits with the broader scheme of Acts in which the apostolic preaching of forgiveness of sins is extended to the Jewish people before the turn to the Gentiles.⁶⁰ Second, other uses of ἀνίστημι with God as subject and Jesus as object in Acts are consistently references to the resurrection.⁶¹ Third, the concluding appeal to repent in speeches in Acts is often closely linked to a proclamation of the resurrection; this is a truncated version of these more elaborate examples.⁶² Fourth, O'Toole has pointed out that the speech's beginning and end have a number of parallels, suggesting a deliberate *inclusio*: Abraham is mentioned in vv. 13, 25; Jesus is referred to with the title παῖς in vv. 13, 26;⁶³ conforming to this pattern, O'Toole suggests that the speech begins and ends with references to the resurrection.⁶⁴ Fifth, the hermeneutical principle in Luke-Acts that the proclamation of the prophets points ahead to the events of Easter (cf. Luke 24:46–47) favors understanding Deut 18:15 as a reference to the resurrection.⁶⁵

---

close inspection suggests reasons for its awkwardness. It places great emphasis on faith and on Jesus' name as the keys to the healing of the lame man."

59 Robert O'Toole, "Some Observations on Anistēmi, 'I Raise,' in Acts 3:22, 26," *Science et Esprit* 31 (1979): 85–92 points to Acts 26:23 as evidence that Luke considers the risen Christ to be actively involved in post-resurrection proclamation (90–91). There Paul says that the Messiah would rise from the dead "in order to proclaim light, both to our people and to the Gentiles (φῶς μέλλει καταγγέλλειν τῷ τε λαῷ καὶ τοῖς ἔθνεσιν)."

60 Cf Acts 13:46, "it was necessary that the word of God should be spoken first (πρῶτον) to you." On 3:26, see Tannehill, *Narrative Unity*, 56: "Saying 'to you first' implies a progressive mission, the mission traced in the rest of Acts." So also Conzelmann, *Acts*, 30; Haenchen, *Acts*, 212; Dillon, *Eyewitnesses*, 135n91.

61 See 2:24, 32; 13:33, 34; 17:31; cf also 10:41, 17:3. It is possible but not necessary to interpret this case as an an anomalous usage (so Fuller, *Foundations*, 168: "only here in Acts is ἀναστήσας ["having raised"] used of Jesus' historical mission, rather than of the resurrection. The word is taken directly from Deut 18:15").

62 See 2:32–38; 13:30–39; 17:30–31; cf also 26:23. O'Toole, "Anistēmi in Acts 3," 86, presents a longer list of parallels, but some are not germane.

63 Johnson, *Acts*, 67, relates the title to Moses typology, which would seem attractive in view of the earlier arguments in this monograph for a strong overlap between these titles in the Hebrew Bible. But for the author of Acts, it can equally be used in Davidic christology (Acts 4:24–27).

64 O'Toole, "Anistēmi in Acts 3," 86–87.

65 O'Toole, "Anistēmi in Acts 3," 88–89.

I conclude, then, that Luke applies Deut 18:15 to Jesus not only as the eschatological prophet like Moses, but also as a cryptic prophecy of the resurrection.[66] Indeed, as the narrative continues, the speech can be summarized in a phrase as a proclamation of resurrection:

> While Peter and John were speaking to the people, the priests, the captain of the temple, and the Sadducees came to them, much annoyed because they were teaching the people and proclaiming that in Jesus there is the resurrection of the dead (ἐν τῷ Ἰησοῦ τὴν ἀνάστασιν τὴν ἐκ νεκρῶν).
> Acts 4:1–2

This thesis makes good sense of the data in Luke-Acts, in which this verse is not directly quoted in the gospel of Luke, but only in the apostolic proclamation in Acts. As we will see, there are allusions to the promised prophet like Moses in Luke's gospel narrative, but Luke postpones explicit citation until after the resurrection has confirmed the identification of this prophet with Jesus. Indeed, Luke "must wait" to cite this verse, as Dillon points out,[67] because it is only after the risen Lord opened the apostles' minds that they could understand the full meaning of the Scriptures (cf. Luke 24:45). According to Luke, it is only now, in the mouth of Peter, that Deut 18:15 receives its full and deeper interpretation.[68] Indeed, the annoyance of the chief priests is due not only to their skepticism regarding the concept of resurrection, but also because the apostles are portrayed as assuming the priestly prerogative of teaching the people and providing authoritative scriptural interpretation. Thus, in Acts 3:22–24, Luke understands Deut 18:15 to refer to the succession of prophets following Moses, beginning with Samuel, but particularly to reach its fulfillment in the resurrected prophet Jesus.

3.3 The Rejected Prophet: Acts 7:37
3.3.1 Stephen's Speech in Narrative Context

The second citation occurs in Stephen's speech, in essentially the same form as it occurred in Acts 3:22:

---

66 So also McWhirter, *Rejected Prophets*, 68.
67 Dillon, *Eyewitnesses*, 122n56: "Mosaic-prophet Christology is important to Luke, but he must wait until Easter and afterward to instill it fully into his narrative."
68 The notion that prophetic oracles are inherently cryptic and therefore require specialized interpreters to divine their meaning is practically ubiquitous in the ancient world. Elsewhere in the NT, cf 1 Pet 1:10–12.

(a) οὗτός ἐστιν ὁ Μωϋσῆς ὁ εἴπας τοῖς υἱοῖς Ἰσραήλ·(b) προφήτην ὑμῖν (c) ἀναστήσει ὁ θεὸς (d) ἐκ τῶν ἀδελφῶν ὑμῶν ὡς ἐμέ.

This is the Moses who said to the children of Israel: "A prophet for you God will raise from your brothers, like me."
Acts 7:37

In its immediate context, the identification of this promised prophet with Jesus is not made explicit, which is in keeping with the rhetoric of the section on Moses as a whole. Nowhere does Stephen explicitly claim that Moses was a "type" of Christ,[69] but the way that Moses' story is narrated—in particular the episodes that are selected—leave no doubt that Luke intends to draw parallels between the rejection of Moses as "leader and judge" and the rejection of Jesus.

In the narrative context, the speech's content and rhetorical strategy is related to the trial setting. Stephen is charged with a two-fold accusation, speaking against Moses and the temple (6:11, 13–14). Many scholars—committed to the view that ascribes the theology of Stephen's speech *not* to Luke, but to early Christian "Hellenists"[70]—have been scornful of the relationship between the speech and these charges. So Haenchen comments: "it is incomprehensible that the judges did not interrupt Stephen after the first few sentences and order him to keep to the point."[71] Dibelius puts the matter even more sharply: "The irrelevance of most of this speech has for long been the real problem of exegesis."[72] On the basis of this contextual incoherence, the speech has been

---

69 Barrett notes the absence of specific reference to Jesus (*Acts*, 1:337): in the "polemical sections there is material that cried aloud for Christian elaboration but did not receive it. Thus the rejection of Moses in vv. 25, 27 could have been used to point directly to the story of Jesus." Barrett therefore concludes that the speech came from a pre-Lukan Jewish source. This seems wholly unlikely; rather, the speech's typology is deliberately understated in order for Stephen to be portrayed as arguing from premises with which his opponents would (in theory) agree.

70 For a thorough review of this tradition, see Todd Penner, *In Praise of Christian Origins: Stephen and the Hellenists in Lukan Apologetic Historiography* (New York: T&T Clark, 2004), particularly 1–59. See also the critique of the Hellenist hypothesis by Craig Hill, *Hellenists and Hebrews: Reappraising Division within the Earliest Church* (Minneapolis: Fortress, 1992). Johnson, *Acts*, 119 is biting in his critique of this tradition: "we must listen to the speech as the creation of Luke and as serving his literary goals. It is futile and even fatuous to seek to find in these words the special theological outlook of the historical 'Hellenists' represented by Stephen." "Fatuous" is perhaps a bit strong, but the point is well taken.

71 Haenchen, *Acts*, 288: so also Fitzmyer, *Acts*, 364.

72 Dibelius, *Studies*, 167.

considered pre-Lukan, and great ingenuity has been applied to the task of hypothesizing as to the nature and extent of Luke's source.[73]

These critiques are vastly overstated. Though the speech admittedly begins with what might have *seemed* to be an irrelevant historical review (7:2–16),[74] it does ultimately deal with the subjects of Moses (7:17–44) and the temple (7:44–53) in turn.[75] The speech defends Stephen against the accusations by, paradoxically, issuing an indictment of the Jewish leaders as the ones that both reject Moses and the prophets and rely on the temple as a guarantee of the divine presence in their midst.[76] There is no rejection of law or even temple in the speech;[77] indeed, even the reminder that reminder that no physical building (cf. χειροποίητος, v. 48) is guaranteed to be a permanent abode for the divine finds precedent in such temple-affirming passages as Solomon's prayer of dedication (cf 1 Kgs 8:27). Rather, Stephen's trial becomes a "trial" of the Jewish leaders: in condemning Stephen, they condemn themselves, so that Stephen prays that they be delivered from judgment (7:60).

---

73 See, e.g., Haenchen, *Acts*, 289; Barrett, *Acts*, 1:337.
74 I say "seemed" because, although it is outside the scope of this investigation, Luke's treatment of the promises to Abraham are not irrelevant to his larger literary goals, as is clear in the way these promises are also important in the speech in Acts 3 (cf 3:13, 25). Moreover, 7:7 ("worship me in this place") introduces the theme of the Temple, and indeed, as in speeches such as Jer 7, the point of the historical review is to remind the hearers that they have not always possessed this "place," and their continued stay in it depends on obedience (here, Luke has the events of 70 CE in view).
75 Pervo, *Acts*, 187: "The relationship between the speech and the charges of 6:11–14 is Lucan and shrewd. Although the charges are labeled as false, Stephen does attend to each in due course." Verse 44 is the transitional verse between these subjects, concluding Stephen's discussion of the life of Moses and beginning his discussion of the sanctuary. It should be noted that the speech has a sustained interest in chronology (vv. 6, 17, 20, 23, 30, 36, 45), and the discussions of Moses and the temple have been rooted in this framework. See also David Peterson, *The Acts of the Apostles*, PNTC (Grand Rapids: Eerdmans, 2009), 265.
76 Peterson, *Acts*, 244: "The main intention of this prophetic-type utterance is to 'turn the tables' on his opponents by presenting an extensive indictment against them."
77 Rightly, Terence Donaldson, "Moses Typology and the Sectarian Nature of Early Christian Anti-Judaism: a Study in Acts 7," *JSNT* 12 (1981): 27–52; here 30–31: "the theme of the speech is not a radical rejection of law and temple. Law and temple come into the discussion only as illustrations of the real theme, that Israel has consistently resisted and rejected both God's will and his messengers"; Fredriksen, *From Jesus to Christ*, 197: "[T]o Luke, the Temple represented a tangible link between the redemptive revelation of scripture and the revelation of Christ. To be sure, the Jewish authorities had failed to see this connection. They consequently misunderstood the Temple's true purpose.... Luke, through Stephen, criticizes them on this account.... Despite its misuse, however, the Temple is and was holy; Jesus himself called it 'my Father's house' (Lk 2:49)."

In a stimulating article, Maxine Grossman has underscored the priestly context of Stephen's speech in Acts 7. Grossman emphasizes that references to the priesthood reflect "interpretive competition" in Early Judaism and Christianity.[78] She notes priestly themes in the body of Stephen's speech,[79] and points out that the entire narrative is framed by an intriguing comment in Acts 6:7: "The word of God continued to spread; the number of the disciples increased greatly in Jerusalem, and a great many of the priests became obedient to the faith (ὀλύς τε ὄχλος τῶν ἱερέων ὑπήκουον τῇ πίστει)." She observes: "By stressing the diversity of the Christian community, and the presence of actual priests in its midst, the text provides a ground for Stephen's speech."[80] This verse also links the Stephen speech to the broader narrative as Luke has constructed it: it is the final act in the Jerusalem scene, before the "word of God" continues its dramatic spread to Samaria (8:14) and the nations (13:46).[81] Jerusalem, of course, remains an important locale throughout Acts, as the home of the apostles and the central authority [cf. ch. 15], but after Stephen's speech it is no longer on the forefront of the "growth" of the "word of God," to use Lukan terminology.[82]

3.3.2   Parallels between Acts 3 and Acts 7

Table 21 lists the parallels between the speeches in Acts 3 and 7, and includes relevant parallels elsewhere in Luke-Acts.[83] These show that the overlap between the speeches goes beyond the citation of Deut 18:15, and demonstrate their thoroughly Lukan character.[84] Most importantly for our purposes, in Acts

---

78   Maxine Grossman, "Priesthood as Authority: Interpretive Competition in First-Century Judaism and Christianity," in *The Dead Sea Scrolls as Background to Postbiblical Judaism and Early Christianity: Papers from an International Conference at St Andrews in 2001*, ed. James Davila, STDJ 46 (Leiden: Brill, 2003), 117–131.
79   Grossman, "Priesthood as Authority," 123.
80   Grossman, "Priesthood as Authority," 123.
81   Conzelmann, *Acts*, 57: "The speech relates the martyrdom to Luke's whole view of history and furnishes the theoretical preparation for the transition to the mission to the Gentiles"; Fitzmyer, *Acts*, 368: "The story of Stephen and especially this speech represent the beginning of Luke's account of the break of Christianity from its Jewish matrix."
82   The difference may be illustrated by the two accounts of the apostles' miraculous deliverance from prison by an angel: in 5:19–25 the apostles are freed precisely to preach in the temple; in 12:6–17 Peter's deliverance concludes with his leaving for another place (cf 12:17, καὶ ἐξελθὼν ἐπορεύθη εἰς ἕτερον τόπον).
83   The first ten parallels are primarily between Acts 3 and 7, while the last four are between the portrayal of Moses in Acts 7 and that of Jesus elsewhere in Luke-Acts. A number of these are found in Allison, *New Moses*, 98–100; Robert F. O'Toole, "The Parallels between Jesus and Moses," *BTB* 20 (1990): 22–29; here 25–26.
84   Compare the rather odd statement by Allison, *New Moses*, 97n10: "The recent tendency,

3 Jesus is presented as a prophet who was rejected due to ignorance (3:17), but sent again with power to his people (3:26), which also serves as a précis of Luke's account of Moses' career in 7:17–40 (esp. 7:25, 35).[85] If the table establishes the thematic resonances which inform the carefully constructed speeches of Acts 3 and 7, it is not meant to deny the substantial differences between them. The most prominent of these is the *pathos* or emotional quality, which is dictated by Luke's conception of the audience.[86] Acts 3, like Acts 2, strikes a much more positive tone with respect to Israel than Acts 7: the people have failed on account of their ignorance (3:17), but now have an opportunity to repent and turn from their evil deeds (3:26). Stephen's speech begins with a seemingly innocuous recital of history, but increasingly develops a hostile tone (most commentators note a shift in v. 35).[87] The accusatory rhetoric in 7:51–53 is the culmination of the speech. The audience of the first speech is the people who were at the temple, whom Peter addresses as fellow Israelites (ἄνδρες Ἰσραηλῖται, 3:12), whereas Stephen's charged speech is directed at the leaders, who are held to be more directly responsible for Jesus' death (cf Luke 24:20, Acts 13:27).[88]

---

altogether justified, to attribute to Lukan redaction more and more in the speeches of Acts, goes too far when it denies that Acts 3 and 7 were based on pre-Lukan speeches." If the "recent tendency" is indeed "altogether justified," why does it go too far here? One suspects that this is due to Allison's desire to root Moses-typology in the very early stages of the tradition. See *New Moses*, 106: "Because we cannot believe that one author, then another, and then another, just happened upon the idea that Jesus' significance should be gauged by placing him beside Moses, we may justly speak of a tradition: Moses' utility as a type was an item of *paradosis*. Further, that item clearly entered the tradition very near the birth of the church, perhaps even in the pre-Easter period." In line with this perspective, Allison asserts (but does not prove) that the speeches in Acts 3, 7 "preserve pieces of old Christian apologetic" (*New Moses*, 97).

85 This has been particularly emphasized by Johnson, *Literary Function*, 70–76; McWhirter, *Rejected Prophets*, 66–68.
86 Craig Keener, *Acts: An Exegetical Commentary*, 4 vols. (Grand Rapids: Baker Academic, 2012–2015), 1:267–268, provides references to the ancient historiographic convention that speeches were composed with a view to their setting and audience.
87 Pervo, *Acts*, 187, "encomium" style "erupts"; Johnson, *Acts*, 128, "The speech takes a dramatic rhetorical turn"; Haenchen, *Acts*, 289, therefore takes v. 35 as the beginning of Lukan additions to a "neutral" source.
88 To be sure, 3:17 specifies that the leaders acted in ignorance; even here, however, they are explicitly mentioned as significant agents in Jesus' death, leading to a certain tension in the verse. The remarks of Dillon are apposite (*Eyewitnesses*, 130; emphasis original): "The sundering process within Jewish ranks that is recorded in Lk's narrative has the formation of a *true, redeemed Israel* as the object of the *argumentum* …. The prototypical impenitence of the ἄρχοντες consigns them to unbelieving Judaism, which will have no part in the Israel of the restoration. The is suggested when Peter … mentions the *unknowing* agency of *both* leaders and people in the παθεῖν of God's messiah, but seems to extend the oppor-

TABLE 21   Parallels between the Speeches in Acts 3 and Acts 7

Parallel	Peter's Speech	Stephen's Speech	Luke-Acts (if relevant)
Citation of Deut 18:15	v. 22	v. 37	–
Promises to Abraham	vv. 25–26	v. 17	Lk 1:55, 73; Acts 13:32, 26:6
"the God of Abraham and Isaac and Jacob"	v. 13	v. 32 (citation of Exod 3:6)	Lk 20:37 (citation of Exod 3:6)
References to the "fathers"	vv. 13, 25	vv. 11, 12, 15, 19, 32, 38, 39, 44, 45, 51, 52	Lk 6:23, 26; 11:47, 48 ("fathers" reject "prophets")
God "sends" a leader, ἀποστέλλω	Jesus, v. 26 (and v. 20)	Moses, vv. 34, 35	Lk 11:49
The leader is "denied," ἀρνέομαι[a]	Jesus, vv. 13, 14	Moses, v. 35	Lk 12:9
Similar terms for "leader"[b]	ἀρχηγός, v. 15	ἄρχων, vv. 27, 35	Acts 5:31
The prophets "foretell," προκαταγγέλλω	v. 18, suffering of the Christ	v. 52, coming of the righteous one	Nowhere else in NT
Jesus is "the Righteous One"[c]	v. 14	v. 52	Lk 23:47; Acts 22:14
Ignorance as excuse	v. 17	v. 60 (?)	Acts 17:30; [Lk 23:34]
"Mighty in words and deeds"[d]	–	v. 22, Moses was δυνατὸς ἐν λόγοις καὶ ἔργοις αὐτοῦ	Lk 24:19, Jesus was προφήτης δυνατὸς ἐν ἔργῳ καὶ λόγῳ
"visitation"[e]	–	v. 23, Moses "visits" his people	Lk 1:68; 7:17; 19:44; God, through Jesus
"redemption"[f]	–	v. 35, Moses sent as λυτρωτής	Lk 24:21, "we had hoped that he was the one to redeem [λυτρόω] Israel"
"wonders and signs"	–	v. 36, performed by Moses	Performed by Jesus, Acts 2:22; apostles, 2:43, 4:30, 5:12; Stephen, 6:8; Barnabas and Saul, 14:3, 15:12

a   So Dillon, *Eyewitnesses*, 138; Fuller, *Foundations*, 168; Peterson, *Acts*, 257.
b   Johnson, *Acts*, 129: "*archōn* is very close to *archēgos*"; so also Haenchen, *Acts*, 282; Dillon, *Eyewitnesses*, 138; Fuller, *Foundations*, 168.
c   Fuller, *Foundations*, 168.
d   Dillon, *Eyewitnesses*, 138.
e   John P. Meier, *A Marginal Jew: Rethinking the Historical Jesus*, 5 vols., AYBRL (New Haven: Yale University, 1991–2016), 2:850–851, notes the importance of the concept for Luke.
f   Haenchen, *Acts*, 282; Dillon, *Eyewitnesses*, 131.

In fact, this difference between the speeches is the proverbial exception that proves the rule; that is, it provides further confirmation that Stephen's speech

tunity of repentance and conversion only to the people." This is perhaps correct for Acts 3, but note Acts 6:7, 15:5, where priests and Pharisees respectively are described as believers in Christ. Indeed, Paul himself was a Jewish leader.

was deliberately constructed in order to build upon Peter's. The difference in tone is related to the broader narrative contexts of each: whereas the apostles met with considerable success in their proclamation (cf Acts 4:4, 5000 men),[89] Stephen meets with rejection and martyrdom.

Luke's two citations of Deut 18:15 are therefore related to his conviction that Israel has become "the divided people of God": many have "listened" to the prophet and so experienced blessing (cf 3:26), but many have also rejected the prophet.[90] *The "raised up" prophet is the rejected prophet*: this is the movement from Acts 3 to 7. Luke prepares his readers for the transition from the success of the apostolic proclamation to Stephen's rejection and martyrdom by filling out in more detail what the identification of Jesus as the prophet like Moses means: Moses is the paradigmatic rejected prophet, and therefore Jesus' followers ought not to be surprised at rejection either.[91] This is the goal that governs Luke's presentation of the life of Moses in Acts 7. In that sense, though Luke is indebted to standard Hellenistic and Roman era tropes in this "life of Moses,"[92] his retelling of Moses' story is highly creative. A seemingly minor incident such as his killing of the Egyptian (Exod 2:11–15) is given a central role because of its potential for establishing Moses as the "prophet like Jesus,"[93] rejected by his own people.

3.3.3   Use of the Citation in Stephen's Speech

Luke's interpretation of Deut 18:15 in Acts 7 includes the following features, which I will now examine in greater detail: first, Luke attributes a messianic self-understanding to Moses *before* his call in Exodus 3 and highlights the failure of Moses' contemporaries to understand this; second, Luke seizes upon two Pentateuchal citations in which Israelite(s) give voice to criticism of Moses

---

[89]   Pervo, *Acts*, 112: "This is the last time Luke provides specific numbers, possibly intimating the end of an era."

[90]   Jervell, *Theology*, 35–37: "When the Messiah arrives the people of God is in a crisis. Messiah reinforces the crisis and brings it to a climax, dividing the people into two parts .... Israel has not rejected the gospel, but has become divided over the issue .... The identity of the church, then, is clear: it is Israel, the one and only. The Christians are heirs to the promises to Israel, and they are so as Jews."

[91]   On this theme, see McWhirter, *Rejected Prophets*, 57–74, 95–109.

[92]   See Boesenberg, "Moses in Luke-Acts," 360–366 for parallels to the description of Moses as "exposed" (ἐκτίθημι), as "beautiful to God," and as educated "in all the wisdom of Egypt" in such varied sources as Philo, Josephus, Ezekiel the Tragedian, Artapanus, the Wisdom of Solomon, and the epistle to the Hebrews.

[93]   Many have observed that Moses is portrayed in terms of Jesus, rather than the reverse. Kraus, "Dtn 18," 160: "Es handelt sich somit präzise um eine Christus–Mose–Christus–Typologie."

(Exod 2:14 in vv. 27, 35; Exod 32:1, 23 in v. 40); third, Luke's citation of Deut 18:15 is preceded by mentioning the "signs and wonders" performed by Moses (v. 36); fourth, Luke demonstrates awareness of the Pentateuchal context of the appointment of the prophet like Moses, namely, the request of the people for a covenant mediator.

Luke's presentation of Moses' life is chronological, divided into three forty-year periods (vv. 20–22; vv. 23–29; vv. 30–44). Luke concludes the first of these by signaling his real interest: the attentive reader of Luke-Acts knows that describing Moses as "powerful in deeds and words (δυνατὸς ἐν λόγοις καὶ ἔργοις αὐτου)" is reminiscent of Jesus (Luke 24:19).[94] This description prepares for the second section, with its surprising attribution of a messianic consciousness to Moses in the episode of the killing of the Egyptian. That Moses' motivations for the heinous deed were in fact noble is indicated by the verb "to visit" in v. 23[95] and expanded on in v. 25: "He supposed that his kinsfolk would understand (συνιέναι) that God through him was rescuing them, but they did not understand (οἱ δὲ οὐ συνῆκαν)" (7:25). The author of Luke-Acts, like his contemporaries,[96] is interested in justifying Moses, but his strategy is different than theirs. Luke uses the opportunity to link his account of Moses to the theme of "understanding," which is of considerable importance in his two-volume work.[97] As proof that the Israelites did not understand Moses' offer of salva-

---

94   So McWhirter, *Rejected Prophets*, 68.
95   The text states that Moses decided to "visit his brothers, the Israelites (ἐπισκέψασθαι τοὺς ἀδελφοὺς αὐτοῦ τοὺς υἱοὺς Ἰσραήλ)" (7:23). Pervo, *Acts*, 185: "the verb 'to visit' here 'refers to redemptive action.'" See Luke 1:68, 7:16. I wonder if the description of "the sons of Israel" as Moses' "brothers" is a proleptic reference to Deut 18:15. In any case, it emphasizes Moses' kinship with the Israelites.
96   Johnson, *Acts*, 127, demonstrates that contemporary Jewish exegetes had a distinct interest in downplaying this event (Josephus [*Ant*. 2.254–256] does not mention it) or finding justifications for Moses' action: often, the murder becomes one of self-defense, understanding Pharaoh's ill will towards Moses (Exod 2:15) as actually *prior* to Moses' killing of the Egyptian; see Artapanus, *On the Jews*, frag. 3; Philo, *Life of Moses*, 1.43–46.
97   Based primarily on Isa 6:9, the verb συνίημι plays a thematic role in Luke's presentation of the response of Israel to Jesus and the apostolic preaching. This lack of "understanding" is itself a fulfillment of prophecy (Luke 8:10; cf. Isa 6:9). Prior to the resurrection, the apostles also fail to "understand" Jesus and his mission (Luke 18:34), a theme for which Luke is also indebted to Mark (Mark 8:17, 21). However, unlike in Mark, Luke records the moment of apostolic illumination: when Jesus appears after the resurrection, "he opened their minds to understand (συνιέναι) the Scriptures" (Luke 24:45). This is the direct precursor to the transformation of the apostles in Acts into inspired interpreters of scriptural testimony, which occurs throughout its narrative (see, e.g., 17:2–3: Paul was "explaining and proving from the Scriptures" that the Christ must suffer and rise from the dead). Luke's two-volume work concludes with two more usages of this verb (28:26–27), again drawing on Isa 6:9–10.

tion, Luke fixates on the rebuff of Moses by the anonymous Israelite (cf Exod 2:14): "who made you a ruler and judge over us?" Luke puts particular emphasis on this challenge to Moses' authority, quoting it in 7:28 and again in 7:35. Because Luke attributes a messianic self-understanding to Moses prior to his call in Exodus 3, the answer to this question is *already* "God." For Luke, then, Moses (like Jesus; cf Luke 4:16–30) is the object of initial rejection in his salvation mission.[98]

Luke's second usage of Exod 2:14 occurs at the beginning of the paragraph that extends from 7:35–40, which is marked by emphatic repetition of the demonstrative pronoun, so that all the emphasis is placed on the person of Moses:[99]

> (35) **This** is the Moses (Τοῦτον τὸν Μωϋσῆν), whom they denied, saying, "Who appointed you ruler and judge?"—**this one** (τοῦτον) God sent as ruler and deliverer by means of the angel who appeared to him in the bush. (36) **This one** (οὗτος) led them out, performing wonders and signs (τέρατα καὶ σημεῖα) in Egypt and at the Red Sea and in the wilderness for forty years. (37) **This** is the Moses (οὗτός ἐστιν ὁ Μωϋσῆς) who said to the Israelites, "A prophet for you God will raise up from among your brothers, like me." (38) **This** (οὗτός) is the one who was among the assembly in the wilderness when the angel spoke to him on Mount Sinai, and with our ancestors, who received living oracles to give to us (ὃς ἐδέξατο λόγια ζῶντα δοῦναι ἡμῖν), (39) whom our fathers did not want to obey; but they pushed him aside and turned in their hearts to Egypt, (40) saying to Aaron, "Make for us gods who will go before us. For **this Moses** (Μωϋσῆς οὗτος), who brought us out from Egypt, we do not know what happened to him."
>
> Acts 7:35–40

For Luke, this prophecy of Isaiah and in particular its assertion that Israel will not "understand" provides an explanation of how it is that Israel has become divided: that many did not accept the Messiah was for Luke a divine necessity, revealed in the prophecies of Isaiah, as part of the plan for the salvation of the nations. On this theme, see McWhirter, *Rejected Prophets*.

98 Johnson, *Acts*, 136, therefore speaks of a "double sending" of Moses: "Moses 'visits' his people a first time, but because of their ignorance, they reject him, and he must depart into exile. But while in exile, he encounters God and is empowered by him to be 'sent with a commission' to his people once more. In this 'second visitation,' Moses works 'wonders and signs' in unmistakable fashion as he 'led them out.'"

99 Haenchen, *Acts*, 282: "Now we have an abrupt change of style. The placid flow of historical narrative gives way to passionate, rhetorically heightened indictment."

TABLE 22   The prophet's rejection and vindication in Acts

Acts 2:23–24a (Jesus)	Acts 3:15a (Jesus)	Acts 7:35a (Moses)
τοῦτον τῇ ὡρισμένῃ βουλῇ καὶ προγνώσει τοῦ θεοῦ ἔκδοτον διὰ χειρὸς ἀνόμων προσπήξαντες ἀνείλατε, (24) ὃν ὁ θεὸς ἀνέστησεν	τὸν δὲ ἀρχηγὸν τῆς ζωῆς ἀπεκτείνατε ὃν ὁ θεὸς ἤγειρεν ἐκ νεκρῶν	Τοῦτον τὸν Μωϋσῆν ὃν ἠρνήσαντο εἰπόντες· τίς σε κατέστησεν ἄρχοντα καὶ δικαστήν; τοῦτον ὁ θεὸς ἄρχοντα καὶ λυτρωτὴν ἀπέσταλκεν

In v. 35, Luke repeats the quotation of Exod 2:14 to create an *inclusio* with the concluding quotation of Exod 32:1: the paragraph begins and ends with Israelite rejections of Moses. Furthermore, in 7:35 we have Luke's hermeneutical starting point for understanding the identity of the prophet like Moses: *rejected by humanity, vindicated by God*. The pattern is that of Acts 2:23–24; 3:15a (Table 22). These statements all have the same structure: the prophet is the (grammatical) object of the people's rejection and God's vindication, related in that order.[100]

The citation of Deut 18:15 occurs in the center of this paragraph. On an initial reading it may not seem well integrated into its context, especially if this section is taken to be a string of observations about Moses focused on Israel's rejection of him.[101] If one grants, however, that Luke understood Deut 18:15 as a retrospective reference by Moses to a promise made by Yhwh at Horeb in response to Israel's request for a covenant mediator (Deut 18:16–18//Exod 20:18–19), then the speech in Acts 7 follows a chronological order of presentation, extending from Exodus 3–32:[102]

---

100   See Johnson, *Literary Function*, 74: "The initial rejection of Moses by his brothers is not definitive; he is sent to them again by God, this time with power …. This corresponds exactly to the pattern we have seen used of Jesus in the discourses."

101   Boesenberg, "Moses in Luke-Acts," 382–383, has argued that the strict chronological presentation which hitherto has governed the speech is here abandoned for thematic statements about the rejection of Moses.

102   A similar list, with some variations, is presented in Dillon, *Eyewitnesses*, 255. Dillon connects this to the unnecessary hypothesis of Luke's usage of the Samaritan Pentateuch (since that tradition transfers the promise of the prophet like Moses to follow the Ten Commandments). The harmonization made in the Samaritan Tradition, however, could easily be made by other readers of Deuteronomy (as the evidence of harmonistic texts such as 4Q Reworked Pentateuch establishes). Further, there are significant reasons to

v. 35b: sending through the revelation at the burning bush (Exod 3:2)
v. 36: attestation of prophet by "signs and wonders" (Exod 7:3; 14:21)
v. 37: Promise of a covenant mediator (Deut 18:15–18//Exod 20:19)
v. 38: Mediator as transmitter of God's word to people (Exod 20:22–23:33; 25–31)
v. 39–40: Rejection of mediator, incident with golden calf (Exod 32:1, 23)

The paragraph recounts the sending, attestation, work and rejection of Israel's covenant mediator. Other than the comment that Moses performed "wonders and signs" throughout the whole forty year wilderness period (v. 36),[103] it proceeds chronologically. That this makes good sense of the speech's structure is confirmed by the fact that Stephen goes on to speak about the tabernacle, which was in the wilderness with the Israelites (7:44); that is, he progresses beyond the golden calf incident to the construction of the tabernacle. This structure relates the promise of the prophet like Moses to two themes in particular: the attestation of the prophet by "signs and wonders" (v. 36) and the prophet's mediatorial function (vv. 38–39).

The association of "signs and wonders" with Moses' prophetic status is established in Moses' epitaph (Deut 34:10–12), which states that there has never since arisen in Israel a prophet like Moses, in terms of the "signs and wonders" that he performed. The importance of "signs and wonders" for potential prophetic claimants is evident elsewhere in the gospel tradition and Josephus.[104] For Luke, "signs and wonders" have an important role to play in attesting to the credibility of the narrative's key characters. This is clear in Luke's citation of Joel in Acts 2:[105]

καὶ δώσω τέρατα ἐν τῷ οὐρανῷ καὶ ἐπὶ τῆς γῆς αἷμα καὶ πῦρ καὶ ἀτμίδα καπνοῦ
Joel 3:3 LXX [Eng. 2:30]

---

doubt the Samaritan provenance of Stephen's speech, not least the significant role played by the prophets in it.

103 Note, however, that Exod 16:35 contains an initial reference to the forty-year period, well before its narrative realization, in connection with the provision of manna. So this too could be understood as part of Luke's recitation of Exod 3–32.

104 Hahn, *Titles*, 379, associates the request for a sign in the gospel tradition (Mark 8:11–12//Matt 16:1–4 [12:38–39]//Luke 11:16, 29; John 6:30; cf 1 Cor 1:22) with the expected prophet like Moses; with respect to the messianic prophets mentioned in Josephus, he points out: "attestation by miracle played a decisive role precisely in the case of the agitators of that time who appeared as eschatological prophets." See also the discussion of "signs and wonders" in connection with Moses' prophetic status in Lierman, *New Testament Moses*, 52–63.

105 See Johnson, *Literary Function*, 44–45; Steyn, *Septuagint Quotations*, 84–86.

καὶ δώσω τέρατα ἐν τῷ οὐρανῷ ἄνω καὶ **σημεῖα** ἐπὶ τῆς γῆς **κάτω**, αἷμα καὶ πῦρ καὶ ἀτμίδα καπνοῦ
Acts 2:19

Luke introduces the term σημεῖον into his quotation of Joel to emphasize that "wonders and signs" function "as accrediting signs of the eschatological prophecy."[106] These "wonders and signs" are then ascribed in Peter's Pentecost speech to Jesus: Jesus of Nazareth was "a man attested to you by God with deeds of power, wonders, and signs that God did through him among you, as you yourselves know (ἄνδρα ἀποδεδειγμένον ἀπὸ τοῦ θεοῦ εἰς ὑμᾶς δυνάμεσι καὶ τέρασι καὶ σημείοις οἷς ἐποίησε δι' αὐτοῦ ὁ Θεὸς ἐν μέσῳ ὑμῶν, καθὼς καὶ αὐτοὶ οἴδατε)" (2:22).[107] Luke's scriptural precedent for this description of Jesus is none other than Deut 34:10–12, both in terms of its piling up of synonyms for "miracle," and in terms of its emphasis on the public character of these wondrous deeds (cf. Deut 34:12, "before all Israel").[108] Luke goes on to associate "wonders and signs" with the apostles (2:43, 4:30, 5:12), Stephen (6:8), and Barnabas and Saul (14:3, 15:12)—that is, the main protagonists of his narrative.[109] Moses is paradigmatic for Jesus, the eschatological prophet like Moses, who in turn provides the template by which the apostles and church leaders are accredited.[110]

The other feature associated here with the prophet like Moses is Stephen's claim that Moses "received living oracles (λόγια ζῶντα) to give to us." In both Acts 3:22–23 and 7:37–38, the citation of Deut 18:15 is followed by a paraphrase of Deut 18:18b–19. In both cases Luke mentions the words that God gave Moses, and the response of the people to Moses. This consistent structure suggests that Luke was invoking the broader context within Deuteronomy, in which the Israelites, fearful that hearing the divine voice directly will result in their death, designate Moses for this dangerous task (Exod 20:19; Deut 18:16). This is why Stephen goes on to specify, after citing Deut 18:15, that Moses was "among the

---

106   Dillon, *Eyewitnesses*, 126, emphasis removed.
107   "Among you (ἐν μέσῳ ὑμῶν)" appears to be an allusion to the raising up of the prophet like Moses "in your midst."
108   So Johnson, *Literary Function*, 61; McWhirter, *Rejected Prophets*, 67.
109   On the legitimating function of "wonders and signs" for the main characters in Acts, see McWhirter, *Rejected Prophets*, 100–104, 113.
110   See also *Ps. Clem. Rec.* 1:57 (as cited in Allison, *New Moses*, 104): "as Moses wrought signs and wonders, so also did Jesus. And there is no doubt but that the likeness of the signs proves Him to be that prophet of whom he said that He should come, 'like himself.'"

TABLE 23   The structure of Deut 18:15, 18–19; Acts 3:22–23; 7:37–39

	Deut 18:15, 18–19	Acts 3:22–23	Acts 7:37–39
Promise Prophet receives words from God	Deut 18:15, 18a [Cf. Deut 18:16, τῇ ἡμέρᾳ τῆς ἐκκλησίας] (18b) I will put my words in his mouth, who shall speak (λαλήσει) to them everything that I command.	Acts 3:22a (22b) You must listen to him, according to all which he speaks (λαλήσῃ) to you.	Acts 7:37 (38) This is the one who was among the assembly (ἐν τῇ ἐκκλησίᾳ) in the wilderness when the angel spoke (τοῦ λαλοῦντος) to him on Mount Sinai, and with our ancestors; who received living oracles (λόγια ζῶντα) to give to us,
People's Response to the Prophet	(19) Anyone who does not listen to (ἐὰν μὴ ἀκούσῃ) the words that the prophet shall speak in my name, I myself will hold accountable.	(23) And it will be that everyone who does not listen (ἐὰν μὴ ἀκούσῃ) to that prophet will be utterly rooted out of the people.	(39) whom our ancestors were unwilling to obey (ὑπήκοοι), but they pushed him aside and in their hearts they turned back to Egypt

assembly in the wilderness" before receiving "living oracles to give to us":[111] the emphasis is on Moses as the chosen intermediary between God and the people (Table 23).

A notable difference between Acts 3 and 7 is the description of the people's response to the prophet. In both Deut 18:19 and Acts 3:23, a conditional phrase is used to warn the people about the consequences of not listening to the prophet. In Acts 7:39, Luke explicitly states that the people did not want to obey Moses, utilizing the golden calf episode as the evidence for this. That Luke has that episode in mind as a parade example of a history of failing to listen to Moses

---

111   The phrase "living oracles" (λόγια ζῶντα) deserves further comment. Though the terminological parallel is inexact, there is a conceptual parallel with the instruction to the imprisoned apostles in Acts 5. They also receive a message from an angel (5:19), who frees them from prison and commands them: "Go, stand in the temple, and speak (λαλεῖτε) to the people all the words of this life (πάντα τὰ ῥήματα τῆς ζωῆς ταύτης)" (5:20). As with the performance of "signs and wonders," so with the "living words": Luke constructs a chain of tradition that extends from Moses and the prophets to Jesus and the apostles.

and his prophetic successors is established by the citation of Amos 5:25–27 in 7:42–43 and Isa 66:1–2 in 7:49–50. Again, evidence for the eschatological interpretation of Deut 18:15 in Acts 3 and 7 is weaker than is typically assumed; the primary referent of the concept of the prophet like Moses for Luke in both passages has to do with Moses and his prophetic successors. The rejected prophets are not just Moses and Jesus, but include Amos and Isaiah as well. Overall, the transition from Acts 3 to Acts 7 is a transition from an appeal to listen to Moses' authorized successors in Peter's speech to an indictment of Israel's leaders for their history of failing to do so in Stephen's. This makes it apparent why Deut 18:15 does so much work for Luke: rather than the early Christian community rejecting Torah and Moses (per the charges against Stephen), Luke claims via Deut 18:15 that Israel's leaders have failed to listen to the prophets, and in so doing, are themselves the ones who reject Moses.

4 Listening to the Resurrected Prophet in Luke

The thorough integration of the quotations of Deut 18:15 into the overall purpose of the speeches in Acts demonstrates that these citations are not vestiges of a pre-Lukan source, foreign to Luke's own thought; rather they are important for Luke in shaping his account of the early church. This hypothesis, however, bears testing by a consideration of the gospel of Luke. In what follows, I offer some comments on how Luke has prepared for his distinct interpretation of Deut 18:15 in the first volume of his work.

Luke's redactional interest in increasing the emphasis on Jesus' prophetic profile is clear from his adaptations to his base texts. For example, he transfers the story of Jesus' rejection at Nazareth to the beginning of Jesus' ministry (Luke 4:16–30; cf Mark 6:1–6). In this narrative, Luke amplifies the prophetic profile of Jesus found in his Markan source only in the proverb quoted by Jesus (Mark 6:4//Luke 4:24).[112] He does this by means of the citation of Isa 61:1–2 (4:18–21), and by invoking the examples of Elijah and Elisha (4:25–27).[113] Inter-

---

112 Verheyden, "Calling Jesus a Prophet," 186, notes that this aphorism is linked to another in its context, "Physician, heal yourself" (4:23), and on this basis argues against taking it as a reference to Jesus' prophetic status: "The former of course does not turn Jesus into a physician, and for that reason the latter does not make him a prophet." This argument is weak because the proverb about the prophet is clearly intended to refer directly to Jesus' own homecoming; that is, ἐν τῇ πατρίδι refers in v. 23 to Nazareth, and in v. 24 is used in the proverb: the only conclusion available is that Jesus (obliquely) refers to himself as a prophet.
113 So also Croatto, "Jesus, Prophet like Elijah," 455–456; McWhirter, *Rejected Prophets*, 48–49.

preting Isa 61:1–2, Jesus says to his home-town crowd: "Today this Scripture has been fulfilled in your ears (ἐν τοῖς ὠσὶν ὑμῶν)" (4:21).[114] The emphasis on the *hearing* of the words of Jesus recalls the function of the prophet like Moses, and the attempt of the crowd to kill Jesus perhaps reflects their awareness of a prophetic claim (4:29).[115]

There are also revisions of Mark that specifically include allusions to Deut 18:15. In the the Transfiguration account, Luke detected an allusion to Deut 18:15 in the words of the heavenly voice, "listen to him" (Mark 9:7//Luke 9:35). He therefore re-ordered Mark's wording to match Deut 18:15 (that is, "to him you will listen").[116] This is the only allusion to Deut 18:15 in this passage, but there are further indications that Luke wanted to emphasize Jesus' role as the prophet like Moses:[117] instead of saying that Jesus was "transformed" (μετεμορφώθη, Mark 9:2), Luke speaks about the appearance of Jesus' *face* changing (τὸ εἶδος τοῦ προσώπου αὐτοῦ ἕτερον, 9:29), and twice uses the term δόξα, "glory," to describe Jesus, Moses, and Elijah's appearance (vv. 31, 32), lacking in Mark. Both of these changes evoke Moses' glorified appearance (cf. δοξάζω, Exod 34:29, 30 LXX).[118] Moreover, Luke answers the burning question of the more inquisitive of Mark's readers—just what were they talking about on that mountain?—by specifying that Moses and Elijah were speaking with Jesus about his "exodus" (τὴν ἔξοδον αὐτοῦ, ἣν ἤμελλεν πληροῦν ἐν Ἰερουσαλήμ, 9:29).[119] Finally, Fitzmyer has noted the importance Luke's narrative of the Transfiguration places on not

---

114 Bart J. Koet, *Five Studies on Interpretation of Scripture in Luke-Acts*, SNTA XIV (Leuven: Leuven University Press, 1989), 38, notes the connection to Stephen's indictment of the leaders as "uncircumcised in hearts and ears" (Acts 7:51), and points out the "remarkable parallels" between Luke 4:16–30 and Acts 7: both involve an inspired individual explaining the Scriptures and facing a negative, violent reaction from his audience.

115 So Tiede, *Prophecy and History*, 46–47:
   [N]o great risk is involved in the interpretation of Luke 4 to suggest that it represents a Christian response to the charge that Jesus was a false prophet. The question of whether the people will hear or listen to what is spoken "in their ears" is clearly a question of Israel's faithfulness or obduracy, that is, as asked from the viewpoint of those who have already accepted Jesus as the prophet like Moses … It is crucial to note that those same traditions … also require faithful Israel to refuse to listen to the false prophet and demand his death.

116 So Barbara E. Reid, *The Transfiguration: A Source- and Redaction-Critical Study of Luke 9:28–36*, CahRB 32 (Paris: Gabalda, 1993), 73. Matt 17:5 also makes this change; see Allison, *New Moses*, 244.

117 See also O'Toole, *Luke's Presentation*, 36–37.

118 Matt 17:2 independently inserts a reference to the shining of Jesus' face: the presence of Moses typology was evidently clear to ancient readers of Mark and demanded further elaboration. See Allison, *New Moses*, 243–248; Boesenberg, "Moses in Luke-Acts," 453–454.

119 This could be a reference to Jesus' death (cf 2 Pet 1:15 for this use of the term), or a broader

only the appearing, but also the *withdrawal* (διαχωρίζω, 9:33) of Moses and Elijah: "Heaven's word thus substitutes Jesus, its chosen messenger and Son, for the withdrawing figures of old."[120] Peter attempts to detain Moses and Elijah, but to no avail, and the voice designates Jesus, the chosen one, as the authorized recipient of the prophetic tradition and therefore the one who is to be obeyed.[121]

More significant for our purposes is the way Luke has edited Mark's reports of people's opinions about Jesus in the direction of Deut 18:15 (see Table 24 below). In both Mark and Luke, this opinion is a third option, after proposed identifications of Jesus with John the Baptist and Elijah. Mark's formulation of this third proposal in 6:15 seems tautologous (is not a prophet by definition "like" other prophets?). Luke's reformulations of Mark seem to be an allusion to Deut 18:15.[122] Indeed, it is likely that Luke wanted to make more explicit what was implicit in Mark's account, based on Mark's usage of the term ὡς, "like."[123] Luke turns Mark's echo of Deut 18:15 into an allusion by utilizing the key verb ἀνίστημι, which we have already seen particularly struck Luke as a cryptic reference to the resurrection (cf ἀνίστημι in Acts 3:22, 26). Here, Luke utilizes the language of Deut 18:15 to have the crowds express the idea that Jesus was an ancient prophet *redivivus*.[124] He offers no evaluative comment on the crowds' identifi-

---

reference to the entire complex of Easter events (death-resurrection-ascension), in which Jesus' "exodus" refers to his accomplishing of salvation and "assumption" (cf. Luke 9:51) of glory in the heavenly realm.

120 Joseph Fitzmyer, *The Gospel according to Luke: Introduction, Translation, and Notes*, 2 vols., AB 28–28A (Garden City, N.Y.: Doubleday, 1981–1985), 1:803.

121 Croatto, "Jesus, Prophet like Elijah," 461: "Moses and Elijah disappear. This is quite significant. From this moment on, the risen Jesus (anticipated in the transfiguration) will be the only mediator, interpreter, and teacher for the Christian community. The risen Jesus will replace both the prophet-teacher Moses and the prophet Elijah."

122 It is considered an allusion by McWhirter, *Rejected Prophets*, 67; Moessner, "Luke 9:1–50," 590.

123 See Joel Marcus, *Mark 1–8: A New Translation with Introduction and Commentary*, AYB 27 (New Haven: Yale University Press, 2000), 393: "There were other 'prophets' in first-century Palestine.... The second phrase, 'like one of the prophets,' distinguishes Jesus from these contemporary prophets and links him with *the* prophets, i.e. those of the Old Testament, whose line was considered to have ceased." The echo is also recognized by Hans F. Bayer, *Das Evangelium des Markus*, HTA 5 (Giessen: Brockhaus, 2008), 252; Robert H. Stein, *Mark*, BECNT (Grand Rapids: Baker Academic, 2008), 301. See also the discussion of Adela Yarbro Collins, *Mark: A Commentary*, Hermeneia (Minneapolis: Fortress, 2007), 44–52.

124 François Bovon, *Luke 1: A Commentary on the Gospel of Luke 1:1–9:50*, Hermeneia (Minneapolis: Fortress, 2002), 250: "Mark only emphasized the similarity..., but Luke describes public opinion as identifying Jesus with a resurrected ... prophet. The possibility of this popular belief does not bother him." Fitzmyer (*Luke*, 1:759) expresses doubt as to whether

TABLE 24   Luke's modification of Mark 6:15b; 8:28d

Mark 6:15b, 8:28d	Luke 9:8c, 19c
προφήτης ὡς εἷς τῶν προφητῶν	προφήτης τις τῶν ἀρχαίων ἀνέστη
εἷς τῶν προφητῶν	προφήτης τις τῶν ἀρχαίων ἀνέστη
"a prophet like one of the prophets"	"a prophet, one of the ancients, has arisen"
"one of the prophets"	"a prophet, one of the ancients, has arisen"

cations of Jesus, though the impression one receives from Peter's confession (Jesus is τὸν χριστὸν τοῦ θεοῦ, 9:20) is that they are "probably half-truths."[125] For Luke, the crowds' identification of Jesus as the return of an ancient prophet was a garbled understanding of Deut 18:15. Indeed, the arrival and withdrawal of Moses and Elijah on the Mount of Transfiguration shows that Luke did not consider this opinion to be accurate, and wants to correct it: Jesus could not be one of the "ancient prophets" after all, because the most prominent of these have now promptly entered and exited Luke's gospel.[126] It is not the case that Luke was reluctant to apply Deut 18:15 to Jesus; however, he considered that Deut 18:15 referred to Jesus as a *resurrected* prophet like Moses, not as Moses *redivivus*. Thus he prepares the ground for debate over the proper identification of the prophet like Moses to be a matter of qualified scriptural interpretation. The crowds are unreliable in their understanding of what it means to expect such a prophet, and the full revelation of the meaning of Deut 18:15 must await the resurrection of Jesus and the opening of the disciples' minds to understand the Scriptures.

Luke begins the process of correcting his readers' understanding of Deut 18:15 in the gospel account, preparing for the identification of Jesus as the "raised up" prophet in Acts. He does this in two significant places, first, in the

---

the idea is of a resurrected ancient prophet, or merely of the "raising up" of such a prophet, as God promised in Deut 18:15: regarding resurrection, he says, "the verb need not have that connotation here [i.e. of resurrection] (or in 9:19), although one cannot exclude it either"; allusion to the "prophet like Moses" in 9:8 is also "not certain." Luke's account is indeed (deliberately?) ambiguous.

125   Bovon, *Luke 1*, 350.

126   Verheyden, "Calling Jesus a Prophet," 193–194, is right to say that in the Transfiguration story "it is demonstrated that Jesus is not Elijah *redivivus*, nor Moses, or for that, any other prophet of the past" but he is wrong to argue further that the allusion to Deut 18:15 (which he accepts) "does not turn Jesus into a prophet."

parable of the rich man and Lazarus (16:19–31); second, in his account of the travelers to Emmaus and the subsequent appearance of Jesus to the apostles (24:13–49). The parable of the rich man and Lazarus is unique to Luke. It is doubtful that it is entirely a Lukan creation; rather, it seems that a parable focused on eschatological reversal was taken up by Luke and used to make another theological point, one pertaining to listening to Moses and prophets.[127] The plea of the rich man that Lazarus might go and warn his brothers (his altruism having been "kindled" all too late), in particular, takes the parable in this latter direction, and should be regarded as a Lukan addition:[128]

> (27) He said, "Then, father, I beg you to send him to my father's house— (28) for I have five brothers—that he may testify to them (ὅπως διαμαρτύρηται αὐτοῖς), so that they will not also come into this place of torment." (29) Abraham replied, "They have Moses and the prophets; let them listen to them (ἔχουσι Μωϋσέα καὶ τοὺς προφήτας· ἀκουσάτωσαν αὐτῶν)." (30) He said, "No, father Abraham; but if someone goes to them from the dead, they will repent." (31) He said to him, "If they do not listen to Moses and the prophets, neither will they be convinced even if someone rises from the dead (εἰ Μωϋσέως καὶ τῶν προφητῶν οὐκ ἀκούουσιν, οὐδ' ἐάν τις ἐκ νεκρῶν ἀναστῇ πεισθήσονται)."
> Luke 16:27–31

The rich man asks that Lazarus "testify" to his brothers. The verb διαμαρτύρομαι occurs fifteen times in the NT, ten of which are in Luke-Acts.[129] In the LXX,

---

[127] The Q-sayings which Luke included before the parable (16:16–18) also demonstrate his redactional interest in the claims of Moses and the prophets here. Though McWhirter, *Rejected Prophets*, 100–101, does not comment on the original unity of the parable, she points out that the "second chance" parable is a Lukan device, and directly connects the offer of a second chance to Luke's concept of the prophet like Moses, as manifest in Stephen's speech in Acts 7, in which Moses is portrayed as making two offers of salvation to Israel.

[128] For a discussion of scholarship on the parable (and a defense of its unity), see Klyne R. Snodgrass, *Stories with Intent: A Comprehensive Guide to the Parables of Jesus* (Grand Rapids: Eerdmans, 2008), 425–433. The position taken here, that vv. 27–31 represent a later addition, was argued by Rudolf Bultmann, *The History of the Synoptic Tradition*, trans. John Marsh, rev. ed. (New York: Harper & Row, 1976), 178. François Bovon, *Luke 2: A Commentary on the Gospel of Luke 9:51–19:57*, Hermeneia (Minneapolis: Fortress, 2013), 476–485, argues that there are two successive developments, vv. 27–29 being an "L" addition to the original parable, while vv. 30–31 are Lukan. In my judgment, positing three stages of tradition is unnecessarily complex.

[129] Only here in Luke. Other occurrences are Acts 2:40; 8:25; 10:42; 18:5; 20:21, 23, 24; 23:11; 28:23; 1 Thess 4:6; 1 Tim 5:21; 2 Tim 2:14; 4:1; Hebr 2:6.

it is the language of juridical testimony, and is associated particularly with the function of prophets.¹³⁰ The rich man is therefore asking Abraham to "raise up" Lazarus *as a prophet* in order to warn his brothers. Abraham's response echoes Deut 18:15: "They have Moses and the prophets. Let them listen to them (ἀκουσάτωσαν αὐτῶν)" (16:29).¹³¹ Here, Luke's interpretation of Deut 18:15 is a standard one: there has been an authorized Mosaic prophetic succession, whom the people are commanded to obey. The rich man objects: if one returns from the dead, his brothers will repent! And at this point Luke's unique interpretation of this passage again emerges, in Abraham's rebuttal: "If they do not listen (οὐκ ἀκούουσιν) to Moses and the prophets, neither will they be convinced even if someone rises (ἀναστῇ) from the dead" (16:31).¹³²

On its face, Abraham's statement is clearly questionable. It seems that the resurrection of Lazarus would be a significant sign, which might cause the rich man's brothers to reconsider! But Luke is not syllogizing, he is theologizing, and thinking not of Lazarus's resurrection but of Jesus's.¹³³ The rich man's "brothers," from the perspective of the author, represent those Jews who have not believed in Christ.¹³⁴ Luke's claim is that failure to "listen" to the "raised up" prophet like Moses (i.e., Jesus) is a direct consequence of their failure to "listen" to the prophets whom God "raised up" (i.e., the Mosaic prophetic succession). The failure, then, is hermeneutical, just as it is when Jesus—the resurrected prophet—upbraids the travelers on the road to Emmaus ("how foolish, and how slow of heart to believe all that the prophets have spoken," 24:25). This is the manner in which Luke claims continuity for the early Christian movement with "Moses and the prophets": Moses himself spoke of resurrection (cf Luke 20:37), and promised that God would send a resurrected prophet.

This discussion has thus brought us to the second important context to consider, Luke's resurrection narrative, in which Jesus appears as a resurrected prophet like Moses, the one with the hermeneutical authority to "open" both the Scriptures (24:32) and the minds of the apostles (24:45), in order that the latter might understand the eschatological meaning of the former.¹³⁵ It is par-

---

130   Cf. 2 Kgs 17:13; Jer 6:10; Ezek 16:2, 20:4; 2 Chr 24:19; Neh 9:26.
131   Verheyden, "Calling Jesus a Prophet," 194, recognizes the allusion to Deut 18:15 here.
132   Boesenberg, "Moses in Luke-Acts," 450, rightly notes the dependence of Luke's language on the thought of Deut 18:15.
133   Fredriksen, *From Jesus to Christ*, 33, speaks of the passage as a "clumsy foreshadowing that borders on anachronism."
134   See McWhirter, *Rejected Prophets*, 103, who argues that Luke has figures such as Gamaliel and the Jerusalem council in mind (cf. Acts 5:33–39).
135   See Croatto, "Jesus, Prophet like Elijah," 460: "Through his resurrection, he becomes not only the glorious Messiah but also the interpreter of Scripture, as it is clearly stated in

ticularly significant in this account that Jesus coordinates *his* words to those of Scripture:

> Εἶπεν δὲ πρὸς αὐτούς· οὗτοι οἱ λόγοι μου οὓς ἐλάλησα πρὸς ὑμᾶς ἔτι ὢν σὺν ὑμῖν, ὅτι δεῖ πληρωθῆναι πάντα τὰ γεγραμμένα ἐν τῷ νόμῳ Μωϋσέως καὶ τοῖς προφήταις καὶ ψαλμοῖς περὶ ἐμοῦ.

> He said to them, "These are my words which I spoke to you while I was with you, that it is necessary that all that is written about me in the law of Moses and in the Prophets and in the Psalms be fulfilled."
> Luke 24:44

Jesus' opening words are reminiscent of Deut 1:1:[136]

> οὗτοι οἱ λόγοι οὓς ἐλάλησεν Μωυσῆς ...
> Deut 1:1

> οὗτοι οἱ λόγοι μου οὓς ἐλάλησα
> Luke 24:44

In coordinating his own speaking (λαλέω) to scriptural testimony, Jesus is performing precisely the function of the prophet like Moses of Deut 18:15, who, like Moses, "speaks" (λαλέω, 18:18) the words of God.[137] Thus what might seem to be worded redundantly ("my words which I spoke") is part of Luke's presentation of Jesus as the resurrected prophet like Moses. Hooker points out that a further aspect of Jesus' characterization as Mosaic prophet lies in his conformity to the test of Deut 18:21–22: he has been vindicated as a prophet, because his words about the suffering and vindication of the Messiah have come to pass.[138]

---

two references: Luke 24:27 ('he explained [διερμήνευσεν] to them in all the Scriptures the things concerning himself') and 24:45 ('then he opened their minds to understand the Scriptures')."

136 So O'Toole, "Parallels," 24; Allison, *New Moses*, 100.
137 On λαλέω in Luke-Acts, see Koet, *Five Studies*, 67: "it is possible that, when λαλέω is used, we are dealing with a prophetic message. We can find this peculiar use of it elsewhere in Luke [Koet refers to 1:64, 67, 70; 2:33, 38; Acts 2:4; 19:6; cf 1 Cor 14:29]. ... λαλέω may perhaps reflect a special way of speaking i.e. a kind of prophetic message, and as such it is related to (divinely) inspired speaking and learning."
138 Morna Hooker, "'Beginning from Moses and from all the Prophets,'" in *From Jesus to John: Essays on Jesus and New Testament Christology in Honour of Marinus de Jonge*, ed. M.C. de Boer, JSNTSup 84 (Sheffield: JSOT Press, 1993), 216–230, at 227.

From this perspective, the narrative of Acts is the further fulfillment of the prophet like Moses' announcement that forgiveness of sins is to be preached to all nations (cf. vv. 46–47).

5 Conclusion

Luke's distinctive interpretation of Deut 18:15–19, then, may be summed up with the following conclusions: (1) Although Luke holds that Jesus is the eschatological prophet like Moses, he displays familiarity with the priestly-scribal concept of a Mosaic prophetic succession, and this is the primary meaning that is emphasized in his citations of Deut 18:15, 18–19 in Acts 3 and 7. (2) The cryptic meaning of Deut 18:15 is that the prophet like Moses will be "raised" from the dead, which is hinted at in Luke's gospel, but fully revealed only in the apostolic interpretation in Acts. (3) Both Jesus and Moses suffered initial rejection by their people, who did not understand their mission, but were raised in power by God, "sent" to bring salvation and attested by "wonders and signs." (4) As covenant mediators, both Moses' and Jesus' proclamations are decisive for the future of Israel, and Israel's blessing or curse rests upon whether they will listen to the prophets raised up by God. (5) As was the case already in Deuteronomy, the concept of the prophet like Moses is used by Luke in order to construct a normative tradition that extends from Moses and prophets to Jesus and the apostles: the apostles, too, are like Moses in speaking "living words" to the people and in performing "wonders and signs."

Thus, the identification of Jesus as the eschatological prophet like Moses was no mere vestige of early christology unthinkingly retained by Luke, but was important to the author's own goals. For Luke, the use of this trope is related to his claim that Jesus and the apostles are the heirs of Moses and the prophets, that is, he wants to construct a normative tradition. This conclusion is interesting, precisely because it shows that Luke did not "proof-text" Deut 18:15, but in some ways recapitulated its creation of a genealogical model for prophecy. His use of the concept of the Mosaic prophetic succession in *speeches* of authoritative characters makes the continuity with Dtr historiography all the more remarkable: Peter and Stephen are exponents of Mosaic Discourse, and, like Jeremiah, represent a prophetic warning to Israel to repent before it is too late (here, Luke has the events of 70 CE in mind).[139]

---

[139] See Tiede, *Prophecy and History*, 1–3, on the calamity of the destruction of the temple and its importance for Luke-Acts: "As always, the vanquished were pitted against each other

Luke thus authorizes the early Christians as legitimate recipients of the Mosaic prophetic succession, and, more ominously, warns that those who do not listen to Jesus and the apostles are to be excluded from the people of God (Acts 3:23). On the one hand, this leads to the recognition that Luke-Acts is indeed a deeply Jewish text, writing from within a particular scribal interpretive tradition. Peter and Stephen are portrayed as priestly interpreters of the prophetic oracles, in ways strikingly analogous to figures such as the Righteous Teacher known from Qumran.[140] On the other hand, we are faced here with the limitations of the genealogical model of prophecy: by constructing a sole authorized channel for the continuation of the Mosaic prophetic succession, it must be acknowledged that Luke-Acts provides a conceptual basis that would lead to anti-Semitic interpretation of the NT. There is a danger of appropriating these texts as referring to a Jewish "other"[141]—an anachronistic reading that

---

and burdened with the question, 'Why?'... the extensive testimony of the deuteronomistic historians ... required that Israel's fortunes be correlated directly to its obedience to God and that Israel's suffering be viewed as the result of failure or refusal to heed the prophets sent to it .... Those who stood *within* this scriptural tradition, therefore, were at least provided with certain time-honored categories and theological concepts for interpreting their experience."

140   Grossman, "Priesthood as Authority," 122, captures this dynamic in Acts as well as other early Jewish and Christian texts:
For first-century Jews and Christians, the image of the priesthood represented a number of important ideas: that there was an ancient covenant between God and Israel, that the community of Israel had important responsibilities for maintaining such a covenant, and that certain members of the community might take on a leadership role (or an otherwise exclusive responsibility) in ensuring the continuity of the covenant. "Priesthood," as a concept, provided language for arguments about which community was maintaining the ancient covenant (or enacting a new one to replace one that had become corrupted). It provided language for talking about how that covenant might be maintained, as well as a way of distinguishing between those people who were maintaining the covenant and those who had gone astray.
This is a fitting summation of the significance of Luke's representation as Peter and Stephen as priestly interpreters of prophetic oracles.

141   Luke's polemic is not necessarily more heated than that found in the texts from Qumran—and in that case, the anachronism of the unhelpful label "anti-Semitic" is apparent. Critique *from within* is firmly rooted within Judaism. Tiede, *Prophecy and History*, 7, characterizes Luke-Acts as involved in an *"intra-family* struggle"; see also Donaldson, "Moses Typology," and the helpful comments of McWhirter, *Rejected Prophets*, 6–7. For an alternate approach to Luke-Acts, which see it as anti-Semitic, see Jack T. Sanders, *The Jews in Luke-Acts* (Philadelphia: Fortress, 1987). Sanders has been criticized by Günter Wasserberg, *Aus Israels Mitte—Heil für die Welt: eine narrativ-exegetische Studie zur Theologie des Lukas*, BZNW 92 (Berlin: de Gruyter, 1998), 13–30. Note also Levine's strong language, "Luke and the Jewish Religion," 401: "For Luke's Gospel, the 'Jewish religion' consists of a bankrupt and soon to be defunct temple, synagogues of violence, leaders who per-

has been all too common throughout history—but Luke has no such concept: there is for him one people of God, which includes many Jews and is embracing the Gentile world. He utilizes Deut 18:15 to identify Jesus and the apostles as the normative continuation of the prophetic tradition, and so aligns the young Christian community with the covenantal people of God.

> vert the tradition, and halakhic practices that lack scriptural warrant or that prove either misguided or irrelevant." Fredriksen, *From Jesus to Christ*, 191–198, makes a contrasting argument (at 192): "An unrelieved and mutual hostility between Jesus and his Jewish contemporaries, such as Matthew and Mark portray, would compromise Luke's vision of the continuity and historicity of the salvation revealed in scripture .... For Luke, this means that Jesus was a Jewish leader with Jewish followers, and so he portrays them in his gospel and Acts."

PART 3

Mosaic Prophecy and Logos-Theology:
The Triumph of Mosaic Discourse

CHAPTER 11

Moses, the Prophetic Nature: The Incomparability of Moses in the Writings of Philo

1 Introduction: The Triumph of Mosaic Discourse

In the final two chapters of this book, I investigate two authors in which the charismatic model of prophecy re-asserts itself, but now influenced by Deuteronomy's concept of the prophet like Moses. These authors, Philo of Alexandria and the anonymous author of the Fourth Gospel, are deeply influenced by Deuteronomy's concept of likeness to Moses, but they interpret that similarity more in terms of the vertical axis of divine revelation—the prophet is the one in whose mouth God puts God's word (τὸ ῥῆμά μου; Deut 18:18)—than in terms of the horizontal axis of genealogical and historical succession. The approach to Mosaic prophecy in these authors could therefore be described from a variety of analytical perspectives. On the level of interpretation of Deuteronomy, it represents the triumph of Deut 34:10–12: Moses is held to be the supreme prophet, separated from his prophetic successors, and the primary scriptural touchstone for understanding the divine Logos (and its embodiment, in John). On the sociological level, it might be speculated that these authors deploy a charismatic rather than genealogical model as a mode of self-authorization, as both in certain respects are positioned at some distance from the central religious authorities in their respective communities. Although Philo of Alexandria was a person of some standing and reputation, his entire intellectual project is certainly distinctive. And, in contrast with the author of Luke-Acts, who stands in the broad stream of early Christian tradition (related as his work is to Mark, Q, and Pauline traditions), the Johannine literature is marked by the independence of its thought within early Christianity. In these authors, the charismatic model of prophecy re-emerges, in authors who made distinctive cases for their construals of the importance of Mosaic Discourse in early Judaism and nascent Christianity.

2   Philo of Alexandria and Mosaic Prophecy

Among the authors, texts, and traditions considered in this study, Philo of Alexandria is unique for several reasons. First, he is one of the few to offer explicit interpretive commentary on Deut 18:9–22; thus, unlike authors such as Josephus, his understanding of the passage need not be gleaned from incidental remarks and implicit evidence. Second, he stands outside of the historiographic tradition, in which the prophetic commission of Moses and the raising up of prophets like him were understood to be a manifestation of the divine commitment to Israel, and an integral feature of its covenantal story. Rather than focus on the horizontal axis ("like Moses"), Philo's interest is almost exclusively in the vertical relationship, in which God promises to put God's word in the mouth of the prophet. Somewhat paradoxically, for Philo Moses himself is not a prophet like Moses, since Moses' experience as a prophet is completely unsurpassed. Nevertheless, there are hints in his writings of Deuteronomy's model of prophecy, in which prophetic legitimation depends on a genealogical relationship to Moses.

This discussion of Philo's view of Mosaic prophecy will begin with his commentary on the prophet-law of Deut 18:9–22 in his *On the Special Laws*. After this, I will consider Philo's portrayal of Moses as a prophet, and finally turn to the slender references to a succession of Mosaic prophets in Philo's writings. Though Philo is unique in some respects, his writings do share features with other authors and traditions in Second Temple Judaism, notably the elevation of Moses' status to that of prophet *par excellence* and the widespread tendency to reserve προφήτης and associated terms for scriptural, and not contemporary, figures.

2.1   Philo's Commentaries on Deut 18:9–22

John Levison has argued not only that Philo accepted the possibility of contemporary prophecy, but that he considered himself to be one. Moreover, he situates this claim in terms of the broader debate about the so-called cessation of prophecy in Second Temple Judaism:

> While the dogma of the cessation of prophecy may have lost its stranglehold, the task of unmasking the error of this dogma remains integral to our understanding of formative Judaism and Christianity because the dogma of the cessation of prophecy has the unfortunate effect of accentuating the vitality of early Christianity at the expense of an allegedly lifeless Judaism. Yet this task will not be complete until the writings of Philo Judaeus are brought front and center to the discussion, and that is where they belong because Philo, more than any other Jewish author

of Greco-Roman antiquity, provides indispensable autobiographical evidence that prophecy was not relegated to the past or left to the eschatological future.[1]

Levison declares that scholars who assert a temporary cessation in prophecy are theologically motivated and anti-Jewish; the terminology used ("dogma," "unmasking," "error") suggests that Levison is equally motivated by theological considerations.[2] Levison's statement fails to question adequately the main problem in such scholarship, namely, its assumption of an anachronistic dichotomy between earliest Christianity and Second Temple Judaism.[3] My interaction with Levison's contribution is twofold: first, in agreement, I affirm that evidence from Philo is problematic for any general theory of the cessation of prophecy; second, towards the end of my discussion of Philo, I will come back to a point of disagreement on whether Philo provides autobiographical evidence for the persistence of prophecy.

With regard to the first of these, it must be stated that Philo's commentaries on Deut 18:9–22 make it clear that he considers prophecy a live possibility. Philo's interpretation of Deut 18:9–22 is found in his treatise *On the Special Laws*, where he deals with the prophet-law in two places, first in relation to the nature of God (*Spec.* 1.59–65), and second in relation to the commandment to not bear false witness (*Spec.* 4.48–52). There are four features of Philo's interpretation that are particularly interesting and worthy of comment.

First, in both places Philo demonstrates awareness of the mantic context of the prophet-law, following Deuteronomy by juxtaposing prophecy to all

---

[1] John R. Levison, "Philo's Personal Experience and the Persistence of Prophecy," in *Prophets, Prophecy, and Prophetic Texts in Second Temple Judaism*, ed. M.H. Floyd and R. Haak, LHB/OTS 427 (New York: T&T Clark, 2006), 194–209; here 195.

[2] I would not deny that some exponents of the traditional view of prophecy's cessation may have done so based on negative assumptions about Judaism; the specific topic I am interested in, however, is a view about the Mosaic prophetic succession that was itself articulated by various ancient Jews.

[3] Levison's statement is problematic on two levels. Even if ancient Christianity claimed to experience a renewal of prophecy (which, in some quarters, it clearly did), this should be understood as one aspect of the diverse "vitality" of Early Judaism. But why should we accept the view that ancient Jewish authors and groups that rejected contemporary prophecy or prophetic claimants were "lifeless"? It is the unspoken association of "prophecy" and "vitality"—itself dependent on categories that go back to Wellhausen—that is more deeply problematic. (There is a certain Protestant bias operative here, since the priestly character of Second Temple Judaism, thought by Wellhausen to represent the stifling authority of Law, also is reflective of anti-Catholic tendencies in Protestant scholarship.) Levison's acceptance of those terms animates his agenda, which aims at demonstrating the persistence of prophecy (and, therefore, "vitality") of ancient Judaism more generally.

other forms of divination. He says Moses "forbids them to use any of its forms and expels from his own commonwealth all its fawning followers, haruspices, purificators, augurs, interpreters of prodigies, incantators, and those who put their faith in sounds and voices" (*Spec.* 1.60; trans. LCL).[4] The prophet is contrasted to these other modes of divination as the sole legitimate means to know the future (*Spec.* 1.64).

Second, Philo departs from Deuteronomy by supplying an alternate rationale for the prohibition on divination. In Deuteronomy, the contrast between prophecy and divination is rooted in the contrast between Israel and the nations. For Philo, however, Moses' ban on divinatory practices is based on their uncertain character:[5]

> But since a longing to know the future is ingrained in all men, which longing makes them turn to haruspication and the other forms of divination in the prospect of finding certainty thereby (ὡς δι' αὐτῶν τὸ σαφὲς ἀνευρήσοντες), though actually they are brimful of uncertainty and constantly convict themselves of falsehood (τὰ δ' ἀσαφείας γέμει πολλῆς καὶ ἐξ ἑαυτῶν ἀεὶ διελέγχεται)—while he very earnestly forbids them to follow such, yet he tells them that if they do not swerve from piety they will not be denied the full knowledge of the future (οὐκ ἀμοιρήσουσι τῆς τῶν μελλόντων ἐπιγνώσεως).
> *Spec.* 1.64; trans. LCL

In one sense, Philo's interpretation departs from Deuteronomy, but in another sense, it is consistent with the fundamental concern of the prophet-law for normativity in revelation. That is, Philo is superficially opposed to Deut 18:9–22, but deeply in concord with it. Congruent with this theme, Philo reiterates the emphasis on divination's status as mere conjecture and full of uncertainty in his later discussion of the prophet-law (*Spec.* 4.50–52).

Third, Philo is intrigued by Deuteronomy's description of the prophet as the one in whose mouth God will put God's word (Deut 18:18), which he interprets

---

4 Levison, "Philo's Personal Experience," 199, accurately notes Philo's strong contrast between prophecy and divination, and points out that it also occurs with reference to Balaam in *Mos.* 1.277, but does not observe that Philo is dependent on Deuteronomy for this contrast.

5 See also earlier (*Spec.* 1.61; trans. LCL): "For all these are but guessing at what is plausible and probable, and the same phenomena present to them ideas which differ at different times because the things on which they are based have no natural stability nor has the understanding acquired any accurate touchstone by which the genuine can be tested and approved."

as divine commandeering of the rational faculty. His description of prophecy as an alternative to divination is set forth below:

> ἀλλά τις ἐπιφανεὶς ἐξαπιναίως προφήτης θεοφόρητος θεσπιεῖ καὶ προφητεύσει, λέγων μὲν οἰκεῖον οὐδέν—οὐδὲ γάρ, εἰ λέγει, δύναται καταλαβεῖν ὅ γε κατεχόμενος ὄντως καὶ ἐνθουσιῶν,—ὅσα δ' ἐνηχεῖται, διελεύσεται καθάπερ ὑποβάλλοντος ἑτέρου· ἑρμηνεῖς γάρ εἰσιν οἱ προφῆται θεοῦ καταχρωμένου τοῖς ἐκείνων ὀργάνοις πρὸς δήλωσιν ὧν ἂν ἐθελήσῃ.

> A prophet possessed by God will suddenly appear and give prophetic oracles. Nothing of what he says will be his own, for he that is truly under the control of divine inspiration has no power of apprehension when he speaks but serves as the channel for the insistent words of Another's prompting. For prophets are the interpreters of God, Who makes full use of their organs of speech to set forth what He wills.
> *Spec.* 1.65, trans. LCL

For Philo, Deuteronomy's description of the prophet as one through whom God speaks means that divine inspiration overwhelms and takes control of the prophet's rational faculties; the prophet's words are not their own but God's.[6] This is also an important feature of his later description of prophecy:

> For no pronouncement of a prophet is ever his own; he is an interpreter prompted by Another in all his utterances, when knowing not what he does he is filled with inspiration (καθ' ὃν χρόνον ἐνθουσιᾷ γεγονὼς ἐν ἀγνοίᾳ), as the reason withdraws and surrenders the citadel of the soul (μετανισταμένου μὲν τοῦ λογισμοῦ καὶ παρακεχωρηκότος τὴν τῆς ψυχῆς ἀκρόπολιν) to a new visitor and tenant, the Divine Spirit which plays upon the vocal organism and dictates words which clearly express its prophetic message.
> *Spec.* 4.49; trans. LCL

Philo indicates in these passages a contrast between the rational and the prophetic that is important for his philosophy of revelation; indeed, prophecy is necessary precisely because its deliverances go beyond those which can be attained by reason.[7]

---

6 For parallels in Greek literature, see particularly David Winston, "Two Types of Mosaic Prophecy according to Philo," *JSP* 2 (1989): 49–67.

7 See *Mos.* 2.6: ἀναγκαίως καὶ προφητείας ἔτυχεν, ἵν' ὅσα μὴ λογισμῷ δύναται καταλαμβάνειν, ταῦτα

Fourth and finally, Philo omits from his summary of Deut 18:9–22 the notion that the prophet will be "like Moses." In fact, as Winston and Levison have shown, there are important ways in which this hypothetical prophet is not like Moses for Philo.[8] Philo omits any suggestion that the prophet of Deut 18:15, 18 will be like Moses because he inherits and amplifies the tradition, found in Num 12:6–8 and Deut 34:10, that Moses is vastly superior to all other prophets. It is these latter passages, and not Deut 18:15, 18, that Philo cites when supplying evidence that Moses was a prophet (*Her.* 262). This brings us to a discussion of Moses' prophetic status in Philo's writings.

2.2 Moses' Prophetic Status in Philo

Philo's portrait of Moses is rich and complex:[9] he is the best man that ever was (*Mos.* 1.1), and in a certain sense can even be understood as divine.[10] For Philo, Moses is the "man of many names" (*Mut.* 125), endowed with "all legislative and prophetic skill" (*Congr.* 132). Four titles for Moses in particular are important to him: king, legislator, priest, and prophet.[11] His biography of Moses is explicitly structured around these offices (*Mos.* 1.334; 2.1–3, 292), which leaves discussion of Moses' role as prophet for last (*Mos.* 2.187–291). For Philo, Moses is the supreme prophet or "arch-prophet."[12] Indeed, over half of the usages of the noun "prophet" in his extant writings occur in reference to Moses.[13] Philo

---

προνοίᾳ θεοῦ εὕροι; cf. also *Her.* 249, where he describes prophecy as the best form of mania; *Her.* 259.

8   Winston, "Two Types;" John R. Levison, "Two Types of Ecstatic Prophecy according to Philo," *SPhiloA* 6 (1994): 83–89.

9   The most comprehensive survey is provided by Louis H. Feldman, *Philo's Portrayal of Moses in the Context of Ancient Judaism*, CJAS 15 (Notre Dame: University of Notre Dame Press, 2007).

10 See Exod 7:1. The scholarly discussion on this point, however, is entangled in terminological debates about the definition of "divine." For a thorough discussion with references to the literature, see M. David Litwa, "The Deification of Moses in Philo of Alexandria," *SPhiloA* 26 (2014): 1–27.

11 One wonders if there is some connection to the four offices of the Deuteronomic constitution in Deut 16:18–18:22 (judge, king, priest, and prophet). Philo's discussion of Moses' kingship seems to portray him as the ideal version of Deut 17:14–20 (see *Mos.* 1.148–154; in particular, note his lack of dependency on cavalry [1.148], his refusal to accumulate gold or silver [1.152, οὐ χρυσὸν οὐκ ἄργυρον ἐθησαυρίσατο], and his strict adherence to the guidance of Torah [1.154]). If there is a connection to the Deuteronomic constitution, it could explain why Philo leaves his discussion of Moses' prophetic status for last.

12 ἀρχιπροφήτης: *Mut.* 103, 125; *Somn.* 2.18.

13 He uses the term προφήτης or προφῆτις 96 times in his extant writings, 49 in reference to Moses: *Leg.* 2.1, 3.173; *Sacr.* 130; *Gig.* 49, 56; *Migr.* 15, 151; *Her.* 4, 262; *Congr.* 170; *Fug.* 140; *Mut.* 11; *Somn.* 2.277; *Mos.* 1.57, 1.156, 2.3, 2.76, 2.187, 2.188, 2.209, 2.213, 2.246, 2.250, 2.257,

makes liberal usage of superlatives to describe Moses's greatness as a prophet: he was "the most illustrious (δοκιμώτατος) of prophets" (*Mos.* 2.187); "the most pious man that ever was (ὁσιώτατον τῶν πώποτε γενομένων)" (*Mos.* 2.192); "the most perfect of the prophets (τοῦ τελειοτάτου τῶν προφητῶν)" (*Decal.* 175); "the most holy (ἱερώτατος) prophet" (*Virt.* 119). In certain respects, Moses is prophecy *itself* for Philo; he describes Moses as "the prophetic word (ὁ προφήτης λόγος)" (*Congr.* 170) and even "the prophetic nature (τὸ προφητικὸν γένος)" (*Fug.* 147).[14]

In view of this exalted rhetoric, Philo's summary of Moses' role as prophet in *Mos.* 2.187–291 strikes the reader as somewhat disappointing. In this extended discussion, Philo retells eight biblical narratives. The first four have to do with "question and answer" prophecy (in which Moses inquired of God about what should be done in a particular situation, and received an oracular response),[15] the next four provide examples of prophecy proper, in which Moses was ecstatically inspired and predicted the future.[16] For Philo, these instances represent not the summit of Mosaic prophecy; rather, they are the most ordinary instances of Moses' career as prophet, when he mostly closely resembles other prophets. Yet, even in these cases, Mosaic prophecy is superior to all others, so that Moses is more unlike than like other prophets.

Philo provides a justification for the episodes of Mosaic prophecy that he has chosen to relate by developing a typology of three different kinds of prophecy. The gradation of prophecy that he envisages depends on the nature of the interaction between the divine being and the prophetic agent:

> Now I am fully aware that all things written in the sacred books are oracles delivered through Moses; but I will confine myself to those which are more especially his (λέξω δὲ τὰ ἰδιαίτερα), with the following preliminary remarks. Of the divine utterances, some are spoken by God in His

---

2.262, 2.269, 2.275, 2.278, 2.280, 2.284, 2.292; *Decal.* 18, 19, 175; *Spec.* 1.345, 3.125; *Virt.* 51, 119; *Praem.* 1, 2, 55, 123; *Contempl.* 64, 87; *QG* 1.24, 1.28; *QE* 2.16, 2.46, 2.49.

14 For these and other titles for Moses in Philo, see John Lierman, *The New Testament Moses: Christian Perceptions of Moses and Israel in the Setting of Jewish Religion*, WUNT 2/173 (Tübingen: Mohr Siebeck, 2004), 44.

15 The four cases of question and answer prophecy are based on narratives from Lev 24:10–23 (*Mos.* 2.192–212), Num 15:32–36 (*Mos.* 2.213–220), Num 9:1–14 (*Mos.* 2.222–232), and Num 27:1–11; 36:1–12 (*Mos.* 2.233–245).

16 The four episodes selected are Moses' promise to the Israelites that they would be saved at the crossing of the Sea (Exod 14:13–14; *Mos.* 2.246–257), Moses' three prophecies concerning manna (Exod 16; *Mos.* 2.258–269), Moses' summoning of the Levites to kill those responsible for the sin of the golden calf (Exod 32:25–29; *Mos.* 2.270–274), and finally Moses' prediction that the earth would open up and provide divine vindication of Moses against Korah's rebellion (Num 16:28–30; *Mos.* 2.275–287).

own Person with His prophet for interpreter, in some the revelation comes through question and answer, and others are spoken by Moses in his own person, when possessed by God and carried away out of himself (τὰ δ' ἐκ προσώπου Μωυσέως ἐπιθειάσαντος καὶ ἐξ αὐτοῦ κατασχεθέντος).

> *Mos.* 2.188; trans. LCL

The first kind of prophecy is the highest, and it involves a direct communion of minds, in which God's mind and that of the prophet are as one. Moses' mediation of divine Torah would appear to be an example, as Philo claims that this type of prophecy has an ethical orientation.[17] Philo says, however, that he is not going to discuss this kind of prophecy:

> Now, the first kind must be left out of the discussion. They are too great to be lauded by human lips (μείζω γάρ ἐστιν ἢ ὡς ὑπ' ἀνθρώπου τινὸς ἐπαινεθῆναι); scarcely indeed could heaven and the world and the whole existing universe worthily sing their praises. Besides, they are delivered through an interpreter, and interpretation and prophecy are not the same thing (ἑρμηνεία δὲ καὶ προφητεία διαφέρουσι). (*Mos.* 2.191a; trans. LCL)

In *Spec.* 1.65, Philo said that "prophets are the interpreters of God," so his usage of terminology is inconsistent. Nevertheless, his meaning here is that prophecy, in the technical sense, involves displacement of human reason by the divine spirit (ecstasy). The higher form of prophecy—hermeneutical or noetic prophecy—involves direct mind-to-mind communication, too great to be understood by humans. I would venture the claim that for Philo, *only Moses* has experienced this form of prophecy, in his receiving of the Torah and in the commands to build the tabernacle.[18] The second form of prophecy involves

---

17 Cf *Mos.* 2.189: it is this prophecy "by which He incites all men to noble conduct, and particularly the nation of His worshippers."
18 See, for example, *Mos.* 2.76: "So the shape of the model was stamped upon the mind of the prophet (ὁ μὲν οὖν τύπος τοῦ παραδείγματος ἐνεσφραγίζετο τῇ διανοίᾳ τοῦ προφήτου)." Winston, "Two Types," 54 claims that the giving of the Decalogue "must serve us as the paradigm for prophey through the divine voice." Rather, it seems that the giving of the Decalogue is not prophecy at all, but unmediated experience of God (see *Spec.* 3.7). Rather, with Levison, "Philo's Personal Experience," 205, this form of prophecy should be understood as Moses' mediation of the special laws (later, at 56, Winston acknowledges that these laws would be a part of this form of prophecy). But, it should be observed that there is a marked difference between the Decalogue and all other law in the Pentateuch: the former is given by God directly, and all of the latter is communicated through Moses' mediation.

interaction between human reason and divine prompting (μῖξιν ἔχει καὶ κοινωνίαν, *Mos.* 2.190), and the third form, which is prophecy proper (as Philo has described it in *Spec.* 1.65; 4.49), involves ecstatic possession, "in which the speaker appears under that divine possession in virtue of which he is chiefly and in the strict sense considered a prophet (ἐν ᾧ τὸ τοῦ λέγοντος ἐνθουσιῶδες ἐμφαίνεται, καθ' ὃ μάλιστα καὶ κυρίως νενόμισται προφήτης)" (*Mos.* 2.191, trans. LCL). It is these latter two forms of prophecy that Philo goes on to illustrate in his account of the life of Moses.

For Philo, it is only the last four narratives that provide instances in which Moses acted as an ecstatic prophet, or a prophet in the technical sense.[19] For example, at the Crossing of the Sea, Philo says of Moses: "the prophet, seeing the whole nation entangled in the meshes of panic, like a draught of fishes, was taken out of himself by divine possession and uttered these inspired words (οὐκέτ' ὢν ἐν ἑαυτῷ θεοφορεῖται καὶ θεσπίζει τάδε)" (*Mos.* 2.250; trans. LCL). Moses goes on to predict God's salvation of the Israelites, which highlights another feature of prophecy in the technical sense: it is principally concerned with prediction.[20] For Philo, the Crossing of the Sea represented the beginning of Moses' career as an inspired prophet.[21] In the account of manna in Exodus 16, Philo discovers three prophecies of Moses: first, that the Israelites should not leave any for the next day (*Mos.* 2.258–2.262), second, that the manna would be doubled on the sixth day (*Mos.* 2.263–267), and third, that there would be no manna on the Sabbath (*Mos.* 2.268–269). To Philo, these Mosaic announcements—not marked as prophecies in the scriptural text—are all predictions, even though their fulfillment is almost immediate.[22] The fourth narrative, the account of Korah's rebellion, also fits with the more limited definition of prophecy as prediction; indeed, Philo specifies that it was fulfilled immediately.[23] The only case that fits this pattern imprecisely is Moses' summoning of the Levites to kill their compatriots. Philo acknowledges the anomalous character of this instance, admitting that Moses' words "may be thought to

---

19 See *Mos.* 2.246 (trans. LCL): "I will proceed next to describe those delivered by the prophet himself under divine inspiration (ἑξῆς δηλώσω τὰ κατ' ἐνθουσιασμὸν τοῦ προφήτου θεσπισθέντα λόγια)."

20 This is also the case in *Spec.* 1.65; 4.49; *Her.* 260.

21 *Mos.* 2.258, trans. LCL: "It was thus that Moses began and opened his work as a prophet possessed by God's spirit (Τοῦτ' ἐστὶ τῆς κατ' ἐνθουσιασμὸν προφητείας Μωυσέως ἀρχὴ καὶ προοίμιον)."

22 Levison, "Philo's Personal Experience," 200–201, shows how Philo transforms the LXX text into prophetic predictions.

23 *Mos.* 2.275, trans. LCL: "it was fulfilled not long afterwards but at the very time when the prediction was given (τελειωθὲν οὐ μακροῖς χρόνοις ὕστερον, ἀλλ' εὐθὺς ὅτ' ἐχρησμῳδεῖτο)."

resemble exhortations rather than oracular sayings (καίτοι δόξαντα ἂν παραινέσεσιν ἐοικέναι μᾶλλον ἢ χρησμοῖς)" (*Mos.* 2.270, trans. LCL). Philo may have included this episode because Moses prefaces his summon to the Levites with the prophetic formula, "Thus says the Lord, the God of Israel" (Exod 32:27). Alternatively, Philo may have believed there was an element of supernatural prediction at work, if only because the Levites were able to slaughter their compatriots without meeting the slightest resistance (αὐτοβοεί, *Mos.* 2.274): Moses told the Levites to "mow them down" (*Mos.* 2.273), and so they did.

This third mode of prophecy—which is prophecy proper, ecstatic, and principally concerned with prediction—is the lowest grade of Moses' experience of the divine, and is that which connects him to others who can be called prophets. Nevertheless, even here his experience of prophecy is superior to other prophets. Indeed, David Winston and John Levison have demonstrated that in these four narratives Moses' own thinking and emotions are portrayed as important precursors to his reception of the prophetic spirit and are not completely overridden by the experience of inspiration. As Winston says,

> [I]t is now evident that not only is Moses' legislative prophetic activity unique, but even his predictive prophecy, a gift he otherwise shares with Noah and the Patriarchs (*Her* 260–261), is likewise unique in character, since it is not, as with the latter, a product of psychic invasion and displacement.[24]

Levison builds on Winston's claim with a detailed analysis of the portrayal of Moses in the narratives mentioned above; in each case Moses' experience of ecstasy does not override but concurs with his own judgments about the situations he encounters.[25] Winston and Levison conclude that Moses experiences "a milder form of ecstatic prophecy,"[26] one "which preserves rather than displaces his human abilities."[27] Moreover, Levison notes the contrast between Moses' experience of prophecy and Philo's description in *Spec.* 1.65, 4.49, where prophecy involves complete psychic displacement.[28] Thus, paradoxically, for Philo Moses himself is not a prophet like Moses, since Moses' own experience

---

[24] Winston, "Two Types," 54.
[25] Levison, "Two Types," 84–87. In his article, Levison demonstrates (84): "Philo portrays a unified experience which includes: (1) Moses' emotional response to a situation; (2) his experience of possession; and (3) his subsequent oracular utterance."
[26] Winston, "Two Types," 53; cf Levison, "Two Types," 86.
[27] Levison, "Two Types," 86.
[28] Levison, "Two Types," 86–87.

of prophecy is far greater than that of the prophet described in his paraphrase of the prophet-law of Deut 18:9–22.

Before leaving Philo's *Life of Moses*, it is worth noting that he actually mentions seven occurrences in which Moses prophesies the future. It is undoubtedly significant that four and seven are the main numbers utilized in his discussion of Mosaic prophecy. One can arrive at seven because Philo explicitly notes three predictions in the second of his four instances (*Mos.* 2.268), and because he appends to the four main narratives Moses' prediction of his death and burial (thus, 1+3+1+1+1=7). Philo sums up Moses' prophetic prowess at the end of his life by saying that some of his predictions were continuing to be fulfilled, even up to his days (*Mos.* 2.288). Moses is thus superior to all other prophets in having a long-range prowess. Philo is also awestruck that Moses was able to prophesy the story of his own death and burial (*Mos.* 2.291), presumably taking the view that Moses was the author of all of Deuteronomy 34.[29]

2.3 Philo and the Mosaic Prophetic Succession

Philo does not provide explicit evidence for an interpretation of Deut 18:15, 18 in terms of a Mosaic prophetic succession, but his writings do contain some hints that prophetic claims involve being classified among "disciples" or "companions" of Moses. Thus, even though the model of relating Moses to prophecy developed in Numbers 11–12 is dominant in Philo, Deuteronomy's genealogical model plays a minor role as well.

Philo uses the term προφήτης or προφῆτις ninety-six times in his extant writings; as mentioned above, just over half (forty-nine) occurrences are in reference to Moses. The remaining forty-seven occurrences are divided as follows: twenty refer to other biblical figures;[30] thirteen are a part of references to biblical texts or books;[31] four are in reference to reason or speech,[32] three are used in the discussion of the definition of prophecy;[33] three are used to refer

---

29   A view from which the rabbis demurred; see *b. B. Bathra* 14b.
30   Noah (*Her.* 259); Abraham (*Her.* 258, 266; *Virt.* 218); Abraham's guests as potential prophets (*Abr.* 113); Miriam (*Contempl.* 87); Aaron (*Det.* 39; *Migr.* 84, 169); Balaam posing as a prophet (*Mos.* 1.266); Hannah (*Somn.* 1.254); Samuel (*Ebr.* 143); David as psalmist (*Agr.* 50); Elijah (*Deus* 136, 138); Hosea (*Plant.* 138); Isaiah (*Somn.* 2.172; *Praem.* 158; *QG* 2.26); Jeremiah (*Cher.* 49).
31   Scriptural texts in general (*Contempl.* 25); Gen 20:7 (*Her.* 258); Num 12:6 (*Leg.* 3.103; *Her.* 262); Deut 13:1 (*Spec.* 1.315 [2×]); Deut 18:15 (*Spec.* 1.65 [2×], 4.49); Deut 34:10 (*Her.* 262); 1 Sam 9:9 (*Deus* 139; *Migr.* 38; *Her.* 78).
32   Reason (*Cher.* 17; *Deus* 138); Speech (*Det.* 40; *Migr.* 84).
33   *Mos.* 2.190, 191, 192.

to the good person (one who raises himself above the material world);³⁴ one refers to the translators of the LXX;³⁵ three are miscellaneous usages.³⁶ The only humans not mentioned in the scriptures to whom Philo explicitly ascribes prophetic status and activity are the translators of the LXX (*Mos.* 2.37, 2.40). This is suggestive of the widespread sensibility in Early Judaism that prophetic terminology is best reserved for individuals from or closely related to Israel's scriptural heritage. In four instances, Philo specifies that later biblical figures are to be considered in relation to or dependence upon Moses:³⁷ the Psalmist is designated "one of the disciples of Moses (τῶν Μωυσέως γνωρίμων τις)" (*Conf.* 39); later, the book of Zechariah is referred to as coming from one of the "disciples of Moses (τῶν Μωυσέως ἑταίρων τινός)" (*Conf.* 62); Prov 3:11–12 is attributed to Solomon, who is called "one of Moses' disciples (τις τῶν φοιτητῶν Μωυσέως)" (*Congr.* 177);³⁸ finally, the Psalmist is designated as "one of Moses' company (τις τῶν ἑταίρων Μωυσέως)" (*Somn.* 2.145).

Philo does not provide evidence for the tradition developed above, in which Joshua is Moses' heir in the prophetic office (Sir. 46:1), and thus the first prophet like Moses. However, in his account of Joshua's accession to leadership (*Virt.* 51–70), Philo does refer to Joshua as Moses' successor (διάδοχος: *Virt.* 56, 64, 68, 70), and, importantly, he combines this with several references to Moses' function as a model (παράδειγμα: *Virt.* 51, 70; cf. *Mos.* 1.158). He begins the account of Joshua's succession of Moses by noting that Moses "used to incite and train all his subjects to fellowship, setting before them the monument of his own life like an original design to be their beautiful model (παράδειγμα καλόν)" (*Virt.* 51, trans. LCL). Moses therefore did not practice nepotism or favoritism, but awaited God's appointment of his successor (*Virt.* 53–65). Joshua is described as the disciple and imitator of Moses (*Virt.* 66: ὁ φοιτητὴς αὐτοῦ καὶ μιμητὴς τῶν ἀξιεράστων ἠθῶν Ἰησοῦς). Philo concludes the account by claiming that Moses provides a model for all who would rule: "Thus all future rulers would find a law to guide them right by looking to Moses as their archetype and model (ἵνα τοῖς ἔπειτα γένηται κανὼν καὶ νόμος ἅπασιν ἡγεμόσι πρὸς ἀρχέτυπον παράδειγμα Μωυσῆν ἀποβλέπουσι)" (*Virt.* 70, trans. LCL). Though Philo does not claim that

---

34   *Gig.* 61; *Her.* 259; *Spec.* 4.192.
35   *Mos.* 2.40.
36   God spoke without one (*Spec.* 3.7); priest as prophet (*Spec.* 4.192); Mercury as a prophet (*Legat.* 99).
37   The first three of these are noted by John Barton, *Oracles of God: Perceptions of Ancient Prophecy in Israel after the Exile* (London: Darton, Longman & Todd, 1986), 280nn24–26.
38   In the near context, Philo describes Moses as "the prophet-word (ὁ προφήτης λόγος)" (*Congr.* 170).

Joshua was the first prophet like Moses, he uses the key term διάδοχος in close connection with the concept of imitation of Moses as a supreme example.

From this overview one can draw the following conclusions. First, Philo displays reticence to apply prophet-terminology to non-scriptural figures; thus, he provides indirect evidence for the scripturalization of the Mosaic prophetic succession. In a few instances, he does portray the authors of scripture as being members of a broader class that could be known as "the company of Moses," though for him membership in this class is not bound up with genealogical succession. For Philo, all prophets are Moses' disciples; not all of Moses' disciples, however, are prophets.

Does Philo accept contemporary prophets? Though Philo does not deny the possibility of prophecy, he does not attribute prophetic status to any of his contemporaries, including himself.[39] John Levison has argued that Philo provides autobiographical evidence for the persistence of prophecy based on his descriptions of experiencing some form of divine inspiration (*Migr.* 34–35; *Cher.* 27–29; *Somn.* 2.252). There is certainly an analogy between the experiences Philo discusses and his understanding of prophecy, but Philo does not claim to be a prophet or draw significantly upon any of his standard prophetic terminology in these passages.[40] Moreover, Philo displays a marked awareness of requiring a significant justification to deploy the title prophet, as even a luminary like Abraham can be said to be a prophet in part because of the scriptural precedent (cf Gen 20:7): "Yet it is not merely this experience which proves him a prophet, but we have also the actual word written and recorded in the holy Scriptures (ἀλλὰ καὶ γράμμα ῥητὸν ἐστηλιτευμένον ἐν ἱεραῖς βίβλοις)" (*Her.* 258, trans. LCL). Philo thus indicates that the explicit use of prophetic terminology is an important index for him in relation to the establishing of a prophetic claim, and he does not use this terminology for his own ecstatic experiences. Furthermore, the fact that "prophecy" in the technical sense is a fairly circumscribed activity for Philo, principally having to do with prediction of the future, casts further doubt on Levison's case.

Most astonishingly, Levison claims that Philo considers himself to be not just a prophet, but a prophet like Moses, who experiences both hermeneuti-

---

39 He does use the significant verb ἐνθουσιάζω in relation to the Essenes, which may suggest prophetic experience (*Contempl.* 12).

40 In addition to προφήτης and cognates, one might note that key terms such as θεσπίζω, ἐνθουσιάω, θεοφόρεω, κατοκωχή, ἔκστασις are regularly used by Philo in connection with prophecy, but do not occur in autobiographical passages. Unable to rely on close terminological parallels, Levison, "Philo's Personal Experience," 199, draws on concepts such as "suddenness" and an experience of light—general observations that do not sustain the view that Philo makes a prophetic claim.

cal (noetic) and ecstatic inspiration: "Philo's claim to both forms of inspiration is nothing short of remarkable, for with such claims he puts himself on a par with Moses, the prophet *par excellence*."[41] In view of all that has been said about Philo's view of Moses' role as supreme and unsurpassed prophet, this interpretation surely misses the mark. As much as Philo's "inspired" experience as an interpreter of Scripture might be analogous to prophecy, it does not constitute an actual claim by him to be a prophet, and certainly he does not place himself on the level of Moses, who is "the prophetic logos" himself.[42]

3   Conclusion

Philo's strikingly independent reflections on prophecy and Mosaic prophecy almost entirely emphasize the vertical axis—God placing God's word in the mouth of the prophet—rather than the horizontal axis ("like Moses" as genealogical or historical succession). Moreover, for Philo, Moses is the supreme prophet, the prophetic Logos itself. Another first-century Jewish text in which the vertical—and not the horizontal—understanding of assimilation to Moses is emphasized is the gospel of John. Like Philo, the author of the Fourth Gospel incorporates his understanding of Deut 18:15, 18 into a Logos-theology. Unlike Philo, the author also reflects upon and interacts with a contemporary eschatological interpretation of the concept of the prophet like Moses. To John's gospel we now turn.

---

41 Levison, "Philo's Personal Experience," 207.
42 See Hindy Najman, *Seconding Sinai: The Development of Mosaic Discourse in Second Temple Judaism*, JSJSupS 77 (Leiden: Brill, 2003), 106, "Philo's own interpretive activity can be regarded as copying the interpretive activity of Moses himself. Similarly, Philo describes his interpretations as—at least occasionally—inspired, using terms similar to those he employs to characterize the inspiration of Moses. But Philo never ascribes to himself the highest level of inspiration, attained by Moses: total displacement of reason by the divine spirit." This is correct in terms of the Philo-Moses comparison, but not in terms of Najman's description of the highest level of inspiration.

CHAPTER 12

Like and unlike Moses: The Interpretation of Deut 18:15–18 in the Gospel according to John

1 Introduction

The focus on Moses as supreme revelatory agent that we have seen in 4Q377 and in the writings of Philo is also an important feature of the gospel according to John. Like Philo, the author of John's gospel has a Logos-theology that focuses on the vertical axis of divine-human communication; the horizontal axis of historical and genealogical relationships is only of subsidiary interest to him.[1] For John's gospel, authorizing Jesus as the promised prophet like Moses does not mean, as in Luke-Acts, situating Jesus as the culmination of a historical succession of prophets, and authorizing the apostles as Moses' inspired and authorized interpreters. Rather, the author of the Fourth Gospel works with a charismatic rather than genealogical conception of prophecy, and his authorization of Jesus and the disciples (not "apostles," in John)[2] has to do with their charismatic reception of divine revelation. There are a few places in John where the horizontal plane of genealogical succession to Moses re-emerges, as we will see below, but by far the main imagery John uses in understanding Jesus' identity as the promised Mosaic prophet has to do with the vertical axis of his identity as the Revealer.[3]

There are two features of John's gospel that suggest the fruitfulness of an investigation into the interpretation of Deut 18:15–22 by the author. First, more

---

[1] Paula Fredriksen, *From Jesus to Christ: The Origins of the New Testament Images of Christ*, 2nd ed. (New Haven: Yale University Press, 2000), 200, captures the dynamic that my discussion will explore with respect to the concept of the prophet like Moses: "through his Christology, John rotates the axis of Christian tradition ninety degrees, away from the historical, horizontal poles of Past/Future to the spiritualizing, vertical poles of Below/Above."

[2] See Raymond Brown, *The Community of the Beloved Disciple: The Life, Loves, and Hates of an Individual Church in New Testament Times* (New York: Paulist, 1979), on the ecclesiology of John and how it compares to the apostolic/Petrine tradition.

[3] See, most famously, Rudolf Bultmann, *Theology of the New Testament*, trans. K. Grobel, 2 vols. (New York: Scribner's Sons, 1951–1955), 2:49–69, and the famous saying (undoubtedly one-sided, but one that captures the essential Christological thrust of John) at 2:66 (emphasis original): "Thus it turns out in the end that Jesus as the Revealer of God *reveals nothing but that he is the Revealer.*"

than the synoptic gospels, John demonstrates familiarity with a contemporary eschatological interpretation of Deut 18:15, in which a figure known as "the Prophet" is expected. Second, the author is intensely interested in the figure of Moses as revelatory agent. Indeed, as Bultmann influentially argued, revelation is a major theme in John's theology; a corollary of this, not emphasized by Bultmann,[4] is that Moses plays a major role in the gospel. Moses is the scriptural character named more often than any other in this gospel,[5] and is consistently appealed to in terms of his identity as agent of revelation. "Moses" is thus virtually synonymous with that which is normative and binding.[6]

In this chapter, I will focus on the use, influence, and interaction with Deut 18:15, 18 by the writer of the fourth gospel towards the close of the first century. As I will show, the author's perspective on the interpretation of Deut 18:15, 18 and the Moses-Jesus relationship was highly nuanced. Jesus is like Moses in that he takes on the functions and embodies the role of "the Prophet," but he is unlike Moses in that, according to the author, he is the very Logos, the mediating principle between God and creation. Moses is revealer and prophet, but Jesus—for this gospel—is both the revealer and that which is revealed. In terms

---

4   John Ashton, *Understanding the Fourth Gospel* (2nd ed.; Oxford: Oxford University, 2007), 184, remarks:
   In his great commentary, Bultmann allows the Old Testament to be jostled and frequently elbowed out by huge numbers of other ancient texts. This fits in with his own perspective: by minimizing the influence of the Old Testament, he can highlight the independence and the novelty of the revelation of Jesus. But it also involves a serious misreading of the Gospel, which remains faithful to its source in its insistence that Jesus fulfils in every respect the eschatological expectations of the Jews. For all the mysteriousness and otherness of his person, he is set firmly in the context of a living tradition.
5   For the breadth and consistency of his role in the gospel, Moses is the scriptural character that outstrips all others in importance. He is mentioned 12× (1:17; 45; 3:14; 5:45 [2×]; 6:32; 7:19; 7:22–23 [3×]; 9:28 [2×]). (A thirteenth is found in the *pericope adulterae* [8:5]). Abraham is mentioned 9×, but all occur in John 8:33–58. For a narratological approach to Moses' role in the gospel, see Stan Harstine, *Moses as a Character in the Fourth Gospel: A Study of Ancient Reading Techniques*, JSNTSup 229 (Sheffield: Sheffield Academic, 2002).
6   Because Moses represents the locus of revelatory authority, any normative practice, such as circumcision, can be ascribed to him, even though the author or redactor of John hastens to clarify that it actually comes from the patriarchs (John 7:22–23). For the distinction between the author and the redactor, see Rudolf Bultmann, *The Gospel of John: A Commentary*, trans. G.R. Beasley-Murray, R.W.N. Hoare and J.K. Riches (Philadelphia: Westminster, 1971), 10–11 (who influentially posited a major rearrangement of material by the final editor); Raymond Brown, *The Gospel According to John: Introduction, Translation, and Notes*, 2 vols. AB 29–29A (New York: Doubleday, 1966–1970), 1:xxxiv–xxxix; Andrew Lincoln, *The Gospel According to Saint John*, BNTC 4 (London: Continuum, 2005), 50–59. Bultmann's theory of extensive rearrangement is no longer widely held, though there seems to be places in the gospel where relocations of material have occurred, as we will see below.

of Deut 18:18 ("I will put my word in his mouth"), Jesus is both the prophet who speaks and the "word" or revelation delivered to humanity.[7]

2 Previous Assessments of the Importance of the Prophet like Moses in John

It is fair to say that the view that I will develop in this chapter—that the conception of Jesus as prophet like Moses and Logos are closely related for the author of the gospel—has not been widely held. In introductions to major commentaries on the gospel, Jesus' identification as the prophet like Moses is hardly emphasized, if it is even mentioned.[8] Craig Keener devotes forty pages to Christology,[9] but just one paragraph is focused on Mosaic themes. Keener acknowledges the gospel's development of the "new Moses expectation of early Judaism," but concludes:

---

7 See the conclusion of Adele Reinhartz, "Jesus as Prophet: Predictive Prolepses in the Fourth Gospel," *JSNT* 36 (1989): 3–16, at 10: "The Johannine Jesus is not only the prophet, but the prophesied, not only the mouthpiece for the divine word but the content of the message itself." Reinhartz's article illustrates this claim primarily with respect to Jesus' prophetic predictions in John; I will consider how it informs John's understanding of the Moses-Jesus relationship.

8 Lincoln's section on christology (*John*, 59–70), makes no mention of the prophet like Moses theme, though interestingly Lincoln does touch on it briefly in the next section of his introduction, titled "Relation to Judaism," 70–81 (see 75–76). Rudolf Schnackenburg, *The Gospel according to St. John*, trans. Kevin Smyth, 3 vols. (New York: Seabury, 1980 [Vol 1 and 2]; New York: Crossroad, 1982 [Vol 3]), 1:154–156, also does not mention Jesus' prophetic status in his brief treatment of christology. In his five-page section on John's Christology, Barrett says only this on the prophet like Moses (*The Gospel According to St. John: An Introduction with Commentary and Notes on the Greek Text*, 2nd ed. [Philadelphia: Westminster, 1978], 74):

> Another Christological type that has been found in John is that of the prophet-king, which Judaism found in Moses. That this figure plays some part especially in the background of John 6 is probably true; that it is the major constituent in John's Christology is a proposition much harder to prove.

J. Ramsey Michaels, *The Gospel of John*, NICNT (Grand Rapids: Eerdmans, 2010), 39–42, has a section on "theological contribution," which makes no mention of Jesus' potential status as prophet like Moses. See also the summary of the state of scholarship on John's christology in Raymond Brown, *An Introduction to the Gospel of John*, ed. F.J. Moloney, ABRL (Doubleday: New York, 2003), 249–265. Brown mentions the theme of the prophet like Moses in passing, as one proposed "key" motif (252), but elaborates further on the title "Son of Man" (252–259) and Wisdom motifs (259–265).

9 Craig Keener, *The Gospel of John: A Commentary*, 2 vols. (Peabody, Mass.: Hendrickson, 2003), 1:280–320.

> [W]hile Jesus is to some degree a new Moses in John, this Christology is as inadequate as 'the prophet' Christology …. Jesus is much more one greater than Moses, the divine glory which Moses witnessed; it is his disciples, rather than Jesus himself, who most directly parallel Moses (1:14; 14:8; 15:15).[10]

For Keener, a 'prophet' Christology is thought to be deficient, and unworthy of the gospel's view of Jesus. This is curious: Philo of Alexandria has an exalted view of Moses, and has no difficulty speaking of him in the categories of prophet, Logos, and even in terms of the divine being. It may be that the perceived tension between these views of Jesus is more of a problem for modern scholars than it was for the author of the gospel of John.

A second view in Johannine scholarship is that the identification of Jesus as the prophet like Moses was important either as a part of the gospel's pre-history in the life of the Johannine community,[11] or in early stages of the gospel's formation (especially, the putative "Book of Signs"), but that in later versions of the gospel it was eclipsed by the high christology that identified Jesus with the very being of God.[12] Like the preceding view, this reflects the assumption that a

---

10   Keener, *John*, 1:291; see also 1:277–278. Keener is rather innovative in his commentary in repeatedly stressing that the disciples (and not Jesus) parallel Moses. There is some truth to this (both the disciples and Moses "see" the "glory"; cf Exod 33–34; John 1:14; 2:11), but it does not do justice to the main thrust of the gospel's reflection on Moses, which is as a revelatory authority who is in some way to be compared to Christ.

11   Brown, *Community of the Beloved Disciple*, 26–58, posits a development from "low" to "high" christology in community's development prior to the gospel's composition. John Ashton, *The Gospel of John and Christian Origins* (Minneapolis: Fortress, 2014), 136, says the identification of Jesus as the prophet like Moses "was already present hidden deep in the origins of Johannine Christianity."

12   So, e.g., Urban von Wahlde, *The Earliest Version of John's Gospel: Recovering the Gospel of Signs* (Wilmington, Del.: Michael Glazier, 1989), 161–171; see especially 166, on the title "the Prophet": "This concentration on the identification of Jesus with the prophet is all the more striking in the light of the fact that such identification occurs only in John (and only in the signs material!)." Brown, *Introduction*, 71–72, discusses the theory of Georg Richter, "Präsentische und futurische Eschatologie im 4. Evangelium," in *Gegenwart und kommendes Reich: Schulergabe Anton Vögtle zum 65. Geburtstag*, ed. P. Fiedler and D. Zeller (Stuttgart: KBW, 1975), 117–151, who argues that "Mosaic-prophet Christians" were responsible for the *Grundschrift* of the gospel; see also A.J. Mattill, "Johannine Communities Behind the Fourth Gospel: Georg Richter's Analysis," *TS* 38 (1976): 294–315. On the low christology of a "Books of Signs," see Robert Fortna, *The Gospel of Signs: A Reconstruction of the Narrative Source Underlying the Fourth Gospel*, SNTSMS 11 (Cambridge: Cambridge University, 1970), 228–234; and see idem, *The Fourth Gospel and its Predecessor: From Narrative Source to Present Gospel* (Philadelphia: Fortress, 1988), 225–234, on the relationship between the christology of the source and that of the author. With respect to the prophet

prophet-christology is a low christology, and therefore properly belongs in the earlier stages of the gospel tradition. As we saw earlier, this historical schematization has been applied to Luke-Acts as well.[13] With respect to John, if a "Book of Signs" existed—I confess to some skepticism[14]—the author's creativity has made recovery of such a source a highly speculative endeavor, and it is unlikely that the ideological profile of this source can be delineated with the specificity claimed by this approach's leading proponents. More importantly, I believe that there is clear evidence that the question of Jesus' relationship to Moses was pressing at the time of the gospel's composition, so that appeals to a source are unnecessary in the context of Jesus' potential identification as the prophet like Moses.

In contrast to the minimalist approaches charted above, a number of scholars have argued that Deut 18:15–18 was of constitutive and fundamental important for the author. In 1963, T.F. Glasson published a short monograph, *Moses in the Fourth Gospel*, in which he argues that representing Jesus as the fulfillment of Deut 18:15 is an "important" part of the author's christology, and briefly

---

like Moses, Fortna believes there has been a "typological deepening and transcending of the Moses image" (*Fourth Gospel*, 232; cf 230) in the movement from the source to the gospel. Marie-Émile Boismard, *Moses or Jesus: An Essay in Johannine Christology*, trans. B.T. Viviano, BETL 84-A (Leuven: Leuven University, 1993), 127–133, believes that the earliest document behind the gospel (which he calls Document C) presented Jesus as "a new Moses, implicitly referring to the text of Deut 18:18" (127). See the brief summary in Tom Thatcher, "Remembering Jesus: John's Negative Christology," in *The Messiah in the Old and New Testaments*, ed. S. Porter, MNTS (Grand Rapids: Eerdmans, 2007), 165–189 (at 168): "Fortna, along with other source critics, thus solves the christological puzzle of the Fourth Gospel by arguing that the conflicting statements about Jesus' identity must originate in two different places."

13 See François Bovon, *Luke the Theologian: Fifty-Five Years of Research (1950–2005)*, 2nd rev. ed., (Waco: Baylor University Press, 2006), 203: "I have no trouble believing that Luke underscores Jesus' prophetic function, but how can one explain … that this interest emerges at a time when the Christology of Christ the prophet was losing momentum?" It is noteworthy that scholars of Luke-Acts and John have independently developed complex theories of diachronic development of these texts (the early speeches in Acts; the "Book of Signs" in John) based on a historical schematization (the so-called "development" of Christology) that is a scholarly construct. In fact, there is no evidence that a prophet-Christology was "losing momentum" at the end of the first century; Luke-Acts and John both develop Jesus' prophetic profile. See the sharp critique of this scholarly tradition by Fredriksen, *From Jesus to Christ*, 19, who speaks of the "false impression" that the gospels' "images of Jesus evolved in some sort of ordered development."

14 My skepticism is rooted in the nature of Jesus' signs in John. John provides a limited set of signs which point to Jesus' creative powers, and thus are closely allied to the theological conception established by the prologue.

develops a number of suggestive parallels to Moses-traditions in John.[15] A more influential study, however, was Wayne Meeks' *The Prophet-King*. Meeks' study took its starting point in the problem posed by John 6:14–15:

> (14) When the people saw the sign that he had done, they began to say, "This is indeed the prophet who is to come into the world." (15) When Jesus realized that they were about to come and take him by force to make him king, he withdrew again to the mountain by himself.

Meeks asks: "Why is it so self-evident that 'the prophet' is to be made 'king'?"[16] To answer this question, Meeks articulated his "working hypothesis" as follows: "Certain traditions about Moses provided for the Fourth Gospel not only the figure of the eschatological prophet, but the figure who combines in one person both royal and prophetic honor and functions."[17] Meeks concludes that the fourth gospel was written in a Jewish context in which veneration of Moses was practiced, and that this provided the background for the author's claims about Jesus.[18] Meeks' study remains programmatic in certain respects and will often be referred to in what follows; nevertheless I chart a different course, as I argue that the author's interest in Moses and prophecy is a more a feature of his Logos-theology than of his view of Jesus as royal Messiah.

Maximalist positions regarding the dependence of John's thought on Deut 18:15–22 are found in the work of Marie-Émile Boismard and Paul N. Anderson. Boismard says that Deut 18:18–19 "holds an essential place in the gospel of John

---

15   T.F. Glasson, *Moses in the Fourth Gospel*, SBT (Naperville, Ill.: Alec R. Allenson, 1963), 29–30. Wayne A. Meeks, *The Prophet-King: Moses Traditions and the Johannine Christology*, NovTSup 14 (Leiden: Brill, 1967), 287n3, comments that Glasson's work provides "an example of the extraordinary number of allusions to Moses that an imaginative reader can discover in John," and, more critically (24n4), "Glasson's monograph has many imaginative suggestions, to which I am indebted. On the whole, however, his interest is more homiletical than historical, and he exercises little exegetical control over the allusions which occur to him."

16   Meeks, *Prophet-King*, 1.

17   Meeks, *Prophet-King*, 29.

18   Meeks, *Prophet-King*, 286–319. Meeks' hypothesis is possible but not strictly necessary, since "Moses" had enough normative weight generally in Second Temple Judaism that one need not seek the context of a particular Moses-exalting group to explain the gospel's interest. A similar approach to Meeks' is taken by John Lierman, "The Mosaic Pattern of John's Christology," in *Challenging Perspectives on the Gospel of John*, ed. J. Lierman, WUNT 2/219 (Tübingen: Mohr Siebeck, 2006), 210–234, who concludes (233–234): "When John's christological portrait is analyzed as a whole, no one besides Moses even comes close as a precedent for what John has to say about Jesus, and it turns out that Moses comes a lot closer than many would imagine."

since it governs most of its Christology."¹⁹ He sums up its influence with the following points: Jesus is God's emissary; the purpose of his mission is to transmit the words of God; he offers signs as authenticating proofs of his divine mission; the reaction to Jesus' words is a matter of life and death.²⁰ For his part, Anderson has gone beyond any other in unearthing references and allusions to Deut 18:15–22 across the gospel. He notes that the key terms of this passage play "significant thematic roles" in John,²¹ and proposes some twenty-four parallels between Deut 18:15–22 and John's gospel, divided under eight themes.²² On the basis of these parallels, Anderson concludes that Deut 18:15–22 provides a "foundational typological schema" for John's gospel.²³ This passage has therefore achieved an extraordinary prominence in Anderson's work.²⁴

---

19 Boismard, *Moses or Jesus*, 1.
20 Boismard, *Moses or Jesus*, 59–66.
21 Paul N. Anderson, "The Having-Sent-Me Father: Aspects of Agency, Encounter, and Irony in the Johannine Father-Son Relationship," *Semeia* 85 (1999): 33–57; here 37. He refers to προφήτης, ἀδελφός, ἀνάστασις, ἀκούω, ῥῆμα, λαλέω, ἐντέλλομαι, ὄνομα, and γινώσκω.
22 Anderson, "Having-Sent-Me," 38–40. The themes that Anderson distills are the following: 1) Deut 18:15a, 18a—God will raise up a prophet like Moses; Jesus is written about by Moses (John 1:45; 5:45–47) and identified as being a prophet like him (John 4:19; 6:14–15; 7:40; 9:17); 2) Deut 18:15:15b—Listen to him; Jesus passes on what he has heard from Father (e.g., John 5:19, 30; 15:15); *hearing* the Son is stressed (John 3:36; 5:24; 6:45; 8:51); 3) Deut 18:18b—God will put his words in the prophet's mouth; cf John 3:11, 34; 6:63, 68; 7:16–18, 28; 8:28, 38, 55; 12:44–50; 14:24, 31; 4) Deut 18:18c—he speaks what God *commands*; Jesus' carries out the Father's command (John 10:18; 12:49–50; 14:31; 15:10) and issues a new command (John 13:34; 14:15, 21; 15:10–17); 5) Deut 18:19—those who do not listen will be held accountable; Those not receiving the Son have been judged (John 3:16–18; 12:47); the words of the Son produced judgment (John 12:47); 6) Deut 18:20—prophets who speak falsely shall die; Jesus is accused of deceiving the crowd (John 7:12, 47), and the Jewish leaders seek to kill him (John 5:16, 18; 7:1; etc.); 7) Deut 18:22a—the fulfillment criterion; Jesus' words about his own departure and glorification are fulfilled (John 2:19–22; 3:14; 4:50–53; etc.); Jesus employs the criterion, declaring what will happen so they know he is from God (John 13:18–19; 14:28–29; 16:2–4; 18:8–9, 31–32); 8) Deut 18:22b—do not fear the presumptuous prophet; ironically, those tending to be "feared" are the Jewish leaders (John 7:13; 9:22; 12:42) rather than God or the Prophet like Moses.
23 Anderson, "Having-Sent-Me," 40.
24 His study of John's christology includes some hyperbolic claims, e.g., see his *The Christology of the Fourth Gospel: Its Unity and Disunity in the Light of John 6*, WUNT 2/78 (Tübingen: Mohr Siebeck, 1996), 175: "It would not be an exaggeration to say that much of John's theology, christology, pneumatology, and ecclesiology is based on an understanding of Deuteronomy 18:18, which promises that God will continue his redemptive dialogue with humanity by means of the prophet(s) like Moses who speak all that God commands"; see also *Christology*, 192 (emphasis original): "The underlying christology of John 6 (and most of the Gospel) is the Prophet-like-Moses typology based on Deuteronomy 18:15–22, and this typology accounts for much of John's christological unity and disunity, *in and of itself*."

If some scholarship has devalued the importance of Moses and Deut 18:15–22 in relation to John's gospel, Anderson's corrective swings the pendulum too far in the other direction. Methodologically, the problem with Anderson's claims is that key terms in Deut 18:15, 18 (προφήτης, ἀκούω, ῥῆμα, λαλέω, ἐντέλλομαι) are fairly common, and usage of these words cannot in itself satisfy the requirement of an allusion, so the omnipresence of this particular passage as the intertextual key that unlocks John's gospel cannot be affirmed. More importantly, on an interpretive level, Anderson's overstatement of the case fails to see the way the gospel writer's approach to the Moses-Jesus is highly nuanced. Against the minimalist traditions cited above, the question of Jesus' relationship to Moses was a pressing concern for the author of the Fourth Gospel. Against the maximalist tradition, there are important respects in which Jesus remains *unlike* Moses for the author. In fact, as we will see, the author uses a series of scriptural images to carefully integrate the Moses-Jesus parallel into his Logos theology. The approach that I will develop below is most indebted to the work of J. Louis Martyn, who says with respect to the identification of Jesus as the prophet like Moses: "John's stand on this question is neither a simple affirmation of the typology nor a simple denial of it."[25] I now turn to a brief summary of Martyn's thesis, and indicate the ways in which his discussion of the Moses-Jesus relationship remains programmatic for contemporary research.

3 Martyn and the Moses-Jesus Relationship

J. Louis Martyn's monograph *History and Theology in the Fourth Gospel* was one of the most influential contributions to Johannine studies in the twentieth century. Martyn famously read John as a two-level drama: on one level the gospel claims to be about Jesus and the events of his day; on the second level, the gospel narrates the dramatic confrontation and split between the Johannine community and the synagogue in the late first century. Aspects of Martyn's thesis have come under attack, but his work remains programmatic for modern study of John in several ways. His emphasis on the sociological character

---

Anderson makes such claims because the key terminology from Deut 18:15–22 is ubiquitous in John, also later with respect to the community (e.g., 17:8) and the Paraclete (e.g., 16:13). But his identification of which passages from John are dependent on Deut 18:15–22 lacks sufficient methodological control.

25 J. Louis Martyn, *History and Theology in the Fourth Gospel*, 3rd ed., NTL (Louisville: Westminster John Knox, 2003), 101–143, here 125 (the chapters are entitled, "From the Expectation of the Prophet-Messiah like Moses …" and "… To the Presence of the Son of Man").

of John's gospel has led to scholarly inquiry into the nature and history of the so-called Johannine community. It has also caused theories of a non-Jewish background for the gospel, influentially advanced by figures such as Bultmann, to be completely displaced: it is recognized today that the gospel is a Jewish text and is best understood in the context of the diverse panoply of late Second Temple Judaism.[26]

The point of entry into Martyn's theory is his exegesis of John 9:28, which is part of a dispute between Jewish leaders (identified as Pharisees, 9:13, 15, 16, 40; and with the more general appellation "the Jews," 9:18, 22) and a blind man healed by Jesus. In this debate, the Jewish leaders claim that being a disciple of Moses is incompatible with being one of Jesus. They are provoked to this statement by the healed man, who, wearying of their repeated requests regarding how his sight was restored, grows confrontational: "I have told you already, and you would not listen (οὐκ ἠκούσατε). Why do you want to hear it again? Do you also want to become his disciples?" (John 9:27). In response the leaders assert the incompatibility of being a disciple of both Moses and Jesus: "Then they reviled him, saying, 'You are a disciple of that one, but we are disciples of Moses. We know that God has spoken (λελάληκεν) to Moses, but as for this man, we do not know where he comes from'" (John 9:28–29). The dissociative rhetoric is clear in the Pharisees' charge that the formerly blind man is a disciple of "that one" (ἐκείνου). On 9:28, Martyn comments:

> This statement is scarcely conceivable in Jesus' lifetime, since it recognizes discipleship to Jesus not only as antithetical, but also as somehow comparable, to discipleship to Moses. It is, on the other hand, easily understood under circumstances in which the synagogue has begun to view the Christian movement as an essential and more or less clearly distinguishable rival.[27]

Martyn understood the unique Johannine term "from the synagogue" (ἀποσυνάγωγος, 9:22; cf 12:42; 16:2) to refer to a specific historical excommunication from the synagogue in the late first century CE, and connected it to the rabbinic *Birkat ha-Minim*. This speculative reconstruction has rightly been criticized.[28]

---

26 For the preceding, see the assessment of Martyn's contribution by D. Moody Smith, "The Contribution of J. Louis Martyn to the Understanding of the Gospel of John," in Martyn, *History and Theology*, 1–23.
27 Martyn, *History and Theology*, 47.
28 For reviews of the literature on this question, see Adele Reinhartz, *Befriending the Beloved Disciple: A Jewish Reading of the Gospel of John* (New York: Continuum, 2005), 37–53;

Nevertheless, Martyn's contribution has been to point out that the antithetical construction of the Jesus-Moses relationship in 9:28 reflects a theological conflict that stems not from the life of the historical Jesus, but from the circumstances of the gospel's composition.[29] This relationship had evidently become a neuralgic point in discussions between synagogue members who believed that Jesus was the Messiah and those who did not. It was therefore important, even pressing, for the author to delineate precisely the appropriate mode of relating Jesus to Moses. In my view, the author adopts a quite nuanced view of the way Jesus both is and is not the prophet like Moses, and develops these reflections as an elaboration or clarification of the implications of the gospel's Logos theology. The author's conviction is that discipleship to Moses and to Jesus is not incompatible, but not strictly speaking commensurate.

4   The Interpretation of Deut 18:15–18 in John's Gospel

4.1   *References to "The Prophet" in John's Gospel*

Like the synoptic gospels, the gospel of John reports the opinions of various constituencies about Jesus (the Jewish leaders, the crowd, the disciples) and develops its own viewpoint in implicit dialogue—both polemical and conciliatory—with these diverse constructions of Jesus' identity. Unlike the synoptics, however, John's gospel makes a clear distinction between regular prophets and an eschatological figure known as "the Prophet," to whom he refers on at least four (John 1:21, 25; 6:14; 7:40) and possibly five occasions (7:52).[30] In other gospels, we find the suggestion that Jesus is *a* prophet, but

---

Jonathan Bernier, *Aposynagōgos and the Historical Jesus in John: Rethinking the Historicity of the Johannine Expulsion Passages*, BINS 122 (Leiden: Brill, 2013), 27–76.

29   See Smith, "The Contribution," 6; Ashton, *Understanding*, 6, who says that with Martyn "a new note is sounded." Later (*Understanding*, 32–33), Ashton points out: "In putting so much stress on the relationship between the Birkath ha-Minim and the expulsion of the Jesus group from the synagogue, Martyn lays himself open to the complete rejection of his theory.... This is unfortunate, because as I observed fifteen years ago his reading of John 9 is not built upon his interpretation of the Eighteen Benedictions: 'at most it is buttressed by it.'"

30   The early papyri P[66] and P[75vid] read ὁ προφήτης in 7:52. Bruce Metzger, *A Textual Commentary on the Greek New Testament* (United Bible Societies, 1971), 219, points out that that this reading was already conjecturally proposed in the late eighteenth century. It is impossible to know whether it is original or not—it could easily represent a scribal correction or assimilation to 7:40 (so Barnabas Lindars, *The Gospel of John*, NCB [London: Marshall, Morgan, and Scott, 1972], 305; Barrett, *John*, 333)—but it is an indisputably early reading, and possibly original. Brown, *John*, 1:325 accepts the reading of the early papyri "for the

there is no use of the expression "the Prophet."[31] Most scholars agree that this expression reflects an eschatological interpretation of Deut 18:15, so that by "the Prophet," the coming Mosaic prophet is meant.[32]

Does the author intend the readers to apply the title to Jesus? The fact that references to Jesus as "the Prophet" occur in the mouth of sympathizers (6:14, 7:40) or opponents (7:52) means that its suitability for Jesus cannot simply be assumed.[33]

The first two references occur in the context of an interview of John the Baptist by representatives of the priestly authorities regarding his status as eschatological figure. John repudiates three titles: the Messiah, Elijah,[34] and the Prophet. Brown and others have argued that part of the context for John's gospel—at some stage of its composition—involved polemical interaction with disciples of John the Baptist, who were claiming messianic status for him.[35] The emphatic character of John's denial of messianic titles ("he confessed and did not deny, but confessed [καὶ ὡμολόγησεν καὶ οὐκ ἠρνήσατο, καὶ ὡμολόγησεν]," 1:20) may reflect this agenda, as does the author's insistence on John's role as witness when he is introduced in the gospel (cf 1:8). This may

---

Johannine concept of *the* Prophet-like-Moses could easily have been misunderstood in the process of copying." Schnackenburg, *John*, 2:161 also accepts the reading, claiming it solves the difficulty of the verse (because regular prophets did in fact come from Galilee). This, however, could also be an argument against its originality.

31 For Jesus as "a prophet," see, e.g., Matt 11:9; 13:57; 16:14; 21:11; Mark 8:28; Luke 7:16, 39; 9:8, 19; 24:19; von Wahlde, *Earliest Version*, 166n10. The definite article is used in Matt 21:11, but this exceptional usage is because Jesus is specified as "the prophet, the one from Nazareth in Galilee (ὁ προφήτης Ἰησοῦς ὁ ἀπὸ Ναζαρὲθ τῆς Γαλιλαίας)"; it does not constitute a true parallel to the Johannine usage.

32 Ashton, *Understanding*, 159, says this identification is "universally agreed"; though Bultmann, *John*, 89–90, expresses some reservation (in keeping with his tendency to downplay the influence of the OT on John), and suggests that the gnostic "Revealer" is possibly what is meant. See also Michaels, *John*, 98–99.

33 Lierman, "Mosaic Pattern," 211, too quickly concludes that such references "depict Jesus as the Prophet like Moses" without distinguishing between the author's perspective and that of characters within the narrative.

34 John's repudiation of the title Elijah is a crux. This title is ascribed to him in the Synoptic tradition (Mark 9:13//Matt 17:12–13), though Luke downplays it, eliminating the interchange between Jesus and his disciples found in Mark (cf Luke 9:36–37). This denial may thus involve polemical interaction with the synoptic tradition about John, and not be related to Jesus' potential status as Elijah.

35 See Brown, *John*, 1:lxvii–lxx. Brown, *John*, 1:46 notes that such a context does not mean that the gospel's traditions about the Baptist are historically worthless—there is nothing inherently implausible in a delegation from Jerusalem inquiring of John who he was claiming to be—but it does imply that the author's theological agenda is to the fore here.

imply that John's denial of the title "the Prophet" is due to the fact that the author wishes to reserve it for Jesus.

A positive confirmation of this implication might be deduced from the next section of the chapter (1:35–51), as disciples of John become followers of Jesus (cf 1:37). In particular, Philip tells Nathanael: "we have found him about whom Moses in the law and also the prophets wrote (ὃν ἔγραψεν Μωϋσῆς ἐν τῷ νόμῳ καὶ οἱ προφῆται εὑρήκαμεν), Jesus son of Joseph from Nazareth" (John 1:45).[36] Boismard and others have argued that this is a specific reference to Deut 18:15, 18.[37] First, in this scene the prophetic profile of Jesus is developed as one with superhuman knowledge who was able to see Nathanael under the fig tree (1:48). Second, Nathanael's objection to Jesus' status as eschatological figure—that Jesus comes from Nazareth in Galilee—anticipates the later rejection of Jesus' status as "the Prophet" by the Jewish leaders, who say that "the Prophet" does not come from Galilee (7:52). Third, Jesus has been designated the Messiah in the near context, and the titles "Messiah" and "Prophet" or "King" and "Prophet" are closely linked elsewhere in the gospel (6:14–15; 7:40–41). Finally, an indirect argument could be made from the abundance of Messianic titles in this pericope. Jesus is referred to as Messiah (1:41), Son of God (1:49), King of Israel (1:49), and Son of Man (1:51). The force of the passage is that Jesus is the fulfillment of traditional eschatological expectations. In this light, it seems possible to understand the phrase "the one about whom Moses wrote in the law" in 1:45 as a claim that Jesus is also the fulfillment of Deut 18:15.[38]

The next reference to "the Prophet" occurs in John 6:14–15, after the feeding of the five thousand:

---

36   It is striking that the phrase "and the prophets" is added somewhat obtrusively and ungrammatically to Philip's claim in 1:45. Stretching the bounds of what can be confidently affirmed, some have argued that these three words were added to refer to Mal 4:5—the prophecy of Elijah's return. Taking the one about whom the prophets wrote as Elijah is "tempting," says Brown (*John*, 1:86), for "we would then have the disciples of John the Baptist recognizing Jesus under the same three titles that John the Baptist had disclaimed—but this is perhaps too neat."

37   Boismard, *Moses or Jesus*, 25–30; also Lincoln, *John*, 120; Michaels, *John*, 128n42; Norman Peterson, *The Gospel of John and the Sociology of Light: Language and Characterization in the Fourth Gospel* (Valley Forge, PA: Trinity Press, 1993), 30.

38   Ashton, *Understanding*, 169 (emphasis original): "here we have a Jesus who is *presented* to the Jews as the one who has come to fulfill all their hopes: he is the promised Messiah, he is Elijah returned to earth, he is the eschatological prophet foretold by Moses, he is the Chosen One, the Son of God, the King of Israel." The text Ashton is interpreting, however (as is clear from the reference to Elijah), is his reconstruction of the author's source, which inserts an identification of Jesus as Elijah in 1:43 (see *Understanding*, 156).

(14) When the people saw the sign (σημεῖον) that he had done, they began to say, "This is indeed the prophet who is to come into the world (οὗτός ἐστιν ἀληθῶς ὁ προφήτης ὁ ἐρχόμενος εἰς τὸν κόσμον)." (15) When Jesus realized that they were about to come and take him by force to make him king (βασιλέα), he withdrew again to the mountain by himself.

The crowd's conclusion is that Jesus is not just any ordinary prophet, but *the* prophet, the one "coming into the world."[39] That the people are not entirely correct in their assessment of Jesus, however, is indicated by their misguided attempt to make him king. Here the author resists an interpretation of Deut 18:15 which would associate "the Prophet" with the political messianism of a revolutionary movement, perhaps along the lines of later figures such as Theudas or the Egyptian.[40] Meeks argues that the author wishes to retain the titles for Jesus used here, while rejecting the meaning of those titles assigned by the crowd: "The identification of Jesus as this prophet-king is by no means denied by Jesus' 'flight' to the mountain; only the time and the manner in which the men seek to make him king are rejected."[41] This is correct as far as it goes, but the author has left the precise relationship of Jesus and "the Prophet" somewhat ambiguous.

There are two references to "the Prophet" in John 7, one positive and one hostile. At the Feast of Booths, Jesus calls people to come to him for "living water" (7:37–38). There are Mosaic associations with such an offer,[42] and it

---

39   Cf John 11:27; Lindars, *John*, 244.
40   On the relationship between John 6:1–15 and these movements, see Paul Barnett, "The Jewish Sign Prophets—A.D. 40–70: Their Intentions and Origin," *NTS* 27 (1980–1981): 679–697; C.H. Dodd, *Historical Tradition in the Fourth Gospel* (Cambridge: Cambridge University, 1963), 214–215, who comments (214): "Whether therefore it is historically veracious or not, John's account has dramatic verisimilitude. Further, it fits perfectly what we know of the situation in Palestine, and the popular mood, about the time." If John is responding to such an interpretation, this passage is a clue that the eschatological interpretation of Deut 18:15 was perhaps more widespread in first century Judaism than the limited evidence allows us to affirm confidently.
41   Meeks, *Prophet-King*, 99. For an alternate perspective, see Barrett, *John*, 277: "It is doubtful whether John should be thought of as defending the Mosaic prophetic understanding of Messiahship against the royal political understanding implied by v. 15. Neither is adequate for his Christological purposes, though each contributes something, both positively and negatively."
42   See Exod 17:1–7; Ps 78:16; note discussion in Brown, *John*, 1:327–329, Lincoln, *John*, 254–258, and particularly Hannah S. An, "The Prophet like Moses (Deut 18:15–18) and the Woman at the Well in Light of the Dead Sea Scrolls," *ExpTim* 127 (2016): 469–478, who argues that water imagery was associated with the prophet like Moses both in the Dead Sea Scrolls as well as here and elsewhere in John's gospel (cf. 4:10–19).

again provokes discussion and dissension concerning which eschatological figure Jesus claims to be:

> (40) When they heard these words (ἀκούσαντες τῶν λόγων τούτων), some in the crowd said, "This is really the prophet (οὗτός ἐστιν ἀληθῶς ὁ προφήτης)." (41) Others said, "This is the Messiah." But some asked, "Surely the Messiah does not come from Galilee, does he? (42) Has not the scripture said that the Messiah is descended from David and comes from Bethlehem, the village where David lived?"[43] (43) So there was a division in the crowd because of him. (44) Some of them wanted to arrest him, but no one laid hands on him. (45) Then the temple police went back to the chief priests and Pharisees, who asked them, "Why did you not arrest him?" (46) The police answered, "Never has anyone spoken like this (οὐδέποτε ἐλάλησεν οὕτως ἄνθρωπος)!" (47) Then the Pharisees replied, "Surely you have not been deceived too, have you (μὴ καὶ ὑμεῖς πεπλάνησθε)? (48) Has any one of the authorities or of the Pharisees believed in him? (49) But this crowd, which does not know the law—they are accursed." (50) Nicodemus, who had gone to Jesus before, and who was one of them, asked, (51) "Our law does not judge people without first giving them a hearing to find out what they are doing, does it?" (52) They replied, "Surely you are not also from Galilee, are you? Search and you will see that no prophet is to arise from Galilee (ἐκ τῆς Γαλιλαίας [ὁ] προφήτης οὐκ ἐγείρεται)."

Meeks points out that "in a broad sense" the structure of this section is chiastic: Jesus is identified as the Prophet (v. 40), the Christ (v. 41) and then subsequently rejected as the Christ (v. 40b–42) and the Prophet (v. 47, 52).[44] The

---

43 There is an extensive scholarly debate over whether John 7:41–42 represents an instance of Johannine irony (so, the author knows and affirms the Bethlehem tradition, and the crowd unwittingly testifies to the truth about Jesus; see, e.g., Barrett, *John*, 330; Keener, *John*, 1:730–731; Lincoln, *John*, 258; Michaels, *John*, 470–471) or whether the author is ignorant of the Bethlehem tradition, and rejects such criteria in view of the essential affirmation that Jesus is "from above" or "from God" (see, e.g., Bultmann, *John*, 306n6: "the Evangelist knows nothing, or wants to know nothing of the birth in Bethlehem"; Meeks, *Prophet-King*, 21, 35–41). Schnackenburg, *John*, 2:158–159, remains undecided. Fredriksen, *From Jesus to Christ*, 25, thinks the question may have been "irrelevant" to the author ("John can therefore acknowledge forthrightly that Jesus comes from Nazareth, not the messianically correct town of Bethlehem .... Jesus' earthly point of origin is irrelevant, because his true point of origin is beyond this cosmos, with the Father").

44 Meeks, *Prophet-King*, 34. So also Richard Bauckham, "Messianism According to the Gospel of John," in *Challenging Perspectives on the Gospel of John*, ed. J. Lierman, WUNT 2/219 (Tübingen: Mohr Siebeck, 2006), 34–68 (at 52).

"titles are treated in an exactly parallel manner;" thus, for Meeks, "the Prophet" no less than "Messiah" is from the writer's perspective appropriately affirmed of Jesus.[45] As an additional consideration, Meeks appeals to the use of the term ἀληθῶς in 7:40.[46] Indeed, this term is important for John 7's discussion of Jesus' potential identification as the prophet like Moses. The debate between people and leaders occurs in the context of stark oppositions: Jesus is either a true and accredited Mosaic prophet, or he is the deceiving prophet of Deut 13, and therefore to be rejected.[47] This provokes an epistemological crisis that is indebted to Deuteronomy's framework for evaluating prophetic claimants, as reflected in the terminology of both people and leaders (ἀληθῶς, 7:40 [cf 6:14]; πλανάω, 7:12, 47). More generally, the employment of scriptural and traditional criteria in order to test messianic claims is a motif that recurs throughout the chapter (7:27, 31, 41–42, 52). The authorities regard themselves as adjudicators of such claims (by virtue of their interpretive finesse), and Jesus' Galilean origin disqualifies him from messianic titles.

The basis of the authorities' rejection of Jesus in John 7:52 poses several interpretive problems. It is framed as a challenge: "search and you will see (ἐραύνησον καὶ ἴδε)." It is unclear, however, what passage would preclude a Galilean origin for a (or the) prophet. In fact, the prophet Jonah came from Galilee (2 Kgs 14:25). Some interpreters consider this to be an instance of Johannine irony: the teachers do not even know the scriptures to which they appeal![48] This reading is overly subtle. More promising is Martyn's suggestion that the attributes of the Messiah are assimilated to the Prophet,[49] so that the non-Galilean origin of the former is predicated of the latter, but it is difficult to follow him in his view that the Messiah and Prophet are thought to be identical figures, here or elsewhere in John (cf 1:21–25). Though I have not seen it proposed, it seems plausible that the phrases "from your midst, from your brothers" (מקרבך מאחיך) in Deut 18:15 could have been interpreted as criteria regarding the prophet's origin.[50] This

---

45 See Meeks, *Prophet-King*, 34–35.
46 Meeks, *Prophet-King*, 33–34: "Is the identification of Jesus as 'the Prophet' also a proper Christian affirmation? The use of the adverb ἀληθῶς already suggests that it is."
47 As Meeks himself shows in great detail; see *Prophet-King*, 42–61. See also Reinhartz, *Befriending the Beloved Disciple*, 94–95, for later rabbinic references to Jesus in terms of Deut 13.
48 So Keener, *John*, 1:734–735; Lincoln, *John*, 79: "The authorities engage in a searching of Scripture that excludes the possibility of their listening to Jesus and in the process show themselves in fact to be more ignorant than the despised crowd, because Scripture does talk of a prophet from Galilee (cf 2 Kings 14:25)"; cf also 259–260.
49 Martyn, *History and Theology*, 109–111.
50 *Contra* Bauckham, "Messianism," 52, who rejects this possibility.

suggestion is tentative, because it remains uncertain how these clauses would rule out a Galilean origin, unless "your brothers" was understood to refer specifically to Judeans or even Levites (like Moses).

The foregoing survey of the uses of the title "the Prophet" in John's gospel is inconclusive. It is applied to Jesus by characters whose understanding of him may be inadequate, even if it is positive. The title is not denied by the author, and one could perhaps infer from his strong repudiation of it for John the Baptist that he wants to reserve it for Jesus, but the claim that Jesus is the eschatological prophet like Moses is not directly made in the gospel. That said, the claim that Jesus is the prophet like Moses is a claim that may be implicitly made. This can be seen both by Jesus' prophetic characterization throughout the narrative (regardless of specific dependance on Deut 18:15–18) as well as via allusions to Deut 18:15–18 in the gospel.

4.2 *The Prophetic Characterization of Jesus in John*

Though some have doubted the propriety of the designation,[51] Reinhartz avers: "There is no doubt that the Johannine Jesus, in addition to being the Christ, Son of God, Son of Man, and King of Israel, is also a prophet."[52] Characters that the gospel writer views with sympathy use the designation "a prophet," for Jesus, perhaps attesting that it is indeed appropriate (the Samaritan woman, 4:19; the man born blind, 9:17).[53] More importantly, Jesus displays the super-human knowledge that is characteristic of prophets throughout the gospel.[54] He knows the thoughts of his interlocutors, and on several occasions he surprises and discomfits them by disclosing knowledge of their personal circumstances.[55] He regularly makes predictions,[56] and also draws out the implications of their ful-

---

[51] Marinus de Jonge, *Jesus: Stranger From Heaven and Son of God: Jesus Christ and the Christians in Johannine Perspective*, ed. and trans. John. E. Steely, SBLSBS 11 (Missoula, Mont.: Scholars Press, 1977), 50, calls attention to the fact that in the narratives of John 4 and 9 the designations of Jesus as "a prophet" function as initial perceptions, which are modified by further encounters with Jesus. He concludes: "Obviously 'prophet' is neither the most suitable nor the final title for Jesus"; cf. 61, 64–65. Clearly Jesus has a number of designations in John; my claim that "prophet" is suitable does not mean it is complete or final.

[52] Reinhartz, "Jesus as Prophet," here 3.

[53] An, "Prophet like Moses," 469–470, argues that even the designation "a prophet" in John 4:19 is a reference to Deut 18:15–18, based on Samaritan expectation of such a figure.

[54] John 1:48; 2:24–25; 4:16–19; 5:6; 6:6, 53, 61, 64, 70–71; 7:1; 13:1, 21, 26, 38; 18:4.

[55] See in particular John 1:48; 4:16–19.

[56] Reinhartz, "Jesus as Prophet," 3–9, provides a full survey of predictions that Jesus makes in John, referring to John 1:51; 2:19; 3:14; 3:36; 4:21; 5:26–29; 6:70; 7:37–38; 11:4; 13:21; 13:38; 14:2–3, 12, 13, 16, 18–21, 26; 15:20, 26; 16:2, 7, 13. It should be noted that the predictions in 4:21 and 7:38 are connected to an identification of Jesus as a/the prophet (4:19; 7:41).

fillment for his disciples. Indeed, on several occasions Jesus appears to employ the criterion of fulfillment from Deut 18:21–22:

> I tell you this now, before it occurs, so that when it does occur, you may believe that I am he.
>   John 13:19

> And now I have told you this before it occurs, so that when it does occur, you may believe.
>   John 14:29

> But I have said these things to you so that when their hour comes you may remember that I told you about them.
>   John 16:4

With respect to such passages, Anderson remarks:

> To remove all doubt, Jesus *declares ahead of time what is to take place* so that it will be acknowledged that he is sent from God .... The typological embodiment of Deut 18:22 could not be put any clearer; Jesus is the true Prophet like Moses because all of his words—as well as the testimony about him—come true.[57]

Indeed, the narrator also explicitly indicates ways in which Jesus' words are fulfilled with editorial asides that refer to his resurrection (2:21–22), the pouring out of the Spirit (7:39), the flight of the disciples (18:9), and the mode of Jesus' death (18:32).[58] Reinhartz spells out the implications for John's christology:

> The demonstration that Jesus' prophecies come true supports the assertion that Jesus' words come from God (14.10; 17.8, 14, 17) and therefore that Jesus himself is truly a prophet, as some of the characters in the story label him (4.19; 6.14). Because his prophecies come to pass, the Johannine Jesus fulfils at least one of the criteria of the Prophet-like-Moses described in Deut. 18.15–21, though no explicit mention of this passage appears in the Gospel.[59]

---

57 Anderson, "Having-Sent-Me Father," 40, referring to John 13:18–19; 14:28–29; 16:2–4; 18:8–9, 31–32.
58 On 18:32, see Reinhartz, "Jesus as Prophet," 5.
59 Reinhartz, "Jesus as Prophet," 9–10.

Reinhartz correctly notes that Deut 18:15, 18 is not quoted by the author, but two of the passages she notes here also among those identified by Meeks and Boismard as allusions to the thought of Deut 18:15, 18.[60] This again raises the question of whether the identification of Jesus as the prophet like Moses is implicitly made by the author of this gospel, and brings us to a consideration of allusions to Deut 18:15–18 in John.

TABLE 25   Allusions to and echoes of Deut 18:15, 18 in John's gospel[a]

Concept from Deut 18:15, 18	Allusions to/Echoes of Concept in John
"Words" of God are put in prophet's mouth; cf ῥῆμα, λαλέω in 18:18	3:34a: ὃν γὰρ ἀπέστειλεν ὁ θεὸς τὰ ῥήματα τοῦ θεοῦ λαλεῖ (see also ἀκούων αὐτοῦ in 3:29; and compare 3:35–36 with Deut 18:19)
Jesus "speaks" the words that the Father "gives" him; cf δίδωμι, λαλέω in 18:18	8:28: εἶπεν οὖν αὐτοῖς ὁ Ἰησοῦς· ὅταν ὑψώσητε τὸν υἱὸν τοῦ ἀνθρώπου, τότε γνώσεσθε ὅτι ἐγώ εἰμι, καὶ ἀπ' ἐμαυτοῦ ποιῶ οὐδέν, ἀλλὰ καθὼς ἐδίδαξέν με ὁ πατὴρ ταῦτα λαλῶ.
"Hearing" the "words" of God; cf ἀκούω in 18:15, ῥῆμα in 18:18	8:47: ὁ ὢν ἐκ τοῦ θεοῦ τὰ ῥήματα τοῦ θεοῦ ἀκούει· διὰ τοῦτο ὑμεῖς οὐκ ἀκούετε, ὅτι ἐκ τοῦ θεοῦ οὐκ ἐστέ
"Hearing" Jesus' "words" is a criterion for judgment (Deut 18:15, 18, 19); Jesus speaks the "words" of the Father, who has "given" him a "commandment"	12:47–50: (47) καὶ ἐάν τίς μου ἀκούσῃ τῶν ῥημάτων καὶ μὴ φυλάξῃ, ἐγὼ οὐ κρίνω αὐτόν· οὐ γὰρ ἦλθον ἵνα κρίνω τὸν κόσμον, ἀλλ' ἵνα σώσω τὸν κόσμον. (48) ὁ ἀθετῶν ἐμὲ καὶ μὴ λαμβάνων τὰ ῥήματά μου ἔχει τὸν κρίνοντα αὐτόν· ὁ λόγος ὃν ἐλάλησα ἐκεῖνος κρινεῖ αὐτὸν ἐν τῇ ἐσχάτῃ ἡμέρᾳ. (49) ὅτι ἐγὼ ἐξ ἐμαυτοῦ οὐκ ἐλάλησα, ἀλλ' ὁ πέμψας με πατὴρ αὐτός μοι ἐντολὴν δέδωκεν τί εἴπω καὶ τί λαλήσω. (50) καὶ
Cf ἀκούω in Deut 18:15; ῥῆμα, δίδωμι, λαλέω, ἐντέλλομαι in Deut 18:18	οἶδα ὅτι ἡ ἐντολὴ αὐτοῦ ζωὴ αἰώνιός ἐστιν. ἃ οὖν ἐγὼ λαλῶ, καθὼς εἴρηκέν μοι ὁ πατήρ, οὕτως λαλῶ.

a This is my list based on the criteria above. Similar lists are given by Meeks, *Prophet-King*, 45–46 and de Jonge *Stranger from Heaven*, 56. Meeks' list is slightly more expansive and also includes 10:3 and 18:37, both of which contain a reference only to "hearing" Jesus and are therefore too general to refer to Deut 18:15. Meeks and de Jonge also both posit that Deut 18 lies behind 7:14–18, which is certainly possible, though impossible to demonstrate decisively.

60   Meeks, *Prophet-King*, 45–46; Boismard identifies 17:8 as such, *Moses or Jesus*, 17–18.

TABLE 25   Allusions to and echoes of Deut 18:15, 18 in John's gospel (*cont.*)

Concept from Deut 18:15, 18	Allusions to/Echoes of Concept in John
The "words" Jesus "speaks" are not his own, but the Father's; cf ῥῆμα, λαλέω in 18:18	14:10: οὐ πιστεύεις ὅτι ἐγὼ ἐν τῷ πατρὶ καὶ ὁ πατὴρ ἐν ἐμοί ἐστιν; τὰ **ῥήματα** ἃ ἐγὼ λέγω ὑμῖν ἀπ' ἐμαυτοῦ οὐ **λαλῶ**, ὁ δὲ πατὴρ ἐν ἐμοὶ μένων ποιεῖ τὰ ἔργα αὐτοῦ.
The "words" the Father has "given" Jesus; cf ῥῆμα, δίδωμι in Deut 18:18	17:8: ὅτι τὰ **ῥήματα** ἃ **ἔδωκάς** μοι **δέδωκα** αὐτοῖς, καὶ αὐτοὶ ἔλαβον καὶ ἔγνωσαν ἀληθῶς ὅτι παρὰ σοῦ ἐξῆλθον, καὶ ἐπίστευσαν ὅτι σύ με ἀπέστειλας.

A methodological hurdle with identifying allusions to Deut 18:15–18 is that the key terms in the passage are fairly common, and usage of these words cannot in itself satisfy the requirement of an allusion.[61] What is required is that these terms be used in such a way that they provide a clear *conceptual* parallel to the governing idea of the passage, which is that God puts words in the mouth of the prophet, so that the prophet speaks what God commands. When one prioritizes this conceptual parallel, the list of possible allusions to and echoes of Deut 18:15, 18 in the gospel of John is relatively restricted (Table 25). Of these proposed allusions, 12:47–50 is surely the most impressive; Lincoln claims the influence of Deut 18:15–19 here is "unmistakable":[62]

> (47) I do not judge anyone who hears my words and does not keep them, for I came not to judge the world, but to save the world. (48) The one who rejects me and does not receive my word has a judge; on the last day the word that I have spoken will serve as judge, (49) for I have not spoken on my own, but the Father who sent me has himself given me a commandment about what to say and what to speak. (50) And I know that his commandment is eternal life. What I speak, therefore, I speak just as the Father has told me.
> John 12:47–50

---

61   Eg., προφήτης, ἀκούω, ῥῆμα, λαλέω, ἐντέλλομαι. This is the problem with Anderson's exhaustive list of potential parallels ("Having-Sent-Me," 38–40).

62   Meeks, *Prophet-King*, 46, says the allusion is "fairly plain." Lincoln, *John*, 361: "Jesus' words contain unmistakable allusions to Deut 18:18–19."

The passage contains the confluence of several specific ideas: the theme of hearing Jesus' words, Jesus' claim that his words are not his own but that the Father "has given him a command what I should say and what I should speak," and that he speaks only what the Father tells him. The theme of judgment in 12:47–48 can be connected to Deut 18:19, and the notion that the "commandment" is "life" also has a Deuteronomic background (12:50; cf., e.g., Deut 30:15; 32:46–47).[63] Lincoln concludes: "As the one who speaks the words that God has commanded and to which all will be held accountable, Jesus' assertion is that, far from being a false prophet, he fulfills all the criteria for the true prophet like Moses."[64] This passage is placed at a significant juncture in John, concluding the gospel's account of Jesus' ministry prior to the passion. Interestingly, the prophet in view in the near context is not Moses but Isaiah (12:37–41); that said, Isaiah is discussed precisely in terms of his likeness to Moses (12:41: "Isaiah said this because he saw his glory and spoke about him [αὗτα εἶπεν Ἡσαΐας, ὅτε εἶδε τὴν δόξαν αὐτοῦ, καὶ ἐλάλησε περὶ αὐτοῦ]"; cf. 1:14; Exod 33:18; 34:5–7). Thus, at the transition to the passion narrative, the author positions Jesus as the fulfillment of both Moses' and Isaiah's words.

The dialogue at the Feast of Booths in John 7–8 is the only place in the gospel that combines references to Jesus' proposed identity as "the Prophet" (7:40, 52) with later allusions in Jesus' own words to the key concepts of Deut 18:18 (8:28, 47). Above, we saw that John 7 contains debate between various constituencies about Jesus' identity. Jesus' own intervention into the intractable dispute occurs in John 8:12–58. Jesus' opening words, "I am the light of the world," set in the context of the Feast of Booths, allude to the divine presence that accompanied the Israelites in the wilderness.[65] They fit within a pattern in John 6–8 in which Jesus compares himself to the gifts that sustained the Israelites on their wilderness journeys (ch. 6: manna; ch. 7: water; ch. 8: fire).[66] In these instances, Jesus is identified not with Moses, but with the divine gifts bestowed through Moses' activity. In this context, there are two allusions to the thought of Deut 18:15, 18:

> John 8:28b: "I do nothing on my own own, but I speak these things as the Father instructed me [καθὼς ἐδίδαξέν με ὁ πατὴρ ταῦτα λαλῶ]."

---

63 So Boismard, *Moses or Jesus*, 65–66.
64 Lincoln, *John*, 361.
65 So, e.g., Keener, *John*, 1:739; Brown, *John*, 1:343–344.
66 Glasson, *Moses in the Fourth Gospel*, 10, attributes this observation to F.B. Meyer, *The Light and Life of Men* (1891). See also Bauckham, "Messianism," 49–50.

John 8:47: "Whoever is from God hears the words of God. The reason you do not hear them is that you are not from God [ὁ ὢν ἐκ τοῦ θεοῦ τὰ ῥήματα τοῦ θεοῦ ἀκούει· διὰ τοῦτο ὑμεῖς οὐκ ἀκούετε, ὅτι ἐκ τοῦ θεοῦ οὐκ ἐστέ]."

"Speaking" the words that God "gives" or "commands" and "hearing" the words that God speaks are central concepts in Deut 18:15, 18. Again, it is noteworthy that the author of the Fourth Gospel is more interested in the vertical axis posited in Deut 18—the notion that God puts God's word in the mouth of the prophet—than the horizontal axis of genealogical succession to Moses. Jesus attributes to himself the function of the prophet like Moses, even as his self-description is as the one who is "from above" (8:23) and from the Father (8:26–27, 42). Jesus' interlocutors intuit the vaunted claims he is making, but reframe it in terms of historical or genealogical succession: "Are you greater than our father Abraham, who died? The prophets also died. Who do you claim to be?" (John 8:53). Jesus' reply, "Before Abraham was, I am," (8:58) is illustrative of this gospel writer's approach to authorizing Jesus, which does not depend on historical succession or descent (there are no genealogies in John), but draws upon the vertical axis of Jesus' identity as the divine Logos.[67]

To draw the threads of the preceding discussion together, we are faced with the following situation: the author of John's gospel is aware of an eschatological figure known as "the Prophet," allows diverse groups to raise the possibility of this figure's identification with Jesus, does not directly affirm that identification, but seems to implicitly affirm it by developing a prophetic profile for Jesus and by alluding several times to key concepts from Deut 18:15,18 in Jesus' own words. A rather delicate balance is being struck. The issues, for the author, are hermeneutical: the Moses-Jesus relationship is of great importance, but is easily misunderstood. Indeed, in my view, the avoidance of the title "the Prophet" for Jesus is due to potential misunderstanding of Jesus' identity in terms of a political or revolutionary messianism (cf. 6:15; 18:36), which is a theological analogue for the motif of literalist and "physical" misunderstandings of Jesus' teachings throughout the narrative (cf. 3:4; 4:15; 6:34, 52). The author must respond to the perceived incompatibility of discipleship to Moses and Jesus (9:28–29), but he does so with a highly modulated and nuanced portrayal of the way Jesus is both like and unlike Moses. To illustrate this claim, it is necessary to consider four passages that function as controlling statements delineating the contours of the Moses-Jesus relationship in the gospel. These statements are

---

67 Fredriksen, *From Jesus to Christ*, 23, comments that for John, "the cross is literally the sole intersection of the 'horizontal' context of mundane history ... and the 'vertical' context of heavenly reality."

not directly germane to the interpretation of Deut 18:15, 18, and so cannot be treated in as much depth and detail as they deserve. Nevertheless, they provide *prima facie* evidence that a precise articulation of the Moses-Jesus relationship was a pressing concern for the author.

4.3 The Moses-Jesus Relationship in John: Four Controlling Passages

I begin with John's famous prologue, which concludes with the author's deft articulation of his nuanced perspective on the Moses-Jesus relationship: "The law was given through Moses; grace and truth came through Jesus Christ (ὅτι ὁ νόμος διὰ Μωϋσέως ἐδόθη, ἡ χάρις καὶ ἡ ἀλήθεια διὰ Ἰησοῦ Χριστοῦ ἐγένετο)" (John 1:17). This passage (along with the rest of the prologue) has attracted voluminous commentary; I cannot do justice to the history of this interpretation in the confines of this discussion. Ashton is a representative of the interpretive tradition that has seen the thrust of these verses as highlighting the discontinuity between Moses and Jesus. He expresses himself forcefully: "the uncompromising rejection of Moses and the law in favor of the grace and truth brought by Christ is stated in the prologue."[68] Indeed, Ashton believes that these verses represent the birth of Christianity as a movement distinct from Judaism, a claim which goes beyond the evidence.[69]

In John 1:17, Jesus is both like and unlike Moses. Jesus and Moses are alike as mediators of divine revelation (both names are governed by the preposition διά). Moreover, the essential content of the revelation Jesus brings ("grace and truth") is an allusion to the theophany given to Moses (Exod 33–34).

---

68   Ashton, *Gospel of John*, 10; cf 20–22; 167; so also Lincoln, *John*, 107, who says this is an "antithetically structured parallelism." Severino Pancaro, *The Law in the Fourth Gospel: The Torah and the Gospel, Moses and Jesus, Judaism and Christianity According to John*, NovTSup 42 (Leiden: Brill, 1975), 534–546, also interprets the parallelism as primarily antithetical. He bases this upon drawing an inference that goes beyond what John states (see 539–540: "If the words are taken at their face value, one must hold that Jn in no way implies that ἡ χάρις καὶ ἡ ἀλήθεια also came to be through the Law"). This is not, strictly speaking, relevant: even if the Law served positively to point toward the embodiment of ἡ χάρις καὶ ἡ ἀλήθεια in Jesus, the parallelism would not be antithetical.

69   Ashton, *Gospel of John*, 22: "In attributing grace and truth to Christ rather than to Moses, the author of this sentence knew—cannot but have known—that he was dissociating himself from Judaism in any of its forms." So also Fredriksen, *From Jesus to Christ*, 25: "This radical divorce from Judaism—its people, its history, and in a more complicated way, its scripture—liberates the evangelist stylistically and theologically from composing his gospel around biblical testimonia …. This gospel, in other words, is written by someone who consciously placed himself outside, if not against, Judaism." As comments on the text, these statements lack precision. As historical claims, they are anachronistic and fail to capture the highly modulated claims of the author of the Fourth Gospel.

There is no strong antithetical parallelism between "the law" and "grace and truth," since "grace and truth" is attested to in the Law of Moses.[70] Thus, law (ὁ νόμος) should not be understood as having a negative valence or connotation in 1:17, in contrast to the positive associations of grace and truth. Rather, as Pancaro has shown, "the law" in John's gospel is equivalent to Torah.[71] The author has deliberately left the relationship between the clauses ambiguous: there is no δέ or ἀλλά, which would imply a contrasting or antithetical relationship;[72] moreover, the verb "to give" (δίδωμι) has positive connotations, so that Brown's interpretive translation is not unjustified: "For while the law was a gift through Moses, this enduring love came through Jesus Christ."[73] Brown represents the contrasting (and I think, more persuasive) exegetical tradition, which understands the relationship between Moses and Jesus here to be primarily one of continuity.[74] Nevertheless, a difference is posited: the law was *given* through Moses; grace and truth *came into being* through Jesus Christ. As Michaels says:

> The coming of "grace and truth" is a kind of new creation, and the Word though whom all things came to be finally has a name—"Jesus Christ". Because of the differing verbs, therefore, the phrases "through Moses" and "through Jesus Christ" are not strictly parallel. Jesus is not a new Moses receiving and delivering a new law, but the Word in human flesh, calling "grace and truth" into being.[75]

---

70 As is commonly recognized, ἡ χάρις καὶ ἡ ἀλήθεια translates חסד ואמת, important attributes of the divine identity as it was proclaimed to Moses (Exod 34:6). Even Ashton, *Gospel of John*, 20, recognizes this allusion, though it does no work in his interpretation.

71 With regard to 1:17, Pancaro, *Law*, 515, defines "law" as "the body of teaching revealed to Moses which constitutes the foundation of the whole social-religious life and thought of Israel." Later, Pancaro, *Law*, 517, comments (emphasis original): "even when Jn refers to a particular aspect or text of the Law, *it is always the Law as a whole, as the body of divine revelation given to Moses,* passed on from generation to generation *and constituting the foundation of Judaism, which lurks* [?] *in the background*." See also his summary of results, 514–534.

72 As pointed out by many commentators, e.g., Schnackenburg, *John*, 1:276.

73 Brown, *John*, 1:4.

74 Michaels, *John*, 90: "The accent is rather on continuity. The law is itself grace from God, 'given through Moses' as a preparation for more and greater grace to come [cf. v. 16, χάριν ἀντὶ χάριτος]." Lindars, *John*, 98 concludes: "It really is a case of synthetic parallelism (so J. Jeremias): *just as* the law was given through Moses, *so* grace and truth (which the law prefigures) came into being (*egeneto*) through Jesus Christ." So also Schnackenburg, *John*, 1:227.

75 Michaels, *John*, 91.

The prologue concludes by indicating that the ways Jesus is like and unlike Moses will be a major theme of the gospel's narrative, and closely ties the gospel's Moses-Jesus comparison to its Logos theology.

The next passage to be considered is Jesus' cryptic statement comparing the "Son of Man" to the serpent Moses lifted up in the desert (Num 21:5–9): "And just as (καθὼς) Moses lifted up the serpent in the wilderness, so (οὕτως) must the Son of Man be lifted up, that whoever believes in him may have eternal life" (John 3:14–15). As Meeks points out, it is not Moses, but the gift of life that came through Moses, that is paralleled in Jesus.[76] In this passage then, the accent is on how the Son of Man is *unlike* Moses,[77] in being the embodiment of gifts that were available through him in an anticipatory fashion.

A third passage, which provides the clearest evidence of synonymous parallelism between Moses and Jesus in the gospel, occurs at the end of Jesus' speech in chapter 5. In this speech, Jesus has pointed to the various "testimonies" that he has, from John (5:33–35), from his deeds (5:36), and more importantly, from the Father (5:37–38). The final witness that Jesus summons is Moses:

> (39) You search the scriptures because you think that in them you have eternal life; and it is they that testify on my behalf …. (45) Do not think that I will accuse you before the Father; your accuser is Moses, on whom you have set your hope. (46) If you believed Moses, you would believe me, for he wrote about me (εἰ γὰρ ἐπιστεύετε Μωϋσεῖ, ἐπιστεύετε ἂν ἐμοί· περὶ γὰρ ἐμοῦ ἐκεῖνος ἔγραψεν). (47) But if you do not believe what he wrote, how will you believe what I say (πῶς τοῖς ἐμοῖς ῥήμασιν πιστεύσετε)?
>
> John 5:39, 45–47

Many have argued that Jesus' words, "Moses wrote about me," contains a reference to Deut 18:15, 18.[78] Jesus' concluding question places the emphasis on his "words": "if you do not believe what he wrote, how will you believe my words

---

76   Meeks, *Prophet-King*, 292.
77   Meeks, *Prophet-King*, 301, argues that the dissimilarity between Jesus and Moses is also behind the preceding verse: "the statement 'No one has ascended to heaven' would in this context carry the pointed implication 'Not even Moses'."
78   See Boismard, *Moses or Jesus*, 27–28; Meeks, *Prophet-King*, 239; Brown, *John*, 1:226; Schnackenburg, *John*, 2:129; Michaels, *John*, 337n157: "[The Johannine] Jesus may have a number of specific written texts in mind, but perhaps especially Deuteronomy 18:15–18." Keener, *John*, 1:662, takes it as a reference to Exod 33–34: "Moses saw the glory of Jesus on Sinai when he received Torah (Exod 33–34; John 1:14–18)." This seems unlikely; Jesus' emphasis here is not that Moses *saw* him (contrast Abraham, John 8:56; Isaiah, John 12:41), but that Moses *wrote* about him.

(τοῖς ἐμοῖς ῥήμασιν)?"⁷⁹ Jesus' "words" are here placed in parallel with and in succession to Moses' "writings." Atkins points out: "Thus, in the very same sentence in which Jesus says, 'he wrote about me,' Jesus also implies, 'I am like Moses.'"⁸⁰ Indeed, the logic of the statement, "if you believed Moses, you would believe me," is that Jesus is the rightful heir and exponent of Mosaic Discourse. This is an indisputably positive view of Moses, one that calls into question the attempt of Ashton and others to consider Moses as a negative foil for Jesus throughout the gospel.⁸¹ The language used calls for comparison with Exod 14:31 and John 14:1:

Exod 14:31bβ LXX:	καὶ ἐπίστευσαν τῷ θεῷ καὶ Μωυσῇ τῷ θεράποντι αὐτοῦ
John 5:46:	εἰ γὰρ ἐπιστεύετε Μωϋσεῖ, ἐπιστεύετε ἂν ἐμοί
John 14:1b:	πιστεύετε εἰς τὸν θεὸν καὶ εἰς ἐμὲ πιστεύετε.

Exodus 14:31 and John 14:1 make parallel claims for Moses and Jesus respectively: believing in God involves believing them as God's accredited salvific agents.⁸² John 5:46 serves as a middle term between these passages, making explicit on the horizontal plane what one would infer from the vertical relationships between God and Moses/Jesus posited in these texts. (This, it should be noted, is one of the author's only appeals to the horizontal axis of genealogical succession.) In these verses Jesus situates himself as the legitimate heir of Moses, stating that his words provide the continuation of the function of the prophet like Moses of Deut 18:15, 18.⁸³

That said, for the author of the Fourth Gospel, Jesus' words "[Moses] wrote about me," have a broader reference than just to Deut 18:15, 18.⁸⁴ John 3:14–15 has already pointed to one way this might be the case: the Son of Man is like the serpent, which Moses lifted up so that the Israelites who looked at it might

---

79   See Boismard, *Moses or Jesus*, 27.
80   J.D. Atkins, "The Trial of the People and the Prophet: John 5:30–47 and the True and False Prophet Traditions," *CBQ* 75 (2013): 279–296; here 295.
81   Because Ashton, *Gospel of John*, interpreted 1:17 in terms of "uncompromising rejection of Moses and the law" (see above), he is forced (somewhat lamely) to say that the use of Moses as a positive witness in 5:46 "conceals a real opposition he [the author] is not yet prepared to disclose" (14).
82   On the allusion to Exod 14:31 in John 14:1, see Keener, *John*, 1:291, 2:931; Lierman, "Mosaic Pattern," 214–216.
83   Atkins, "Trial of the People and the Prophet," comments on some of the motifs that have been addressed above, e.g., the theme of "hearing" the prophet (289–291), which he uses to shed light on 5:37. More speculatively, he argues that Deut 13:4 lies behind 5:42 (291–294).
84   So, e.g., Lincoln, *John*, 208: "Jesus is the fulfillment of everything in the law"; Lindars, *John*, 233.

have life. Moreover, John 6, which was in all probability placed before John 5 in an earlier version of the gospel,[85] has now been moved after these words of Jesus in order to function as an interpretive commentary on the way that Scripture (5:39) and Moses (5:45–47) testify about Jesus.[86] It cannot be coincidental that after saying "he wrote about me," the gospel proceeds with the most Mosaic of Jesus' "signs" (the feeding of the five thousand, 6:1–13), reports the crowd's interpretation of that sign in terms of Jesus' potential identity as the Mosaic prophet, an interpretation that Jesus resists (6:14–15), and goes on to correct the reader's understanding of the significance of the sign in the Bread

---

85   The arguments in favor of rearrangement are succinctly stated by Bultmann, *John*, 209–210. The main basis for this is in the locales of the various chapters:

> John 4: Jesus travels through Samaria to Galilee, ends up in Cana, and heals the son of an official from Capernaum
>
> John 5: Jesus in Jerusalem
>
> John 6:1: "After this Jesus went to the *other side* of the Sea of Galilee, also called the Sea of Tiberias."
>
> John 7:1: "After this Jesus went about in Galilee. He did not wish to go about in Judea because the Jews were looking for an opportunity to kill him."

A reference to going to the "other side" of the Sea of Galilee makes better sense after healing an official's son near Capernaum than it does when Jesus is in Jerusalem; therefore, the "after this" in John 6:1 more naturally refers to the events of John 4 than John 5. Moreover, the "after this" that begins John 7:1 naturally follows on John 5: after his vitriolic confrontation with the Jewish leaders, Jesus went about in Galilee and not Judea (where he was in John 5), because the Jewish leaders wanted to kill him (cf John 5:18). Brown, *John*, 1:235, observes:

> Nowhere has the theory of rearrangements in John (see Introduction, p. xxvi) had more following than in the reversal chapters v and vi. Not only those who practice rearrangement on a large scale (Bernard, Bultmann), but even those who make little of rearrangement in general (Wikenhauser, Schnackenburg) reverse these chapters.

Further arguments to support this include John 7:19–23, which clearly looks back to John 5, and knows nothing of the "works" Jesus has done (cf. "one work," 7:19) in the intervening chapter. Thus, there are compelling reasons to understand the original order of the gospel as 4–6–5–7. This poses the question: who rearranged the material, and why? Ashton, *Understanding*, 44–48, argues (following Lindars, *John*, 50) that John 6 was inserted by the author himself in the second edition of the gospel (so, the original order is 4–5–7; we have to do not with transposition but insertion). Moreover, the motivation for this insertion was precisely so the author could clarify what it means that "Moses wrote about me"; it serves as an "illustration" of "the interpretation of the Scriptures" (so Peder Borgen, "John 6: Tradition, Interpretation, and Composition," in *Critical Readings of John 6*, ed. R.A. Culpepper, BINS 22 [Leiden: Brill, 1997], 95–114, here 112). In my view, transposition rather than insertion seems the most likely scenario [because why would an insertion not take into account the events of John 5?], but the reason is that highlighted by Ashton and Borgen.

86   See Lindars, *John*, 234: "the present position of it is particularly suitable because of the way in which it serves as an illustration of Jesus' claim in 5:39, 46 f."

of Life discourse (6:32–58). That is, John 6 contains both a potential misinterpretation and a corrective of what it means to say that Moses wrote about Jesus. It therefore seems that its current position in the gospel is due to the author's attempt to clarify exactly how Jesus is both like and unlike Moses. The author interprets "Moses wrote about me" not just in terms of Jesus' identity as prophet like Moses, but also with respect to his role as the bread of life.[87]

With these observations, I arrive at the fourth and final text to be considered on the Moses-Jesus relationship, which Martyn understands to contain "the line of thought most important for our understanding of John's attitude to the hope for the Mosaic Prophet."[88] The crowd, having identified Jesus as the prophet like Moses, requests a repetition of the miracle (perhaps on the assumption that if Moses did it for forty years, surely this fellow can do it at least twice), or another sign confirming his status as *the* eschatological prophet (John 6:30–31). In reply, Jesus focuses on the contrast between him and Moses:

> (32) Then Jesus said to them, "Very truly, I tell you, it was not Moses who gave (οὐ Μωϋσῆς δέδωκεν) you the bread from heaven, but it is my Father who gives you (ἀλλ᾽ ὁ πατήρ μου δίδωσιν) the true bread from heaven. (33) For the bread of God is that which comes down from heaven and gives life to the world."
>
> John 6:32–33

Jesus goes on to refer to himself as this bread (6:35, 48, 51, 58). Once again, the parallel is not between Jesus and Moses, but between Jesus and the gift of life mediated by Moses.[89] As with the lifted-up serpent (3:14–15), the scriptural imagery to which the author is drawn has to do more with the vertical axis of divine-human communication than the horizontal axis of genealogical succession. The author therefore refines the sense in which "Moses wrote about me" (5:46). On one level, this refers to Jesus fulfilling the description of the prophet like Moses; on another level, this refers to the identification of Jesus as the serpent (3:14), the bread (6:32–33), the living water (7:37–38), and the light of the world (8:12), which allude to divine gifts imparted in connection with the

---

87   See the summary in Borgen, "John 6," 113–114.
88   Martyn, *History and Theology*, 121.
89   See Keener, *John*, 1:680: "Thus the real giver of bread from heaven is God, and what they should seek is not a wilderness prophet like Moses but the gift of God which is greater than the earthly manna in the wilderness." Borgen, "John 6," 104 paraphrases Jesus' reply as follows: "You have misunderstood the manna miracle. It was not given by Moses, nor now by the prophet-like-Moses, but it was the gift from heaven, given by the Father, and I am (myself) the manna/bread."

Israelites' travels in the wilderness. Building on the work of Borgen,[90] Martyn emphasizes the hermeneutical function of the passage; that is, he argues that it represents the author's attempt to change the terms of the debate in which the relationship between Moses and Jesus is conducted.[91] Jesus is like Moses, but also unlike him, and like the life-giving benefactions mediated through Moses.

5 Conclusion: John and Luke-Acts on Deut 18:15–18

In terms of early Christianity, I have now examined the influence and interaction with Deut 18:15–22 by two creative late-first century writers, the authors of Luke-Acts and John respectively. It remains to consider briefly the similarities and differences between their respective construals. In terms of similarities, Luke and John are the two gospel writers that show themselves to be familiar with an eschatological interpretation of Deut 18:15, and thus reflect on this passage and its context in developing their views of Jesus. Significantly, they both reflect the discourse of normativity that was an animating factor for the original authors of Deuteronomy; in different ways, they both attempt to position

---

[90] See Peder Borgen, *Bread from Heaven: An Exegetical Study of the Concept of Manna in the Gospel of John and the Writings of Philo*, NovTSup 10 (Leiden: Brill, 1965), 61–68, who takes John 6:32 as an example of correcting the text. According to Borgen, John 6:32 is commenting on Exod 16:4, 15, and providing direction in how to read it. The contrasts might be rephrased as follows: "do not read 'Moses' as subject, but read 'God' as subject, and do not read 'gave' (נתן), but 'gives' (נותן)." Borgen demonstrates similar techniques in Palestinian midrash (see, e.g., *Mek.* to Ex 16:15).

[91] Martyn, *History and Theology*, 123, distills three main points from the passage (the quotation marks are supplied by Martyn, as his distillation of the gospel's engagement with its interlocutors):
  1. "You are wrong in your identification of the type. It was not Moses but rather God who provided the manna." ...
  2. "The correspondence between type and antitype is fixed by God in his sovereign freedom." ...
  3. "The issue is not to be defined as an argument about an ancient text. It is not a midrashic issue. By arguing about texts you seek to evade the present crisis. God is *even now* giving you the true bread from heaven, and you cannot hide from him in typological speculation or in any other kind of midrashic activity. You must decide now with regard to this present gift of God." ... John allows Jesus paradoxically to employ a form of midrashic discussion in order to terminate all midrashic discussion!

  On this, see also Paul N. Anderson, "The *Sitz im Leben* of the Johannine Bread of Life Discourse and Its Evolving Context," in *Critical Readings of John 6*, ed. R.A. Culpepper, BINS 22 (Leiden: Brill, 1997), 1–60.

Jesus as the authorized exponent of Mosaic Discourse. This is a part of their broader struggle to legitimate late first-century Christian communities as legitimate recipients of Israel's scriptures and traditions.

Their strategies for doing so, however, are remarkably different. As I showed earlier, Luke's treatment involves an imaginative reinterpretation of "to raise up" (ἀνίστημι), and recapitulates the logic of Deut 18:15–22 by claiming that Jesus and the apostles represent the normative continuation of Moses and the prophets. Luke has a thorough-going prophet christology, and straightforwardly affirms Jesus' status as the prophet like Moses. His two-volume work consistently places Jesus within the framework of salvation-history and that of Mosaic prophecy. Thus, Luke provides an early Christian analogue to Josephus' historiographic interpretation of the Mosaic prophetic succession.[92] In many ways this is the sort of apologetic that will be typified in the second century by Justin Martyr's *Dialogue with Trypho*: it locates Jesus within a framework of promise-fulfillment, and consequently supposes that interpretation of the scriptures is the ground over which debates about Jesus' identity are to be conducted.[93]

The locus of John's reflection, in contrast, is in the concept of God putting God's word in the mouth of the prophet, who serves as the authorized agent of revelation between God and humanity. Indeed, John's portrait of Jesus has distinct similarities with Philo's portrayal of Moses, particular in relation to his supreme status as revelatory agent. As the Logos, John's Jesus cannot be confined to the bounds of historical succession (cf. John 8:58). This theological perspective, developed programmatically in John's prologue, creates the tension which ultimately causes Jesus to be both like and unlike Moses in John.

[92] See the apt comparison between Luke-Acts and John in Fredriksen, *From Jesus to Christ*, 27: "If the prologue to the Fourth Gospel evokes the timelessness of the upper realm, the prologue to the Third evokes exactly the opposite: a world of eyewitnesses to past events, chains of transmission, researched narrative—in brief, the horizontal plane of human history that John's double context devalues. Luke, conscious of standing in an extended tradition, writes like a historian ...." My argument, in a sense, unpacks how this general observation illuminates their respective engagements with the concept of the prophet like Moses.

[93] Cf, e.g., Acts 17:2–3; 26:27–28; 28:23.

Conclusion: Retrospect and Prospect

This book has traced the story of the prophet like Moses from its origin in the seventh century BCE to its reception in a variety of Jewish and early Christian texts from the late first century CE. The journey has been somewhat winding, as I have endeavored to respect the creativity and independence of the various ancient sources in their interaction with Deut 18:15–22. Nevertheless, a common thread has been the deployment of this concept in the construction of normative tradition. Indeed, the main contribution of this study is the way that it contributes to a more granular and precise understanding of the way bids for normativity functioned in Second Temple Judaism, in the era preceding a fixed literary canon. The concept of the prophet like Moses originates as a prophetic office; it is transformed into a prophetic succession; still later, the precise boundaries of the past Mosaic prophetic succession as well as the potential of its future return are both asserted and contested as part of the development of normative discourses within Early Judaism. I now draw some threads together and indicate directions for future research by reflecting on how the argument of the book has made important interventions in relationship to the category of Mosaic Discourse, the so-called "end of prophecy," and the importance of the Moses-Jesus relationship in early Christianity.

First, I have argued that in order to understand the tremendous influence of Mosaic Discourse in Second Temple Judaism, it is crucial to take into account how figures later than Moses are represented as its legitimate exponents. I have thus argued for an expanded definition of Mosaic Discourse, one that is not restricted to Moses-pseudepigrapha, as found in Najman's original articulation of the concept. Deuteronomy's creation of genealogical model for Mosaic prophecy deeply influenced the literary representation of later prophetic claimants, so that individuals such as Jeremiah, Joshua, and Jesus were portrayed as heirs of Moses, as authoritative arbiters of Israel's scriptures, and as tradition-mediating and tradition-generating figures in their own right. This expanded definition of Mosaic Discourse highlights the vitality and influence of Deuteronomy's genealogical model of Mosaic prophecy throughout this time-period. Indeed, though I have limited my focus to texts and authors that explicitly interpret Deut 18:15–22, I have been mindful that readers may object that there are other texts and traditions that could or perhaps should have been included in the book (*Jubilees*, the gospel of Matthew, and *Fourth Ezra* come to mind). This observation only further underlines the importance of Mosaic Discourse as the basic unit of religious normativity throughout this time-period. Indeed, in terms of future research, it would be of interest to explore a variety of apocalyptic and pseudepigraphic texts through the lens of Deuteronomy's genealogical model of prophecy, considering the relationship of the "authors" of these works to the Mosaic prophetic succession, and whether their location within it (e.g., Ezra, Baruch) or outside of it (e.g., Enoch, Abraham, the Sibyl) clarifies their overall goals and theological orientation.

Second, the book makes a contribution to the scholarly debate regarding the so-called "end of prophecy." Many of the texts that used to be understood as evidence for the "end of prophecy" in Second Temple Judaism should be understood more precisely as referring to a (perhaps temporary) cessation of the Mosaic prophetic office established in Deut 18:15–22. The boundaries constructed for Mosaic prophecy reflects a priestly-scribal tradition of interpretation in which prophecy in general did not cease, but prophecy as an authorized national institution did. In my engagement with scholarship, I have consistently emphasized that the boundary-drawing in view for prophecy is chronological and not canonical. There are robust traditions of scholarly interpretation understanding Deut 34:10–12, or the scroll of Jeremiah, or Mal 3:22–24, or Ben Sira's *Laus Patrum* as indicating an "end of prophecy" and as positing literary or canonical boundaries. With respect to such texts, I have argued that the scribal class is engaged in a historiographic and antiquarian project, more precisely drawing the chronological boundaries of Mosaic prophecy in the past and asserting interpretive control over the Mosaic prophetic tradition in the present. The thesis of a chronological and not canonical boundary also helps to clarify the dynamics of religious normativity in Second Temple Judaism, in which there was continuous production of texts claiming scriptural and authoritative status, even as the construct of the past Mosaic prophetic succession exerted normative pressure.

Third, the book makes an important contribution to the study of early Christian literature and the identification of Jesus as the prophet like Moses. Debate and reflection on the concept of prophet like Moses is not a prominent feature of earliest Christianity, as many scholars have assumed. Rather, intense reflection on the concept of the prophet like Moses is found in the late first-century, in Luke-Acts and John, and is a part of early Christianity's emerging self-understanding vis-à-vis its Jewish context. In the case of John, I have argued that it is not to be understood as a "low" Christology, but is part and parcel of this gospel's development of a Logos-theology. Importantly, both of these authors situate their claims for Jesus within the normative framework for prophetic claims operative within Second Temple Judaism, and thereby validate the self-understanding of early Christian communities as authorized recipients of Israel's scriptural traditions. In certain respects, this represents a retrieval of Deuteronomy's own polemical character. In its time, Deuteronomy also made a bid—successfully, as it happens—to be considered the normative continuation of Mosaic tradition. On the one hand, this feature of the project provided a striking confirmation of my thesis that the concept of the prophet like Moses is bound up with normativity, both in its origin and in its reception. On the other hand, it was discomfiting and jarring to find myself working with some of the most vitriolic portions of the NT (Acts 7; John 8). These polemical passages, in which the Jewish authorities are sharply castigated for rejecting Moses, the prophets, and the prophet like Moses, have their own devastating reception in the history of Christian anti-semitism. My interest in the concept of the prophet like Moses had been in the way that it was used to *include* later figures in the penumbra of Mosaic authority, but here I was faced with its deployment to *exclude*. When the coordination of later figures to Moses is contested, the genealogical model of prophecy excludes those who do not "listen" to the prophet. This points to the limitations in construing prophetic succession on the horizontal, genealogical plane, and perhaps emphasizes the ongoing relevance of the non-Deuteronomic, charismatic model of prophecy, that is, the recognition of the divine prerogative to continue to speak in fresh and "unauthorized" ways.

This dialectic of inclusion and exclusion, however, lies at the heart of why the concept of the prophet like Moses functions as a building block of normative tradition. All throughout the history of the prophet like Moses (and the history of scholarship on it), readers have responded to this dynamic. To cite a few examples: scholars on Jeremiah have argued that his representation as prophet like Moses functions either to *include* Jeremiah as Moses' equal successor or to *exclude* later post-Jeremianic prophetic claimants from a hearing; the end of Malachi *includes* the future coming of Elijah while *excluding* contemporary Mosaic prophetic claimants; Josephus *includes* a past succession of prophet-historians as successors of Moses and *excludes* contemporary figures such as Theudas, the Egyptian, and other "charlatans." Though I ended my investigation at a major juncture in the emergence of Christianity, one could go on to consider how the genealogical model of Mosaic prophecy with its dynamic of inclusion and exclusion exercises influence in rabbinic texts, Samaritan texts, and still later in the emergence of Islam. The deployment of Deuteronomy's strategy of linking later authoritative prophetic claims to Mosaic authority has never ceased in the history of Judaism and Christianity; in that sense, there can be no "end of prophecy" from a scholarly perspective. I began thinking about this project about a decade ago, aware of the eschatological interpretations of Deut 18:15, 18 at Qumran and in early Christianity, but with some trepidation about whether there would be enough to write about for a dissertation. Little did I realize that as I would bring this project to an end, I am keenly conscious

CONCLUSION: RETROSPECT AND PROSPECT   323

of how much more there is to say. It is my hope that this study of the origin and impact of Deut 18:9–22 provides reflections that will be helpful in exploring how its model of Mosaic prophecy contributed to the dynamic character of Early Judaism and nascent Christianity.

Bibliography

Achenbach, Reinhard. "'A Prophet like Moses' (Deuteronomy 18:15)—'No Prophet like Moses' (Deuteronomy 34:10): Some Observations on the Relation between the Pentateuch and the Latter Prophets." Pages 435–458 in *The Pentateuch: International Perspectives on Current Research*. Edited by T.B. Dozeman, K. Schmid, and B. Schwarz. Forschungen zum Alten Testament 78. Tübingen: Mohr Siebeck, 2011.

Achenbach, Reinhard. *Die Vollendung der Tora: Studien der Redaktiongeschichte des Numeribuches im Kontext von Hexateuch und Pentateuch*. Beihefte zur Zeitschrift für Altorientalische und Biblische Rechtsgeschichte 3. Wiesbaden: Harrassowitz Verlag, 2003.

Albertz, Rainer. *The History of Israelite Religion in the Old Testament Period*. Translated by John Bowden. Louisville, Ky.: Westminster/John Knox Press, 1994.

Albertz, Rainer. *Israel in Exile: The History and Literature of the Sixth Century BCE*. Translated by David Green. Society of Biblical Literature 3. Atlanta: Society of Biblical Literature, 2003.

Allen, Leslie. *Jeremiah: A Commentary*. Old Testament Library. Louisville, Westminster John Knox, 2008.

Allison, Dale C. *The New Moses: A Matthean Typology*. Minneapolis: Fortress Press, 1993.

Allison, Dale C. "Q's New Exodus and the Historical Jesus." Pages 395–428 in *The Sayings Source Q and the Historical Jesus*. Edited by A. Lindemann. Leuven: Leuven University, 2001.

Amir, Yehoshua. "Josephus on the Mosaic 'Constitution'." Pages 13–27 in *Politics and Theopolitics in the Bible and Postbiblical Literature*. Edited by H.G. Reventlow et al. Journal for the Study of the Old Testament Supplement Series 171. Sheffield: Sheffield Academic, 1994.

An, Hannah S. "The Prophet like Moses (Deut 18:15–18) and the Woman at the Well in Light of the Dead Sea Scrolls." *Expository Times* 127 (2016): 469–478.

Andersen, Francis I. and David Noel Freedman. *Amos: A New Translation with Introduction and Commentary*. Anchor Bible 24A. Garden City, N.Y.: Doubleday, 1989.

Andersen, Francis I. and David Noel Freedman. *Hosea: A New Translation with Introduction and Commentary*. Anchor Bible 24. Garden City, N.Y.: Doubleday, 1980.

Anderson, Paul N. *The Christology of the Fourth Gospel: Its Unity and Disunity in the Light of John 6*. Wissenschaftliche Untersuchungen zum Neuen Testament. 2 Reihe 78. Tübingen: Mohr, 1996.

Anderson, Paul N. "The Having-Sent-Me Father: Aspects of Agency, Encounter, and Irony in the Johannine Father-Son Relationship." *Semeia* 85 (1999): 33–57.

Anderson, Paul N. "The *Sitz im Leben* of the Johannine Bread of Life Discourse and Its Evolving Context." Pages 1–60 in *Critical Readings of John 6*. Edited by R.A. Culpepper. Biblical Interpretation Series 22. Leiden: Brill, 1997.

Ashton, John. *The Gospel of John and Christian Origins*. Minneapolis: Fortress, 2014.

Ashton, John. *Understanding the Fourth Gospel*. Second edition. Oxford: Oxford University, 2007.

Assis, Elie. "Moses, Elijah, and the Messianic Hope: A New Reading of Mal 3:22–24." *Zeitschrift für die alttestamentliche Wissenschaft* 123 (2011): 207–220.

Atkins, J.D. "Reassessing the Origins of Deuteronomic Prophecy: Early Moses Traditions in Deuteronomy 18:15–22." *Bulletin of Biblical Research* 23 (2013): 323–341.

Atkins, J.D. "The Trial of the People and the Prophet: John 5:30–47 and the True and False Prophet Traditions." *Catholic Biblical Quarterly* 75 (2013): 279–296.

Auld, Graeme. *Amos*. Old Testament Guides. Sheffield: JSOT Press, 1986.

Auld, Graeme. *Amos*. Old Testament Guides. "Jeremiah–Manasseh–Samuel: Significant Triangle? Or Vicious Circle?" Pages 1–9 in *Prophecy in the Book of Jeremiah*. Edited by H.M. Barstad and R.G. Kratz. Beihefte zur Zeitschrift für die alttestamentliche Wissenschaft 388. Berlin: Walter de Gruyter, 2009.

Auld, Graeme. "Prophets and Prophecy in Jeremiah and Kings." *Zeitschrift für die alttestamentliche Wissenschaft* 96 (1984): 66–82.

Aune, David E. *Prophecy in Early Christianity and the Ancient Mediterranean World*. Grand Rapids: Eerdmans, 1983.

Aune, David E. "The Use of ΠΡΟΦΗΤΗΣ in Josephus." *Journal of Biblical Literature* 101 (1982): 419–421.

Baden, Joel. *The Composition of the Pentateuch: Renewing the Documentary Hypothesis*. Anchor Yale Bible Reference Library. New Haven: Yale, 2012.

Barnett, Paul W. "The Jewish Sign Prophets—A.D. 40–70: Their Intentions and Origin." *New Testament Studies* 27 (1981): 679–697.

Barrett, C.K. *A Critical and Exegetical Commentary on the Acts of the Apostles*. Two volumes. International Critical Commentary. Edinburgh: T&T Clark, 1998.

Barrett, C.K. *The Gospel According to St. John: An Introduction with Commentary and Notes on the Greek Text*. Second edition. Philadelphia: Westminster, 1978.

Barstad, Hans M. "Prophecy at Qumran?" Pages 104–120 in *In the Last Days: On Jewish and Christian Apocalyptic and its Period*. Edited by K. Jeppesen, K. Nielsen, and B. Rosendal. Aarhus: Aarhus University, 1994.

Barstad, Hans M. "The Understanding of the Prophets in Deuteronomy." *Scandinavian Journal of the Old Testament* 8 (1994): 236–251.

Barton, John. *Oracles of God: Perceptions of Ancient Prophecy in Israel after the Exile*. London: Darton, Longman & Todd, 1986.

Bauckham, Richard. "Messianism According to the Gospel of John." Pages 34–68 in *Challenging Perspectives on the Gospel of John*. Edited by J. Lierman. Wissenschaftliche Untersuchungen zum Neuen Testament. 2 Reihe 219. Tübingen: Mohr Siebeck, 2006.

Bayer, Hans F. *Das Evangelium des Markus*. Historisch-Theologische Auslegung 5. Giessen: Brockhaus, 2008.

Becker, Adam H. and Annette Y. Reed, eds. *The Ways that Never Parted: Jews and Christians in Late Antiquity and in the Early Middle Ages.* Minneapolis: Fortress Press, 2007.

Beentjes, Pancratius. *The Book of Ben Sira in Hebrew: A Text Edition of All Extant Hebrew Manuscripts and a Synopsis of all Parallel Hebrew Ben Sira Texts.* Vetus Testamentum Supplement Series 68. Leiden: Brill, 1997.

Beentjes, Pancratius. "Prophets and Prophecy in the Book of Ben Sira." Pages 207–229 in *"Happy the One who Meditates on Wisdom" (Sir. 14,20): Collected Essays on the Book of Ben Sira.* Contributions to Biblical Exegesis and Theology 43. Leuven: Peeters, 2006.

Bernier, Jonathan. Aposynagōgos *and the Historical Jesus in John: Rethinking the Historicity of the Johannine Expulsion Passages.* Biblical Interpretation Series 122. Leiden: Brill, 2013.

Berthelot, Katell. "4QTestimonia as a Polemic Against the Prophetic Claims of John Hyrcanus." Pages 99–116 in *Prophecy after the Prophets? The Contribution of the Dead Sea Scrolls to the Understanding of Biblical and Extra-biblical Prophecy.* Edited by K. de Troyer and A. Lange. Contributions to Biblical Exegesis and Theology 52. Leuven: Peeters, 2009.

Berthelot, Katell. "The Image of Joshua in Jewish Sources from the Second Temple Period." *Meghillot* 8–9 (2010): 97–112. [Hebrew]

Bilde, Per. "*Contra Apionem* 1.28–56: Josephus' View of his Own Work in the Context of the Jewish Canon." Pages 94–114 in *Josephus' Contra Apionem: Studies in its Character and Context with a Latin Concordance to the Portion Missing in Greek.* Edited by L.H. Feldman and J.R. Levison. Arbeiten zur Geschichte des antiken Judentums und des Urchristentums 34. Leiden: Brill, 1996.

Bilde, Per. "Josephus and Jewish Apocalypticism." Pages 35–61 in *Understanding Josephus: Seven Perspectives.* Edited by Steve Mason. Journal for the Study of the Pseudepigrapha Supplement Series 32. Sheffield: Sheffield Academic, 1998.

Blenkinsopp, Joseph. *A History of Prophecy in Israel.* Revised and Enlarged edition. Louisville, Ky: Westminster John Knox Press, 1996.

Blenkinsopp, Joseph. "Judaeans, Jews, Children of Abraham." Pages 461–482 in *Judah and the Judaeans in the Achaemenid Period: Negotiating Identity in an International Context.* Edited by O. Lipschits, G. Knoppers, and M. Oeming. Winona Lake, Ind.: Eisenbrauns, 2011.

Blenkinsopp, Joseph. *Prophecy and Canon: A Contribution to the Study of Jewish Origins.* Center for the Study of Judaism and Christianity in Antiquity 3. University of Notre Dame Press, 1977.

Blenkinsopp, Joseph. "Prophecy and Priesthood in Josephus." *Journal of Jewish Studies* 25 (1974): 239–262.

Blenkinsopp, Joseph. " 'We Pay No Heed to Heavenly Voices': the 'End of Prophecy' and the Formation of the Canon." Pages 19–31 in *Biblical and Humane: A Festschrift for*

John F. Priest. Edited by L.B. Elder, D.L. Barr, and E.S. Malbon. Atlanta: Scholars Press, 1996.

Bloch, René. "Mose und die Scharlatane: Zum Vorwurf γόης καὶ ἀπατεών in *Contra Apionem* 2:145.161." Pages 142–157 in *Internationales Josephus-Kolloquium, Bruxelles 1998*. Edited by F. Siegert and J.U. Kalms. Münsteraner judaistische Studien 4. Münster: Lit, 1999.

Boesenberg, Dulcinea. "Moses in Luke-Acts." PhD dissertation. University of Notre Dame, 2013.

Boismard, Marie-Émile. *Moses or Jesus: An Essay in Johannine Christology*. Translated by B.T. Viviano. Bibliotheca ephemeridum theologicarum lovaniensium 84-A. Leuven: Leuven University, 1993.

Bond, Helen K. "Josephus and the New Testament." Pages 147–158 in *A Companion to Josephus*. Edited by H.H. Chapman and Z. Rodgers. Blackwell Companions to the Ancient World. Chicester, West Sussex, UK: John Wiley & Sons, 2016.

Borgen, Peder. *Bread from Heaven: An Exegetical Study of the Concept of Manna in the Gospel of John and the Writings of Philo*. Novum Testamentum Supplement Series 10. Leiden: Brill, 1965.

Borgen, Peder. "John 6: Tradition, Interpretation, and Composition." Pages 95–114 in *Critical Readings of John 6*. Edited by R.A. Culpepper. Biblical Interpretation Series 22. Leiden: Brill, 1997.

Bosman, H.L. "Redefined Prophecy as Deuteronomic Alternative to Divination in Deut 18:9–22." *Acta Theologica* 16 (1996): 1–23.

Bosshard, Erich and Reinhold G. Kratz. "Maleachi im Zwölfprophetenbuch." *Biblische Notizen* 52 (1990): 27–46.

Bovon, François. *Luke 1: A Commentary on the Gospel of Luke 1:1–9:50*. Hermeneia. Minneapolis: Fortress, 2002.

Bovon, François. *Luke 2: A Commentary on the Gospel of Luke 9:51–19:57*. Hermeneia. Minneapolis: Fortress, 2013.

Bovon, François. *Luke the Theologian: Fifty-Five Years of Research (1950–2005)*. Second, revised edition. Waco: Baylor University Press, 2006.

Bowley, James E. "Moses in the Dead Sea Scrolls: Living in the Shadow of God's Anointed." Pages 159–181 in *The Bible at Qumran: Text, Shape, and Interpretation*. Edited by P. Flint. Studies in the Dead Sea Scrolls and Related Literature. Grand Rapids: Eerdmans, 2001.

Boyarin, Daniel. *Border Lines: The Partition of Judaeo-Christianity*. Philadelphia: University of Pennsylvania Press, 2004.

Brin, Gershon. "The Laws of the Prophets in the Sect of the Judaean Desert: Studies in 4Q375." *Journal for the Study of the Pseudepigrapha* 10 (1992): 19–51.

Brooke, George J. "Moses in the Dead Sea Scrolls: Looking at Mount Nebo from Qumran." Pages 209–221 in *La Construction de la Figure de Moïse/The Construction of the*

Figure of Moses. Edited by T. Römer. Supplément no. 13 à *Transeuphratène.* Paris: Gabalda, 2007.

Brooke, George J. "Prophecy and Prophets in the Dead Sea Scrolls." Pages 151–165 in *Prophets, Prophecy, and Prophetic Texts in Second Temple Judaism.* Edited by M. Floyd and R. Haak. Library of Hebrew Bible/Old Testament Studies 427. New York: T&T Clark, 2006.

Brown, Raymond. *The Community of the Beloved Disciple: The Life, Loves, and Hates of an Individual Church in New Testament Times.* New York: Paulist, 1979.

Brown, Raymond. *The Gospel According to John: Introduction, Translation, and Notes.* Two volumes. Anchor Bible 29, 29A. New York: Doubleday, 1966–1970.

Brown, Raymond. *An Introduction to the Gospel of John.* Edited by F.J. Moloney. Anchor Bible Reference Library. Doubleday: New York, 2003.

Brueggemann, Walter. *A Commentary on Jeremiah: Exile and Homecoming.* Grand Rapids: Eerdmans, 1998.

Brueggemann, Walter. *Deuteronomy.* Abingdon Old Testament Commentary. Nashville: Abingdon Press, 2001.

Buber, Martin. *Moses: The Revelation and the Covenant.* New York: Harper, 1958.

Budd, Philip J. *Numbers.* Word Biblical Commentary 5. Waco: Word, 1984.

Bultmann, Rudolf. *The Gospel of John: A Commentary.* Translated by G.R. Beasley-Murray, R.W.N. Hoare and J.K. Riches. Philadelphia: Westminster, 1971.

Bultmann, Rudolf. *The History of the Synoptic Tradition.* Translated by John Marsh. Revised edition. New York: Harper & Row, 1976.

Bultmann, Rudolf. *Theology of the New Testament.* Translated by Kendrick Grobel. Two volumes. New York: Charles Scribner's Sons, 1951.

Calvin, John. *Commentary on the Acts of the Apostles.* Translated by H. Beveridge. Reprint. Two volumes. Grand Rapids: Baker, 1979 [1848].

Carr, David M. *The Formation of the Hebrew Bible: A New Reconstruction.* New York: Oxford, 2011.

Carroll, Robert P. "The Elijah-Elisha Sagas: Some Remarks on Prophetic Succession in Ancient Israel." *Vetus Testamentum* 19 (1969): 400–415.

Carroll, Robert P. *Jeremiah: A Commentary.* Old Testament Library. Philadelphia: Westminster, 1986.

Carroll, Robert P. *When Prophecy Failed: Cognitive Dissonance in the Prophetic Traditions of the Old Testament.* New York: Seabury Press, 1979.

Chapman, Stephen B. "A Canonical Approach to Old Testament Theology? Deuteronomy 34:10–12 and Malachi 3:22–24 as Programmatic Conclusions." *Horizons in Biblical Theology* 25 (2003): 121–145.

Chapman, Stephen B. "The Canon Debate: What It Is and Why It Matters." *Journal of Theological Interpretation* 4 (2010): 273–294.

Chapman, Stephen B. *The Law and the Prophets: a Study in Old Testament Canon Formation.* Forschungen zum Alten Testament 27. Tübingen: Mohr Siebeck, 2000.

Charles, R.H. *The Apocrypha and Pseudepigrapha of the Old Testament.* Two volumes. Oxford: Clarendon Press, 1913.

Charlesworth, James H. "Challenging the *Consensus Communis* Regarding Qumran Messianism (1QS; 4QS MSS)." Pages 120–134 in *Qumran-Messianism: Studies on the Messianic Expectations in the Dead Sea Scrolls.* Edited by J. Charlesworth, H. Lichtenberger, and G. Oegema. Tubingen: Mohr Siebeck, 1998.

Childs, Brevard. *Introduction to the Old Testament as Scripture.* Philadelphia: Fortress, 1979.

Clements, Ronald E. *Deuteronomy.* Old Testament Guides. Sheffield: JSOT Press, 1989.

Clements, Ronald E. *Prophecy and Tradition.* Atlanta: John Knox, 1975.

Coats, George W. *Moses: Heroic Man, Man of God.* Journal for the Study of the Old Testament Supplement Series 57. Sheffield: JSOT Press, 1988.

Coggins, R.J. *Haggai, Zechariah, Malachi.* Old Testament Guides. Sheffield: JSOT Press, 1987.

Coggins, R.J. "Prophecy—True and False." Pages 80–94 in *Of Prophets' Visions and the Wisdom of Sages: Festschrift for R.N. Whybray.* Edited by H.A. McKay and D.J.A. Clines. Journal for the Study of the Old Testament Supplement Series 162. Sheffield: JSOT Press, 1993.

Collins, Adela Yarbro. *Mark: A Commentary.* Hermeneia. Minneapolis: Fortress, 2007.

Collins, John J. *Apocalypse, Prophecy, and Pseudepigraphy: On Jewish Apocalyptic Literature.* Grand Rapids: Eerdmans, 2015.

Collins, John J. *The Scepter and the Star: Messianism in Light of the Dead Sea Scrolls.* Second Edition. Grand Rapids: Eerdmans, 2010.

Conzelmann, Hans. *Die Mitte der Zeit.* Tübingen: J.C.B. Mohr (Paul Siebeck), 1953. ET: *The Theology of St. Luke.* Translated by Geoffrey Buswell. New York: Harper & Row, 1961.

Cook, L. Stephen. *On the Question of the "Cessation of Prophecy" in Ancient Judaism.* Texts and Studies in Ancient Judaism 145. Tübingen: Mohr Siebeck, 2011.

Corley, Jeremy. "Canonical Assimilation in Ben Sira's Portrayal of Joshua and Samuel." Pages 57–77 in *Rewriting Biblical History: Essays on Chronicles and Ben Sira in Honor of Pancratius C. Beentjes.* Edited by J. Corley and H. van Grol. Deuterocanonical and Cognate Literature Series 7. Berlin: De Gruyter, 2011.

Corley, Jeremy. "A Numerical Structure in Sirach 44:1–50:24." *Catholic Biblical Quarterly* 69 (2007): 43–63.

Crenshaw, James L. *Prophetic Conflict: Its Effect upon Israelite Religion.* Berlin and New York: De Gruyter, 1971.

Croatto, J. Severino. "Jesus, Prophet like Elijah, and Prophet-Teacher like Moses in Luke-Acts." *Journal of Biblical Literature* 124 (2005): 451–465.

Cross, Frank M. *Canaanite Myth and Hebrew Epic.* Cambridge: Harvard University Press, 1973.

Cullmann, Oscar. *The Christology of the New Testament*. Tranlated by S.C. Guthrie and C.A. Hall. Revised edition. Philadelphia: Westminster, 1963.

Damgaard, Finn. "Brothers in Arms: Josephus' Portrait of Moses in the 'Jewish Antiquities' in the Light of His Own Self-Portraits in the 'Jewish War' and the 'Life.'" *Journal of Jewish Studies* 59 (2008): 218–235.

Daniels, Dwight R. *Hosea and Salvation History: The Early Traditions of Israel in Prophecy of Hosea*. Beihefte zur Zeitschrift für die alttestamentliche Wissenschaft 191. Berlin: de Gruyter, 1990.

Dearman, J. Andrew. *The Book of Hosea*. New International Commentary on the Old Testament. Grand Rapids: Eerdmans, 2010.

De Troyer, Kristin, Armin Lange and Lucas Schulte, eds. *Prophecy after the Prophets? The Contribution of the Dead Sea Scrolls to the Understanding of Biblical and Extra-biblical Prophecy*. Contributions to Biblical Exegesis and Theology 52. Leuven: Peeters, 2009.

Dexinger, Ferdinand. "Der 'Prophet wie Mose' in Qumran und bei den Samaritanern." Pages 97–111 in *Mélanges bibliques et orientaux en l'honneur de M Mathias Delcor*. Edited by A. Caquot, S. Légasse, and M. Tardieu. AOAT 215. Kevelaer: Butzon und Bercker; Neukirchen-Vluyn: Neukirchener Verlag, 1985.

Dexinger, Ferdinand. "Reflections on the Relationship between Qumran and Samaritan Messianology." Pages 83–99 in *Qumran-Messianism: Studies on the Messianic Expectations in the Dead Sea Scrolls*. Edited by J.H. Charlesworth, H. Lichtenberger, and G.S. Oegema. Tübingen: Mohr Siebeck, 1998.

Dibelius, Martin. *Studies in the Acts of the Apostles*. Translated by Mary Ling. London: SCM Press, 1956.

Di Lella, Alexander. "Ben Sira's Praise of the Ancestors of Old (Sir 44–49)." Pages 151–170 in *History and Identity: How Israel's Later Authors Viewed its Earlier History*. Deuterocanonical and Cognate Literature Yearbook. Berlin: de Gruyter, 2006.

Dillon, Richard J. *From Eye-Witnesses to Ministers of the Word: Tradition and Composition in Luke 24*. Analecta Biblica 82. Rome: Biblical Institute Press, 1978.

Dillon, Richard J. "The Prophecy of Christ and his Witnesses according to the Discourses of Acts." *New Testament Studies* 32 (1986): 544–556.

Dimant, Devorah. "Two Discourses from the Apocryphon of Joshua and Their Context (4Q378 3 i–ii)." *Revue de Qumran* 23 (2007): 43–61.

Dodd, C.H. *The Apostolic Preaching and its Developments*. London: Hodder, 1936.

Dodd, C.H. *Historical Tradition in the Fourth Gospel*. Cambridge: Cambridge University, 1963.

Donaldson, Terence. "Moses Typology and the Sectarian Nature of Early Christian Anti-Judaism: a Study in Acts 7." *Journal for the Study of the New Testament* 12 (1981): 27–52.

Driver, Samuel R. *A Critical and Exegetical Commentary on Deuteronomy*. International Critical Commentary. Edinburgh: T&T Clark, 1895.

Edenburg, Cynthia and Reinhard Müller. "A Northern Provenance for Deuteronomy? A Critical Review." *Hebrew Bible and Ancient Israel* 4 (2015): 148–161.

Eichrodt, Walther. *Theology of the Old Testament.* Translated by J.A. Baker. 2 volumes. Old Testament Library. London: SCM Press, 1961.

Epp-Tiessen, Daniel. *Concerning the Prophets: True and False Prophecy in Jeremiah 23:9–29:32.* Eugene, Ore.: Pickwick, 2012.

Eynikel, Erik. "The Portrait of Mannaseh and the Deuteronomistic History." Pages 233–261 in *Deuteronomy and Deuteronomic Literature: Festschrift C.H.W. Brekelmans.* Edited by M. Vervenne and J. Lust. Louvain: Peeters, 1997.

Fabry, Heinz-Josef. "Mose, der 'Gesalbte JHWHs': Messianische Aspekte der Mose-Interpretation in Qumran." Pages 129–142 in *Moses in Biblical and Extra-Biblical Traditions.* Edited by A. Graupner and M. Wolter. Beihefte zur Zeitschrift für die alttestamentliche Wissenschaft 372. Berlin: de Gruyter, 2007.

Fallon, F. "Eupolemus: A New Translation and Introduction." In *The Old Testament Pseudepigrapha.* Edited by J. Charlesworth. Two volumes. Garden City: Doubleday, 1983. Volume 2: 861–872.

Farber, Zev I. "Images of Joshua: the Construction of Memory in Cultural Identities." Ph.d. Dissertation. Emory, 2013.

Farber, Zev I. *Images of Joshua in the Bible and Their Reception.* Beihefte zur Zeitschrift für die alttestamentliche Wissenschaft 457. Berlin: De Gruyter, 2016.

Feldman, Ariel. *The Rewritten Joshua Scrolls from Qumran: Texts, Translations, and Commentary.* Beihefte zur Zeitschrift für die alttestamentliche Wissenschaft 438. Berlin: De Gruyter, 2013.

Feldman, Ariel. "The Sinai Revelation according to 4Q377 (*Apocryphal Pentateuch B*)." *Dead Sea Discoveries* 18 (2011): 155–172.

Feldman, Louis H. *Judean Antiquities 1–4, Translation and Commentary.* Volume 3 of *Flavius Josephus: Translation and Commentary.* Edited by S. Mason. Leiden: Brill, 2000

Feldman, Louis H. "Parallel Lives of Two Lawgivers: Josephus' Moses and Plutarch's Lycurgus." Pages 209–242 in *Flavius Josephus and Flavian Rome.* Edited by J. Edmondson et al. Oxford: Oxford University, 2005.

Feldman, Louis H. *Philo's Portrayal of Moses in the Context of Ancient Judaism.* Christianity and Judaism in Antiquity Series 15. Notre Dame: University of Notre Dame Press, 2007.

Feldman, Louis H. "Prophets and Prophecy in Josephus." *Journal of Theological Studies* 41 (1990): 386–422.

Finsterbusch, Karin. *Deuteronomium: Eine Einführung.* Göttingen: Vandenhoeck & Ruprecht, 2012.

Fischer, Georg. "Jeremiah—'The Prophet like Moses?'" Pages 45–66 in *The Book of Jeremiah: Composition, Reception and Interpretation.* Edited by Jack Lundbom, Craig

A. Evans and Bradford Anderson. Supplements to Vetus Testamentum 178. Leiden: Brill, 2018.

Fishbane, Michael. *Biblical Interpretation in Ancient Israel*. Oxford: Oxford University, 1988.

Fitzmyer, Joseph. *The Acts of the Apostles*. Anchor Bible 31. New York: Doubleday, 1998.

Fitzmyer, Joseph. *The Gospel according to Luke: Introduction, Translation, and Notes*. Two Volumes. Anchor Bible 28–28A. Garden City, N.Y.: Doubleday, 1981–1985.

Fletcher-Louis, Crispin H.T. *All the Glory of Adam: Liturgical Anthropology in the Dead Sea Scrolls*. Studies in the Texts of the Desert of Judah 42. Leiden: Brill, 2002.

Floyd, Michael H. *Minor Prophets, Part 2*. Forms of Old Testament Literature 22. Grand Rapids: Eerdmans, 2000.

Floyd, Michael H. "The Production of Prophetic Books in the Early Second Temple Period." Pages 276–297 in *Prophets, Prophecy, and Prophetic Texts in Second Temple Judaism*. Edited by M.H. Floyd and R.D. Haak. Library of Hebrew Bible/Old Testament Studies 427. New York: T&T Clark, 2006.

Floyd, Michael H. and Robert D. Haak, eds. *Prophets, Prophecy, and Prophetic Texts in Second Temple Judaism*. Library of Hebrew Bible/Old Testament Studies 427. New York: T&T Clark, 2006.

Forbes, Christopher. *Prophecy and Inspired Speech in Early Christianity and its Hellenistic Environment*. Wissenschaftliche Untersuchungen zum Neuen Testament. 2 Reihe 75. Tübingen: Mohr Siebeck, 1995.

Fortna, Robert. *The Fourth Gospel and its Predecessor: From Narrative Source to Present Gospel*. Philadelphia: Fortress, 1988.

Fortna, Robert. *The Gospel of Signs: A Reconstruction of the Narrative Source Underlying the Fourth Gospel*. Society of New Testament Studies Monograph Series 11. Cambridge: Cambridge University, 1970.

Fredriksen, Paula. *From Jesus to Christ: The Origins of the New Testament Images of Christ*. Second Edition. New Haven: Yale University Press, 2000.

Freedman, David N. "Headings in the Books of the Eighth-Century Prophets." Pages 9–26 in *Festschrift in Honor of Leona Glidden Running*. Edited by W.H. Shea. Andrews University Seminary Studies 25. Berrien Springs, Mich.: Andrews University Press, 1987.

Fuller, Reginald H. *The Foundations of New Testament Christology*. New York: Charles Scribner's Sons, 1965.

García López, Félix. "Deut 34, Dtr History and the Pentateuch." Pages 47–61 in *Studies in Deuteronomy: In Honour of C.J. Labuschagne on the Occasion of His 65th Birthday*. Edited by Florentino García Martínez et al. Vetus Testamentum Supplement Series 53. Leiden: Brill, 1994.

Glasson, T.F. *Moses in the Fourth Gospel*. Studies in Biblical Theology. Naperville, Ill.: Alec R. Allenson, 1963.

Glazier-McDonald, Beth. *Malachi: The Divine Messenger*. Society of Biblical Literature Dissertation Series 68. Atlanta: Scholars Press, 1987.

Goldstein, Jonathan. *1Maccabees: A New Translation with Introduction and Commentary*. Anchor Bible 41. Garden City, N.Y.: Doubleday, 1976.

Goodman, Martin. "Texts, Scribes, and Power in Roman Judaea." Pages 99–108 in *Literacy and Power in the Ancient World*. Edited by A. Bowman and G. Woolf. Cambridge: Cambridge University, 1994.

Goshen-Gottstein, Alon. "Ben Sira's Praise of the Fathers: A Canon-Conscious Reading." Pages 235–267 in *Ben Sira's God: Proceedings of the International Ben Sira Conference Durham—Ushaw College 2001*. Edited by O. Kaiser. Beihefte zur Zeitschrift für die alttestamentliche Wissenschaft 321. Berlin: de Gruyter, 2002.

Grabbe, Lester L. "Thus Spake the Prophet Josephus ...: The Jewish Historian on Prophets and Prophecy." Pages 240–247 in *Prophets, Prophecy, and Prophetic Texts in Second Temple Judaism*. Edited by M.H. Floyd and R.D. Haak. Library of Hebrew Bible/Old Testament Studies 427. New York: T&T Clark, 2006.

Gray, George B. *A Critical and Exegetical Commentary on Numbers*. International Critical Commentary. Edinburgh: T&T Clark, 1903.

Gray, John. *I & II Kings: A Commentary*. Second revised edition. Old Testament Library. Louisville: Westminster/John Knox Press, 1971.

Gray, Rebecca. *Prophetic Figures in Late Second Temple Jewish Palestine: The Evidence from Josephus*. New York: Oxford University Press, 1993.

Greenspahn, Frederick E. "Why Prophecy Ceased." *Journal of Biblical Literature* 108 (1989): 37–49.

Grossman, Maxine. "Priesthood as Authority: Interpretive Competition in First Century Judaism and Christianity." Pages 117–131 in James Davila (ed.), *The Dead Sea Scrolls as Background to Postbiblical Judaism and Early Christianity: Papers from an international conference at St Andrews in 2001*. Studies on the Texts of the Desert of Judah 46. Leiden and Boston: Brill, 2003.

Gunneweg, Antonius H.J. "Das Gesetz und die Propheten: Eine Auslegung von Ex 33,7–11; Num 11,4–12,8; Dtn 31,14 f.; 34,10." *Zeitschrift für die alttestamentliche Wissenschaft* 102, no. 2 (1990): 169–180.

Haenchen, Ernst. *The Acts of the Apostles: A Commentary*. Translated by Bernard Noble and Gerald Shinn. Philadelphia: Westminster, 1971.

Hahn, Ferdinand. *The Titles of Jesus in Christology: Their History in Early Christianity*. Translated by Harold Knight and George Ogg. London: The Lutterworth Press, 1969.

Halpern Amaru, Betsy. "The Killing of the Prophets: Unraveling a Midrash." *Hebrew Union College Annual* 54 (1983): 153–180.

Hamori, Esther J. *Women's Divination in Biblical Literature: Prophecy, Necromancy, and Other Arts of Knowledge*. Anchor Yale Bible Reference Library. New Haven: Yale University Press, 2015.

Haran, Menahem. *Temples and Temple-Service in Ancient Israel: an Inquiry into the Character of Cult Phenomena and the Historical Setting of the Priestly School*. Oxford: Clarendon Press, 1977.

Harnack, Adolf von. *The Mission and Expansion of Christianity in the First Three Centuries*. Translated by James Moffatt. Two volumes. Second edition. New York: G.P. Putnam's Sons, 1908 [German original 1902].

Harrington, Daniel J. "Pseudo-Philo: A New Translation and Introduction." In *The Old Testament Pseudepigrapha*. Edited by J. Charlesworth. Garden City: Doubleday, 1983. Volume 2:297–377.

Harstine, Stan. *Moses as a Character in the Fourth Gospel: A Study of Ancient Reading Techniques*. Journal for the Study of the New Testament Supplement Series 229. Sheffield: Sheffield Academic, 2002.

Heller, Roy L. *Power, Politics, and Prophecy: The Character of Samuel and the Deuteronomistic Evaluation of Prophecy*. Library of Hebrew Bible/Old Testament Studies 440. London: T&T Clark, 2006.

Hengel, Martin. *Acts and the History of Earliest Christianity*. Translated by John Bowden. Philadelphia: Fortress, 1980.

Hengel, Martin. *Judaism and Hellenism: Studies in their Encounter in Palestine during the Early Hellenistic Period*. Translated by J. Bowden. Two volumes. Philadelphia, Fortress Press, 1974.

Henze, Matthias. "Invoking the Prophets in Zechariah and Ben Sira." Pages 120–134 in *Prophets, Prophecy, and Prophetic Texts in Second Temple Judaism*. Edited by M. Floyd and R. Haak. Library of Hebrew Bible/Old Testament Studies 427. New York: T&T Clark, 2006.

Hibbard, James T. "True and False Prophecy: Jeremiah's Revision of Deuteronomy." *Journal for the Study of the Old Testament* 35 (2011): 339–358.

Hill, Andrew E. *Malachi: A New Translation with Introduction and Commentary*. Anchor Bible 25D. New York: Doubleday, 1998.

Hill, Craig. *Hellenists and Hebrews: Reappraising Division within the Earliest Church*. Minneapolis: Fortress, 1992.

Hobbs, T.R. *2 Kings*. Word Biblical Commentary 13. Dallas: Word, 1986.

Holladay, William L. "Background of Jeremiah's Self-Understanding: Moses, Samuel, and Psalm 22." *Journal of Biblical Literature* 83 (1964): 153–164.

Holladay, William L. *A Concise Hebrew and Aramaic Lexicon of the Old Testament*. Grand Rapids: Eerdmans, 1988.

Holladay, William L. "Elusive Deuteronomists, Jeremiah, and Proto-Deuteronomy." *Catholic Biblical Quarterly* 66 (2004): 55–77.

Holladay, William L. *Jeremiah 1: A Commentary on the Book of the Prophet Jeremiah Chapters 1–25*. Hermeneia. Philadelphia: Fortress, 1986.

Holladay, William L. *Jeremiah 2: A Commentary on the Book of the Prophet Jeremiah Chapters 26–52*. Hermeneia. Minneapolis: Fortress, 1989.

Holladay, William L. "Jeremiah and Moses: Further Observations." *Journal of Biblical Literature* 85 (1966): 17–27.

Hooker, Morna. "'Beginning from Moses and from all the Prophets.'" Pages 216–230 in *From Jesus to John: Essays on Jesus and New Testament Christology in Honour of Marinus de Jonge*. Edited by M.C. de Boer. Journal for the Study of the New Testament Supplement Series 84. Sheffield: JSOT Press, 1993.

Horsley, Richard A. "'Like One of the Prophets of Old': Two Types of Popular Prophets at the Time of Jesus." *Catholic Biblical Quarterly* 47 (1985): 435–463.

Horsley, Richard A. "A Prophet like Moses and Elijah: Popular Memory and Cultural Patterns in Mark." Pages 166–190 in *Performing the Gospel: Orality, Memory, and Mark*. Edited by R.A. Horsley, J.M. Draper, and J.M. Foley. Minneapolis: Fortress, 2006.

Horsley, Richard A. *Scribes, Visionaries, and the Politics of Second Temple Judea*. Louisville: Westminster John Knox, 2007.

Horsley, Richard A. and John S. Hanson. *Bandits, Prophets, and Messiahs: Popular Movements in the Time of Jesus*. New Voices in Biblical Studies. Minneapolis: Winston Press, 1985.

Hossfeld, Frank Lothar and Ivo Meyer. *Prophet gegen Prophet: Eine Analyse der alttestamentlichen Texte zum Thema: Wahre und falsche Propheten*. Biblische Beitrag 9. Fribourg: Verlag Schweizerisches Katholisches Bibelwerk, 1973.

Hugenberger, Gordon P. "The Servant of the Lord in the 'Servant Songs' of Isaiah." Pages 105–140 in *The Lord's Anointed: Interpretation of Old Testament Messianic Texts*. Edited by P.E. Satterthwaite, R.S. Hess, and G.J. Wenham. Carlisle: Paternoster, 1995.

Hurvitz, Avi. "The Linguistic Status of Ben Sira as a Link between the Biblical and the Mishnaic Hebrew: Lexicographical Aspects." Pages 71–85 in *The Hebrew of the Dead Sea Scrolls and Ben Sira*. Edited by T. Muraoka and J.F. Elwolde. Studies on the Texts of the Desert of Judah 26. Leiden: Brill, 1997.

Hyatt, J. Philip. "The Deuteronomic Edition of Jeremiah." Pages 247–267 in *A Prophet to the Nations: Essays in Jeremiah Studies*. Edited by L.G. Perdue and B.W. Kovacs. Winona Lake: Eisenbrauns, 1984.

Hyatt, J. "Jeremiah and Deuteronomy." Pages 113–127 in *A Prophet to the Nations: Essays in Jeremiah Studies*. Edited by L.G. Perdue and B.W. Kovacs. Winona Lake: Eisenbrauns, 1984 [first published 1942].

Isser, Stanley J. *The Dositheans: A Samaritan Sect in Late Antiquity*. Studies in Judaism in Late Antiquity 17. Leiden: Brill, 1976.

Jacobson, Howard. *A Commentary on Pseudo-Philo's* Liber Antiquitatum Biblicarum: *With Latin Text and English Translation*. Two volumes. Arbeiten zur Geschichte des antiken Judentums und des Urchristentums 31. Leiden: Brill, 1996.

Jaffee, Martin S. *Torah in the Mouth: Writing and Oral Tradition in Palestinian Judaism, 200 BCE–400 CE*. Oxford: University Press, 2001.

Janzen, J. Gerald. *Studies in the Text of Jeremiah.* Harvard Semitic Monographs 9. Cambridge: Harvard University Press, 1973.

Jassen, Alex P. *Mediating the Divine: Prophecy and Revelation in the Dead Sea Scrolls and Second Temple Judaism.* Studies on the Texts of the Desert of Judah 68. Leiden; Boston: Brill, 2007.

Jassen, Alex P. "The Presentation of the Ancient Prophets as Lawgivers at Qumran." *Journal of Biblical Literature* 127 (2008): 307–337.

Jeremias, Joachim. "Μωυσῆς." *Theological Dictionary of the New Testament.* Edited by G. Kittel and G. Friedrich. Translated by G.W. Bromiley. 10 vols. Grand Rapids, 1964–1976. Volume 4: 848–873.

Jervell, Jacob. *The Theology of the Acts of the Apostles.* Cambridge: Cambridge University, 1996.

Jobling, David. *The Sense of Biblical Narrative: Three Structural Analyses in the Old Testament (1 Samuel 13–31, Numbers 11–12, 1 Kings 17–18).* Journal for the Study of the Old Testament Supplement Series 7. Sheffield: University of Sheffield, 1978.

Johnson, Luke Timothy. *The Acts of the Apostles.* Sacra Pagina 5. Collegeville: Liturgical Press, 1992.

Johnson, Luke Timothy. *The Literary Function of Possessions in Luke-Acts.* Society of Biblical Literature Dissertation Series 39. Missoula, Mont.: Scholars Press, 1977.

Jones, Barry Alan. *The Formation of the Book of the Twelve: A Study in Text and Canon.* Society of Biblical Literature Dissertation Series 149. Atlanta: Scholars Press, 1995.

Jones, Gwilym H. *1 & 11 Kings.* Two volumes. New Century Bible Commentary. Grand Rapids: Eerdmans, 1984.

Jong, Matthijs J. de. "The Fallacy of True and False in Prophecy Illustrated by Jer 28:8–9." *Journal of Hebrew Scriptures* 12.10 (2012): 1–29.

Jong, Matthijs J. "Why Jeremiah is Not Among the Prophets: An Analysis of the Terms נביא and נבאים in the Book of Jeremiah." *Journal for the Study of the Old Testament* 35 (2011): 483–510.

Jonge, Marinus de. *Jesus: Stranger From Heaven and Son of God: Jesus Christ and the Christians in Johannine Perspective.* Edited and translated by John. E. Steely. Society of Biblical Literature Sources for Biblical Study 11. Missoula, Mont.: Scholars Press, 1977.

Jülicher, A. *Einleitung in das Neue Testament.* Grundriss der Theologischen Wissenschaften 3/1. Fifth/Sixth editions. Tubingen: J.C.B. Mohr (Paul Siebeck), 1913.

Kaufmann, Yehezkel. *History of the Religion of Israel.* Translated by C.W. Efroymson. Four volumes. New York: Ktav, 1977.

Keener, Craig. *Acts: An Exegetical Commentary.* Four volumes. Grand Rapids: Baker Academic, 2012–2015.

Keener, Craig. *The Gospel of John: A Commentary.* Two volumes. Peabody, Mass.: Hendrickson, 2003.

Kelle, Brad E. "Hosea 4–14 in Twentieth-Century Scholarship." *Currents in Biblical Research* 8 (2010): 314–375.

Kessler, Rainer. *Maleachi*. Herders Theologische Kommentar zum Alten Testament. Freiburg: Herder, 2011.

Kingsbury, Jack Dean. "Jesus As the 'Prophetic Messiah' in Luke's Gospel." Pages 29–42 in *The Future of Christology: Essays in Honor of Leander E. Keck*. Edited by A.J. Malherbe and W.A. Meeks. Philadelphia: Fortress, 1993.

Klawans, Jonathan. *Josephus and the Theologies of Ancient Judaism*. New York: Oxford University, 2012.

Knibb, Michael A. "Apocalypticism and Messianism." Pages 403–432 in *The Oxford Handbook of the Dead Sea Scrolls*. Edited by T.H. Lim and J.J. Collins. Oxford: Oxford University, 2010.

Knohl, Israel. *The Sanctuary of Silence: The Priestly Torah and the Holiness School*. Minneapolis: Fortress Press, 1995.

Knohl, Israel. "Two Aspects of the 'Tent of Meeting'." Pages 73–79 in *Tehillah le-Moshe: Biblical and Judaic Studies in Honor of Moshe Greenberg*. Edited by Mordechai Cogan, Barry L. Eichler, and Jeffrey H. Tigay. Winona Lake, Ind: Eisenbrauns, 1997.

Knoppers, Gary N. "The Deuteronomist and the Deuteronomic Law of the King: A Reexamination of a Relationship." *Zeitschrift für die alttestamentliche Wissenschaft* 108 (1996): 329–346.

Knoppers, Gary N. "The Northern Context of the Law-Code in Deuteronomy." *Hebrew Bible and Ancient Israel* 4 (2015): 162–183.

Knoppers, Gary N. "Rethinking the Relationship between Deuteronomy and the Deuteronomistic History: The Case of Kings." *Catholic Biblical Quarterly* 63 (2001): 393–415.

Knoppers, Gary N. " 'There Was None Like Him': Incomparability in the Books of Kings." *Catholic Biblical Quarterly* 54 (1992): 411–431.

Knoppers, Gary N. *Two Nations under God: The Deuteronomic History of Solomon and the Dual Monarchies*. Two volumes. Harvard Semitic Monographs 52–53. Atlanta; Scholars Press, 1993–1994.

Koet, Bart J. *Five Studies on Interpretation of Scripture in Luke-Acts*. Studiorum Novi Testamenti Auxilia 14. Leuven: Leuven University Press, 1989.

Kraus, Wolfgang. "Die Bedeutung von Dtn 18,15–18 für das Verständnis Jesu als Prophet." *Zeitschrift für die neutestamentliche Wissenschaft* 90 (1999): 153–176.

Lamb, David T. " 'A Prophet Instead of You' (1 Kings 19.16): Elijah, Elisha, and Prophetic Succession." Pages 172–187 in *Prophecy and Prophets in Ancient Israel*. Edited by John Day. Library of Hebrew Bible/Old Testament Studies 531. London: T&T Clark, 2010.

Lange, Armin. *Vom prophetischen Wort zur prophetischen Tradition: Studien zur Traditions- und Redaktionsgeschichte innerprophetischer Konflikte in der Hebräischen Bibel*. FAT 34. Tübingen: Mohr Siebeck, 2002.

Leivestad, Ragnar. "Das Dogma von der prophetenlosen Zeit." *New Testament Studies* 19 (1973): 288–299.

Leuchter, Mark. "Samuel: A Prophet Like Moses or a Priest Like Moses?" Pages 147–168 in *Israelite Prophecy and the Deuteronomistic History: Portrait, Reality, and the Formation of a History*. Edited by Mignon R. Jacobs and Raymond F. Person Jr. Ancient Israel and its Literature 14. Atlanta: Society of Biblical Literature, 2013.

Levine, Amy-Jill. "Luke and the Jewish Religion." *Interpretation* 68 (2014): 389–402.

Levine, Baruch A. *Numbers 1–20: A New Translation with Introduction and Commentary*. Anchor Bible 4. New York: Doubleday, 1993.

Levinson, Bernard. *Deuteronomy and the Hermeneutics of Legal Innovation*. New York: Oxford, 1997.

Levinson, Bernard. "The Reconceptualization of Kingship in Deuteronomy and the Deuteronomistic History's Transformation of Torah." *Vetus Testamentum* 51 (2001): 511–534.

Levison, John R. "Did the Spirit Withdraw from Israel? An Evaluation of the Earliest Jewish Data." *New Testament Studies* 43 (1997): 35–57.

Levison, John R. "Philo's Personal Experience and the Persistence of Prophecy." Pages 194–209 in *Prophets, Prophecy, and Prophetic Texts in Second Temple Judaism*. Edited by M. Floyd and R. Haak. Library of Hebrew Bible/Old Testament Studies 427. New York: T&T Clark, 2006.

Levison, John R. "Prophecy in Ancient Israel: The Case of the Ecstatic Elders." *Catholic Biblical Quarterly* 65 (2003): 503–521.

Levison, John R. *The Spirit in First Century Judaism*. Arbeiten zur Geschichte des antiken Judentums und des Urchristentums 29. Leiden: Brill, 1997.

Levison, John R. "Two Types of Ecstatic Prophecy according to Philo." *Studia Philonica Annual* 6 (1994): 83–89.

Lierman, John. "The Mosaic Pattern of John's Christology." Pages 210–234 in *Challenging Perspectives on the Gospel of John*. Edited by J. Lierman. Wissenschaftliche Untersuchungen zum Neuen Testament. 2 Reihe 219. Tübingen: Mohr Siebeck, 2006.

Lierman, John. *The New Testament Moses: Christian Perceptions of Moses and Israel in the Setting of Jewish Religion*. Wissenschaftliche Untersuchungen zum Neuen Testament. 2 Reihe 173. Tübingen: Mohr Siebeck, 2004.

Lim, Timothy H. *The Formation of the Jewish Canon*. Anchor Yale Bible Reference Library. New Haven: Yale University, 2011.

Lincicum, David. *Paul and the Early Jewish Encounter with Deuteronomy*. Wissenschaftliche Untersuchungen zum Neuen Testament. 2 Reihe 384. Tübingen: Mohr Siebeck, 2010.

Lincoln, Andrew. *The Gospel According to Saint John*. Black's New Testament Commentary 4. London: Continuum, 2005.

Lindars, Barnabas. *The Gospel of John*. New Century Bible. London: Marshall, Morgan, and Scott, 1972.

Litwa, M. David. "The Deification of Moses in Philo of Alexandria." *Studia Philonica Annual* 26 (2014): 1–27.

Lohfink, Norbert. "Das Deuteronomium: Jahwegesetz oder Mosegesetz?" *Theologie und Philosophie* 65 (1990): 387–391.

Lohfink, Norbert. "Die Sicherung der Wirksamkeit des Gotteswortes durch das Prinzip der Schriftlichkeit der Tora und durch das Prinzip der Gewaltenteilung nach dem Ämtergesetzen des Buches Deuteronomiums (Dt 16,18–18,22)." Pages 143–155 in *Testimonium Veritati: Festschrift W. Kampf*. Edited by H. Wolter. Frankfurter Theologische Studien 7. Frankfurt am Main: Knecht, 1971.

Lohfink, Norbert. "Was There a Deuteronomistic Movement?" Pages 36–66 in *Those Elusive Deuteronomists: The Phenomenon of Pan-Deuteronomism*. Edited by L.S. Schearing and S.L. McKenzie. Journal for the Study of the Old Testament Supplement Series 268. Sheffield: Sheffield Academic, 1999.

Long, Burke O. *2 Kings*. Forms of Old Testament Literature 10. Grand Rapids: Eerdmans, 1991.

Lübbe, John. "A Reinterpretation of 4QTestimonia." *Revue de Qumran* 12 (1986): 187–197.

Lundbom, Jack. *Deuteronomy: A Commentary*. Grand Rapids: Eerdmans, 2013.

Lundbom, Jack. *Jeremiah 21–36: A New Translation with Introduction and Commentary*. Anchor Bible 21B. New York: Doubleday, 2004.

MacDonald, Nathan. "Issues in the Dating of Deuteronomy: A Response to Juha Pakkala." *Zeitschrift für die alttestamentliche Wissenschaft* 122 (2010): 431–435.

Mack, Burton L. *Wisdom and the Hebrew Epic: Ben Sira's Hymn in Praise of the Fathers*. Chicago Studies in the History of Judaism. Chicago: University of Chicago, 1985.

MacIntosh, A.A. *A Critical and Exegetical Commentary on Hosea*. International Critical Commentary. Edinburgh: T&T Clark, 1997.

Maier, Christl. *Jeremia als Lehrer der Tora: Soziale Gebote des Deuteronomiums in Fortschreibungen des Jeremiabuches*. Forschungen zur Religion und Literatur des Alten und Neuen Testaments 196. Göttingen: Vandenhoeck & Ruprecht, 2002.

Maier, Christl. "Jeremiah as Teacher of Torah." *Interpretation* 62 (2008): 22–32.

Makiello, Phoebe. "Was Moses Considered to be an Angel by those at Qumran?" Pages 115–127 in *Moses in Biblical and Extra-Biblical Traditions*. Edited by A. Graupner and M. Wolter. Beihefte zur Zeitschrift für die alttestamentliche Wissenschaft 372. Berlin: de Gruyter, 2007.

Marcus, Joel. *Mark 1–8: A New Translation with Introduction and Commentary*. Anchor Yale Bible 27. New Haven, Yale University Press, 2000.

Markl, Dominik. "Moses Prophetenrolle in Dtn 5; 18; 34. Structurelle Wendepunkte von rechtshermeneutischem Gewicht." Pages 51–68 in *Deuteronomium—Tora für eine neue Generation*. Edited by G. Fischer, D. Markl, and S. Paganini. Beihefte zur Zeitschrift für Altorientalische und Biblische Rechtsgeschichte 17. Wiesbaden: Harrassowitz Verlag, 2011.

Maronde, Christopher A. "Moses in the Gospel of John." *Concordia Theological Quarterly* 77 (2013): 23–44.
Marshall, I. Howard. *The Book of Acts: An Introduction and Commentary*. Tyndale New Testament Commentaries. Downers Grove: InterVarsity, 1980.
Martyn, J. Louis. *History and Theology in the Fourth Gospel*. Third edition. New Testament Library. Louisville: Westminster John Knox, 2003.
Mason, Rex. *The Books of Haggai, Zechariah, and Malachi*. Cambridge: Cambridge University, 1977.
Mason, Steve. "Introduction: Josephus as Author and Thinker." Pages 11–18 in *Understanding Josephus: Seven Perspectives*. Edited by Steve Mason. Journal for the Study of the Pseudepigrapha Supplement Series 32. Sheffield: Sheffield Academic, 1998.
Mason, Steve. "Josephus and His Twenty-Two Book Canon." Pages 110–127 in *The Canon Debate*. Edited by L.M. McDonald and J.A. Sanders. Peabody, Mass.: Hendrickson, 2002.
Mason, Steve. *Josephus and the New Testament*. Second edition. Peabody, Mass.: Hendrickson, 2003.
Mason, Steve. " 'Should Any Wish to Enquire Further' (*Ant*. 1.25): The Aim and Audience of Josephus' *Judean Antiquities/Life*." Pages 64–103 in *Understanding Josephus: Seven Perspectives*. Edited by Steve Mason. Journal for the Study of the Pseudepigrapha Supplement Series 32. Sheffield: Sheffield Academic, 1998.
Mastnjak, Nathan. *Deuteronomy and the Emergence of Textual Authority in Jeremiah*. Forschungen zum Alten Testament. 2 Reihe 87. Tübingen: Mohr Siebeck, 2016.
Mattill, A.J. "Johannine Communities Behind the Fourth Gospel: Georg Richter's Analysis." *Theological Studies* 38 (1976): 294–315.
Mayes, Andrew D.H. *Deuteronomy*. New Century Bible Commentary. Grand Rapids: Eerdmans, 1981.
McBride, S. Dean. "Polity of the Covenant People: The Book of Deuteronomy." *Interpretation* 41 (1987): 229–244.
McLaren, James S. "Josephus and the Priesthood." Pages 273–281 in *A Companion to Josephus*. Edited by H.H. Chapman and Z. Rodgers. Blackwell Companions to the Ancient World. Chicester, West Sussex, UK: John Wiley & Sons, 2016.
McKane, William. *A Critical and Exegetical Commentary on Jeremiah*. Two volumes. International Critical Commentary. Edinburgh: T&T Clark, 1986–1996.
McKeating, Henry. "Ezekiel the 'Prophet Like Moses'." *Journal for the Study of the Old Testament* 61 (1994): 97–109.
McWhirter, Jocelyn. *Rejected Prophets: Jesus and his Witnesses in Luke-Acts*. Minneapolis: Fortress, 2013.
Meeks, Wayne A. *The Prophet-King: Moses Traditions and the Johannine Christology*. Novum Testamentum Supplement Series 14. Leiden: Brill, 1967.
Meier, John P. *A Marginal Jew: Rethinking the Historical Jesus*. Five volumes. Anchor Yale Bible Reference Library. New Haven: Yale University, 1991–2015.

Metso, Sarianna. *The Community Rule: A Critical Edition with Translation*. Early Judaism and its Literature 51. Atlanta: SBL Press, 2019.

Metso, Sarianna. *The Textual Development of the Qumran Community Rule*. Studies in the Texts of the Desert of Judah 21. Leiden: Brill, 1997.

Metzger, Bruce. *A Textual Commentary on the Greek New Testament*. United Bible Societies, 1971.

Meyer, Rudolf. "Prophecy and Prophets in the Judaism of the Hellenistic-Roman Period." *Theological Dictionary of the New Testament*. Edited by G. Kittel and G. Friedrich. Translated by G.W. Bromiley. 10 vols. Grand Rapids, 1964–1976. Volume 6: 812–828.

Meyers Carol L. and Eric M. Meyers. *Haggai, Zechariah 1–8: A New Translation with Introduction and Commentary*. Anchor Bible 25B. New York: Doubleday, 1987.

Michaels, J. Ramsey. *The Gospel of John*. New International Commentary on the New Testament. Grand Rapids: Eerdmans, 2010.

Milgrom, Jacob. *Numbers = [Ba-midbar]: The Traditional Hebrew Text with the New JPS Translation*. Jewish Publication Society Torah Commentary 4. Philadelphia: Jewish Publication Society, 1990.

Miller, David M. "Luke's Conception of Prophets Considered in the Context of Second Temple Literature." PhD dissertation: McMaster University, 2004.

Miller, David M. "Whom Do You Follow? The Jewish Politeia and the Maccabean Background of Josephus's Sign Prophets." Pages 173–183 in *Common Judaism: Explorations in Second Temple Judaism*. Edited by A. Reinhartz and W. McCready. Minneapolis: Fortress, 2008.

Miller, Patrick D. "Moses My Servant: The Deuteronomic Portrait of Moses." *Interpretation* 41 (1987): 245–255.

Moberly, R.W.L. *Prophecy and Discernment*. Cambridge and New York: Cambridge University Press, 2006.

Moessner, David P. "Good News for the 'Wilderness Generation': The Death of the Prophet like Moses according to Luke." Pages 1–34 in *Good News in History: Essays in Honor of Bo Reicke*. Edited by L. Miller. Atlanta: Scholars Press, 1993.

Moessner, David P. *Lord of the Banquet: The Literary and Theological Significance of the Lukan Travel Narrative*. Minneapolis, Fortress, 1989.

Moessner, David P. "Luke 9:1–50: Luke's Preview of the Journey of the Prophet like Moses of Deuteronomy." *Journal of Biblical Literature* 102 (1983): 575–605.

Moessner, David P. "Paul and the Pattern of the Prophet like Moses in Acts." *Society of Biblical Literature Seminar Papers* 22 (1983): 203–212.

Montgomery, James. *A Critical and Exegetical Commentary on the Books of Kings*. Edited by H.S. Gehman. International Critical Commentary. Edinburgh: T&T Clark, 1951.

Mowinckel, Sigmund. *Zur Komposition des Buches Jeremia*. Kristiania: Jacob Dybwad, 1914.

Mroczek, Eva. *The Literary Imagination in Jewish Antiquity*. Oxford: Oxford University Press, 2016.

Najman, Hindi. *Seconding Sinai: The Development of Mosaic Discourse in Second Temple Judaism*. Journal for the Study of Judaism Supplement Series 77. Leiden: Brill, 2003.

Nasrallah, Laura. *An Ecstasy of Folly: Prophecy and Authority in Early Christianity*. Harvard Theological Studies 52. Cambridge, Mass.: Harvard University Press, 2004.

Neef, Heinz-Dieter. *Die Heilstraditionen Israels in der Verkündigung des Propheten Hosea*. Beihefte zur Zeitschrift für die alttestamentliche Wissenschaft 169. Berlin: de Gruyter, 1987.

Nelson, Richard D. *Deuteronomy: A Commentary*. Old Testament Library. Louisville, Ky.: Westminster John Knox Press, 2002.

Nelson, Richard D. *The Double Redaction of the Deuteronomistic History*. Journal for the Study of the Old Testament Supplement Series 18. Sheffield: JSOT Press, 1981.

Newsom, Carol. "Apocryphon of Joshua." Pages 237–288 in *Qumran Cave 4 XVII: Parabiblical Texts, Part 3*. Discoveries in the Judaean Desert 22. Oxford: Clarendon, 1996.

Nicholson, Ernest W. "Deuteronomy 18.9–22, the Prophets and Scripture." Pages 151–171 in *Prophecy and Prophets in Ancient Israel*. Edited by John Day. Library of Hebrew Bible/Old Testament Studies 531. London: T&T Clark, 2010.

Nicholson, Ernest W. *Deuteronomy and the Judaean Diaspora*. Oxford: Oxford University, 2014.

Nicholson, Ernest W. *Deuteronomy and Tradition*. Philadelphia: Fortress, 1967.

Nicholson, Ernest W. *Preaching to the Exiles: A Study of the Prose Tradition in the Book of Jeremiah*. New York: Schocken Books, 1970.

Nickelsburg, George. "Enochic Wisdom: An Alternative to the Mosaic Torah?" Pages 123–132 in *Ḥesed ve-Emet: Studies in Honor of Ernest S. Frerichs*. Edited by J. Magness and S. Gitin. Brown Judaic Studies 320. Atlanta: Scholars Press, 1998.

Nihan, Christophe. "The Holiness Code Between D and P: Some Comments on the Function and Significance of Leviticus 17–26 in the Composition of the Torah." Pages 85–100 in *Das Deuteronomium zwischen Pentateuch und Deuteronomistischem Geschichtswerk*. Edited by E. Otto and R. Achenbach. Forschungen zur Religion und Literatur des Alten und Neuen Testaments 206. Göttingen: Vandenhoeck & Ruprecht, 2004.

Nihan, Christophe. " 'Moses and the Prophets': Deuteronomy 18 and the Emergence of the Pentateuch as Torah." *Svensk exegetisk årsbok* 75 (2010): 21–55.

Nissinen, Martti. "The Dubious Image of Prophecy." Pages 26–41 in *Prophets, Prophecy, and Prophetic Texts in Second Temple Judaism*. Edited by M.H. Floyd and R.D. Haak. Library of Hebrew Bible/Old Testament Studies 427. New York: T&T Clark, 2006.

Nissinen, Martti. "The Socio-religious Role of the Neo-Assyrian Prophets." Pages 89–114 in *Prophecy in its Ancient Near Eastern Context: Mesopotamian, Biblical, and Arabian*

Perspectives. Edited by M. Nissinen. Society of Biblical Literature Symposium Series 13. Atlanta: Society of Biblical Literature, 2000.

Nogalski, James. *Literary Precursors to the Book of the Twelve*. Beihefte zur Zeitschrift für die alttestamentliche Wissenschaft 217. Berlin: de Gruyter, 1993.

Nogalski, James. *Redactional Processes in the Book of the Twelve*. Beihefte zur Zeitschrift für die alttestamentliche Wissenschaft 218. Berlin: de Gruyter, 1993.

Noort, Ed. "Joshua: The History of Reception and Hermeneutics." Pages 199–215 in *Past, Present, Future: The Deuteronomistic History and the Prophets*. Edited by J.C. de Moor and H.F. van Rooy. Oudtestamentische Studiën 44. Leiden: Brill, 2000.

Noth, Martin. *A History of Pentateuchal Traditions*. Translated by Bernhard W. Anderson. Englewood Cliffs, N.J.: Prentice-Hall, 1972. Repr., Chico, Cal.: Scholars Press, 1981.

Noth, Martin. *Numbers: A Commentary*. Old Testament Library. Philadelphia: Westminster, 1968.

Noth, Martin. *Überlieferungsgeschichtliche Studien*. Tübingen: Niemeyer, 1943.

O'Brien, Julia M. *Nahum, Habakkuk, Zephaniah, Haggai, Zechariah, Malachi*. Abingdon Old Testament Commentaries. Nashville: Abingdon, 2004.

O'Brien, Mark A. "Deuteronomy 16.18–18.22: Meeting the Challenge of Towns and Nations." *Journal for the Study of the Old Testament* 33 (2008): 155–172.

O'Kane, Martin. "Isaiah: A Prophet in the Footsteps of Moses." *Journal for the Study of the Old Testament* 69 (1996): 29–51.

Olson, Dennis T. *Deuteronomy and the Death of Moses: A Theological Reading*. Minneapolis: Fortress Press, 1994.

Ossandón Widow, Juan Carlos. *The Origins of the Canon of the Hebrew Bible: An Analysis of Josephus and 4 Ezra*. Supplements to the Journal for the Study of Judaism 186. Leiden: Brill, 2018.

Osuji, Anthony C. *Where is the Truth?: Narrative Exegesis and the Question of True and False Prophecy in Jer 26–29 (MT)*. Bibliotheca ephemeridum theologicarum lovaniensium 214. Leuven: Peeters, 2010.

O'Toole, Robert F. *Luke's Presentation of Jesus: A Christology*. Subsidia biblica 25. Rome: Pontificio Istituto Biblico, 2004.

O'Toole, Robert F. "The Parallels between Jesus and Moses." *Biblical Theology Bulletin* 20 (1990): 22–29.

O'Toole, Robert F. "Some Observations on Anistēmi, 'I Raise,' in Acts 3:22, 26." *Science et Esprit* 31 (1979): 85–92.

Otto, Eckart. *Das Deuteronomium im Pentateuch und Hexateuch: Studien zur Literaturgeschichte von Pentateuch und Hexateuch im Lichte des Deuteronomiumrahmens*. Forschungen zum Alten Testament 30. Tübingen: Mohr Siebeck, 2000.

Otto, Eckart. *Deuteronomium 1–11: Erster Teilband: 1,1–4,43*. Herders Theologischer Kommentar zum Alten Testament. Freiburg: Herder, 2012.

Otto, Eckart. *Deuteronomium 12–34: Erster Teilband: 12,1–23,15*. Freiburg: Herder, 2016.

Pakkala, Juha. "The Date of the Oldest Edition of Deuteronomy." *Zeitschrift für die alttestamentliche Wissenschaft* 121 (2009): 388–401.

Pancaro, Severino. *The Law in the Fourth Gospel: The Torah and the Gospel, Moses and Jesus, Judaism and Christianity According to John*. Novum Testamentum Supplement Series 42. Leiden: Brill, 1975.

Pearce, Sarah J.K. "Josephus as Interpreter of Biblical Law: The Representation of the High Court of Deut 17:8–12 according to Jewish Antiquities 4.218." *Journal of Jewish Studies* 46 (1995): 30–42.

Pearce, Sarah J.K. *The Words of Moses: Studies in the Reception of Deuteronomy in the Second Temple Period*. Texts and Studies in Ancient Judaism 152. Tübingen: Mohr Siebeck, 2013.

Penner, Todd. *In Praise of Christian Origins: Stephen and the Hellenists in Lukan Apologetic Historiography*. New York: T&T Clark, 2004.

Perlitt, Lothar. "Mose als Prophet." *Evangelische Theologie* 31 (1971): 588–608.

Person Jr., Raymond F. *The Deuteronomic School: History, Social Setting, and Literature*. Society of Biblical Literature 2. Atlanta: Society of Biblical Literature, 2002.

Pervo, Richard. *Acts: A Commentary*. Hermeneia. Minneapolis: Fortress, 2009.

Petersen, David L. "The Ambiguous Role of Moses as Prophet." Pages 311–324 in *Israel's Prophets and Israel's Past: Essays on the Relationship of Prophetic Texts and Israelite History in Honor of John H. Hayes*. Edited by B.E. Kelle and M.B. Moore. Library of Hebrew Bible/Old Testament Studies 446. New York: T&T Clark, 2006.

Petersen, David L. *Haggai and Zechariah 1–8: A Commentary*. Old Testament Library. London: SCM Press, 1984.

Petersen, David L. *Late Israelite Prophecy: Studies in Deutero-Prophetic Literature and in Chronicles*. Society of Biblical Literature Monograph Series 23. Missoula, Mont: Scholars Press, 1977.

Petersen, David L. *Zechariah 9–14 and Malachi: A Commentary*. Old Testament Library. Louisville: Westminster John Knox, 1995.

Peterson, David. *The Acts of the Apostles*. Piller New Testament Commentary. Grand Rapids: Eerdmans, 2009.

Peterson, Norman. *The Gospel of John and the Sociology of Light: Language and Characterization in the Fourth Gospel*. Valley Forge, PA: Trinity Press, 1993.

Petitjean, A. *Les Oracles du Proto-Zacharie*. Etudes bibliques. Paris: Gabalda, 1969.

Peursen, Wido van. "Who was Standing on the Mountain? The Portrait of Moses in 4Q377." Pages 99–114 in *Moses in Biblical and Extra-Biblical Traditions*. Edited by A. Graupner and M. Wolter. Beihefte zur Zeitschrift für die alttestamentliche Wissenschaft 372. Berlin: de Gruyter, 2007.

Philonenko, M. " 'Jusqu'à ce que lève un prophète digne de confiance' (1 Maccabées 14,41)." Pages 95–98 in *Messiah and Christos. Studies in the Jewish Origins of Christianity Presented to David Flusser*. Edited by I. Gruenwald, S. Shaked, and G. Stroumsa. Tübingen: Mohr Siebeck, 1992.

Poirier, John C. "The Endtime Return of Elijah and Moses at Qumran." *Dead Sea Discoveries* 10 (2003): 221–242.

Polzin, Robert. *Moses and the Deuteronomist: a Literary Study of the Deuteronomic History*. New York: Seabury Press, 1980.

Priest, J. "Testament of Moses: A New Translation and Introduction." In *The Old Testament Pseudepigrapha*. Edited by J. Charlesworth. Two volumes. Garden City: Doubleday, 1983. Volume 1:920–934.

Rad, Gerhard von. *Deuteronomy: a Commentary*. Translated by D. Barton. OTL. Philadelphia: Westminster Press, 1966.

Rad, Gerhard von. *Old Testament Theology*. Translated by D.M.G. Stalker. 2 vols. New York: Harper & Row, 1962.

Rad, Gerhard von. *Studies in Deuteronomy*. Translated by D.M.G. Stalker. London: SCM Press, 1953.

Redditt, Paul. "The Book of Malachi in its Social Setting." *Catholic Biblical Quarterly* 56 (1994): 240–255.

Reid, Barbara E. *The Transfiguration: A Source- and Redaction-Critical Study of Luke 9:28–36*. Cahiers de la Revue biblique 32. Paris: Gabalda, 1993.

Reinhartz, Adele. *Befriending the Beloved Disciple: A Jewish Reading of the Gospel of John*. New York: Continuum, 2005.

Reinhartz, Adele. "Jesus as Prophet: Predictive Prolepses in the Fourth Gospel." *Journal for the Study of the New Testament* 36 (1989): 3–16.

Reis, Pamela Tamarkin. "Numbers XI: Seeing Moses Plain." *Vetus Testamentum* 55 (2005): 207–231.

Richter, Georg. "Präsentische und futurische Eschatologie im 4. Evangelium." Pages 117–151 in *Gegenwart und kommendes Reich: Schulergabe Anton Vögtle zum 65. Geburtstag*. Edited by P. Fiedler and D. Zeller. Stuttgart: KBW, 1975.

Richter, Sandra Lynn. "The Question of Provenance and the Economics of Deuteronomy." *Journal for the Study of the Old Testament* 42 (2017): 23–50.

Römer, Thomas C. "The Formation of the Book of Jeremiah as a Supplement to the So-called Deuteronomistic History." Pages 168–183 in *The Production of Prophecy: Constructing Prophecy and Prophets in Yehud*. Edited by D.V. Edelman and E. Ben Zvi. London: Equinox, 2009.

Römer, Thomas C. "How Did Jeremiah Become a Convert to Deuteronomistic Ideology?" Pages 189–199 in *Those Elusive Deuteronomists: The Phenomenon of Pan-Deuteronomism*. Edited by L.S. Schearing and S.L. McKenzie. Journal for the Study of the Old Testament Supplement Series 268. Sheffield: Sheffield Academic, 1999.

Römer, Thomas C. "Moses, Israel's First Prophet, and the Formation of the Deuteronomistic and Prophetic Libraries." Pages 129–146 in *Israelite Prophecy and the Deuteronomistic History: Portrait, Reality, and the Formation of a History*. Edited by Mignon R. Jacobs and Raymond F. Person Jr. Ancient Israel and its Literature 14. Atlanta: Society of Biblical Literature, 2013.

Römer, Thomas, and Marc Zvi Brettler. "Deuteronomy 34 and the Case for a Persian Hexateuch." *Journal of Biblical Literature* 119 (2000): 401–419.

Rossi, Benedetta. "Conflicting Patterns of Revelation: Jer 31,33–34 and its Challenge to the Post-Mosaic Revelation Program." *Biblical* 99 (2018): 202–225.

Rossi, Benedetta. "Reshaping Jeremiah: Scribal Strategies and the *prophet like Moses*." *Journal for the Study of the Old Testament* 44 (2020): 575–593.

Rudolph, Wilhelm. *Haggai, Sacharja 1–8, Sacharja 9–14, Maleachi*. Kommentar zum Alten Testament 13/4. Gutersloh: Mohn, 1976.

Rütersworden, Udo. *Von der politischen Gemeinschaft zur Gemeinde: Studien zu Dt 16,18–18,22*. Bonner biblische Beiträge 65 Frankfurt am Main: Athenäum, 1987.

Sanders, Ed P. *Judaism: Practice and Belief, 63 BCE–66 CE*. London: SCM/Philadelphia: Trinity, 1992.

Sanders, Jack T. *The Jews in Luke-Acts*. Philadelphia: Fortress, 1987.

Schearing, Linda S. and Stephen L. McKenzie, eds. *Those Elusive Deuteronomists: The Phenomenon of Pan-Deuteronomism*. Journal for the Study of the Old Testament Supplement Series 268. Sheffield: Sheffield Academic, 1999.

Schmid, Konrad. "Deuteronomy within the 'Deuteronomistic Histories' in Genesis–2 Kings." Pages 8–30 in *Deuteronomy in the Pentateuch, Hexateuch, and the Deuteronomistic History*. Edited by K. Schmid and R.F. Person Jr. Forschungen zum Alten Testament Second Series 56. Tübingen: Mohr Siebeck, 2012.

Schmid, Konrad. "The Late Persian Formation of the Torah: Observations on Deuteronomy 34." Pages 237–250 in *Judah and the Judeans in the Fourth Century BCE*. Edited by O. Lipschits, G.N. Knoppers, and R. Albertz. Winona Lake, Ind.: Eisenbrauns, 2007.

Schmidt, Brian. "Canaanite Magic vs. Israelite Religion: Deuteronomy 18 and the Taxonomy of Taboo." Pages 242–259 in *Magic and Ritual in the Ancient World*. Edited by Paul A. Mirecki and Marvin W. Meyer. Religions in the Graeco-Roman World 141. Leiden: Brill, 2002.

Schmidt, Werner H. "Das Prophetengesetz Dtn 18:9–22 im Kontext erzählender Literature." Pages 55–69 in *Deuteronomy and Deuteronomic Literature: Festschrift C.H.W. Brekelmans*. Edited by M. Vervenne and J. Lust. Bibliotheca ephemeridum theologicarum lovaniensium 133. Leuven: Leuven University Press, 1997.

Schmitt, Hans-Christoph. "Dtn 34 als Verbindungsstück zwischen Tetrateuch und Deuteronomistischem Geschichtswerk." Pages 181–192 in *Das Deuteronomium zwischen Pentateuch und Deuteronomistischem Geschichtswerk*. Edited by E. Otto and R. Achenbach. Forschungen zur Religion und Literatur des Alten und Neuen Testaments 206. Göttingen: Vandenhoeck & Ruprecht, 2004.

Schnackenburg, Rudolph. *The Gospel according to St. John*. Translated by Kevin Smyth. Three volumes. Volume 1 and 2: New York: Seabury, 1980. Volume 3: New York: Crossroad, 1982.

Schniedewind, William M. "The Textualization of Torah in the Deuteronomic Tradition." Pages 153–167 in *Das Deuteronomium zwischen Pentateuch und Deuteronomistischem Geschichtswerk*. Edited by Eckart Otto and Reinhard Achenbach. Forschungen zur Religion und Literatur des Alten und Neuen Testaments 206. Göttingen: Vandenhoeck & Ruprecht, 2004.

Schofield, Alison. *From Qumran to the Yaḥad: A New Paradigm of Textual Development for The Community Rule*. Studies in the Texts of the Desert of Judah 77. Leiden: Brill, 2009.

Schott, Martin. "Die Jacobpassagen in Hosea 12." *Zeitschrift für Theologie und Kirche* 112 (2015): 1–26.

Schuller, Eileen M. "4QNon-Canonical Psalms B." Pages 87–172 in *Qumran Cave 4 VI: Poetical and Liturgical Texts, Part 1*. Discoveries in the Judaean Desert 11. Oxford: Clarendon, 1998.

Schuller, Eileen M. *Non-Canonical Psalms from Qumran: a Pseudepigraphic Collection*. Harvard Semitic Studies 28. Atlanta: Scholars Press, 1986.

Schwartz, Daniel. "Josephus's *Jewish Antiquities*." Pages 36–58 in *A Companion to Josephus*. Edited by H.H. Chapman and Z. Rodgers. Blackwell Companions to the Ancient World: Chicester, West Sussex, UK: John Wiley & Sons, 2016.

Schwartz, Daniel. "Josephus on Jewish Constitutions and Community." *Scripta Classica Israelica* 7 (1983–1984): 30–52.

Seitz, Christopher R. "The Prophet Moses and the Canonical Shape of Jeremiah." *Zeitschrift für die alttestamentliche Wissenschaft* 101 (1989): 3–27.

Sharp, Carolyn J. *Prophecy and Ideology in Jeremiah: Struggles for Authority in Deutero-Jeremianic Prose*. Old Testament Studies. London; New York: T&T Clark, 2003.

Singh, David E. "Muḥammad, 'the Prophet like Moses'?" *Journal of Ecumenical Studies* 43 (2008): 545–561.

Skehan, Patrick and Alexander Di Lella. *The Wisdom of Ben Sira: A New Translation with Notes, Introduction, and Commentary*. Anchor Bible 39. New York: Doubleday, 1987.

Smend, Rudolf. *Biblische Zeugnisse: Literatur des Alten Israel*. Fischer-Verlay, 1967.

Smend, Rudolf. *Die Weisheit des Jesus Sirach erklärt*. Berlin: Reimer, 1906.

Smith, D. Moody. "The Contribution of J. Louis Martyn to the Understanding of the Gospel of John." Pages 1–23 in J. Louis Martyn, *History and Theology in the Fourth Gospel*. Third edition. New Testament Library. Louisville: Westminster John Knox, 2003.

Smith, J.M.P. *A Critical and Exegetical Commentary on Haggai, Zechariah, Malachi, and Jonah*. International Critical Commentary. Edinburgh: T&T Clark, 1912.

Smith, Steve. *The Fate of the Jerusalem Temple in Luke-Acts: An Intertextual Approach to Jesus' Laments over Jerusalem and Stephen's Speech*. Library of New Testament Studies 553. London: T&T Clark, 2017.

Snaith, John G. "Biblical Quotations in the Hebrew of Ecclesiasticus." *Journal of Theological Studies* 18 (1967): 1–12.

Snodgrass, Klyne R. *Stories with Intent: A Comprehensive Guide to the Parables of Jesus*. Grand Rapids: Eerdmans, 2008.

Soards, Marion. *The Speeches of Acts: Their Content, Context, and Concerns*. Louisville, Ky.: Westminster/John Knox, 1994.

Sommer, Benjamin D. "Did Prophecy Cease? Evaluating a Reevaluation." *Journal of Biblical Literature* 115 (1996): 31–47.

Sommer, Benjamin D. "Reflecting on Moses: The Redaction of Numbers 11." *Journal of Biblical Literature* 118 (1999): 601–624.

Sommer, Benjamin D. *Revelation and Authority: Sinai in Jewish Scripture and Tradition*. Anchor Yale Bible Reference Library. New Haven: Yale University Press, 2015.

Sonnet, Jean-Pierre. "Redefining the Plot of Deuteronomy—From End to Beginning. The Import of Deut 34:9." Pages 37–49 in *Deuteronomium—Tora für eine neue Generation*. Edited by G. Fischer, D. Markl, and S. Paganini. Beihefte zur Zeitschrift für Altorientalische und Biblische Rechtsgeschichte 17. Wiesbaden: Harrassowitz Verlag, 2011.

Sperling, S. David. "Miriam, Aaron and Moses: Sibling Rivalry." *Hebrew Union College Annual* 70 (2000): 39–55.

Spilsbury, Paul. *The Image of the Jew in Flavius Josephus' Paraphrase of the Bible*. Texts and Studies in Ancient Judaism 69. Tübingen: Mohr Siebeck, 1998.

Stackert, Jeffery. *A Prophet Like Moses: Prophecy, Law, and Israelite Religion*. New York: Oxford, 2014.

Stackert, Jeffery. "Mosaic Prophecy and the Deuteronomic Source of the Torah." Pages 47–63 in *Deuteronomy in the Pentateuch, Hexateuch, and the Deuteronomistic History*. Edited by K. Schmid and R.F. Person Jr. Forschungen zum Alten Testament Second Series 56. Tübingen: Mohr Siebeck, 2012.

Stadelmann, Helge. *Ben Sira als Schriftgelehrter: Eine Untersuchung zum Berufsbild des vor-makkabäischen Sōfēr unter Berücksichtigung seines Verhältnisses zu Priester-, Propheten- und Weisheitslehrertum*. Wissenschaftliche Untersuchungen zum Neuen Testament Second Series 6. Tübingen: Mohr [Paul Siebeck], 1980.

Steck, Odil Hannes. *Israel und das gewaltsame Geschick der Propheten: Untersuchungen zur Überlieferung des deuteronomistischen Geschichtsbildes im Alten Testament, Spätjudentum und Urchristentum*. Wissenschaftliche Monographien zum Alten und Neuen Testament 23. Neukirchen-Vluyn: Neukirchener Verlag, 1967.

Stegemann, Harmut. "Some Remarks to 1QSa, to 1QSb, and to Qumran Messianism." *Revue de Qumran* 17 (1996): 479–505.

Stein, Robert H. *Mark*. Baker Exegetical Commentary on the New Testament. Grand Rapids: Baker Academic, 2008.

Sterling, Gregory E. *Historiography and Self-Definition: Josephos, Luke-Acts, and Apologetic Historigraphy*. Novum Testamentum Supplement Series 64. Leiden: Brill, 1992.

Steyn, Gert J. *Septuagint Quotations in the Context of the Petrine and Pauline Speeches of the Acta Apostolorum*. Contributions to Biblical Exegesis and Theology 12. Kampen: Kok Pharos, 1995.

Stoellger, Phillip. "Deuteronomium 34 ohne Priesterschrift." *Zeitschrift für die alttestamentliche Wissenschaft* 105 (1993): 26–51.

Strelan, Rick. *Luke the Priest: The Authority of the Author of the Third Gospel*. London: Routledge, 2016.

Strugnell, John. "4QApocryphon of Moses[a.]" Pages 121–136 in *Qumran Cave 4 XIV: Parabiblical Texts, Part 2*. Discoveries in the Judaean Desert 19. Oxford: Clarendon, 1995.

Strugnell, John. "Moses-Pseudepigrapha at Qumran: 4Q375, 4Q376, and Similar Works." Pages 221–256 in *Archaeology and History in the Dead Sea Scrolls: The New York University Conference in Memory of Yigael Yadin*. Edited by L.H. Schiffman. Journal for the Study of the Pseudepigrapha Supplement Series 8. Sheffield: JSOT Press, 1990.

Stulman, Louis. *Jeremiah*. Abingdon Old Testament Commentary. Nashville: Abingdon, 2005.

Stulman, Louis. *The Prose Sermons of the Book of Jeremiah: A Redescription of the Correspondences with Deuteronomistic Literature in the Light of Recent Text-Critical Research*. Society of Biblical Literature Dissertation Series 83. Atlanta: Scholars Press, 1986.

Sundberg, Albert C. *The Old Testament of the Early Church*. Harvard Theological Studies 20. Cambridge, MA: Harvard University Press, 1964.

Sweeney, Marvin. *The Twelve Prophets*. Two volumes. Berit Olam. Collegeville, Minn.: Liturgical Press, 2000.

Tannehill, Robert C. *The Narrative Unity of Luke-Acts: A Literary Interpretation*. Two volumes. Minneapolis: Fortress, 1990.

Tarrer, Seth B. *Reading with the Faithful: Interpretation of True and False Prophecy in the book of Jeremiah from Ancient Times to Modern*. Journal of Theological Interpretation Supplement Series 6. Winona Lake, In.: Eisenbrauns, 2013.

Teeple, Howard Merle. *The Mosaic Eschatological Prophet*. Journal of Biblical Literature Monograph Series 10. Philadelphia: Society of Biblical Literature, 1957.

Tengström, Sven. "Moses and the Prophets in the Deuteronomistic History." *Scandinavian Journal of the Old Testament* 8 (1994): 257–266.

Tervanotko, Hanna. "Speaking in Dreams: the Figure of Miriam and Prophecy." Pages 147–167 in *Prophets Male and Female: Gender and Prophecy in the Hebrew Bible, the Eastern Mediterranean, and the Ancient Near East*. Edited by Jonathan Stökl and Corrine Carvalho. Ancient Israel and Its Literature 15. Atlanta: SBL Press, 2013.

Thatcher, Tom. "Remembering Jesus: John's Negative Christology." Pages 165–189 in *The Messiah in the Old and New Testaments*. Edited by S. Porter. McMaster New Testament Series. Grand Rapids: Eerdmans, 2007.

Thelle, Rannfrid I. "MT Jeremiah: Reflections of a Discourse on Prophecy in the Persian Period." Pages 184–207 in *The Production of Prophecy: Constructing Prophecy and Prophets in Yehud*. Edited by D.V. Edelman and E. Ben Zvi. London: Equinox, 2009.

Thelle, Rannfrid I. "Reflections of Ancient Israelite Divination in the Former Prophets." Pages 7–33 in *Israelite Prophecy and the Deuteronomistic History: Portrait, Reality, and the Formation of a History*. Edited by Mignon R. Jacobs and Raymond F. Person Jr. Ancient Israel and its Literature 14. Atlanta: Society of Biblical Literature, 2013.

Thiel, Winfried. *Die deuteronomische Redaktion von Jeremia 1–25*. Wissenschaftliche Monographien zum Alten und Neuen Testament 41. Neukirehen: Neukirchener Verlag, 1973.

Thiel, Winfried. *Die deuteronomische Redaktion von Jeremia 26–45*. Wissenschaftliche Monographien zum Alten und Neuen Testament 52. Neukirehen: Neukirchener Verlag, 1981.

Tiede, David L. *Prophecy and History in Luke-Acts*. Philadelphia: Fortress, 1980.

Tigay, Jeffrey H. *Deuteronomy = [Devarim]: The Traditional Hebrew Text with the New JPS Translation*. Jewish Publication Society Torah Commentary 5. Philadelphia: Jewish Publication Society, 1996.

Tollington, Janet E. *Tradition and Innovation in Haggai and Zechariah 1–8*. Journal for the Study of the Old Testament Supplement Series 150. Sheffield: JSOT Press, 1993.

Toorn, Karel van der. *Scribal Culture and the Making of the Hebrew Bible*. Cambridge, MA: Harvard University Press, 2007.

Torrey, C.C. *The Second Isaiah*. New York: Charles Scribner's Sons, 1928.

Ulrich, Eugene C. *The Dead Sea Scrolls and the Origins of the Bible*. Studies in the Dead Sea Scrolls and Related Literature. Grand Rapids: Eerdmans, 1999.

Ulrich, Eugene C. "The Bible in the Making: The Scriptures Found at Qumran." Pages 51–66 in *The Bible at Qumran: Text, Shape, and Interpretation*. Edited by P. Flint. Studies in the Dead Sea Scrolls and Related Literature. Grand Rapids: Eerdmans, 2001.

Ulrich, Eugene C. "The Notion and Definition of Canon." Pages 21–35 in *The Canon Debate*. Edited by L.M. McDonald and J.A. Sanders. Peabody, Mass: Hendrickson Publishers, 2002.

Unnik, Willem C. van. *Flavius Josephus als historischer Schriftsteller*. Franz Delitzsch Vorlesungen 1972. Heidelberg: Verlag Lambert Schneider, 1978.

Urbach, Ephraim. "When Did Prophecy Cease?" *Tarbiz* 17 (1946): 1–11. [Hebrew]

VanderKam, James C. *The Dead Sea Scrolls and the Bible*. Grand Rapids: Eerdmans, 2012.

VanderKam, James C. *From Revelation to Canon: Studies in the Hebrew Bible and Second Temple Literature*. Journal for the Study of Judaism Supplement Series 62. Leiden; Boston; Cologne: Brill, 2000.

VanderKam, James C. "Messianism in the Scrolls." Pages 211–234 in *The Community of the New Covenant*. Edited by E. Ulrich and J.C. VanderKam. Notre Dame, IN: University of Notre Dame, 1994.

VanderKam, James C. "Questions of Canon Viewed through the Dead Sea scrolls."

Pages 91–109 in *The Canon Debate*. Edited by L.M. McDonald and J.A. Sanders. Peabody, Mass: Hendrickson Publishers, 2002.

VanderKam, James C. and Monica Brady. "4QApocryphal Pentateuch B." Pages 205–217 in *Qumran Cave 4 XXVIII: Miscellanea, Part 2*. Discoveries in the Judaean Desert 28. Oxford: Clarendon, 2001.

VanderKam, James C. and Peter Flint. *The Meaning of the Dead Sea Scrolls: Their Significance for Understanding the Bible, Judaism, Jesus, and Christianity*. New York: HarperCollins, 2002.

Verheyden, Joseph "Calling Jesus a Prophet, as Seen by Luke." Pages 177–210 in *Prophets and Prophecy in Jewish and Early Christian Literature*. Edited by. J. Verheyden, K. Zamfir, and T. Nicklas. Wissenschaftliche Untersuchungen zum Neuen Testament. 2 Reihe 286. Tübingen: Mohr Siebeck, 2010.

Vermes, Geza. *Jesus the Jew: A Historian's Reading of the Gospels*. Philadelphia: Fortress, 1973.

Vermes, Geza. *An Introduction to the Complete Dead Sea Scrolls*. Minneapolis: Fortress, 1999.

Vermes, Geza. "The Leadership of the Qumran Community: Sons of Zadok—Priests—Congregation." Pages 375–384 in *Geschichte, Tradition, Reflexion: Festschrift für Martin Hengel zum 70. Geburtstag*. Edited by Peter Schäfer et al. Tübingen: Mohr Siebeck, 1996

Vriezen Th.C. and A.S. van der Woude. *Ancient Israelite and Early Jewish Literature*. Translated by Brian Doyle. Leiden: Brill, 2005.

Wahlde, Urban von. *The Earliest Version of John's Gospel: Recovering the Gospel of Signs*. Wilmington, Del.: Michael Glazier, 1989.

Wasserberg, Günter. *Aus Israels Mitte—Heil für die Welt: eine narrativ-exegetische Studie zur Theologie des Lukas*. Beihefte zur Zeitschrift für die neutestamentliche Wissenschaft 92. Berlin: de Gruyter, 1998.

Webb, Robert L. *John the Baptizer and Prophet: A Socio-historical Study*. Journal for the Study of the New Testament Supplement Series 62. Sheffield: JSOT Press, 1991.

Weinfeld, Moshe. *Deuteronomy 1–11: A New Translation with Introduction and Commentary*. Anchor Bible 5. New York: Doubleday, 1991.

Weinfeld, Moshe. *Deuteronomy and the Deuteronomic School*. Oxford: Clarendon Press, 1972.

Weippert, Helga. *Die Prosareden des Jeremiasbuches*. Beihefte zur Zeitschrift für die alttestamentliche Wissenschaft 132. Berlin: de Gruyter, 1973.

Wellhausen, Julius. *Prolegomena to the History of Ancient Israel*. Translated by J. Black and A. Menzies. Reprint. Gloucester, Mass.: Peter Smith, 1973 [1885].

Wenzel, Heiko. *Reading Zechariah with Zechariah 1:1–6 as the Introduction to the Entire Book*. Contributions to Biblical Exegesis and Theology 59. Leuven: Peeters, 2011.

Williams, Ronald J. *Hebrew Syntax: An Outline*. Second edition. Toronto: University of Toronto, 1976.

Wilson, Robert R. *Prophecy and Society in Ancient Israel.* Philadelphia: Fortress Press, 1980.

Winston, David. "Two Types of Mosaic Prophecy according to Philo." *Journal for the Study of the Pseudepigrapha* 2 (1989): 49–67.

Wolff, Hans W. *Hosea: A Commentary on the Book of the Prophet Hosea.* Translated by Gary Stansell. Hermeneia. Philadelphia: Fortress, 1974 [German original 1965].

Wright, Benjamin. *No Small Difference: Sirach's Relationship to its Hebrew Parent Text.* Society of Biblical Literature Septuagint and Cognate Studies 26. Atlanta: Scholars Press, 1989.

Xeravits, Géza G. *King, Priest, Prophet: Positive Eschatological Protagonists of the Qumran Library.* Studies on the Texts of the Desert of Judah 47. Leiden: Brill, 2003.

Yoo, Philip Y. "The Four Moses Death Accounts." *Journal of Biblical Literature* 131 (2012): 423–441.

Zahn, Molly M. *Genres of Rewriting in Second Temple Judaism: Scribal Composition and Transmission.* Cambridge: Cambridge University Press, 2020.

Zahn, Molly M. *Rethinking Rewritten Scripture: Composition and Exegesis in the 4QReworked Pentateuch Manuscripts.* Studies in the Texts of the Desert of Judah 95. Leiden; Boston: Brill, 2011.

Zehnle, Richard F. *Peter's Pentecost Discourse: Tradition and Lukan Reinterpretation in Peter's Speeches of Acts 2 and 3.* Society of Biblical Literature Monograph Series 15. Nashville: Abingdon, 1971.

Zimmerli, Walther, and Joachim Jeremias. *The Servant of God.* Studies in Biblical Theology 20. Naperville, Ill.: A.R. Allenson, 1965.

Index of Modern Authors

Achenbach, Reinhard   4n10, 30n1, 35n16
Albertz, Rainer   73–74, 93n53
Allegro, John   196n64
Allen, Leslie   104n19, 107n29, 108n33
Allison, Dale C.   4n12, 4n13, 158n3, 162n17, 228, 230, 237, 238n7, 255n83, 255–256n84, 263n110, 266n116, 266n118, 271n136
Amir, Yehoshua   213n23
An, Hannah S.   303n42, 306n53
Andersen, Francis I.   28n39, 94n55, 94n57
Anderson, Paul N.   296–298, 307, 309n61, 318n91
Ashton, John   292n4, 294n11, 300n29, 301n32, 302n38, 312, 313n70, 315, 316n85
Assis, Elie   161n13, 162n16, 164, 165n37
Atkins, J.D.   56n95, 315
Auld, Graeme   76n16, 91n48, 94
Aune, David   185n26, 186n29, 236n2, 237n7, 239n10

Baden, Joel   32n5
Barnett, Paul W.   226n51, 303n30
Barrett, C.K.   243n24, 246n37, 246n38, 249n52, 250n56, 253n69, 254n73, 293n8, 300n30, 303n41, 304n43
Barstad, Hans M.   131n30, 186–187
Barton, John   7n22, 147, 149n11, 149n13, 152–153, 186n29, 209n9, 209n11, 210n13, 224, 288n37
Bauckham, Richard   229n58, 231n68, 232n69, 304n44, 305n50, 310n66
Bayer, Hans F.   267n123
Becker, Adam H.   243n24
Beentjes, Pancratius   168n45, 170n53, 172, 175n67
Bernier, Jonathan   300n28
Berthelot, Katell   178n2, 197
Bilde, Per   205n1, 210n13
Blenkinsopp, Joseph   1n1, 2–6, 25n28, 26n32, 26n33, 36n21, 47n60, 53–54n84, 93n54, 116, 125–126, 130, 135, 136n43, 138, 158n3, 159–161, 164n27, 205n1, 207n7, 209n10, 221n41
Bloch, René   233

Boesenberg, Dulcinea   245n36, 246n40, 258n92, 261n101, 266n118, 270n132
Boismard, Marie-Émile   295n12, 296, 297n19, 297n20, 302, 308, 310n63, 314n78, 315n79
Bond, Helen K.   229n60
Borgen, Peder   316n85, 317n87, 317n89, 318
Bosman, H.L.   59n111
Bosshard, Erich   166n41
Bovon, François   244n32, 267n124, 268n125, 269n128, 295n13
Bowley, James   187, 188n37
Boyarin, Daniel   243n24
Brady, Monica   188n39, 188n40, 189n43, 190n46, 191n47
Brettler, Mark   126–127, 128n19, 133n34, 139, 140n56, 140n57
Brin, Gershon   201n86, 202n87
Brooke, George J.   187n34, 187n35, 188n36, 188n41
Brown, Raymond   291n2, 292n6, 293n8, 294n11, 294n12, 300n30, 301, 302n36, 303n42, 310n65, 313, 314n78, 316n85
Brueggemann, Walter   69n134, 104n19
Buber, Martin   37n23
Budd, Philip J.   32n5, 36n22, 40n32
Bultmann, Rudolf   242, 269n128, 291n3, 292, 299, 301n32, 304n43, 316n85

Calvin, John   162n17, 248n48
Carr, David M.   35n16, 132n31, 135n41, 176n70
Carroll, Robert P.   25n30, 46n56, 97n1, 104n19, 105n21, 145n1, 158n4
Chapman, Stephen B.   3–4, 6, 7n22, 24n26, 92n49, 125–127, 128n19, 135n42, 136n44, 136n45, 159n5, 159n7, 164n33, 165–167
Charles, R.H.   181n14
Charlesworth, James H.   194–195n59, 197n66
Childs, Brevard   2–3, 164n25
Clements, Ronald E.   65n127, 82n25
Coats, George W.   19n6, 19n7, 23n24
Coggins, R.J.   72, 73n2, 120n73, 164n26
Collins, Adela Yarbro   267n123
Collins, John J.   4n11, 147n7, 197

INDEX OF MODERN AUTHORS

Cook, L. Stephen   115, 148n10, 150, 152n26, 184n23, 186n29, 212, 224
Conzelmann, Hans   243, 251n60, 255n81
Corley, Jeremy   168n47, 171, 172n61, 175, 182n20
Crenshaw, James L.   46n56, 105n23
Croatto, J. Severino   237n4, 243n27, 265n113, 267n121, 270n135
Cross, Frank M.   73n5, 153n58, 196n64
Cullmann, Oscar   228n58, 236, 242

Damgaard, Finn   211n15, 220n37
Daniels, Dwight R.   28n37, 28n38
Dearman, J. Andrew   28n38, 28n39
De Troyer, Kristin   149n11, 150n18, 197n67
Dexinger, Ferdinand   4n11, 5n16
Dibelius, Martin   238n8, 244, 253
Di Lella, Alexander   169n49, 169n50, 173n63
Dillon, Richard J.   243n27, 247n43, 249n53, 250n55, 251n60, 252, 256n88, 257, 261n102, 263n106
Dimant, Devorah   180n8
Dodd, C.H.   244n32, 303n40
Donaldson, Terence   254n77, 273n141
Driver, S.R.   53n83, 54n90, 55, 57, 60n111, 125, 135n42

Edenburg, Cynthia   27n35
Eichrodt, Walther   62n121
Epp-Tiessen, Daniel   105n23
Eynikel, Erik   78

Fabry, Heinz-Josef   191n48
Fallon, F.   179
Farber, Zev I.   178n2, 182n18, 182n19, 183n21
Feldman, Ariel   148n9, 172n60, 179, 180n9, 180n10, 180n11, 180n12, 182n17, 189n42, 191n48, 197
Feldman, Louis   210n13, 212, 213n22, 216n29, 216n30, 217n31, 222, 282n9
Finsterbusch, Karin   56n96
Fischer, Georg   109n36
Fishbane, Michael   87n34, 104n18
Fitzmyer, Joseph   238n8, 245n35, 248n47, 249n51, 253n71, 255n81, 266, 267n120, 267n124
Fletcher-Louis, Crispin H.T.   188n41, 189n43, 190n44
Flint, Peter   209n9

Floyd, Michael H.   115n58, 118n68, 120n74, 121n80, 149n11, 150n18, 164n25, 164n33, 165n37
Forbes, Christopher   239n10
Fortna, Robert   294–295n12
Fredriksen, Paula   241n19, 254n77, 270n133, 274n141, 291n1, 295n13, 304n43, 311n67, 312n69, 319n92
Freedman, David Noel   28n39, 74n8, 94n55, 94n57
Fuller, Reginald   242, 250n56, 251n61, 257

García López, Félix   130n23, 133n33, 140n56
Glasson, T.F.   295, 296n15, 310n66
Glazier-McDonald, Beth   158n3, 162n17, 164n25, 165n34, 166n40
Goldstein, Jonathan   184n23, 185n27, 185n28
Goodman, Martin   155n33
Goshen-Gottstein, Alon   176n70
Grabbe, Lester L.   205n1
Gray, George B.   39n30, 41n37
Gray, John   26n31, 76n15
Gray, Rebecca   205n1, 206n4, 208n8, 209n12, 212–213, 224, 225n50, 226, 228n55, 232n71
Greenspahn, Frederick   149n11, 154n31, 184n23
Grossman, Maxine   255, 273n140
Gunneweg, Antonius H.J.   32, 33n8, 35n16, 36n20, 38n25, 39n30, 45n53, 125n4

Haak, Robert D.   149n11, 150n18
Haenchen, Ernst   246n37, 249n49, 250n56, 251n60, 253, 254n73, 256n87, 257, 260n99
Hahn, Ferdinand   242, 262n104
Halpern Amaru, Betsy   76n17
Hamori, Esther J.   40n33, 41n40, 42n42, 43n47
Hanson, John S.   226n51, 231n67
Haran, Menahem   34–35, 36n20, 130
Harnack, Adolf von   150n14
Harrington, Daniel J.   181n15
Harstine, Stan   292n5
Heller, Roy L.   25n30, 46n56, 47n61
Hengel, Martin   167n44, 170n52, 174n66, 238n8
Henze, Matthias   184n25
Hibbard, James T.   98n2, 105n20

Hill, Andrew E.   158n3, 160n10, 161n13, 162, 163n22, 163n23, 164n29, 166n40
Hill, Craig   253n70
Hobbs, T.R.   76n15, 91n45
Holladay, William   91n44, 97n1, 100n7, 103n16, 104n18, 104n19, 106n26, 107, 108n31, 108n34
Hooker, Morna   271
Horsley, Richard   169n49, 197, 226n51, 230–231
Hossfeld, Frank L.   104n19
Hugenberger, Gordon P.   5n14, 141n59
Hurvitz, Avi   173n63
Hyatt, J. Philip   97n1

Isser, Stanley J.   5n16

Jacobson, Howard   181n15, 182n18, 183n21
Jaffee, Martin S.   146n3
Janzen, J. Gerald   98n2
Jassen, Alex P.   186, 191n47, 193–195, 196n63, 196n64, 198–201, 202–203n89
Jeremias, Joachim   19n6, 228n56, 313n74
Jervell, Jacob   248n46, 258n90
Jobling, David   37n24, 38n28, 42
Johnson, Luke Timothy   243n27, 246n38, 248n47, 249, 251n63, 253n70, 256n85, 256n87, 257, 259n96, 260n98, 261n100, 262n105, 263n108
Jones, Barry Alan   157n2, 160n10, 164n28, 166n39
Jones, Gwilym H.   76n15, 91n46, 91n47
Jong, Matthijs J. de   98n2, 106n25
Jonge, Marinus de   306n51, 308
Jülicher, Adolf   244n31

Kaufmann, Yehezkel   151–152
Keener, Craig   256n86, 293–294, 304n43, 305n48, 310n65, 314n78, 315n82, 317n89
Kelle, Brad E.   26n34, 28n37
Kessler, Rainer   160, 161n12
Kingsbury, Jack Dean   243n28, 244n29
Klawans, Jonathan   223n45
Knibb, Michael A.   199n78
Knohl, Israel   35n19, 60n112
Knoppers, Gary N.   27n35, 54, 73n5, 127n14
Koet, Bart J.   266n114, 271n137

Kratz, Reinhold G.   166n41
Kraus, Wolfgang   247n43, 258n93

Lamb, David T.   145n1
Lange, Armin   116–117, 149n11, 150n18
Leivestad, Ragnar   149n10
Leuchter, Mark   29n45, 45n52
Levine, Amy-Jill   241n18, 273n141
Levine, Baruch A.   38n29, 41n36, 42n43, 44n49
Levinson, Bernard   53n83, 54, 59n108, 59n110, 66
Levison, John R.   38n29, 39n30, 149n11, 149n12, 182n19, 184n23, 186n29, 278–279, 280n4, 282, 284n18, 285n22, 286, 289, 290n41
Lierman, John   237n6, 262n104, 283n14, 296n18, 301n33, 315n82
Lim, Timothy H.   175n66
Lincicum, David   215n25
Lincoln, Andrew   292n6, 293n8, 302n37, 303n42, 304n43, 305n48, 309–310, 312n68, 315n84
Lindars, Barnabas   300n30, 303n39, 313n74, 315n84, 316n85, 316n86
Litwa, M. David   282n10
Lohfink, Norbert   53n81, 59n109, 73n4, 73n7, 74n10, 91n43
Long, Burke O.   91n45
Lübbe, John   193n56
Lundbom, Jack R.   57n103, 103n16

MacDonald, Nathan   56n96
MacIntosh, A.A.   26n33, 27n36, 28, 29n43
Mack, Burton L.   170n52, 174, 176n70
Maier, Christl   100n8, 102, 109–111
Makiello, Phoebe   188n41
Mastnjak, Nathan   97n1, 101n11, 103n16, 105n23, 107n30, 108n34, 110n40, 112–113
Marcus, Joel   267n123
Markl, Dominik   30n1, 47n59, 52n76, 64, 70n136, 71n139, 140
Maronde, Christopher A.   237n3
Marshall, I. Howard   238n8
Mason, Rex   164n28
Mason, Steve   206n3, 208n8, 209–210, 212, 213n23, 215n27, 216n29, 216–217n30, 238n8

Martyn, J. Louis   298–300, 305, 317–318
Mattill, A.J.   294n12
Mayes, Andrew D.H.   51, 60, 134n38, 137n47
McBride, S. Dean   215
McKane, William   97n1, 100n7, 101n9, 103n17, 107n29
McKeating, Henry   5n15
McLaren, James S.   207n6
McWhirter, Jocelyn   237, 239n9, 240n14, 243n27, 244n34, 247n42, 252n66, 256n85, 258n91, 259n94, 260n98, 263n108, 263n109, 265n113, 267n122, 269n127, 270n134, 273n141
Meeks, Wayne A.   4n12, 5n16, 179n6, 199n74, 218–219n34, 220n38, 220n39, 237, 242n22, 296, 303–305, 308, 309n62, 314
Meier, John P.   257
Metso, Sarianna   193n54, 194n59
Metzger, Bruce   300n30
Meyer, F.B.   310n66
Meyer, Ivo   104n19
Meyer, Rudolf   1n2, 149n11, 150, 153
Meyers, Carol L.   74n12, 119–120
Meyers, Eric M.   74n12, 119–120
Michaels, J. Ramsay   293n8, 301n32, 302n37, 304n43, 313, 314n78
Milgrom, Jacob   32n6, 34n13, 36n22, 37n24, 38n26, 38n27, 39n31, 41n35, 41n37, 42n43
Miller, David M.   226n51, 250n56, 250n57
Miller, Patrick D.   138n49
Moberly, R.W.L.   105n23
Moessner, David P.   4n12, 237, 243n27, 267n122
Montgomery, James   81n24
Mowinckel, Sigmund   98n3
Mroczek, Eva   6n20, 6n21, 147n6, 212n16, 225n49
Müller, Reinhard   27n35

Najman, Hindy   1n3, 8–11, 66n131, 290n42, 320
Nasrallah, Laura   239n10
Neef, Heinz-Dieter   27n36, 28n37
Nelson, Richard D.   48n64, 53n83, 54n90, 57–58, 60n115, 64n123, 65n126, 73n5, 77, 80n22, 81, 125n5, 136n44, 137n47, 139n53

Newsom, Carol   171n55
Nicholson, Ernest W.   30n1, 53n81, 55n94, 56n96, 71n139, 82n25, 90, 97n1, 100n7, 104n19, 107–108, 124n1
Nickelsburg, George   147n7
Nihan, Christophe   4n10, 17n2, 18n4, 30n1, 45n52, 45n53, 47, 50n68, 51–53, 55n94, 60n112, 64n125, 70n137, 82n26, 94, 95n58, 134n35, 135n41, 137, 157n1, 158n3, 158n4, 161, 163, 167
Nissinen, Martti   23n23, 52n79
Nogalski, James   74n8, 157n2
Noort, Ed   178n2, 181n16
Noth, Martin   32n7, 38n29, 39n30, 40n33, 44n49, 45n52, 73n6
Novick, Tzvi   82n27, 117n65, 131n25

O'Brien, Julia M.   164n29, 165n35
O'Brien, Mark A.   53n82
O'Kane, Martin   5n14
Olson, Dennis   137n47
Ossandón Widow, Juan Carlos   212n16
Osuji, Anthony C.   104n18, 104n19, 105n23
O'Toole, Robert F.   243n28, 251, 255n83, 266n117, 271n136
Otto, Eckart   47n62, 52n77, 58, 139n53

Pakkala, Juha   56n96
Pancaro, Severino   312n68, 313
Pearce, Sarah J.K.   218, 219n35, 219n36, 222n42
Penner, Todd   253n70
Perlitt, Lothar   17n2, 29, 43, 44n49, 135
Person Jr., Raymond F.   73–74, 118n66
Pervo, Richard   238n8, 254n75, 256n87, 258n89, 259n95
Petersen, David L.   20, 21n11, 23n24, 115n58, 118n67, 120, 121n79, 162n21, 163n22, 164n29
Peterson, David   254n75, 254n76, 257
Peterson, Norman   302n37
Petitjean, A.   121n77
Peursen, Wido van   188n41, 190n45, 191n48
Philonenko, M.   184n24
Poirier, John C.   4n11
Polzin, Robert   64n126, 65, 87, 89–90
Priest, J.   180, 181n14

Rad, Gerhard von   5n14, 21–22, 24, 27n35,
    32n7, 43, 46, 63n122, 81n24, 86–87, 89,
    106n24, 124n1, 141n59
Redditt, Paul   164n26
Reed, Annette Y.   243n24
Reid, Barbara E.   266n116
Reinhartz, Adele   293n7, 299n28, 305n47,
    306–308
Reis, Pamela Tamarkin   33n9
Richter, Georg   294n12
Richter, Sandra Lynn   27n35
Römer, Thomas C.   17n1, 66n132, 85n29,
    97n1, 107n27, 108n31, 126–127, 128n19,
    133n34, 139, 140
Rossi, Benedetta   110–111, 113
Rudolph, Wilhelm   26n33, 164n28, 166–167
Rüterswörden, Udo   51

Sanders, E.P.   229n59, 229n62
Sanders, Jack T.   273n141
Schearing, Linda   73n2
Schmid, Konrad   59n109, 66n130, 125n4, 126,
    128n19, 129n20, 137n47, 137n48, 139,
    140n56, 140n57
Schmidt, Brian   54n88, 60n114, 60n115,
    60n116, 85
Schmidt, Werner   107n30
Schnackenburg, Rudolf   293n8, 301n30,
    304n43, 313n72, 313n74, 314n78,
    316n85
Schniedewind, William M.   65n128
Schofield, Alison   193n54
Schott, Martin   28n37, 28n41
Schuller, Eileen   191–192
Schulte, Lucas   149n11, 150n18, 197n67
Schwartz, Daniel   213n23, 216n30
Scott, James C.   230
Seitz, Christopher   116, 117n62
Sharp, Carolyn J.   101n11, 101n12, 102n13,
    108n34
Singh, David E.   13n33
Skehan, Patrick   169n49, 169n50, 173n63
Smend, Rudolf   76n15, 171n56
Smith, D. Moody   299n26, 300n29
Smith, J.M.P.   165
Smith, Steve   241n18
Snaith, John G.   173n64, 174n65
Snodgrass, Klyne R.   269n128
Soards, Marion   244

Sommer, Benjamin   5, 31n2, 33–34, 36,
    37n24, 44n49, 149n10
Sonnet, Jean-Pierre   47n58, 131
Sperling, S. David   42, 43n47
Spilsbury, Paul   216n28, 216n30, 218n32,
    220n37
Stackert, Jeffery   4n10, 20n10, 22–24, 30n1,
    32n5, 32n6, 35n16, 39–40n31, 42n43,
    43n45, 44n50, 47, 55n93, 56n96, 124n1,
    132n31, 134n36, 135n40, 136n45, 137n47
Stadelmann, Helga   172n61, 173n62
Steck, Odil Hannes   76n17
Stegemann, Harmut   197n66
Stein, Robert H.   267n123
Sterling, Gregory E.   239n11
Steyn, Gert J.   246n38, 246n39, 246n40,
    246n41, 247n44, 262n105
Stoellger, Phillip   130n23
Strelan, Rick   240, 241n17, 241n19
Strugnell, John   201n85, 202n89
Stulman, Louis   101n10, 102n14, 107n29,
    108n35
Sundberg, Albert C.   7n22
Sweeney, Marvin   164n25, 165n37

Tannehill, Robert C.   243n28, 250n58,
    251n60
Tarrer, Seth B.   105n19
Teeple, Howard M.   4n11, 181n14, 236–237,
    241–242
Tengström, Sven   66n130, 71n139, 89n37
Tervanotko, Hanna   41n38, 43n46, 45n52
Thackeray, H. St. J.   207n5, 208n8, 217n31
Thatcher, Tom   295n12
Thelle, Rannfrid   55n92, 60n113, 60n116,
    106n26
Thiel, Winfried   97n1, 107n28
Tiede, David L.   243n27, 244n34, 266n115,
    272n139, 273n141
Tigay, Jeffrey H.   20n10, 21n11, 23n22, 54n90,
    55n91, 57, 58n107, 61, 125n6, 137n47
Tollington, Janet E.   121
Toorn, Karel van der   52–53, 54n86, 56–58,
    153–154, 158
Torrey, C.C.   150n14

Ulrich, Eugene   3, 7n22, 147n4, 234n75
Unnik, Wilhelm C. van   210n13
Urbach, Ephraim   149n11, 150, 153

VanderKam, James   147, 188n39, 188n40, 189n43, 190n46, 191n47, 200n78, 209n9
Verheyden, Joseph   244n29, 265n112, 268n126, 270n131
Vermes, Geza   194, 195n60, 195n61, 197, 198n70, 228n58
Vriezen, Th.C.   27n35

Wahlde, Urban von   294n12, 301n31
Wasserberg, Günter   273n141
Webb, Robert L.   226n51
Weinfeld, Moshe   57, 69n133, 69n134, 129n21
Weippert, Helga   97n1
Wellhausen, Julius   1, 1n1, 5, 115, 115n55, 115n56, 151, 152, 279n3
Wenzel, Heiko   121n78
Williams, Ronald J.   100

Wilson, Robert R.   124n1, 158n4
Winston, David   281n6, 282, 284n18, 286
Wolff, Hans W.   26n33, 28n37
Woude, A.S. van der   27n35
Wright, Benjamin   169n49, 172n57

Xeravits, Géza G.   189n43, 199n78, 200n79, 200n80

Yoo, Philip Y.   124n1, 130n23
Young, Franklin   150

Zahn, Molly M.   6n20, 7n23, 8n24, 69n135, 147n6
Zehnle, Richard F.   243n24
Ziegler, Joseph   168n45
Zimmerli, Walther   19n6, 133n34

Index of Ancient Sources

(Deut 18:15; 18:18; 34:10; 34:10–12 are excluded due to the ubiquity of these references)

Hebrew Bible

Genesis
	127n18, 139, 140n57, 146, 147n6, 148n8
8:21	138n51
9:11	138n51
9:15	138n51
12–13	140
12:1	139; 139n52
12:1–4a	140n56
12:6–8	140n56
12:7	139n53, 140, 140n56
12:7b	139
13:14–17	140n56
13:15	139
17:5	138n51
17:14	247n42, 248n45
18:19	135n39
20:3	41n35
20:6	41n35
20:7	21n14, 181n15, 213n22, 287n31, 289
30:27	61
41:7	41n35
41:19b	136
49:2	41n35

Exodus
	28, 29, 99, 100, 117, 124, 135, 140, 237
1–2	11
1:13	24n27
1:14	24n27
2:1–10	108
2:3	138n50
2:11–12	24n24
2:11–15	258
2:14	259, 260, 261
2:15	259n96
2:23	24n27
3	48n63, 258, 260
3–4	22n19, 25, 47, 135n40
3–32	261, 262n103
3:1–12	22n19
3:2	262
3:6	257
3:12	24n27
4:10	19n6, 24n25, 108
4:23	24n27
5:15	24n27
5:16	24n27
5:21	24n27
6–7	22n19
6:5	24n27
6:5–7	24n27
6:9	24n27
7:1	40n34, 170, 188n36, 213n22, 282n7
7:2	108
7:2a	109
7:3	262
7:10	24n27
7:16	24n27
7:17	21
7:20	24n27
7:26	24n27
8:1	21
8:3	24n27
8:5	24n27
8:7	24n27
8:16	24n27
8:17	24n27
8:20	24n27
8:25	24n27
8:27	24n27
9:1	24n27
9:13	21, 24n27
9:14	24n27
9:20	24n27
9:30	24n27
9:34	24n27
10:1	24n27
10:3	24n27
10:6	24n27
10:7	24n27

10:8	24n27	32:27	286
10:11	24n27	33–34	294n10, 312, 314n78
10:24	24n27	33:5–11	35n16
10:26	24n27	33:7	35
11:3	24n27	33:7–11	35, 169n49
11:8	24n27	33:8	36n20
12	230n63	33:11	36, 36n21, 43, 134,
12:15	247n42		134n38, 139n39,
12:19	247n42, 248n45		169n49, 171n55, 190,
12:30	24n27		190n44
12:31	24n27	33:17	24n24
12:32–36	230n63	33:18	310
13:3	24n27	34:5–7	310
13:14	24n27	34:6	313n70
14:5	24n27	34:29	266
14:13–14	283n16	34:30	266
14:21	262	39:43	23n24
14:31	19n6, 315, 315n82		
15:20	40n34	**Leviticus**	60n113
16	31n3, 283n16, 285	8:14–23	23n24
16:4	318n90	17:4	248n45
16:15	318n90	17:9	248n45
16:35	262n103	17:14	248n45
17:1–7	303n42	18:21	61
18:13–26	31n4	18:29	248n45
18:13–27	217	19:8	248n45
19:9	24n26	19:26	61
20	69n135	19:31	61
20:2	24n27	20:2–5	61
20:18	67, 68	20:6	61
20:18–19	66n132	20:17	248n45
20:18–21	169n50	20:18	248n45
20:19	173n63, 262, 263	20:27	61
20:19–21	66, 67, 68	22:3	248n45
20:20	68, 69n133	23:29	246, 247, 248n45
20:21	170n51, 196, 199	24:10–23	283n15
20:22–23:33	262		
22:18	61	**Numbers**	
23:20	163n22	9:1–14	283n15
24:3	69	9:13	248n45
24:7	67, 68, 69, 69n134,	11	34n14, 43, 44n49,
	131, 190		45n52, 218n33, 223
24:13	171n55	11–12	12, 30, 31, 34, 35n16,
25–31	262		43, 45n52, 46, 70, 131,
30:33	248n45		287
31:14	248n45	11:1–3	31
32:1	259, 261, 262	11:3	31
32:23	259, 262	11:4–10	31, 36n22
32:25–29	283n16	11:4–15	33n9

INDEX OF ANCIENT SOURCES   361

Numbers (*cont.*)

11:4–24a	36	12:4–5	32, 32n6, 36
11:4–35	32, 33, 33n9, 37, 40, 41	12:4–10	35n16
		12:5	36n20
11:4–12:16	31, 36, 44	12:6	41n36, 41n37, 45, 70n137
11:10	36n20	12:6–8	21n11, 32n6, 41, 41n38, 42, 44n50, 45n52, 70n137, 134, 134n38, 135, 135n39, 135n41, 169, 169n49, 282
11:11	19n6		
11:11–12	31, 33n9		
11:11–15	36n22		
11:13	31		
11:14	33n9		
11:14–15	33n9	12:7	19n6, 169, 184, 184n24
11:14–17	31		
11:15	33, 35n19	12:7–8	169n49
11:16	36n20	12:8	41n36, 41n37, 62n120, 71
11:16–17	33n9		
11:16–23	36n22	12:9–16	32, 32n6
11:16–25	217	12:16	31
11:16–29	35n16	13:3	31
11:17	33n9, 37, 38, 38n28	15:30	248n45
11:18–24a	31, 33n9	15:32–36	283n15
11:21–22	37n24	16:28–30	283n16
11:22	33	19:20	248n45
11:23	37, 37n24	21:5–9	314
11:24	36n20, 43	22:38	108n34
11:24–25	31, 38	24:15–17	196
11:24–29	40	27:1–11	283n15
11:24–30	36, 36n22	27:7	69
11:24b	37	27:12–14	130
11:24b–30	31, 33n9	27:15–23	130, 131n26
11:25	37, 38n28	27:18	130, 222
11:26	44	27:18–20	221
11:26–27	31	27:21	222
11:28	171, 171n55	27:23	130
11:29	31, 39, 40n31, 44	36:1–12	283n15
11:30–35	40	36:5	69
11:31–35	31, 33n9, 36n22		
12	40, 40n33, 43, 44n49, 45n52	**Deuteronomy**	
		1–3	57
12:1	32, 41n36, 41n37	1:1	62n119, 271
12:1–2	32n6	1:1–5	57, 57n103
12:1–16	31, 32, 40	1:5	65
12:1aα	32n6	1:6–3:29	64
12:1aβb	32n6	1:9–18	31n4
12:2	32n6, 41, 41n36, 41n37	1:18	62n119
		1:38	129n21
12:2–3	32n6, 41	3:21–22	129n21
12:2–15	32n6	3:24	19n6
12:3	24n24, 42n40, 169	3:28	129n21

INDEX OF ANCIENT SOURCES

4	57, 57n100	7:19	137
4:1	65, 192	8:14	24n27
4:1–40	64	8:19–20	85
4:2	10n31, 64, 64n123, 103n16	9:4	85
		9:5	85
4:5	65, 192	9:10	62n119
4:6	190	10:1–2	117n62
4:10	62n119	10:2	62n119
4:12	62, 62n119, 71	10:4	62n119
4:13	62n119	11:18	62n119
4:14	65, 192	12:1–16:17	57
4:34	137	12:2–3	85
4:36	62n119	12:13–28:44	58n105
4:44	57, 57n104	12:28	62n119
4:44–45	57	12:29–31	51
4:44–49	57, 57n103	12:29–13:6	51
4:44–28:68	57n104	12:31	47, 51, 61, 85
4:45	57	13	202n87, 305
5	51, 57	13–18	47, 51n74
5–26	57, 57n103	13:1	10n31, 64, 64n123, 103n16, 287n31
5:1	64		
5:1–22	64	13:2	47, 47n57, 48, 124n3
5:2–3	58	13:2–3	47
5:4	190n44	13:2–6	29, 46, 47, 48, 51, 137n47, 201, 201n84, 232, 233
5:6	24n27		
5:6–21	58		
5:22	59, 62n119	13:3	47
5:22–31	51	13:4	47, 48, 315n83
5:23	67, 68	13:5	24n27
5:23–27	64, 113n52	13:6	233
5:23–29	66n132	13:10	24n27
5:23–31	21, 66, 169n49, 169n50, 190	15:11	52n78
		16:18–18:22	52, 52n78, 52n79, 53n81, 54n85, 282n11
5:24–31	67, 68		
5:25	170n51	17:8–12	213
5:27	69n134, 131, 170n51	17:8–13	201–202
5:28	68	17:12	52n78, 202n88
5:28–31	64n126	17:13	52n78, 202n88
5:28–29	196	17:14–20	53n84, 54, 216, 282n11
5:29	69, 69n133		
5:31	65, 170n51	17:15	52n78
5:33	112	17:18–20	71n139
6:1	65, 192	17:19	62n119
6:1–2	193	17:20	52n78
6:4–9	57	18:2	52n78
6:6	62n119	18:8–12	51
6:12	24n27	18:9–11	192
7:8	24n27	18:9–12	51, 78, 79
7:12	190	18:9–14	50, 59, 80, 85, 216n29

Deuteronomy (*cont.*)

18:9–15	51, 59, 82, 84, 85	18:18b–19	247
18:9–22	11, 12, 46–52, 55, 56, 58n105, 59, 60n112, 70n137, 71, 71n139, 72, 75, 77, 81, 83, 85, 86, 92, 103, 108, 113n52, 122, 152, 158n4, 214, 216, 278–280, 282, 287, 323	18:19	50n67, 55, 62n119, 81, 248, 264, 297n22, 308, 310
		18:19–20	51
		18:20	51, 52n78, 104, 104n18, 106n26, 202n88, 233, 297n22
		18:20–22	48, 89n37
		18:21	48
18:10	51, 77, 78, 80, 81, 83	18:21–22	47n59, 51, 55n93, 271, 307
18:10–11	78, 80, 84, 85, 216n29		
18:11	80	18:22	52n78, 202n88, 307
18:12	47, 51, 85, 117, 192	18:22a	297n22
18:12–18	192n52	18:22b	297n22
18:12b	192	19–25	57n100
18:13	51	19:19	52n78
18:14	51, 81, 82n27, 95	24:7	52n78
18:14–15	62, 83	26	57
18:14–22	85n29, 89	27	57
18:15–16a	247	27–34	215n25
18:15–18	12, 17, 51, 64, 71n135, 111n44, 123, 125, 191, 192, 199, 201, 262, 295, 300, 306, 306n53, 308, 309, 314n78, 318	27:3	62n119
		27:8	62n119, 65
		27:26	62n119
		28	57, 57n103, 57n104
		28–33	10
		28:2	119n70
18:15–19	48, 56n95, 231n68, 247, 272, 309	28:14	62n119
		28:15	119n70
18:15–20	50	28:45	119n70
18:15–22	3, 3n8, 5, 46, 106, 145n1, 146, 149, 152, 158n3, 185, 187, 203n89, 205, 210, 213n22, 218, 223, 232, 237n7, 238, 239, 291, 296, 297, 297n24, 298, 298n24, 318, 319, 320, 321	28:58	62n119
		28:69	57, 58, 58n107, 59, 62n119
		29	57
		29–30	57
		29:2	137
		29:8	62n119
		29:27	141
		29:28	57
18:16	50n67, 81, 170n51, 263, 264	29:29	62n119, 63
		30	57n100, 57n104
18:16–17	190, 199n76	30:1–10	141
18:16–18	21, 51, 52, 64, 66, 66n132, 67, 68, 113n52, 169n50, 261	30:11–14	63
		30:15	310
		31	57
18:16–22	51	31:1–8	129
18:17	68	31:3	129n21
18:18–19	114, 196, 246, 247, 296, 309n62	31:7–8	129n21
		31:9–13	111n44, 129

INDEX OF ANCIENT SOURCES   365

31:19	65	11:12	19n6
31:12	62n119	11:15	19n6
31:14–15	35n16, 129–130, 222	12:6	19n6
31:22	65	13:8	19n6
31:23	130	13:22	61, 80
31:24	62n119	14:6	19n7
32	221	14:7	19n6
32:45	62n119	18:7	19n6
32:46	62n119	22:2	19n6, 133n34
32:46–47	310	22:4	19n6
32:48–52	130	22:5	19n6
33:1	19n7	24	128n19, 133n34
33:8–11	196, 199	24:17	24n27
34	57, 126, 287	24:25	24n34
34:1	139	24:26	24n34
34:1–3	139	24:29	133, 133n34
34:1–4	140	24:31	133n34
34:1b–4	140n56		
34:2–3	139	**Judges**	73, 172
34:4	127, 139	2:2	81
34:5	19n6, 72, 132, 133	2:8	133, 133n34
34:5–8	130	2:14	138n50
34:7–9	133n34	4:4	224
34:9	129, 130, 131, 132n31	6:8	24n27
34:11	137, 169n49	6:10	81
34:11–12	135, 136, 137	6:11b–17	22n19
34:12	263	6:22	135n39
		6:34	182n19
Joshua	73, 172	7:7–10	224n46
1:1	19n6, 90, 132, 133n33, 171n55	9:37	80
1:1–2	133	**1 Samuel**	73, 172
1:2	19n6, 133n33, 166, 167	1:18	138n50
1:5–6	129n21	3:1	224
1:7	19n6, 129n21, 133n33, 166, 167	3:11	91
		3:15	41n35
1:7–8	133	3:20	184, 213n22
1:8	71n139	6:2	80
1:9	129n21	6:12	100n6
1:13	19n6, 133, 134n38	7:5	21n14
1:15	19n6	9	55, 113n52
1:15b	133	9:9	287n31
2:11	138n50	10:5	38n29
5:1	138n50	10:6	44, 182, 182n18, 182n19
5:12	138n50		
6:24–26	180	10:10–11	38n29
8:31	19n6	10:13	44
8:33	19n6	12:19	21n14
9:24	19n6	12:23	21n14

1 Samuel (cont.)

15:23	61
16:13	52n78
19:20–24	38n29
19:23–24	44n51
27:12	24n26
28:3	61, 80
28:5 f.	55
28:7	80
28:8	80
28:9	80

2 Samuel

	73, 172
3:11	138n50
7:13	86
7:20	135n39
14:10	138n50

1 Kings

	73, 172
1:45–46	185
8:20	86
8:27	254
8:53	19n6
8:56	19n6
10:5	138n50
10:10	138n50
10:10bα	137n46
11:29–39	87
12:15b	87
14:6–16	87
14:11	76
15:29	87
16:4	76
17:1	174
18:4	76
18:13	76
19	34n15, 35
19:4	34n12, 35n19
19:13	163n24
19:15–16	185
19:16	145, 191n48
19:16b	174
19:19	145, 163n24, 171, 182n19
19:21	172
19:21bβ	171
20:33	80
21:19–24	76, 90
21:21–24	87
21:27–29	87
22	55n92
22:10	38n29
22:17	87
22:35–38	87

2 Kings

	73, 172
1:6	87
1:17	87
2:3	249n54
2:5	249n54
2:7	249n54
2:8	163n24
2:9	145
2:11	249n54
2:12	138n50
2:13	163n24
2:14	163n24
2:15	145, 249n54
2:15aβ	174
4:43	172n58
6:15	172n58
9:1–10:17	76
9:7	75, 75n13, 76, 77, 92n52
9:7–10a	76
9:11	41n35
9:22	61
9:26	76
9:36–37	76
10:10	76
10:17	76
14:15–16	90
14:25	305, 305n48
14:27	93n54
16:3	61, 80
17	77, 78, 83, 91n43, 93
17:5–23	75
17:7–12	78
17:9	82n27
17:10	91n44
17:13	75, 75n13, 77, 82n24, 86, 87, 88, 90, 91, 92n49, 92n51, 270n130
17:13–14	77, 81, 158n3, 176n69
17:13–17	82, 83, 85
17:13 ff.	82n25
17:14	81, 82

17:15	91	**Isaiah**	93n53, 98n2, 287n30, 310, 314n78
17:15–16	78		
17:15–17	78	1:1	91
17:17	61, 77, 78, 78n21, 79, 80, 85	2:5–9	60n114
		2:6	61
17:18–20	85	3:2	60n114, 61
17:19	91	6:1–13	22n19
17:22–23	88	6:9	259n97
17:23	75, 75n13, 77, 86, 90, 92n51	6:9–10	259n97
		8:19	60n114, 60n116, 61
17:31	61	8:19–20	60–61
17:40	81	10:14	60n116
18:12	19n6	11:9	134n36
19:1	21n14	19:3	60n114, 61
21	77, 93	28:17	91
21:1–7a	82	29:4	60n114, 60n116, 61
21:1–10	83	29:10	90n42
21:1–15	82, 85	30:10	90n42
21:1–16	75	38:14	60n114
21:2	78, 79, 84	40:1–11	22n19
21:3–5	78	40:3	194
21:3–6a	78	42:19	133n34
21:4	78	47:9	61
21:5	78	47:12	61
21:6	61, 77, 78, 78n21, 79, 80, 83, 84, 85	49:5–6	159n6
		52:7	200, 200n79, 200n81
21:7b–9	82	61:1	191n48, 200, 200n79
21:7–10	84	61:1–2	265, 266
21:8	19n6	61:11	134n36
21:9	81, 83	63:11	152n26
21:10	75, 75n13, 77, 86, 86n30, 90, 92n50	66:1–2	265
		Jeremiah	54, 71n139, 72, 73, 74n12, 75, 92, 98, 98n2, 98n3, 102, 103, 113
21:10–15	77, 82, 85, 87, 88		
21:11–15	91		
21:12	91, 92		
21:14	91, 92	1	107n30, 108, 108n35
22–23	56n96	1–25	99
22:15	86	1:2	108
23:10	61	1:4–9	105n48
23:20	86	1:4–10	22n19, 107
23:24	61, 80	1:5	108, 135n39, 135n40, 136n45
24:2	75, 75n13, 77, 86, 86n30, 90, 92n51	1:6	108
		1:7	107, 108, 108n34
24:2–4	88	1:7c	109
24:18–25:30	116	1:7d	110
25:30	90	1:9	71n139, 107, 108, 108n34, 114

Jeremiah (*cont.*)

1:9c	110
2:5	91
2:20	91n44
5:14	107
6:10 LXX	270n130
6:13 LXX	185n25
7	254n74
7–35	97n1
7:5–8	109n38
7:5–9	110
7:12	103
7:13	102n13
7:14	103
7:16	116
7:22–23	105, 105n48
7:23	112, 113
7:24	102, 102n14
7:25	75n13, 92n51, 98n3, 99, 100, 100n5, 101, 102n13, 105
7:25–26	99, 102
7:26	102n14
11:1–5	105n48
11:7	100, 102n13
11:8	102, 102n14
11:14	116
12:7	91, 92
14:11	116
14:14	61
15:1	19n8, 109, 116
17	109
17:19–27	109n38
17:23	102, 102n14
18:11	120
19:3	92
21:8–10	105n48
22:1–5	109n38
23	117
23:9–40	46, 117n63
25	108n35
25:1	99
25:3	99, 100, 100n5, 102n13, 108
25:3–4	99, 100n9, 101, 102, 108
25:4	75n13, 98n3, 100, 100n5, 102n13, 102n14
25:4–6	92n49, 92n50
25:5	120, 121, 121n78
25:7	121n78
25:11–12	99, 105
26	103
26–29	46
26:2	103n16, 105n48
26:3	105
26:4b–6	103
26:5	75n13, 92n51, 98n3, 102, 102n13, 110
26:6	103
26:10	103n17
26:11	104
26:12	104
26:13	105
26:15	104
26:16	104
26:18	74, 95, 104
26:20	105
26:20–23	105
27:9	61
27:16–22	117n63
28–29	105n23
28:2–4	105
28:8	106, 106n25
28:8–9	106
28:9	106, 106n25
28:10	106
28:28	110
29	95
29:8	61
29:15	47n57, 94, 124n3
29:19	75n13, 92n51, 102, 102n13
29:26	41n35
31:31–34	110, 111n44, 111n46
32:33	102n13
32:35	61
33:7 LXX	185n25
33:8 LXX	185n25
33:11 LXX	185n25
34:9 LXX	185n25
34:13	24n27
34:13–17	109n38
34:14	102, 102n14
35:1 LXX	185n25
35:14	102n13

INDEX OF ANCIENT SOURCES

35:15	75n13, 92n50, 98n3, 102, 102n13, 102n14, 120, 121	2	95
		2:1	94n55
		2:4	91n43
36	117n62	2:9–12	95
36:1 LXX	185n25	2:10	95
36:8 LXX	185n25	2:11	26n32, 47n57, 94, 95, 124n3
36:28	105n48		
37:19	106n25	3:3–8	93, 94
43	116	3:7	75, 75n13, 93, 94n55, 94n56
43:1–7	105n22		
44:4	75n13, 92n50, 98n3, 102n13	3:7–8	92n51
		5:25–27	265
44:4–5	102	7:7–8	91
44:5	102n14	7:14	93, 163n24, 249n54
44:22	138n50	7:14–15	95
52	116	8:11	152n26
		9:8a	93n54

Ezekiel
	98n2	**Obadiah**	
1:1	41n35	1	91
1:1–3:11	22n19		
8:3	41n35	**Jonah**	166
13:6	61	4:3	34n12
13:23	61		
16:2	270n130	**Micah**	73, 95, 103, 104, 106
20:4	270n130	3:6–7	60n114, 61, 152n26
20:31	61	3:11	62n118
22:30	34n13	3:12	104
33:22	138n50	5:2	60n114
38:17	75, 75n13, 92n51, 121n81	5:11	61
		6:4	18n4, 24n27, 26n32
40–48	53n81, 110n40		
40:2	41n35	**Nahum**	
		3:4	61

Hosea
	26, 73	**Zephaniah**	73
6:5	28n38, 29		
9:7	29, 41n35	**Haggai**	74, 74n12, 114, 117, 117n63, 162n18
12:13–14	27		
12:14	18, 19, 25, 27, 28, 28n41, 29, 29n43, 29n45, 45	**Zechariah**	114, 117, 117n63, 162n18, 288
		1–8	74, 74n12

Joel
2:31b	163n22	1:1	120, 120n74
3:1–5	239	1:1–6	118, 119
3:3	262	1:2–3	118n68
		1:2–6	121

Amos 73
1:6	94n55	1:3	118n68
1:13	94n55	1:4	118, 119, 120, 121n78

Zechariah (cont.)

1:4–6	120n73
1:4b	121n79
1:5	120
1:6	74n12, 75, 75n13, 92n51, 118, 119
4	200n78
7–8	118
7:7	118
7:12	118
13:2	185n25
13:2–3	152n26
13:2–6	52n79, 120n73, 160n8, 163
13:4	163n24
13:4–5	163n24
13:5	163n24

Malachi

	13, 151, 153, 155, 176, 186, 234, 322
1:6	164, 164n32
2:6	164
2:6–7	159–160
3:1	162, 162n17, 164, 165
3:1–5	162, 162n17
3:1aα	162, 163
3:5	162
3:7	164
3:19	174
3:19aα	175
3:22	19n6, 164n33, 166
3:22–24	3, 12, 125, 153, 156, 157–158, 158n3, 159, 160, 160n8, 161, 163, 165, 166, 176, 196, 321
3:23	159n6, 162, 163, 164, 302n36
3:23–24	157, 158n3, 158n4, 162, 162n17, 164n33
3:24	156, 164, 174
3:24a	175
4:5 [= 3:23]	302n36

Psalms

18:1	133n34
36:1	133n34
42:2	134n36
58:6	61
74:9	152n26
78:16	303n42
78:18–31	31n3
90:1	19n7
99:6	19
105:15	191n48
105:26	19n6
105:40	31n3
106:23	19, 34n13

Proverbs

3:11–12	288
5:1	103n15
5:13	103n15
16:10	61
22:17	103n15

Lamentations

2:9	152n26

Esther

	224–225

Daniel

1:17	41n35
2:2	61
9	121n81, 192n52
9:2	121n81
9:6	75, 75n13, 92n51, 121n81
9:10	75, 75n13, 92n51, 121n81
9:11	19n6, 121n81, 132n32
9:26	200
12:1	184n23

Ezra

3:2	19n7
9	192n52
9:11	75, 75n13, 92n50, 121n81, 192

Nehemiah

1:7	19n6
1:8	19n6
6:12	168n46
6:14	52n79
9:13–14	192
9:14	19n6
9:20	192
9:24	192

9:26	270n130	9:4	138n50
9:30	192	9:29	91n42, 168n46
10:30	19n6, 132n32	12:15	91n42
		13:20	138n50
1 Chronicles		15:8	168n46
6:34	19n6	24:6	19n6
10:13	61	24:9	19n6
16:22	191n48	24:19	270n130
19:19	138n50	29:25	91n42
23:14	19n7	30:10	19n7
29:29	91n42	33:6	61
		36:15	102n13
2 Chronicles		36:15–16	100
1:3	19n6		

Deuterocanonical Books

Tobit		47:1	170n53, 171, 172n57, 173, 173n63
4:12	249n54	48:1	170n53, 174, 175
Wisdom of Solomon		48:1–10	175n69
11:1	18n5	48:1a	171, 174
		48:8b	171, 173, 174
Sirach		48:10	156, 157, 158n4, 159, 159n6, 174, 196
24:33	174		
44:3	167	48:10abα	175
44:23b–45:5	168	48:12	170n53, 172n57, 173
45:1	169n49	48:12–14	175n69
45:2	170	48:12a	171, 174
45:1–5	168, 169n49	48:15–16	176n69
45:3b–5	168	48:23–25	176n69
45:4	169, 189n43	49:6–7	176n69
45:4–5	169	49:8	176n69
45:4a	169	49:9	175
45:5	170	49:10	156, 176n69
45:7	170	50:27	175n66
45:15	170		
45:25	170	**Baruch**	
46–49	170n53	2:20	121n81
46:1	170n53, 171, 172, 175n67, 222, 288	2:24	121n81
46:1a	222	**Prayer of Azariah**	
46:1–8	175n69	15	152n26
46:1b	172n61		
46:5	182n20	**1 Maccabees**	
46:11–12	175n69	2:29–30	185n27
46:13	170n53, 175n67	2:51–68	185n27
46:13–20	175n69	3:1–9	185n27

1 Maccabees (cont.)

3:18–22	185n27
3:58–60	185n27
4:8–11	185n27
4:17–18	185n27
4:22–25	185n27
4:44–46	183
4:45b–46	152n26, 185n26
4:46	151, 199n74, 223
9:27	152n26, 183, 183–184n23
9:54	184n23
14:41	152n26, 184, 185n26, 199n74

2 Maccabees

1:29	18n5

Pseudepigrapha

Letter of Aristeas
148n8

Jubilees
8, 10, 10n31, 147, 147n6, 148n8, 320

Testament of Moses

1:5	18n5, 180
1:6–7	180
3:11	18n5
10:15	181
11:16	18n5, 180, 181

Martyrdom and Ascension of Isaiah

3:9	18n5

Second Baruch

85:1–3	152n26

Fourth Ezra
320

14:45	211n16

Liber Antiquitatum Biblicarum (Pseudo-Philo)

19:3	181, 217
20:2	182
21:2–6	182
23:3	182
24:6	183
27:10	182n19
28:1	183n22
28:3	183n22
28:6	183n22
30:5	183n22
35:6	181
36:2	182n19
53:8	181

Dead Sea Scrolls and Related Texts

The Community Rule

1QS	195, 198, 199
1:1–3abα	193
1:1–3	121n81, 199
1:2–3	188n37
1:3	193
5:8b–9	194
8:15	188n37
8:15–16	193, 199
8:15b–9:11	196
9:3–9	195
9:4–5	201n83
9:6	201n83
9:9–11	152n26, 195
9:11	195, 198, 199n74, 201
4QS^d	194
4QS^e	196

The Damascus Document
197

5:17–19	187n36
5:21	188n37
5:21–6:1	188n40
7:18	199

1QH^a

4:24	188n38
12:16	185n25

1QpHab
2:6–10	152n26
7:4–5	152n26

The War Rule (1QM)
10:6	188n37

4QReworked Pentateuch
147, 147n6, 261n102

Florilegium (4Q174)
i 11–12	199

Testimonia (4Q175)
148, 172n60, 180, 196–197, 197n67, 198, 198n73, 199
17–18	199n77
23	196

4Q252
frag. 1 4:2	188n37

4Q374
frag. 2 2:6	187n36

Apocryphon of Moses (4Q375)
201–203
B 1:1–9	202
1:4–5	201
1:7	202n87, 203n89

4Q377
187–191, 200n79, 291
frag. 2 2:2–12	188–190
3	190
4	190
5	188, 188n37, 190
6–7	190
10	188
10–11	190
11	188
12	188

Apocryphon of Joshua (4Q378; 4Q379; 5Q22)
148, 172n60, 179–180, 196
4Q378	179
frag. 22 i 2	171n55
frag. 22 i 2–3	180
4Q379	172n60, 179, 180
frag. 18	180n10
frag. 22 7–12	197n67
5Q22	179
frag. 9	180

Non-Canonical Psalms B (4Q381)
191–193
frag. 69 1–5	191–192
1–4	192
4	192

4Q382
frag. 104 2:7	188n38

4QDibHam^a (4Q504)
frag. 1 2:7–10	188n36
frag. 1–2 5:14	188n38
frag. 3 2:16	188n38
frag. 4 2:8	188n38

Messianic Apocalypse (4Q521)
196n65

4Q558
196n65

11QMelchizedek (11Q13)
200, 200n79
2:16–17	200n79
2:17	200n81
2:17–18	200
2:20	200n79

The Temple Scroll (11Q19)
8, 10, 10n31, 147n6

Early Jewish Authors

Artapanus
On the Jews
frag. 3	259n96

Eupolemus
178–179

Josephus
Against Apion
1.6–27	206
1.29	206
1.30–36	207
1.32	207
1.32–34	207
1.36	207
1.37	209n12
1.37–41	206, 208
1.38	211
1.39–40	209n12
1.40–41	224
1.41	152n26, 208n8, 222, 223, 225
1.42–43	211
2.145	233
2.161	233
2.185	217n30

Jewish Antiquities
1.5	214
1.10	213
1.13	214n24, 215n26
1.121	213
1.208	215n26
2.6	213n22
2.18	220n37
2.20	220n37
2.23	220n37
2.24	220n37
2.194	220n37
2.241	210
2.254–256	220n37
2.268	259n96
2.293 ff.	220, 220n37
2.327	213n22
3.2	220
3.11	220n37
3.12	220n37
3.28	220n37
3.65	220n37
3.67	220n37
3.78	220n37
3.84	214n24, 215n26
3.102	220n37
3.105	220n37
3.180	220n37
4.13	220n37
4.45	215n26
4.82	220n37
4.104–130	216n29
4.150	220n37
4.156	220n37
4.156–158	216n29
4.165	221, 222
4.176–193	215n25
4.176–331	215
4.177	217n31
4.181	217
4.184	215n26, 217, 217n31
4.186	216n29, 217, 217n31
4.191	215n26
4.193	215n26
4.194	215n26, 217, 217n31, 220n37
4.194–198	214n24, 215n25
4.195	215n26
4.196	215n26
4.198	215n26
4.199–301	215n25
4.214–218	222n43
4.218	218, 219n35
4.223	215, 215n26, 216, 216n30, 219
4.223–224	214n24, 215
4.230	215n26
4.279	216n29
4.292	215n26
4.301–331	215n25
4.302	214n24, 215n26
4.303	221
4.310	215n26
4.311	222
4.312	215n26
4.312–319	215n25
4.313–314	221
4.317	220n37
4.324	219n36
4.329	220, 220n37
5.15	217n30, 219n36
5.20	223
5.23	217n30
5.43	217n30
5.55	217n30, 219n36
5.57	219n36
5.80	219n36
5.103	219n36
5.119	224

5.120	214n24, 224	6.285	229n62
5.200	224	6.285–287	227
5.285	224	6.286	229n62
5.318	224	6.287	232n70
5.340	224	7.437–450	227
5.345	224	7.450	233n74
5.351	224	*Life*	
6.36	214n24, 215	1–6	207
6.83	214n24	424–425	227
6.84	215	425	233n74
6.268	215		
8.148	206n2	**Philo of Alexandria**	
10.79	221n41	*On the Life of Abraham (Abr.)*	
10.276	221n41	113	287n30
11.184–296	225	*On Agriculture (Agr.)*	
12.142	217n30	50	287n30
13.299	197n67, 210	*On the Cherubim (Cher.)*	
13.311–313	153n27	17	287n32
15.373–379	153n27	27–29	289
17.346–348	153n27	49	287n30
20.97	229, 229n61, 232	*On the Confusion of Tongues (Conf.)*	
20.97–98	226	39	288
20.98	232, 233n74	62	288
20.160	232	*On the Preliminary Studies (Congr.)*	
20.161	233n74	132	282
20.167	232, 233n74	170	282n13, 283, 288n38
20.167–168	226		
20.169	229n61	177	288
20.169–172	226	*On the Contemplative Life (Contempl.)*	
20.170	229	12	289n39
20.171	233n74	25	287n31
20.188	227, 232, 233n74	64	283n13
20.224–251	217n30	87	283n13, 287n30
20.299	215	*On the Decalogue (Decal.)*	
20.261	214n24	18	283n13
Jewish War		19	283n13
1.78–80	153n27	175	283, 283n13
2.159	153n27	*That the Worse Attacks the Better (Det.)*	
2.211–213	153n27	39	287n30
2.258	229n62	40	287n32
2.258–260	226, 233n74	*That God is Unchangeable (Deus)*	
2.261	232	136	287n30
2.261–263	226	138	287n30, 287n32
2.263	233n74	139	287n31
3.351–354	207	*On Drunkenness (Ebr.)*	
3.352–353	153n27	143	287n30
3.399–408	153n27	*On Flight and Finding (Fug.)*	
3.400–403	207	140	282n13
6.284–285	233n74	147	283

On Giants (Gig.)

49	282n13
56	282n13
61	288n34

Who is the Heir? (Her.)

4	282n13
78	287n31
249	282n7
258	287n30, 287n31, 289
259	282n7, 287n30, 288n34
260	285n20
260–261	286
262	282, 282n13, 287n31
266	287n30

Allegorical Interpretation (Leg.)

2.1	282n13
3.103	287n31
3.173	18n5, 282n13

On the Embassy to Gaius (Legat.)

99	288n36

On the Migration of Abraham (Migr.)

15	282n13
34–35	289
38	287n31
84	287n30, 287n32
151	282n13
169	287n30

On the Life of Moses (Mos.)

1.1	282
1.43–46	259n96
1.57	18n5, 282n13
1.148	282n11
1.148–154	282n11
1.152	282n11
1.154	282n11
1.156	282n13
1.158	288
1.266	287n30
1.334	282
2.1–3	282
2.3	18n5, 282n13
2.6	281n7
2.37	288
2.40	288, 288n35
2.76	282n13, 284n18
2.187	282n13, 283
2.187–291	282, 283
2.188	282n13, 283–284
2.189	284n17
2.190	285, 287n33
2.191	285, 287n33
2.191a	284
2.192	283, 287n33
2.192–212	283n15
2.209	282n13
2.213	282n13
2.213–220	283n15
2.222–232	283n15
2.233–245	283n15
2.246	282n13, 285n19
2.246–257	283n16
2.250	282n13, 285
2.257	282n13
2.258	285n21
2.258–262	285
2.258–269	283n16
2.262	283n13
2.263–267	285
2.268	287
2.268–269	285
2.269	283n13
2.270	286
2.270–274	283n16
2.273	286
2.274	286
2.275	283n13, 285n23
2.275–287	283n16
2.278	283n13
2.280	283n13
2.284	283n13
2.288	221n40, 287
2.291	287
2.292	282, 283n13

On the Change of Names (Mut.)

11	282n13
103	282n12
125	282, 282n12

On Planting (Plant.)

138	287n30

On Rewards and Punishments (Praem.)

1	283n13
2	283n13
55	283n13
123	283n13
158	287n30

Questions and Answers on Exodus (QE)
- 2.16 — 283n13
- 2.46 — 283n13
- 2.49 — 283n13

Questions and Answers on Genesis (QG)
- 1.24 — 283n13
- 1.28 — 283n13
- 2.26 — 287n30

On the Sacrifices of Cain and Abel (Sacr.)
- 130 — 282n13

On Dreams (Somn.)
- 1.254 — 287n30
- 2.18 — 282n12
- 2.145 — 288
- 2.172 — 287n30
- 2.252 — 289
- 2.277 — 282n13

On the Special Laws (Spec.)
- 1.59–65 — 279
- 1.60 — 280
- 1.61 — 280n5
- 1.64 — 280
- 1.65 — 281, 284, 285, 285n20, 286, 287n31
- 1.315 — 232, 287n31
- 1.345 — 283n13
- 3.7 — 288n36
- 3.125 — 283n13
- 4.48–52 — 279
- 4.49 — 281, 285, 285n20, 286, 287n31
- 4.50–52 — 280
- 4.192 — 288n34, 288n36

On the Virtues (Virt.)
- 51 — 283n13, 288
- 51–70 — 288
- 53–65 — 288
- 56 — 288
- 64 — 288
- 66 — 288
- 68 — 178n1, 288
- 70 — 288
- 119 — 283, 283n13
- 218 — 287n30

New Testament

Matthew — 11, 236–238, 320
- 7:15 — 185n25
- 11:9 — 301n31
- 11:10 — 162n17
- 11:13 — 152n26, 219n34, 239n12
- 12:38–39 — 262n104
- 13:57 — 301n31
- 16:1–4 — 262n104
- 16:14 — 301n37
- 17:2 — 266n118
- 17:5 — 236, 266n116
- 17:12–13 — 301n34
- 21:11 — 301n37
- 24:11 — 185n25
- 24:24 — 185n25

Mark
- 1:2 — 162n17
- 6:1–6 — 265
- 6:4 — 265
- 6:15 — 152n26, 267
- 6:15b — 268
- 8:11–12 — 262n104
- 8:17 — 259n97
- 8:21 — 259n97
- 8:28 — 301n31
- 8:28d — 268
- 9:2 — 266
- 9:4 — 236
- 9:7 — 236, 266
- 9:13 — 301n34
- 13:22 — 185n25

Luke
- 1:3 — 249n52
- 1:8–23 — 241n19
- 1:55 — 257
- 1:64 — 271n137
- 1:67 — 271n137
- 1:68 — 257, 259n95
- 1:70 — 240, 271n137
- 1:73 — 257
- 1:76 — 239n13
- 2:22–52 — 241n19
- 2:33 — 271n137

Luke (*cont.*)

2:36	150n14, 239n13
2:38	271n137
2:49	254n77
4	266n115
4:16–30	260, 265, 266n114
4:18–21	265
4:21	266
4:24	265
4:25–27	265
4:29	266
6:23	257
6:26	185n25, 257
7:16	240, 240n13, 242n20, 259n95, 301n31
7:17	257
7:26	239n13
7:39	236, 301n31
8:1	249n52
8:10	259n97
9:8	240n13, 301n31
9:8c	268
9:19	240n13, 301n31
9:19c	268
9:20	268
9:29	266
9:31	266
9:32	266
9:33	266
9:35	236, 266
9:36–37	301n34
9:51	267n119
10:24	240
11:16	262n104
11:29	262n104
11:47	257
11:48	257
11:49	257
11:50	239n12
12:9	257
13:28	239n12, 240
16:16	219n34
16:16–18	269n127
16:19–31	269
16:27–29	269n128
16:27–31	269, 269n128
16:29	270
16:30–31	269n128
16:31	270
18:34	259n97
19:44	257
20:6	239n13
20:37	257, 270
23:34	257
23:47	257
24:13–49	269
24:19	257, 259, 301n31
24:20	256
24:21	257
24:25	236, 270
24:27	239n12, 271n135
24:32	270
24:44	271
24:45	252, 259n97, 270, 271n135
24:46–47	251, 272
24:50–53	241n19

John

1:8	301
1:14	294, 294n10, 310
1:14–18	314n78
1:17	292n5, 312–313, 313n71, 315n81
1:20	301
1:21	229n58, 236, 300
1:21–25	305
1:25	300
1:35–51	302
1:37	302
1:41	302
1:43	302n38
1:45	292n5, 297n22, 302, 302n36
1:48	302, 306n54, 306n55
1:49	302
1:51	302, 306n56
2:11	294n10
2:19	306n56
2:19–22	297n22
2:21–22	307
2:24–25	306n54
3:4	311
3:11	297n22
3:13–14	314
3:14	292n5, 297n22, 306n56, 317
3:14–15	314, 315, 317

3:16–18	297n22	6:35	317
3:34	297n22	6:45	297n22
3:34a	308	6:48	317
3:35–36	308	6:51	317
3:36	297n22, 306n56	6:52	311
4	306n51, 316n85	6:53	306n54
4:10–19	303n42	6:58	317
4:15	311	6:61	306n54
4:16–19	306n54, 306n55	6:63	297n22
4:19	297n22, 306, 306n53, 306n56, 307	6:64	306n54
		6:68	297n22
4:21	306n56	6:70	306n56
4:50–53	297n22	6:70–71	306n54
5	314, 316, 316n85	7	303, 305, 310, 316n85
5:6	306n54		
5:16	297n22	7–8	310
5:18	297n22, 316n85	7:1	297n22, 306n54, 316n85
5:19	297n22		
5:24	297n22	7:12	297n22, 305
5:26–29	306n56	7:13	297n22
5:30	297n22	7:14–18	308
5:33–35	314	7:16–18	297n22
5:36	314	7:19	292n5, 316n85
5:37	315n83	7:19–23	316n85
5:37–38	314	7:22–23	292n5, 292n6
5:39	314, 316, 316n86	7:27	305
5:42	315n83	7:28	297n22
5:45	292n5	7:31	305
5:45–47	297n22, 314, 316	7:37–38	303, 306n56, 317
5:46	18n5, 236, 315, 315n81, 317	7:38	306n56
		7:39	307
5:46 f.	316n86	7:40	297n22, 300, 301, 304, 305, 310
6	293n8, 297n24, 310, 316, 316n85, 317		
		7:40–41	302
6–8	310	7:40–52	304
6:1	316n85	7:40b–42	304
6:1–13	316	7:41	304, 306n56
6:1–15	303n40	7:41–42	304n43, 305
6:6	306n54	7:47	297n22, 304, 305
6:14	300, 301, 305, 307	7:52	300, 301, 302, 304, 305, 310
6:14–15	296, 297n22, 302–303, 316		
		8	310, 322
6:15	303n41, 311	8:5	292n5
6:30	262n104	8:12	317
6:30–31	317	8:12–58	310
6:32	292n5, 318n90	8:23	311
6:32–33	317	8:26–27	311
6:32–58	317	8:28	297n22, 308, 310
6:34	311		

John (cont.)
8:28b	310	14:15	297n22
8:33–58	292n5	14:16	306n56
8:38	297n22	14:18–21	306n56
8:42	311	14:21	297n22
8:47	308, 310, 311	14:24	297n22
8:51	297n22	14:26	306n56
8:52	152n26	14:28–29	297n22, 307n57
8:53	311	14:29	307
8:55	297n22	14:31	297n22
8:56	314n78	15:10	297n22
8:58	311, 319	15:10–17	297n22
9	300n29, 306n51	15:15	297n22, 294
9:13	299	15:20	306n56
9:15	299	15:26	306n56
9:16	299	16:2	299, 306n56
9:17	297n22, 306	16:2–4	297n22, 307n57
9:18	299	16:4	307
9:22	297n22, 299	16:7	306n56
9:27	299	16:13	298n24, 306n56
9:28	292n5, 299	17:8	298n24, 307, 308n60, 309
9:28–29	299, 311	17:14	307
9:40	299	17:17	307
10:3	308	18:4	306n54
10:18	297n22	18:8–9	297n22, 307n57
11:4	306n56	18:9	307
11:27	303n39	18:31–32	297n22, 307n57
12:37–41	310	18:32	307, 307n58
12:41	310, 314n78	18:36	311
12:42	297n22, 299	18:37	308
12:44–50	297n22		
12:47	297n22	Acts	
12:47–48	310	1:8	245
12:49–50	297n22, 308, 309	2	256, 262
12:50	310	2–5	241n19
13:1	306n54	2:4	271n137
13:18–19	297n22, 307n57	2:16–21	239
13:19	307	2:19	263
13:21	306n54, 306n56	2:22	257, 263
13:26	306n54	2:23–24	261
13:34	297n22	2:23–24a	261
13:38	306n54, 306n56	2:24	251n61
14:1	315n82	2:32	251n61
14:1b	315	2:32–38	251n62
14:2–3	306n56	2:40	269n129
14:8	294	2:43	257, 263
14:10	307, 309	3	242, 243n24, 249n52, 254n74, 255, 255n83, 256,
14:12	306n56		
14:13	306n56		

INDEX OF ANCIENT SOURCES

	256n84, 257, 257n88, 258, 264, 265, 272	6:11–14	254n75
		6:13–14	253
		7	241n19, 242, 255, 255n83, 256, 256n84, 257, 258, 261, 264, 265, 266n114, 269n127, 272, 322
3:2	245		
3:12	250, 256		
3:12–26	245		
3:13	250, 251, 254n74, 257		
3:14	257		
3:15	257	7:2–16	254
3:15a	261	7:6	254n75
3:16	250, 250n58	7:7	254n74
3:17	256, 256n88, 257	7:11	257
3:18	239n12, 257	7:12	257
3:18–21	250	7:15	257
3:18–26	245–246	7:17	254n75, 257
3:20	257	7:17–40	256
3:21	248	7:17–44	254
3:22	248, 249, 249n53, 250, 251, 252, 257, 267	7:19	257
		7:20	254n75
		7:20–22	259
3:22–23	236, 246, 247, 248n44, 249n53, 263, 264	7:22	257
		7:23	254n75, 257, 259, 259n95
3:22–24	250, 252	7:23–29	259
3:22–26	245	7:25	253n69, 256, 259
3:23	246n37, 264, 273		
3:24	239n12, 249, 249n53	7:27	253n69, 257, 259
		7:28	260
3:25	249, 250, 251, 254n74, 257	7:30	254n75
		7:30–44	259
3:25–26	257	7:32	257
3:26	250, 250n57, 251, 251n60, 256, 257, 258, 267	7:34	257
		7:35	256, 256n87, 257, 259, 260, 261
		7:35–40	260
4:1–2	252	7:35a	261
4:4	258	7:35b	262
4:24–27	251n63	7:36	254n75, 257, 259, 262
4:30	257, 263		
5	264n111	7:37	236, 246n37, 253, 257, 262
5:12	257, 263		
5:19	264n111	7:37–38	263
5:19–25	255n82	7:37–39	264
5:20	264n111	7:38	257, 262
5:31	246n37, 257	7:38–39	262
5:33–39	270n134	7:39	257, 264
5:36	226	7:39–40	262
6:7	255, 257n88	7:40	259
6:8	257, 263	7:42–43	265
6:11	253		

Acts (cont.)

7:44	254n75, 257, 262	20:21	269n129
		20:23	269n129
7:45	257	20:24	269n129
7:44–53	254	21:9	240n13
7:45	254n75	21:10	240, 240n13
7:48	254	21:38	226, 227n54
7:49–50	265	22:14	257
7:51	257, 256n114	23:11	269n129
7:51–53	256	24:14	241
7:52	257	24:22	241
7:60	254, 257	26:6	257
8:14	255	26:22	18n5
8:25	269n129	26:23	251n59, 251n62
9:2	241	26:27–28	319n93
10:41	251n61	27:1–28:16	238n8
10:42	269n129	28:23	18n5, 269n129, 319n93
10:43	239n12		
11:4	249n52	28:26–27	259n97
11:27	240, 240n13		
12:6–17	255n82	1 Corinthians	
12:17	255n82	1:22	262n104
13:1	240n13	11–14	239n10
13:6	185n25	14:29	271n137
13:27	256		
13:30–39	251n62	1 Thessalonians	
13:32	257	4:6	269n129
13:33	251n61	5:20–21	239n10
13:34	251n61		
13:46	251n60, 255	1 Timothy	
14:3	257, 263	5:21	269n129
15	255		
15:5	257n88	2 Timothy	
15:12	257, 263	2:14	269n129
15:32	240n13	4:1	269n129
16:10–17	238n8		
17:2–3	259n97, 319n93	Hebrews	
17:3	251n61	1:1–2	152n26
17:30	257	2:6	269n129
17:30–31	251n62	3:5	18n5
17:31	251n61		
18:5	269n129	1 Peter	
18:23	249n52	1:10–12	252n68
18:25–26	241		
19:2	152n26	2 Peter	
19:6	271n137	1:15	266n119
19:9	241	2:1	185n25
19:23	241		
20:5–21:18	238n8	1 John	
		4:1	185n25

Revelation

16:13	185n25
19:20	185n25
20:10	185n25

Rabbinic Literature

Tosefta

t. Sot. 13:2	149n12
t. Sot. 13:3	152n26

Talmud

y. Sot. 24b	152n26
b. Sanh. 11a	152n26
b. B. Bathra 14b	287n29

Avot de R. Nathan

1	114n54; 152n26

Mekhilta

Vayassa to Exod 16:5	318n90
Bahohesh to Exod 19:9	24n26
Bahodesh to Exod 20:19	173n63

Pesiqta de Rab Kahana

13:6	114
13:14	114, 152n26

Bamidbar Rab.

14:20	134n37

Cant. Rab.

8:9	152n26

S. 'Olam Rab.

30	152n26

Qohelet Rab.

12:7	114n54, 152n26

Vayikra Rab.

1:13	134n37

Sifre Deut 134n37

Early Christian Literature

Justin Martyr, *Dialogue with Trypho*

	319
52:3	218–219n34
53:3–4	152n26

Origen, *Against Celsus*

7.8	152n26

Athanasius, *On the Incarnation*

39–40	152n26

Eusebius
Demonstration of the Gospel

III.2	138n49

Preparation for the Gospel

9.30.1–2	179

Pseudo-Clementine Recognitions

1:57	263n110

Islamic Sources

Qur'ān

2:129	13n33
7:157	13n33

Index of Subjects

Aaron   26, 40–44, 170, 213n22, 217, 287n30
Abraham   139–140, 181n15, 213n22, 240, 246, 251, 254n74, 257, 269–270, 287n30, 289, 292n5, 311, 314n78, 321
Agabus   240
Ahijah   87, 90
Amos   90–91, 93–96, 106, 265
Anna   150n14, 239n13, 240n14

Balaam   80, 108n34, 134n37, 216n29, 280n4, 287n30
Book of Signs   294–295

call narrative   22, 107–109
canon   2–7, 11, 17, 70–71, 147, 320–321
   canon criticism   2–3
   formation of   6–7, 124–129, 140n57, 147–148, 154, 165–167, 172, 175–176, 206–212, 225
   structure of   6–7, 17, 82n25, 127–128, 147–148, 166–167, 172, 176
charisma   *See under* prophecy
Christology   236–237, 242–244, 252, 272, 292–298, 321–322
complaint narrative   31–32

David   8, 133n34, 170, 185, 187n34, 287n30, 304
Day of Yhwh   158, 160, 162–163, 196n65
Deuteronomistic History
   and Josiah's Reform   72–74
   and prophetic succession   72, 77, 86–93, 96
   relation to Jeremiah   98–103, 108–109, 112–113, 116–118, 121–122
Deuteronomy
   and centralization   54, 56, 62–63, 69–71, 130–131
   constitutional polity of   52–54, 213, 215–220
   relationship to pre-Deuteronomic sources   23n24, 26, 44–45, 94–95
   provenance of   26–27
   synchronic interpretation of   138–141
   theology of   59, 62–63
   and *Urdeuteronomium*   26–27, 56–59

divination   50, 55, 59–61, 77–85, 113n52, 280–281

Eldad and Medad   31–32, 39–41, 43–44, 171
elders (seventy)   31–40, 43–44, 217–219
Elijah
   in the books of Kings   25–26, 29, 35, 76, 87, 90, 145, 287n30
   in early Christianity   240n14, 265, 266–268, 301–302
   eschatological return of   156–167, 174–176, 196n65, 322
   as prophet like Moses   158n3, 171, 173–174, 196
Elisha   25–26, 76, 90, 145, 170–174, 240n14, 265
Enoch and Enochic literature   8, 147n7, 188n36, 321
eschatological prophets   *see under* Elijah, *see under* messianism, *see under* prophecy
Ezekiel   5, 41n35, 53n81, 176n69
Ezra   74, 224
exile   73, 77, 80–81, 85–86, 95, 117–118, 141, 148

Hananiah of Gibeon   105–106
Hellenism   145–148, 155, 167, 172–173, 176–177, 184–185n25, 234
   Hellenistic Jewish Christianity   242, 253
historiography   72, 89n37, 129, 146, 154, 178–186, 203, 209, 225, 238–241, 321
Horeb theophany   10, 12, 58–59, 63–71, 95, 113, 192–193
Hosea   26–29, 287n30

Isaiah   91, 93n53, 109, 176n69, 200, 265, 287n30, 310

Jacob   27–28, 41n35, 210, 240
Jesus
   and Logos Christology   *see* Logos theology
   as prophet   265, 306–307

INDEX OF SUBJECTS

as prophet like Moses 228, 236–238, 243–244, 248–272, 293–298, 300–306, 308–311, 314–315
resurrection of 250–252, 267–271, 307
Jeremiah
and Deuteronomy *see* Deuteronomistic History, relationship to Jeremiah
as final prophet 98–103, 114–118
as prophet like Moses 107–113
and the prophetic succession 98–103
temple sermon of 99, 103
John the Baptist 162n17, 239n13, 240, 267, 301–302, 306
John Hyrcanus 197, 210, 225n50
Joshua
as Moses' assistant 39–40, 171–172
as prophet like Moses 131–132, 142, 146, 148, 167, 171–173, 176, 178–183, 203, 212, 217–223, 230–231, 234
as Moses' successor 129–133, 288–289

"The Law and the Prophets." *See under* canon, structure.
Logos theology 277, 283, 290; 291–294, 296, 312–319

messianism
eschatological prophetic movements 226–231
at Qumran 197–203
royal messianism 200n78, 229n58, 296, 302–305, 311
Micah of Moresheth 103–105
Micaiah ben Imlah 87
Miriam 26, 32, 40–45, 287n30
Mosaic Discourse 8–11, 59, 65, 93, 99, 119–121, 147, 179, 192, 272, 277, 315, 319
Moses
epithets for 19–20
as mediator 37, 66–69, 110, 168–169, 187–191, 261–262, 312–313
portrayal in Pentateuchal sources 20–25
portrayal in Early Jewish sources 168–170, 187–190, 220–221, 257–258, 282–287
Nathan 90, 173

Nazirites 26, 94–95
Normativity 5–8, 70–71, 118, 122, 123–129, 147–148, 232–235, 241, 245, 272–274, 280, 292, 318–319

Pentateuch, redaction of 45n52, 126–129, 135, 139–140, 147
Peter 245, 252
Priests and priesthood 23, 146, 148, 152–155, 159, 161, 179–180, 201, 206–208, 240–241, 252, 255, 273, 301
"Messiah of Aaron," 195–196, 199
Zadokites 194–195
prophecy
cessation of 44n50, 114–118, 145, 148–155, 208–211, 278–279, 321
and charisma 25–29, 44–48, 71, 131, 159, 239–240, 277, 281, 284, 290, 291, 311, 317
and prophetic conflict 46–48, 103–106
criteria for 48, 50–51, 103–106, 201–203, 232–234, 271, 305, 307
and divination 23, 55, 61–62, 80–85, 279–281
and prophets of doom 93–95, 105
ecstatic prophecy 38, 41, 285, 289–290
eschatological return of 161–163, 174, 195–203, 226–231, 236–237, 262–263, 300–301, 311
etiology of 21, 64–70
and fulfillment 77, 86–90, 131, 140–141, 221, 245, 252, 285–287, 302, 307, 319
genealogical model of 70–72, 98–102, 119, 170, 193–194, 239–241, 272–274, 287, 291, 311, 315, 319, 320–322
halakhic model of 25, 65, 81–82, 102–103, 109–110, 119, 122, 185–186, 191–196, 199, 203, 223, 263–265
as prediction 10, 86–90, 106, 113n52, 221, 245, 249, 285–287, 289, 306–307
relation to priesthood 152, 154, 159, 183, 186, 201–203, 206–208, 232–234
and "signs and wonders" 127, 136–137, 226–229, 262–264
war prophecy 26
prophet, as designation 19–21, 48, 65, 75, 120, 186–187, 212–214, 239–240, 282–283, 287–289, 306–307

prophetic office   21, 23, 54–55, 62, 72, 116, 146, 151, 167–168, 170–174, 185–186, 213–214, 218, 282, 320
prophetic succession   28, 72, 75, 87, 90–91, 98–102, 118–121, 129–132, 170–177, 206–210, 223–225, 249, 265, 272–273, 287–290, 319
pseudepigraphy   9–10, 58–59, 65, 320

reception history   2–5, 111, 141, 158n3
revelation   5, 9, 35–37, 41–46, 59, 63–65, 70–71, 112–113, 134–135, 194, 277, 291–293, 312–313, 319
Righteous Teacher   *see* Teacher of Righteousness

Samaritans   5, 196, 199, 231n67, 248, 261–262n102, 306
Samuel   19n8, 25–26, 28, 41n35, 44, 90, 94n57, 109, 170–173, 175, 179, 183n22, 213n22, 224, 248–249, 252, 287n30
scribes and scribalism   74, 98, 111–112, 117, 146, 148, 152–155, 157, 167, 176, 183, 203, 214, 234, 239, 241, 321

scripture   7, 71, 126–129, 147–148, 154–155, 174, 206–211, 225, 233–234, 240–241, 252, 270–271, 288–290, 305, 314–316
Second Isaiah   5n14, 141n59
seventy elders   *see* elders
Sinai   *See* Horeb theophany
spirit   29, 37–40, 44, 130–131, 149n12, 174, 182, 192, 194, 200, 221, 281, 284
synagogue   298–300

Teacher of Righteousness   197, 273
temple   , 117, 153–154, 183–185, 227, 240–241, 245, 252–255, 272–273n139, 273n141
temple sermon   99–100, 103, 245, 254n74
theodicy   72, 85–86, 100–103, 272–273n139
Tent of Meeting   34–36, 129–130, 222–223
Torah   *See* Pentateuch; *See also* prophecy, halakhic model of
Transfiguration   237–238, 266–268
typology   11, 237

Urdeuteronomium   *see under* Deuteronomy
Uriah ben Shemaiah   105

Zechariah   118–121